The Great Skiing & Snowboarding Guide 2006

Peter and Felice Hardy

SKI CLUB OF GREAT BRITAIN AND THE GREAT SKIING AND SNOWBOARDING GUIDE

The Ski Club of Great Britain is for skiers and snowboarders of all ages and abilities. Since its creation over one hundred years ago, over 30,000 snowsports lovers a year have taken advantage of the Club's unrivalled knowledge of the skiing and snowboarding world.

It's the only way to stay in the mountains all year round – and now is the perfect time to join…

EXCLUSIVE OFFER
Half-price membership for one year
Individual: £24.50
Family: £37.50

GET WHAT YOU WANT

As a member of the UK's largest and most active snowsports organisation, you will receive hundreds of benefits that are unavailable elsewhere.

UP TO 15% DISCOUNT ON YOUR HOLIDAY
Save on holidays booked with over 90 tour operators

OVER 1000 DISCOUNTS
Get money off in White Stuff, Snow+Rock, Fat Face, Blacks, Ellis Brigham, Cotswold Outdoor and many more outlets; Eurostar, RailEurope, airport car parking, car hire and airport hotels; dry and real slopes and gyms in the UK; resort rental shops and ski schools

SKI CLUB REPS
Ski and board with reps in over 40 premier mountain resorts in Europe and North America

WWW.SKICLUB.CO.UK
Get the latest news, competitions and offers; snow reports and resort information; tour operator search engine, chat, photos, games, and access to the Members Only area

WWW.SKIFRESHTRACKS.COM
Ski with a group of similar ability, meet like-minded people and enjoy an extra level of care on and off the slopes with holiday leaders, mountain guides or instructors on Ski Club tailored holidays

UNBEATABLE INSURANCE
Buy the best on- and off-piste holiday and seasonal insurance cover

INFORMATION AND ADVICE
Get expert guidance on all aspects of snowsports, resorts, and how to maximise on the benefits of membership; snow reports and equipment hire

EVENTS
Enjoy exhibitions across the UK, film premieres, resort events and glittering Summer Balls

PUBLICATIONS
Receive four issues of Ski and Board magazine, Clubtalk newsletter and 'the edge' e-newsletter

This offer is subject to the production of the corner flash on page 1 and to signing a direct debit for second and subsequent subscriptions. The offer expires on 30 April 2006 and may not be used in conjunction with any other offers. For further information, call the Ski Club's Membership Department on 0845 45 807 82 or visit www.skiclub.co.uk.

Grandvalira Andorra

VALLNORD Mountain Park

Vallnord

temps 2019eu

ESPANYA

PORT DE CABÚS
PORT DE COMA PEDROSA 2843m
PLA DE L'ESTANY
PIC DE RACÓFRED 2950m
EST. FO...
PIC DE LES TRÀTER...
PIC DELS LLACS 2749m
EST. DE L'ESTANY
PIC DE CABEYROU 2772m
COSTA 2930m
CREUSSANS
PORT DE RAT
PIC DE GRAPEROIS 2650m
LA COMA 2250m
SECTOR ARINSAL
SECTOR ARCALÍS
SECTOR ORDINO-ARCALÍS
PIC DE L'ESTANY 957m
PIC DEL GUBIL 2383m
PIC D'ENCLAR 2382m
PLA DE LA COT 2029m
PIC DE GALLINA 2335m
ELS CORTALS
PIC D'ARCALÍS 2776m
EST. DE L'ANGONELLA 1470m
PIC DE LA MESQUITA
LES PORTELLES 2353m
ELS PLANELLS
LA CALDANS 1940m
COLL
COLL
ARINSAL 1550m
SECTOR PAL
PIC DEL CAMALL 2601m
PLOT DEL CAMALL
PIC DE LES FONTS 2245m
ANDORRA LA VELLA
BISONY 1770m
LA MASSANA 1300m
LA CORTINADA
ANSALONGA
ORDINO
LES SALINES
ERTS

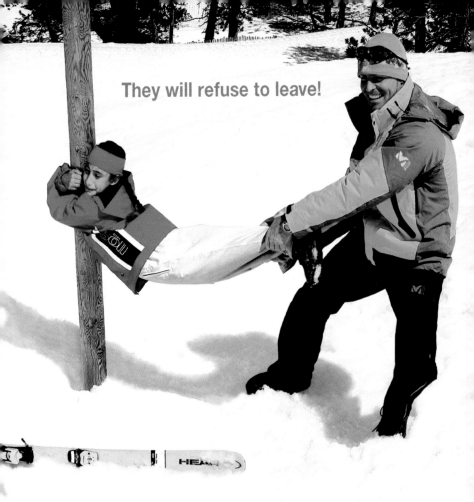

They will refuse to leave!

Austria.
You've arrived!

www.austria.i

Kitzbühel

Mayrhofen

Schermerspitze 3117 m

Wurmkogl 3082 m

Wurmkoglgipfelhaus

Wurmkogl II

Königsjoch 2825 m

Königskogl 3055 m

Ferwalljoch 2908 m

Granatenkogl 3304 m

Hochfirst 3405 m

Liebenerspitze 3400 m

Festkogl 3035 m

Rotmoosgletscher

Rotmoosjoch 3055 m

Hinterer Seelenkogl

Hohe Wilde 3480 m

Vorderer Seelenkogl

Hangerer 3021 m

Karlsruher Hütte 2430 m

Schönwieshütte 2266 m

Hoc 28

K ö n i g s t a l

F e r w a l l t a l

Top Wurmkogl

Speicherteich

Sektion I

Top Express

Verbindungsbahn Obergurgl-Hochgurgl

Vorderer Wurmkogllift

Wurmkoglhütte-Mittelstation

Hochgurglbahn Sektion II

Top Wurmkogl Sektion II

Festkoglhütte

Gipfel-Lift

Mittelstation

Plattachbahn

Hohe Mut 2670 m

Hohe Mut Lift

Hohe Mut Häusl

Nederlift

Speicherteich

Nederhütte

Roßkarbahn

Mittelstation

Roßkarbahn

Festkoglbahn

Ausstieg

Gaisberglift

Bruggenbodenlift

Steinmahbahn

David's Skihütte

Wiesenlift

Bobo's Kinderclub

Skischullift

Mahdstuhllift

OBERGURGL 1930 m

HOCHGURGL 2150 m

Obergurgl

7 km

2 km

$\langle 1 \rangle$ = **Varianten:**

= **Schwarze Abfahrt** = **schwierig**

= mittelschwer

Saalfelden

Saalbach

Ski Welt

M17

M18

St Anton

Mauerkogel 2074 m

Kitzsteinhorn 3203 m

Großglockner 3798 m

Großvenediger 3674 m

Nationalpark Hohe Tauern

Gipfelstation 3029 m

GLETSCHERPLATEAU 2900 m:
Gletscher-Shuttle,
Magnetdepilatte

Glocknerkanzel
Panorama-Tunnel

Bella Vista, Kitz: 3000 m
Terrasse Gletscherwelt

ALPINCENTER 2452 m:
Big Apple, Mix Kids,
Skyline, Paradise
Interport Kitzsteinhorn

Kettenjet

Maurergletscherlifte

Grattbahn

Kitz- und Kneslifte

Schmiedingerlifte

Krefelder Hütte

LANGWIED 1978 m:

Gletscherjet 3

Maiskogel 1675 m

Gletscherjet 2

Maiskogelbahn

Langwiedbahn

Austria
Academy

ORTSKASSA
Tickets

Maiskogelexpress

Glocknerbahn

Schmittenhöhe 2000 m

SCHMITTENHÖHE Bergstation
Panorama-Pfiff
Elisabeth-Kapelle

Kapellenbahn

Gipfelbahn

Platzgumer Hütte

SONNKOGEL Bergstation
Sonnkogel-Pfiff

SONNKOGEL Bergalpel

Sonnschupfbahn

Hochmaisbahn

Schmiedlbahn

Hochzelleralm

Breiteckbahn

Breiteckalm

AREITBAHN III Bergstation
Panorama-Pfiff

Areitbahn III

Schmittenhöhebahn

Glocknerbahn

Sonnalmbahn

Jaga-Alm

Blacksner's

**SCHMITTENHÖHE &
SONNALM** Talstation

Hirschkogel-Express

Areitbahn

Areitbahn II

Trass-Alm

Fischerntal-Bahn

Cambl Mittelstation

cityXpress

cityXpress Talstation

AREITBAHN I Talstation
Pfiffel mit Schirmbar

Salersbach

Schüttdorf

Kaprun

Zell am See

Zell am See

Bruck-Fusch

Thumersbach

Hotel Bellevue bis Camping Süd

Im Gebiet Sonnenalm/Sonnkogel
Beschneiungsanlage
(90% der Pisten beschneit)
Hochmaisbahn (6er-Sesselbahn)
mit Hauben und Sitzheizung
Neue Piste

M19

S		Skischule / ski school
S		Salomon-Station
S		Intersport Servicenetwork
i		Info Service
i		Info Tourismus
B		Buckelpiste / mogul
T		Trainingsgelände / tr
K		Kinderland / children area

leichte Abfahrt / gentle slope
mittlere Abfahrt / intermediary slope
schwere Abfahrt / difficult slope
Skiroute / ski route
Langlaufloipe / cross-country track
Nachtloipe / spot-light night track
Winterwanderweg / winter hiking trail
Beschneite Talabfahrten /
snow making system
Fun Park / Half Pipe
Rennstrecke / race track
Pistenrichtung-Stützpunkt

Banff–Lake Louise

Front Side/South Face

1120 Skiable Acres

Mount Whitehorn
6,760ft
2,672m

SKI & RIDE AREA SAFE

To Back Bowls,
Larch Area and
Temple Lodge

Eagle Ridge
2,530m

Summit Platter

West Bowl

SKI Area Boundary

Top of the World — Pack Express

Whitehorn
Lodge
6,750ft/2,057m

Whiskyjack Lodge
5,400ft/1,646m

Lodge of the Ten Peaks

Mount Redoubt
9,502ft
2,902m

Ptarmigan Peak

To Back Bowls,
Larch Area and
Temple Lodge

Temple Lodge

Overview

N W E S

Front Side

Back Bowls

First Guided Tours

Guest Services

Trail Marker

Ptarmigan/Paradise and Back Bowls

1700 Skiable Acres

"The Jewelry Box"

Mount Victoria
11,365ft
3,464m

Ski Area Boundary

The Diamond Mine

Larch Area

900 Skiable Acres

Ski Area Boundary

Larch

Ptarmigan Bowl

Temple Lodge
6,600ft
2,015m

halet-hotel Alta Vista

Alta Vista lounge

73, High Street, Uppermill, Saddleworth, OL3 6AP
Tel. 01457 821200 email. ski@miquelhols.co.uk
Visit our web site at www.miquelhols.co.uk

:i Miquel offers an eclectic range of resorts, from the exclusive Baquiera to the world nowned Whistler. Specialising in en-suite chalet-hotels offering excellent accommodation th wonderful food including wine & coffee, six day ski guiding programme, well timed ghts and direct transfers to resort.

Featured Resort - Whistler. From only £624 including flight, transfer, half board.
y Direct to Vancouver, enjoy the picturesque 2 hour sea to sky transfer, stay in luxurious commodation and ski one of the worlds top resorts for an unbelievable price. Choose tween our chalet-hotel Alta Vista or one of our luxury chalet's.

Enjoy a Whistler ski holiday- The experience of a lifetime

Whistler

RELAX AS HARD AS YOU LIKE

New tailor-made holiday service for USA and Canada

Want to learn to turn for the first time? Or go racing down a black run? Ski with the kids or let us entertain them? However you relax, whether you're a boarder or skier, beginner or expert, Neilson have the perfect holiday for you. And with our new tailor-made service you can choose individual elements of your trip such as flights, accommodation, lift passes, car hire or ski lessons. You can even enjoy a city break at the end of your trip. So if you want even more flexibility from your holiday, call the Neilson tailor-made team. They'll be happy to help.

Call now on 0870 900 5621
or visit www.neilson.co.uk

SAILING   WINDSURFING   SKI & SNOWBOARDING   YACHTING   WATERSKIING   MOUNTAIN BIKING   DIVING   KIDS' CLUBS

SELECTED CHALETS IN VAUJANY

Ski Peak the Vaujany specialists with catered chalets, including the award winning Saskia, the Hotel Rissiou and the prestigious Oisans Apartments.

Outstanding cuisine and a personal service, good childcare and excellent travel arrangements into Grenoble airport.

T: 01428 608070
F: 01428 608071
W: www.skipeak.com

Ski PEAK

Alpe d'Huez

Portes du Soleil

Les Deux Alpes

M27

M28

MONT-BLANC 4810M

GRANDES JORASSES
4208 M

DENT DU GÉANT
4013 M

DÔME DU GOÛTER
4304 M

AIGUILLE DU GOÛTER
3817 M

BLANC DU TACUL
4248 M

HELBRONNER
3466 M

GOÛTER DU
VALLÉE BLANCHE

AIGUILLE DU MIDI
3842 M

GLACIER
DES BOSSONS

LA SALLE À MANGER

AIGUILLE VERTE
4121 M

PLAN DE L'AIGUILLE
2317 M

LES GRANDS MONTETS
3275 M

AIGUILLE DU
3754 M

MONTENVERS
1913 M

MER DE GLACE

GLACIER D'ARGENTIÈRE

ST-GERVAIS

TRAMWAY DU MONT-BLANC

LE BRÉVENT
2525 M

COLONNEY
CHARLANOZ

PLANPRAZ
1999 M

LES HOUCHES

CHAMONIX
1037 M

LES PRAZ
1060 M

LA FLÉGÈRE
1877 M

LA TRAPPE

ARGENTIÈRE
1252 M

LA JOURAINE

LOGNAN
1972 M

BOCHARD
1765 M

LA HERSE
2595 M

GLACIER DU TOUR

LE TOUR
1462 M

CHARAMILLON
1856 M

AIGUILLETTE
DES POSETTES
2201 M

CHALETS
DE BALME

TÊTE DE BALME
2270 M

VALLORCINE
1264 M

DOMAINE DE BALME
2270 M

Chamonix

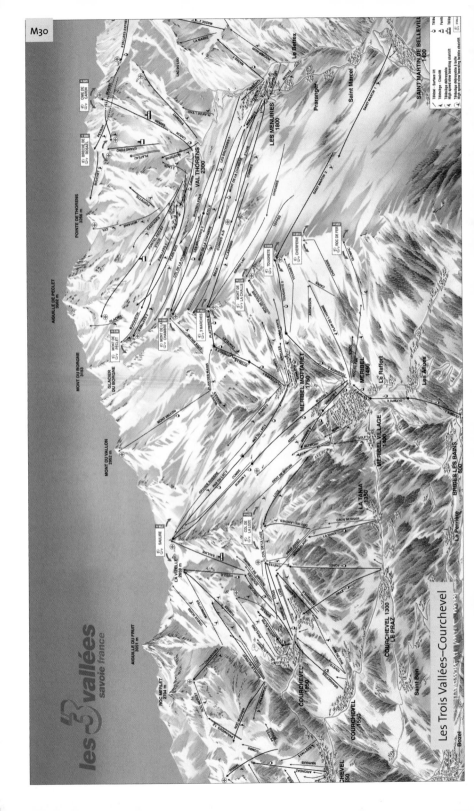

les 3 vallées
savoie france

Les Trois Vallées–Courchevel

Valmorel la Belle, Grand Domaine

Haute Tarentaise

Massif de la Vanoise

Las 3 Vallées

Col du Gollet 1981 m

Le Grand Niélard 2551 m

Col du Mottet 2403 m

Le Cheval Noir 2832 m

Massif des Grandes Rou...

Vallée de

Massif de la Lauzière

Grand Pic 2839 m

LIMITE DE VALIDITÉ DU FORFAIT VALMOREL

2186 m

2650 m

2020 m

1826 m

1520 m

Restaurants

d'Alpage 04 79 09 93 81
Altiporc 04 79 09 86 31
Cogellin 04 79 09 81 58
Pierrafort 04 79 09 97 17

St François Longchamp

Valmorel

La Charmette
Le Pré La Croy

Doucy Combelouvière

DOCUMENT NON CONTRACTUEL

M34

AIG. DE ROSELETTE
2384

CRÊT DU MIDI
1590

LA GIETTAZ

FLUMET

LE PLAN
1200

LE TORRAZ
1930

PRAZ S/ARLY

LE CHRISTOMET
1853

CASSIOZ

AIG. CROCHE
2487

MONT JOLY
2525

LE VILLARD

LE JAILLET
1580

ROCHEBRUNE
1754

LA PRINCESSE

CÔTE 2000

COTE 2000

ALTIPORT

LE PLANAY

MONT JOUX
1958

2353

MONTS ROSSET

LE PLANELLET

MÉGÈVE

MONT D'ARBOIS
1840

LES PETTOREAUX

MONT D'ARBOIS

PONT D'ARBON

VÉVREY

DEMI-QUARTIER

ONMARET

COMBLOUX

L'EPAULE
2112

LES COMMUNAILLES

LE GRATTIER

LES PRAZ

LE PLANAY

LE VERNAY

ST NICOLAS

LE ROSSET

CUPELIN

LE CHATELET

ST GERVAIS
MONT BLANC

Megève

Les Trois Vallées—Méribel

extreme luxury
BY DESCENT INTERNATIONAL

DISCOVER A COLLECTION OF UNIQUE ALPINE CHALETS

paradiski
Savoie – France

M38

Versant SUD / Champagny-en-Vanoise

paradiski
Savoie – France

Discover Paradiski, the massive ski area between the fabulous resorts of La Plagne and Les Arcs in the French Alps, where you can ski 425 exhilarating kilometres of wide, open space - one of the largest and most dramatic ski areas in the world. Served by the super-fast Vanoise Express telecabine, there's even more time for thrills.

Paradiski - pure escapism.

Erna Low   LesArcs   Peisey Vallandry   la Plagne

espace **killy**

le plus bel espace de ski du monde

M40

Val d'Isère–Tignes

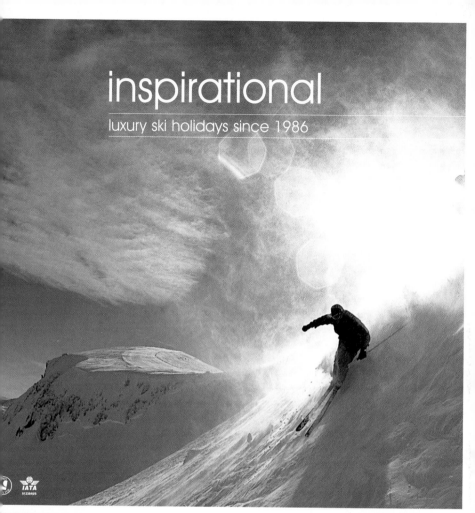

inspirational

luxury ski holidays since 1986

Imagine the ultimate winter holiday...
impeccable service, exquisite food,
outstanding accommodation.
All this and skiing too... perfect.

Scott Dunn

chalets 020 8682 5050
hotels   020 8682 5080
scottdunn.com

Selva / Sella Ronda

VIALATTEA
sciare senza confini

SESTRIERE

SAUZE D'OULX

SANSICARIO

CESANA

CLAVIERE

MONTGENEVRE

www.vialattea.it

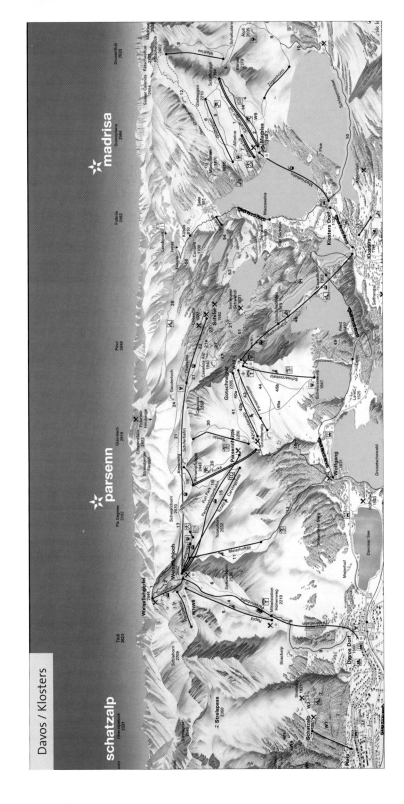

Davos / Klosters

Verbier

Italie
Super-St-Bernard 2350 m.
999 Menouve
98 Plan Syssa
Vichères 1425 m.
Bourg-St-Pierre
Six Blanc 2445 m.
Mont Vélan 3734 m.
Mont Rogneux 3084 m.
Petit Combin 3672 m.
Sembrancher
Bruson 1080 m.
Le Châble 821 m.
Verbier 1500 m.
Pierre-Avoi 2473 m.
Grand Combin 4314 m.
Bec des Rosses 3222 m.
La Chaux 2260 m.
Attelas 2727 m.
Les Ruinettes 2200 m.
Savoleyres 2354 m.
Croix de Coeur 2174 m.
La Tzoumaz Mayens-de-Riddes 1500 m.
Col des Gentianes 2950 m.
Mont-Gelé 3023 m.
Chassoure 2740 m.
Plan-du-Fou 2430 m.
Col des Mines
Vallon d'Arbi
Prarion 1766 m.
Mont-Fort 3330 m.
Tortin 2050 m.
59 Plan-du-Fou
58 Les Fontaines
Tracouet 2200 m.
Dent de Nendaz 2463 m.
Rosablanche 3336 m.
Siviez 1730 m.
Lac de Cleuson 2238 m.
Combatzeline 2238 m.
Nendaz 1400 m.
Veysonnaz 1400 m.
Grepon Blanc 2700 m.
Mont-Rouge 3051 m.
L'Etygeon
64 Greppon Blanc 1
65 Mena
21 Les Chottes
17 Cheminée
14 Combyre
16 Dent
11 Veysonnaz
La Ruinette 3875 m.

St Moritz

Julierpass
Piz Giugia
Piz Julier
3380 m

Piz d'Agnel
Tschima da Flix
Piz Suvretta
Piz Bever
Piz d'Err
Piz Grisch
Piz Güna
Piz Salüver
Corn da Tinizong
Piz Mitgel
Piz Ela
Albulapass

Piz Nair, 3057 m

Fuorcla Griścha
Piz Schlattain
Lej da la Pésch
Fuorcla Schlattain
Val Schlattein
2940 m

Munt da San Murezzan, 2659 m
Clavanova
2040 m

Las Trais/Fuorn
Chantarella Salüver
Alp Salüver
Marguns, 2278 m
Celerina, 1720 m

Corviglia, 2486 m
Salastrains
Alp Laret
Alp Nova
1928–1948
Saluv Runzöl
Chantarella, 2005 m
St. Moritz Dorf, 1856 m

Signal
Trutz
Alp Giop
el paradiso
Chantas
Suvretta
Meierei
Silvaplana
Julierpass
St. Moritz Bad, 1772 m

Val Suvretta

Wengen–Mürren–Grindelwald

Zermatt

M55

SPEN MOUNTAIN

M57

CATHEDRAL PEAK
13,943'

HAYDEN PEAK
13,561'

SUNDECK
11,200'

KRISTI, HYRUP'S AND WALSH'S
SCHEDULED TO CLOSE
AT 3 P.M. DAILY

OTHELLO'S
RAIL RIDERS

WALSH'S
HYRUP'S
KRISTI
LUD'S LANE
NORTH STAR
GENT'S RIDGE
SEIBERT'S
KNOWLTON'S
BACK OF BELL #1
BACK OF BELL #2
BLONDIE'S
PUSSYFOOT
BLAZING STAR
SUMMIT
SUNRISE/SUNSET
HANGING TREE
FACE OF BELL
RIDGE OF BELL
KEITH GLEN
GLADE #1
GLADE #2
GLADE #3
GENTLEMAN'S RIDGE
SHOULDER OF BELL
JACKPOT
BINGO GLADES

PARK
PERCY
BONNIE'S
10,400'
RED'S RUN
F.I.S. TRAIL
F.I.S.
BEAR PAW
S1
INTERNATIONAL
SHORT SNORT
ZAUGG DUMP
PERRY'S PROWL
LAST DOLLAR
RAYBURN'S
SILVER QUEEN
SILVER RUSH
SCHILLER ROAD
RUTHIE'S
SPAR RUN
NORTH AMERICAN
SUMMER ROAD
AZTEC
DIPSEY
PITCH
CORKSCREW
CORKSCREW GULLY
SUPER 8
LIFT LINE
FRANKLIN DUMP
FIS SLALOM HILL
MAGNIFICO
MAGNIFICO ROAD
LAZY 'J' GULLEY
SCHUSS GULLEY
SHADOW MOUNTAIN
TOWER TEN ROAD
5TH AVENUE
NORWAY SLOPE
COMPROMISE MINE
BELL MOUNTAIN
SILVER QUEEN GONDOLA
CORNER
NIAGRA
LITTLE NELL
CLOSED AREA
SUMMER ROAD
TOWER TEN ROAD

CONUNDRUM
VALLEY

WHITE R
NATIONAL

ASPEN MOU
LOCATED IN THE
NATIONAL FOR
UNDER PERMIT
FOREST SERV

TORTILLA
FLATS

PUMP
HOUSE
HILL

SPAR
GULCH

DEER PARK

HANGING
TREE

SUNRISE/SUNSET

BLAZING STAR

GATED TERRAIN: TRAINORS,
RAYBURNS AND BINGO GLADES
ARE AREAS MANAGED ON A DAILY
BASIS. GATES WILL BE OPENED
AND CLOSED DEPENDING ON
SNOW AND WEATHER
CONDITIONS. PLEASE CHECK WITH
SKI PATROL FOR STATUS.

KRISTI, HYRUP'S AND WALSH'S SCHEDULED TO CLOSE AT 3 P.M. DAILY

SKI AREA
BOUNDARY

VATION TOP:	11,212 ft/3,418 m
PICAL RISE:	3,267 ft/996 m
RAIN:	673 acres/273 hectares
GEST RUN:	3 miles/4.83 km
S:	Silver Queen Gondola, 1 high-speed quad,
	1 high-speed double, 2 quads, 3 doubles
CAPACITY:	10,755 riders per hour
RAGE ANNUAL SNOWFALL:	300 inches/762 cm
WMAKING CAPABILITIES:	210 acres/85 hectares
	(33% of area)
EST TERRAIN:	None
RE DIFFICULT TERRAIN:	48%
ST DIFFICULT TERRAIN:	26%
ERT TERRAIN:	26%
SON DATES:	November 25, 2004 – April 10, 2005

ASPEN MOUNTAIN

Trail Map and Terrain Guide

	More Difficult		Closed Area Do Not Enter		Ticketing
	Most Difficult		Ski Patrol		Restaurant
	Expert Only		Restrooms		Picnic Tables
	Extreme Terrain		Public Lockers		Buses
	Lifts		Ski/Snowboard Check		Guest Service Center
	High-Speed Quad		Mountain Photo		TV 16 Live Broadcast
	High-Speed Double		Four-Mountain Sports/D&E	N	NASTAR
	Gondola		Handicapped Access		XC Skiing
	Secondary Lift		Ski/Snowboard School		Snowshoe Trails
	Slow Skiing				Danger
	Flat Catwalk				

THE LITTLE
NELL HOTEL

AJAX TAVERN

RUBEY PARK
TRANSPORTATION CENTER

TOWN OF ASPEN

bols and color codes indicate the relative skiing difficulty
lopes and trails on Aspen Mountain only. For your own
ection, do not start down a trail or slope until you know
egree of difficulty and never ski/ride a CLOSED trail.

TO ASPEN CROSS COUNTRY CENTER

M58

RENDEZVOUS MOUNTAIN 10,450' (3,185 Meters)
Vertical Rise 4,139' (1,261 Meters)

GRAND TETON NATIONAL PARK

APRES VOUS MOUNTAIN
8,481' (2,585 Meters)

Jackson Hole

CROWBAR
PATHFINDER
SARATOGA BOWL
BIG HORN
Symmetry

SHERIDAN BOWL
CRAGS
(ACCESS THROUGH GATES ONLY)

TEEWINOT FACE
MORAN FACE
Twenty-four
Raven Woods
Rock-a-hula

Ashley Ridge
Beaver Tooth
Hanna
Bronco

TETON VILLAGE
ELEVATION 6,311' (1,924 Meters)

CASPER BOWL
(ACCESS THROUGH GATES ONLY)

Sweetwater-Triple Chair
Casper-Bowl-Triple-Chair
Casper-Triple-Chair

Eagle's Rest
Double Chair
Eagle's Rest

Jackson-Face

HEADWALL
9,696' (2,955 Meters)

GONDOLA SUMMIT
9,095' (2,772 Meters)

CIRQUE

Bridger Gondola
Sundance
Slalom

Gros-Ventre

Dicks Ditch

TENSLEEP BOWL
Expert Chutes
Downhill
Broadway
Peanut Brittle
Tensleep Chute

Amphitheater
Lower Tram Line
Elk Alley
Thunder Quad Chair
Tram

Corbet's Cabin

East Ridge
Traverse

LARAMIE BOWL
Flip Point
Alta Chutes
Laramie Traverse

Sublette Quad Chair
Dog Face

RENDEZVOUS BOWL

CHEYENNE BOWL
BERNIES BOWL

CODY BOWL
(ESS THROUGH GATES ONLY)

ROCK SPRINGS BOWL

BRIDGER
TETON
NATIONAL
FOREST

North Colter Ridge
Buffalo Bowl
South Colter Ridge
Rawlins Bowl
Lower Sublette Ridge
Cheyenne Gully
North Hoback
Mouse Creek Quad
Middle Hoback
South Hoback

SKI AREA MAP COVERS
2,500 ACRES
(4 SQUARE MILES)

Riverton Bowl
Gannett
Corbet's Couloir

Vail
Front Side
Back Bowls
Blue Sky Basin

Eagle's Nest™

Wildwood

MidVail

FRONT SIDE

Buffalo's/PHQ

Terrain Park

7 miles (11.3 km)

BACK BOWLS

Two Elk™

Belle's Camp™

BLUE SKY BASIN

Vail

Elegant Resorts

SKI & BOARD

For further information call
01244 897 333 or visit
www.elegantresorts.co.uk/ski

Breckenridge

SKI THE AMERICAN

Dream

THE ORIGINAL
NORTH AMERICAN SKI COMPANY
TAILORING THE FINEST
SKI EXPERIENCES SINCE 1979

TAILOR-MADE SKI AND
SNOWBOARD HOLIDAYS
FROM £499PP

When your carving becomes art...

...you're going to need a very big canvas!

Welcome to skiing in North America!

0870 350 7547
www.skidream.com

ATOL PROTECTED 2856

UNPARALLELED REACH
UNRIVALLED SERVICE
UNMATCHED EXPERTISE

About the authors

Peter and Felice Hardy are both full-time travel writers and acknowledged worldwide as the two most authoritative experts on ski resorts and the ski industry. They met each other in a blizzard on a mountainside in Obertauern in Austria and have spent many years skiing in some 500 resorts around the globe. In an average 18-week winter Peter alone commutes from Britain to some 45 resorts on both sides of the Atlantic. When not up to their knees in fresh powder somewhere in the Alps, the Rockies, or the Andes, you can find them at their rural home in Hampshire with their three children and two dogs, all of whom are expert skiers and accomplished snowboarders (not the dogs).

Peter and Felice are the joint authors of some 20 travel books and they consider *The Great Skiing & Snowboarding Guide 2006* to be by far their most exhaustive work to date, a completely new look at what they consider to be the best resorts in the world. Peter is the ski correspondent of the *Daily Telegraph* and the *Daily Mail* and Felice writes regularly in the *Guardian* and the *Evening Standard*. Their work also appears in an enormous number of lifestyle and travel magazines, including *Condé Nast Traveller* and *Tatler*.

Contents

Cadogan Guides

2nd Floor 233 High Holborn London WC1V 7DN

info@cadoganguides.co.uk

www.cadoganguides.com

Copyright © Peter and Felice Hardy 2005

Cover photograph: TVB Ischgl
Other photographs: p.2 TVB Ischgl; p.3 Stowe,
TVB Ischgl, Lech Zurs; p.24 Avoriaz AgenceNuts,
Avoriaz Pascal Lebeau, Avoriaz AgenceNuts;
p.29 Avoriaz Pascal Lebeau, Avoriaz AgenceNuts,
Avoriaz Christophe Vaury; p.35 Mègeve Nuts.fr,
Courchevel; p. 45 OT Val Thorens/Bruno
Boissère; OT Val Thorens/Gil Marande, Agence
Basile; p.47 Courmayer, Aiat Monte Bianco;
p.51 Verbier; p.53 TVB Ischgl; p.54 OT Méribel/
J.M. Gouédard; TVB Ischgl,TVB Ischgl;
p.56 Stowe; p.59 Jackson Hole/Gilman, Jackson
Hole/McCall; p.61 Jackson Hole/Annerby,
Jackson Hole/McCall, Jackson Hole/Brown;
p.63 Perisher Blue, Stowe; p.64 TVB Ischgl,
Stowe, TVB Ischgl, OT Méribel/J.M. Gouédard

Managing Editor: Natalie Pomier
Editorial Assistant: Nicola Jessop
Research Assistant: Kate Parker
Proofreading: Daphne Trotter
Design: Sarah Gardner
Typesetting: Dorchester Typesetting Ltd

Printed in the Italy by Legoprint

A catalogue record for this book is available
from the British Library

ISBN 1-86011-335-4

The Globe Pequot Press
246 Goose Lane, PO Box 480, Guilford,
Connecticut 06437–0480

The publishers would like to thank the resorts for
the kind provision of maps for this guide.

The author and publishers have made every effort
to ensure the accuracy of the information in this
book at the time of going to press. However, they
cannot accept any responsibility for any loss,
injury or inconvenience resulting from the use of
information contained in this guide.

Please help us to keep this guide up to date. We
have done our best to ensure that the information
in this guide is correct at the time of going to press.
But places and facilities are constantly changing,
and standards and prices in hotels and restaurants
fluctuate. We would be delighted to receive any
comments concerning existing entries or omis-
sions. Authors of the best letters will receive a copy
of the Cadogan Guide of their choice.

Introduction

So what's you favourite resort? It's the question we are always asked and the answer is always the same. We don't have one, we have dozens. Bad ski destinations don't exist – it's just that some are better than others. The greatest ski resort in the world is the one where you find yourself with family or friends on a day when the sky is blue, the snow lies fluffy and deep beneath your feet, and the promise of a fine lunch in some wayside mountain hut dances in the crisp morning air along with a million ice crystals. Some of our greatest days have been spent in world-class wonderlands like Zermatt, Val d'Isère, St Anton, Whistler, and Jackson Hole. Others equally or even more enjoyable have been spent on remote slopes above villages that don't even warrant a lift map of their own.

The trouble with the whole business of skiing and snowboarding is that at every level it is deeply addictive. From the moment you master those first linked turns on the nursery slope, life is never going to be quite the same again. Floating down a white mountainside through deep, light powder induces a loss of gravity and a sensation of physical and spiritual freedom that has no natural parallel. Suspended momentarily between Heaven and Earth, all the worries of life are washed away. It is impossible to think about boss, bank balance, or personal relationships when your brain is entirely focussed on where and when to make the next turn. It is this quality of mental relaxation, coupled with a full glass of physical well-being, that makes a ski or snowboard holiday so much more rewarding than any other.

Where you choose to ski or ride is entirely a matter of personal taste, but with 6,000 resorts in 75 countries it is not always an easy decision. In producing this first edition of *The Great Skiing & Snowboarding Guide* we aim to provide you with informed and detailed assistance.

Together we have spent half a lifetime collecting, collating, and constantly updating information on what we consider to be the most important resorts worldwide. Fortunately for us, the only way to successfully do this is by skiing the runs, staying in the hotels, and lunching and dining in the restaurants, both on and off the mountain. Collectively we have clocked up around five years on snow. Being a ski gypsy has its rewards.

Unlike other guide books, *The Great Skiing & Snowboarding Guide* is heavily opinionated. If we like or dislike a resort for any particular reason, we consider that it is our duty to say so. This is not a policy that pleases every resort director around the world who is used to reading only sugared brochure-style praise rather than a fair and sometimes searching appraisal of his patch. You may not always agree with our opinions, but they do provide a yardstick from which to make your own personal judgement. You will also discover that fine food is a love of ours that lies a close second to snow. Consequently, this book doubles as the Great Ski Food Guide.

Unlike other guide books, we have included the phone number of every ski school, hotel, and restaurant that we mention, along with hotel websites wherever possible. We feel that it's not much good to you to have the name without the means of making a reservation.

The Great Skiing & Snowboarding 2006 Awards

The Great Skiing & Snowboarding Awards are this year judged by a panel of experts including the editors of the guide. These prestigious awards go to the resorts that demonstrate particular merit. Two winners have been selected for each category: one in Europe and the other in North America.

Readers are invited to submit their nominations for The Great Skiing & Snowboarding 2007 Awards. Please send them by email to greatskiing@aol.com

🏆 Ski Resort of the Year
Europe: Val d'Isère, France
North America: Jackson Hole, Wyoming

🏆 Best Family Resort
Europe: Soldeu/El Tarter, Andorra
North America: Vail, Colorado

🏆 Best Small Resort
Europe:Corvara, Italy
North America: Kicking Horse, BC

🏆 Most Chilled Resort
Europe: St Anton, Austria
North America: Sun Valley, Idaho

🏆 Most Improved Resort
Europe: Bansko, Bulgaria
North America: Copper Mountain, Colorado

🏆 Ski Hotel of the Year
Europe: Hotel Rosa Alpina, San Cassiano, Italy
North America: The Four Seasons Resort, Jackson Hole, Wyoming

So what do you two do in the summer? That's the second question we are always asked. When not skiing in the Southern Hemisphere, we write this book, and we would greatly value your assistance. It is simply not possible for us or our team to visit every resort every year. We keep abreast of improvements to resort infrastructure such as new lifts, runs, and ski schools. However hotels, restaurants, and après-ski venues are constantly changing. The bigger the resort, the greater the annual innovations. Please send us your experiences and reviews. We welcome your help on the new, the better – and the worse. Email us at greatskiing@aol.com

The Ski Club of Great Britain icon, which appears in the Top Resort chapters of this guide highlights resorts where you will find a representative of the Ski Club of Great Britain. See page M4 for details of the Ski Club of Great Britain 2006 offer.

The Top Resorts: Andorra

Pal-Arinsal and Ordino-Arcalis

Profile

Friendly area with good nightlife, ideally suited to beginners, intermediates, and families with small children. Atmosphere in Arcalis is more intimate and alpine than in other Andorran resorts

Resorts

The village of Arinsal and the linked ski area of Pal have now joined forces with the valley town of La Massana and the quite separate ski area of Ordino-Arcalis in this corner of Andorra. Together they form the single lift pass region of Vallnord.

It's all part of the dramatic €160 million regeneration of Andorra in recent years as a serious ski destination. It has binned its bargain basement image and the once humble resort of Arinsal, still renowned for its low-cost nightlife, has even managed to twin itself with glitzy Gstaad in Switzerland.

Most skiers and riders choose to stay in Arinsal, an attractive little resort with easy gondola access to some easy beginner and low intermediate pistes.

A sleek 12-person gondola now connects La Massana into the Pal-Arinsal circuit, transforming it into an alternative and convenient place in which to stay. It is also a useful base for the more demanding and much underrated ski area of Ordino-Arcalis, situated a 20-minute drive away up a remote valley.

When the snow is good and the sun is shining the easy, undulating pistes

> ## Essentials
>
> **Altitude**: Pal-Arinsal: 1940m (6,363ft)–2624m (8,609ft) Ordino-Arcalis: 1950m (5,084ft)–2573m (8,442ft)
> **Map**: see page M6
> **Further information**: Pal-Arinsal, t +376 737 000, Ordino-Arcalis, t +376 739 900, *www.vallnord.com* for both
> **Lifts in area**: 38 (3 cableways, 17 chairs, 18 drags) serving 89km of piste
> **Lift pass**: Vallnord adult €120–144, child 6–11yrs €90–108
> **Access**: Toulouse airport 3½hrs, Barcelona airport 3hrs

can match those of any resort. But no amount of investment can give the mountains here the thrilling high-altitude terrain of the Alps.

One of the major reasons to choose the Vallnord region is its proximity to the capital, Andorra La Vella. Here you can shop your heart out on the Avenida Carlemany. Boutiques sell designer names like Versace, Armani, Donna Karan, Ralph Lauren and Dolce & Gabbana at discount prices.

Mountain

Arinsal's skiing begins with a gondola ride from the middle of the village up to the mid-mountain station at 1950m. You can also take a venerable double-chair from the end of the village – or drive up the mountain road.

Lifts from here bring you up towards the 2569m Pic Negre and allow for some smooth novice and easy runs back down to 1950m. In good snow conditions the descent through the trees to the valley is hugely enjoyable.

From the top of Arinsal, a cable-car spans the valley to the Coll de la Botella and the start of the Pal ski area. Runs here are slightly more demanding, but the whole area is best suited to beginners and low intermediates.

Ordino-Arcalis is of considerably more interest for advanced skiers. Its remote position and limited base facilities deter most foreign tourists except the Spanish from across the border. This is where you will find Andorrans skiing at weekends.

A couple of black runs on the front face of the 2552m mountain provide a serious challenge, as well as several long reds served by modern quad-chairs.

Vallnord has a high percentage of riders among its clientele. The FreeStyle Area at Arinsal contains a half-pipe, jumps and other obstacles.

Learn

Arinsal, t +376 737 029, and **Pal**, t +376 737 008, ski schools have lots of experience in teaching foreign skiers. **Arcalis**, t +376 739 600, is the third school.

Children

Babyclub cares for children from 12 months at Comallempla above Arinsal and Els Planells at Pal. **Snowpark** ski kindergarten is from four years at Pal (all t +376 737 014). Ordino-Arcalis has a **Jardin d'enfants**, t +376 739 600.

Lunch

At Arinsal, the midday meal is multicultural. Eat Chinese at **Xina Igloo** and Tex-mex at **MexicObelix**, British burgers at **Panoramix**, and pork 'n' beans in the **Far West**, or pasta at **Bella Italia**, t +376 737 020, for all. **La Borda**, t +376 737 020, at Pal serves chicken tikka, Thai red curry, and authentic Catalan cuisine of sausages and peppery salads. At Ordino-Arcalis **La Coma**, t +376 850 201, specializes in barbecued meat.

Dine

The incomparable **El Rusc**, t +376 838 200, in La Massana is one of the finest restaurants in Andorra. Starters include oyster soup with a hint of saffron, a main course of steamed cod with rosemary, tomato, olives and port wine jus. **La Borda**, mountain restaurant in Pal, t +376 737 020, is also open in the evenings.

Party

Arinsal's nightlife involves sustained drinking in bars such as **El Cau** and **Quo Vadis**. **Surf** and the **Derby** are also popular. In La Massana the action is at **El Cocktail de l'Avi** and **El Xtu en el Complejo Tabola**.

Escaldes-Engordany, on the outskirts of Andorra La Vella, is home to **Caldea**, t +376 800 999, www.caldea.ad, a futuristic spa inspired by Gaudí and made entirely from glass and metal. Inside is a miniature mosque housing Turkish, Roman, Aztec and Icelandic baths, as well as a thermal lagoon.

Sleep

Arinsal:
★★★★Hotel Princesa Park and Princesa Diana, t +376 736 400, www.hotelprincesapark.com, for both, attracts 93 per cent of its visitors from the UK. The establishment is a mélange of eccentric styles, with a bar called The Bog and a room full of kitsch classical statues.
★★★Poblado apartments, t +376 835 122, are recommended.
★★Residencia Janet, t +376 835 088, is a small, family-run apartment building at Erts between Arinsal and La Massana.
La Massana:
★★★★Hotel Rutllan, t +376 835 000, www.hotelrutllan.ad, is the best hotel and ideally situated close to the gondola.

Pas de la Casa

Profile

Frontier town with cheap and unsophisticated nightlife at the foot of Andorra's largest ski area. Suits 20-somethings looking for Ibiza-style partying with piste-bashing

Resort

Over the past four years, Andorra has dramatically reinvented itself as a world-class destination. Pas de la Casa on the French frontier now shares the Grand Valira lift pass with neighbouring El Tarter. The single ski area also extends to Canillo, and outlying Encamp in the middle of the country.

New lifts and hotels abound, but Pas remains largely unchanged, a concrete dormitory with duty-free booze and some of the best skiing in the principality. It is ideal for 20-somethings who want to sandwich some slope time with otherwise uninterrupted inebriation. Other resorts in Andorra are better suited to families and older skiers and riders.

Mountain

Main mountain access from the town is by a choice of chair-lifts that take you up to the ridge overlooking the hamlet of Grau Roig. From here you can either explore the lift-served terrain on either side of the ridge, or take the Cubil quad-chair and work your way across to the wooded slopes above Soldeu. The terrain park is on the Tubs piste at Pas.

Essentials

Altitude: 2095m (6,872ft)–2580m (8,465ft)
Map: see page M5
Further information: Grandvalira, t +376 808 900, www.grandvalira.com
Lifts in area: 58 (4 cableways, 30 chairs, 24 drags) serving 193km of piste
Lift pass: adult €129–186, child 6–11yrs €123–163.50
Access: Toulouse airport 3hrs, Barcelona airport 3hrs

Learn

Pas de la Casa Ski, t +376 871 920, and **Grau Roig,** t +376 872 920, schools both have considerable experience in teaching foreigners to ski and snowboard.

Children

Pas de la Casa, t +376 871 920, and **Grau Roig,** t +376 872 920, crèches care for children from 12 months to three years. Grau Roig also offers an introduction to skiing from three years.

Lunch

Llac de Pessons, t +376 759 015, near Grau Roig, is the best mountain restaurant in Andorra. It serves fine grilled meat and has dramatic views across the lake.

Dine

Chez Paulo, t +376 855 596, offers pizzas and French cuisine. **El Carli,** t +376 855 211, is renowned for its mussels and trout with almonds. **Refugo Calones,** t +376 856 040, has fondues and raclette. **La Tagliatelle,** t +376 750 656, serves pizza and pasta dishes.

Party

Milwaukee is the largest and most crowded bar, while the **Underground, Mulligans Irish Pub, KYU Disco-pub, Havana, The Pirate** and **Kamikaze Surf** all provide serous competition. **The Outdoor Centre** offers paintballing in the snow.

Sleep

****Hotel Himalaia Pas**, t +376 735 515, *www.hotansa.com*, has a pool, sauna and a gym.
****Aparthotel Alaska**, t +376 756 056, was new last season. It is situated in the upper part of town and houses La Tagliatelle restaurant.
****Hotel Font d'Argent**, t +376 739 739, *www.fontdargent.com*, is an attractive boutique hotel.
***Hotel Cristina**, t +376 736 800, is a friendly hotel at the top of town.

Soldeu-El Tarter

Profile

This is the skiing capital of the new Andorra, a village with considerable charm that provides much the most agreeable base in the principality. It suits families and others in search of creature comforts and good, easy skiing. Nightlife is hectic but less brash than in neighbouring Pas de la Casa

Resort

Soldeu is a smart little resort just over the pass from Pas de la Casa, but a world

away in style. The ribbon of stone-and-wood buildings stretching along the main road to adjoining El Tarter has undergone a physical and social transformation.

New lifts and hotels abound, and this winter the resort sees the opening of a five-star with a four-storey spa centre of the kind of proportions you might only otherwise encounter in Ancient Rome.

Like other Andorran resorts, Soldeu is still popular with budget skiers, but you have to ask yourself for how much longer. The new Andorra, recipient of lavish €160 million funding in recent years, is in danger of losing sight of why it was ever popular in the first place – low prices.

Soldeu is part of the Grand Valira, a single ski pass area that includes Pas de la Casa, El Tarter, and the ancient community of Canillo further along the valley. The skiing can also be accessed by a long gondola from the town of Encamp in the middle of the country. In recent years the snow record across Andorra has been excellent.

Mountain

The skiing area is reached by a gondola or chair-lift from Soldeu and by the same choice from El Tarter. From the mid-mountain station of Espiolets, lifts fan out in both directions towards Pas and further down the valley to Canillo.

The undulating terrain above and below the treeline is best suited to beginners and intermediates. However the substantial size of the Grand Valira should keep more advanced skiers fully occupied. Off-piste opportunities down through the trees are particularly good and new snow does not get tracked out within hours.

Recent lift improvements include the €5.3 million 10-person gondola, which takes skiers up the mountain from El Tarter. Bosc Fosc (it means Dark Forest) is a new blue piste leading down to Soldeu.

Learn

Soldeu's ski school, t +376 890 591, deservedly has the reputation of being the best in Andorra and one of the top half-dozen learning academies in Europe.

Much of this is due to the enthusiasm of its veteran teaching director, Yorkshireman Gordon Standeven. Some 100 of the 240 instructors are native English speakers. **Canillo, t** +376 890 691, and **El Tarter, t** +376 890 641, also have good reputations. All of them become very crowded over February half-term.

Children

Mickey Snow Club in Soldeu, **t** +376 890 591, **Canillo, t** +376 890 691, and **El Tarter, t** +376 890 641, cares for non-skiing children aged two to three years and the **Jardin de Neige** ski kindergarten from three years.

Lunch

Roc de les Bruixes, t +376 890 696, above Canillo is warmly recommended along with refurbished **Solanelles, t** +376 759 008, in the Encamp sector. **Gall de Bosc, t** +376 890 607, above Soldeu has mountain Catalan cuisine and spectacular views. Try *faves* (warm bean, pea and ham

salad) or *Trinxat* (bubble-and-squeak topped with slithers of black pudding).

Dine

Soldeu's Cort de Popaire, t +376 851 211, is renowned for its grilled lamb and steaks. **La Fontanella, t** +376 871 787, in the Hotel Piolets serves pasta and pizza. **La Llar del Artesa, t** +376 851 078, just out of town at Bordes d'Envalira, has good-value Catalan mountain dishes. **Borda de l'Horto, t** +376 851 622, outside El Tarter, serves grilled meat and fish and is popular with the locals.

Party

Caldea spa, **t** +376 800 999, in Escaldes-Engordany on the outskirts of the capital Andorra La Vella has a giant 68°C thermal pool and is one of the largest spas in Europe.

Soldeu's main street is lined with shops, bars and restaurants. Nightlife is frenetic all season but, unlike brasher Pas, revellers here are not confined to the 16–25 age bracket. Venues include the **Avalanche, Roc Bar, Aspen, Ice Berg, Pussy Cat** and the popular **Villager** bar. Most atmospheric is **Fat Albert's**, a cavernous barn with videos and live music.

Sleep

All accommodation can be booked through a central reservations office, **t** +376 890 501.
Soldeu:
★★★★★**Sport Hermitage, t** +376 870 500, *www.sporthotelcomplex.com*, under the same ownership as the Sporthotel, is the resort's first five-star opening this winter. It is linked internally to a colossal four-storey spa with 14 treatment rooms and a giant basement pool.

****Sport Village**, t +376 870 500, *www.sporthotelcomplex.com*, has a vast lobby with hacienda-style atrium. The wood-panelled bedrooms are large and comfortable. The main mountain access gondola is actually in the hotel.

****Hotel Piolets Park**, t +376 872 787, *www.ahotels.ad*, has comfortable rooms and contains a steak house, swimming pool and gym.

****Hotel Himalaia Soldeu**, t +376 878 515, *www.hotansa.ad*, has been refurbished and has a recommended buffet-style restaurant.

Canillo:

****Hotel Font d'Argent**, t +376 753 753, *www.fontdargent.com*, in the old town centre, is new.

***Hotel Bonavida**, t +376 851 300, is a cosy place with a swimming pool.

El Tarter:

****Hotel Llop Gris**, t +376 751 515, *www.llopgris.com*, is convenient for the slopes, with squash courts and a swimming pool.

****Hotel Nordic**, t +376 739 500, *www.grupnordic.ad*, has a wood-and-stone decor and an entrance hall dominated by a Rolls-Royce.

***Hotel del Tarter**, t +376 802 080, *www.hotel-eltarter.com*, has a well-regarded restaurant.

***Hotel del Clos**, t +376 851 500, *www.grupnordic.ad*, is ski-in ski-out and modern.

Encamp:

****Hotel Guillem**, t +376 832 133, 500m from the Funicamp lift, has a heated pool, sauna and hot tub.

The Top Resorts: Austria

02

Alpbach

Profile

Typically Tyrolean village with loads of Alpine charm. Family-friendly with good intermediate skiing and some surprisingly varied off-piste possibilities

Resort

Alpbach is officially the prettiest village in Austria, a small friendly resort with enduring charm. The overriding key to its success is that in the early 1970s the wise village fathers took an ice-axe to future development plans in their determination to avoid the commercial path taken by some of its Tyrolean rivals.

Daily life still revolves around the church, which is backed by two buttressed village inns where, between services, drink has been taken and gossip exchanged for 1100 years.

Mountain

With the exception of one nursery slope in the middle of the village, the skiing takes place a five-minute free bus ride away on the Wiedersbergerhorn. Runs here are more challenging than in the better-known nearby resorts. Alpbach still has plenty of novice terrain, but the skiing is best suited to intermediates. Experts will find enticing off-piste opportunities adjacent to the marked runs. The local piste map understates the potential of the region, which includes lifts in the hamlet of Inneralpbach and in neighbouring Reith. The former FIS downhill course tracks the fall-line of the gondola, which provides main access to the Wiedersbergerhorn.

Alpbach has two terrain parks and is a past host of the World Pro Tour. Plans are on the drawing board to link the Alpbach Valley with the adjoining Wildschönau.

Learn

Alpbach-Inneralpbach Ski School, t +43 (0)5336 5515, has a fine reputation and Alpbach Aktiv Ski School, t +43 (0)5336 5351, is the alternative.

Children

Both ski schools operate all-day ski kindergartens for children from four years, with free helmets provided.

Lunch

The choices include **Berggasthaus Hornboden**, t +43 (0)5336 5366, near the top of the access gondola, **Gasthof Almhof** by the Wiedersbergerhorn mid-station, t +43 (0)5336 5379, and **Schihütte Böglalm**, t +43 (0)664 916 1743, at Inneralpbach.

Dine

Try **Gasthof Wiedersbergerhorn**, t +43 (0)5336 5612, at Inneralpbach, or **Jo Margeiter's Hotel Post**, t +43 (0)5336 5203. **Gasthaus Rossmoos**, t +43 (0)5336 5305, and **Gasthof Jakober**, t +43 (0)5336 5171, both have fine food.

Party

The liveliest bars are the **Messnerwirt**, the **Postalm** and the **Waschkuchl**, but Alpbach can be quiet mid-week.

Sleep

★★★★**Romantikhotel Böglerhof, t** +43 (0)5336 52270, *www.boeglerhof.com*, is ski-in ski-out, with a swimming-pool and spa.
★★★★**Hotel Galtenberg, t** +43 (0)5336 5610, *www.galtenberg.com*, has a new restaurant, a children's play area and a swimming-pool.
★★★★**Hotel Alphof, t** +43 (0)5336 5371, *www.hotel-alphof.at*, is in a peaceful location.
★★★**Hotel Post, t** +43 (0)5336 5203, *www.tiscover.at/post.alpbach*, is in the heart of the village, with a popular bar and restaurant.
★★★**Gästehaus Larch, t** +43 (0)5336 5875, *www.gaestehaus-larch.at*, offers B&B or self-catering.

The Gasteinertal

Profile

The skiing is suited to all standards, especially for those wanting to cover a high mileage. The resort is also ideal for non-skiers who like walking, spas and eating

Resort

The ancient watering-hole of Bad Gastein is the original and still the most important of the four resorts dotted along this scenic valley which sits on a giant reservoir of bath-temperature thermal water, a 90-minute drive from Salzburg. The Romans, the Habsburgs, and later the Nazis, viewed it as the ideal holiday hideaway. An impressive 23 million litres of this curative water bubble up each day from 17 springs. This is piped to the leading hotels and to public indoor and outdoor baths. You can enjoy the surreal experience of soaking at the foot of the pistes while snow falls around you.

Johann Strauss and Franz Schubert were both inspired to compose here. Hotel Mozart is named not after the supreme maestro – but after his mother, who was a regular guest. Visitors should be aware that the hotels, an interesting mix of revamped imperial and gleaming modern, are set on extraordinarily steep gradients. If you don't like walking in ski boots, choose your base with care. However, it is possible to leave equipment overnight close to the lifts. The town centre is flanked by smart boutiques and expensive jewellery shops that rely largely for their living on the high number of wealthy non-skiing customers who visit Bad Gastein throughout the year.

Bad Hofgastein, further along the valley, is a modern and spacious resort built at a

Essentials

Altitude: 840m (2,756ft)–2686m (8,810ft)
Map: see page M9
Further information: t +43 (0)6432 3393 0, *www.gastein.com*
Lifts in area: 44 (11 cableways, 18 chairs, 15 drags) serving 201km of piste. Skiverbund Amadé region 276 (30 cableways, 74 chairs, 172 drags) serving 860km of piste
Lift pass: Skiverbund Amadé adult €159–171, child 6–15yrs €81–87, both for 6 days
Access: Salzburg airport 90mins. Station in Bad Gastein

less challenging angle. It shares the main Alpine ski area but is more suited to families and those who enjoy cross-country skiing, snowshoeing, and walking. It also has good ice rinks, a sophisticated sports centre, and its own assortment of thermal pools and accompanying health treatments.

Dorfgastein is contrastingly different – a sleepy farming settlement by the entrance to the valley. It has considerable rural charm as well as some of the best skiing in the area, which stretches across the shoulder of the 2027m Kreuzkogel to link with the village of Grossarl.

Sportgastein, at the head of the valley, is a high-altitude ski area rather than a resort, a lift station built on the site of a medieval gold mine that was briefly reopened by Hermann Goering in the Second World War in the hope of finding fresh natural resources to fund the war machine of the Third Reich. Health-conscious visitors should pay a visit to the nearby Healing Galleries, a naturally heated underground chamber reached by a 2km train journey into the mountain. The Gastein resorts are included in the regional Amadé lift pass.

Mountain

The valley is best suited to high-mileage intermediates looking for a large ski area with plenty of challenges. Advanced skiers and riders should head to Sportgastein and Graukogel, which both have fine off-piste runs in the right conditions. Each resort has its own beginner slopes as well as a good nursery area in the Angertal. However, a general lack of ski convenience does not commend it as an area for absolute novices.

More than €30 million has been spent in recent years on improving the lift system and other mountain facilities including snowmaking in the valley.

Bad Gastein and Bad Hofgastein share the main Stubnerkogel/Schlossalm ski area, reached respectively by gondola and funicular. This complex of constantly updated lifts on both sides of the Angertal is a pleasant intermediate playground with lots of varied blue and red runs both above and below the treeline – and no overtly demanding surprises. When the slopes get crowded on high season weekends wise skiers head across Bad Gastein to the steeper and more peaceful Graukogel ski area, reached by a two-stage chair-lift.

Dorfgastein has the pick of the skiing in the Gasteinertal, although this is not apparent at village level. A modern gondola from just above the village takes you up to the 2000m ridge. From here you can either enjoy the choice of easy blue or more challenging sweeping red runs back towards Dorfgastein, or you can head over to Grossarl in the neighbouring valley.

Sportgastein is considerably higher – the base is at 1590m and the top at 2686m – and usually provides good skiing when cover is thin elsewhere. However, it is a bleak place when the weather suddenly closes in. Ski buses link all the areas. Taxis are plentiful, but expensive.

Learn

Bad Gastein, t +43 (0)6434 2260, **Bad Hofgastein, t** +43 (0)6432 6339, and **Dorfgastein, t** +43 (0)6433 7538, are the three main ski and board schools. Small and friendly **Schlossalm, t** +43 (0)6432 3298, operates from Bad Hofgastein and **Dorf Aktiv, t** +43 (0)6433 20048, has a strong following in Dorfgastein.

Guiding is available through the ski schools or from **L. Kravanja, t** +43 (0)6434 2941, **F. Sendlhofer, t** +43 (0)6434 2879, and **Hans Zlöbl, t** +43 (0)6434 5355.

Children

The geography of the valley with its separate ski areas does not make the Gasteinertal a good choice for a family holiday with small children. The three main ski schools operate ski- and non-ski kindergartens for children from three years with lessons from four years. **Hotel Grüner Baum**, t +43 (0)6434 2516, has a crèche for guests. The **Fun Centre** at the Stubnerkogel lift has a kids' cinema, table tennis, a climbing wall and a ball pond. **Restaurant Angertal 1180**, t +43 (0)6432 7475, in the futuristic Angertal Ski Centre, offers supervised meals for children aged three to 12 years.

Lunch

The Gasteinertal is dotted with welcoming huts serving typical mountain fare. **Aeroplanstadl**, t +43 (0)6432 8603, on the home run to Bad Hofgastein has to be visited not just for its *Apfelstrudl* but for its extraordinarily original *Damen* and *Herren*. We also recommend **The Jungerstube**, t +43 (0)6433 7370, and the **Wengeralm**, t +43 (0)6433 7257, as well as the cosy **Waldgasthof Angertal**, t +43 (0)6432 8418, for its homemade *Gulaschsuppe*.

Dine

Restaurant Thom, t +43 (0)6434 5101, at the Villa Solitude is a favourite of ours, along with the **Fischerstüberl**, t +43 (0)6434 4505, **Orania Stüberl**, t +43 (0)6434 2717, and the **Mediterran**, t +43 (0)6434 30004, by the waterfall. **Gisela & Co**, t +43 (0)6434 225350, and the **Bahnhofrestaurant**, t +43 (0)6434 2166, are also recommended. **Bellevue Alm**, t +43 (0)6434 3881, and the **Hofkeller**, t +43 (0)6434 203 7245, both specialize in fondue. The restaurant in **Hotel Grüner Baum**, t +43 (0)6434 2516 has

won awards as one of the outstanding restaurants in the region.

Party

The bars at and near the Felsentherme outdoor baths are the focal point as skiers return from the slopes. The action moves on to a huge assortment of bars and clubs in town. **Haeggbloms**, **Oslags**, **Silver Bullet**, **Eden's Pub** and the **Gatz Music Club** are among the most popular. **Ritz** in the Salzburgerhof has regular live music, while the British-owned **Tannenburg Hotel** near the top of town claims to have the cheapest beer. Badhofgastein has five discos and a dozen bars.

Sleep

Bad Gastein has an unusually wide range of hotels, pensions and student hostels as befits a resort that caters for wealthy middle-aged bankers, euro-skint British snowboarders, and everybody in between. Some arduous uphill walking is unavoidable although the ski bus operates between 8am and 6pm daily. **Bad Gastein:**
- ★★★★**Arcotel-Elizabethpark**, t +43 (0)6434 2551, *www.arcotel.at*, is modern, central and has an indoor pool and wellness centre.
- ★★★★**Hotel Wildbad**, t +43 (0)6434 3761, *www.hotel-wildbad.com*, is much nearer the lifts and recommended for its half-board cuisine that includes tea as well as dinner.
- ★★★★**Hotel Grüner Baum**, t +43 (0)6434 2516, *www.grunerbaum.com*, is a 19th-century imperial hunting lodge in its own rural hamlet, just outside the resort. The stylish hotel has a spa and a children's club, and attracts a celebrity crowd.
- ★★★★**Villa Solitude**, t +43 (0)6434 5101 is a magnificently restored 19th-century

town house near the casino and the waterfall.

★★★**Hotel Mozart, t** +43 (0)6434 2686, *www.hotelmozart.at*, is conveniently located and reasonably priced.

Bad Hofgastein:

★★★★★**Grand Park Hotel, t** +43 (0)6432 6356, *www.grandparkhotel.at*, is the smartest address as well as being piste-side.

★★★★**Österreichischer Hof, t** +43 (0)6432 62160, *www.oehof.at*, is warmly recommended.

★★★★**Hotel Alte Post, t** +43 (0)6432 62600, *www.bergwelthotels.at*, is a traditional hotel in the town centre.

Dorfgastein:

★★★★**Hotel Römerhof, t** +43 (0)6433 7777, *www.roemerhof.com*, has a pool and spa.

★★★★**Dorfhotel Kirchenwirt, t** +43 (0)6433 7251, *www.kirchenwirt-gastein.at*, is friendly and family run.

★★★**Gasthof Steindlwirt, t** +43 (0)6433 7219, *www.steindlwirt.com*, has a cheerful children's playroom and provides everything from baby baths to bottle warmers.

★★★**Landgasthof Gasteiner Einkehr, t** +43 (0)6433 7248, *www.einkehr.com*, is situated close to the main lift.

★★★**Gasthof Mühlbachstüberl, t** +43 (0) 6433 7367, *www.muehlbachstueberl.com*, has a reputation for fine food.

Ischgl

Profile

The resort is surrounded by beautiful scenery and a large intermediate ski area. It boasts the biggest terrain park in Europe as well as some of the liveliest après-ski. This is not a place for people on a tight budget

Resort

Ischgl is considered by the Germans to be Austria's second most important resort behind St Anton. The two ski centres, which are only 45km apart, developed along parallel lines during the early 20th century. But St Anton found international fame while Ischgl remained largely the private haunt of ski-tourers.

Today it has a sophisticated lift system, and the old farming village houses a collection of sophisticated hotels and cavernous bars. An airport-style pedestrian walkway, cut through the rock around which the town was built, provides easy access to pistes, shops and restaurants – regardless of where you choose to stay.

If St Anton is the skiing capital of Europe, then Ischgl – against strong opposition from its rival – wears the après-ski crown and waves the sceptre of a never-empty Stein of beer. The resort is linked on piste across the Swiss frontier to the duty-free village of Samnaun. It is also connected to the small resort of Galtür by a free shuttle bus during the day.

Essentials

Altitude: 1400m (4,592ft)–2864m (9,394ft)
Map: see page M10
Further information: t +43 (0)5444 5266, *www.ischgl.com*
Lifts in area: 42 (2 funiculars, 3 cableways, 21 chairs, 16 drags) serving 205km in Ischgl-Samnaun
Lift pass: VIP (covers Ischgl/Samnaun) adult €161.50–177.50, child €106.50. Silvretta Regional (covers Galtür, Ischgl, Kappl, Samnaun, See) adult €179–208, child 7–15yrs €118.50. All for 6 days
Access: Innsbruck airport 90mins, Zurich airport 2½hrs. Landeck station 30km, with frequent buses from station

Mountain

The ski area has been hugely improved in recent years with lifts being upgraded and pistes widened on an annual basis. Main mountain access is by three swift gondolas from different parts of town that take you up to Idalp, the mid-mountain station at 2320m that forms the hub of the lift system. Lifts extend up to and over the ridge which forms the territorial frontier with Switzerland. Some of the best skiing is at Palinkopf, which at 2864m is the highest point, reached by two chair-lifts from Idalp. Long red and black runs sweep down into the beautiful Fimbatal on the edge of the ski area. Some of the most rewarding off-piste runs here can be found off the Gampenbahn chair.

However, whenever the day dawns bright and sunny it seems that almost everyone in the resort heads over to Samnaun to indulge in a Swiss mountain lunch and fill their rucksacks with duty-free cigarettes, drink, perfume and electrical goods at supposedly bargain prices.

The return journey begins with a ride on what was the world's first double-decker cable-car. Multiple chair-lifts – Ischgl had the first eight-seater – help to ferry skiers homeward. However, one shortfall of the resort are the final runs down to the village. These are narrow and steep – too difficult from many of Ischgl's habitual clients, but that does not stop them trying and falling in the path of others.

This is a serious snowboarding resort. Boarders Paradise at Idjoch has a half-pipe and over 30 obstacles and is one of the largest in the Alps.

Learn

The **Ischgl School, t** +43 (0)5444 5257, has plenty of good English speakers, but don't expect to pick up any cutting-edge technique from most of the locally born instructors.

Children

The **Ski Kindergarten, t** +43 (0)5444 5257, at Idalp is run by the ski school and provides all-day care with lunch for children aged from three years. Ski lessons start at four years.

Lunch

A new restaurant opens this season in the giant glass-and-steel Pardatschgrat complex at the top of the gondola. **Panorama-Restaurant Alp Trida Sattel**, t +41 (0)81 868 5117, has the recommended Gourmet-Stüberl'n on the first floor. **La Marmotte** in the Bergrestaurant Alp Trida, t +41 (0)81 868 5221, and **Bodenalp, t** +43 (0)5444 5285, in the Fimbertal are also suitable escapes from the ubiquitous self-services.

Across the frontier, the **Samnaunerhof**, t +41 (0)81 861 8181, is good for *Rösti* and **Hotel Chasa Montana, t** +41 (0)81 861 9000, has great pizzas.

Dine

Paznauner Stube, t +43 (0)5444 600, in the Trofana Royal, has a Michelin star. Martin Sieberer, former Austrian Chef of the Year, specializes in gourmet local cuisine. **Feuer & Eis, t** +43 (0)5444 591956, and **Salz & Pfeffer, t** +43 (0)5444 591956, both have good pizzas. **Gasthaus Alt-Paznaun, t** +43 (0)5444 5380, has a comprehensive menu of regional and international dishes.

Hotel Madlein, t +43 (0)5444 5226, serves light Austrian food inspired by the Far East. **The Goldener Adler, t** +43 (0)5444 5217, is known for its baked fresh trout. The rustic **Heidelberger Hütte**, t +43 (0)5444 5418, **Bodenalp, t** +43 (0)5444 5285, and **Vider Alp, t** +43 (0)5444 5385, are mountain huts offering fondue evenings.

Party

By 4pm Germans and Austrians are in full swing, dancing on table-tops to jaded euro anthems and New Wave Oompah while downing litres of beer and shots of schnapps. Go-go girls clad in minimalist parodies of Austrian national dress are an intrinsic part of Ischgl's tea-time scene.

The **Schatzi Bar** in the **Hotel Elisabeth**, **Kitzloch**, **Kuhstall** at the **Sporthotel Silvretta**, **Trofana Alm** and **Niki's Stadl** form the hardcore of this sozzled spectacle. Those still sober enough (and others, too) then tackle the famous toboggan run on Mondays and Thursdays. The track from the top of the Silvrettabahn is a gruelling 7km with a vertical drop of nearly 1000m.

Remaining energy is expended on the late night dance floors of **Pacha** in the **Hotel Madlein**, **Feuer & Eis**, **Hölle**, and **Trofana Arena** in the **Trofana Royal**.

Every winter the resort holds its Top of The Mountain open-air pop concerts at Ischgl Dorfarena featuring some big stars.

Sleep

★★★★★**Trofana Royal**, t +43 (0)5444 600, *www.trofana.at*, has an extensive wellness centre – anti-ageing is the speciality.

★★★★**Hotel Madlein**, t +43 (0)5444 5226, *www.madlein.com*, is a minimalist hotel with Oriental overtones.

★★★★**Hotel Elisabeth**, t +43 (0)5444 5411, *www.ischglelisabeth.com*, is a popular resort meeting-place.

★★★★**The Goldener Adler**, t +43 (0)5444 5217, *www.goldener-adler.at*, is in a 350-year-old building with an ultra-modern interior and a wellness centre.

★★★★**Hotel Jägerhof**, t +43 (0)5444 513650 is conveniently placed for the underground walkway and has a friendly atmosphere.

★★★★**Hotel Seiblishof**, t +43 (0)5444 5425, *www.seiblishof.com*, has a separate children's restaurant.

Kitzbühel

Profile

Architecturally the most beautiful ski resort in Austria, with lots of Alpine charm, scenic intermediate skiing, and lively après-ski

Resort

This attractive silver-mining medieval town, set against the dramatic backdrop of the Wilder Kaiser mountains, has been a ski centre ever since local hero Franz Reisch managed to acquire a pair of long wooden skis from Norway in 1893.

His antics on the Kitzbüheler Horn above the town incited a combination of curiosity and amusement that quickly spread across the Tyrol.

Each January the town is the setting for the Hahnenkamm Downhill, the Blue

Essentials

Altitude: 760m (2,493ft)–2,000m (6,562ft)
Map: see page M12
Further information: t +43 (0)5356 777, *www.kitzbuehel.com*
Lifts in area: 56 (9 cableways, 29 chairs, 18 drags) serving 150km in linked area
Lift pass: Area pass covers Jochberg, Kitzbühel, Kirchberg, Pass Thurn. Adult €147.50–170, child 6–15yrs €85, both 6 days
Access: Salzburg airport 1½hrs, Innsbruck airport 2hrs, Munich airport 2½hrs. Station in Kitzbühel

Riband event of the Word Cup calendar, which attracts a Bacchanalian frenzy among dedicated supporters who party the day and the night away in the pedestrianised centre with its buttressed buildings and delicate frescoes.

This annual flood of publicity gives the erroneous impression that Kitz is for experts only. In fact, as well as having superb nursery slopes, the whole area is best suited to strong intermediates – with few serious piste challenges for experts.

Mountain

The 2000m Hahnenkamm is the main ski area and it is best reached by a six-person gondola from the centre of town. However, at busy times it can make sense to employ one of a number of alternative routes. The Fleckalmbahn gondola near the neighbouring town of Kirchberg takes you directly to the top of the mountain. The Wagstäst chair-lift at Jochberg now provides a back-door into the system, as does the Pengelstein gondola that rises from a car park beyond Kirchberg on the main road to Aschau. A new gondola this season rises from here to the top of Gampen above Westendorf, effectively linking Kitzbühel into the giant SkiWelt circuit.

Last season saw the opening of the long-awaited gondola spanning the valley between Pengelstein and Wurzhöhe. This allows Kitzbühel-based skiers to complete the Ski Safari (just follow the elephant signposts) to Jochberg and Pass Thurn in both directions without a bus link.

The Kitzbüheler Horn, the town's second mountain, is on the far side of the valley and reached from the centre by regular ski bus. A gondola followed by a cable-car brings you to the summit. But the views from top are better than the skiing.

However, the presence of a half-pipe, boardercross course, and a terrain park makes the Horn of major interest to riders and twin-tippers.

The third small ski area of Aurach, reached by a ten-minute bus ride, has only one lift. But in the crowded high season this is where you will find the locals after a fresh snowfall.

A new eight-person gondola links the valley town of Mittersill to the Pass Thurn area.

Learn

We do not consider that any of Kitzbühel's ski schools maintain the high standard that you might expect of a resort of this pedigree. **Rote Teufel/The Red Devils**, t +43 (0)5356 62500, is the original and still the best of the bunch. However, together with its rivals, it too suffers from overcrowding and a consequent fall-off in service at peak times.

The others are **Hahnenkamm Egger**, t +43 (0)5356 63177, **Jochberg**, t +43 (0)5355 5342, **Kitzbüheler Horn**, t +43 (0)5356 64454, **Total**, t +43 (0)5356 72011, **Wagstätt**, t +43 (0)5355 20152, and **Aurach**, t +43 (0)5356 65804. **Alpinschule Kitzbühel**, t +43 (0)5356 73323 takes groups off-piste.

Children

All the ski schools give group lessons and all (except Wagstätt) have ski kindergartens. **Anita Halder**, t +43 (0)5356 75063, provides private childcare.

Lunch

Sohnbühel, t +43 (0)5356 62776 on the Hahnenkamm has a good sun terrace and great food. **Hochkitzbühel**, t +43 (0)5356 6957 230, at the top of the Hahnenkamm gondola, serves typical Austrian dishes and also has a popular sun terrace.

Staudachstub'n, t +43 (0)5357 2084 on the main run down to the Fleckalm gondola is recommended; **Streifalm**, t +43 (0)5356 64690 is famous for its homemade ravioli. **Seidlalm**, t +43 (0)5356 63135 on the Hahnenkamm is renowned for its cheese dishes and has great views of the resort.

Dine

Rosengarten, t +43 (0)5357 2527, in the Hotel Taxacherhof at *Kirchberg*, is one of the finest restaurants in the Tyrol. Acclaimed chef Simon Taxacher has created his own outstanding style of Austrian nouvelle cuisine. **Hotel zur Tenne**, t +43 (0)5356 64444, in Kitzbühel's Vorderstadt, is known for its fresh trout and is a personal favourite of ours. **Huberbräu-Stüberl**, t +43 (0)5356 65677, serves simple dishes at reasonable prices. **La Fonda**, t +43 (0)5356 73673, in the Hinterstadt, serves Mexican food. **Lois Stern**, t +43 (0)5356 74882, has Asian fusion cuisine.

Party

Kitzbühel's long-established British pub, **The Londoner**, takes central stage as the après-ski venue as soon as the lifts close for the day. However it now has a serious British rival in **Brass Monkeys**. Others include the tiny **Waschkuchl**, **Stamperl**, **S'Lichtl**, **Jimmy's**, **Funferl**, **Bergsinn** and **Barrique**. The coolest nightclub is **Club Take Five**. **Olympia** and **Royal** are the alternatives. **Aquarena leisure complex**, t +43 (0)5356 64385, has a 25m pool and offers a full range of spa treatments.

Sleep

★★★★★**Romantikhotel Tennerhof**, t +43 (0)5356 63181, *www.tennerhof.com*, was originally an elegant Tyrolean country house.

★★★★★**Hotel Weisses Rössl**, t +43 (0)5356 625410, *www.weisses-roessl.com*, is the other sophisticated hotel. Its facilities include the two-storey Cheval Blanc spa with an indoor pool and pool-bar.

★★★★**Hotel Goldener Greif**, t +43 (0)5356 64311, *www.hotel-goldener-greif.at*, is warmly traditional.

★★★★**Hotel Jägerwirt**, t +43 (0)5356 64067, *www.hotel-jaegerwirt.at*, has its own Irish pub, Sigi's Sport Bar.

★★★★ The converted hunting lodge of **Schloss Lebenberg**, t +43 (0)5356 6901, *www.tiscover.com/schloss-lebenberg*, on the outskirts, has a medieval-style interior complete with four-poster beds, and a health centre.

★★★★**Hotel Zur Tenne**, t +43 (0)5356 64444, *www.hotelzurtenne.com*, in the town centre, is a comfortable designer hotel. Many bedrooms have open fireplaces, and some suites have whirlpools and steam baths.

★★★★**Villa Mellon**, t +43 (0)5356 66821, *www.villa-mellon.at*, is a private house formerly owned by the banking family. Decorated like a hunting lodge, it offers haute cuisine and beautiful views.

★★★★**Golfhotel Bruggerhof**, t +43 (0)5356 62806, outside town, is recommended for the quality of its food.

Lech and Zürs

Profile

Attractive traditional village on the banks of a river, with a large collection of sumptuous four- and five-star hotels. It is a resort for comfort-seekers who prefer a flattering piste to a tricky challenge. Not for anyone on a tight budget

Essentials

Altitude: Lech 1450m (4,756ft), Zürs 1720m (5,642ft)–2450m (8,036ft)
Map: see page M11
Further information: t +43 (0)5583 2161 229, *www.lech-zuers.at*
Lifts in area: 33 (4 cableways, 18 chairs, 11 drags), serving 110km in Lech/Zürs and 82 lifts serving 280 km in Arlberg ski area
Lift pass: Arlberg Ski Pass adult €175–189 for 6 days, child 7–14yrs €105–113 for 6 days, 6yrs and under €10 for whole season
Access: Innsbruck airport 2hrs, Zurich airport 2½hrs. Langen station 17km by postbus

Resort

The little village of Zürs lies at a snow-sure high altitude on the Flexen Pass in the Arlberg Region, which looks more towards Switzerland than to the rest of Austria and is best reached by car or train from Zurich. It shares its 33-lift ski area with larger Lech in the pretty little valley on the far side of the pass. The circuit is included in the regional Arlberg ski pass.

This is one of the birthplaces of modern skiing. Victor Sohm, a founding father of the original technique, gave the first lessons in Zürs on the open slopes of the Trittkopf and Hexenboden exactly 100 years ago.

His international clients were mainly wealthy British, Swiss and Germans wanting to learn the new sport and relax in beautiful surroundings. In this respect, not much has changed.

Today, the two villages are the most exclusive resorts in Austria with six five-star hotels between them. Both attract a higher age group of visitors than nearby St Anton.

For many years, Princess Caroline of Monaco has been the unofficial patron of Zürs, while Princess Diana was her counterpart in Lech. The Dutch and Jordanian royal families, as well as former tennis champion Boris Becker and Russian president Vladimir Putin, are numbered among the fans of the region.

The terrain here is markedly easier than in St Anton, with plenty of benign cruising runs best suited to intermediates. As a result, large numbers of skiers and riders based in St Anton come here for the day. However, overcrowding is not an issue.

Zürs is no more than a huddle of smart hotels and precious little else. Hotels, restaurants and the slopes are set on either side of the little river that meanders through the centre, past a magnificent onion-domed church.

Oberlech, on the higher summer pastures, provides a traffic-free environment. Winter access is only by cable-car and luggage is cunningly transported to your hotel through a network of tunnels beneath the piste.

Zug, a tiny hamlet reached along a narrow lane through the woods from Lech, offers an alternative tranquil base that is linked into the lift system.

The galleried road across the Flexen Pass is prone to the occasional closure due to avalanche danger. Skiers wanting to explore further afield can join the St Anton ski area by taking a 20-minute bus ride to Alpe Rauz. It is possible for experts to ski home off-piste – with a guide – from the top station of the 2811m Valluga.

Mountain

Zürs and Lech provide a pleasant playground of three mountains that can be skied in a clockwise direction only. The more challenging slopes are at the Zürs end of the circuit and on the Kriegerhorn and Zuger Hochlicht. The easiest runs are on the sunny meadows surrounding Oberlech.

From Lech, the circuit begins with a ride up the twin Rüfikopf cable-cars.

A combination of easy pistes takes you over the Schüttboden and Hexenboden and down into Zürs.

From Zürs, you take either the Seekopf or Zürsersee chairs followed by the Madloch chair for the long itinerary run down to Zug and on towards Lech.

It is worth noting that unpatrolled ski itineraries are marked by orange triangles and either orange or black broken lines. Most of these runs are so well skied that they are effectively pisted, but you should check the small print of your insurance policy to ensure that you are covered.

In good snow conditions the area has sufficient challenge for accomplished skiers. Zürs has the steep black Sonnenberg, but otherwise the most challenging routes are all marked as itineraries.

Off-piste skiing through the woods is forbidden for environmental reasons and anyone caught doing is liable to forfeit their lift pass.

Beginners have good nursery slopes at Oberlech as well as a dedicated area behind the church in Lech. The Boarderland terrain park on the Schlegelkopf in Lech has a half-pipe, a quarter-pipe and a wide range of obstacles.

Learn

For a resort that has produced a clutch of ski champions, the ski schools at **Lech**, t +43 (0)5583 2355, **Oberlech**, t +43 (0)5583 200 and **Zürs**, t +43 (0)5583 2611, are disappointing. If you come away with the impression that jobs are passed from father to son, you may not be far wrong.

It is a reflection of their financial status that some 80 per cent of visitors to Zürs and 50 per cent to Lech choose to take private rather than group lessons. What they get for their money is year-to-year continuity, but this is by no means the

home of the kind of cutting-edge technique that wins medals for Austria. Guiding can be arranged through the ski schools and heli-skiing with **Wucher Heli-skiing**, t +43 (0)5583 2950.

Children

Children six years and under ski for €10 for the whole season. **Kinderland Oberlech**, t +43 (0)5583 2007, takes children aged from four-and-a-half years. **Miniclub Lech**, t +43 (0)5583 3530, provides a programme of play and skiing for children from three years. **Little Zürs Kindergarten**, t +43 (0)5583 2245 15, also takes children from three years.

Lunch

The pick of the lunch spots are attached to hotels. **Alter Goldener Berg**, t +43 (0)5583 2205 at Oberlech is recommended, along with the nearby **Bergkristall**, t +43 (0)5583 2678, **Montana**, t +43 (0)5583 2460, and the **Sonnenburg**, t +43 (0)5583 2147. In Zürs, **Gasthof Seekopf**, t +43 (0)5583 2143, and the **Trittalm**, t +43 (0)5583 2831, are also rated.

Dine

Most of the best restaurants are in the hotels. These include the **Post**, t +43 (0)5583 2206, **Arlberg**, t +43 (0)5583 2134, and **Brunnenhof**, t +43 (0)5583 2349 in Lech, as well as the **Rote Wand**, t +43 (0)5583 3435, in Zug, the **Albona Nova**, t +43 (0)5583 2341, and **Chesa** in Hotel Edelweiss, t +43 (0)5583 2662, in Zürs.

Other restaurants in Lech include tiny **Hüs Nr. 8**, t +43 (0)5583 33220, opposite the Post, serving grilled meat and light regional cooking with a superb wine list. **Fux**, t +43 (0)5583 2992, offers Asian fusion dishes. **Don Enzo Due**, t +43 (0)5583 2225, has great pizzas.

Party

In Lech, the evening gets under way with drinking at the ice bar outside the **Tannbergerhof** and 5pm tea-dancing inside the hotel. The **Schneggarei** bar by the Schlegelkopf lift catches the crowd as they come off the slopes. Later on the action switches to **Klausur** in the **Almhof Schneider**, **Fux** and **Pfefferköndl**. **Archiv** is a new bar open until 2am. You can dance at the **Tannbergerhof**, **Hotel Krone** and **Egon Zimmerman's Scotch Club**.

In Zürs, **Vernissage** in **Skiclub Alpenrose**, the bar in the **Hotel Hirlanda**, and **Kaminstübel** in the **Schweizerhaus** are all popular.

Disco Zürsserl in **Sporthotel Edelweiss** is the late-night venue.

A collective taxi service called 'James' runs until 4am and will take you home to your hotel for a flat fee.

Sleep

*****Schneider-Almhof**, t +43 (0)5583 3500, *www.almhof.at*, has rooms decorated with natural materials, wooden furniture and stone-made accessories.

*****Hotel Gasthof Post**, t +43 (0)5583 22060, *www.postlech.com*, is small but sumptuous and attracts an older clientele.

*****Hotel Arlberg**, t +43 (0)5583 2134, *www.arlberghotel.at*, is on the edge of the piste and has comfortable suites and a gourmet restaurant.

****Sporthotel Kristiania**, t +43 (0)5583 2561, *www.kristiania.at*, is a boutique hotel founded by 1952 Olympic champion Othmar Schneider.

****Hotel Pension Haldenhof**, t +43 5583 24440, *www.haldenhof.at*, is friendly and family-run.

****Romantik-Hotel Krone**, t +43 (0)5583 2551, *www.ronantikhotelkronelech.at*, is

on the riverbank opposite the church and has a Moroccan-influenced spa.

****Hotel Tannbergerhof**, t +43 (0)5583 3313, *www.tannbergerhof.com*, is a principal resort rendezvous.

Oberlech:

****Hotel Sonnenburg**, t +43 (0)5583 2147, *www.sonnenburg.at*, is the best hotel in the hamlet. Facilities include an indoor swimming-pool and two saunas with 'fog grottos'.

Zug:

****Hotel Rote Wand**, t +43 (0)5583 3435, *www.rotewand.com*, has a swimming-pool, indoor golf, wellness centre and a minimalist apartment wing.

Zürs:

*****Thurnhers Alpenhof**, t +43 (0)5583 21910, *www.thurnhersalpenhof.com*, is our favourite and a member of Leading Hotels of the World.

*****Hotel Lorünser**, t +43 (0)5583 22540, *www.loruenser.at*, is worthy of its rating.

*****Hotel Zürserhof**, t +43 (0)5583 25130, *www.zuerserhof.at*, continues to have a popular following.

****Arlberghaus**, t +43 (0)5583 2258, *www.arlberghaus.com*, has a roof-top curling-rink.

****Sporthotel Edelweiss**, t +43 (0)5583 26620, is convenient for the nightlife.

Mayrhofen

Profile

Large intermediate ski area with a well-regarded ski school make it a good place to learn and to take children. Nightlife is noisy. This is not a resort for advanced skiers and riders or for people looking for skiing convenience

Essentials

Altitude: 630m (2,066ft)–2500m (8,202ft)
Map: see page M14
Further information: t +43 (0)5285 6760,
    www.mayrhofen.at
Lifts in area: 49 in Zillertal 3000 (8
    cableways, 17 chairs, 27 drags) serving
    175km of piste, 590km in the whole
    Zillertal area
Lift pass: Zillertal Superskipass
    adult €168, child 6–15yrs €84, both for
    6 days
Access: Innsbruck airport 1hr, Munich and
    Salzburg airports 2½hrs. Station in resort

Resort

The once quaint village of Mayrhofen
was one of the original migration points
for British skiers back in the 1970s and
early 1980s. In those days, Austria in
general and the Tyrol in particular
attracted more British skiers than
anywhere else in the world.

The mass market has long since
deserted its rivals in favour of the more
demanding slopes of France, but curiously
the allure of Mayrhofen has never faded.
An unfettered nightlife, reasonable
accommodation, as well as good tuition
and childcare gloss over the fact that this
is one of the worst resorts for skiing
convenience in the Alps – with heavy
high- season queues to go up and down
the main access lift. Its big plus point is
that outlying hamlets have been
incorporated into the ski area branded as
Zillertal 3000, making it the largest
complex in the valley and, regardless of
the vagaries of nature, you can ski on the
glacier at Hintertux, at the end of the
valley, throughout the year. However,
overcrowding on the glacier can be a
serious problem when Mayrhofen
and other resorts in the region are short
on snow.

The Zillertal Superskipass covers all 11
different villages in the valley. Buses are
frequent and a free train goes down the
valley to Zell am Ziller and to the mainline
station at Jenbach.

Mountain

Mayrhofen's own ski area is split
between two mountains. Beginners must
make their way to the edge of town to the
Ahorn, a 2000m peak served by a 25-year-
old cable-car. This was due for
replacement this season, but work may
not be completed in time because of
construction difficulties. The top is given
over to snow-sure nursery runs. The 5.5km
black Ebenwald piste from the top also
gives more accomplished skiers and riders
a reason to explore Ahorn.

The main skiing takes place on higher
slopes on the other side of the valley,
reached by the modern Penkenbahn
gondola from the centre of town.
Unfortunately the topography dictates
that there is no home run and skiers and
riders must return by lift at the end of the
day. Alternative access is provided by
gondolas from Finkenberg and
Vorderlanersbach further up the valley,
and from Schwendau further down the
Zillertal. You can – snow conditions
permitting – ski back down to these bases
but must then take a usually overcrowded
peak hour bus back to Mayrhofen. The
resort gets a minus point for skiing
convenience.

The terrain park, with a 150m half-pipe
and served by a dedicated four-person
chair, has been voted the best in the
German-speaking Alps.

If you can't leave your work behind on
holiday or need to commune with iTunes,
it is worth noting that one of the first
wireless hotspots in a ski area is situated
on Penken.

Learn

Five schools with over 100 instructors between them cope with the annual influx of predominantly beginner and lower intermediate clients as well as a few experts who are drawn to the recommended **Mount Everest** ski school, **t** +43 (0)5285 62829. Its charismatic owner, Peter Habeler, climbed Everest without oxygen in 1978. His school teaches all standards and he personally guides off-piste tours with overnight stops in a mountain hut. The other schools are: **Roten Profis**, **t** +43 (0)5285 63800, **Mayrhofen Total**, **t** +43 (0)5285 63939, **Mike Thanner/Mayrhofen 3000**, **t** +43 (0)5285 64015.

Children

Back in the 1970s, Mayrhofen pioneered the first ski kindergarten in the Alps. The resort maintains its long tradition of childcare, which remain as good as any in the Alps. **Wuppy's Kinderland**, **t** +43 (0)5285 63612, takes children from three months to seven years. **Roten Profis**, **t** +43 (0)5285 63800, looks after children from 12 months, and **Max Rahm's Mayrhofen Total**, **t** +43 (0)5285 63939, accepts children from two years.

Lunch

Some 28 huts are dotted on the mountain-side. **Ahornhütte** on the Ahorn is owned by ex-World Cup racer Uli Spiess. **Josef's Biohütte**, **t** +43 (0)5285 62309, has organic fare. **Schneekarhütte**, **t** +43 (0)5285 64940, is renowned for its fresh prawns and salmon steaks. On Penken, the **Penkentenne**, **t** +43 (0)5285 62115, and **Hilde's Skitenne**, **t** +43 (0)664 3857 574, are recommended. **Grillholfalm**, **t** +43 (0)664 3126 426, by the terrain park, has good pizzas. **Christa's Skialm**, **t** +43 (0)5285 63033, and **Schiestl's Sunnalm**, **t** +43 (0)5282 4182, are both popular.

Dine

Most visitors to Mayrhofen eat at their hotels. **Ciao**, **t** +43 (0)5285 63299, is a friendly Italian. **Café Dengg**, **t** +43 (0)5285 64866, has fine pizzas. The modern **Sport Bar Grill**, **t** +43 (0)5285 6705, in Hotel Strass serves international food until 2am. **Bruggerstube**, **t** +43 (0)5285 63793, and the **Eckartauerhof**, **t** +43 (0)5285 62435, is atmospheric.

Party

Après-ski starts up the mountain at Penken before spreading to the **Ice Bar** at the foot of Penken gondola and the new **Speak Easy** in the **Sporthotel Strass**, **Happy End**, **Niki's Schirmbar**, **Mo's** and the **Piccadilly Pub**. **Schlüsselalm** and **Sport's Arena** are the discos.

The **Erlebnis Mayrhofen** swimming pool complex is one of the leading waterparks in this corner of Austria.

Sleep

*******Elisabethhotel**, **t** +43 (0)5285 6767, *www.elisabethhotel.com*, at the entrance to the village, sets the pace. This is a charming, traditional Tyrolean hotel with a fine pool and spa.

******Fun & Spa Hotel Strass**, **t** +43 (0)5285 6705, *www.hotelstrass.com*, is next to the Penken lift.

******The Waldheim**, **t** +43 (0)5285 62211, *www.waldheim.at*, is recommended.

******Hotel Berghof**, **t** +43 (0)5285 62254, *www.berghof.cc*, has three indoor tennis courts.

******Alpenhotel Kramerwirt**, **t** +43 (0)5285 6700, *www.kramerwirt.at*, was established by the Kröll family in 1624 and is stylishly traditional.

*****Hotel-Gasthof Perauer**, **t** +43 (0)5285 62566, *www.perauer.at*, is a converted Tyrolean hotel. It offers regional, international and vegetarian cuisine.

Neustift and the Stubaital

Resort

Neustift with its ornately frescoed church is the most important community in this broad valley between Innsbruck and the Brenner Pass to Italy. It lies between Fulpmes and the remote glacier. The villages of Schönberg, Mieders, and Telfes are dotted along the valley and act as further bed-bases.

Mountain

Apart from the glacier, situated a 20-minute drive away, Neustift has its own little ski area that stretches over undulating pastures. Schlick 2000 at Fulpmes is in a sheltered bowl on the 2230m Sennjoch. Both areas are ideal for families with young children.

The Stubai Glacier is served by twin gondolas that form part of a network of 21 lifts serving 110km of piste. It is a popular out-of-season training area for racers that now closes from the middle of June until the last week in September.

Learn

Neustift has two ski schools: **Neustift Stubaier Gletscher, t** +43 (0)5226 8108, and **Neustift Olympia, t** +43 (0)5226 3682. Fulpmes has the **Stubai ski school, t** +43 (0)664 333 2222.

Essentials

Altitude: Fulpmes 937m (3,074ft)–2200m (7,218ft), Neustift 1000m (3,281ft)–3200m (10,499ft)
Further information: Fulpmes, t +43 (0)5225 62235, *www.stubai.at*, Neustift, t +43(0)5226 2228, *www.neustift.com*
Lifts in area: 24 (9 cableways, 16 chairs, 34 drags) serving 149km
Lift pass: Superskipass Stubai adult €162–198, child 10–14yrs €105.30–128.70
Access: Innsbruck airport 15mins, Munich airport 1½hrs

Children

The **Micky Mouse Ski Club, t** +43 (0)5226 8108, on the glacier, is for kids from four years to learn to ski while having fun. Non-skiers from three years are cared for in the slope-side **Micky Mouse Clubhouse**.

Lunch

Fulpmes has 10 self-service restaurants on the mountain at Schlick 2000. There are five eateries on the **Stubai Glacier, t** +43 (0)5226 8141.

Dine

In Neustift, **Grillstube, t** +43 (0)5226 3147, has great steaks. **Café Anni Platzl, t** +43 (0)5226 3613, has good pizzas. Restaurants in Fulpmes include the hip **Kla4vier, t** +43 (0)5225 63744, which serves Tex-Mex.

Party

Bierfassl and **Harry's Pub** in Neustift are popular meeting places. The **Mutterberg, Hully Gully**, and **Rumpl** discos are the late-night spots. In Fulpmes, **Café Corso, Platzwirt, Jump-In** and the **Dorfalm** provide the action.

Sleep

*****Hotel Jagdhof & Spa**, t +43 (0)5226 2666, *www.hotel-jagdhof.at*, in Neustift, is one of Austria's finest spa hotels.

****Alpenhotel Tirolerhof**, t +43 (0)5226 3278, *www.alpenhoteltirolerhof.com*, is family-run, with a wellness centre and a traditional Tyrolean interior.

****Sporthotel Neustift**, t +43 (0)5226 2510, *www.sporthotelneustift.at*, has a wellness suite and an entire floor for non-smokers.

****Alpenhotel Mutterberg**, t +43 (0)5226 8116, *www.stubaital.at/mutterberg*, is a comfortable hotel for keen skiers who prefer to stay at the base of the Stubai lifts.

****Alpenhotel Tirolerhof**, t +43 (0)5225 62422, *www.tirolerhoffulpmes.at*, in Fulpmes has been recently refurbished.

****Sporthotel Cristall**, t +43 (0)5225 634240, *www.sporthotelcristall.at*, is also recommended.

Niederau

Resort

Niederau is a modest traditional village in the Wildschönau region, which includes the surrounding Tyrolean communities of Thierbach, Oberau, and Auffach. Together they have acted as a winter playground for overseas visitors for 70 years. Much of the appeal has been based on lower-than-average prices and benign but beautiful slopes. Plans have been approved to connect the Wildschönau to the neighbouring and perceivedly smarter Alpbach valley, a move that should be beneficial to both.

Mountain

All the villages are linked by free ski-bus. Main mountain access from Niederau is by a modern eight-person gondola. From the summit of the Markbachjoch you have a choice of three pisted and one unpisted run back to the valley.

Auffach has the pick of the skiing. A gondola takes you through the woods to a network of five drag-lifts and a chair. Oberau has eight short drags, and skiing in Thierbach is confined to just two drag-lifts. Riders congregate in Auffach, which has a terrain park with a half-pipe.

Learn

Niederau has two ski and board schools: **Aktiv**, t +43 (0)5339 2701, and **Wildschönau**, t +43 (0)5339 2200. English is widely spoken in both.

Children

Niederau crèche cares for children from two years. The Wildschönau ski school runs **Bobo's Kinderclub** for two- to six-year-olds.

Lunch

In Niederau, **Anton-Graf-Hütte**, t +43 (0)5339 2547, and **Markbachjochalm**, t +43 (0)5339 8202, offer wholesome fare. In Oberau, try **Achentalalm**, t +43 (0)5339

8578, and **Zauberwinkel**, t +43 (0)5339 8126.

Dine

Hotel Austria, t +43 (0)5339 8188, houses the most popular restaurant in Niederau. There are two Italian eateries, **Ferrari**, t +43 (0)5339 2733, in Niederau, and **Italia 90**, t +43 (0)5339 8109, in Oberau.

Party

Bobo's Heustadl at the gondola base in Niederau and the **Gruttn-Bar** in Auffach draw skiers off the slopes long before the lifts stop for the day. **Sno Blau** in **Hotel Tirolerhof** and the **Starchentstüberl** are the hotspots in Oberau. The **Cave Bar**, **Alm Pub** and **Dorfstub'n** provide late-night entertainment in Niederau.

Sleep

Niederau:
★★★★**Hotel Sonnschein**, t +43 (0)5339 8353, *www.harmony-hotels.com*, has an indoor swimming-pool, playroom and good-sized bedrooms.
★★★★**Hotel Wastlhof**, t +43 (0)5339 8247, *www.tiscover.at/wastlhof*, is less conveniently located on the cross-country skiing track. It has a new spa.
Oberau:
★★★★**Hotel Silberberger**, t +43 (0)5339 8407, *www.silberberger.at*, is charming and traditional.
★★★**Hotel Tirolerhof**, t +43 (0)5339 81180, *www.hoteltirolerhof.at*, is ski-in ski-out and the main resort meeting place.
★★★**Gasthof Kellerwirt**, t +43 (0)5339 8116, *www.kellerwirt.alpinerose.net*, is a former monastery.
Auffach:
★★★**Auffacher Hof**, t +43 (0)5339 8837, *www.auffacherhof.at*, is in the village centre.

Obergurgl-Hochgurgl

Profile

Charming high-altitude family resort with magnificent glacial scenery, a long ski season that stretches to Easter and beyond, cheerful après-ski and good ski-touring

Resort

Obergurgl is a traditional village set around its church at 1930m in the high Ötz Valley close to the frontier with Italy, an easy drive from Innsbruck. Back in 1931, Swiss aviation pioneer Auguste Piccard first put Obergurgl on the ski map when he landed his hot-air balloon on the Gurgler-Ferner glacier after achieving a world altitude record of 16000m. In a triumphant rescue operation, local guide Hans Falkner led the explorers across to crevasses to safety and glory. More recently, Oetzi, the 5,300-year-old hunter whose perfectly preserved body was found on one of the 23 glaciers above the resort, has brought renewed fame to the valley.

Essentials

Altitude: 1930m (6,330ft)–3080m (10,104ft)
Map: see page M15
Further information: t +43 (0)5256 6466, *www.obergurgl.com*
Lifts in area: 23 (4 cableways, 12 chairs, 7 drags) serving 110km of piste
Lift pass: adult €169–190, child 9–16yrs €110, both 6 days
Access: Innsbruck airport 1½hrs. Ötztal station 54km, with regular buses

Higher Hochgurgl is a collection of ski-in ski-out hotels perched on the mountainside and linked by gondola to Obergurgl. Much of the appeal of the joint resort lies in secure snow conditions that last from November to the end of April. Obergurgl has a few shops and an open-air ice rink.

Mountain

This is an easy family ski area with few challenges on piste but plenty of opportunities for guided excursions into magnificent terrain leading up to the Italian frontier.

The skiing takes place in three topographically separate, but lift-linked, areas spread across the north-western side of the Ötztal. Obergurgl's main Festkogel sector is reached either by a gondola at the beginning of the village or by a two-stage chair-lift from the centre. From the top you can reach two further lifts and together these give access to a pleasant choice of blue and red cruising runs as well well as a couple of steeper blacks.

From mid-mountain, the 3.6km Top Express gondola spans two valleys to reach Hochgurgl. The glacial terrain here is much more extensive with plenty of long, mainly blue, descents. The two-stage Hochgurglbahn gondola allows swift access from the valley to the modest collection of drag-lifts and chairs – including a new six-seater – and a continuous vertical drop of 1500m.

The third smaller area of Gaisberg lies to the south of Obergurgl and is reached by chair-lift from the village centre. Gaisberg offers delightful blue runs as well well as three more challenging reds between the trees, served by the swift six-person Steinmannbahn chair. A glorious off-piste route begins from the Hohe Mut and ends up near the Schönwieshütte.

Learn

Obergurgl, t +43 (0)5256 6305, and **Hochgurgl**, t +43 (0)5256 6265, schools have been successfully teaching the basics to international visitors for generations, but don't expect to learn cutting-edge technique here.

Children

Bobo's Kinderclub, t +43 (0)5256 6305 provides care for non-skiing children from three years. The ski school accepts children as young as three years. The resort allows children aged nine and under to ski for free – a higher age limit than in many other resorts. A number of hotels operate their own crèches, usually free of charge. These include **Alpina**, **Austria**, **Bellevue**, **Bergwelt**, **Crystal** and **Hochfirst** as well as **Hotel Edelweiss & Gurgl** and **Top Hotel Hochgurgl**.

Lunch

Hohe Mut Häusl, t +43 (0)699 1141 4045, is a popular lunch venue with magnificent views at the top of the Gaisberg sector. It is reached by chair-lift but the only route down is a unclassified itinerary run. Less accomplished skiers are advised to take the lift back down. The **Schönwieshütte**, t +43 (0)664 4428 113 is a touring refuge renowned for its *Gulaschsuppe* and *Kaiserschmarren* (plum pancakes).

David's Skihütte, t +43 (0)5256 6332, at the bottom of the Steinmannlift, is a popular lunch venue with good food and lively après-ski. **Festkoglalm**, t +43 (0)5256 6370, and **Nederhütte**, t +43 (0)5256 6425, are also recommended.

In Hochgurgl, the **Wurmkoglhütte**, t +43 (0)5675 6100, offers traditional mountain fare.

Dine

With only a handful of exceptions, restaurants in both Obergurgl and Hochgurgl are located within the hotels. **Dorf-Alm, t** +43 (0)5256 6570, offers regional dishes and cheese fondue. **Pizzeria Romantika** in the Hotel Madeleine, **t** +43 (0)5256 63550, and **Pizzeria Belmonte, t** +43 (0)5256 6533, both have good pizzas.

Party

The **Nederhütte** and other mountain restaurants start the ball rolling with music and dedicated drinking in the late afternoon. Later on the **Josl-Keller** has the best atmosphere. **Krump'n'Stadl** is crowded and noisy. **Austria-Keller** in Obergurgl and **African Bar** in Hochgurgl have dancing and stay open into the early hours.

Sleep

Obergurgl:
★★★★**Hotel Deutschmann, t** +43 (0)5256 6594, *www.hotel-deutschmann.com*, at the entrance to the village, is warmly recommended. It is named after the family that own it.
★★★★**Hotel Austria, t** +43 (0)5256 6282, *www.austria-bellevue.com*, dates back to 1561.
★★★★**Hotel Crystal, t** +43 (0)5256 6454, *www.hotel-crystal.com*, is a monster of a building, but extremely comfortable.
★★★★**Hotel Bergwelt, t** +43 (0)5256 6274, *www.hotelbergwelt.com*, is a traditional hotel with great ambience and a good pool.
★★★★**Hotel Edelweiss & Gurgl, t** +43 (0)5256 6223, *www.edelweiss-gurgl.com*, in the centre, is one of the resort's original hotels.

★★★★**Hotel Jenewein, t** +43 (0)5256 6203, *www.hotel-jenewein.com*, offers exceptional half-board cuisine.
★★★★**Hotel Madeleine, t** +43 (0)5256 63550, *www.hotel-madeleine.com*, has been recently refurbished.
★★★**Haus Schönblick, t** +43 (0)5256 6251, *www.tiscover.at/schoenblick.obergurgl*, has large rooms and excellent breakfasts.
Hochgurgl:
★★★★★**Top Hotel Hochgurgl, t** +43 (0)5256 6265, *www.tophotelhochgurgl.com*, leads the field in Hochgurgl and has a crèche and health club.
★★★★**Hotel Riml, t** +43 (0)5256 6261, *www.hotel-riml.com*, is on the piste. Owner Gerold Riml has turned the hotel into a well-balanced energy zone with a colour scheme designed for relaxation, and strategically-placed 'energy pyramids'.
★★★**Alpenhotel Laurin, t** +43 (0)5256 6227, *www.laurin.at*, serves first-rate food.

Obertauern

Profile

Purpose-built resort with convenient snow-sure skiing. Not suitable for non-skiers or committed party-goers

Essentials

Altitude: 1740m (5,708ft)–2313m (7,587ft)
Further information: t +43 (0)6456 7252, *www.obertauern.com*
Lifts in area: 26 (1 cableway, 18 chairs, 7 drags) serving km of piste
Lift pass: adult €162.50–174.50, children up to 15yrs €81.50, both for 6 days
Access: Salzburg airport 90km. Radstadt station 20km

Resort

When snow cover is light elsewhere in Austria, this high-altitude ski area has virtually guaranteed conditions. Its position on a mountain pass in the Niedere Tauern mountain range, 90km south of Salzburg, attracts a favourable micro-climate.

Until local ski enthusiasts 'colonized' the pass in the early 1930s the only building was Hotel Tauernpasshöhe. During the intervening decades a straggle of hotels and bars has sprung up along the roadside to give Obertauern more of an American ski resort atmosphere.

Mountain

The peaks on both sides of the road rise to over 2200m and the lifts complete a circuit that can be skied in either direction. There is plenty of novice terrain close to the village centre as well as a couple of testing blacks. The area provides plenty of variety as well as some sensational off-piste.

Learn

Competition among teaching academies is healthily high. Of the five main schools **Krallinger, t** +43 (0)6456 7258, is most favoured by tour operators. **CSA Willi Grillitsch, t** +43 (0)6456 7462, **Frau Holle, t** +43 (0)6456 7663 84, **Koch, t** +43(0)6456 72285, and **Top, t** +43 (0)6456 7678, are worthy contenders. **Blue Tomato, t** +43 (0)6456 20036, is for boarders. **Vertical, t** +43 (0)6456 7594, is the guiding company.

Children

Petzi-Bär crèche, t +43 (0)6456 7252, cares for children from three. **CSA Willi Grillitsch** has a non-skiing kindergarten,

t +43 (0)6456 7462. All the ski schools run ski kindergartens.

Lunch

The resort has over 20 enticing restaurants. **Lürzer Alm, t** +43 (0)6456 7289, and **Hochalm, t** +43 (0)6456 7318 522 have good food. **Almrausch, t** +43 (0)6456 7407, is also open in the evening. Also try **Flubachalm, t** +43 (0)6456 7217, and **Edelweiss Hütte, t** +43 (0)6456 7653.

Dine

Bacchuskeller, t +43 (0)6456 7561, and **Restaurant Sailer, t** +43 (0)6456 7328, are both recommended. **Edelweiss-Stüberl, t** +43 (0)6456 7245, and **Wagner Stub'n, t** +43(0)6456 7256, have reasonable prices.

Party

The **Edelweisshütte** and the **Achenrainhütte** are lively in the late afternoon. **Der Turm** and **Römerbar** are popular. The **Lürzer Alm** is central to the evening action, which progresses to **Monkey's Heaven** in Hotel Rigele Royal.

Sleep

Sporthotel Edelweiss, t +43 (0)6456 7245, *www.luerzer.at*, is situated beside the village nursery slope.

Sporthotel Cinderella Spa & Resort, t +43 (0)6456 7589, *www.cinderella.at*, is decorated true to its fairytale name. The dining room has low turreted walls painted with pastel frescoes.

Alpenhotel Römerhof, t +43 (0)6456 72380, *www.roemerhof.at*, has a traditional interior and a piste-side terrace.

Sportinghotel Marietta, t +43 (0)6456 7262, *www.marietta.at*, is a lavish place at the foot of the slopes.

Saalbach-Hinterglemm

Profile

These adjoining villages share an extensive ski circuit with confidence-building slopes, reliable snow cover and a modern lift system. Great for ski-to-lunchers and night-owls, but not for anyone who is early-to-bed

Resort

The villages of Saalbach and Hinterglemm, which lie in the Glemm Valley a short drive from Zell am See, are attractive bases for some of the best skiing in Austria outside the Arlberg. This fact has not been lost on generations of mainly Dutch and British visitors who return here each year in numbers proportionate to their respective economies. Euro-free British skiers and riders are currently in ascendance.

The 10 peaks that rise on both sides of the valley are lined with an impressive array of modern lifts that can be skied equally well in both directions.

Essentials

Altitude: 1000m (3,280ft)–2096m (6,877ft)
Map: see page M16
Further information: t +43 (0)6541 680068, www.saalbach.com
Lifts in area: 55 (14 cableways, 16 chairs, 25 drags) serving 200km of piste.
Lift pass: Area (Saalbach-Hinterglemm and Leogang) adult €173, child 7–15yrs €86.50, 16–18yrs €138.40, all for 6 days
Access: Salzburg airport 1½hrs. Zell am See station 19km

In terms of ski convenience, choice of base is relatively unimportant. Saalbach has a wider variety of hotels, shops, restaurants and nightlife. Hinterglemm is much more tranquil and consequently popular with families, although it still has plenty of après-ski.

The village of Leogang in the adjoining valley is linked into the ski area by a modern gondola and three high-capacity chairs. It provides a more rural alternative base.

Mountain

The skiing here is ideal for adventurous intermediates who want to feel that they are travelling somewhere each day rather than skiing the same stretch of mountainside over and over again. The main circuit is made up of easy blue and undemanding red runs that can be tackled by anyone who can ski parallel. Unlike a lot of other circuits, such as the Sella Ronda in Italy, you don't have to complete it – just descend to the valley floor and hop home on a free ski-bus.

Whether you start from Saalbach or Hinterglemm you move seamlessly into the 200km circuit – few areas in Austria can match the modern lift system. The clockwise circuit from Saalbach starts with a two-stage gondola ride to Schattberg Ost. From Hinterglemm the new Westgipfelbahn gondola also provides greatly improved access. On the other side of the valley the Bernkogel triple-chair, followed by one of the few remaining drag-lifts, brings you up to the 1740m summit of Bernkogel and the start of the anti-clockwise circuit.

This is a big resort for snowboarding, with a terrain park situated just above Hinterglemm and another served by the six-person Asitzmuldenbahn between Vorderglemm and Leogang. The nearby quad Polten lift gives access to a boardercross course, while the half-pipe is beneath the Bernkogel chair. The valley offers considerable opportunities for cross-country and the resort has three dedicated toboggan runs. The north side of the valley offers some outstanding powder runs.

Learn

Saalbach has no fewer than seven competing ski schools and Hinterglemm has three. The continual survival of all of them gives an indication of the popularity of the Glemmtal during the main holiday period. In Saalbach we recommend **Aamadall Snowacademy**, t +43 (0)6541 668256, and **Fürstauer**, t +43 (0)6541 8444. In Hinterglemm, **Snow & Fun Thomas Wolf**, t +43 (0)6541 7634640, has an enduring reputation. Off-piste guiding is available through **Sepp Mitterer**, t +43 (0)6541 7008.

Childcare

Snow & Fun Thomas Wolf, t +43 (0)6541 7634640, operates a ski kindergarten for children from three years. In Hinterglemm, **Hotel Lengauerhof**, t +43 (0)6541 7255, and **Hotel Glemmtalerhof**, t +43 (0)6541 71350, both have crèches. **Annaliese Kröll**, t +43 (0)6541 7183, and **Manuela Griesler**, t +43 (0)664 376 2553, provide babysitting.

Lunch

The ski circuit is dotted with 41 huts that vary from proper restaurants to the simplest of snackbars. **Pfefferalm**, t +43 (0)6541 6325, an ancient farmhouse above Hinterglem, is a favourite of ours. Try *Speckknödel* (bacon dumplings) and *Kasnock'n* (shank of pork).

Rosswaldhütte, t +43 (0)6541 6959, situated beside the Rosswald lift, has good food and staff in traditional dress. **Sportalm**, t +43 (0)6541 7972, **Thurner Alm**, t +43 (0)6541 8418, **Gerstreit Alm**, t +43

(0)6541 6565, and the **Maisalm**, t +43 (0)6541 7409, are all recommended.

Dine

In Saalbach, **La Trattoria Italiana** and **Vitrine Asia Wok** are both in the Alpenhotel, t +43 (0)6541 6666, and make a change from traditional Austrian mountain fare. **Bäckstättstall**, t +43 (0)6541 7652, is the best smart eaterie.

In Hinterglemm we recommend the **Fuhrmannstube** in Hotel Dorfschmiede, t +43 (0)6541 740862. **Restaurant Kendler**, t +43 (0)6541 6225, has a rustic atmosphere. Signature dishes include roast venison and sole.

Party

Late afternoon comes to alcoholic life in **Hinterhagalm** above Saalbach and at **Bauer's Schialm** by the church. It is equally noisy at the rustic **GoassStall** and **Hexenhäusl** in Hintgerglemm. The snow bar outside **Hotel Dorfschmiede** is always busy as the lift closes.

Later on, attention in Saalbach focuses on **King's Disco** and the **Kuhstall**. The **Crazy Bear** and **Zum Turn** (a converted jail) are lively. In Saalbach the **Glemmerkeller**, **Road King** and **Tanzhimmel** attract the late-night crowd.

The Nightliner bus service operates along the valley road between the two villages until late evening during the week and until 2.30am on Saturdays.

Sleep

Saalbach:
****Kunst-Hotel Kristiana**, t +43 (0)6541 6253, *www.kunsthotel.at*, in Saalbach, has a typically Tyrolean interior transformed by a modern art collection.
****Gartenhotel Theresia**, t +43 (0)6541 74140, *www.hotel-theresia.co.at*, is a

stylish hotel filled with contemporary art. It has won awards for 'the use of natural and organic produce' in its kitchen and offers especially good family facilities.

****Saalbacher Hof, t +43 (0)6541 7111, *www.saalbacherhof.at*, has a swimming-pool surrounded by rocks.

****Alpenhotel, t +43 (0)6541 6666, *www.alpenhotel.at*, is a multiple nightlife centre.

Hinterglemm:

****Sport & Vitalhotel Ellmau, t +43 (0)6541 7226, *www.sporthotel-ellmau.at*, has an impressive spa, and a kitchen specializing in healthy cuisine including Ayurvedic food. The hotel has a children's funpark with tubing, snowmobiling, a children's gym and sauna.

****Hotel Glemmtalerhof, t +43 (0)6541 7135, *www.alpinparadies.at*, is long established and conveniently situated in the village centre.

****The Blumenhotel Tirolerhof, t +43 (0)6541 64970, *www.blumenhotels.at*, has a wellness centre, and a heated outdoor pool.

****Hotel Dorfschmiede, t +43 (0)6541 74080, also in Hinterglemm village centre, has outstanding half-board cuisine and comfortable rooms.

St Anton

Profile

A lively town with some of the most challenging skiing and nightlife in Europe. This is not a place for beginners or wobbly intermediates. Not recommended for beginners or anyone of a nervous disposition

Resort

The Arlberg is the major European home of skiing. While the Swiss caught on to the idea of what were called 'Norwegian snow shoes' at the start of the 1890s, they had little idea what to do with them. It was ski instructors in St Anton who perfected the original technique that not only allowed you to go downhill – but to turn (almost) at will. The first races were held in the neighbouring hamlet of St Christoph in 1903. But it wasn't until 1921 that the great Hannes Schneider opened his Arlberg Ski School on the slopes below Galzig, and St Anton began to shape the history of modern skiing.

Back in the 1950s, St Anton earned itself a place among the top five ski resorts in the world. It is remarkable, given the enormous development of the sport in both hemispheres over the past half century, that it easily holds on to its position. In the hall of fame, St Anton rubs shoulders with Chamonix, Val d'Isère/Tignes, Verbier, Zermatt, Jackson Hole and Whistler as one of the world's Truly Greats.

Anyone going for the first time should be aware that the terrain here varies from

Essentials

Altitude: 1304m (4,278ft)–2811m (9,222ft)

Map: see page M18

Further information: +43 (0)5446 22690, *www.stantonamarlberg.com*

Lifts in area: 82 on Arlberg Ski Pass (10 cableways, 38 chairs, 35 drags) serving 260km of piste

Lift pass: Arlberg Ski Pass (covers Klösterle, Lech and Zürs, Pettneu, St Anton, St Christoph, Stuben) adult €175–189, child 7–14yrs €105–113, both for 6 days

Access: Innsbruck airport 1hr, Friedrichshafen airport 1½hrs, Zurich airport 2–3hrs, Munich airport 3–4hrs. Station in resort quite steep to the near sheer. It is not a place for novices and certainly not a place for wobbly second-weekers looking for a little confidence-building. St Anton is popular with experienced snowboarders, but if you can't manage steep moguls, then stay away.

The village itself is a blend of old and new, much improved by the relocation of the railway line that used to bisect it. The attractive centre is pedestrianized during day time with a modest selection of sports shops and boutiques, as well as some fine old hostelries and modern bars.

The village stretches in both directions, to the outlying and popular alternative bed-base of Nasserein as well as in the west towards Mooserkreuz. A ski-bus runs throughout the day and a night bus until 2am, but some walking is inevitable. However, it is possible to leave skis and boots overnight in storage near the bottom of the Galzig cable-car.

Mountain

Much has been done to update St Anton's once antiquated lift system. Most of this effort was concentrated into the build-up of the 2001 Alpine World Championships. The Nasserein gondola was a major improvement as was the scrapping of the venerable Gampen funicular. But the fact remains that when the hotel beds are full in high season, queuing is still a way of life that has become unacceptable in comparable resorts. One reporter complained that in early January he faced 30-minute queues on three successive lifts on his way up the mountain.

The ski area is in two sections, one on either sides of the St Anton Valley. Rendl, the smaller and easier of these is a pleasant sun trap with a choice of red and blue runs reached by a gondola which rises inconveniently a short bus ride or awkward walk in boots from outside the

village. Rendl has a terrain park and is popular with riders.

However, most skiers head each morning for the opposite side of the valley. A quad-chair followed by a six-pack take you up Gampen and Kapall for the easiest intermediate skiing in the main area. That said, the long black descent from the top follows the course used for the downhill races in the World Championships.

This sector connects – by piste and chair from Gampen, or by cable-car from St Anton – with 2185m Galzig, the true hub of the ski area. From here you can ski down to the charming hamlet of St Christoph and to *Stuben* at the foot of the Flexen Pass and the road to *Zürs* and *Lech*. Alternatively you can take the cable-car up to the 2811m Valluga, the highest point in the ski area. From the top station it is possible to ski off the back down to Zürs, but you have to be accompanied by a guide.

It is fair to describe almost all St Anton's skiing as difficult and the standard of skier and rider is high. The main runs become bumped up within hours of a major snowfall. The powder skiing is sensational, with unlimited possibilities. This is high Alpine sking, avalanche danger is ever present, and a guide is essential when straying beyond the ropes.

Learn

The two ski schools retain their separate identities but are under the same ownership. The original **Arlberg Ski School**, t +43 (0)5446 3411, founded by Hannes Schneider, has 250 instructors. **Franz Klimmer's St Anton**, t +43 (0)5446 3563, has 60 teachers. Both offer an outstanding level of tuition, although standards can fall during peak weeks. British-run **Piste to Powder Mountain Guided Adventures**, t +43 (0)6641 7462 820, or t +44 (0)1661 824318, teaches

Children

Kinderwelt, t +43 (0)5446 2526, run by the Arlberg school, has a kindergarten at the ski school meeting-place, on the Gampen, in Nasserein, and at St Christoph. Small skiers are accepted once they are out of nappies. Kiki Club, t +43 (0)5446 3563, operated by the St Anton school, runs ski classes for older children.

Lunch

Best mountain meal in the Arlberg is at Galzig in the Verwall Stube, t +43 (0)5446 2352501, for modern Austrian cuisine with an emphasis on fresh fish and seafood. Also recommended are Kaminstube, t +43 (0)5446 2681, and Rodelhütte, t +43 (0)5446 22690, as well as Albona-Grat, t +43 (0)5582 761, and Ulmerhütte, t +43 (0)5446 30200, on the descent from the Schindler Spitze. Sennhütte, t +43 (0)5446 2048, has live music.

Our favourite lunchspot is the sunny terrace of the Arlberg-Hospiz-Alm, t +43 (0)5446 2611, in St Christoph, where waiters wear Austrian national dress and descent to the loo is by a helter-skelter slide. The Maiensee Stube, t +43 (0)5446 2804, also in St Christoph, and the Hotel Post, t +43 (0)5582 761, in Stuben have a warm atmosphere and good food.

Dine

By night the Werner family's Arlberg-Hospiz-Alm, t +43 (0)5446 2611, in St Christoph puts on the tablecloths and becomes a serious gourmet restaurant with an astonishing wine cellar.

In St Anton, warehouse-style Benvenuto, t +43 (0)5446 30203, serves mainly Oriental dishes. Family-run Floriani, t +43 (0) 5446 2330, is recommended, as is Hazienda, t +43 (0)5446 2968, which serves excellent steaks and seafood. The Museum, t +43 (0)5446 2475, is like eating in someone's large private home. Sportcafé Schneider, t +43 (0)5446 2548, is in the pedestrian zone. Café Aquila, t +43 (0)5446 2217, is decorated in 1960s style. The Funky Chicken, t +43 (0)664 4043360, is popular with snowboarders and has some of the best value food in town. The Brunnenhof, t +43 (0)5446 2293, in St Jakob is one of the top eateries in the area. Nasserein's San Antonio, t +43 (0)5446 3474, is a popular pizzeria.

Party

The afternoon warms up with a Glühwein at the Sennhütte before the descent into degenerate behaviour at the infamous Krazy Kanguruh and/or the Mooserwirt on the meadow above the resort. The party gets truly under way with raucous music and much drinking and dancing as the light fades. Most make it back down the nursery slope in one piece, ready for a full evening of entertainment ahead. Hotspots include the Piccadilly, Bar Cuba, Hazienda, Train and Vino. Scottie's Bar in the Hotel Rosanna is a popular meeting place. The Kandahar comes to life in the early hours as other establishments close.

Sleep

★★★★★Hotel Arlberg-Hospiz, t +43 (0)5446 2611, www.hospiz.com, in St Christoph, counts President Putin of Russia among its patrons.

★★★★★Hotel St Antoner Hof, t +43 (0)5446 2910, www.st.antonerhof.at, is comfortable and modern.

★★★★Hotel Post, t +43 (0)5446 2213, www.hotel-post.co.at, is convenient for the lifts.

****Hotel Alte Post, t +43 (0)5446 2553, *www.hotel-alte-post.at*, is the original coaching inn. It is well located and has a good spa.

****Hotel Karl Schranz, t +43 (0)5446 25550, *www.arlberg.com/hotel.karl.schranz*, owned by the former world champion, has pleasant rooms and good food but is slightly out of town.

****Hotel Arlberg, t +43 (0)5446 22100, *www.arlberg.com*, has a relaxed atmosphere and is furnished in traditional Tyrolean style.

****Hotel Tyrol, t +43 (0)5446 2340, *www.tyrolhotel.com*, near the church, is a pleasant place to stay but the wrong end of the village for the skiing.

****Hotel Bergschlossl, t +43 (0)5446 2220, *www.bergschloessl.at*, is well located next to the Galzig cable-car and is owned by Johanna Moosbrugger, whose brother owns Gasthof Post in Lech. Bedrooms are spacious and individually decorated.

A large number of visitors to the resort choose to stay in catered chalets.

St Johann in Tirol

Profile

Unpretentious Tyrolean village of frescoed houses surrounded by less attractive suburbs. A modern lift system and benign slopes suit beginners and families

Resort

St Johann in Tirol found popularity with foreign visitors in the 1970s and 1980s

before fading from the frame. But now, thanks to new lifts and a reaffirmed sense of identity, it is enjoying a fresh lease of winter life.

The pretty Tyrolean village with its ornately frescoed inns and old coaching inns is marred by heavy traffic and industrial estates on the outskirts, but the centre retains considerable charm.

Mountain

This is a particularly good area for beginners, with a series of dedicated nursery slopes on the gentle meadows behind the station and in the hamlet of Eichenhof.

Main mountain access is by a two-stage gondola, which brings you up to the 1700m summit of Harschbichl. A modern, eight-seater gondola, which rises from Penzing on the edge of Oberndorf, has greatly enhanced the ski area and added a considerable challenge. The resort has a terrain park beneath the Penzing chair and a half-pipe at Eichenhof. Cross-country skiing is extensive with 275km of prepared tracks just outside the village.

Learn

St Johann has four ski schools: **St Johann, t** +43 (0)5352 64777, **Eichenhof,**

Essentials

Altitude: 670m (2,198ft)–1,700m (5,576ft)
Further information: t +43 (0)5352 63335, *www.st.johann.tirol.at*
Lifts in area: 17 lifts (3 cableways, 4 chairs, 10 drags) serving 60km of piste. 60 lifts and 170km of piste in linked Schneewinkel area
Lift pass: Schneewinkel adult €134–157, child €67–79, both for 6 days
Access: Innsbruck airport 1hr. Station in resort

t +43 (0)65930 61548, **Wilder Kaiser**, t +43 (0)5352 64888, and **Ski-Akademie** St Johann in Tirol, t +43 (0)5352 624888.

Children

St Johann ski school, t +43 (0)5352 64777, runs **Bobo's** ski kindergarten, which accepts children from four years. Eichenhof school's **Kinderland**, t +43 (0)65930 61548, also cares for children from four years. Babysitters can be booked through the tourist office, t +43 (0)5352 63335.

Lunch

The **Harschbichlhütte**, t +43 (0)5352 64671, has great *Gulaschsuppe*. **Koasaburg**, t +43 (0)65063 94001, has home-cooked food and a sunny terrace. **Grander Schupf**, t +43 (0)5352 63925, and **Bassgeigeralm**, t +43 (0)5352 62117, are recommended.

Dine

Lange Mauer, t +43 (0)5352 62174, serves Chinese cuisine. **La Rustica-Antonio**, t +43 (0)5352 62843, and **Rialto**, t +43 (0)5352 64168, are pizzerias. **Edelweiss**, t +43 (0)05352 63580, serves unpretentious mountain dishes.

Party

Popular bars include **Bunny's**, **Humungus**, **Max's** and **Rogi's Stad**. Rainer and the **Scala-Bar Club** provide the late-night entertainment.

Sleep

****Sporthotel Austria**, t +43 (0)5352 62507, *www.sporthotelaustria.at*, is traditional and in a central yet quiet location. Facilities include an indoor pool

and family apartments with two adjoining bedrooms.

****Hotel Gasthof Park**, t +43 (0)5352 62226, *www.park.at*, is near the gondola.

***Hotel Post**, t +43 (0)5352 62230, *www.hotel-post.tv*, dates from 1225 and is beautifully frescoed on the outside, with each room individually decorated.

***Hotel Fischer**, t +43 (0)5352 62332, *www.hotel-fischer.com*, is in the pedestrian area and has comfortable rooms.

Schladming

Profile

Large intermediate playground that is included in the 270-lift Ski Verbund Amadé lift pass, which covers 25 areas in this corner of Austria. Nearby glacier skiing and extensive cross-country tracks, but the terrain is not suited to advanced skiers

Resort

Schladming is a fine medieval town with an industrial and cultural life of its

Essentials

Altitude: 745m (2,224ft)–2,015m (6,609ft)
Further information: t +43 (0)3687 22777, *www.schladming-rohrmoos.com*
Lifts in area: 81 (8 cableways, 23 chairs, 47 drags) serving 115km of piste. Skiverbund Amadé region 276 (30 cableways, 74 chairs, 172 drags) serving 860km
Lift pass: Skiverbund Amadé adult €171, child €87, both 6 days
Access: Salzburg airport 1hr, Munich airport 2½hrs. Station in resort

own rather than a village that has expanded into a ski resort. It has two beautiful Romanesque and Gothic churches and a magnificent 18th-century town square. In earlier times the whole town was enclosed by heavily buttressed walls. But, apart from one gateway, these were removed during bitter social unrest in 1525, that culminated in a peasants' revolt.

The town makes a charming base from which to explore not just the rather banal skiing immediately around the town, but also the other areas such as Flachau/ Wagrain and the Gasteinertal. All are included in the regional lift pass and are situated just a short drive away.

This is a resort much loved by the Austrians, and the slopes can be very crowded during the national school holidays in February.

Mountain

The central Planai ski area is reached by a gondola that rises from the edge of town. Alternatively you can drive up an all-weather road to a car park just below the mid-station. A network of modern mainly high-capacity chairs serve easy blue and red runs that wind down between the trees.

Pistes and chair-lift provide links to the peaks of Hauser Kaibling on one side and Hochwurzen and Reiteralm on the other. Fageralm, a few kilometres further along the valley towards Radstadt and Salzburg, is another small but enjoyable ski area.

In the other direction towards Linz and Graz lies the pretty farming village of Haus-im-Ennstal, which is flanked by two gondolas that rise to the top of Hauser Kaibling. Beyond Haus the 1986m Galsterbergalm above Pruggern provides marginally more demanding terrain. Schladming is not a place for off-piste skiers. Leaving the marked piste is positively discouraged on the main ski

area above the resort. Planai and the Dachstein Glacier both have good half-pipes.

The Ramsau plateau, situated just a few minutes' drive from Schladming, is one of Austria's most scenic cross-country areas, and a former venue for the World Championships with 145km of snow-sure marked tracks between 1100m and 1300m.

High-altitude skiing is possible on the adjoining Dachstein Glacier, reached by cable-car from Turlwand.

Learn

Hopl, t +43 (0)3687 23582, and Tritscher, t +43 (0)3687 22137, provide the full range of ski and snowboard lessons. Blue Tomato, t +43 (0)3687 24223, is the specialist board school. Off-piste guiding is available from Helli Team Bedarfsflug, t +43 (0)3687 81323.

Children

Meine Kleine Schule, t +43 (0)3687 24407, and Frau Ladreiter, t +43 (0)3687 61313, are the resort's two non-ski kindergartens.

Trischer ski school operates a highly acclaimed ski kindergarten.

Lunch

Schladming has an abundance of friendly huts scattered across the mountainside and should win a prize for being one of the only resorts in the world to list its mountain restaurants with telephone numbers on the piste map.

Seiterhutte, t +43 (0)3687 61615, below the summit of Hochwurzen, has a welcoming sun terrace. Märchenwiesenhütte, t +43 (0)3687 61251, near the lift of the same name, has reliable home cooking. Onkel Willy's Hütte, t +43 (0)03687 23105, has live music and a sunny terrace. The **Eiskarhütte**, t +43 (0)6454 7234, at Reiteralm, is recommended.

Dine

L'**Osteria da Giorgio**, t +43 (0)3687 23173, and **Va Bene**, t +43 (0)3687 23226, provide an Italian alternative to Austrian mountain fare along with **Giovanni's Pizza & Pasta**, t +43 (0)3687 24638. **Planaistub'n Charly Kahr**, t +43 (0)3687 23544, is a favourite of Californian governor Arnold Schwarzenegger when he returns to these parts. **Arnoldstub'n Charly Kahr**, t +43 (0)3687 23544, is under the same ownership. The **Rôtisserie Royer Grill**, t +43 (0)3687 200, in Sporthotel Royer, is recommended. **Kirchenwirt**, t +43 (0)3687 22435, has good-quality food, a warm atmosphere and excellent service. **China Restaurant Peking**, t +43 (0)3687 22688, rings the changes.

Party

Onkel Willy's Hütte on Planai and the Schirmbar draw a large crowd long before the lifts close. Later on the action moves to **Charly's Treff** which is a resort meeting point, along with **La Porta**, **Das Beisl**, **Mariah's Mexican**, the **Hanglbar**, **Ferry's**, **Twister Bar**, **Siglu** and the **Sonderbar** disco. The 8km toboggan run from the top of Hochwurzen is open in the evenings.

Sleep

******Sporthotel Royer**, t +43 (0)3687 200, www.royer.at, has a swimming-pool, indoor tennis and squash, bowling alley and a wellness centre. It is crowded with Russians in January.
******Hotel-Restaurant Alte Post**, t +43 (0)3687 22571, www.alte-post.at, is an old coaching inn in the main square, with a fine restaurant and wellness centre.

******Hotel zum Stadttor**, t +43 (0)3687 24525, www.hotelzumstadttor.at, is a family-run hotel next to the church.
*****Appartment-Hotel Ferienalm**, t +43 (0)3687 23517, www.ferienalm.com, has a panoramic view of Schladming and the Planai ski area and is five minutes by ski bus from the Planai gondola.
*****Gasthof zum Kaiserweg**, t +43 (0)3687-22038, www.members.a1.net/kaiserweg, is in a quiet position five minutes from the centre. It has simple rooms, and a good restaurant with all fresh ingredients and everything home-made.

Seefeld

Profile

Attractive old town with elegant hotels and a sophisticated nightlife. This is the cross-country ski capital of the Austrian Alps, with the downhill variety best suited to beginners and intermediates

Resort

Seefeld is a mini-Kitzbühel with 280km of cross-country tracks and a much more

Essentials

Altitude: 1200m (3,937ft)–2100m: (6,890ft)
Further information: t +(0)43 5212 2313, www.seefeld.at
Lifts in area: 24 (1 mountain railway, 2 cableways, 7 chairs, 24 drags) serving 30km of piste
Lift pass: adult €159.50, child 7–15yrs €96, both for 6 days
Access: Innsbruck airport 20mins. Station in resort

modest amount of downhill skiing, set around a large village with frescoed medieval architecture above the Inn Valley.

Visitors come here not just for the skiing, but for an all-round winter holiday complete with sleigh rides, skating, tobogganing, exotic spa treatments, a casino and a clutch of superlative hotels and restaurants.

Mountain

The serious skiers here are Langlaufers who want to explore the 280km of marked tracks in the area. The 2km floodlit loipe opens four evenings a week.

Downhill skiers have three small areas. Novices congregate at Geigenbühel. Gschwandtkopf is a hill next to the cross-country track used mainly by the ski school, while Rosshütte is the more extensive area with some more challenging runs, a long off-piste trail, night skiing and a snowboard park.

Learn

Seefeld, t +43 (0)5212 2412, is the largest school and has a good reputation. **Sport Aktiv, t** +43 (0)699 1461 0000, in *Reith* is based in the Gschwandtkopf area. **Mösern, t** +43 (0)5212 4736, has a beginner slope in the hamlet of the same name and also teaches on the Gschwandtkopf.

Children

The resort kindergarten, **t** +43 (0)5212 3220 is in the Olympia Sport and Congress Centre. **Ski School Seefeld, t** +43 (0)5212 2412 offers childcare as well as a games zone and designated pistes.

Lunch

Sonnenalm, t +43 (0)5212 2490 is an enticing mountain restaurant on the Gschwandtkopf. **Rosshütte, t** +43 (0)5212 24160, has been completely refurbished.

Dine

Gourmets can try the **Alte Stube** in the Casinohotel Karwendelhof, **t** +43 (0)5212 2655. **Café Nanni, t** +43 (0)5212 2229622, and **Café Moccamühle** in the Hotel Elite, **t** +43 (0)5212 2901, are popular for après-ski. The gourmet restaurant in the **Klosterbräu, t** +43 (0)5212 26210, has a 500-year-old cellar housing 9,000 bottles.

Party

Batzenhäusl, hotels **Royal**, **Kaltschmid** and **Karwendelhof** all have live music. The **Tenne** has tea-dancing, **Siglu** is always crowded, and late-night entertainment is focused on the **Jeep** and **Buffalo** discos.

Sleep

*****Dorint Vital Royal & Spa, t** +43 5212 44310, *www.sofitel.com*, has a large pool and a spa specializing in Chinese treatments.

*****Hotel Klosterbräu, t** +43 (0)5212 26210, *www.seefeld.klosterbraeu.com*, is a former sixteenth-century monastery with sumptuous bedrooms.

****Hotel A-Vita Viktoria, t** +43 (0)5212 4441, *www.viktoria.at*, has suites with apt names such as Laura Ashley, La Dolce Vita and St Paul de Vence.

****Casinohotel Karwendelhof, t** +43 (0)5212 2655, *www.karwendelhof.com*, is in the pedestrian precinct.

****Hotel Kaltschmid, t** +43 (0)5212 2191, *www.kaltschmid.info*. Free kindergarten.

****Gartenhotel Tümmlerhof, t** +43 (0)5212 2571, *www.tuemmlerhof.at*, offers daycare.

Sölden

Profile

High-altitude destination for all standards and for those who want jolly après-ski. Two glaciers offering snow-sure skiing and boarding throughout a long season

Resort

High-altitude Sölden is renowned for reliable snow cover and unfettered nightlife, two products that endear it to substantial numbers of fun-loving visitors who ski hard and party even harder. This is not a place to experience the tranquil ambience of a rural Austrian village.

Hochsölden is a car-free satellite set on summer pastures above the village with a handful of ski-in ski-out hotels and panoramic views of the Ötztal.

Mountain

Sölden's reputation for snow-sure skiing hinges on the presence of the adjoining Tiefenback and Rettenbach glaciers. These were incorporated six years ago into the resort's mainstream terrain by the addition of a gondola that spans the Rettenbach Valley.

However, the resort's own skiing goes up to 3058m, allowing for an impressive vertical drop of 1680m. Sölden's skiing is suited to all standards, with plenty of intermediate terrain and a few testing blacks.

Main mountain access is by two gondolas, one at either end of the village. Giggijoch terrain park, reached by the Hainbachkar chair, has a half-pipe and a boardercross course. Another terrain park is built each autumn on the Rettenbach glacier.

Learn

Sölden has four ski schools: **Sölden-Hochsölden**, t +43 (0)5254 2364, **Yellow Power**, t +43 (0)664 4424866, **Skiaktiv**, t +43 (0)5253 6313, and **Vacancia Total**, t +43 (0)5254 3100. All have established reputations.

Children

Sölden-Hochsölden, t +43 (0)5254 2364, has a non-ski kindergarten for children from six months. It also runs **Bobo's Ski Kindergarten** for children from three years. **Yellow Power**, t +43 (0)664 4424866, operates **Fiddel Bambini Club** ski kindergarten on Giggijoch for little ones from three years.

Lunch

Mountain huts are in abundance. **Gampe Thaya**, t +43 (0)5254 5010 has plenty of atmosphere. **Heide Alm**, t +43 (0)5254 508 875, offers beautiful views.

Dine

Mangia Bene, t +43 (0)5254 5010, is a new eatery serving pasta and fish. **La Tavola**, t +43 (0)5254 2674, has pizzas and Austrian specialities. **Pizzeria Gusto**, t +43 (0)5254 2272, and **Gasthof Waldcafé**, t +43

(0)5254 2319 are recommended, along with the **Schnalser Stube** in the **Hotel Liebe Sonne, t** +43 (0)5254 2203.

Party

Après-ski begins at **Top Ok, Felsenstüberl, Grüner's Almstube, Kuhstall** and at **Philipp** at Innerwald. Later on some 12 nightclubs, including the new **Bierhimml,** keep visitors on their feet until the early hours. In Hochsölden the action centres around **Eugens Obstlerhütte.**

Sleep

★★★★★**Central Sölden, t** +43 (0)5254 22600, *www.central-soelden.at,* has a vast spa.
★★★★**Hotel Regina, t** +43 (0)5254 2301, *www.hotel-regina.com,* has a swimming-pool and is convenient for the Gaislachkoglbahn.
★★★★**Hotel Stefan, t** +43 (0)5254 2237, *www.hotel-stefan.at,* is close to the Giggijoch lift station and has good food.
★★**Gasthof Sonnenheim, t** +43 (0)5254 2276, *www.kraxner.com/sonnenheim,* is a recommended budget option.

Söll and the SkiWelt

Profile

Large linked ski area that is good value for money. Best for beginners, families and skiers on a budget. This is not the place to come if you're looking for other activities besides skiing and nightlife

Resort

By virtue of being the largest bed-base in the region, Söll is the uncrowned capital of what is still Austria's largest interconnected ski area. The network of lifts spans the mainly gently mountainsides surrounding seven resorts near Kitzbühel. Two further resorts, Westendorf and Kelchsau, are linked into the system only by bus but consider themselves part of the network and are included in the lift pass.

This is prime cruising country over undulating summer pastureland, best suited to skiers who have progressed from the nursery slopes and are in need of daily confidence-building mileage to progress.

Söll is a large, friendly village set around an onion-domed church in the middle of a wide valley. The ski area is 1km away and best reached by ski-bus.

Back in the 1980s the resort was an annual mustering point for British and Dutch youth who did more drinking than skiing. However, it has long since shrugged off its overtly laddish image and is now popular with families and couples of all ages.

Après-ski still plays an important role, but the resort along with its clientele has matured to the point of respectability but not sophistication.

Mountain

Mountain access is by a two-stage gondola, which brings you swiftly up to Hohe Salve, the high point of the linked area. The other linked villages of Going, Ellmau, Scheffau, Itter, Hopfgarten and Brixen-im-Thale all line the valley around the dome-shaped massif. Each of these resorts provides alternative access into the system, either by gondola or by funicular from Ellmau or by quad-chair from Going.

Essentials

Altitude: 703m (2,306ft)–1829m (6,001ft)
Map: see page M17
Further information: t +43 (0)5358 505,
www.skiwelt.com.
Lifts in area: 93 (1 funicular, 10 cableways,
38 chairs, 44 drags) serving 250km of
piste in the SkiWelt.
Lift pass: SkiWelt adult €139–161.50, child
6–16yrs €83.50–97, both for 6 days
Access: Innsbruck airport 45mins. Wörgl
station 10mins

The resorts are linked on the main road
by post-bus, but not by free ski-bus, so in
the afternoon it is advisable to keep an
eye on your watch.

All of them, except south-facing
Hopgarten and Brixen, have dedicated
nursery slopes at the bottom of the
mountain. Scheffau, our favourite here, is
set back on the other side of the valley
and has its novice area on a sloping
meadow beneath the church.

The home run back to Söll is marked red
on the piste map. It is covered by snow-
cannon, but lack of natural cover can lead
to difficult icy conditions. Regular blue run
skiers are advised to return to the valley
by gondola.

This is not a place for advanced skiers
who, despite the beauty of the scenery,
will soon tire of the lack of challenge.
Lärchenhang, on the north side of Hohe
Salve, is a short and testing pitch. Other
steep terrain as well as some rewarding
off-piste can be found with the help of a
guide. The terrain park and half-pipe at
Söll are situated above Salvenmoos.

If you don't want to ski alone the
SkiWelt has introduced a find-a-ski-mate
scheme. The area has seven fixed meeting
points and you are given an appropriate
sticker for your jacket. Further information
at *www.skiwelt.at.*

Learn

The various ski schools here have now
amalgamated into the **Söll-Hochsöll,**
t +43 (0)5333 5454, which over the past 40
years has acquired considerable
experience in teaching foreigners to ski.
As a place to get to grips with the basics,
we warmly recommend it. However, like a
lot of Austrian ski schools in major
beginner and intermediate resorts, there
seems to be little emphasis on adapting
teaching methods to encompass the
newer generation of skis.

Children

Bobo's Kinderclub, t +43 (0)5333 5454, is
run by the school and cares for children
from five years. Small guests at the
Alphotel can join the **Smiley Tiny Tots Ski
School, t** +43 (0)5517 5449, from two years.

Lunch

The mountainside is dotted with
welcoming huts and larger self-service
restaurants. **Gründalm, t** +43 (0)5333
5060, and **Gipfelrestaurant Hohe Salve,**
t +43 (0)5335 2216, are both
recommended.

Schernthannstuberl, t +43 (0) 5333 5273,
is a welcome spot on a cold day.
Stöcklalm, t +43 (0)5333 5127, and
Kraftalm, t +43 (0)5332 75152, are both
extremely busy from 11.30am onwards.

Dine

Most restaurants are in the hotels.
Giovanni, t +43 (0)5333 57050, **Venezia,**
t +43 (0)5333 6191, and **Hexenalm, t** +43
(0)5333 5544, are all good pizzerias.
Schindlhaus, t +43 (0)5333 516136, offers
more gourmet fare. **Panoramabad Café,**
t +43 (0)5333 544212, is out the way but
worth the walk for coffee and cakes.

Party

Whisky Mühle is the original and still the best bar/disco here, a resort institution that receives rave reviews from visitors, with live music most nights including UK bands. Après-ski begins much earlier at **Hexenalm** by the gondola station, and at **Hexenkessel** and **Salvenstadl**. The **Moonlight Bar** is a noisy pub and the **Sports Bar** shows Premier League football and has Guinness on tap.

Sleep

★★★★**Hotel Postwirt**, t +43 (0)5333 5081, *www.hotel-postwirt-soell.at*, in the village cenre has an outdoor swimming-pool heated to 33°C.

★★★★**Hotel AlpenSchlössl**, t +43 (0)5333 6400, *www.hotel-alpenschloessl.com*, is more luxurious, with an indoor pool complex and frescoed Sleeping Beauty Tower Rooms.

★★★★**The Alphotel**, t +43 (0)5517 5449, *www.alphotel.at*, is a member of Kinderhotels, which offer indoor 'splash pools', children's menus and organized activities, a children's ski school and soft drinks round the clock.

★★★**Hotel Feldwebel**, t +43 (0)5333 5224, is a newly converted traditional building in the village centre, recommended for its rooms and half-board food.

★★**Hotel Gänsleit**, t +43 (0)5333 5471, is a five-minute walk from the village centre and welcomes children.

Wagrain and the Salzburger Sportwelt

Profile

Large intermediate ski area covering a dozen villages within easy reach of Salzburg. The main resorts are linked by lift, while regular buses serve the outlying corners of the ski area. Towns and villages vary considerably in character, so choose your base with care

Resort

This easily accessible ski area is extremely popular with Austrians from Salzburg and elsewhere, but much underrated by overseas visitors. St Johann im Pongau is the regional capital of this corner of the country and is a ski resort in its own right. However the cathedral city was burnt to the ground in 1852 and lacks the medieval charm of Salzburg or Innsbruck. It has its own small ski area and from the pistes above the town you get a panoramic view of the cathedral.

Of far more interest to the skier are the outlying villages of Alpendorf, Wagrain, Kleinarl, Flachau and Zauchensee, which are linked from valley to valley by a complex network of modern lifts. Other resorts including Radstadt/Altenmarkt and Filzmoos add extra variety and alternative places in which to stay. All are included in the regional Ski Verbund Amadé lift pass.

Essentials

Altitude: 650m (2,132ft)–2188m (7,177ft)
Further information: t +43 (0)6457 2929,
  www.sportwelt-amade.com
Lifts in area: 93 (12 cableways, 34 chairs,
  48 drags) serving 350km of piste.
  Skiverband Amadé region 276 (30
  cableways, 74 chairs, 172 drags) serving
  865km
Lift pass: Skiverbund Amadé adult €171,
  child €87, both 6 days
Access: Salzburg airport 45mins

Wagrain and Flachau are the most centrally placed and convenient resorts. Altenmarkt and Radstadt, linked by piste and lift across the 1677m Kemahdhöhe, are pleasant little market towns. Their main ski area of Zauchensee is a few minutes' bus ride away. Filzmoos, hot-air balloon capital of the Alps and a winter bolthole for Viennese aristocracy in the first years of the 20th century, shares its ski area with neighbouring Neuberg, just off the edge of the circuit.

Mountain

The whole Wagrain region comprises a dozen resorts served by 93 lifts covering undulating pastures and woodland as well as a handful of rounded 2000m summits. Runs here are of limited challenge to true experts, although that did nothing to arrest the development of Austrian downhill hero Hermann Maier who was raised and still lives in Flachau. However the area should prove enormously enjoyable for the vast majority of skiers. Lifts are mainly fast and modern, allowing you to travel a considerable distance from scenic valley to valley in a single day. The post-bus service is efficient, but it makes sense to keep track of time when venturing far from home.

Learn

Each of the resorts has at least one ski school. Wagrain has **Skischule Wagrain**, t +43 (0)6413 7100. Flachau has six including **Hermann Maier, t** +43 (0)6457 2812. St Johann has four including **Alpendorf, t** +43 (0)6412 8455, and its board school, **Vitamin B**.

Schools in Altenmarkt include **Der Erste S, t** +43 (0)6452 60700. In Zauchensee the choice is between **Happy Maier, t** +43 (0)6452 4315, and **Radstadt Pichler, t** +43 6452 7382.

Children

Wagrain **ski kindergarten, t** +43 (0)6413 7100 cares for children from three years. In Flachau the ski schools accept children from four years. **Miniclub Flachau** is the non-ski kindergarten, t +43 (0)6457 3134. **Altenmarkt's Balla** kindergarten, t +43 (0)6452 4737, cares for children from three years. In Alpendorf **Wellness & Sporthotel Alpina, t** +43 (0)6412 8282, runs a supervised activity programme for its small guests.

Lunch

The mountainside is dotted with welcoming huts. In the Flachau area try **Hoflalm, t** +43 (0)6457 2332, **Hubertusalm**, t +43 (0)6457 2756, and the **Griessenkar Hütte, t** +43 (0)6457 2575. In the Wagrain area **Almstadl, t** +43 (0)6413 7444, is recommended. In Zauchensee both **Arlhofhüt**te, t +43 6452 54856, and **Hochnössleralm, t** +43 (0)6452 6242, have plenty of atmosphere.

Dine

In Wagrain, **Gasthof Kalkhofen, t** +43 (0)6413 8206, dates back to the 16th century and serves tradititional

Salzburgerland dishes. **Haar-Trog Alm,**
t +43 (0)6413 7286, has pasta and Asian
fusion cuisine.

Mennerhäusl, t +43 (0)6413 8965, is
recommended. **H.C. Andersen,** t +43
(0)6413 8170, specializes in fresh fish.

In Flachau, **Alter Jagdhof,** t +43 (0)6457
2228, is a family restaurant serving mainly
Italian cuisine. **Rustic Hoagascht–Das
Restaurant,** t +43 (0)6457 32490, has
Asian, Italian and Austrian dishes. **Hotel
Schartner,** t +43 (0)6452 5469, in
Altenmarkt, is famed for its modern
Austrian cuisine.

Party

Wagrain's returning skiers head for the
outdoor Schirmbar at the end of the day.
The **Haar-Trogg Alm** and the **Kuhstall** are
both extremely lively, while the **Point** has
live music and karaoke. You can dance on
the floor or on the tables at the **Tenne.**

In Flachau, **Franzl's Schirmbar,
Dampfkessel, Bergwerk, Ema's Pub** and
Double Dutch are the hotspots. Late-
nighters dance at **Burg** and **Yeti's
Partyhaus.** Altenmarkt's après spots
include **Napa Valley, S'Kessei,** and
Webers Bar.

Sleep

Wagrain:
★★★★**Wagrainerhof,** t +43 (0)6413 8204,
www.wagrainerhof.com, has good half-
board food and welcomes children.
★★★★**Hotel Alpenhof Edelweiss,** t +43
(0)6413 8447,
www.tiscover.com/alpenhof.edelweiss,
has a relaxed atmosphere and the
restaurant uses local organic produce.
★★★★**Hotel Alpina,** t +43 (0)6413 8337,
www.hotelalpina.at, has a large
swimming-pool and spa.
★★★**Hotel Sonne,** t +43 (0)6413 8242,
www.wagrain.at/hotel/sonne, is a

pleasant establishment with a sauna,
gym and a sun terrace.
Flachau:
★★★★**Vierjahreszeiten,** t +43 (0)6457 2981,
www.vierjahreszeiten.co.at, has a central
but quiet location.
★★★★**Hotel Tauernhof,** t +43 (0)6457 2311,
www.tauernhof.at, calls itself 'a four-star
base camp for sporty guests'.
★★★★**Flachauerhof,** t +43 (0)6457 2225,
www.flachauerhof.at, is a comfortable
traditional establishment in the village
centre.
★★★**Hotel Wieseneck,** t +43 (0)6457 2276, is
in a peaceful, ski-in ski-out position.
Altenmarkt:
★★★★**Hotel Alpenrose,** t +43 (0)6452 4027,
www.hotel-alpenrose.at, has a wellness
and fitness centre, and serves 'creative
cuisine'.
Alpendorf:
★★★★**Wellness & Sporthotel Alpina,** t +43
(0)6412 8282,
www.sporthotel-alpina.com, contains
apartments, a playroom, and an
impressive indoor swimming-pool.

Westendorf

Profile

**Appealing village with lots of Tyrolean
atmosphere. The resort has its own
modest beginner and intermediate
skiing, and is linked by bus into the giant
SkiWelt circuit and to Kirchberg and
Kitzbühel**

Resort

Westendorf has the best and highest
skiing in the SkiWelt, a network of 93 lifts
covering nine villages. However
Westendorf is one of the two resorts (the

other is Kelchsau) that is linked only by bus into the system. This attractive village has plenty of atmosphere and has been popular with foreign skiers since the 1960s. The village is popular with families, but après-ski can last well into the night.

Mountain

Lazy skiers avoid the 1km walk or bus ride to the gondola, the only means of mountain access, by riding the Schneebergbahn quad up the nursery slope and traversing to the main lift station. The two-stage gondola takes you up to a small network of high-capacity chairs that bring you to the peak of Fleiding, the highest point in the SkiWelt.

A new gondola this season from the top of 1956m Gampen links Westendorf to Kirchberg, creating a seamless circuit of 400km and 150 lifts but a bus still links Brixen-im-Thale to the rest of SkiWelt.

Learn

Westendorf has three ski schools: **Ideal**, t +43 (0)5334 2919, **Top**, t +43 (0)5334 6737, and **Westendorf**, t +43 (0)5334 6181.

Children

All the ski schools accept children. **Kindergruppe Simba**, t +43 (0)5334 20603, cares for non-skiing children from 18 months to four years.

Lunch

Alpenrosenhütte, t +43 (0)5334 6488, and **Bergrestaurant Choralpe**, t +43 (0)5334 61290, have plenty of atmosphere. **Jausenstation Alte Mittel**, t +43 (0)5334 2324, beneath the gondola, is also recommended.

Dine

Most of the restaurants are in hotels, with the **Vital-Landhotel Schermer**, t +43 (0)5334 6268, providing gourmet cuisine. **Liftstüberl**, t +43 (0)5334 30014, serves Italian food. **Marcel's**, t +43 (0)5334 30111, is recommended along with **Gasthof Maierhof**, t +43 (0)5334 6412, and **Gery's Inn**, t +43 (0)5334 6334.

Party

The après-ski atmosphere is extremely lively. The hotel bars and the **Village Pub** are the main meeting points, while **Bruchstall** is a new après-ski bar next to the nursery slope. The **Wunderbar** disco stays open until 6am.

Sleep

****Hotel Jakobwirt**, t +43 (0)5334 6245, www.jakobwirt.at, is on the edge of the piste and is warmly recommended for its food and facilities.
****Vital-Landhotel Schermer**, t +43 (0)5334 6268, www.vitalhotelschermer.at, is on the edge of the village with a major

wellness centre offering Thalasso treatments.

***Vital Hotel Sportalm, t** +43 (5334) 6495, *www.sportalm-schwaigeralm.at*, is next to the Alpenrose piste and has a spa.

***Hotel Post, t** +43 (0)5334 6202, *www.hotelpost.co.at*, built in 1593, has 40 rooms, including some that sleep six.

Zell am See and Kaprun

Profile

A pretty resort (Zell) on the shore of Austria's most scenic lake. It offers substantial intermediate skiing backed up by snow-sure glacial skiing on the Kitzsteinhorn at nearby Kaprun. Also summer skiing, good nightlife and plenty of Alpine atmosphere

Resort

Zell is one of those rare places where in summer you can ski in the morning and sunbathe, swim and sail in the afternoon. The lakeside town acts as the tourist gateway to the Gross Glockner, Austria's highest mountain, and attracts a year-round clientele that is as sedate in summer as it is lively in winter.

Above it rises the dome of the 2000m Schmittenhöhe, a charming and mainly wooded ski area best suited to intermediates but with dedicated learning areas at base and mid-mountain.

Zell was first established by a monastic order in the eighth century and had considerable commercial importance in medieval times. The legacy of fine old buildings has been transformed over the

years into a seaside Kitzbühel. It has smart hotels and boutiques as well as lakeside villas that are the holiday homes of wealthy Salzburgers.

Less cosmopolitan Kaprun, 8km up the road, is much more of a traditional ski village, with its own little mountain. However, focus here is up the valley on the 3000m Kitzsteinhorn Glacier where skiing continues throughout the year, except for a fortnight in June.

Mountain

A modern gondola rises from Zell, but the quickest way to the top of the mountain is by ski-bus to Schüttdorf and a three-stage gondola. Alternatively, you can catch a bus and join the cable-car from Schittental, the base of the main ski area, but this is prone to overcrowding at peak times.

A glance at the piste map gives the erroneous impression that the skiing here is testing. While the western shoulder of the mountain is given over to easy blue and red runs, the front face features seven blacks. In fact, in many other resorts most of these would be graded as moderate reds.

The severe classification is only barely justified in icy conditions when cover is thin. The whole area is ideally suited to intermediates.

Kaprun has its own winter area on Maiskogel, reached by cable-car or a combination of drag and chair-lift. The glacier is served by twin cableways that take you up to the Alpincenter mid-mountain hub at 2452m. A network of lifts fan out between here and the 3029m top statlon. In winter conditions you can ski all the way down to the cable-car station at Langwied. Terrain parks are located on the Kitzsteinhorn and at Jumping City on the Schmittenhöhe, where there is also a half-pipe.

Learn

Of the 10 schools in both resorts, **Sport-Alpin** Zell am See, t +43 (0)664 4531419, receives the most praise along with **Kitzsteinhorn**, t +43 (0)6547 8621 363, in Kaprun. **Ski Safari**, t +43 (0)6643 361487, teaches off-piste and has a strong reputation. **Snowboard Academy**, t +43 (0)6642 530381, is the dedicated riding school.

Children

The **Sport-Alpin**, t +43 (0)664 4531419, and **Zell-am-See**, t +43 (0)6542 56020, schools in Zell, and five schools in Kaprun offer lessons to children from four years. **Play & Fun**, t +43 (0)6542 56020, is the non-ski kindergarten.

Lunch

On Schmittenhöhe try **Ebenbergalm**, t +43 (0)664 3512307, **Jaga Alm**, t +43 (0)6542 72969, for local game dishes **Schmiedhofalm**, t +43 (0)6542 72868, for

Pinzgauer specialities and panoramic views, and **Hochzeller Alm**, t +43 (0)6542 72113, for home cooking.

On Maiskogel, **Weisssteinalm**, t +43 (0)6547 7439, has plenty of atmosphere. On Kitzsteinhorn, **Gletschermühle**, t +43 (0)6547 8621371, is popular.

Dine

Nearly all the restaurants here are in hotels. In Zell, the **Steinerwirt**, t +43 (0)6542 72502, is recommended along with the **Kupferkessel**, t +43 (0)6542 72768. **Hotel St Georg**, t +43 (0)6542 7680, **Zur Einkehr**, t +43 (0)6542 72363, **Landhotel Erlhof**, t +43 (0)6542 566370, and the **Salzburgerhof**, t +43 (0)6542 765, are all worth a visit.

In Kaprun, **Hotel Orgler**, t +43 (0)6547 8205, has some of the best food in the village and **China**, t +43 (0)6547 8246, makes a change from the ubiquitous *Wienerschnitzel.*

Party

In Zell, **Crazy Daisy** and **Diele** are the long-time hotspots. **Sunrise** disco and the **Rock-Bar** are also important hang-outs. In Kaprun nightlife is more muted. **Kitsch & Bitter** has regular live bands.

The **Optimum** sports centre contains an indoor pool, sauna and fitness centre, as well as a giant outdoor water-slide.

Sleep

Zell:
★★★★★Hotel Salzburgerhof, t +43 (0)6542 765, *www.salzburgerhof.at*, is the most comfortable base and has a good spa.
★★★★Romantikhotel Zum Metzgerwirt, t +43 (0)6542 72520, *www.romantik-hotel.at*, has pastel-decorated bedrooms, with a fireplace and waterbed in one of the suites.

****Alpin Sporthotel**, t +43 (0)6542 769, *www.alpinhotel.at*, has modern rooms.

****Hotel Alpenblick**, t +43 (0)6542 5433, *www.alpenblick.at*, has wood-panelled rooms and studios.

****Hotel St Georg**, t +43 (0)6542 768, *www.grossglockner.co.at/stgeorg*, has traditional rooms and views of the lake.

****Hotel Berner**, t +43 (0)6542 779, *www.bernerhotel.com*, is in a quiet position and has a heated outdoor pool.

****Kinderhotel Hagleitner**, t +43 (0)6542 571870, *www.kinderhotel-hagleitner.at*, at Schüttdorf, is good for young families.

***Hotel Bellevue**, t +43 (0)6542 73104, *www.zellamsee.at/bellevue*, is on the lakeside.

Kaprun:

****Hotel Orgler**, t +43 (0)6547 8205, *www.hotel-orgler.at*, in Kaprun, has comfortable rooms.

****Hotel Sonnblick**, t +43 (0)6547 8301, *www.hotel-sonnblick.at*, is decorated in modern Tyrolean style.

****Active by Leitner's**, t +43 (0)6547 8782, *www.active-kaprun.at*, is a 1960s-style hotel run like an action-packed club. As well as skiing and snowboarding, the owners arrange tobogganing and snowball-throwing parties.

The Top Resorts: Canada

03

Banff-Lake Louise, Alberta

Profile

Lake Louise is a peaceful village surrounded by stunningly beautiful scenery, while the historic town of Banff has a lively nightlife. The snow-sure slopes offer great skiing variety and few queues. This is a resort for skiers and riders on a budget, but not for those who dislike low temperatures

Resort

It is a triumph of successful Canadian marketing that two such totally different resorts in Alberta so far apart from each other should be bracketed together, not to mention similarly separate Sunshine Village which sits on a mountain top between them.

'Banff is an ordinary little tourist resort,' wrote the First World War poet Rupert Brooke in the year before his death, 'but Lake Louise – Lake Louise is of another world.' Ninety winters later, his description is still apt. Banff is a busy but bland little town just inside the gates of the Banff National Park. This is a traditional summer destination for thousands of North Americans, but not until relatively recently one that excited much interest in wintertime. It has its own little ski area of Mount Norquay nearby which it has unsuccessfully tried to brand as SkiBanff@Norquay.

Since hoteliers discovered that overseas skiers would pay to fill their empty beds during the closed season, Banff has

Essentials

Altitude: 5,350ft (1631m)–8,650ft (2637m)
Map: see page M20
Further information: t +1 403 762 4421, www.skibig3.com
Lifts in area: 24 (2 cableways, 20 chairs, 2 drags) serving 7,558 acres in area: 4,200 acres at Lake Louise, 3,168 acres at Sunshine Village, 190 acres at Ski Banff@Norquay
Lift pass: adult CDN$347.75–363.80, child 5–12yrs CDN$171.20, youth 13–17yrs CDN$325, all for 5 days
Access: Calgary airport 90mins

become an important destination for temporary migrants from the slopes of Andorra and Austria in search of fresh low-cost ski fields and an equally frenetic nightlife.

Lake Louise lies 56km away across the park down the Trans-Canadian highway, which is dotted with little bridges so that elk and other animals can cross in safety. It is so small that 'village' is an exaggeration, a handful of hotels and a couple of shops that originally owed their *raison d'être* to the Canadian Pacific railway line. It built the splendid Victorian hotel, the Château Lake Louise, here so that passengers could rest in comfort while drinking in one of most dramatic glacial vistas of the Rockies. Lake Louise has its own substantial ski area situated an inconvenient five-minute bus ride away from the 'village' and hotels.

Sunshine Village is again not a 'village', but the name of the third ski area sandwiched between the two, 16km from Banff and 24km from Lake Louise. Its skiing rivals that of Lake Louise, but the only place to stay is in a hotel at the mid-mountain base, reached by gondola and far from any serious hope of evening entertainment beyond a glass of wine with dinner.

We recommend visitors stay in Banff and commute to the ski areas. All three share a regional lift pass and are connected by a regular bus service. However, renting a car adds considerable convenience and avoids any hanging around in what can be mind-numbingly low temperatures in mid-winter.

Mountain

Mount Norquay is much more than a local hill, but you didn't cross the Atlantic to spend a week or ten days riding three quad-chairs. Nevertheless we spent an enjoyable morning here repeatedly cruising beautifully groomed, but short trails cut through the trees. The pitch dictates whether each is classified as easy or intermediate. Four of them correctly get a double-black-diamond rating.

Lake Louise is far more exciting. A multi-mountain area with every type of terrain from gentle tree-lined trails to steep chutes and awesome open bowls. It is all challenging stuff, but less confident skiers should not be scared away. An easy run descends from every lift. The Larch Express Quad gives access to a couple of easy motorways as well as four hugely enjoyable blue trails.

For strong intermediates as well as advanced skiers and riders, the pick of the action is off the backside. A host of demanding or downright impossible chutes are reached along the heavily corniced ridge from the top of the Summit Platter lift and the Top of the World Express. On a big powder day the locals just ski lap after lap here. The new Grizzly Express gondola accesses some steep double-diamond-graded tree-skiing that is served on the backside by the Ptarmigan quad.

The whole area is popular with snowboarders and we rate the terrain park as one of the best we have ever experienced.

Sunshine Village has three separate mountains. Mount Standish is a rounded, exposed peak with a mixture of terrain for all standards. Look Out Mountain suits strong intermediates and more advanced skiers, while Goat's Eye Mountain is the domain of the hardcore.

Delirium Dive is a classic steep here. While not in the same league as Corbet's in Jackson Hole, it is spoken off in reverentially hushed tones by the cognoscenti. The ski patrol adds to the hype by insisting that you wear a transceiver and have shovel and probe in your backpack. In fact, the idea is to confine this pitch to dedicated off-piste enthusiasts who are already sufficiently experienced enough to have bought their own gear – you can't rent a transceiver anywhere nearby. After a usually tricky entrance it opens into a steep bowl with a choice of exits: the more direct involves a walk-out, while a lengthy traverse to the skier's right offers more powder and a speedier return to a lift.

Learn

Lake Louise, t +1 403 522 1333, **Banff@Norquay, t** +1 403 760 7717, and **Sunshine Village, t** +1 403 762 6560, ski and snowboard schools all offer group and private lessons. **Club Ski/Snowboard, t** +1 403 760 7731, runs three-day courses for groups of similar ability, with guided tours of all three resorts.

Children

At Lake Louise, **Telus Play Station, t** +1 403 522 1333, takes babies from three weeks old. **Club Ski Junior programme, t** +1 403 760 7731, offers a cool mix of guiding and instruction. **Tiny Tigers Daycare, t** +1 403 762 6560, at Sunshine Village and **The Kids' Place, t** +1 403 760 7717, at SkiBanff@Norquay offers daycare from 19 months.

Lunch

At Mount Norquay, Cascade Lodge houses the **Lone Pine** restaurant, t +1 403 762 4421, serving hearty mountain fare.

At Lake Louise, **Sawyers Nook** upstairs at the Temple Lodge, t +1 403 522 3555, has waiter-service food and an intimate atmosphere. **Kokanee Kabin**, t +1 403 522 3555, at the base has barbecues and beer. **Lodge of the Ten Peaks**, t +1 403 522 3555, and the **Whisky Jack Lodge**, t +1 403 522 3555, house a cafeteria. **The Great Bear Room**, t +1 403 522 3555 has self-service dining with soups, pasta and roast beef.

At Sunshine, all the restaurants are at the mid-mountain base area, t +1 403 762 4421, for all. **Lookout Bistro** on the top floor of the Day Lodge has a full menu and a warm fireplace. We recommend **The Eagle's Nest** in Sunshine Inn for a long, relaxed lunch. **Mad Trapper's Saloon** in Old Sunshine Lodge is a Western-style saloon on two floors with the ubiquitous burger.

Dine

Banff has a wonderfully wide choice of restaurants that reflect its multi-cultural clientele. **Maple Leaf Grille**, t +1 403 760 7680, is essentially Canadian with an emphasis on elk, bison, duck and lobster. **Melissa's**, t +1 403 762 5511, is a rustic log cabin with great steaks and BBQ ribs. **Le Beaujolais**, t +1 403 762 2712, is French, romantic and regularly wins Canadian culinary awards. **Giorgio's Trattoria**, t +1 403 762 5114, is Italian. Try the *osso buco* with *polenta*. **El Toro**, t +1 403 762 2520, is Greek. **The Silver Dragon**, t +1 403 762 3939, serves Cantonese and Peking cuisine. **Pad Thai**, t +1 403 762 4911, is Thai, and **Miki**, t +1 403 286 2860, is Japanese.

In Lake Louise Village, the **Post Hotel**, t +1 403 522 3989, and **Deer Lodge**, t +1 403 522 3747, are the pick of a limited choice. **Timber Wolf Pizza** at the **Lake Louise Inn**, t +1 403 522 3791 is recommended. **The**

Fairmont Chateau Lake Louise, t +1 403 522 3511, has four restaurants including the **Walliser Stube Wine Bar**, t +1 403 522 1817. **Mountain Restaurant**, t +1 403 522 3573 serves Asian fusion cuisine and pasta.

Party

Après-ski in Banff largely revolves around the enormous number of bars scattered along Banff Avenue. These include **Tommy's Neighbourhood Pub**, The **Magpie & Stump**, **Rose & Crown**, and **St James's Gate** – an Irish pub originally built in Dublin and shipped over in pieces to Canada. **Wild Bill's** has Country and Western bands, and the **Barbary Coast** has live rock. bands. **Hoodoo Lounge** and **Aurora** are both popular nightclubs. The nightlife at Lake Louise is considerably quieter and restricted to a few hotel bars.

Sleep

Luxury:
Banff:
Fairmont Banff Springs, t +1 403 762 2211, *www.fairmont.com/banffsprings*, Château Lake Louise's majestic 'sister' hotel, is designed to look like a Scottish castle with one of the best spas in Canada.
Rimrock Resort Hotel, t +1 403 762 3356, *www.rimrockresort.com*, is elegant and modern, located on Sulphur Mountain a short walk from Banff's natural hot springs.
Lake Louise:
Fairmont Château Lake Louise, t +1 403 522 3511, *www.fairmont.com/lakelouise*, is in a quiet wilderness setting with spectacular views over the frozen lake.
The Post Hotel, t +1 403 522 3989, *www.posthotel.com*, also in Lake Louise, is a luxuriously elegant recreation in 1900s style.

Moderate/Budget:

Banff:

Buffalo Mountain Lodge, t +1 403 410 7417, *www.crmr.com/lodgebuffalo.php*, is ruggedly luxurious, with open fires and beams.

The Mount Royal, t +1 403 762 3331, *www.mountroyalhotel.com*, is ideally placed for the nightlife of Banff.

Banff Caribou Lodge, t +1 403 762 5887, *www.bestofbanff.com*, is a 15-minute walk from downtown and is in rustic Western style.

The Banff King Edward, t +1 403 762 2202, is the town's second oldest hotel.

Siding 29 Lodge, t +1 403 762 5575, *www.bestwesternsiding29.com*, is a no-frills hotel with an indoor pool.

The Rundle Manor Hotel, t +1 403 762 5544, is a good-value apartment-style hotel.

Juniper Inn, t +1 403 762 2281, *www.decorehotels.com/juniper*, has newly renovated chalets and suites.

Lake Louise:

Deer Lodge, t +1 403 522 3747, *www.crmr.com/lodgedeer.php*, is two minutes' walk from the lake shore, and ideal for those wanting a quiet retreat. It has a roof-top hot tub.

Sunshine Village:

Sunshine Village Inn, t +1 403 762 6564, *www.skibanff.com/accommodation/inn.html*, is reached by a 15-minute gondola ride from Sunshine base and is the area's only on-mountain accommodation.

Big White, BC

Profile

Attractive village with doorstep skiing for intermediates and powder skiers. More suited to families than party-goers,

---

Essentials

Altitude: 4,950ft (1508m)–7606ft (2319m)
Further information: t +1 250 765 3101, *www.bigwhite.com*
Lifts in area: 13 (1 cableway, 9 chairs, 3 drags) serving 85km of trails
Lift pass: adult CD$330, child 6–12yrs CD$162, both for 6 days
Access: Kelowna airport 35 miles (56km), Vancouver airport 4½hrs

---

with a lack of mountain restaurants and après-ski venues

Resort

Big White is a big hitter among the more recently developed clutch of Canadian resorts that have successfully sought international acclaim on the coat-tails of Whistler. It is hidden away in BC in the beautiful Okanagan Valley, the country's equally successful wine-growing region.

Big White takes its name from the sometimes all-enveloping humid cloud cover, which creates a phantom forest of snow-ghosts – trees frozen into eerie monster-like shapes. It is under the same Australian ownership as nearby Silver Star.

Mountain

This is much more than the local hill for Kelowna, a small but testing intermediate area with magical charm. Beginners congregate around the Humming Bird quad below the village, while others head directly for the Ridge Rocket Express which gives smooth access to the main network of runs. Best off-piste is between the snow-ghosts in Sun Ripe Bowl. Riders meet at Telus Park, which has a 500ft super-pipe, a half-pipe and all the usual toys.

Learn

Big White's **Ski and Snowboard School**, **t** +1 250 491 6113, incorporates **Telus Heavy Metal Flight School**, which teaches terrain park technique.

Children

The Kids' Centre, t +1 250 418 6118, provides ski and non-ski daycare from 18 months, and is warmly recommended.

Lunch

The West Ridge Warming Hut, Day Lodge and **Happy Valley Lodge, t** +1 250 765 3101, for all, provide limited alcohol-free options. Wise skiers return to the resort. Try **Frank's Chinese Laundry, t** +1 250 765 7866.

Dine

Snowshoe Sam's, t +1 250 491 765 1416, has good steaks and burgers. **Kettle Valley, t** +1 250 491 0130, has the best gourmet fare. **The Swiss Bear, t** +1 250 491 7750, has authentic fondues.

Party

Snowshoe Sam's is the main resort rendezvous, with pool tables and a dance floor.

Sleep

All the accommodation adjoins the piste and includes a range of condos. Further details **t** +1 250 765 8888, *www.bigwhite.com*
Luxury:
Chateau Big White is the resort's best address at the top of the village. It has a small spa.

Big White Condos throughout the resort, including Firefight Lodge, first phase of 14 new mountain rental homes which opens this season.
Moderate/budget:
Inn at Big White is the only hotel here, with a pool.
White Crystal Inn is in a good location with large family rooms.

Fernie, BC

Profile

Good-value, but remote ski-in ski-out resort with uncrowded slopes, extensive piste grooming, a friendly atmosphere and a good snow record. Well-suited to families, very limited nightlife

Resort

Fernie has been likened to Argentière without glaciers, a wonderfully challenging ski area in a remote corner of BC that has the topographical potential to become the new Whistler. International powderhounds tend to rate Fernie in their top five destinations in North America. Few destinations can offer such premium pistes and powder within the infrastructure of a modern ski village that

Essentials

Altitude: 3,500ft (1068m)–6,316ft (1925m)
Map: see page M21
Further information: **t** +1 250 423 4655, *www.skifernie.com*
Lifts in area: 10 (6 chairs, 4 drags) serving 2,504 acres of terrain
Lift pass: adult CDN$348, child 6–12yrs CDN$120, both for 6 days
Access: Calgary airport 3½hrs

is backed by all the charm and historical association of an attractive Victorian railway town.

Over the past ten years this small and once unfashionable resort has achieved pipe-dream fame as luxurious apartment blocks and mountain homes sprouted around the ski village.

Real estate developers have now started on a CDN$1.5 billion development between the ski area and the old town that is the setting for a Greg Norman championship golf course due to open in 2007. To their surprise and delight 30 of the first 50 homes attracted British buyers. Nearby Cranbrook airport has got the go-ahead to increase its runway to take large airliners, and the whole region looks set for its biggest boom since the 19th-century gold rush.

But where are the new lifts? Fernie's ski area has somehow managed its metamorphosis from ugly duckling to swan with six chairs – none of them covered and only two of them quads. Fernie now belongs to Resorts of the Canadian Rockies, which also owns Banff-Lake Louise, Kimberley, Stoneham and Mont-Sainte-Anne. An initial CDN$6 million investment over two years has resulted in new base facilities but so far no fresh uphill transport.

Despite all the comfortable living accommodation, it is foolish to suppose that international skiers will continue to support Fernie unless it dramatically overhauls its antiquated lift system. Go-ahead Kicking Horse is waiting in the wings to grab Whistler's crown, while two major new resorts are under construction in BC.

Visitors have the choice of staying in ski-convenient hotel rooms and condos at the base area or in the old town of Fernie, three miles below the resort. By slumbering with minimal change throughout the 20th century it has managed to retain its considerable Victorian charm. A regular bus service operates between the mountain village and the town.

Mountain

This is one of these rare resorts that truly suits all levels, and its compact size lends itself particularly well to families. It has a good beginner area at the base, and plenty of tree-skiing for all standards. However the real action is found in the series of five deep powder bowls that stand side by side beneath the 2000m peaks of Elephant Head, Polar Peak and Grizzly Peak. These provide an astonishing variety of challenging terrain that will keep a strong intermediate or advanced skier happy for a whole season.

Main mountain access is by two successive quads from the base area that take you up into Lizard Bowl, setting for the notorious Face Lift. This meat-hook tow, which would be more at home on a Kiwi club field, needs to be treated with considerable respect. The slow and cold Timber Bowl Express quad from the base area brings you to the steep terrain of Siberia Bowl at the other end of the ski area. Fernie is popular with riders. It has a terrain park reached by the Timber chair-lift, and a half-pipe on Bambi trail, close to the base area.

Learn

Fernie Alpine Resort Winter Sports School, t +1 250 423 4655, is warmly recommended for lessons in alpine skiing, snowboarding and telemark. Backcountry excursions can be arranged through **Fernie Wilderness Adventures Snowcat Skiing, t** +1 250 423 6704, **Island Lake Lodge** and **Powder Cowboy Cat Skiing, t** +1 250 423 3700, and **RK Heli-ski** in nearby Panorama, **t** +1 250 342 3889.

Children

Telus Resort Kids Daycare, t +1 250 423 4655, looks after small babies and toddlers. The children's ski programme is extensive. The Freeriders Programme is aimed at experienced teenagers.

Lunch

The Wood on the Hill, t +1 250 423 4597, is the best proper lunch option. **Kelsey's**, t +1 250 423 2444, in the Cornerstone Lodge in the village centre has English-style fish and chips and Mexican dishes. **Lizard Creek Lodge**, t +1 250 423 205, has a reasonably priced bar menu.

Dine

Lizard Creek Lodge, t +1 250 423 205, has the finest food in the ski village. **River Rock Bistro**, t +1 250 423 6871, in Park Place Lodge is recommended for steaks and local trout. **Gabriella's**, t +1 250 423 7388, is Italian and serves good-value pasta dishes. The **Alpine Lodge**, t +1 250 423 4237, above the base area, is Asian fusion. In old Fernie, **Yamagoya**, t +1 250 430 0090, serves sushi. **The Old Elevator**, t +1 250 423 7115, features Ahi tuna carpaccio and pan-seared venison rack. **Rip 'n' Richard's Eatery**, t +1 250 423 3002, has more basic Canadian fare. The historic **Royal Hotel**, t +1 250 423 7743, features modern Australian cuisine.

Party

The **Griz Bar** is where the après-ski starts, but dog-sledding and *ski-jöring* take precedence over Alpine Oompah here. Try your hand at ice-skating or curling in the old town. **Eldorado Lounge**, **Grand Central Hotel & Bar** and the **Royal Hotel** are popular meeting places with regular live music.

Sleep

Luxury:
Lizard Creek Lodge, t +1 250 423 205, *www.lizardcreek.com*, is the best address on the mountain, with spacious condos, a gym, swimming-pool and hot tub. The bar serves snacks while you sit in squashy sofas around the open fire.
Moderate/budget:
Fernie Alpine Lodge, t +1 250 423 4237, *www.alpinelodge.com*, is a ski-in ski-out B&B with a warm atmosphere.
Cornerstone Lodge, t +1 250 423 6855, *www.cornerstonelodge.ca*, is at the foot of Deer chair and houses Kelsey's Restaurant.
Park Place Lodge, t +1 250 423 6871, *www.parkplacelodge.com*, is in the old town and has modern rooms.
The Old Nurses Residence, t +1 250 423 3091, *www.oldnurse.com*, is a B&B built in 1908, with large and attractively restored rooms.
Royal Hotel, t +1 250 423 7750, *www.fernieroyalhotel.com*, is Victorian and has great atmosphere.

Kicking Horse, BC

Profile

Rugged terrain best suited to good skiers and riders wanting serious challenges without having to ignore creature comforts. KH has the best mountain restaurant in North America and new, comfortable accommodation at its base. Not suited to easy cruisers

Essentials

Altitude: 3,902ft (1190m)–8,037ft (2450m)
Further information: t +1 250 439 5424,
  www.kickinghorseresort.com
Lifts in area: 4 (1 cableway, 3 chairs)
  serving 2,750 acres
Lift pass: adult CDN$309, child 7–12yrs
  CDN$134, both for 6 days
Access: Calgary airport 3hrs

Resort

When it opened five years ago, Kicking Horse was billed as the first new resort in the world to be built in a generation. This was not strictly true, but after a tricky start in a bad-snow winter the ski area in a remote corner of BC has far exceeded all expectations and become one of our favourite resorts on both continents. It now has world-class ranking with tough terrain comparable to Whistler and Jackson Hole.

The secret of its international appeal lies in an agreeable blend of Canadian know-how and European sophistication, coupled with substantial Dutch finance. Backbone of KH is a high-speed gondola, which gives a respectable 1260m vertical drop on a ski mountain of near perfect shape. The bottom third of the mountain used to be the old community ski hill of White Tooth above the valley town of Golden. Certainly it needed vision to choose this remote spot.

This is no quaint Victorian mining town awaiting a little gentrification, but a busy blue-collar railway junction awkwardly sprawled across both sides of the tracks and lacking even an ounce of charm.

But having completed the gondola, the stroke of European-inspired genius was to build, at the top of it, the best mountain restaurant in North America.

However, no one would willingly choose to spend a week or a fortnight in a Golden roadside motel. Therefore commensurate accommodation had to be constructed. So far this has taken the form of delightful mountain homes and new guest lodges that ring the base area.

Mountain

Either through lack of finance or foresight, the developers failed to build a half-way station for the Golden Eagle Express gondola. The number of cabins has now been doubled, but queues inevitably develop at peak times. A nearby quad-chair serves the beginner area and an old fixed-grip double gives access to some easy and advanced runs on the lower half of the mountain. But Eagle's Eye on the summit is why you make the effort to travel all this way.

Unlike Jackson Hole's aerial tram, the gondola does offer an easy route down for those who have either eaten and drunk too much in the restaurant – or lost their nerve when they began to discover the nature of the terrain.

The choice of *entrées* starts right outside the door of the Eagle's Eye restaurant. Wicked black-diamonds fall away from both sides of the ridge to produce some sensational tree- and bowl-skiing. Some of this is steep by any standards, and for anyone lacking in confidence it pays to study the topography before immediately committing yourself to runs that may test your ability to its limits.

Stairway to Heaven, a detachable-quad on the far side of the ski area, takes you up to Blue Heaven, highest point on the mountain. More steep runs follow down through the trees on one side of Redemption Ridge. The other leads down into Feuz Bowl, a glorious powder cache after a fresh fall. Kicking Horse's 2,600-acre ski area is now larger than Breckenridge and this season has 10 new marked runs.

Learn

Kicking Horse Snow School, t +1 866 754 5425, has already established a reputation as a worthy powder academy. Heli-skiing can be arranged through **Purcell Heli Skiing**, t +1 250 344 5410.

Children

No kindergarten facilities. The ski school teaches children from three years.

Lunch

Corks, t +1 250 344 7644, in the Copper Horse Lodge serves pasta and pizza. **Glacier Lodge** has a new sushi bar and café, t +1 250 439 1160. A mid-mountain yurt – called **Heaven's Door** – serves sushi. The base lodge has a self-service restaurant but the **Eagle's Eye**, t +1 250 439 5400, at the gondola summit, has a roaring log fire, floor-to-ceiling windows, and wooden rafters which all add to the atmosphere. Local game is the culinary speciality.

Dine

The Eagle's Eye, t +1 250 439 5400, is open on weekend evenings.

Corks, t +1 250 344 7644 and **Sushi Bar & Café** in Glacier Lodge, t +1 250 439 1160 are both open for dinner. Golden boasts a number of coffee shops, bars and cafés, such as the smoky **Mad Trapper Pub**, t +1 250 344 2330, and the **Dogtooth Café**, t +1 250 344 3660. **Cedar House**, t +1 250 344 4679, on the edge of town, is strongly recommended. **The Kicking Horse Grill**, t +1 250 344 2330, which has a Dutch chef/owner, is highly recommended for its atmospheric log-cabin setting and adventurous cuisine.

Party

The **Mad Trapper Pub** in Golden has been the only establishment to rise to the evening needs of skiers and snowboarders. However, the new **Vagabond Lodge**, near the ski area base, has a bar and games room.

Sleep

Luxury:
The Eagle's Eye restaurant, t +1 250 439 5400, *www.kickinghorseresort. com/eagleseye* has two suites where you can stay after dinner and make 'first tracks' down in the morning.
The ski-in ski-out chalets, t +1 250 439 5424, at the area base are beautifully equipped with large rooms and modern kitchens, outdoor hot-tubs and garages.
Copper Horse Lodge, t +1 250 344 7644, *ww.copperhorselodge.com*, is a 10-room boutique hotel housing Corks restaurant.
Glacier Lodge, t +1 250 439 1160, is just 100ft from the Eagles Express gondola and comprises a health club, sushi bar and ski shop.
Vagabond Lodge, t +1 250 344 2622, *www. vagabondlodge.ca*, opens this season with 10 suites and a lounge with fireplace.
About 45km away on the other side of Kicking Horse Pass, **Emerald Lake Lodge**, t +1 403 410 7417, *www.crmr.com/ lodgeemerald.php*, is a lakeside mountain retreat built of hand-hewn timber and featuring massive stone fireplaces. Accommodation is in 24 cabin-style buildings.
Budget:
Golden, a ten-minute drive away, has half-a-dozen B&Bs, and a handful of motels and lodges.
The Ramada Golden, t +1 250 439 1888, *www.ramadagolden.com*, has an indoor swimming pool.
The Prestige Inn, t +1 250 344 7990, *www.prestigeinn.com*, has simple rooms.

Panorama, BC

Profile

Purpose-built village close to some of Canada's best heli-skiing. The piste skiing best suits intermediates and families

Resort

Panorama is an attractive village built by resort developer Intrawest, with comfortable accommodation and good skiing for all standards. It lies a two-hour drive to the south-west of Banff and is on the edge of the Bugaboos.

Mountain

The mainly easy and intermediate terrain here received a major boost a few years ago when the old T-bars on the front face were replaced by three quad-chairs. The enjoyable trails cut through the trees offer few challenges but are ideal for anyone wanting the Canadian ski experience in a thoroughly agreeable environment. Taynton Bowl, off the backside with 1,000 acres of chutes, gullies and difficult tree-skiing,

is a worthy off-piste playground for more advanced skiers.

The resort is included in the Canadian Rockies Super Pass covering eight other resorts, including Banff-Lake Louise, Fernie, Nakiska and Kimberley.

Learn

The School of Skiing and Snowboarding, t +1 250 342 6941, organizes group and private lessons.

Children

Wee Wascals, t +1 250 341 3041, provides daycare for children from 18 months. **Snowbirds ski kindergarten, t** +1 250 342 6941, accepts children from three years.

Lunch

The Summit Hut, t +1 250 342 0217, has a limited menu but great views. **Scott Nordic Centre, t** +1 250 342 6941 x3840 has a restaurant and is at the base of Sunbird chair.

Dine

Wildfire Grill, t +1 250 342 6941, is relaxed and reasonably priced, serving burgers, salads and ribs. **Ferrari's on Toby Creek, t** +1 250 341 3056, has affordable family dining. **Earl Grey Lodge, t** +1 250 341 3641, specializes in French and Italian dishes. You can also eat at the **Heli-Plex restaurant, t** +1 250 342 6941, where the local heli-skiing is based.

Party

This is not a great resort for partying. The **Crazy Horse Saloon** and **Jackpine Pub** are the main rendezvous points. The **Glacier Nightclub** is for music and dancing. You can relax at the **Panorama**

Essentials

Altitude: 3,800ft (1158m)–7,800ft (2360m)
Further information: t +1 250 342 6941, *www.panoramaresort.com*
Lifts in area: 8 (1 cableway, 5 chairs, 2 drags) serving 2,847 acres of terrain
Lift pass: adult CDN$299, child 7–12yrs CDN$139, both for 6 days
Access: Calgary airport 4hrs

Springs outdoor waterpark, or take the shuttle bus to the valley town of Invermere to bathe in the radium hot springs.

Sleep

Luxury:
For all accommodation contact Resort Reservations, **t** +1 250 342 6941.
Riverbend Townhomes on Toby Creek have easy access to the Village gondola.
Wolf Lake Townhomes are in a ski-in ski-out position by the Sunbird chair-lift.
Gold Premium Lodging is in condos in the Upper Village.
Earl Grey Lodge, t +1 250 341 3641, *www.earlgreylodge.com*, is a privately-owned boutique hotel situated 200m from the main mountain access lift.
Moderate/budget:
Silver Lodging is at Creekside.
Bronze Lodging is at the Pine Inn at the base of the Mile 1 chair.

Red Resort, BC

Profile

Rough and tough skiing for accomplished intermediates to advanced skiers and boarders. Accommodation choice lies between small ski base area and historic valley town

Resort

Red is under potentially dynamic new ownership and it has dropped the 'Mountain' from its name. For a while back in 2004 it looked as if this cult resort in

BC, with a rugged reputation for some of the steepest terrain in Canada, was going to go out of business. But to the delight of the people of the nearby distressed Victorian mining town of Rossland, Red was saved in the nick of time by a businessman from San Diego in California.

What he is going to do with it still remains to be seen, but he has begun with a major property development around the base area. Retro-chic is what Red has traded upon for a generation – a last frontier of Canadian machismo where slow lifts, mighty moguls and big drop-offs were the name of the game. But commercial reality is that retro-chic makes money for no one.

Mountain

Red and adjoining Granite Mountains can be skied 360 degrees on all faces that are served by only six lifts. Together they offer 83 trails of which a high 45 per cent is graded at least black-diamond. The vertical drop is only 887m but the longest run – Long Squaw – is a respectable 7km. The off-piste opportunities down through the trees are endless and the overall quality of the skiing is nothing short of phenomenal. Red's terrain park on the T-bar slope has 15 rails, funboxes, and table-tops.

Learn

Red Snowsports School, t +1 800 663 0105, offers lessons and guiding.

Children

Club Red Kindercare, t +1 800 663 0105, accepts children from 18 months, and combines skiing with childcare for three-to-six-year-olds.

Lunch

Paradise Lodge has been revamped and provides simple but good food. Rafters Lounge at the base lodge is recommended. For information contact, t +1 800 663 0105.

Dine

Mountain Gypsy Café, t +1 250 362 3342, in Rossland has good fusion cuisine.

Party

The laid-back town of Rossland has little more than bars with pool and air-hockey tables. The Powder Keg Pub in the Prestige Mountain Resort is the town's hot spot.

Sleep

Moderate/budget:
The former Uplander has become Prestige Mountain Resort-Rossland, t +1 250 362 7375, and has simple rooms.
Black Bear B&B, t +1 250 362 3398, *www.blackbearinn.ca*, is five minutes' drive from Red, was built in 1898 and has an outdoor hot-tub.
The Ram's Head Inn, t +1 250 362 9577, *www.ramshead.bc.ca*, a pleasant B&B, is almost ski-in ski-out, with communal breakfast dining and a hot-tub.

Silver Star, BC

Profile

Intriguing neo-Victorian village with convenient skiing for intermediates and advanced skiers and riders. Recommended ski school

Resort

Silver Star is one of a trio of resorts in the heart of the the scenic wine-growing country of BC that has come to prominence over the past five years. It's not big, but combined with Big White, its Australian-owned stablemate, this area makes for a great holiday.

At first sight, the nine-lift resort near Vernon suggests that it is a restored *fin de siècle* mining town. In fact the 'old' vividly painted townhouses and streets lit with soft sodium lamps are a complete sham. For a purpose-built resort it has considerable panache, but it is not a place for non-skiers.

Mountain

The ski area, our favourite in the Okanagan Valley, is underrated. The front face comprises the usual North American menu of gladed easy and intermediate runs. However, the backside is much more

Essentials

Altitude: 3,780ft (1155m)–6,280ft (1915m)
Further information: t +1 250 542 0224, *www.skisilverstar.com*
Lifts in area: 9 (5 chairs, 4 drags) serving 2,725 acres of terrain
Lift pass: adult CDN$349, child 6–12yrs CDN$157, both for 6 days
Access: Kelowna airport 55mins

demanding. Double-diamond runs such as vertiginous Freefall and the infamous Cowabunga are of sufficiently steep pitch to make even the most jaded powderhound think edge control. The terrain park is one of the most highly rated in BC.

Learn

Silver Star Snowsport School, t +1 250 558 6065, has a strong reputation for teaching cutting-edge ski and snowboard technique.

Lunch

Paradise Camp, t +1 250 558 6087, near the top of the Powder Gulch Express, offers the only on-mountain lunch. Longjohn's Pub, t +1 250 549 2992, is back in the village.

Children

Star Kids Center, t +1 250 558 6065, accepts little ones from newborn to six years old, skiers and riders from four years.

Dine

The Italian Garden Restaurant, t +1 250 558 1448, has pizzas and pasta, Clementine's, t +1 250 545 3208, has live piano at weekends, and the Silver Lode Restaurant, t +1 250 549 5105, serves international cuisine. The Craigellachie Room at Putnam Station Inn, t +1 250 542 2459, is warmly recommended.

Party

Après-ski here is what you make it. Beyond Wrapture Mind and Body Care Day Spa is one place in which to relax, while the tubing park is another. The

action then shifts rather slowly to a pre-dinner drink in the Wine Cellar below Putnam Station followed by the pool table in the Saloon.

Sleep

Luxury:
Victorian Vacation Homes range from simple studios to five-bedroom townhouses with private hot-tubs, t +1 250 542 0224.
Moderate:
Bookings for all, t +1 250 558 6083.
The Silver Star Club Resort is a complex of three buildings in a ski-in ski-out position.
Creekside Condos are beside the tubing park and suitable for families.
Putnam Station is a colourful wooden building with rustic charm.
Silver Lode Inn is a European-style property with simple rooms in a good location.

Sun Peaks, BC

Profile

Upmarket resort with comfortable accommodation, good restaurants and nightlife, and doorstep skiing for all standards. Not the place for non-skiers

Resort

Sun Peaks has come a long way in the 13 years since a Japanese company bought Tod Mountain outside the BC mining town of Kamloops. Lying as it does nearly four hours by road from Vancouver, it seemed an unlikely location for an international resort .

But Nancy Greene, the *grande dame* of Canadian skiing who won Olympic gold in Grenoble, was summoned to give her opinion on the terrain. 'It took me rather less than 30 minutes to say "yes",' she said. Nancy set about promoting newly-named Sun Peaks while owners Nippon Cable Company stomped up CDN$225 million. The result is a delightful three-mountain ski area set around a well-designed purpose-built village with world-class accommodation.

Mountain

The skiing is suited to strong intermediates who will enjoy the mainly short but searching runs on Sundance and on Mount Tod. Advanced skiers will find plenty to keep them busy on steeper trails served by the Burfield quad. But the real excitement is the well-organized cat-skiing on the upper reaches of Mount Todd.

Novices and wobbly second-weekers will find their ski legs on Mount Morrisey, where the gentlest of scenic trails have been cut through the trees. Sun Peaks has a terrain park and a 100m half-pipe.

Learn

Sun Peaks Snowsports School, t +1 250 578 5505, is for group and private lessons.

Children

Sundance Playschool, t +1 250 578 5433, cares for babies from 18 months. **Sun Tots** gives private ski lessons from three years, and **Sun Kids Adventure Club, t** both +1 250 578 5505, accepts children from six years for skiing and eight years for snowboarding.

Lunch

Mountain eating is limited to the grim **Sunburst Self-service, t** +1 250 578 7222, at the top of the Sunburst Express.

Dine

Sun Peaks Village has an Asian restaurant called **Toro, t** +1 250 578 7870. **The Val, t** +1 250 578 8111 in Sun Peaks Lodge and **Macker's Bistro & Bar, t** +1 250 578 7894, in Nancy Green's Cahility Lodge, are both recommended. **Powderhounds Restaurant, t** +1 250 578 0014, in the Fireside Lodge offers a European/ Canadian menu.

Party

Macdaddy's, in the Delta Sun Peak Resort, is the liveliest nightspot.

Sleep

Luxury:
Delta Sun Peaks Resort, t +1 250 578 6000, *www.deltasunpeaks.bcresorts.com,* is one of the country's finest ski hotels.
Moderate:
Nancy Greene's **Cahilty Lodge, t** +1 250 578 7454, *www.cahiltylodge.com,* is ski-in ski-out.
Fireside Lodge, t +1 270 578 7842, *www.woodlandsatsunpeaks.com/Lodges Fireside.html,* condos have fully equipped kitchens.

Hearthstone Lodge, t +1 250 578 8588, *www.hearthstonelodgeatsunpeaks.com*, is a charming boutique hotel.
The Ice Palace Hotel, t +1 604 328 2663, *www.icepalacehotel.com*, featuring themed ice rooms, ice bar, ice chapel and ice sculptures, is new for this season.

Essentials

Altitude: 870ft (265m)–3,001ft (915m)
Further information: t +1 819 681 2000, *www.tremblant.ca*
Lifts in area: 9 (1 cableway, 8 chairs) serving 628 acres of terrain
Lift pass: CDN$257.75–346.27, children 6–12yrs CDN$147.28–209.70, both for 6 days
Access: Montréal airport 1½hrs

Tremblant, Québec

Profile

State-of-the-art lift system, beautifully groomed slopes, extensive snowmaking, attractive purpose-built village, and *québeçois* cuisine. Bitterly cold mid-winter temperatures might deter some people

Resort

Tremblant has achieved phenomenal success. A decade has slipped by since developer Intrawest began pumping in tens of millions of dollars in one of its first lucrative explorations of the relationships between real estate, ski areas and golf courses.

What's surprising is that the company behind Whistler in BC and Arc 1950 in France chose such a modest mountain in chilly Québec rather than the Rockies. What's even more surprising is that Tremblant now ranks close to Whistler as the most popular destination in Canada for European skiers.

Tremblant lies in the Laurentian Mountains, 150km north-west of Montréal. Intrawest retained the original village of Vieux-Tremblant while creating a new one of steeply terraced streets with painted wooden buildings modelled on the old quarter of Québec City. A visit here is a chance to appreciate *québeçois* culture and cuisine in contrived but charming surroundings. The ambience is warm, but the same cannot be said about the air temperature in mid-winter. European February half-term is the most popular time to visit, but for families with young children the temperature can be too low for enjoyable skiing.

Mountain

The nine-lift ski area stretches in four sectors across both faces of the mountain. The main Équilibre beginner area lies just above the village, and most of the easy intermediate terrain is also on the South Side. The heated gondola ride up from the village to the Grand Manitou temporarily shelters you from the reality of skiing in a cold climate. But low temperatures do not necessarily equate with high snowfall. To compensate for nature's not infrequent failure, Tremblant has Canada's largest artificial snowmaking system.

The North Side receives little sunshine in winter – a fact you may well feel, or rather not feel, in your fingers – and consequently retains good cover throughout the winter. It offers considerably more scope for strong intermediates and advanced skiers and riders. A couple of trails have short sharp pitches of 42 degrees and call for a high level of technique in the often-icy conditions.

The Edge, served by its own quad-chair, is an area set aside for accomplished skiers and riders. Haute-Tension, an expert run that follows the fall line beneath the lift, is guaranteed to raise blood pressure.

The main terrain park, Nintendo Park, on the North Side, has a super-pipe, quarter-pipe and a variety of obstacles. Two further parks on the South Side are for experts and beginners. The nearby intermediate runs of Réaction and Sensation wind down through the frozen spruces and provide a dramatic introduction to tree-skiing.

Learn

The Tremblant Snow School, t +1 819 681 5666, has a first-rate reputation but new visitors to this part of Canada may be surprised to discover that not all instructors are necessarily fluent English speakers.

Children

Kidz Club, t +1 819 681 5666, at the base of the slopes provides daycare for non-skiing children from 12 months, and runs ski programmes from three years of age.

Lunch

Mountain eating includes a wide range of cafeteria-style places, including **Le Grand Manitou, t** +1 819 681 3000, at the summit. **Le Refuge du Trappeur, t** +1 450 533 1091, on the Versant Soleil is a log cabin that serves soups and drinks by the fireplace.

Dine

The cost of eating out in Tremblant is high at the eclectic choice of restaurants from pizzas and cuisine *québeçois* to sushi. **Aux Truffes, t** +1 819 681 4544, is for truffles, *foie gras* and game, and La Forge has steaks and grills. **La Grappe à Vin, t** +1 819 681 4727, is an intimate eatery serving creative French cuisine with an extensive wine list. **Coco-Pazzo, t** +1 819 681 4774, offers Italian and vegetarian food, and **Crêperie Catherine, t** +1 819 681 4888, specializes in Breton crêpes. **Restaurant U, t** +1 819 681 4141, combines sushi with international creations. **Mexicali Rosa's, t** +1 819 681 2439, is Californian-Mexican. **Loup-Garou** in the Fairmont Tremblant, **t** +1 819 681 7685, offers 'daring Québec cuisine'.

Party

Bar Café d'Époque is a main resort meeting place, open from mid-afternoon until 3am with a DJ and dancing. **Octobar** has rock, **Le P'tit Caribou** in Vieux-Tremblant offers a more intimate atmosphere.

Microbrasserie La Diable brews its own beer and is a popular bar before dinner. The pool at **La Source Aquaclub** provides good family entertainment. **Spa Le Scandinave** is a relaxing wellness centre a few kilometres out of town. **Hammam Vaporium** and **Slope-Side Spa** are more convenient. Other activities nearby include dog-sledding, sleigh rides, ice-climbing, tubing, snow mobiling and moonlit snowshoe hikes.

Sleep

All accommodation, unless otherwise stated, can be booked through central reservations, **t** +1 819 681 2000.

Luxury/moderate:

Fairmont Château Mont Tremblant, t +1 819 681 7000, on the edge of the piste, with a large spa and outdoor pool, is still the premier hotel address.

Le Westin Resort & Spa, t +1 819 681 8000, is a comfortable hotel with a choice of restaurants.

Hilton Homewood Suites are in the Town Square, just a short walk from the lifts.

Le Lodge de la Montagne is a ski-in ski-out condo hotel next to La Source Aquaclub.

Le Tour des Voyageurs, at the entrance to the village, has both hotel rooms and condos. A people-mover lift links it to the ski area.

Outside Tremblant Village:

Club Tremblant, t +1 819 425 8781, is 10 minutes' drive away on the shore of Lake Tremblant, with fine views over the lake and to the ski slopes.

Le Grand Lodge, t +1 819 425 2734, also 10 minutes away, is a smart log-cabin-style hotel close to the Gray Rocks ski area.

Whistler, BC

Profile

Still the top resort in North America. Twin mountains with an enormous vertical act as showcases for every conceivable type of terrain from glacier to glade and from steep to deep. Its Pacific Rim position makes it a melting pot of different nationalities. Whistler has a vibrant atmosphere, excellent accommodation and restaurants as well as a buzzing nightlife.

Resort

Whistler is the setting for the next Winter Olympics after Sestriere and it is

Essentials

Altitude: 2,140ft (652m)–7,494ft (2284m)
Map: see page M22
Further information: t +1 604 664 5625, *www.whistlerblackcomb.com*
Lifts in area: 33 (3 cableways, 18 chairs, 12 drags) serving 7,071 acres of terrain
Lift pass: adult CDN$408, child 7–12yrs CDN$216, both for 6 days
Access: Vancouver airport 2hrs

right that what is still indisputably Number One in North America has been given the honour of hosting the games. Whistler and Blackcomb mountains have the longest vertical drop on the continent, awesome terrain and a cosmopolitan atmosphere. You can stay and eat here better than in almost any other resort in either Canada or the USA. It's just a shame about the weather.

Normally the village, which lies at an altitude of only 652m – but on the same latitude as Labrador – attracts abundant winter precipitation. Much of this falls as rain in the resort and as powder on the top half of the mountain. The number of blue-sky days is significantly lower than in Colorado, but the snow quality is usually excellent. However the winter of 2004–5 was the worst in Whistler's history. Other resorts in BC also suffered, but Whistler was the sacrificial victim. A much lower-than-average snowpack was pummeled by violent wind, and periodic heavy rain at altitude, while record high temperatures thwarted snowmaking. Let's hope last winter was a one-off, but inevitably this has temporarily dented public confidence in a resort that has always seemed so snow-secure.

In normal circumstances, mid-winter temperatures can be chilly, although not as low as in Banff-Lake Louise and the central Rockies. Whistler suits all standards of skier and rider. Glacier skiing continues on Blackcomb throughout most of the summer.

Mountain

Whistler and Blackcomb provide equally enjoyable intermediate and advanced skiing on their gladed lower slopes, but the top halves of both offer contrastingly different experiences. While Whistler is given over to a succession of glorious powder bowls, Blackcomb has steep couloirs and long glacial descents. Both offer thrilling top-to-bottom skiing on long cruising trails, and part of the enjoyment of a stay here is deciding which to choose each morning. Both are reached from adjoining lifts in Whistler Village. Plans to provide a mid-mountain gondola link are on the drawing board but show no signs off progressing to the pylon stage.

Whistler Village gondola provides the main two-stage access to mid-mountain Roundhouse Lodge. At peak times wise skiers take the much underused Fizsimmons Express quad-chair beside it. This links to a second quad that provides a trouble-free backdoor into the system. Creekside, down Highway 99 from Whistler, is an alternative accommodation base with car parks designed to attract the large numbers of day visitors from Vancouver and deter them from clogging up Whistler itself. Access from here to the Roundhouse and top lifts is by the Creekside gondola, followed by the Big Red Express quad.

Blackcomb Mountain is accessed by the Excalibur gondola from Whistler Village or by the Wizard Express chair from Upper Village, formerly called Blackcomb Village. You can ski from Blackcomb mountain to Whistler Village but not vice versa.

Blackcomb has nursery slopes served by a chair-lift just above the village.

Whistler has dedicated higher beginner terrain reached by the first stage of the Village gondola.

Whistler is considered to be among the top snowboarding resorts in North America, with sophisticated terrain parks on both mountains, and a Nintendo super-pipe and snowcross track on Blackcomb. The Chipmunk Park on Whistler is for expert riders and skiers. Entry requires a separate pass and a helmet is compulsory.

Numerous heli-ski companies operate in and around Whistler, including **Blackcomb Helicopters, t** +1 604 938 1700, **Coast Range Heliskiing, t** +1 604 894 1144, **Helico Presto, t** +1 604 938 2927, **Spearhead Mountain Guides, t** +1 604 932 8802, **TLH Heliskiing, t** +1 250 558 5379, **Whistler Alpine Guides Bureau, t** +1 604 932 4040, and **Whistler Heli-skiing, t** +1 604 932 4105.

Learn

Whistler Blackcomb Ski and **Snowboard School, t** +1 604 932 3434, is an established academy for cutting-edge ski and riding instruction. Make use of the free daily tours of the piste hosted by volunteers who include some of Canada's greatest skiers. **Extremely Canadian, t** +1 604 932 4105, provides guiding and powder instruction, while **Lauralee Bowie Ski Adventures, t** +1 604 689 7444, offers tuition with video.

Childcare

Whistler Kids, t +1 604 932 3434, looks after children from three months with all-day care and lessons for appropriate ages. It also runs special classes for teenagers. Evening babysitting in your hotel or condo can be arranged through **The Nanny Network, t** +1 604 938 2823.

Lunch

A lack of good mountain restaurants is Whistler's only true failing.

On Whistler Mountain the **Roundhouse Lodge, t** +1 604 932 3434, offers hamburgers, Asian stir-fry, and pasta in cavernous and compellingly unpleasant self-service surroundings. **Steeps, t** +1 604 932 3434, in the same building, has waiter-service West Coast cuisine. **Garibaldi Lift Company, t** +1 604 905 2220, has good hamburgers and a warm atmosphere. **Ravens Nest, t** +1 604 905 2176, at the top of Creekside gondola, offers soups and stews. **Dusty's, t** +1 604 905 2171, at Creekside base, has barbecued burgers and plenty of ambience.

On Blackcomb, **Christine's Restaurant, t** +1 604 938 7437, in Rendezvous Lodge, is the resort's best shot at a waiter-service mountain restaurant with international cuisine – but standards of cuisine and service seem to yo-yo. **The River Rock Grill, t** +1 604 938 7417, upstairs at the Glacier Creek Lodge, is a good self-service. **Monks Grill, t** +1 604 932 9677, in the Upper Village, is highly recommended.

Dine

In Whistler Village, **Bearfoot Bistro, t** +1 604 932 3433 specializes in French and other European cuisine. **Il Caminetto di Umberto, t** +1 604 932 4442, and **Trattoria di Umberto, t** +1 604 932 5858, are Italian. **Araxi, t** +1 604 932 4540, and **Apres, t** +1 604 935 0200, have seafood and Pacific Rim cuisine. **Zueski's Taverna, t** +1 604 932 6009, is good-value Greek. **Teppan Village, t** +1 604 932 2223, is a Japanese steakhouse.

In Upper Village, try **La Rua, t** +1 604 932 5011, for West Coast cuisine or **Thai One On, t** +1 604 932 4822, for Thai. In Village North **Sushi-Ya, t** +1 604 905 0155, has great sushi.

In Whistler Creek, **The Rim Rock Cafe, t** +1 604 932 5565, has seafood and fine European dishes. **Zen Whistler, t** +1 604 932 3667, is Japanese.

Party

Après-ski begins noisily at the **Dubh Linn Gate** Irish pub, and **Longhorn**, at the base of the Excalibur and Whistler Village gondolas. **Garibaldi Lift Co** in Whistler and **Merlin's** at Blackcomb base have live bands. The shopping – which continues until 10pm – is a core part of the evening entertainment. Zip wiring is a new sport for Whistler and an exhilarating way to spend the afternoon.

Later on the action switches to **Garfinkel's**, the **Savage Beagle, Tommy Africa's** and **Maxx Fish. Moe Joes's** is smaller and more intimate. Buffalo Bill's attracts the over-30s. Citta's Bar in the Village Square is a friendly hang-out for a quiet drink. The Mallard Bar in the Château Whistler is more sophisticated and expensive

Sleep

Luxury:

Fairmont Château Whistler, t +1 604 938 8000, *www.fairmont.com/whistler*, is one of the world's great ski hotels, right on the piste at Blackcomb base, with a good restaurant, heated outdoor pools and the outstanding Vida spa.

The Four Seasons Resort, t +1 604 935 3400, *www.fourseasons.com/whistler*, is slightly less well positioned, but a true contender for Whistler's most luxurious hotel.

The Westin Resort & Spa, t +1 604 905 5000, *www.westinwhistler.com*, at Whistler Mountain base, has a shopping mall and is conveniently located.

Whistler Chalets, t +1 604 905 5287, *www.whistlerchalets.com*, offers a portfolio of luxury self-catering homes.

Moderate:

Delta Whistler Village Suites, t +1 604 905 3987, *www.deltahotels.com*, has a rustic mountain atmosphere.

Pan Pacific Lodge, t +1 604 905 2999, *whistler.panpacific.com*, offers apartments with fireplaces and floor-to-ceiling windows.

Timberline Lodge, t +1 604 932 5211, *www.whistler-timberline.com*, is comfortable and well situated.

Crystal Lodge, t +1 604 932 2221, *www.crystal-lodge.com*, is conveniently located.

Listel Hotel Whistler, t +1 604 932 1133, *www.listelhotel.com*, has a heated outdoor pool and is a short walk from the shops.

Summit Lodge, t +1 888 913 8811, *www.summitlodge.com*, in the heart of Whistler Village North, has a spa and free in-room yoga.

Budget:

Alpine Springs B&B, t +1 604 905 2747, *www.bc-bed-and-breakfast.com*, is in a peaceful setting.

Blue Spruce Lodge B&B, t +1 604 932 3508, *www.bluesprucelodgewhistler.com*, sleeps eight to ten people and is good value.

Shoestring Lodge, t +1 604 932 3338, *www.shoestringlodge.com*, has simple, clean rooms.

The Top Resorts: Eastern Europe

04

Bansko, Bulgaria

Profile

Best-developed ski resort in Eastern Europe, an attractive old town with a modern lift system and hotels of international standard

Resort

Bansko is the only resort in Eastern Europe to have taken a full step forward in the 16 years since the collapse of the Iron Curtain. Substantial investment of €130 million has been made in new mountain facilities – sufficient to lure the Kempinski hotel group into opening a magnificent new five-star hotel on the edge of the piste.

The resort has a long season that usually runs from mid-December until mid-May and it is now recognized as the best resort in Bulgaria.

This fine medieval town lies at the foot of 2915m Mount Vihren in the scenic Pirin mountain range, close to the Macedonian and Greek frontiers. On a clear day you can see the Aegean Sea.

Essentials

Altitude: 936m (3,079ft)–2560m (8,399ft)
Further information: t +359 (0)7443 8060,
www.banskoski.com
Lifts in area: 14 (1 cableway, 7 chairs, 6 drags) serving 65km of piste
Lift pass: adult €179, child €105, both for 6 days
Access: Sofia airport 160km

Mountain

A new 'village' of modern hotels is being built just above the town around the Doppelmayr gondola that forms the backbone of the lift system. The gondola takes you up to the mid-mountain area at 1725m, where a small network of lifts takes you up to the highest point at 2560m. This gives a huge vertical drop of 1570m, and the run to the valley is supposedly 17km long. The final 7km is floodlit and covered by snow-cannon. Bansko has an electronic hands-free lift pass and Bulgaria's first terrain park with half-pipe.

Learn

The Ulen school, t +359 (0)7443 8060 is recommended and most instructors speak good English.

Children

The Ulen school runs its own ski kindergarten and has a dedicated beginner area with a magic carpet.

Lunch

Mountain restaurants serving simple local dishes at reasonable prices are located at the foot of the gondola and at mid-mountain.

Dine

Beli Noshti, t +359 (0)7443 5088, and **Kamenitsa, t** +359 (0)7443 4635, are recommended, along with **Georgeo's Pizzeria, t** + 359 (0) 7443 2948, **Steak House, t** + 359 (0)7443 2416, and **Come Prima** in the Kempinski, **t** +359 (0)7443 8933, which has gourmet Italian cuisine.

Party

Traditional Bansko taverns offer Bulgarian wines and live folk music. The best include the new **Glazne** as well as the **Bansko, Bishine, Bunare, Vakanova** and **Valevitsata**. The **Torino** cabaret bar attracts smart Sofian weekenders. **Art, No Name, Country, Retro** and **Diana-4** feature among a host of nightclubs.

Sleep

★★★★★**Kempinski Grand Arena,** t +359 (0)7443 8933, *www.kempinski.com,* is a smart new establishment opposite the gondola station. It has an indoor pool, two restaurants and a spa.

★★★★**Hotel Glazne,** t + 359 (0)7443 8021, *www.glazne.bansko.bg,* has a sports centre and separate villas for families.

★★★★**Hotel Tanne,** t + 359 (0)7443 8100, *www.hotel-tanne.com,* is decorated in authentic Bulgarian style. Its Tavern restaurant has live music.

★★★★**Hotel Bansko,** t +359 (0)7443 8054, *www.hotelbansko.bansko.bg,* is popular with the locals and has huge rooms with intricate wood-carved ceilings.

Bohinj, Slovenia

Profile

Beginner and limited intermediate skiing in a retro-Austrian atmosphere with beautiful scenery, low prices, excellent tuition and a high standard of food and hotels

Essentials

Altitude: 512m (1,680ft)–1800m (5,905ft)
Further information: Vogel, t +386 (0)4572 4236, Kobla, t +386 (0)4574 7100, *www.bohinj.si*
Lifts in area: 18 (1 cableway, 7 chairs, 10 drags) serving 65km of piste
Lift pass: adult €113, child €80, both for 6 days
Access: Ljubljana airport 60mins

Resort

Bohinj is pronounced 'Bocking' and lies just 27km beyond the beautiful lakeside town of Bled, which is dominated by a fairytale castle and an enchanting island church. This is the most entertaining of Slovenia's 26 ski areas. Slovenia is reminiscent of neighbouring Austria as it was a couple a decades ago. Imagine, for a moment, a ski holiday in quaint traditional Alpine surroundings where a lift pass costs €18 a day, a three-course meal with wine €14, and a pint of beer €1.75.

Mountain

Bohinj's three separate ski areas are 10-minutes' drive apart in the rugged mountains above Lake Bohinj. Vogel is reached by a cable-car, which rises over cliffs from the far end of Lake Bohinj. The 18km area is much larger than its statistics suggest, and you can ski around the shoulder of the mountain back down to the cable-car station.

Kobla, the second area and the country's original ski resort, is our favourite. Its three antiquated double chair-lifts add to, rather than detract from, its charm as you rise slowly over farmland from the village to the mountain top.

The steep and long run down the front face has the pedigree of the FIS downhill course it once was. The third little area of Soriska Planina has three drag-lifts and 3km of nursery slopes.

Learn

Vogel, t + 386 (0)4572 1451, Kobla, t +386 (0)4574 7100, and Soriska Planina, t +386 (0)4511 7835, schools all offer friendly tuition at a low price.

Children

No special facilities.

Lunch

Mountain huts in Vogel and Kobla provide a good range of hot dishes. Vogel Bar, t +386 (0)5063 7921, at Vogel, is recommended for pizzas and grilled meat.

Dine

Rupa, t +386 (0)4572 3401, at Sednja Vas, has good home-cooked food. Erlah, t +386 (0)4572 3309, at the Vogel end of the lake, is renowned for its fresh trout and *struklji* (cheese- or nut-filled buckwheat dumplings).

Party

Bohinj has a few bars that liven up at weekends. Nearby Bled has a disco and a famous casino.

Sleep

Bohinj:
★★★★Hotel Bohinj, t +386 (0)4572 6000, *www.alpinum.net*, is new and highly recommended.
★★★★Hotel Jezero, t +386 (0)4572 9100, *www.bohinj.si*, overlooks the lake and is convenient for both main ski areas.

★★★Hotel Zlatorog, t +386 (0)4572 3381, is in a beautiful setting just back from the lake.
Bled:
★★★★★Grand Hotel Toplice, t +386 (0)4579 1000, *www.hotel-toplice.com*, is a traditional hotel.
★★★★Vila Bled, t +386 (0)4579 1500 has an intimate atmosphere.

Borovets, Bulgaria

Profile

Antiquated lift system and unimaginative food are offset by an appealing forest setting, low prices, a lively nightlife and good beginner instruction

Resort

Borovets is the oldest resort in Bulgaria. Skiing started here as long ago as 1896 and cynics would argue that the lift system has scarcely improved since. The village was originally the site of a hunting lodge for the Bulgarian royal family. It is

Essentials

Altitude: 1323m (4,339ft)–2540m (8,333ft)
Further information: t +359 (0)2987 9778 or t +359 (0)7226 6171, *www. bulgariaski.com*
Lifts in area: 8 (1 cableway, 1 chair, 6 drags) serving 40km of piste
Lift pass: adults €120, child €60
Access: Sofia airport 60mins

situated in a pine forest at the foot of Mount Moussala, 73km from Sofia.

It developed into a popular ski resort in the 1970s and, after the fall of Communism in Eastern Europe, Borovets looked set to attract overseas investment. But it never happened and Bansko has now stolen its title of top ski destination in Bulgaria. Despite its mountain shortcomings, Borovets has a lively atmosphere and continues to attract a large number of overseas skiers, from Britain in particular.

Mountain

The antiquated lift system is headed by an ageing gondola and an assortment of fixed-grip chair-lifts and equally venerable drag-lifts. Inevitably, high-season lift queues are irritatingly long. The skiing is divided into two separate sectors, linked by a long walk on an ice-rutted road. The Markoudjik sector, reached by a 1970s gondola, offers the best of the resort's skiing, which is mainly above the tree-line with a highest ski point of 2540m. All the nursery slopes are located at the base of the separate Martinovi Baraki area. In good conditions there are plenty of off-piste opportunities, including low-cost heli-skiing.

Learn

Borovets ski and snowboard school, t +359 (0)7128 2441, has a strong reputation for teaching the basics in a friendly and efficient manner. Ski classes do not have priority on the lifts.

Children

The ski school's kindergarten, t +359 (0)7128 2441, in the Rila Hotel accepts non-skiers from 12 months to four years old and skiers from four to eight years.

Lunch

A couple of snack bars are located on the mountain, but it is best to return to the resort.

Dine

Reporters repeatedly comment that half-board hotel food should be avoided. Small restaurants abound serving burgers, pasta and pizzas as well as Bulgarian fare. Chips are big here in Bulgaria's biggest potato-growing region. Try **The Hungry Horse**, **Mamacita's**, **The White Horse**, **Franco's**, **Blue Café** and **White Magic**. (Telephone numbers not available.)

Party

The Buzz Bar is the main resort rendezvous. **The Samakov** and the **Rila** hotels both have nightclubs.

Sleep

★★★★**Ice Angels Hotel**, *www.bulgariaski.com*, is the newest and smartest hotel in Borovets, situated in the centre.

★★★★**Samokov Hotel**, t +359 (0)7128 2306, *www.samokov.com*, has comfortable rooms and a good range of facilities including a swimming-pool, bowling alley and nightclub.

★★★★**Hotel Rila**, t +359 (0)7128 2441, *www.bulgariaski.com*, is convenient for the skiing, but the rooms are small.

Poiana Brasov, Romania

Essentials

Altitude: 1021m (3,350ft)–1775m (5,823ft)
Further information: t +40 (0)286 550443,
www.poiana-brasov.com
Lifts in area: 10 (3 cableways, 7 drags)
serving 14km of piste
Lift pass: adult €80, child €52, both for
6 days
Access: Bucharest airport 186km

Profile

Budget beginner skiing with competent and friendly tuition, but blighted by a primitive lift system. High standard of hotels and unlimited nightlife in nearby Brasov

Resort

Poiana Brasov opened as a ski resort in 1906 and has slowly grown into a small town at the foot of 1799m Mount Postavaru in the Carpathian mountains. It lies a 13km drive up a mountain road from the attractive medieval town of Brasov with its famous Black Church, Romania's most important cathedral.

Beautiful surroundings, a high standard of accommodation and cuisine, together with the friendliness of the people make this one of our favourite destinations in Eastern Europe.

Mountain

This a pleasant beginner and lower intermediate area for anyone who wants to get to grips with the basics without breaking the bank.

Mount Postavaru is accessed by a gondola and two ancient cable-cars. Nursery slopes are located by the Sport and Bradul hotels.

Learn

The six ski schools teach modern technique and are all of a similar high standard. **Ana Hotels**, t +40 (0)268 407330, **Club Montana Schi**, t +40 (0)722 269411, **Euro Inter Ski**, t +40 (0)268 151735, **Impera International**, t +40 (0)744 321065, **Poiana SA**, t +40 (0)268 262310, and **Valona Tour**, t +40 (0)722 269411.

Children

All schools take children from four years. Non-skiing activities include tobogganing, paintballing in the woods and excursions to **Dracula's Castle** and to **Peles Castle** at Sinaia.

Lunch

Two mountain restaurants, **Cristianu Mare** and **Postavaru**, serve pizzas, burgers, soup and sandwiches at wonderfully low prices.

Dine

In Poiana Brasov, **Sura Dacilor**, t +40 (0)268 262327, has Romanian cuisine and folk music. **Coliba Haiducilor**, t +40 (0)268 2621370, also known as **The Outlaws' Hut**, has barbecued bear and traditional dancing. **Vanatorul**, t +40 (0)268 2623540, serves venison, pheasant and wild boar.

In Brasov, **Le Stradivari, t** +40 (0)268 476945 is Italian and specializes in seafood. **Pepper Jack, t** +40 (0)268 417349 has Mexican and Transylvanian cuisine.

Party

In Poiana the **Ciucas**, **Alpin**, **Bradul** and **Poiana** hotel bars are the liveliest. In Brasov, try **Festival 39**, **Cabana** and **Blue Night**. **Blitz** is the new late-night hotspot. Other discos are **Pro-Club**, **Hacienda** and **No Problem**.

Sleep

★★★**Hotel Miruna, t** +40 (0)268 262120, *www.mirunahotel.ro*, built three years ago, is recommended.

★★★**Piatra Mare, t** +40 (0)268 262029, *www.piatramare.ro*, has a good restaurant.

★★★**Sport Hotel, t** +40 (0)268 407330, *www.anahotels.ro*, is convenient for the nursery slopes.

★★★**Tirol Hotel, t** +40 (0)268 262460, has a good restaurant.

★★★**Alpin Hotel, t** +40 (0)268 262111, has a swimming-pool and a gym.

★★**Hotel Bradul, t** +40 (0)268 407330, *www.anahotels.ro*, adjoins the Sport and is well located.

The Top Resorts: France

Alpe d'Huez

Profile

A large and architecturally unattractive resort with plenty of high-altitude, snow-sure skiing from before Christmas until after Easter. The lift system extends down to Vaujany and other smaller and more pleasing resorts in neighbouring valleys

Resort

Alpe d'Huez is one of France's oldest resorts and is the hub for the fifth largest ski circuit in the country. Back in 1934, a young engineer called Pomagalski invented the drag-lift here just days ahead of a rival in Davos. It was also a venue for the 1968 Winter Olympics. However, Alpe d'Huez is better known to millions of cycle fans each July when the approach road becomes one of the most energy-sapping climbs of the Tour de France.

Over the years the resort has grown without design along a sunny balcony above the beautiful Oisans Valley, reached by 22 hairpin bends. Lifts link the various sectors of the village, which provides a utilitarian base for some excellent skiing for all standards.

Mountain

Alpe d'Huez is one of the few resorts that five years ago started quietly responding to the threat of global warming – and it has paid huge dividends. The lift company took the decision to develop the summer ski area on the glacier above the resort. The plan was to ensure that, even in the worst winters, skiers and riders would have plenty of snow-sure terrain at high altitude.

Essentials

Altitude: 1120m (3,674ft)–3330m (10,922ft)
Map: see page M25
Further information: t +33 (0)4 76 11 44 44, www.alpedhuez.com
Lifts in area: 85 (16 cableways, 24 chairs, 42 drags) serving 240km of piste
Lift pass: Area (covers linked resorts, 2 days in Les Deux Alpes, 1 day in La Grave, The Milky Way, Puy-St-Vincent and Serre Chevalier) adult €187, child 5–15yrs €133, both for 6 days
Access: Grenoble airport 1½hrs, Lyon airport 2hrs

Two quad-chairs now serve long runs on the glacier, which can be reached by a new extension of the Marmottes gondola at one end of the resort and by the Pic Blanc cable-car at the other.

Skiers and riders must return to mid-mountain by lift unless they are capable of descending the notoriously difficult and often icy Tunnel run down the front face or the 16km Sarenne that leads into the Sarenne Gorge below the resort.

Alpe d'Huez-based skiers tend to congregate on the easy and intermediate runs directly above the resort, which are served by gondolas from either end. In fact the best skiing is to be found off both sides leading down to the neighbouring villages of Oz, Vaujany and Auris-en-Oisans, as well as the lower satellites of Villard-Reculas, and Huez.

The 3330m Pic Blanc is the starting point for a number of off-piste itineraries. These include the Grand Sablat, the Combe du Loup and a long, tricky descent via the Couloir de Fare. A 20-minute climb from the cable-car station takes you to the top of La Pyramide. From here you can ski more than 2000m of vertical down to Vaujany. Alpe d'Huez has a half-pipe on the Signal piste as well as a terrain park at Plat des Marmottes.

Learn

The **ESF**, t +33 (0)4 76 80 94 23, has a number of English-speaking instructors. The **ESI**, t +33 (0)4 76 80 42 77, offers smaller classes and tuition in English, while **British Masterclass**, t +33 (0)4 76 80 93 83, is strongly recommended. Guiding is available through the **Bureau des Guides**, t +33 (0)4 76 80 42 55, while **SAF Isère Heliskiing**, t +33 (0)4 76 80 65 49, is for the most adventurous.

Children

The **ESF**, t +33 (0)4 76 80 94 23, accepts children from four years and guarantees 10 or fewer pupils per class, although we have seen up to 16 during high season. The **ESI**, t +33 (0)4 76 80 42 77, teaches children from three-and-a-half, and **Les Eterlous**, t +33 (0)4 76 80 67 85, alternates skiing and games for little ones from two-and-a-half years. **Les Crapouilloux**, t +33 (0)4 76 11 39 23, is a crèche for children from two-and-a-half years. **Les Intrépides**, t +33 (0)4 76 11 21 61, is the alternative for non-skiers aged six months to three years.

Lunch

La Cabane du Poutat, t +33 (0)4 76 80 42 88, beneath the Marmottes gondola, has a serious gourmet menu. **La Bergerie**, t +33 (0)4 76 80 36 83, on the way down to Villard-Reculas, is an Alpine museum with simple dishes. **Auberge de l'Alpette**, t +33 (0)4 76 80 70 00, above Oz, has the best omelettes and salads on the mountain. **The Chalet du Lac Besson**, t +33 (0)4 76 806 537, on the cross-country trail, has an open fireplace and a large sun terrace. **L'Altibar**, t +33 (0)4 76 804 115, beside the altiport runway, is a local favourite. **Le Signal**, t +33 (0)4 76 803 954, offers panoramic views. **La Forêt de Maronne**, t +33 (0)4 76 80 00 06, has wonderful home-cooked cuisine.

Dine

Alpe d'Huez has a fine choice of restaurants. **Au P'tit Creux**, t +33 (0)4 76 806 283, is one of the best restaurants but expensive, while **Passe Montagne**, t +33 (0)4 76 113 153, is good value. **Les Caves**, t +33 (0)4 76 80 92 44, has fine food and wine. **Le Génépi**, t +33 (0)4 76 80 36 22, was praised by reporters.

Party

Alpe d'Huez has a vibrant atmosphere and après-ski lasts well into the early hours at **The Underground** and **Le Sporting**. Others recommended include **Sphere Bar**, **Les Caves**, **Zoo Music Bar**, **Freeride Café** and **L'Etalon**. **Magoos**, **The O Bar**, **The Last Bar** and **O'Sharkeys** are all popular venues.

Sleep

- ★★★★**Royal Ours Blanc**, t +33 (0)4 76 80 35 50, *www.eurogroup-vacances.com*, has an an indoor swimming-pool.
- ★★★★**Au Chamois d'Or**, t +33 (0)4 76 80 31 32, *www.chamoisdor-alpedhuez.com*, is at the top of the village, with some delightful wood-panelled suites.
- ★★★★**Pierre et Vacances Les Bergers**, t +33 04 76 80 85 00, *www.pierreetvacances.com*, are the best apartments in the resort.
- ★★★**Le Christina**, t +33 (0)4 76 80 33 32, *www.lechristina-alpedhuez.com*, is a chalet-style building with a restaurant serving local cuisine.
- ★★★**Hotel Le Pic Blanc**, t +33 (0)4 76 11 42 42, *www.hmc-hotels.com*, is a very welcoming place.
- ★★★**Le Printemps de Juliette**, t +33 (0)4 76 11 44 38, *www.leprintempsdejuliette.com*, is a delightful hotel with just four rooms and four suites.

Les Arcs

Profile

Part of the giant Paradiski area linking the resort with La Plagne and providing snow-sure, high-altitude skiing in purpose-built villages. Good terrain for all standards and abundant off-piste opportunities

Resort

Les Arcs was one of France's great new areas developed during the boom years of the 1960s. This was a time when every Parisian and quite a few others flocked to the Alps for at least one week each winter in search of snow, sunshine and a shoebox-sized apartment they could call their own.

Local skier, Robert Blanc, conceived the idea of building a series of villages at different altitudes on the mountain above his home town of Bourg-St-Maurice. Ex-Olympic champion, Emile Allais, lent his name to the project and the first village of Arc 1600 opened in 1968. Les Arcs has come a long way since then.

Villages at 1800 and 2000 were followed much more recently by the development of another at 1950. Intrawest, the giant North American resort developer, chose Les Arcs for the first of what are planned as a number of property-led commercial forays in the Alps.

Arc 1950 continues to expand and building will continue until 2008. it provides sympathetic architecture and reasonablypriced apartments finished to a level not previously found in the French Alps.

The timing of initial construction coincided with the creation of Paradiski, the new name for the now combined ski

Essentials

Altitude: 1200m (2,788ft)–3226m (10,581ft)
Map: see page M38
Further information: t +33 (0)4 79 07 12 57, www.lesarcs.com
Lifts in area: 141 in Paradiski (1 mountain railway, 16 cableways, 66 chairs, 58 drags) serving 425km of piste
Lift pass: Paradiski adult €225 (covers linked Les Arcs/La Plagne area and one day in each of Val d'Isère/Tignes, Pralognan-La Vanoise, Les Saisies), child 6–13yrs €169, both for 6 days
Access: Chambéry airport 2hrs, Geneva airport 2½hrs, Lyon airport 2½hrs. Bourg-St-Maurice station (for Eurostar) 15km, with buses and funicular to Arc 1600

area of Les Arcs and adjoining *La Plagne*. Both resort lift companies are under the same ownership of the Compagnie des Alpes, who decided to link two of France's largest ski areas together to provide a rival to the Trois Vallées.

After years of discussion and oiling of the cogs of French bureaucracy, the 200-passenger double-decker Vanoise Express cable-car was built at a cost of €16 million across the deep Ponturin gorge that separates the two resorts. From the beginning, the lift company admitted that the number of visitors in either centre who would use the lift in any one week would not exceed 30 per cent. In reality the figure is much lower.

Nevertheless, skiers in both Les Arcs and La Plagne now have the daily choice of a quite stupendous amount of terrain. The hamlets of Vallandry, Peisey Nancroix and higher Plan-Peisey beside the new lift have also developed as resorts in their own right.

The original village Arc 1600 remains the most compact and child-friendly. Arc 1800 is the largest and liveliest, soulless

2000 has guaranteed snow-cover but precious little else to commend it. Arc 1950 is the brave new heart of the resort. Les Arcs founder Robert Blanc would be proud of it had he lived to see it. Sadly he died in an avalanche in 1980.

Mountain

The 425km of skiing in Paradiski covers every conceivable type of terrain, but most of it is given over to enjoyable red and blue motorway pistes that are ideal intermediate terrain. Long runs start above the tree-line and descend through the woods to outlying hamlets, and in good mid-winter conditions you can ski all the way down to Bourg-St-Maurice at 850m.

The easy pistes above Arc 1800, served by the Transarc gondola and a whole series of chairs spread across the mountainside attract the crowds – but more enterprising skiers and riders will explore further afield.

A gondola and a cable-car from Arc 2000 take you up to the 3226m Aiguille Rouge, the highest point in the ski area and starting point for some classic steep runs including a 7km descent down to Le Planay or Le Pré. The area is so large that even accomplished skiers must work at travelling by lift and piste in a single day from Le Pré at one end of Paradiski to Champagny-en-Vanoise at the other – and back again. Each of the Arc villages has its own dedicated nursery slopes, but the best are found at 1800.

Les Arcs is famous for its speed-skiing track above Arc 2000, the setting over the years for a number of world records. For a modest €12.50 anyone is allowed to have a go from a lower starting point that keeps your speed down to a sensible level. Les Arcs was a pioneer of snowboarding in Europe. The terrain park is situated between Arc 1800 and Arc 1600 with a half-pipe and snowcross course.

Learn

The **ESF**, t +33 (0)4 79 07 40 31, has a branch in each village. We recommend **Arc Aventures**, t +33 (0)4 79 07 41 28, in Arc 1800 and **Spirit 1950**, t +33 (0)4 79 04 25 72, in Arc 1950. **Initial Snow**, t +33 (0)6 12 45 72 91, is a small school based in Bourg-St-Maurice with meeting points in Les Arcs. **Privilege**, t +33 (0)4 79 07 23 38, is another small school in Arc 1800. **Darentasia**, t +33 (0)4 79 04 16 81, specializes in off-piste. Guiding can also be arranged through the **Bureau des Guides**, t +33 (0)4 79 07 71 19.

Children

In Arc 1600, **Hotel La Cachette**, t +33 (0)4 79 07 70 50, cares for children from four months to two years and has a mini-club for under-12s.

In Arc 1800, **Les Pommes des Pins**, t +33 (0)4 79 04 24 31, looks after children from 12 months to six years.

In Arc 200, **Les Marmottons**, t +33 (0)4 79 07 64 25, provides a mix of daycare and lessons, but not lunch.

Lunch

The Aiguille Grive, t +33 (0)4 79 07 43 97, has good food in a panoramic setting. **Chalet de Luigi**, t +33 (0)6 08 57 23 36, at 1950 is renowned for its ham-based gourmet cuisine. **Bélliou La Fumée**, t +33 (0)4 79 07 29 13, is a 500-year-old hunting lodge in Pré-St-Esprit below Arc 2000. **Les Chalets de l'Arc 2000**, t +33 (0)4 79 04 15 40, has a warm atmosphere and serves traditional Savoyarde cuisine.

Dine

In Arc 1600, **La Rive** in the Hotel La Cachette, t +33 (0)4 79 07 70 50, is

recommended, along with **Pizza 1600**,
t + 33 (0)4 79 04 27 73.

In Arc 1800, try **Casa Mia**, t +33 (0)4 79 07 05 75, **La Marmite**, t +33 (0)4 79 07 44 28, **L'Equipe**, t +33 (0)4 79 07 49 34 and **Le Chalet Bouvier**, t +33 (0)4 79 04 14 68.

In Arc 1950, **Chalet de Luigi**, t +33 (0)6 08 57 23 36, is the focal point for fine dining.

In Arc 2000, **El Latino Loco**, t +33 (0)4 79 07 79 49, has some of the best food.

In Bourg-St-Maurice, **L'Hostellerie du Petit Saint Bernard**, t +33 (0)4 79 07 04 32, is the kind of old-fashioned *bourgeois* French restaurant that serves snails, frogs' legs and wonderful steaks.

Party

This is definitely not a place for lively après-ski. At the end of the day the French seem to disappear into their self-catering apartments and do not reappear until morning. Apart from a few busy bars, the main action – what there is of it – is found in **Apokalypse** and **L'Igloo** at Arc 1800. **Chalet de Luigi** at 1950 has a new night club, which is building a reputation as the best in the resort.

Sleep

Most accommodation is in self-catering apartments. Arc 1950 has the newest and the best, t +33 (0)4 79 07 68 00 or t +44 (0)20 7584 2841, *www.ernalow.co.uk*, for all.
Arc 2000:
****Les Chalets des Neiges**, t +44 (0)20 7244 8764, is a complex containing chalet-apartments sharing an indoor pool and bar. They include **Chalet Turia** and **Chalet Charvet**, which sleep 10 people each.
Arc 1800:
****Les Alpages du Chantel apartments**, t +33 (0)1 58 21 58 21, *www.residences mgm.com*, are piste-side and have a swimming-pool, sauna and massage.

***Hotel du Golf Maeva**, t +33 (0)4 79 41 43 43, *www.maeva.com*, is the village's original hotel with sloping walkways rather than staircases.
***Hotel Mercure Coralia**, t +33 (0)4 79 07 65 00, *www.mercure.com*, makes up for in efficiency what it lacks in character.
Arc 1600:
***Hotel La Cachette**, t +33 (0)4 79 07 70 50, *www.lesarcs.com*, has a deserved reputation as one of the best hotels in the Alps for families with small children.
Hotel Béguin, t +33 (0)4 79 07 72 61, *www.lesarcs.com*, is small and simple.
Hotel Explorers, t +33 (0)4 79 04 16 00, *www.lesarcs.com*, provides cheerful accommodation.
Bourg-St-Maurice:
Hostellerie du Petit-St-Bernard, t +33 (0)4 79 07 04 32, has a celebrated restaurant.
Hotel La Petite Auberge, t +33 (0)4 79 07 05 86, on the edge of town, has clean rooms and good restaurant.

Avoriaz

Profile

Part of the vast Portes du Soleil ski area, this car-free resort is in a dramatic clifftop setting offering skiing and snowboarding for all standards

Resort

The Portes du Soleil, a trans-frontier alliance of a dozen ski villages in France and Switzerland, largely came into being as a consequence of the 1960 Olympics which were held 8000km away in Squaw Valley in California.

Jean Vuarnet won gold in the downhill for France and on his return was asked to oversee the creation of a high-altitude station de ski above his native Morzine. At the same time it was suggested he might try linking his new ski area to Champéry in Switzerland.

He called the new resort Avoriaz and the Portes du Soleil now includes 206 lifts, which serve a mighty 650km of piste covering a large area of mountainside above Lac Léman.

Ironically Vuarnet is better-known today for his sunglasses than for his speed on snow, but it is a tribute to him that his vision all those years ago remains as futuristic-looking today as it did then.

Avoriaz clings to the cliff face at the top of the cable-car that brings you up from Les Prodains in the Morzine Valley. The French government has already correctly listed it as a Landmark of the Twentieth Century.

Most of the original 'shoebox' résidence buildings have been completely gutted to provide a smaller number of decent-sized apartments. Other new ones in the Falaise and Festival quartiers fulfill the much more luxurious expectations of present-day skiers who can't remember cable bindings and leather ski boots – and have spent summer holidays in much more spacious surroundings in Florida. But the concept remains unchanged: a series of apartment buildings on different levels that are linked by exterior boulevard

Essentials

Altitude: 1000m (3,280ft)–2466m (8,090ft)
Map: see page M26
Further information: t +33 (0)4 50 74 02 11, www.avoriaz.com
Lifts in area: 206 in Portes du Soleil area (14 cableways, 82 chairs, 110 drags) serving 650km of piste
Lift pass: Portes du Soleil (covers 14 resorts) adult €179, child 5–16yrs €120, both for 6 days
Access: Geneva airport 2hrs

pistes and interior stairs, lifts and walkways.

You can also drive up to Avoriaz, but the covered parking is expensive and in a pedestrianized resort you have no need for your own transport. Baggage is conveyed to your apartment or hotel by horse-drawn sleigh or snow tractor.

Avoriaz is the best place to base yourself in the Portes du Soleil, which falls short of being one of the world's outstanding ski circuits only because of uncertainty of snow cover. The top of the ski area, in this the highest resort in the region, only goes up to 2466m which is simply not high enough in these variable winters. When cover is poor or non-existent elsewhere, the overcrowding here can become unacceptable.

The resort has been a champion of snowboarding since the boards arrived here in the 1970s, and in 1993 it was the first resort in France to build a dedicated terrain park and half-pipe. The resort now has three terrain parks, including La Chapelle park, which is designed for beginners. The Tête aux Bœufs, which is 120m long and 4.5m high, plays host to a number of international snowboard competitions.

A constantly updated lift system allows you to explore the main villages of the Portes du Soleil and return to base by evening. A few such as St-Jean-d'Aulps and Abondance, remain entirely independent and require a separate excursion.

As with Sella Ronda in Italy, completing the actual tour of the principal French and Swiss resorts in a single day restricts the amount of time spent going downhill, with most of your day taken up riding lifts. It makes more sense to explore one sector of the area at a time.

Decide where you want to go and the quickest way of getting there. Despite vast improvements over the years to both piste signposts and lift maps, this is not always an easy task. Unfortunately the maps for each sector are only available from individual tourist offices or from lift stations on the way. This can result in a chicken-and-egg situation – you need a map to get there, but you can't get the map until you get there. It makes sense to acquire a full set before you leave home.

Border controls are extremely unusual, but not unheard of. We strongly advise you to carry your passport as well as euros and Swiss francs. If you, or one of your party, has an accident along the way, you could be stranded overnight or for much longer in another country.

Border guards on skis are increasingly a rarity and few goods are so much cheaper in one country than the other that it pays to lug them them home in a rucksack. However, Switzerland is not part of the EU and restrictions apply as to what you may take from one country to the other without paying duty.

Both currencies are widely accepted, but you will find the exchange rate more favourable if you tender the appropriate one for lunch or goods purchased.

Mountain

Avoriaz is suited to all levels of skier and rider, but in particular to intermediates who will enjoy the feeling of 'going somewhere' each day rather than being forced to repeatedly ski the same slopes over and over again for the whole week. Part of the charm of the resort is that the village streets are pistes – making this the definitive destination for doorstep skiing. The main nursery slopes are above the village and a number of different lifts serve a series of pleasant green runs that connect to lifts coming up from the valley town of Morzine.

Most of Avoriaz's own intermediate terrain lies on the lift-served slopes leading up to the ridge that marks the Swiss border as well as in the adjoining Les Hauts Forts sector, accessed by a chair-lift near the lower 'gate' of Avoriaz. Skiers here can explore some outstanding blue and red runs above and below the tree-line with lots of off-piste variations that are superb after a fresh snowfall. A long and testing black run descends from Le Plan Brazy follow ing the basic steep line of the FIS downhill course and brings you down eventually – by bus or green run in good snow conditions over the last bit – to Les Prodains where you can take the cable-car directly back to Avoriaz.

Aventurous skiers or riders will soon want to explore further afield either by taking the Chaux Fleurie chair to the Col de Bassachaux and Châtel beyond, or by tackling the notorious Wall and heading into Switzerland for a cheesy lunch.

The Wall – its correct name is La Chavanette – has achieved considerable notoriety over the years as one of the most difficult descents marked as a black run on any piste map. In reality its bark is usually much worse than its bite, although the toxicity of the latter is dependent on the quality of the snow. A piste sign at the top warns that the run should be attempted only by experts. At the start, the angle of descent does not allow you to see what lies ahead. But once you have completed the first half-dozen turns, it eases into a relatively straight-forward and heavily mogulled run.

More lifts take you up to a point above Les Crosets, Champéry and the rest of the Portes du Soleil. If conditions are hard-packed and you don't like what you see – or rather don't see – at the top of The Wall, then you are strongly advised to ride the chair down. In off-piste conditions alternative descents from the ridge are much more enjoyable. There are also other, easier routes into Switzerland.

The hamlet of Les Crosets is little more than a few holiday homes and a hotel that doubles as a lift station. It is surrounded by wide north-facing pistes served by lifts leading back up in the direction of Avoriaz. It's worth spending some time exploring this sector.

A chair-lift to the Pointe de l'Au takes you deeper into the Portes du Soleil in the direction of little Champoussin and Morgins beyond. Morgins has an enjoyable north-facing run that takes you down through the woods to the village. On the far side, a lift takes you up to Super-Châtel over the Pas de Morgins and back into France. Alternatively you can ski down into Switzerland again to the remote purpose-built village of Torgon.

At Châtel you have to cross the village by bus to take the gondola up to Linga and the series of lifts and piste beyond here that complete the circuit to Avoriaz. Plan your day carefully and allow plenty of time. If for some reason you don't manage to finish your tour before the lifts close, you must decide between an expensive taxi ride or an unscheduled overnight stay.

The best powder runs are found on both sides of the Swiss border. The area is prone to considerable avalanche danger, and the services of a qualified guide are essential. **Mont Blanc Helicopters, t** +33 (0)4 50 74 22 44, will take you heli-skiing.

Learn

Avoriaz has the **ESI Ecole de Glisse, t** +33 (0)4 50 74 02 18, which received favourable comments from reporters, and the **ESF, t** +33 (0)450 74 05 65. Both schools also teach snowboarding, in healthy competition with **Emery Snowboard School, t** +33 (0)4 50 74 12 64, and **Free Ride, t** +33 (0)4 50 74 00 36. **The British Alpine Ski and Snowboarding School, t** +44 (0)1237 451099, is warmly recommended.

Childcare

Le Village des Enfants/Le Village Snowboard, t +33 (0)4 50 74 04 46, cares for children from three years in a dedicated area in the centre of the resort, using methods developed by the celebrated French ski champion, Annie Famose. **Les P'tits Loups, t** +33 (0)4 50 74 00 38, cares for non-skiing children.

Lunch

The main self-service restaurants are prone to overcrowding during high season or when snow-cover is poor elsewhere. It pays to seek out one of the authentic mountain huts. **Coquoz, t** +41 (0)24 479 1255, at Planachaux has a circular open fireplace and good food. The goat-farming hamlet of Les Lindarets has a number of enticing eateries including **La Crémaillère, t** +33 (0)4 50 74 11 68. **L'Abricotine, t** +33 (0)4 50 74 17 43, at Les Brochaux and **Les Crêtes de Zorre, t** +33 (0)4 50 79 24 73, are also recommended.

Dine

Avoriaz has a wide choice of restaurants. **La Table du Marché** and **Restaurant Gastronomique**, both **t** +33 (0)4 50 74 08 11, are in Les Dromonts hotel. **Le Bistro, t** +33 (0)4 50 74 14 08, opposite Le Village des Enfants, is good but expensive. **La Réserve, t** +33 (0)4 50 74 02 01, has wonderful lamb dishes. **Chez Flo, t** +33 (0)4 50 74 19 24, and **Le Petit Dru, t** +33 (0)4 50 74 02 24, are also recommended.

Party

The Place, Le Shooter's and **Le Globe Trotters Café** are all popular international pubs with live music. **Le Tavaillon-Pub** attracts predominantly young British customers. **Le Fest** and **Pub Le Choucas** are the late-night venues.

Sleep

Most visitors to Avoriaz stay in apartments. Bookings can be made through **Pierre et Vacances, t** +33 (0)8 25 82 08 20, **Agence Immobilière des Dromonts, t** +33 (0)4 50 74 00 03, **Agence Immobilière des Hauts Forts, t** +33 (0)4 50 74 16 08, and **Selectis, t** +33 (0)4 50 74 13 33. As all the skiing is from your door, it makes little difference where you stay.

★★★**Hotel Dromonts, t** +33 (0)4 50 74 08 11, *www.christophe-leroy.com/dromont.htm*, has a Thalgo spa and a handy children's playroom.

★★★**Hotel Neige & Roc, t** +33 (0)4 50 79 03 21, *www.neige-roc.com*, is down at Les Prodains.

Chamonix and Argentière

Profile

Strikingly beautiful glacial scenery and rugged off-piste beneath the soaring peaks of the Mont Blanc massif. This is a high Alpine area best suited to strong intermediate and expert skiers and riders looking for new challenges. Beginners and nervous skiers should steer clear. Vibrant après-ski scene, a cosmopolitan ambience, and easy airport access

Resort

Chamonix first ventured into tourism in 1741 when two English explorers, William Windham and Richard Pococke, took three days rather than the present 60 minutes to reach the valley from Geneva. Pococke, for reasons best known to himself, was dressed as an Arab.

They gazed up at the ice fields of Mont Blanc, but it was another 45 years before the highest peak in Western Europe was successfully conquered by local crystal collector Jacques Balmat. Since then it has become the climbing – and more recently – skiing capital of the world.

The little town with its *fin de siècle* villas and grand hotels acts as a magnet for powderhounds. They are attracted by the extraordinarily steep and awe-inspiring terrain that takes no prisoners.

After a fresh ovenight snowfall you must rise with the sun to cut first tracks. By mid-morning not a bowl or a single gully will be left unsullied by the passage of ski and board.

There are plenty of groomed pistes, but they are much steeper than in most other resorts. This is not a good resort for families or groups of mixed abilities.

Essentials

Altitude: 1035m (3,396ft)–3842m (12,605ft)
Map: see page M28
Further information: t +33 (0)4 50 53 00 24, *www.chamonix.com*
Lifts in area: 46 (1 funicular, 12 cableways, 17 chairs, 16 drags) serving 150km of piste; 729km in Mont Blanc ski area
Lift pass: Cham'Ski (covers Chamonix valley except Les Houches) €186, child adult 4–15yrs €130–158. Ski Pass Mont Blanc (covers all local resorts including Courmayeur, Les Houches, Megève) adult €216, child 4–15yrs €173–184, all for 6 days
Access: Geneva airport 1hr. Station in resort

Mountain

Chamonix is dominated by the 3842m Aiguille du Midi, reached by cable-car from the southern side of town. This is the starting point for the famous Vallée Blanche, a glorious 22km descent past yawning crevasses and house-sized *séracs* (ice boulders) all the way back to Chamonix. Anyone who can ski parallel and who is not afraid of heights can tackle the easiest of the four main routes, but you must take a guide.

At the start you have to negotiate the ice steps cut into the spine of the ridge leading down from the cable-car station. They are not difficult, but the 2000m sheer drop to your left can have an unsettling psychological effect. The return to Chamonix is by rack-and-pinion railway from Montenvers or via a short climb and a long descent down a narrow path and piste to a cowbell factory on the outskirts of Chamonix.

But the town's main skiing is on the other side of the valley, reached either from the outskirts of the resort or from a lift station at Les Praz higher up the valley. Linked Le Brévent and La Flégère provide plenty of scope for intermediate and strong skiers.

However, for powderhounds the main course is to be found at the little village of *Argentière*, where an 80-person cable-car and a quad-chair give access to Lognan. From this mid-mountain station a cable-car (not included in the lift pass) rises to the 3275m Grands Montets, one of the world's greatest ski mountains. The descents from here through the glacier are as staggeringly beautiful as they are demanding. Pas de Chèvre, a run from the top of Bochard via one of several extreme couloirs down to the Mer de Glace is a Chamonix classic.

At the head of the valley, Le Tour offers some good novice terrain as well as rewarding runs on the Col de Balme and a long descent to *Vallorcine*. The Grands Montets and Le Tour both have terrain parks but the majority of snowboarders here are usually busy elsewhere, climbing up or riding down a vertiginous couloir.

Learn

The **ESF**, t +33 (0)4 50 53 22 57, offers traditional tuition. **Sensation Ski Ecole Internationale**, t +33 (0)4 50 53 56 46, takes a more offbeat approach. **Evolution 2**, t +33 (0)4 50 55 90 22, is strongly praised by reporters. The ESF also has a branch in **Argentière**, t +33 (0)4 50 54 00 12, and **Summit Ski Montagne**, t +33 (0)4 50 54 05 11, is the specialist board school. Other schools include **Kailish Adventure**, t +33 (0)450 53 18 99, and **Stages Bernard Muller**, t +33 (0)4 50 53 18 99.

Guiding is available through **Association Internationale des Guides du Mont-Blanc**, t +33 (0)4 50 53 27 05, **Compagnie des Guides de Chamonix**, t +33 (0)4 50 53 00 88, **Mont Blanc Ski Tours**, t +33 (0)4 50 53 82 16, **Roland Stieger**, t +33 (0)4 50 55 84 77, **Sensation Ski Ecole Internationale**, t +33 (0)4 50 55 94 26, **Stages Vallençant**, t +33 (0)4 50 54 05 11, and **Yak & Yeti**, t +33 (0)4 50 53 53 67.

Children

Two ski areas, Les Planards and Le Savoy, are reserved for children. The **ESF Piou Piou Club**, t +33 (0)4 50 53 22 57, cares for children from three years. The **ESF** runs its **Panda Club** ski kindergarten in **Chamonix**, t +33 (0)4 50 55 86 12, and in **Argentière**, t +33 (0)4 50 54 04 76. Both provide daycare and tuition from three years. **Halte Garderie**, t +33 (0)4 50 53 36 68, the municipal crèche, looks after non-skiing children from 18 months. **Evolution 2** gives lessons from three years at **Chamonix**, t +33 (0)4 50 55 93 03, and at **Argentière**, t +33 (0)4 50 54 21 36.

Lunch

At Lognan, **La Crèmerie du Glacier**, t +33 (0)4 50 55 90 10, in the woods above the base station of the Lognan cable-car, is one of the only restaurants not owned by the lift company. It is renowned for its *croûte fromage*. **Plan Joran**, t +33 (0)4 50 53 05 42, has good food and a sunny terrace.

We recommend **La Bergerie de Planpraz**, t +33 (0)4 50 53 93 40, at Brévent and **La Chavanne** at Flégère, t +33 (0)4 50 53 06 13.

In Chamonix, **Le Robinson**, t +33 (0)4 50 53 45 87, on the cross-country track, has a great atmosphere and serves mountain cuisine.

Dine

La Maison Carrier, t +33 (0)4 50 53 05 09, has outstanding Savoyard cuisine. **L'Auberge du Bois Prin**, t +33 (0)4 50 53 33 51, is also warmly recommended along with **Hotel Eden in Les Praz**, t +33 (0)4 50 53 18 43. **Atmosphere**, t +33 (0)4 50 55 97 97, serves gourmet food. **La Calèche**, t +33 (0)4 50 55 94 68, specializes in traditional Savoyard dishes. **Le Satsuki**, t +33 (0)4 50 53 21 99, has sushi. **The Rusticana**, t +33 (0)4 50 55 88 28, in Argentière offers fish and chips and Irish stew.

Party

Chamonix has better and more lively après-ski than in almost any other French resort. Start the evening with cocktails at **Chambre Neuf**, **Le Choucas**, **Le Privilege**, **Jekyll** or **Expedition**. Rue du Docteur Paccard is paved with welcoming bars. Real late-nighters end up at the **BPM**, or the **Garage** in Chamonix Sud.

In Argentière, **The Office** is a resort institution where you can drink, eat, listen to live music – or even stay.

Sleep

Chamonix offers the full spectrum, from youth hostels to four-star hotels, plus a wide choice of chalets and apartments. All bookings can be made through **Chamonix Reservations Centre**, t +33 (0)4 50 53 23 33. ★★★★**Le Hameau Albert 1er**, t +33(0)4 50 53 05 09, *www.hameaualbert.fr*, is a stylish and atmospheric hotel owned by the Carrier brothers.

★★★★**L'Auberge du Bois Prin**, t +33(0)4 50 53 33 51, *www.boiprin.com*, has considerable charm and a fine restaurant.

★★★★**Balcons du Savoy**, t +33(0)4 50 55 32 32, *www.lesbalconsdusavoy.com*, are the resort's prime apartments.

★★★★**Grand Hotel des Alpes**, t +33 (0)4 50 55 37 80, *www.grandhoteldesalpes.com*, is new and extremely comfortable.

★★★**Hotel Gustavia**, t +33 (0)4 50 53 00 31, *www.hotel-gustavia.com*, is lively and central.

★★★**Park Hotel Suisse**, t +33 (0)4 50 53 07 58, *www.chamonix-park-hotel.com*, is friendly and was rated 'superb' by reporters.

★★**Hotel Richemond**, t +33 (0)4 50 53 08 85, *www.richemond.fr*, is an old favourite in the town centre.

The Clubhouse, t +33 (0)4 50 90 96 56, *www.thebigfriendlyhouse.com*, opened last winter and doesn't have a star rating. It is a contemporary boutique hotel inside an Art Deco mansion built in 1927. Accommodation is in custom-built bunkhouses. Each has a plasma screen, Xbox, and 'rainforest' shower.

Argentière:

Hotel Le Dahu, t +33 (0)4 50 54 01 55, *www.hotel-le-dahu.com*, is warmly recommended.

Le Lavancher:

★★★★**Hotel Jeu de Paume**, t +33 (0)4 50 54 03 76, *www.jeudepaumechamonix.com*, is a romantic boutique hotel with an outstanding gourmet restaurant.

***Les Chalets de Philippe, t +33 (0)4 50 54 56 35, are tiny but stylishly converted wood-and-stone *mazots* (ancient barns).

La Clusaz

Profile

One of the closest resorts to Geneva airport with lots of low-level intermediate skiing, good mountain restaurants and modest hotels

Resort

La Clusaz has been a resort since 1908 when local lad Pierre-Noël Vittoz experimented wth skis and an invention called *Le Paret*, the first-ever snowbike. The attractive village is built around an early 19th-century church and a mountain stream.

Mountain

The skiing is divided into five sectors. Access to Beauregard and L'Aiguille is by lifts from the resort centre. The other areas (Balme, L'Etale and Croix-Fry/Merdassier) are reached by ski-bus. Most of the skiing is ideal for intermediates. The terrain park on Aiguille receives much praise from reporters.

Learn

ESF, t +33 (0)4 50 02 40 83, is rated excellent, while the ESI Sno-Académie, t +33 (0) 4 50 32 66 05, and Aravis Challenge, t +33 (0)4 50 02 81 29, are recommended. The others are Evolution 2, t +33 (0)4 50 23 52 77, Alter Ego, t +33 (0)6 07 39 72 53, and Dimension Freeride, t +33 (0)4 50 03 54 39.

Essentials

Altitude: 1100m (3,608ft)–2600m (8,528ft)
Further information: t +33 (0)4 50 32 65 00, www.laclusaz.com
Lifts in area: 88 in Aravis (8 cableways, 27 chairs, 53 drags) serving 220km of piste
Lift pass: Aravis (covers La Clusaz, Le Grand-Bornand, Manigod and St-Jean-de-Sixt) adult €155, child 5–15yrs €114
Access: Geneva airport 60mins. Station at Annecy 30mins

Children

The ESF and ESI provide lessons. Club des Mouflets is the non-ski kindergarten, Club des Champions offers daycare with optional ski lessons, and – unusually – there is a cross-country ski kindergarten for children from four years, t +33 (0)4 50 02 40 83 for all.

Lunch

Try Altitude 1647, t +33 (0)4 50 02 44 00, in the Beauregard area, and Chalet des Praz, t +33 (0)4 50 02 59 84, an atmospheric Savoyard chalet built in 1792 on the Crêt du Merle pistes. Le Bercail, t +33 (0)4 50 02 43 75, on the Massif de L'Aiguille, is a fine lunching experience.

Dine

Au Cochon des Neiges, t +33 (0)4 50 02 62 62, serves Savoyard cuisine. La Calèche, t +33 (0)4 50 02 42 60, is renowned for its fresh fish and home-made foie gras. L'Arbé, t +33 (0)4 50 02 60 54, has a chalet ambience. Le Symphonie in Hotel Beauregard, t +33 (0)4 50 32 68 00, is gastronomic.

Party

Après-bars include **La Grolle, Les Caves du Paccaly** and **La Braise**. **Le Pressoir** is the haunt of snowboarders and **Le Grenier** attracts the locals. **L'Ecluse** nightclub has a glass dance-floor over the river, and at **Club 18** you can dance until the early hours.

Sleep

★★★**Hotel Beauregard**, t +33 (0)4 50 32 68 00, *www.hotel-beauregard.fr*, has an attractive interior and a swimming-pool.
★★★**Hotel L'Alpage de Tante Pauline**, t +33 (0)4 50 02 63 28, *www.chaletalpage.com*, has ten rooms.
★★★**Hotel Vieux Chalet**, t +33 (0)4 50 02 41 53, *www.levieuxchalet.fr*, is even smaller, with eight rooms.
★★**Hotel Les Sapins**, t +33 (0)4 50 63 33 33, *www.clusaz.com*, is in a good position.

Courchevel

Profile

At its highest level, Courchevel is the most chic and the most expensive resort in France, and it also happens to have outstanding skiing. But that is just the top bit. Courchevel is made up of four quite separate villages at different altitudes and has something to suit everybody. You just need to know your geography

Resort

Courchevel has been reigning supreme since 1946 as the resort closest to the heart of Parisians. Ever since the Mounier family first cashed in their cow pastures and agreed to the construction of the first lift, Courch' as the locals call it, has caught the eye of capital café society. In present-day terms what we are talking about is Courchevel 1850, the highest of these villages with direct links to Méribel and the other resorts of the Trois Vallées.

Courchevel 1850 is the only centre here with Le Jet Set appeal, a purpose-built portfolio of extraordinarily hedonistic hotels and private chalets perched on the mountainside above the still unspoilt valley town of Bozel. It has few Alpine rivals for comfort and cuisine – and none for cost. It caters for an international clientele that includes Russians, and now Chinese and Bollywood, who frankly don't give a damn what it costs to stay, ski and eat here as long as they enjoy themselves. That's 1850.

Some 200 vertical metres down the mountain in both altitude and social standing comes Courchevel 1650, a more authentic French mountain village with reasonable restaurant prices and affordable chalet accommodation. It also has the best skiing.

Courchevel 1550, which is geographically directly below 1850 and now served by a new six-person chair, is becoming a serious satellite of its sophisticated sister, while 1650 retains a less affluent and earthy character entirely of it own.

At the bottom of the mountain lies the original farming village of Le Praz or Courchevel 1300. This is a delightful place to stay with good accommodation, one of the best restaurants in the area, and easy access by gondola to the other Courchevels. However, it is inevitable that resort-level snow-cover here throughout an increasingly larger proportion of the season will be limited.

Mountain

The number of lifts and the sheer scale of the skiing in the Trois Vallées is simply staggering. Mere statistics mean nothing, you have to see it for yourself. It is worth noting that the resort lift map takes considerable licence with the compass. Courchevel appears to be the most westerly resort in the region, when in fact it is the most easterly, a fact to be borne in mind when searching for sunshine or north-facing slopes.

From the hub of La Croisette at 1850 a network of gondolas and a cable-car take you up to 2738m Saulire. You can either ski down the far side to Méribel and further into the Trois Vallées, or return towards Courchevel. The main arterial run back down to 1850 can become horrendously overcrowded and it pays to spend time around adjoining 2659m where most slopes are slightly more challenging and therefore less popular.

For accomplished skiers and riders, the black Les Suisses is particularly enjoyable. In the right snow conditions it is possible to ski from Saulire all the way down to Bozel below Courchevel – a vertical drop of over 2000m.

Courchevel is famed for its Couloirs, three ribbons of snow between the rocks that unfurl from the ridge on the right-hand side of the top station of the cable-car. Grand Couloir, Sous le Télépherique and Emile Allais can be extremely demanding when icy. However, in good mid-winter snow conditions they

should present no great problem to an experienced skier or rider. Catch them as soon as they are declared open after a major dump. They quickly become bumped up with some awkward VW-sized moguls in the high reaches. If you fall here, it is a long way down, but there are no obstacles and the likelihood of serious injury is small. However, you should treat the often icy approach route from the cable-car with considerable caution.

The Altiport sector of Courchevel just to the east of 1850 is ideal beginner terrain with green and easy blue runs that are ideal for building confidence before heading further afield. Topographically, the Trois Vallées is the perfect ski area. The links between different sectors are natural rather than contrived. This allows for more real ski time rather than hours wasted on paths. From almost everywhere there is an easy way down and anyone who can vaguely ski parallel can explore far afield.

During peak high season the cognoscenti head for Courchevel 1650 – unless they are already staying here. Its own extensive ski area beneath a trio of peaks is off the Trois Vallées beaten track. The runs on Col de Chanrossa, Signal and Bel Air above the village are suited to all standards and are some of the most enjoyable in the whole region. From Roc Merlet you can ski off-piste on the higher slopes of the Vallée des Avals on a glorious itinerary that brings you back down to 1650.

Snowboarders will find a good supply of natural hits throughout Courchevel. The terrain park at Plantrey has a half-pipe. Riders also congregate at Les Verdons and Biolley.

Essentials

Altitude: 1300m (4,265ft)–2738m (8,983ft)
Map: see page M30
Further information: t +33 (0)4 79 08 00 29, www.courchevel.com
Lifts in area: 167 in Trois Vallées (40 cableways, 69 chairs, 58 drags) serving 600km of piste
Lift pass: Trois Vallées adult €204, child 5–13yrs €153.50, both for 6 days
Access: Chambéry 2hrs, Lyon 2½hrs, Geneva 3hrs, Moûtiers station 25km

Learn

Ski lesson are big businees in Courchevel and there is intensive rivalry between the various schools. Large number of 'blacks' – unqualified ski bums – also tout for business and should be avoided. The **ESF**, t +33 (0)4 79 08 07 72, has branches in all the villages and, with over 700 teachers working during peak February, the quality of instruction is a lottery. We recommend **New Generation/Le Ski School**, t +33 (0)4 79 01 03 18, owned and operated by **British BASI instructors. Supreme**, t +33 (0)4 79 08 27 87, is another long-established British school. **Ski Académie**, t +33 (0)4 79 08 11 99, has a strong reputation. **Magic in Motion**, t +33 (0)4 79 01 01 81, is a favourite with tour operators. Guiding can be arranged through the ski schools or the **Bureau des Guides**, t +33 (0)4 79 01 03 66.

Children

Courchevel has the French government's *P'tits Montagnards* award for childcare. The **ESF** runs non-ski and ski kindergartens that come in for criticism during peak holiday times when they are stretched to capacity.

In 1850, **Village des Enfants**, t +33 (0)4 79 08 08 47, provides all-day care and an introduction to skiing from three years. **Magic in Motion**, t +33 (0)4 79 01 01 81, runs English-only classes for four- to six-year-olds. **Ski Académie**, t +33 (0)4 79 08 11 99, has morning classes for children from four years as well as dedicated classes for children aged 10 to 13 years and 14 to 16 years. **Supreme**, t +33 (0)479 08 27 87, has classes for children aged six to 12 years during school holidays.

In 1650, **Les Pitchounets**, t + 33 (0)479 08 33 69, is a dedicated play area for small children. **Le Club des Oursons**, t +33 (0)479 08 26 08, teaches children from three years. The **Garderie**, t +33 (0)6 20 66 37 23, cares for children under 18 months. In 1550, **Le Club des Piou-Piou**, t +33 (0)4 79 08 21 07, takes children from three to five years for a mix of lessons and snow fun.

Lunch

Courchevel has lots of overpriced self-services and a portfolio of elegant piste-side eateries that cater for a clientele that sees a gourmet lunch and a €50 bottle of wine as a basic component of the skiing day. Booking is essential. Best value is **Bel-Air**, t +33 (0)4 79 08 00 93, at the top of the Courchevel 1650 gondola. It serves traditional Savoyard cuisine in a beautiful setting, with friendly and attentive staff.

Le Cap Horn, t +33 (0)4 79 08 33 10, by the Altiport, offers seafood and Asian dishes served by liveried waiters. **Chalet de Pierres**, t +33 (0)4 79 08 18 61, on the descent from Saulire, is a comfortable but costly resort institution with a sunny terrace, more liveried waiters, and an enticing display of desserts. In 1650, **Le Petit Savoyard**, t +33 (0)4 79 08 27 44, and **L'Eterlou**, t +33 (0)4 79 08 25 45, both serve pizzas.

Dine

In 1850, double Michelin-starred **Le Bateau Ivre**, t +33 (0)4 79 08 36 88, in Hotel Pomme de Pin, has inspirational cooking that stands head and shoulders above its many rivals. **Hotel Le Chabichou**, t +33 (0)4 79 08 00 55, has a similar Red Guide accolade. **La Saulire** (known as **Jacques' Bar**), t +33 (0)4 79 08 07 52, is our favourite here; it has an impressive menu and wine list, intimate surroundings and impeccable, friendly service.

In 1650, prices are considerably lower. We recommended **L'Eterlou**, t +33 (0)4 79 08 25 45, and **La Montagne**, t +33 (0)4 79 08 09 85. In 1550, **L'Œil de Bœuf**, t +33 (0)4 79 08 22 10, is in an old mountain barn. In Le Praz, **La Table de mon Grand-Père** in Hotel Les Peupliers, t +33 (0)4 79 08 41 47, offers traditional cooking using fresh ingredients and is one of the finest

restaurants in the region. L'Ecurie,
t +33 (0)4 79 00 28 14 is in a 300-year-old
converted stable in St Bon and is full
of atmosphere.

Party

At **Prends Ta Luge et Tire-toi** in
Courchevel 1850 you can check your
emails, have a drink or buy a snowboard.
The iniquitously expensive **Le Pyggys Pub**
is popular, and **The Purple** is a new
'fashion bar' with a DJ. **Les Caves** is the
shockingly expensive, late-night venue.

In 1650, the British celebrate and check
their emails in **Le Bubble**. **Le Plouc** is an
intimate late-night bar. In 1550, après-ski
centres around the friendly **Taverne**, the
Glacier Bar, **Le Barouf** and **Chanrossa**.
Family-oriented **Le Praz** (Courchevel 1300)
falls asleep early.

Sleep

Courchevel 1850:
★★★★*deluxe* Hotel Les Airelles, t +33 (0)4 79
09 38 38, *www.airelles.fr*, is tastefully
discreet.
★★★★*deluxe* Hotel Byblos Courchevel, t +33
(0)4 79 00 98 00 attracts celebrities and
has a sister hotel in St Tropez.
★★★★*deluxe* Hotel Kilamandjaro, t +33 (0)4
79 01 46 46, *www.hotelkilimandjaro.com*,
is a collection of chalets grouped around
a central building with restaurant and a
La Prairie spa.
★★★★*deluxe* Hotel Lana, t +33 (0)4 79 08 01
10, has a spa with swimming-pool.
★★★★*deluxe* Le Mélézin, t +33 (0)4 79 08 01
33, *www.amanresorts.com*, is the stylish
Alpine headquarters of Amanresorts,
with a gym and swimming-pool.
★★★★*deluxe* Hotel Le Saint-Joseph, t +33
(0)4 79 08 16 16, in the heart of the
village, offers understated luxury
combined with a retro style in its 11
rooms and three apartments.

★★★★Hotel Chabichou, t +33 (0)4 79 08 00
55, *www.chabichou-courchevel.com*, is in
a large chalet-style building, and offers
weekly cookery courses.
★★★★Hotel des Neiges, t +33 (0)4 79 03 03
77, has a gastronomic restaurant and a
Banyan Spa.
★★★★La Sivolière, t +33 (0)4 79 08 08 33,
has recently been upgraded to four-star
status.
★★★★Hotel Trois Vallées, t +33 (0)4 79 08
00 12, has panoramic views.
★★★Ducs de Savoie, t +33 (0)4 79 08 03 00,
has a swimming-pool and is in the
Jardin Alpin residential area.
★★★La Loze, t +33 (0)4 79 08 28 25,
www.la-loze.com, has a library that
doubles as a bar.
Courchevel 1650:
★★★Hotel du Golf, t +33 (0)4 79 00 92 92,
www.hoteldugolf-courchevel.fr, is ski-in
ski-out.
★★★Le Seizena, t+33 (0)4 79 01 46 46,
www.hotelseizena.com, is a new B&B
for this winter with 20 attractive and
minimalist rooms.
★★★Chalet Rikiki is right on the edge of
the piste, and **Chalet Les Sorbiers** has
great views, both t +44 (0)870 754 4444,
www.leski.com.
Le Praz:
★★★Hotel Les Peupliers, t +33 (0)4 79 08 41
47, *www.lespeupliers.com*, is a delightful
place to stay.

Les Deux Alpes

Profile

Large ski area with snow-sure glacial slopes served by a modern lift system. Suited to novices, intermediate cruisers, families and off-piste skiers in search of fresh challenges. The nightlife is some of the most frenetic in France

Essentials

Altitude: 1650m (5,412ft)–600m (11,808ft)
Map: see page M27
Further information: t +33 (0)4 76 79 22 00, *www.les2alpes.com*
Lifts in area: 51 (1 funicular, 6 cableways, 23 chairs, 19 drags) serving 220km of piste
Lift pass: Area (includes 1 free day in Alpe d'Huez, La Grave, The Milky Way, Puy-St-Vincent, Serre Chevalier) adult €165, child 6–13yrs €123.80, both for 6 days
Access: Grenoble airport 90mins, Lyon airport 2hrs

Resort

Les Deux Alpes lies between Grenoble and Briançon in a remote corner of the Dauphiné. It biggest asset is its high altitude, which allows skiing to continue throughout much of the year and makes it a popular venue for out-of-season ski and snowboard camps. It has been a ski resort since 1939 when a primitive rope-tow was installed. Unfortunately this fell down 15 minutes after the opening ceremony. Hostilities with Germany then got in the way of any further development plans until the late 1950s when a gondola paved the way for Les Deux Alpes to become an important French resort.

The purpose-built village was conceived as a *station de ski* on the sunny balcony above the ancient community of Venosc to which it is connected by gondola but not by piste. Venosc, with its cobbled lanes, craft shops and enticing restaurants provides a welcome contrast and a tranquil alternative bed-base to the functional ski factory above it.

L2A sprawls along a narrow ledge below what were once the high summer pastures of sheep and goat farmers. The village lacks aesthetic appeal but is by no means an architectural eyesore on the scale of Tignes, Les Menuires and other French resorts that developed during the the 1960s.

L2A is suited to all levels of skier and rider. However, lower intermediates should note that on the main mountain the gradient here is 'reversed'. Some of the easiest skiing is higher up on and around the glacier. The benefit of this is that complete beginners can learn against the panoramic backdrop of the high Alps rather than on a shaded slope tucked away on the outskirts of a village. The downside is that newcomers and other inexperienced skiers will find the much steeper final descent to L2A beyond their capabilities. The alternative is to follow a narrow and often icy green path. This is not made easier by the number of better skiers whizzing by. Until you have gained sufficient confidence it makes sense to download by gondola.

Advanced skiers will want to explore the glacial terrain of La Meije, reached by a 20-minute hike from the top of the ski area to the 3568m Dome de la Lauze. From here you can ski all the way down to the ancient climbing village of La Grave.

Here and elsewhere in the L2A area it is important always to be aware that you are in high mountains where the weather can change within minutes. It is the kind of territory where anyone who goes off-piste without a qualified local mountain guide is risking their life. Even then, it is up to the individual to take overall responsibility for his or her own safety. Mountain guides, like everyone else, are fallible.

Mountain

A choice of gondolas and cable-cars provides main mountain access. The most important of these, the Jandri Express jumbo gondola, takes you to an underground funicular station at 3200m for the final ride to the top of the glacier. The whole journey from the village takes around 45 minutes, a practical indication of the enormous vertical drop here. The bulk of the skiing revolves around the hubs of Les Crêtes at 2100m and Toura at 2600m. The terrain flattens out on the lower reaches of the glacier to provide easy pistes where the snow quality is always excellent.

La Fée sector, off the shoulder below Toura, is usually uncrowded and offers some of the best blue and black runs on the mountain. On the other side of the resort, the Pied Moutet sector provides gentle sunny blue runs served by three lifts. From here, snow conditions permitting, you can also ski down to the village of Bons at 1300m.

L2A is an important resort for riders and each October hosts the World Snowboard Meeting. The terrain park has a 120m half-pipe and is one of the most sophisticated in Europe.

Learn

The **ESF**, t +33 (0)4 76 79 21 21, and **ESI St Christophe**, t +33 (0)4 76 79 04 21, are the main teaching establishments. The British-run **European Ski School**, t +33 (0)4 76 79 74 55, offers tuition in English for

classes of up to four pupils. **Ski Privilège**, t +33 (0)4 76 79 23 44, and new British-run **Easiski**, t +33 (0)6 82 79 57 34, are alternatives. **Primitive**, t +33 (0)6 07 90 71 35, and **Burton Connexion**, t +33 (0)6 15 07 94 42, are the dedicated snowboard academies. Race-training is with **Stages Pierre Alain Carrel**, t +33 (0)4 76 80 51 99, and **Stages Damien Albert**, t +33 (0)4 76 79 50 38. Guiding is through **Bureau des Guides ESF**, t +33 (0)4 76 79 50 12.

Children

L2A has the coveted *Les P'tits Montagnards* award from the Fench government for excellence in childcare. **Crèche Les 2 Alpes 1800**, t+33 (0)4 76 79 02 62, cares for children aged six months to two years. **Garderie Le Bonhomme de Neige**, t +33 (0)4 76 79 06 77, looks after children aged two to six years. **Espace Luge** is a children's play area at the base of the mountain with animal characters, a trampoline, slalom course, snow-biking, tobogganing, tubing and an inflatable bob-run.

The **ESF**, t +33 (0)4 76 79 21 21, runs ski kindergartens in the village, at Champamé, and at les Crêtes with lessons for little ones from three years combined with fun in the snow and indoor play and videos. **ESI St Christophe**, t +33 (0)4 76 79 04 21, is for children up to eight years. **The European**, t +33 (0)4 76 79 74 55, also runs classes for children.

Lunch

La Molière, t+ 33 (0)4 76 80 18 99, is at the foot of the pistes, and **Le Diable au Coeur**, t +33 (0)4 76 79 99 50, at 2400m has an open fireplace and well-prepared regional cuisine. Both are recommended. **Les Glaciers**, t +33 (0)4 76 79 21 36, at 3200m is a new self-service that also has separate gastronomic restaurants with 40 covers. **Le Panoramic, t** +33 (0)4 76 79 06 75, at 2600m is a mountain hut with a great atmosphere and some of the best mountain fare in the resort.

Dine

The gourmet choices are the **Bel Auberge, t** +33 (0)4 76 79 57 90, which is 'Austrian style' with inventive cuisine, and **Le P'tit Polyte, t** +33 (0)4 76 80 56 90 , which has an excellent wine list. **L'Abri, t** +33 (0)4 76 79 21 41, has an Alpine ambience. **La Spaghetteria, t** +33 (0)4 76 79 05 77, is recommended for pasta, and **Tribeca Caffé, t** +33 (0)4 76 80 58 53, for pizzas. **Blue Salmon, t** +33 (0)4 76 79 29 56, serves simple fish dishes, and **Il Caminetto, t** +33 (0)4 76 79 51 54, is a typical Italian restaurant. **Thai Alloi, t** +33 (0)6 18 58 39 24, is authentic Thai, while **Smokey Joe's, t** +33 (0)4 76 79 21 70, offers good-value Tex-Mex. **La Patate, t** +33 (0)4 76 79 23 55, serves raclette and fondue in an Alpine atmosphere. **Hotel-Chalet Mounier, t** +33 (0)4 76 80 56 90, has reasonable prices and romantic surroundings.

Party

'The nightlife is amazing', says one reporter. Popular watering holes include **The Irish Bar, Pub Le Windsor, Smokey Joe's,** the **Secret** and **Le Pressoir. L'Opéra** is the recommended disco. **L'Avalanche** and **La Casa** also have a strong following.

Sleep

Most of the accommodation is in apartments.
- ★★★★**Alpina Lodge, t** +33 (0)4 76 79 75 17, *www.les2alpes.com*, contains some very comfortable apartments for two to ten people.
- ★★★★**Les Balconnes de Sarenne, t** +33 (0)4 76 79 57 97,

www.lesbalconnesdesarenne.com, are luxury apartments.
- ★★★★**Hotel La Bérangère, t** +33 (0)4 76 79 24 11, *http://berangerehotel.free.fr* is ski-in ski-out, with indoor and outdoor heated pools, games room and gym.
- ★★★★**Hotel La Farandole, t** +33 (0)4 76 80 50 45, *www.utaf.com/lafarandole*, is a traditional chalet with gastronomic restaurant and a piano bar.
- ★★★**Hotel Le Souleil'Or, t** +33 (0)4 76 79 24 69, *www.le-souleil-or.fr*, is a modern hotel with friendly owners and lots of Alpine character.
- ★★★**Hotel-Chalet Mounier, t** +33 (0)4 76 80 56 90, *www.chalet-mounier.com*, was a mountain refuge and Alpine farm back in 1879. Today it is attractively decorated, and has a swimming-pool and spa.
- ★★★**Hotel Muzelle Sylvana, t** +33 (0)4 76 80 50 93, *www.skisystem.net*, is 50m from the Diable cable-car and has a good wine cellar.

Flaine

Profile

Large ski area with an excellent snow record near the Mont Blanc massif. Suitable for all standards of skier and rider looking for a no-frills holiday in delightful Alpine surroundings. A short airport transfer and piste-side accommodation makes it popular with families

Resort

Flaine's 37-year history as a major ski resort has been marked by more troughs and crests than anywhere else, and after a decade in the doldrums it is suddenly once again about to become the hottest property in the Alps.

Canadian resort developer Intrawest, the force behind the creation of the successful new Arc 1950 village at Les Arcs, has announced that Flaine is the choice for its next 2,500-bed property investment in the Alps. The area around the main gondola base station is to be completely redeveloped and a new 'village' will be constructed below the present Scandinavian-style hamlet.

The first units go on sale in 2006 and completion will be in stages between 2008 and 2012. Canny skiers who did not buy in Les Arcs will be reaching for their cheque books, for Flaine has just as much to offer.

Despite its modest altitude, Flaine has a more reliable snow record than any comparable resort in Europe, thanks to the fridge-effect micro-climate created by nearby Mont Blanc. Good snow-cover is virtually guaranteed from early December until late April.

Equally important is the high quality of the ski terrain, which extends to the traditional villages of Samoëns, Morillon, Les Carroz and Sixt. In all some 73 lifts serve the 265km of piste in the area known as the Grand Massif.

The opportunities for off-piste are enormous. Famous French guide Yves

Détry, the first person to ski the north face of the Aiguille du Midi, says he prefers Les Carroz's skiing to that of Chamonix. However, it is important to be aware that the area is full of natural hazards. What begins as a gentle cruise through the powder in the trees all too often ends in an abrupt little cliff. The services of a local guide are essential.

Flaine opened to a fanfare of publicity in 1968. Sculptures by famous artists such as Picasso adorned the open spaces in the new ski village designed in grey concrete in the manner of the Bauhaus school of architecture.

But the years have not been kind. Financial insolvency beckoned in the 1980s and the works of art were sold off. Most of the original cramped apartment blocks and resort-owned hotels were in desperate need of renovation when the Compagnie des Alpes bought the lift system and launched a €28 million rescue plan. The Intrawest project should breathe new life into a resort that has so far never managed to achieve its full potential.

Flaine is currently divided into higher and lower villages connected by people-mover lifts. There is also a separate much more attractive Scandinavian-inspired chalet village just outside the resort and served by a free bus. The area below it is one of the two sites chosen by Intrawest for its new development.

Essentials

Altitude: 1600m (5,248ft)–2480m (8,134ft)
Map: see page M32
Further information: t +33 (0)4 50 90 80 01, *www.flaine.com*
Lifts in area: 73 in Le Grand Massif (7 cableways, 28 chairs, 38 drags) serving 265km of piste
Lift pass: Grand Massif (covers Les Carroz, Flaine, Morillon, Samoëns, Sixt) adult €168, child 5–15yrs €123–135, both for 6 days
Access: Geneva airport 90mins. Station at Cluses 25km, frequent bus service to resort

Mountain

Main mountain access is by gondola, which takes you up to the Grandes Platières at 2480m. This is the starting point for a whole series of runs graded blue, red and black leading down into the main bowl of Flaine. The natural amphitheatre is rimmed by a series of lifts all going up to around 2500m. Good nursery slopes are located in and outside the village, making it an ideal spot for families with young children. But for more adventurous skiers and riders Flaine is a base for exploring further afield into the Grand Massif.

The main link out of the bowl is a fast eight-person chair. From the 2204m summit of the Tête des Saix, north-facing runs drop down steep mogul slopes towards Samoëns. Alternatively you can choose easier cruising runs that bring you all the way down to Morillon or to Les Carroz. The ancient village of Sixt has its own small ski area and is directly linked into the Grand Massif via a piste, but ski-buses provide the only return.

Anyone who can ski parallel can enjoy day-long excursions to the far corners of the Grand Massif and enjoy the experience. But the lift system is prone to high-season bottlenecks in the afternoon when everyone is heading for home and you need allow plenty of time.

Flaine was one of the first resorts in France to embrace snowboarding. The 1500m Jam-Park has a half-pipe and snowcross course. Fantasurf has a half-pipe for children.

Learn

The ESF, t +33 (0)4 50 90 81 00, has a large presence. Anglo-Saxon visitors tend to favour the ESI, t +33 (0)4 50 90 84 41, which has small classes of six to seven pupils. We have good reports of **Moniteurs Independants**, t+ 33 (0)6 07 19 56 09, a co-operative of individual teachers run by veteran instructor Guy Pezet. They offer group and private instruction for adults and children. **Stages Francois Simond**, t +33 (0)4 50 90 80 97, and **Stages Flaine Super Ski**, t +33 (0)6 81 06 19 06, both offer race training. Guiding is available through the ski schools.

Children

All the ski schools offer lessons, with **La Souris Verte/ESI**, t +33 (0)4 50 90 84 41, putting children into small groups. The **ESF Rabbit Club**, t +33 (0)4 50 90 81 00, is more Gallic. Both offer a collection and drop-off service. **MMV** in Hotel Aujon and **Le Flaine**, t +33 (0)4 92 12 62 12, have mini-clubs for four to 11 years and a youth club for 12 to 14 years. **Club Med**, t +33 (0)4 50 90 81 66, has childcare for its small residents. Hotel Totem's **Whizz Kids**, t +44 (0)870 160 6040, was rated 'first class' by reporters. **Les P'tits Loups**, t +33 (0)4 50 90 87 82, accepts children from six months to three years.

Lunch

Blanchot, t +33 (0)4 50 90 82 44, is renowned for its onion soup. **Epicéa**, t +33 (0)4 50 90 83 79, between Flaine Forêt and Forum, has good pasta. **L'Eloge**, t +33 (0)4 50 90 85 91, by the Flaine gondola, provides a simple food and service with a smile. **L'Igloo**, t +33 (0)4 50 90 14 31, at the top of the Morillon chair, has reasonable food at good prices. The **Oréade**, t +33 (0)4 50 90 03 61, at the top of the Kédeuse gondola, has local mountain dishes. **Le Bissac**, t +33 (0)4 50 90 81 32, is a busy self-service with a good range of lunchtime dishes.

Dine

In Flaine Forum, try friendly **Chez La Jeanne**, t +33 (0)4 50 90 81 87, for excellent pizzas. **The White Grouse Pub**, t +33 (0)4 50 90 84 76, is a resort institution with a good restaurant serving burgers, pizzas and fondue. **L'Auroch**, t +33 (0)4 50 90 12 83, and **Le Grain de Sel**, t +33 (0)4 50 90 80 49, serve traditional French cuisine. **Chez Daniel**, t +33 (0)4 50 90 81 87 has a warm Alpine ambience. **La Pizzeria Chez Pierrot**, t +33 (0)4 50 90 84 56, has the best pizzas in town. **Les Chalets du Michet, t** +33 (0)4 50 90 80 08, has plenty of atmosphere. In Flaine Forêt, **La Perdrix Noire, t** +33 (0)4 50 90 81 81, specializes in Savoyard cuisine and has a fine reputation.

Party

'Ideal family resort – too quiet for a boys' holiday,' said one reporter. Certainly other resorts have livelier après-ski, but the **White Grouse** has a great atmosphere. The **Flying Dutchman** has karaoke and **Le Diamant Noir** is busy at weekends and in high season. You can also try your hand at driving a saloon car on ice. **The Motoring School t**+ 33 (0)4 50 90 44 07, is one of the most famous in France.

Sleep

All the original hotels are now run by French or British tour operators; accommodation can also be booked through **Flaine Reservations, t** +33 (0)4 50 90 89 09, *www.flainereservations.com*.
★★★Le Hameau de Flaine, t +33 (0)4 50 90 40 40, on the mountain at 1800m, has Scandinavian-inspired chalets.
★★Cap'Vacances Les Lindars, t +33 (0)4 71 50 80 88, *www.capvacances.com*, is in the centre, with a sun terrace and a theatre.
★★The Totem, t +44 (0)870 160 6040, is runs by Crystal and has good-sized rooms. 'The food was 10/10' said one reporter.
★★Hotel-Club Le Flaine MMV, t +33 (0)4 50 90 47 36, *www.mmv.fr*, has spacious rooms and good food.
★★Hotel-Club Aujon MMV, t +33 (0)4 50 90 80 10, *www.mmv.fr*, has comfortable, clean rooms.
★★Résidence de la Forêt, t +33 (0)4 50 90 86 99, situated at the top of the resort, has old-style Pierre et Vacances apartments.

La Grave

Profile

For experts only. Rugged off-piste skiing on the glacial slopes of the mighty 4000m La Meije, tenuously linked to Les Deux Alpes

Resort

La Meije, which rises above the rugged little village of La Grave between Grenoble and Briançon, was the last great peak of the Alpes to be conquered. Local guide Pierre Gaspard finally reached the 3982m summit in 1877. This corner of L'Oisans is one of poorest, least populated, and most wildly beautiful areas of France, a place of jagged peaks and rushing waterfalls.

La Grave has some of the most demanding high-altitude skiing and snowboarding in Europe, with an extraordinary vertical drop of 2200m through dramatic glacial scenery.

The top of the ski area can be reached by a long gondola and drag-lift from La Grave or by a 20-minute hike from the top of the ski area at *Les Deux Alpes*.

Mountain

The old but efficient gondola takes half an hour to climb from the village of La

Essentials

Altitude: 1450m (4,757ft)–3550m (11,647ft)
Further information: t +33 (0)4 76 79 90 05, *www.lagrave-lameije.com*
Lifts in resort: 4 (2 cableways, 2 drags) serving 5km of piste
Lift pass: adult €158, child under 16yrs €138, both for 6 days
Access: Grenoble airport 2hrs

Grave to the top station. You must then find your own way down between the giant *séracs* and yawning crevasses. The main routes are clearly indicated but stray from the well-beaten path and you may enounter some spectacular couloirs. Runs at le Pan de Rideau start with a traverse along the edge of cliffs that requires a certain degree of concentration even for the most experienced powderhound.

From the top of the ski area you can either descend to the valley or ski off the backside with a guide to the remote village of of St-Christophe-en-Oisans. You can take a taxi back to Venosc below Les Deux Alpes, climb through the lift system to the glacier, and return to La Grave down the front face of La Meije.

Learn

This is not teaching terrain. You can hire a guide from the **Bureau des Guides, t** +33 (0)4 76 79 90 21, but the only tuition is with the **ESF, t** +33 (0)4 76 79 92 86, five km away at **Le Chazelet.**

Children

The **ESF** in Le Chazelet accepts children from four years. Babysitting can be arranged through the tourist office.

Lunch

The area has three mountain refuges, but most people have lunch in the village.

Dine

La Meije, t +33 (0)4 76 79 21 27, is a new pizzeria close to the tourist office. The other restaurants are in the hotels.

Party

La Grave itself has little to offer anyone who does not climb or ski off-piste.

Sleep

***Hôtel les Chalets de la Meije, t +33 (0)4 76 79 97 97, has double, triple and quadruple rooms, and a restaurant.

**Hotel Edelweiss, t +33 (0)4 76 79 90 93, *www.hotel-edelweiss.com*, has a bar and restaurant.

La Roche Meane, t +33 (0)4 76 79 91 43, *www.rochemeane.com*, is a charming and good-value B&B that was once an old stone barn. It has five bedrooms.

Les Houches

Profile

Family-friendly resort in the Chamonix Valley with good tree-skiing for all standards and a revered World Cup downhill course. Ski area linked by lift but not by piste to St-Gervais

Essentials

Altitude: 1000m (3,281ft)–1860m (6,102ft)
Further information: t +33 (0)4 50 55 50 62, *www.leshouches.com*
Lifts in area: 19 (1 mountain railway, 2 cableways, 4 chairs, 12 drags) in Les Houches serving 55km of piste; 729km in Mont Blanc ski area
Lift pass: Chamoni-Mont Blanc adult €210, child 5–11yrs €168. Ski Pass Mont Blanc (covers all local resorts including Courmayeur, Chamonix, Megève) adult €216, child 4–15yrs €173–184, all for 6 days
Access: Geneva airport 1hr, station in resort

Resort

Les Houches is a pleasant family resort with the best tree-skiing in the Mont Blanc region. It has a FIS World Cup downhill course considered by racers to be second only to the Hahnenkamm in Kitzbühel in technical difficulty.

Mountain

Main mountain access is by an old cable-car from the village, or by an equally venerable four-person gondola from just outside it. However the gondola is being replaced by modern eight-person cabins for 2006–7. Don't be surprised to see a railway carriage slowly crossing the pistes near the cable-car top station. The rack-and-pinion Mont Blanc Tramway, which comes up from St-Gervais, opened in 1904 and is still going strong.

The pistes offer a wide variety of skiing for all levels with some excellent trails winding through the woods. The slopes are used by the **British Ski Academy, t** +44 (0)20 8399 1181, a skiing school for young British hopefuls, based in Les Houches.

Learn

ESF, t +33 (0)4 50 54 48 79, and **Evolution 2, t** +33 (0)4 50 54 31 44, are the two schools. The **Compagnie des Guides de Chamonix, t** +33 (0)4 50 47 21 68, has a branch in Les Houches.

Children

The **ESF Jardin des Neiges, t** +33 (0)4 50 54 48 79, is for skiers from three years. **La Garderie des Chavants, t** +33 (0)4 50 54 48 19, looks after little ones from three months.

Lunch

Try **Les Vieilles Luges, t** +33 (0)6 84 42 37 00, at Maisonneuve, **Le Prarion, t** +33 (0)4 50 54 40 07, at Prarion and **Le Courant d'Air, t** +33 (0)4 50 55 99 65, on the Col de Voza.

Dine

La Sabaudia, t +33 (0)4 50 54 47 72, **Le Kandahar, t** +33 (0)4 50 54 26 34, and **La Ferme des Agapes, t** +33 (0)4 50 54 50 69, offer regional specialities.

Party

Nightlife is restricted to a couple of quiet bars. If you require after-dinner entertainment, it is best to head into Chamonix.

Sleep

★★★**Hotel Beau-Site, t** +33 (0)4 50 55 51 16, *www.hotel-beausite.com*, is in the heart of the village with a restaurant and swimming-pool.

★★★**Hotel Chris-Tal, t** +33 (0)4 50 54 50 55, *www.chris-tal.fr*, has a games room and swimming-pool.

★★★**Hotel du Bois, t** +33 (0)4 50 54 50 35, *www.hotel-du-bois.com*, is decorated in traditional chalet style, and houses Le Caprice restaurant.

La Ferme d'en Haut, t +33 (0)4 50 54 74 87, *www.lafermedenhaut.fr*, is an early 19th-century farmhouse with four bedrooms.

Megève

Profile

A smart ski town near Chamonix that is much loved by Parisians. It has Alpine ambience, superlative designer hotels, Michelin-rated restaurants and sophisticated nightlife. It's best suited to families, intermediates and non-skiers

Resort

Megève vies with Courchevel 1850 for the title of France's smartest resort. It was founded in 1914 by Baroness de Rothschild who, during the years following First World War, turned it into her own winter salon for European aristocracy. The rich and famous built houses here and, at one point, the resort liked to boast that it was the winter home to more kings and queens – both crowned and uncrowned – than any other resort in Europe.

Its heyday was in the 1950s and 1960s when artist and author Jean Cocteau, as well as celebrities such as Charles Aznavour, Sacha Distel, Johnny Halliday and Brigitte Bardot, made it the focus of Parisian café society.

Patronage has continued from other influential families such as Citroën, Taittinger and Benetton. However, the only royals left these days are the House of Saudi who have a lavish chalet just above the town.

Megève's position, just an hour's drive from Geneva airport, makes it popular with weekenders and families wanting to avoid long transfers. Its only downside is that low altitude can restrict snow-cover in the village.

The focal point of Megève is a central square surrounded by mellow 18th-century buildings, a fine medieval church,

Essentials

Altitude: 1113m (3,651ft)–2350m (7,708ft)
Map: see page M34
Further information: t +33 (0)4 50 21 27 28, www.megeve.com
Lifts in area: 113 in Evasion Mont Blanc (11 funicular, 13 cableways, 38 chairs, 60 drags) serving 450km of piste; 729km in Mont Blanc ski area
Lift pass: Ski Pass Mont Blanc (covers all local resorts including Chamonix, Courmayeur, Les Houches) adult €216, child 4–15yrs €173–184, all for 6 days
Access: Geneva airport 1hr. Station at Sallanches 10km, regular bus service to resort

and the Aallard department store where the world's first ski trousers were tailored.

Brightly painted sleighs driven by local farmers ply for hire to reach the lift stations and hotels. They are more fun but more expensive that the free ski-buses and regular services to Chamonix and other resorts in the region covered by the extensive Evasion Mont Blanc lift pass.

Mountain

This enormous ski area extends from the spa town of St-Gervais and the village of Saint-Nicolas-de-Véroce through Mègeve and on to the little resort of La Giettaz where wooded slopes lead down to Praz-sur-Arly in the Val d'Arly. The next step will be for Mègeve to join the new 73-lift Espace Diamant circuit here that includes Flumet, Notre-Dame-de-Bellecombe, Les Saisies and Crest-Voland.

For the present, Megève's skiing is divided into three sectors with two of them, Mont d'Arbois and Rochebrune, joined by cableways.

A gondola from the town centre or a cable-car from the outskirts takes you up to Rochebrune. The area offers the most attractive runs in the resort and is usually less crowded than Mont d'Arbois. From the top of the gondola, a sequence of further lifts and pistes lead up to Côte 2000, which has some of the most challenging runs in the region.

The main beginner and intermediate area of Mont d'Arbois is reached by cable-car and gondola from Rochebune or by a choice of two gondolas from the other side of town. A network of green and blue pistes provide easy skiing back towards Megève, or you can venture almost endlessly further afield. From 1958m Mont Joux you cruise wood-fringed pastures to Le Bettex and St-Gervais, or you can tackle higher and more demanding exposed terrain at 2350m on Mont Joly.

Le Jaillet, Megève's third and least-known area, is reached by gondola from the edge of town. The front face, leading back to the resort, has a good variety of mainly red runs and usually remains uncrowded even in high season. A new six-seater chair takes you up to the 1853m summit of Christomet where you can ski down to La Giettaz. Some outstanding off-piste can be found on the wooded slopes beneath the Tête de Bonjournal, as well as runs from La Torraz into the Val d'Arly.

Megève is popular for cross-country skiers with four circuits totalling 70km, including a long, scenic track from the Mont d'Arbois cable-car to Le Bettex and Saint-Nicolas-de-Véroce.

The resort's only terrain park is at Mont Joux, and there is a snowcross course at Rochebrune.

Learn

Both the **ESF, t** +33 (0)4 50 21 00 97, and the **ESI, t** +33 (0)4 50 58 78 88, are warmly recommended, but reporters reserve their most lavish praise for British-run **White Sensations, t** +33 (0)4 50 91 14 25. **Ecole Freeride, t** +33 (0)4 50 93 03 52, and **Summits, t** +33 (0)4 50 93 03 52, are the

alternatives. Guiding can be arranged through the long-established **Bureau des Guides de Megève, t** +33 (0)4 50 21 55 11.

Children

Megève has a justified reputation for providing good childcare. The non-ski kindergarten, **Meg Accueil, t** +33 (0)4 50 58 77 84, situated next to the Palais des Sports, cares for children from 12 months. **Club Piou-Piou, t** +33 (0)4 50 58 97 65, accepts skiers from three to five years. **La Princesse, t** +33 (0)4 50 93 00 86, looks after skiers from two-and-a-half years. All the ski schools offer children's classes. **Ecole Freeride, t** +33 (0)4 50 93 03 52, limits the class size to six.

Lunch

You can eat better on the mountain in Megève than in any other resort in France, but you will pay for the privilege. At Rochebrune, **L'Alpette, t** +33 (0)4 50 21 03 69 ,has been a lunchtime institution since 1935. **Côte 2000, t** +33 (0)4 50 21 31 84, is also praised. At Mont d'Arbois, **Les Mandarines, t** +33 (0)4 50 21 31 27, and **L'Igloo, t** +33 (0)4 50 93 05 84, both have good food. At Le Jaillet, **Auberge du Christomet, t** +33 (0)4 50 21 11 34, is warmly recommended.

Dine

Chef Marc Veyrat's **La Ferme de Mon Père, t** +33 (0)4 50 21 01 01, has three Michelin stars and is one of the top restaurants in France. **Le Cintra, t** +33 (0)4 50 21 02 60, is famed for its seafood. **Flocons de Sel, t** +33 (0)4 50 21 49 99, has a Michelin star. **L'Alpage, t** +33 (0)4 50 21 30 39, has a good ambience and serves Savoyard specialities. Delightfully named **Le Sapin Chaud, t** +33 (0)4 50 91 08 88, is in an old wooden chalet. **Le Prieuré, t** +33

(0)4 50 21 01 79, and **Mirtillo**, t +33 (0)4 50 21 69 33, are both recommended.

Party

Après-ski is taken just as seriously as the skiing, with window-shopping for jewellery, antiques and designer clothing a major part of the early evening entertainment. **Club de Jazz Les Cinq Rues**, off the church square, is both an apéritif and late-night focal point. Its cosy surroundings draw some of the biggest names in jazz from both sides of the Atlantic. **Bar Tabac St-Paul** attracts the locals. The **Palo Alto** houses two popular discos. The **Casino**, originally a 1930s bus station, also has a restaurant. **Le Pallas** is popular with the young crowd. **Bar des Alpes**, opposite the Post Office, is an Internet café. **Wake Up** is a cocktail and tapas bar.

The **Palais des Sports** has an outdoor Olympic-size skating-rink and a swimming-pool. Electric-powered ice bumper-cars are an unusual sport on the skating-rink.

Sleep

The standard of Megève's four-stars is outstanding.

★★★★**Chalet Hotel du Mont d'Arbois** , t +33 (0)4 50 21 25 03, *www.chalet-montarbois.com*, used to be the Rothschild family home and is located close to the Mont d'Arbois cable-car. The hotel also has a separate chalet, **Le Réfuge du Planay**, with four double rooms.

★★★★**Le Fer à Cheval**, t +33 (0)4 50 21 30 39, *www.feracheval-megeve.com*, is attractively decorated and serves a good English breakfast.

★★★★**Les Fermes de Marie**, t +33 (0)4 50 93 03 10, *www.c-h-m.com*, ten minutes' walk from the centre, is an exquisite place to stay, based around an ancient cowshed and other farm buildings. A swimming-pool is set into rocks and the spa is one of the finest in Europe.

★★★★**Le Hameau du Maverin**, t +33 (0)4 50 91 48 70, *www.hameaudemavarin.com*, is a collection of five deluxe chalets and four apartments offering hotel service.

★★★★**Lodge Park**, t +33 (0)4 50 93 05 03, *www.c-h-m.com*, looks like a private club decorated in hunting-shooting-fishing style.

★★★★**Le Manège**, t +33 (0)4 50 21 41 09, *www.hotel-le-manege.com*, is small and chalet-style with 30 rooms.

★★★★**Mont Blanc**, t +33 (0)4 50 21 20 02, *www.c-h-m.com*, is perfectly placed in the centre of the pedestrian district and is one of the best small hotels in the Alps.

★★★★**Chalet Saint Georges**, t +33 (0)4 50 93 07 15, *www.hotel-chaletstgeorges.com*, provides excellent accommodation.

★★★★**Le Chalet Saint Philippe et Son Hameau**, t +33 (0)4 50 91 19 30, *www.chalet-saint-philippe.com*, are four luxury chalets with hotel service.

★★★**Hotel Coin du Feu**, t +33 (0)4 50 21 04 94, *www.coindufeu.com*, is a delightful small hotel.

★★★**La Grange d'Arly**, t +33 (0)4 50 58 77 88, *www.grange-darly.com*, is a comfortable place to stay.

★★★**Au Vieux Moulin**, t +33 (0)45 0 21 22 29, *www.vieuxmoulin.com*, is tastefully decorated, with excellent food.

★★**La Chauminé**, t +33 (0)4 50 21 37 05 is a B&B with 11 rooms.

★★★★ **La Ferme du Châtel and La Ferme d'Hauteluce**, t +33 (0)4 50 93 03 10, *www.c-h-m.com*, are two beautiful chalets, the latter with an indoor swimming-pool.

Les Menuires

Profile

Large sunny purpose-built resort in the giant Trois Vallées area favoured by the budget-conscious who want to ski Méribel and Courchevel without the high cost of staying there. Suits all standards of skier and rider

Resort

The ugly ducking of French ski resorts from the 1960s has grown positively handsome in middle age. A swan it is not, but Les Menuires has long since matured from the low-cost concrete dormitory that it once was into a comfortable and convenient ski base that lies 450 vertical metres short of Val Thorens up the winding road from Moûtiers.

The original eyesore of La Croisette had a makeover for the Albertville Olympics (the slalom events took place here) and then a couple of years ago the worst *résidence* was bulldozed to make way for a gleaming new MGM apartment block that has completely changed the aspect of the resort. The construction of a church also gave it physical, if not spiritual, soul providing a focal point for the real village that Les Menuires had finally become.

Much of the new development is concentrated on the pleasant satellites of Reberty, Les Bruyères and Preyerand, slightly higher up the hill, which have really become a resort in their own right with restaurants, shops, and bars (but no pharmacy – the only one is in La Croisette).

Inevitably the downside of this grand metamorphosis is that Les Menuires is no

longer the bargain basement it once was. However, accommodation prices remain significantly lower than in the more fashionable big-name resorts of the Trois Vallées. Val Thorens, St-Martin-de-Belleville and Méribel are easily reached on skis. A trip to the lower reaches of Courchevel is more of an expedition – a full day out with scarcely time to grab a quick lunch before beginning the homeward journey. Missing the last lift connections involves an expensive taxi ride home.

Mountain

The skiing takes place on both sides off the valley. Les Menuires has its own challenging and usually uncrowded ski area on the 2805m Pointe de la Masse, reached from the village by gondola and chair. Runs down the front face include the infamous black Dame Blanche, which can be tricky in icy conditions. The summit is the starting point for several off-piste itineraries towards the Lac du Lou and Val Thorens, as well as down the valley towards St-Martin.

On the other side of Les Menuires, an assortment of gondolas and chairs take you up to Roc des 3 Marches and Mont de

Essentials

Altitude: 1850m (6,068ft)–3300m (10,827ft)
Map: see Méribel page M36
Further information: Les Menuires, t +33 (0)4 79 00 73 00, *www.lesmenuires.com*
Lifts in area: 167 in Trois Vallées (40 cableways, 69 chairs, 58 drags) serving 600km of piste
Lift pass: Trois Vallées adult €204, child 5–13yrs €153.50, both for 6 days
Access: Chambéry airport 2hrs, Lyon airport 2½hrs, Geneva airport 3hrs. Moûtiers station 25km

la Chambre above the Méribel Valley. The new Les Granger six-seater chair has replaced two old drag-lifts here. The enormous area of open slopes leading back down to Les Menuires provide the sunniest and some of the most enjoyable skiing in the Trois Vallées. A huge battery of snow-cannon usually manage to maintain cover on the lower slopes into April, although inevitably they suffer from their south-facing aspect. Riders have a new terrain park and a snowcross course in the Combes-Becca sector.

Learn

The **ESF, t** +33 (0)4 79 00 61 43, is the only ski school in Les Menuires. Most – but not all – instructors speak reasonable English.

Children

Village des Schtroumpfs, t +33 (0)4 79 00 63 79, cares for non-skiers from three months at La Croisette, and those from two-and-a-half years can go to the **Village des Piou Piou, t** +33 (0)4 79 00 69 50, in Bruyères. The **ESF, t** +33 (0)4 79 00 61 43, gives lessons from three years.

Lunch

Le Grand Lac, t +33 (0)4 79 08 25 78, is a new gourmet restaurant at the bottom of Les Granges chair. **Chalet 2000, t** +33 (0)4 79 00 60 57, at Reberty, is warmly recommended. **Chalet des Neiges, t** +33 (0)4 79 00 60 55, above St-Martin, has good food and a sunny terrace, and **Quatres Vents, t** +33 (0)4 79 00 64 44, at Les Bruyères, maintains a high standard.

Dine

Eateries include **La Marmite du Géant, t** +33 (0)4 79 00 74 75, and **Les Sonnailles, t** +33 (0)4 79 00 74 28, which are both in

Les Bruyères. **La Trattoria, t** +33 (0)4 79 00 74 23, in **La Croisette** and **La Ferme de Reberty, t** +33 (0)4 79 00 77, 01 are also recommended.

Party

Après-ski in Les Menuires is fairly muted, with most French families keeping to their apartments. **The Tilbury, L'Oisans** and **Crazy Bar** are popular watering holes. **Le New Pop** at La Croisette and **Le Leeberty** at Les Bruyères are the late-night venues. Night-time tubing takes place on two 200m-long pistes equipped with a moving carpet. Swimming and skating are the other après-ski activities.

Sleep

Les Menuires is mainly apartment territory. All can be booked through the reservations office, **t** +33 (0)4 79 00 79 79. **Reberty/Les Bruyères:**
****Les Montagnettes 3 Vallées, t +33 (0)4 79 00 20 51, *www.montagnettes.com*, is a collection of spacious chalets and apartments.
****MGM Hameau des Marmottes, t +44 (0)870 750 6820, *www.ernalow.co.uk*, are extremely comfortable apartments.
****Les Alpages de Reberty, t +33 (0)4 79 01 35 35, is a smart Pierre et Vacances complex.
***Les Bruyères, t +33 (0)4 79 00 75 10, *www.latitudeshotels.com*, in Les Bruyères offers some good-value accommodation.
***Hotel Le Menuire, t +33 (0)4 79 00 60 33, *www.le-menuire.fr*, has family-sized rooms with satellite TV.
***L'Ours Blanc, t +33 (0)4 79 00 61 66, *www.hotel-ours-blanc.com*, has a lounge with an open fireplace and a rustically decorated bar.
**Chalet 2000, t +33 (0)4 79 00 60 57, *www.hotel-chalet2000.fr*, has double, triple and quadruple rooms.

Méribel

Profile

Méribel is a sprawling chalet-style resort built originally by an Englishman on the mountainside above the valley town of Moûtiers. The most central and convenient base for fully exploring the giant Trois Vallées ski area. It offers an enormous amount of intermediate skiing and the widest choice of luxury chalets of any resort in Europe

Resort

Méribel vies with Val d'Isère for the title of the most popular resort in Europe for English-speaking skiers. It was founded in the late 1930s by British skier Colonel Peter Lindsay who, like other international racers, had boycotted St Anton in Austria and was looking for a new resort when he stumbled upon the scenic Les Allues Valley.

The first lift was installed after the Second World War when Lindsay began developing the area in conjunction with French racer Emile Allais. He decreed that all buildings must be made of stone and wood with slate roofs in order to blend into their beautiful mountain environment. Méribel today has grown into a ski city that he would not begin to recognize. It stretches in different *quartiers* up the mountain from Méribel Village at 1400m to the top of Méribel Mottaret at 1800m. But, miraculously, his building regulations have been vigorously adhered to and, with the exception of the original buildings of Mottaret, Méribel avoided the concrete architectural horrors of the 1960s. The main village is connected to the valley by a long gondola that climbs from the spa resort of *B*rides-les-Bains.

Heart of the resort is Méribel 1450, which houses most of the shops,

restaurants, and the lift hub of La Chaudanne. The bi-weekly street market provides colour. Other communities are situated off the dead-end road leading to the Altiport and on the edge of the wooded pistes leading into the resort. Confusingly, Méribel Village is not the main village but a modern satellite situated a 2km drive away from 1450, but linked by chair-lift into the ski area.

Méribel Mottaret is a higher satellite situated at 1750m on the road above Méribel 1450, and is a convenient base for anyone wanting doorstep skiing and the best snow-cover. The different sectors of town are served by a ski-bus which reporters complain is oversubscribed. Some walking is inevitable. Before booking accommodatlon – particularly for families with young children – it is important to find out where your hotel or chalet is located.

From Méribel a mighty network of lifts link Courchevel, La Tania, Les Menuires and Val Thorens to form one of the world's greatest intermediate playgrounds. However, so many English-speakers congregate here during the winter months that you could be forgiven for thinking that this was some sloping suburb of south-west London rather than a top French ski resort.

Essentials

Altitude: 1400m (4,593ft)–2952m (9,685ft)
Map: see page M36
Further information: t +33 (0)479 08 60 01, *www.meribel.net*
Lifts in area: 167 in Trois Vallées (40 cableways, 69 chairs, 58 drags) serving 600km of piste
Lift pass: Trois Vallées adult €204, child 5–13yrs €153.50, both for 6 days
Access: Chambéry airport 2hrs, Lyon airport 2½hrs, Geneva airport 3hrs. Eurostar to Moûtiers, 18km

Mountain

You need a whole season to explore every corner of the Trois Vallées, and Méribel is the best place to start. From the Chaudanne lift centre at 1450 and from Méribel Mottaret higher up the valley, lifts rise on either side. To the east, gondolas take you up to 2738m at Saulire for a choice of descents towards Courchevel and La Tania. The mountainside back down to the resort is criss-crossed with mainly blues, benign reds and an assortment of chairs. To the west, more gondolas and chairs rise to the long ridge that separates the valleys of Les Allues and Belleville. From the top you can ski towards Les Menuires, St-Martin-de-Belleville and Val Thorens. Alternatively you can explore the dozens of lifts and runs down to 1450 and Méribel Mottaret.

Accomplished skiers and riders head for the more challenging terrain off the Mont de la Chambre, Mont Vallon and the Col du Fruit at the head of the valley. The sheer volume of skiers funnelling into both 1450 and Mottaret at peak times means that some queuing is inevitable, but the lift system is extremely efficient. One of the greatest assets of the Trois Vallées is that anyone who can ski parallel can travel far afield without ever leaving blue runs, while better skiers can find a route to the same destination almost entirely on reds. The seemingly endless range of runs has produced a whole generation of skiers who never go anywhere else.

Méribel has good nursery slopes with easy green runs around the Altiport and back to the resort. However they tend to suffer from through-traffic, particularly at lunchtime and at the end of the day. This can be unnerving – with the ever-present risk of collision from out-of-control skiers and riders. Méribel has two terrain parks: the 1200m Moon Park and the Snowpark des Plattières at Mottaret.

Learn

The **ESF, t** +33 (0)4 79 08 60 31, has 400 teachers and the standard of instruction varies enormously. Ian and Susan Saunders are BASI instructors who work for the ESF and have their own company, **Ski Principles, t** +33 (0)4 79 00 52 71. British-run **New Generation, t** +33 (0)4 79 01 03 18, is much praised by reporters. **Magic in Motion, t** +33 (0)4 79 08 53 36, is the other mainstream option. The British ski school, **Parallel Lines, t** +44 (0)1702 589580, has BASI instructors and small classes. **Snow Systems, t** +33 (0)4 79 00 40 22, receives praise. Off-piste guiding is through the **Bureau des Guides, t** +33 (0)4 79 00 30 38.

Children

Les Saturnins, t +33 (0)4 79 08 66 90, is the non-ski kindergarten for children aged 18 months to three years. The tourist office, **t** + 33 (0)4 79 08 60 01, also has a list of babysitters who will care for infants in your hotel or apartment. **Les P'tits Loups** ski kindergarten cares for children aged three to five years at **La Chaudanne, t** +33 (0)4 79 08 60 31 and at **Mottaret, t** +33 (0)4 79 00 49 49.

Lunch

Eating on the mountain is iniquitously expensive anywhere in the Trois Vallées. **Les Castors, t** +33 (0)4 79 08 52 79, is an old favourite at the foot of the Truite run in Méribel. **Les Rhododendrons, t** +33 (0)4,79 00 50 92, at the top of the Rhodos gondola and **Restaurant Le Rond Point, t** +33 (0)4 79 00 37 51, are both recommended. **Bibi Phoque, t** +33 (0)4 79 00 30 93, at Chaudanne has reasonably priced pancakes. **The Altiport Hotel, t** 33 (0052 32 has a sunny terrace. **Chalet de Tougniat, t** +33 (0)4 79 00 45 11, at the top of the Combes chair out of Mottaret, is off the beaten track.

Dine

Most visitors here eat in their chalets, which accounts for the low number of good restaurants in proportion to the size of the resort. **Chez Kiki**, t +33 (0)4 79 08 66 68, specialises in meat cooked over an open fire. **La Taverne**, t +33 (0)4 79 00 32 45, in Hotel Le Roc offers pizzas and Savoyard cuisine. **Le Refuge**, t +33 (0)4 79 08 61 97, has a warm atmosphere and **Le Croix Jean-Claude**, t +33 (0)4 79 00 61 05, is good value with excellent food and wine.

In Mottaret, **Côte Brune**, t +33 (0)4 79 00 40 97, is an old favourite. Try **Au Temps Perdu**, t +33 (0)4 79 00 36 64, for a wide choice of crêpes, or **Pizzeria du Mottaret**, t +33 (0)4 79 00 40 50. **Le Ty Sable**, t +33 (0)4 79 00 43 32, is also recommended.

Party

Jack's Bar and **Le Rond Point** are busy in the late afternoon as the lifts close. **Le Loft**, located above the ice-rink, has live music, a fun atmosphere and stays open late. **Dick's Tea-Bar** in 1450 and **Le Privilège** in Mottaret are also late-night venues.

Sleep

★★★★**Hotel Le Grand Coeur**, t +33 (0)4 79 08 60 03, *www.legrandcoeur.com*, was one of Méribel's first hotels and remains its finest. Excellent food and service.

★★★★**Hotel Le Mont Vallon**, t +33 (0)4 79 00 44 00, *www.hotel-montvallon.com*, is a stylishly decorated hotel in Mottaret, with family rooms, split-level suites, a swimming-pool and fitness centre.

★★★★**Chalet Le Brames**, t +44 (0)20 7384 3854, *www.descent.co.uk*, set above the village, is the most sumptuous chalet here. It sleeps 20 and has a huge open-plan living room, gym, cinema and outdoor hot-tub.

★★★**Chalet-Hotel Marie Blanche**, t +33 (0)4 79 08 65 55, *www.marieblanche.com*, has wood-panelled bedrooms and a restaurant serving traditional Savoyard dishes.

★★★**Hotel Le Yeti**, t +33 (0)479 00 51 15, *www.hotel-yeti.com*, has large, south-facing bedrooms and an attractive lounge with log fire.

★★★**Chalet-Hotel Parc Alpin**, t +33 (0)4 79 08 29 63 has been completely rebuilt with 12 instead of 23 rooms and now has a pool and a sauna.

Montgenèvre

Profile

Sole French component of the otherwise Italian Milky Way circuit, an unpretentious French border town with lots of charm, but blighted by road traffic

Resort

The ancient village on the Italian frontier, the only French component of the Milky Way, plays Cinderella this winter at the XX Winter Olympics. The 88-lift ski area may be a fine example of European sporting *entente*, but the Games are strictly an Italian affair. However, it is much the best base for those who want

Essentials

Altitude: 1860m (6,102ft)–2800m (9,186ft)
Further information: t +33 (0)492 21 52 52, *www.montgenevre.com*
Lifts in area: 88 in Milky Way (5 cableways, 38 chairs, 45 drags) serving 400km of piste
Lift pass: Milky Way (covers Montgenèvre, Sestriere, Sauze d'Oulx and other smaller resorts) adult €145–163, child 8–12yrs €72.50–81.50, both for 6 days
Access: Turin airport 75mins

to ski over and look at the Olympic venues, although on race days Sestriere's lift system will be restricted to racers and their entourage.

Mountain

Skiing takes place on both sides of the main road leading to the frontier. Montgenèvre's own area, beneath 2680m Le Chalvet, holds considerable charm and challenge, with runs for all standards leading back down to the village and across the border to Claviere. Snow-cannon have been added to provide secure training slopes for the Olympic teams.

On the other side of the road, a gondola and a quad-chair provide direct access towards the Monti della Luna and the long runs to Cesana Torinese. Montgenèvre has a terrain park with a half-pipe in the Gondrans area.

Learn

The **ESF, t** +33 (0)4 92 21 90 46, and **Apeak**, **t** +33 (0)4 92 21 83 30, are the choices.

Children

Halte Garderie, t +33 (0)4 92 21 52 50, is for six months to six years, **Club Piou Piou, t** +33 (0)4 92 21 90 46, introduces three, to five-year-olds to skiing, and **Apeak, t** +33 (0)4 92 21 83 30, runs a children's programme.

Lunch

Try **Les Chalmettes, t** +33 (0)4 92 21 93 04, **Les Anges t** +33 (0)6 14 61 97 52, and **La Bergerie, t** +33 (0)4 92 21 81 06.

Dine

Le Jamy, t +33 (0)4 92 21 92 62 has the best food and is renowned for its fondues. **La Ca del Sol, t** +33 (0)4 92 21 87 08, **Pizzeria Le Transalpin, t** +33 (0)6 63 48 38 15, and **Le Refuge, t** +33 (0)4 92 21 92 97 are all recommended.

Party

Le Graal Café and **La Ca del Sol** are the resort meeting places. **Le Blue Night** is the disco. Montgenèvre has a natural skating-rink at the bottom of the slopes.

Sleep

- ***Hotel Napoléon, t** +33 (0)4 92 21 92 04, *www.hotel-napoleon.com,* is the original inn.
- ***Hotel Valérie, t** +33 (0)4 92 21 90 02, *www.hotel-montgenevre.com,* near the church, is comfortable.
- **Hotel Alpis Cottia, t** +33 (0)4 92 21 50 00, is reasonably priced.

Morzine and Les Gets

Profile

These traditional resorts are two of the dozen towns and villages that form the Portes du Soleil, a giant linked ski area that straddles the French border with Switzerland above Lac Léman. Morzine is a bustling market town, while Les Gets is a traditional Savoyard village

Resort

Morzine has been a ski resort since before the First World War, and during the mid-1920s it established a reputation as an important international holiday centre. Wealthy guests arrived to spend the winter at the comfortable Grand Hotel, which boasted central heating and fine cuisine. They passed their days ice-skating on the frozen lake and skiing on the rolling summer pastures of Pleney. The first cable-car was installed in 1934, but the Second World War put a stop to further development. It wasn't until 1960 that the winter sports industry began to eclipse the cattle and sheep farming which, together with forestry, still forms part of the local economy.

The catalyst for this was Jean Vuarnet, a young *Morzinois*, who was packed off to the USA that February with the expectations of the entire town on his shoulders. He came home from the VIII Winter Olympics in Squaw Valley clutching the gold medal for the downhill.

As a reward he was given the task of creating the more snow-sure satellite of Avoriaz on the clifftop above the town and of linking this new purpose-built village and Morzine to other resorts in the region – not only in France but also across the border with Switzerland.

The task proved every bit as difficult as beating Hanspeter Lanig of Germany and fellow Frenchman Guy Perillat down the mountain in California. But, with a winning combination of guile and charm, he finally persuaded a dozen villages to bury differences which in some cases stretched back centuries, and create the Portes du Soleil. The first link was built in 1968 and the single lift pass – now electronic – was introduced in 1974. The ski area is named after a mountain pass above Les Crosets, on the Swiss side of the frontier, that catches the first rays of sunlight each morning. Ironically, Vuarnet

is already better remembered for his sunglasses than his sunny ski area, which now has 206 lifts and 650km of piste.

Not every farmer was converted to harvesting the lucrative annual snow crop, and the attractive town of Morzine continues to be what it always was – a regional agricultural centre with a life that exists outside tourism.

The town sits in a wooded basin marked by the confluence of several mountain streams and covers a large area on both sides of the river gorge. The principal street runs from the village centre up to the foot of Le Pleney where many of the hotels are located. The various sectors of the town, and the lift stations, are linked by a road-train and free buses.

Morzine's low altitude means that snow-cover in the village is by no means always reliable. Avoriaz usually has the best snow in the region, but this is not the best corner of the Alps for certain snow at Christmas or Easter. Avoriaz usually has the best skiing, but in these uncertain winters of global warming even its 2466m top station is simply not high enough. If only the mountains here were elevated by 1000m, the Portes du Soleil would be

Essentials

Altitude: 1000m (3,280ft)–2466m (8,090ft)
Map: see page M26
Further information: Morzine t +33 (0)4 50 74 72 72, *www.morzine-avoriaz.com*; **Les Gets** t +33 (0)4 50 75 80 80, *www.lesgets.com*
Lifts in area: 206 in Portes du Soleil area (14 cableways, 82 chairs, 110 drags) serving 650km of piste
Lift pass: Portes du Soleil (covers 14 resorts) adult €179, child 5–16yrs €120, both for 6 days
Access: Geneva airport 1½hrs. Station at Thonon les Bains 31km, Cluses 25km

classed as one of the greatest circuits of the world.

Morzine is linked across 1550m Pleney to the traditional dairy farming village of Les Gets, a community that dates back to the 12th century. The two holiday bases are only 6km apart by road, but contrastingly different. Les Gets is a pleasing mix of old Savoyard chalets and more modern wooden-and-stone buildings constructed in keeping with their beatiful Alpine surroundings. This is a family resort with a relaxed atmosphere and good links into the Portes du Soleil.

Mountain

A cable-car from the hamlet of Les Prodains, reached by free ski-bus from Morzine, provides the quickest and direct link to Avoriaz.

Alternatively, a gondola from Morzine takes you up to Super-Morzine where you can work your way up through the lift system to Avoriaz, or over to the pretty little goat-farming hamlet of Les Lindarets for access to Châtel and other resorts in the Portes du Soleil. The blue runs above Super-Morzine provide plenty of confidence-building cruising terrain.

From the other side of town, linked by a free road-train, a side-by-side gondola and cable-car rise to Pleney. Blue, red and black runs served by a sequence of chair-lifts, all lead back over the undulating pastureland to the town. You can also drop off the backside of the ridge and follow a long, gentle blue run down into Les Gets.

Skiing takes place on the wooded slopes on both sides of the Les Gets valley, which is criss-crossed with further lifts that extend to 1850m Le Ranfoilly and 1665m La Rosta at the far end. On the north-western side of Les Gets, a gondola and a chair lead up to Mont Chéry. This is the location for dedicated slalom and snowcross courses, as well as a terrain

park. Morzine has a large floodlit area with skiing, tubing and big-air that remains open until 10pm.

Anyone who can ski parallel can complete in a day the Portes du Soleil circuit, which takes you to most but not all the resorts. However, most of the time is spent on lifts rather than going downhill. It makes more sense to fully explore one sector at a time.

Learn

In Morzine, the **ESF, t** +33 (0)4 50 79 13 13, has a sound reputation for teaching modern technique in a friendly manner. **British Alpine Ski and Snowboarding School, t** +33 (0)4 50 74 78 59 or **t** +44 (0)871 7801500, is warmly recommended. **Ski, Snowboard et Aventures, t** +33 (0)4 50 79 05 16, has limited-size classes. Guiding is through **Bureau de la Montagne, t** +33 (0)4 50 79 03 55, and **Maison de la Montagne, t** +33 (0)4 50 75 96 65.

In Les Gets, the **British Alpine Ski and Snowboarding School, t** +33 (0)4 50 79 85 42 or **t** +44 (0)1485 572596, receives equal praise. The **ESF, t** +33 (0)4 50 75 80 03, has a strong presence. **360 International, t** +33 (0)4 50 79 80 31, and **ESI Ski Plus, t** +33 (0)4 50 75 86 01, are the others.

Children

Morzine's **L'Outa, t** +33 (0)4 50 79 26 00, accepts little ones from three months to six years and was recommended by reporters. **Le Club des Piou-Piou, t** +33 (0)4 50 79 13 13, provides daycare with ski lessons for children from three to 12 years.

In Les Gets, which has the French government's *P'tits Montagnards* award for childcare, **Les Fripouilles, t** +33 (0)4 50 79 84 84, welcomes children from six months. The **ESF Jardins des Neiges, t** +33 (0)4 50 75 80 03, takes children from three to five years for a mix of lessons and play.

The **ESF Club des P'tits Montagnys, t** +33 (0)4 50 75 80 03, gives lessons to children aged four to 12 years. **Ile des Enfants** ski school, **t** +33 (0)4 50 75 84 47 gives lessons from three years.

Lunch

Try **Les Crêtes de Zorre, t** +33 (0)4 50 79 24 73, at Super-Morzine, **Les Mines d'Or, t** +33 (0)4 50 79 03 60, in the Vallée de la Manche and **The Belvédère, t** +33 (0)4 50 79 81 52, a welcoming mountain hut at Mont Chéry.

Dine

In Morzine, **Le Tremplin, t** +33 (0)4 50 79 12 31, is rated by reporters. **L'Etale, t** +33 (0)4 50 79 09 29, serves regional cuisine in a mountain ambience, and **La Grange, t** +33 (0)4 50 75 96 40, is for a special occasion. **La Chamade, t** +33 (0)4 50 79 13 91, receives mixed reports: 'most delightful – the taste and presentation were special', and 'not so nice any more'. **Le Matafan, t** +33 (0)4 50 79 27 79, is said to be 'absolutely the best place for dinner'. **Le Mas de la Coutettaz, t** +33 (0)4 50 79 08 26, provides chalet-style communal dining in a centuries-old dining room.

In Les Gets, **Le Flambeau, t** +33 (0)4 50 79 80 66, and **Le Tourbillon, t** +33 (0)4 50 79 70 34, are both recommended, along with **Le Vieux Chêne, t** +33 (0)4 50 79 71 93, and **Le Peau de Vache, t** +33 (0)4 50 75 86 64.

Party

Morzine has a large ice rink where you can skate and watch French league hockey matches. Other activities include tobogganing and snowmobiling. **Le Paradis du Laury's** is a popular disco. **L'Opéra**, the other late-night venue, becomes a teens-only haunt one evening each week during the school holidays. The

Cavern Bar has a young and funky atmosphere and **The Boudha Café** is recommended for people-watching.

In Les Gets, the leisure centre has a swimming-pool and a range of other facilities. **Bar Bush** and **Le Boomerang** are highly rated. For dancing, **The Iglu** is a small but fun nightclub.

Sleep

Morzine has a plentiful supply of hotels in each price bracket. In Les Gets, much of the accommodation is in chalets.
Morzine:
★★★**Hotel Les Airelles, t** +33 (0)4 50 74 71 21, *www.les-airelles.com*, is recently refurbished with comfortable rooms.
★★★**Hotel Le Dahu, t** +33 (0)4 50 75 92 92, *www.dahu.com*, an old favourite, has tastefully decorated rooms and duplex family suites, along with delicious food.
★★★**Hotel Neige Roc, t** +33 (0)4 50 79 03 21, *www.neige-roc.com*, at Les Prodains, is convenient for the cable-car to Avoriaz.
★★★**Hotel Le Tremplin, t** +33 (0)4 50 79 12 31, *www.hotel-tremplin.com*, at the foot of the slopes, has a great view of the night-skiing and snowboarding.
★★**Hotel Fleur des Neiges, t** +33 (0)4 50 79 01 23, *www.fleurdesneiges.com*, is rustic, has a heated pool, and a restaurant serving French country cuisine.
Le Mas de la Coutettaz, t +33 (0)4 50 79 08 26, *www.thefarmhouse.co.uk*, is an 18th-century manor house with eight delightful bedrooms.
Les Gets:
★★★★**Ferme de Moudon, t** +33 (0)20 7384 3854, *www.descent.co.uk*, is a 17th-century chalet three minutes' drive from the village centre. Inside, ancient timbers blend with modern design.
★★★★**Ferme de Montagne, t** +33 (0)4 50 75 36 79, *www.fermedemontagne.com*, is a luxuriously renovated farmhouse set above the village.

***Le Boomerang II, t** +33 (0)4 50 79 80 65, *www.leboomerang2.com*, is a little piece of Australia in the French Alps. The food is impressive.

***Chalet-Hotel Les Alpages, t** +33 (0)4 50 75 80 88, *www.hotel-alpages.com*, has a swimming-pool and spa.

***Chalet-Hotel Crychar, t** +33 (0)4 50 75 80 50, *www.crychar.com*, on the piste, has cosy bedrooms, and a restaurant with a log fire and home-cooked food.

***Chalet-Hotel La Marmotte t** +33 (0)4 50 75 80 33, *www.hotelmarmotte. com* is a 1930s chalet on the edge of the village. Facilities include a swimming-pool, spa and crèche.

***Hotel Mont-Chéry, t** +33 (0)4 50 75 80 75, *www.hotelmontchery.com*, in the town centre, has a swimming-pool, and a restaurant serving 'inventive cuisine'.

***Hotel Nagano, t** +33 (0)4 50 79 71 46, *www.hotel-nagano.com*, has a swimming-pool and is across the road from the ice rink.

****Alpen'Sports Hotel, t** +33 (0)4 50 75 80 55, *www.alpensport-hotel.com*, has five simple chalets in its grounds sleeping from four to 17 people.

La Plagne

Profile

The giant ski area is made up of 10 mainly purpose-built villages set at different altitudes above the valley town of Aime. The skiing is linked by cable-car to Les Arcs and together they form Paradiski, one of the largest ski circuits in the world. Suits high-mileage cruisers, beginners, families and off-piste skiers. Alpine charm is in short supply in a couple of the higher villages

Resort

La Plagne tries to be all things to all people. The lower villages of Montchavin, Montalbert, Les Coches and Champagny-en-Vanoise have varying degrees of rustic farmland appeal, while the six higher holiday centres major on ski convenience. On paper, La Plagne is the perfect ski destination with a long vertical drop, snow-sure high-altitude runs, ski-in ski-out hotels and apartments, and a sophisticated lift system. Runs below the tree-line are delightful. However, the endless acres of exposed and often bland snowfields higher up and the architecture of some of the dormitory villages are not to everyone's taste.

Paradiski – its combined ski area with Les Arcs – is so vast that even an experienced skier will be hard put to travel from one end to the other and back in a single day. The double-decker Vanoise Express, which spans the Ponturin gorge that separates the two resorts, cost €16 million to build and is a remarkable feat of engineering. However, both La Plagne and Les Arcs are so enormous in their own right that only a small proportion of

Essentials

Altitude: 1250m (4,100ft)–3250m (10,660ft)

Map: see page M38

Further Information: t+ 33 (0)479 09 79 79, *www.la-plagne.com*

Lifts in area: 141 in Paradiski (1 mountain railway, 16 cableways, 66 chairs, 58 drags) serving 425km of piste

Lift pass: Paradiski (covers La Plagne/Les Arcs area and one day in each of Val d'Isère/Tignes, Pralognan-La Vanoise, Les Saisies) adult €225, child 6–13yrs €169, both for 6 days

Access: Chambéry airport 2hrs, Geneva airport 2½hrs, Lyon airport 2½hrs. Eurostar station at Bourg-St-Maurice visitors to either make use of it. The main beneficiaries are skiers who choose to stay in Monchavin or Les Coches. Instead of hiking up through the lift system on the La Plagne side, they can explore the equally rewarding terrain above Vallandry and Arc 1800.

The original high-altitude resort of Plagne Centre (1970m) is outwardly a monument to the Alpine architectural atrocities of the 1960s but it has undergone a complete makeover down the years and functions well as a holiday centre. Aime-la-Plagne (2100m) resembles a battleship stranded on a white mountainside. Belle-Plagne (2050m) is easier on the eye with a pleasant village centre. Plagne-Bellecôte (1930m) is high-rise and plain. Plagne-Villages (2050m), Plagne-Soleil (2050m) and Plagne-1800 are much more agreeable wood-clad complexes built in sympathy with their glorious scenic surroundings.

Lower down the mountain, Montchavin and Champagny-en-Vanoise are rich in cowshed kitsch. These are old farming villages that have long since been won over to tourism, but they make excellent and attractive bases from which to explore the region.

Mountain

Wide-open motorway skiing above the tree-line and gladed trails through the forest below it are the main features of the ski area. These are coupled with gentle beginner pistes and some truly outstanding off-piste if you know where to find it. You need a guide to discover the long, sweeping descent from the Glacier de Bellecôte down to Les Bauches, as well as the challenging Cul du Nant run from the back of the glacier into the Champagny-le-Haut valley.

The disadvantage of staying in the lower and much more pleasing villages is that you tend to spend an inordinate amount of time working your way up through the lift system before doing any actual skiing. Champagny (1250m) is the most convenient of these. Just two long lifts take you all the way to Plagne Centre, whereas from Montchavin you need to ride six to reach the same place.

We favour basing yourself in Plagne-Villages or Plagne-Soleil, the two villages that come closest to marrying charm with convenience. From here it is easy to reach the open skiing from the Roche de Mio and the Glacier de Bellecôte.

Scenic routes wind down through the forest to Montchavin, Les Coches, Champagny and Montalbert. Queues are generally not a feature of La Plagne, although the closure in bad weather of an arterial lift can have a knock-on effect across the entire area. The old, slow Arpette chair-lift out of Plagne-Bellecôte has long been a notorious bottleneck, but it has been upgraded this season to an eight-person chair. Terrain parks are located at Plagne-Bellecôte, Montchavin-Les Coches and Champagny. Belle-Plagne now also has the Pro Snowpark with a big S reserved for expert riders.

Learn

The **ESF, Plagne-Centre, t** +33 (0)4 79 09 00 40, **Plagne-Villages, t** +33 (0)4 79 09 04 40, has around 500 instructors working from branches in each of the ten villages.

In Plagne-Centre, **Oxygène, t** +33 (0)4 79 09 03 99, has a good reputation. **Evolution 2** in **Montchavin, t** +33 (0)4 79 07 81 85, and **Les Coches, t** +33 (0)4 79 04 20 83, is recommended. In Plagne-1800, **Reflex, t** +33 (0)4 79 09 16 07, is a small independent school. In Belle-Plagne, **El Pro, t** +33 (0)4 79 09 01 33, is the alternative to the ESF. **Antenne Handicap, t** +33 (0)4 79 09 13 80, in Aime-la-Plagne, teaches disabled skiers.

Children

Most villages have both non-ski and ski kindergartens. In Plagne-Centre, **Les P'tits Bonnets**, t +33 (0)4 79 09 00 83, cares for infants from 10 weeks to three years.

In Montchavin, **Le Chat Bleu**, t +33 (0)4 79 07 82 82, provides daycare. At Montalbert, **Les Bambins**, t +33 (0)4 79 09 77 24, looks after children from 18 months to six years. In Champagny, **Les Cabris**, t +33 (0)4 79 55 06 40, and **Garderie Marie-Christine**, t +33 (0)4 79 09 11 81, accept children from two years.

At Belle-Plagne the **ESF nursery**, t +33 (0)4 79 09 06 68, cares for children from 18 months. At Plagne-Village, the **ESF nursery**, t +33 (0)4 79 09 04 40, accepts children from two years. In Aime-la-Plagne, **La Garderie des Lutins**, t +33 (0)4 79 09 04 75, takes children from two years. At Plagne-Bellecôte, **La Garderie Mini-club**, t +33 (0)4 79 09 05 91, cares for children from two years.

The **ESF**, t +33 (0)4 79 09 00 40, runs ski kindergartens in Montalbert, Champagny, Plagne-Centre, Plagne-Villages, Plagne-Soleil, Aime-la-Plagne, Plagne-Bellecôte, Belle-Plagne and Plagne-1800.

Lunch

You can eat well particularly if you are prepared to wait until the midday–2pm rush-hour is over. Try **Au Bon Vieux Temps**, t +33 (0)4 79 09 20 57, below Aime-la-Plagne. **Le Forperet**, t +33 (0)4 79 55 51 27, is on the piste down to Montalbert. **Auberge de Montagne chez Pat du Sauget**, t +33 (0)4 79 07 83 51, is just above the Vanoise Express cable-car station. **Loup Garou**, t +33 (0)4 79 09 20 17, and **Le Petit Chaperon Rouge**, t +33 (0)4 79 09 09 39, above 1800 are both recommended. **La Rossa**, t +33 (0)4 79 08 28 03, is at the top of the Champagny gondola. **Les Borseliers**, t +33 (0)6 07 54 96 19, in Champagny is

known for *tartiflette* and other rustic Savoyard dishes.

Dine

In Montchavin, **La Boule de Neige**, t +33 (0)4 79 07 83 30, and **La Ferme de Cézar**, t +33 (0)4 79 07 85 31, are both recommended.

In Plagne-Centre, try **La Métairie**, t +33 (0)4 79 09 11 08, and **Le Refuge**, t +33 (0)4 79 09 00 13. In Belle-Plagne, **Le Matafan**, t +33 (0)4 79 09 09 19, is an old favourite. **Le Loup Blanc**, t +33 (0)4 79 09 13 61, in Plagne-1800 has good local cuisine at reasonable prices.

Party

La Plagne is not a place for a busy nightlife. Bars such as **Monica's Pub** in Plagne-Soleil, **Le Mine** in Plagne-1800 and **No Blem Café** in Plagne-Centre are busy after skiing. Most of the action later on lies in Plagne-Centre at **Jet 37** and in Plagne-Bellecôte at **Saloon**. **Le Bleu Night** disco in Aime-la-Plagne is packed in high season. Champagny has **Le Galaxy** disco, and high-decibel **Oxygène** in rural Montchavin keeps the cows awake until the early hours.

La Plagne hosted the bobsleigh in the 1992 Winter Olympics and anyone can take a ride down the 1.5km serpentine track. A trip on an 80km/hr **bob raft** costs €33pp while a 100km/hr run on a real bobsleigh with a pro driver costs €100pp (details t +33 (0)4 79 09 12 73).

Sleep

★★★★**Résidence Aspen**, t +33 (0)4 79 55 75 75, in Plagne-Village receives glowing reports.

★★★★**Les Montagnettes apartments**, t +33 (0)4 79 55 12 00, are extremely comfortable.

****Les Balcons de Belle Plagne
apartments, t +33 (0)4 79 55 76 76, in
Belle-Plagne are favourites among
reporters.

****MGM's Les Hauts Bois apartments,
t +44 (0)870 750 6820 in Aime-la-Plagne
are among the most luxurious in the
resort. Residents have use of a stylish
swimming-pool, sauna and steam room.

****Les Chalets du Bouquetin, t +33 (0)4
79 55 01 13, are in Champagny.

***Paladien Terra Nova, t +33 (0)4 79 55 79
00, in Plagne-Centre has 'a great location
and good food, though a bit impersonal'.

**Hotel Mercure, t +33 (0)4 79 09 12 09,
formerly the Eldorador, in Belle-Plagne is
being refurbished.

Risoul

Profile

This convenient little resort is good
value for money and is usually free of lift
queues. There is little choice of nightlife,
but Risoul now tends to attract students
and school groups who have added to the
liveliness of the place

Essentials

Altitude: 1850m (6,068ft)–2750m
(9,020ft)

Further information: t +33 (0)4 92 46 02
60, www.risoul.com

Lifts in area: 55 (1 cableway, 14 chairs, 39
drags) serving 180km of piste

Lift pass: Forêt Blanche (covers Risoul and
Vars) adult €143.50, child 5–11yrs €124.50,
both for 6 days

Access: Grenoble airport 2½hrs,
Marseille airport 3½hrs. Station at
Montdauphin-Guillestre 17km

Resort

Risoul shares its substantial ski area
with Vars 1850 and they jointly market
themselves as the Domaine de la Forêt
Blanche. Risoul was purpose-built in the
ski boom years of the 1970s as a budget-
conscious no-frills family ski resort
looking for a French rather than an
international market. Its continued
popularity at home and abroad is largely
dependent on its reputation for low prices
and reliable snow. When resorts
elsewhere are suffering from a lack of
cover at the beginning or towards the end
of the season Risoul usually has metres of
the stuff from before Christmas until after
Easter. The resort used to be extremely
popular with the British, but the clientele
has changed in recent years. Visitors from
Eastern Europe now outnumber the
British among the 30 per cent of skiers
and riders who are not French.

The downside of choosing Risoul is the
airport transfer from Grenoble or
Marseille, which in adverse winter
weather conditions can be considerably
longer than advertised. The silver lining of
its isolated position is the absence of day-
trippers and weekenders.

Accommodation is in appealing wood-
and-stone apartment complexes,
although the small shopping area suffers
from a profusion of billboards and a lack
of proper pavements. Other activities
include snowmobiling, guided snowshoe
excursions, parapente, winter horse-
riding, and skating on the natural ice rink.

Mountain

Lifts rise from the village to 2571m Razi
for connections to Vars-Sainte-Marie and
Vars-Les-Claux, while a new six-seater
chair takes you up to the second smaller
ski area of Peyrefolle. The third sector of
L'Homme de Pierre is reached by a
sequence of drag-lifts – despite major

improvements to the lift system in recent years the region still suffers from a predominance of these.

Risoul has a wide diversity of terrain for all standards. The green runs around the base area provide some of the best novice terrain in France, while more confident skiers will find that they can go far afield without ever being forced to stray from blue runs.

Experts will enjoy the ridge run reached by the Chabrières drag from the Col de Crevoux. This takes you to the starting point for the KL speed ski track where a number of world records have been set over the years. Other descents from different points along the cornice are of sufficient gradient to test the nerve of even the most accomplished. The long runs down to Vars-Sainte-Marie from 2580m La Mayt are usually uncrowded and provide perfect cruising terrain.

Vars has also its own ski area on 2273m Peynier on the far side of the town but reached on skis from Vars-Les-Claux. The black Ecureil, which follows the fall-line down the wooded slopes from the top, is one of the most enjoyable in the region. However, most of the ten black runs are graded more for their lack of grooming than their gradient.

After a big dump, Risoul and Vars offer some outstanding off-piste opportunities between the trees. A natural half-pipe in the back bowl off the Col de Valbelle is an attraction for both skiers and riders. The Surfland terrain park on L'Homme de Pierre has a super-pipe, jumps and rails, as well as a dedicated area for board novices.

Learn

The **ESF**, t +33 (0)4 92 46 19 22 and the rival **ESI**, t +33 (0)4 92 46 20 83 both have a sound reputation.

Children

Risoul has the French govenment's *P'tit Montagnards* award for good childcare. **The Garderie**, t +33 (0)4 92 46 02 60, cares for children from six months to six years. **Les Marmottes s'amusent**, t +33 (0)4 92 46 29 37, is a ski-kindergarten for three to six year olds and provides babysitters.

Lunch

Serious mountain lunchers are in the wrong place. Try **Le Vallon**, t +33 (0)4 92 46 05 75, and **Le Tetras**, t +33 (0)4 92 46 09 83, or descend to either resort.

Dine

La Dalle en Pente, t +33 (0)4 92 46 05 40, has traditional mountain cuisine including fondue, raclette and *pierrade*. **Le Plante de Baton**, t +33 (0)4 92 46 06 38 is also recommended. **La Cherine**, t +33 (0)4 92 46 01 80, under Les Mélèzes apartments, has good food at reasonable prices. **Snowboard Café**, t +33 (0)4 92 46 18 65, has cheap daily specials.

Party

Nightlife is limited to a few bars and the late-night **Le Morgan** disco. The resort centre can be extremely noisy and we advise families to choose accommodation in a quieter location away from the bars and restaurants.

Sleep

Most visitors opt to stay in self-catering apartments.
★★★★Balcons de Sirius, t +33 (0)4 92 46 03 47 are new apartments.
★★Au Bon Logis, t +33 (0)4 92 45 14 47, *www.aubonlogis.fr*, is in the hamlet of Gaudissard, 10 minutes from Risoul.

La Bonne Auberge, t +33 (0)4 92 45 02 40, *www.labonneauberge-risoul.com*, is a chalet-style hotel that has been run by the same family for 30 years.
Le Chardon Bleu, t +33 (0)4 92 46 07 27, *http://lechardonbleu.free.fr*, is a clean and modern hotel overlooking the piste.

La Rosière

Profile

The French half of an intermediate ski area shared with La Thuile in Italy's Aosta Valley. A quiet village with uncrowded slopes, recommended for families

Resort

La Rosière is an important resort in the Haute Tarentaise above the valley town of Bourg-St-Maurice. It provides an easy winter link – on skis – to the Aosta Valley in Italy where it shares its ski area with La Thuile. Most probably the Carthaginian general Hannibal came this way in 247 BC en route to Rome. The current lift system would have no problem in ferrying his 26,000 men across the Petit-St-Bernard Pass by detachable quad-chair, but 38 war elephants might be quite another matter.

Essentials

Altitude: 1200m (3,937ft)–2650m (8,694ft)
Further information: t +33 (0)4 79 06 80 51, *www.larosiere.net*
Lifts in area: 37 (1 cableway, 17 chairs, 19 drags) serving 150km of piste
Lift pass: Area (includes La Thuile) adult €151, child 5–12yrs €105.50, both for 6 days
Access: Geneva and Lyon airports 2½hrs. Station at Bourg-St-Maurice 30mins

The lift company – it also owns Val d'Isère's mountain transport – is spending €33 million on improving facilities. First steps have been a remodelling of the base area and two new six-person lifts to provide swift mountain access.

The skiing is on wide, open slopes and is best suited to adventurous intermediates. The 500m-long terrain park is reached by the Poletta drag.

Learn

The **ESF, t** +33 (0)4 79 06 86 21, has a worthy reputation and most instructors speak good English. The other choices are **ESI, t** +33 (0)4 79 06 81 26, and **Evolution 2**, t +33 (0)4 79 40 19 80.

Children

The **ESI, t** +33 (0)4 79 06 81 26, is recommended for its friendly instructors and we also have good reports of **Evolution 2, t** + 33 (0)4 79 40 19 80. The **ESF, t** +33 (0)4 79 06 86 21, is said to be excellent – 'our children loved the instructors' Harry Potter display after the torchlight descent'. **Le Club des Galopines** cares for skiers and non-skiers from 18 months and **Club Loisirs** from three years, both t +33 (0)4 79 06 89 67.

Lunch

Try **La Traversette, t** +33 (0)6 11 70 51 07, **Le Plan du Repos, t** +33 (0)4 79 06 87 92, and **L'Ancolie, t** +33 (0)4 79 06 86 71.

Dine

Le Relais du Petit-St-Bernard, t +33 (0)4 79 40 19 38, **L'Ancolie, t** +33 (0)4 79 06 86 71, and **Le Chalet, t** +33 (0)4 79 06 80 79, are recommended. **Le Turia, t** +33 (0)4 79 06 13 65, has fine cuisine at reasonable prices.

Party

Le P'tit Relais and Le Petit Danois are busy as the lifts close. **Clay's** is a piano-bar. **Le Pub** provides the late-night action.

Sleep

****Les Granges de La Rosière**, t +44 (0)870 750 6820, *www.ernalow.co.uk*, are smart MGM apartments.
****The Relais du Petit-St-Bernard**, t +33 (0)4 79 06 80 48, *www.petit-saint-bernard.com*, is well placed at the foot of the slopes.
****Le Solaret**, t +33 (0)4 79 06 80 47, *www.hotelsolaret.com*, is family-run.

Sainte-Foy

Profile

Burgeoning station de ski above an old village in the Haute Tarentaise, with lots of new chalets but as yet limited lifts. Renowned for its superb off-piste skiing

Resort

Sainte-Foy *station* is the purpose-built ski base above the old village of Sainte-

Foy, on the road up to Tignes and Val d'Isère from Bourg-St-Maurice. In recent years it has been the centre of a speculative building boom, with a large development of attractive traditional-style chalets. Resort developer MGM is banking on the premise that the amount of new accommodation will force the French authorities to allow more lifts to be built. Permission has already been given for a new six-person chair at Camp Filleul to the west of the present ski area.

Mountain

Sainte-Foy is a ski secret that has been long known to Val and Tignes habitués, who come here for the superb powder quality. Three quad-chairs take you up to 2612m Col de l'Aiguille, starting point for a choice of red or black pistes, while the second chair serves less demanding tree-lined terrain. Off-piste itineraries include the 1700m descent of the north face of Fogliettaz and a long powder run to the farming hamlet of Le Monal.

Learn

The **ESF**, t +33 (0)4 79 06 96 76, receives rave reviews from reporters.

Children

Les P'tits Trappeurs, t +33 (0)4 79 06 97 92, accepts children from three to 11 years.

Lunch

Try **Les Brevettes**, t +33 (0)6 88 21 08 79, and **Chez Léon**, t+ 33 (0)6 09 57 23 88, at the top of the first chair, and **Maison à Colonnes**, t +33 (0)4 79 06 94 80, at the bottom of the lifts. **Chez Mérie**, t +33 (0)4 79 06 90 16, at Le Miroir serves hearty peasant fare.

Essentials

Altitude: 1550m (5,084ft)–2620m (8,596ft)
Further information: t +33 (0)4 79 06 95 22, *www.saintefoy.net*
Lifts in resort: 3 (3 chairs) serving 25km of piste
Lift pass: adult €105, child 7–11yrs €81, for 6 days
Access: Chambéry, Geneva and Lyon airports 2hrs. Station at Bourg-St-Maurice 20km

Dine

La Bergerie, t +33 (0)4 79 06 25 51 is a gastronomic restaurant at the foot of the piste. **Maison à Colonnes**, t +33 (0)4 79 06 94 80, and **La Grange** in Hotel Le Monal, t +33 (0)4 79 06 90 07, are both good.

Party

The resort is quiet in the evening, with a choice of the **Pitchouli** for a drink after skiing and the bar of **Hotel Le Monal**.

Sleep

****Les Fermes de Sainte-Foy, t +33 (0)4 50 33 10 96 is a new MGM hotel complex of three- and four-room apartments opening this season.

****Yellow Stone Chalet, t +33 (0)4 79 06 96 06, *www.yellowstone-chalet.com*, is run as a B&B for eight people. It has an indoor pool, a sauna and hot tub.

**Auberge sur la Montagne, t +33 (0)4 79 06 95 83, *www.aubergemontagne. co.uk*, in the hamlet of La Thuile, is warmly recommended.

**Hotel Le Monal, t +33 (0)4 79 06 90 07, *www.le-monal.com*, is in the old village.

St-Gervais

Profile

Traditional spa town with modestly priced accommodation, linked by gondola and piste into the giant Megève ski area, 4km from a station and autoroute exit

Resort

This attractive small spa town has been a resort ever since the first tourists arrived here to take the waters in 1806. It lies at the head of a dramatic river gorge midway between Chamonix and Megève and serves as the gateway to two important ski areas encompassing the villlages of Le Fayet, Le Bettex and Saint-Nicolas-de-Véroce.

Mountain

The main skiing to the east of the town, reached by a fast 20-person gondola from the outskirts, is linked across the slopes of Mont d'Arbois to Megève. The area has a terrain park and a half-pipe. On the other side of town, the venerable Mont Blanc Tramway, a rack-and-pinion railway dating back to 1904, takes you to the top of the neighbouring ski area of Les Houches.

Learn

Lessons are provided by the **ESF St-Gervais/Le Bettex**, t +33 (0)4 50 47 76 21, **ESF Saint-Nicolas-de-Véroce**, t +33 (0)4 50 93 21 61, and the **Mont Blanc Ecole de Ski**, t +33 (0)4 50 93 16 78, at Bettex.

Essentials

Altitude: 860m (2,821ft)–2350m (7,708ft)
Map: see Megève page M34
Further information: t +33 (0)4 50 47 76 08, *www.st-gervais.net*
Lifts in area: 113 in Evasion Mont Blanc (11 funicular, 13 cableways, 38 chairs, 60 drags) serving 450km of piste; 729km in Mont Blanc ski area
Lift pass: Ski Pass Mont Blanc (covers all local resorts including Chamonix, Courmayeur, Les Houches) adult €216, child 4–15yrs €173–184, all for 6 days
Access: Geneva airport 45mins. TGV station at Sallanches 4km, regular buses to resort

Children

Garderie des Neiges, t +33 (0)4 50 93 14 81, cares children aged six months to six years in Le Bettex. **Crèche Halte-Garderie**, t +33 (0)4 50 93 23 90, is for ages two to six years in Saint-Nicolas-de-Véroce. The two **ESF** branches provide lessons from four years.

Lunch

Try **Hotel-Restaurant L'Igloo**, t +33 (0)4 50 93 05 84, at Mont d'Arbois and **Le Prarion**, t +33 (0)4 50 54 41 99, above Les Houches.

Dine

St-Gervais itself has some 35 restaurants. For crêpes try **4 Epices**, t +33 (0)4 50 47 76 08, and for pizzas **L'Eterle**, t +33 (0)4 50 93 64 30. **Le Four**, t +33 (0)4 50 93 14 16, and **A Robinson**, t +33 (0)4 50 93 59 00, serve local specialities.

Party

This is not a party town but there is a good selection of bars, a skating rink, casino and **La Nuit des Temps** disco.

Sleep

★★★**Hotel Restaurant Le Carlina**, t +33 (0)4 50 93 41 10, *www.carlina-hotel.com*, is ski-in ski-out with a traditional restaurant and an indoor pool.
★★★**Hotel-Restaurant L'Igloo**, t +33 (0)4 50 93 05 84, *www.ligloo.com* is a chalet-style hotel set on the piste.
La Maison du Vernay, t +33 (0)4 50 47 07 55, *www.lamaisonduvernay.com*, is a B&B with five wood-panelled bedrooms, each with a different flower theme.

St-Martin-de-Belleville

Profile

Offbeat and attractive old village with direct link in the huge Trois Vallées area. Excellent accommodation and restaurants, but limited après-ski

Resort

St-Martin-de-Belleville is a charming old village situated before Les Menuires on the road up from Moûtiers. It has an entirely different and more relaxed rural atmosphere than any of the better-known purpose-built resorts in the Trois Vallées. Most of the ancient stone and wood barns have been converted into chalets, but farmhouse cheese is still made here and you can still buy fresh milk by the pail.

Mountain

St-Martin's only fault used to be in the inordinate amount of time that it took to link into the rest of the skiing in the Trois Vallées. But all that changed with the

Essentials

Altitude: 1450m (4,757ft)–3300m (10,827ft)
Map: see Méribel page M36
Further information: t +33 (0)4 79 00 20 00, *www.st-martin-de-belleville.com*
Lifts in area: 167 in Trois Vallées (40 cableways, 69 chairs, 58 drags) serving 600km of piste
Lift pass: Trois Vallées adult €204, child 5–13yrs €153.50, both for 6 days
Access: Chambéry airport 2hrs, Lyon airport 2½hrs, Geneva airport 3hrs. Eurostar to Moûtiers, 33km away

construction of a gondola and a fast chair that swiftly convey you up to the Tougnette Ridge for runs down to Les Menuires, or over the far side towards Méribel. In fresh powder conditions the runs from the ridge back to St-Martin are glorious – acres of undulating pastures followed by tree-skiing.

Learn

There's an **ESF** branch, t +33 (0)4 79 00 61 43. **Compagnie des Guides**, t +33 (0)4 79 01 04 15, organizes off-piste excursions.

Children

Piou Piou, t +33 (0)4 79 08 91 15, cares for both non-skiing and skiing children from two-and-a-half years. Not all the staff speak English.

Lunch

Le Corbeley, t +33 (0)4 79 08 95 31 has a sunny terrace and good food, while **L'Etoile des Neiges**, t +33 (0)4 79 08 92 80, is a lunchtime favourite.

Dine

L'Eterlou, t +33 (0)4 79 08 94 07, is recommended, and **La Montagnarde**, t +33 (0)4 79 01 08 40, is in an old hayloft. **La Voutte**, t +33 (0)4 79 08 91 48, serves good pizzas. **L'Etoile des Neiges**, t +33 (0)4 79 08 92 80, uses fresh produce for its local specialities. Chef René Meilleur's **La Bouitte**, t +33 (0)4 79 08 96 77, at nearby St-Marcel, has a much-deserved Michelin star and an intimate atmosphere.

Party

St-Martin has a few bars, including **Pourquoi Pas** piano-bar, **Le Jokker** and **Brewski's**, but is a quiet place by night.

Sleep

★★★Hotel St-Martin, t +33 (0)4 79 00 88 00, *www.hotelsaintmartin.com*, has rooms that have been individually decorated.
★★★Alp'Hôtel, t +33 (0)4 79 08 92 82, *www.alphotel.fr*, is comfortable and traditional.
★★★Hotel Edelweiss, t +33 (0)4 79 08 96 67, *www.hotel-edelweiss73.com*, has 16 cosy rooms and a good restaurant.
La Bouitte, t +33 (0)4 79 08 96 77, *www.laboitte.com*, in the nearby hamlet of St-Marcel, is full of character.

Serre Chevalier

Profile

The collective name for a dozen linked villages that share a large ski area with the garrison town of Briançon. Attractive tree-lined slopes and some varied off-piste. Suited to all standards of skier and rider looking for a combination of

Essentials

Altitude: 1200m (3,936)–2800m (9,184ft)
Map: see page M42
Further information: t +33 (0)4 92 24 98 98, *www.serre-chevalier.com*
Lifts in area: 74 (9 cableways, 19 chairs, 46 drags) serving 250km of piste
Lift pass: Grande Serre Che (covers all centres as well as 1 day in each of Alpe d'Huez, Les Deux Alpes, La Grave, Montgenèvre, Puy-St-Vincent) adult €170, child 6–12yrs €124, both for 6 days
Access: Turin airport 1½hrs, Grenoble airport 2hrs, Lyon airport 3hrs. Station at Briançon, regular bus service to villages

purpose-built and traditional resort with good-value accommodation and food

Resort

Serre Chevalier is not a single resort but the collective marketing name adopted by a dozen villages that line the main Grenoble–Briançon road between the high mountain pass of the Col du Lauteret and the ancient garrison town, close to the frontier with Italy. Accommodation and the main lifts are centred on Briançon and the quite separate villages of Chantemerle, Villeneuve-Le Bez and the sleepy little spa resort of Monêtier-Les-Bains. Where you choose to stay is dependent on your holiday priorities. The old walled town has considerable charm and a wonderful choice of restaurants. But while it is directly linked to the mountain, it lacks the traditional atmosphere of a ski resort.

Chantemerle is the nearest village to Briançon, Villeneuve and the rustic hamlet of Le Bez beside it is the most convenient and charming village base with the most central access to the skiing that is spread along the wall of the valley. Monêtier-Les-Bains (also known as Serre Chevalier 1500) is a picturesque spa village that has been a resort since Victorian times.

The giant Milky Way area, venue for the 2006 Winter Olympics, is a short drive away. From Montgenèvre you can ski over to Sauze d'Oulx and Sestriere, the setting for the main Alpine events. La Grave and Les Deux Alpes can both easily be reached across the Col du Lauteret. Puy-St-Vincent, near Briançon, is also worth a visit.

Mountain

Lots of new lifts have been introduced in recent years as Serre Che continues to compete with its rivals further north in the Alpine chain, despite a series of difficult winters for snow-cover. The Clot Gautier chair above Villeneuve has been upgraded to a six-pack, as has the one from Aravet 2000 to Plateau Rouge.

The linked runs that stretch for more than 19km down the southern side of the valley provide a playground that will test the most advanced skier and rider. But at the same time there is an easy route down to the valley from each lift. Of the different sectors, Monêtier is the most appealing and usually the least crowded. This is the best end of the circuit for accomplished skiers and riders although the link with Villeneuve can sometimes suddenly close in bad weather and you may be forced to take the bus home if staying in Chantemerle or Briançon.

Isolée is an exciting black, which starts on the ridge from L'Eychauda at 2659m and plunges down towards Echaillon. Tabuc is a long black run through the woods with a couple of steep and narrow pitches. The Casse du Bœuf, a sweeping ridge through the trees back to Villeneuve, is one of our favourite runs.

This is considered to be one of the most friendly resorts in France for riders. The snowpark at Monêtier is open until 9pm, as is the half-pipe at L'Aravet in Villeneuve. Chantemerle has a snowcross course with seven bends. Monêtier has a dedicated Big Air arena at Pré Chabert.

Learn

The **ESF** has branches in Chantemerle, t +33 (0)4 92 24 17 41, and Villeneuve, t +33 (0)4 92 24 71 99; they have a reputation for both friendliness and quality of instruction. In Chantemerle, **Evasion**, t +(0)4 92 24 02 41, and **Génération Snow**, t +33 (0)4 92 24 21 51, are recommended. **Buissonnière ESI**, t +33 (0)4 92 24 78 66, in Villeneuve is praised by reporters. **Altitude**, t +33 (0)6 08 02 51 82, provides the alternative. In Monêtier, **EurekaSki**, t +33 (0)6 89 31 66 56, or t +44 (0)1326 375710, is a British-owned ski school run by BASI instructors with an excellent reputation.

Children

In Chantemerle, **Les Poussins**, t +33 (0)4 92 24 03 43, takes children from eight months. In Villeneuve, **Les Schtroumpfs**, t +33 (0)4 92 24 70 95, cares for children from six months. **Les Petit Aigles**, t +33 (0)4 92 24 29 31, also take non-skiing children from three years. In Monêtier, **Les Eterlous**, t +33 (0)4 92 24 45 75, accepts children aged from six months (18 months during French school holidays). The **ESF Jardin des Neiges**, t +33 (0)4 92 20 30 57, in Briançon, Chantemerle, t +33 (0)4 92 24 17 41, Villeneuve, t +33 (0)4 92 24 71 99, and in Monêtier, t +33 (0)4 92 24 42 66, provides a mix of tuition and play for children from three years. In Chantemerle, **Génération Snow**, t +33 (0)4 92 24 21 51, offers lessons to children aged seven to 11 years.

Lunch

Above Chantemerle, **Café Soleil**, t +33 (0)4 92 24 17 39, has carefully prepared food and a great atmosphere. **La Bergerie du Grand Alpe**, t +33 (0)6 81 34 34 14, serves local mountain cuisine.

Above Villeneuve, **The Pi Maï**, t +33 (0)4 92 24 83 63, has considerable charm, good food and attentive service as you sit by a roaring log fire. Remote **L'Echaillon**, t +33 (0)4 92 24 05 15, is also recommended. **D'Abord-L'Aravet 2000**, t +33 (0)4 92 24 97 67, is good value and has breathtaking views. **Le Bivouac de la Casse**, t + 33 (0)4 92 24 87 72 is at the top of the Casse du Bœuf chair-lift.

Above Monêtier, **Peyra Juana**, t +33 (0)6 81 11 40 26, is a mountain hut with some of the best food in the ski area. Try also **Le Bachas**, t +33 (0)4 92 24 50 66.

Dine

In Briançon, **Le Passé Simple**, t +33 (0)4 92 21 37 43, specialises in mountain dishes and cuisine from the seventeenth century.

In Chantemerle, try **Le Bistrot de Serre Che**, t +33 (0)4 92 24 15 16, and **Le Loup Blanc**, t +33 (0)4 92 24 14 27.

In Villeneuve, **La Pastorale**, t +33 (0)4 92 24 75 47, is recommended, **Le Bidule**, t +33 (0)4 92 24 77 80 in the hamlet of Le Bez has a warm atmosphere and enticing seafood and fish dishes.

In Monêtier **L'Antidote**, t +33 (0)4 92 44 09 74, and **Chalet Auberge des Amis**, t +33 (0)4 92 24 43 27 are recommended.

Party

This is not a party resort, with nightlife limited to local bars and the occasional very Gallic disco. **Le QG** in Chantemerle, **Le Bab Bam** and **La Baïta** in Villeneuve are the main focal points. **Le Lièvre Blanc** in Villeneuve is a riders' hangout with weekly live music. **Le Yeti** in Chantemerle is strongly recommended. **Bar Alpin** is said to have a great atmosphere, as has the **Bar Le Que Tal**. In Chantemerle, the **Altiforme** fitness centre offers massage and beauty treatments. Villeneuve has a pool and fitness centre. **Les Bains de Monêtier** is a thermal spa with bath-temperature spring water.

Sleep

Most of Serre Chevalier's lodging is in apartments, and all accommodation can be booked through **Serre Chevalier Reservations**, t +33 (0)4 92 24 98 80. **Briançon:**
***Hotel Le Vauban**, t +33 (0)4 92 21 12 11, *www.hotel-vauban.fr*, has a restaurant that uses fresh local produce. Specials include *foie gras* and *gigot d'agneau*.
***Parc Hotel**, t +33 (0)4 92 20 37 47, *www.monalisahotels.com*, is 300m from

the gondola. Its restaurant serves Alsace cuisine.

****Chalet Chez Bear, t** +33 (0)4 92 21 11 70, in the hamlet of Belvoir just outside Briançon, is the area's most luxurious chalet and run by a British couple.

Chantemerle 1350:

***Hotel Plein Sud, t** +33 (0)4 92 24 17 01, *www.hotelpleinsud.com*, is 250m from the lifts and has a pool.

Grand Hotel, t +33 (0)4 92 24 15 16, is more modest than its name, with a restaurant serving traditional mountain cuisine.

Villeneuve:

***Hotel du Mont Thabor, t** +33 (0)4 92 24 74 41, *www.mont-thabor.com*, was new last season, and has a swimming-pool and games room.

Chalet-Hotel Le Pi Maï, t +33 (0)4 92 24 83 63, is in an isolated position up the mountain at 1985m with a warm ambience and good food.

Monêtier:

****Hotel Les Glaciers Bonnabel, t** +33 (0)4 92 24 42 21, *www.hotelbonnabel. com* is on the Col du Lauteret outside the town centre.

***Auberge du Choucas, t** +33 (0)4 92 24 42 73, *www.aubergeduchoucas.com*, is an ancient inn with a renowned restaurant serving delicious food.

Alliey & Spa Hotel de Charme, t +33 (0)4 92 24 44 20, *www.alliey.com*, has an impressive wine cellar, two pools, and children are warmly welcomed.

Les Colchiques, t +33 (0)4 92 24 42 42, *www.les-colchiques.com*, has rooms for two to six people, and good food.

La Tania

Profile

Attractive low-level Trois Vallées alternative to Courchevel and Méribel. Recommended for families and skiers on a budget wanting to explore this giant ski area

Resort

La Tania was originally built as a dormitory for the 1992 Albertville Olympics. But the village, situated a couple of kilometres from Le Praz (Courchevel 1300) quickly evolved into a pleasant little family resort in its own right. It has the skiing of Courchevel and Méribel but without the high prices. Architecture is in traditional mountain style and Le Forêt, a collection of attractive Scandinavian-style chalets set in the woods above the village, contributes to the cosy mountain ambience.

Mountain

A jumbo gondola provides main mountain access and allows skiers to download when village snow-cover is

Essentials

Altitude: 1350m (4,429ft)–3300m (10,825ft)
Map: see Courchevel page M30
Further information: t +33 (0)4 79 08 40 40, *www.latania.com*
Lifts in area: 167 in Trois Vallées (40 cableways, 69 chairs, 58 drags) serving 600km of piste
Lift pass: Trois Vallées adult €204, child 5–13yrs €153.50, both for 6 days
Access: Chambéry airport 2hrs, Lyon airport 2½hrs, Geneva airport 3hrs, Moûtiers station 25km

limited. Lifts and pistes link to Courchevel 1850 as well as to Méribel via the Col de la Loze. When the light is flat, La Tania's own tree-lined skiing is the best place in the Trois Vallées.

Learn

The resort has a branch of the **ESF**, t +33 (0)4 79 08 80 39, as well as **Magic in Motion**, t +33 (0)4 79 01 07 85, and **Olivier Brané**, t +33 (0)4 79 08 24 21, an independent instructor who specializes in Trois Vallées tours.

Children

La Maison des Enfants, t +33 (0)4 79 08 40 40, is for non-skiers from three years, and **Le Jardin des Neiges**, t +33 (0)4 79 08 80 39, is for skiers from four years. Several tour operator chalets have crèches.

Lunch

Le Bouc Blanc, t +33 (0)4 79 08 80 26, at the top of La Tania gondola, provides tasty omelettes and good service. **Le Ski Lodge**, t +33 (0)4 79 08 81 49, in the village, offers great value for money.

Dine

La Tania has five restaurants including **La Taiga**, t +33 (0)4 79 08 80 33, and **La Ferme de La Tania**, t +33 (0)4 79 08 23 25, both of which offer inexpensive Savoyard specialities.

Party

Le Ski Lodge is the main resort rendezvous.

Sleep

****Chalet Titania**, t +44 (0)870 754 4444, *www.leski.com* is in Le Forêt area and has a crèche on the ground floor. Other chalets include one for 22 with a crèche and the other for 19 next door.
***Hotel Montana**, t +33 (0)4 79 08 80 08, in the village centre, is modern with a swimming-pool.
Hotel Le Télémark, t +33 (0)4 79 08 80 32, *www.hoteltelemark.com* is a rustic-style building set in the forest, with 12 rooms ranging from doubles to those sleeping seven.
The Mountain Centre Chalets, t +44 (0)1202 653456, w*ww.themountaincentre.com* consist of two wooden chalets sleeping 32 and 40 in twin and triple rooms. Arrival and departure is on any day of the week, and dining arrangements are flexible.

Tignes

Profile

Part of the large well-linked Espace Killy ski area, shared with neighbouring Val

d'Isère. Glacier skiing for most of the year and a reliable snow record. Convenient, but not for those seeking a traditional Alpine village ambience

Resort

This is France's most snow-sure and popular resort with the French and a cosmopolitan melting pot of other nationalities. It remains open for skiing for 10 months of the year and is a mandatory summer destination for national ski teams in training – and for all those who can't last from season to season without snow beneath their feet. The glacier used to be open 365 days a year, but the combination of damage from global warming, and a falling interest in summer skiing over the past decade, has caused the resort to 'rest' from mid-May until mid-June and again from early September until October. During the summer months 13 lifts serve 20km of high-altitude pistes with a respectable vertical drop of 750m.

Tignes is divided into four main areas with the main village also sub-divided into different *quartiers*. The resort lies at the head of the Haute Tarentaise, a 40-minute drive up the valley from Bourg-St-Maurice, and is connected by lifts and pistes to Val d'Isère. Together they form a 96-lift area with 300km of piste that is known as L'Espace Killy and has few equals for the diversity of its skiing and riding.

The main resort, built at 2100m, was a monument to the architectural horrors of the 1960s, a concrete jungle completely out of keeping with its beautiful setting beneath the twin peaks of La Grande Motte and La Grande Casse. However, huge investment in recent years has transformed Tignes into a much more aesthetically pleasing place. New buildings have been constructed in a sympathetic mountain style and the older

beasts are either being re-clad or torn down one by one for redevelopment.

Tignes itself divides into Le Lavachet with its high-rise apartment blocks, and more agreeable and convenient Tignes-le-Lac on the edge of a small lake. Le Lac has undergone a complete make-over in recent years and a tunnel acts as a bypass for through-traffic to the principal lift station still higher up at Val Claret.

This is the most convenient base for the skiing with immediate access to the underground funicular and the link lift to Val d'Isère. The much lower villages of Tignes-les-Boisses and the valley farming community of Tignes-les-Brévières provide a much more rural environment. They are well-linked into the lift system and cannon-assisted snow-cover usually remains sufficient in late April. However, it is a long way up through the lift system to reach La Grande Motte and Val d'Isère.

Mountain

The focal point is the 3656m Grande Motte, reached from Val Claret by an efficient but claustrophobic funicular or by a long two-stage quad-chair. The train takes six minutes to reach the Panoramic mountain restaurant; from there a cable-car takes you to 3456m for the start of some spectacular glacial terrain. You need a local guide to explore the considerable powder opportunities such as the magnificent North Face leading through the séracs. Wide pistes for all standards lead back down to Val Claret. From mid-November until the lifts close in May this involves a vertical drop of 1400m. The terrain off to the sides appears benign but is dotted with crevasses and great care should be taken. A number of steep chutes, including the infamous Couloir Deux, can be reached from the funicular.

From Val Claret and the main village of Tignes other lifts lead up to the Col du Palet, where you can ski off-piste with a guide all the way to Les Arcs and linked La Plagne. The route off the back of the *col* is prone to avalanche and should only be attempted.with a guide. Lifts also bring you up to the 2748m Aiguille Percée, the unusual rock formation that appears on almost every postcard of Tignes. The black La Sache run, which leads from here all the way to Tignes-les-Brévières at 1550m, is the finest in the resort.

The terrain park at Tignes-le-Lac has a beginner half-pipe as well as an expert one, a snowcross course and assorted obstacles. There is a summer terrain park on the glacier and Tignes has two dedicated freeride zones.

Learn

The **ESF Tignes le Lac, t** +33 (0)4 79 06 30 28, and **ESF Val Claret, t** + 33 (0)4 79 06 31 28, are both praised by reporters. **Ecole Henri Authier, t** +33 (0)4 79 06 36 38, is another alternative. **Evolution 2, t** +33 (0)4 79 40 09 04, received some unfavourable comments from reporters. **Snow Fun, t** +33 (0)4 79 06 46 10, is commended for its small classes. **British Alpine Ski & Snowboard School, t** +33 (0)6 79 51 24 05, or **t** +44 (0)7 09 220 6321 specializes in teaching English-speaking pupils.

ESI, t +33 (0)4 79 06 36 15, and **333, t** +33 (0)4 79 06 20 88, at Val Claret, are the ski and snowboard alternatives. **Snocool, t** +33 (0)4 79 40 08 58, **Surf Feeling, t** +33 (0)4 79 06 53 63, and **Kébra Surfing, t** +33 (0)4 79 06 43 37, are the dedicated board schools, **Tetra Hors Piste, t** +33 (0)4 79 41 97 07, at Le Lac, specializes in off-piste. **Bureau des Guides, t** +33 (0)4 79 06 42 76 offers guiding.

Children

Les **Marmottons Tignes le Lac, t** +33 (0)4 79 06 51 67, and **Les Marmottons Val Claret, t** +33 (0)4 79 06 37 12, accept children from three and a half years, but staff are said to be rather Gallic in attitude. The **ESF, t** +33 (0)4 79 06 30 28, offers lessons from four years, and the **ESI, t** +33 (0)4 79 06 36 15, from five. **Evolution 2, t** +33 (0)4 79 06 43 78, accepts children from three years and provides free helmets.

Lunch

Upstairs at L'Arbina, t +33 (0)4 79 06 34 78, in Le Lac is a gastronomic experience with a good-value daily *formule skier* menu. Specialities include *rognons de veau* and *coquilles St Jacques*, but you must book in advance.

Le Panoramic, t +33 (0)4 79 06 60 11, at the top of the Grande Motte funicular, has a good restaurant as well a large self-service with reasonable fare. **La Pignatta, t** +33 (0)4 79 06 32 97, in Val Claret has good pizzas, fresh pasta, and a sunny terrace.

Dine

In Le Lac, **Upstairs at L'Arbina, t** +33 (0)4 79 06 34 78, continues to be the best gourmet restaurant in the area. **Le Clin d'Œil, t** +33 (0)4 79 06 59 10, is small and intimate. **Le Brasero, t** +33 (0)4 79 06 30 60 ,serves meat dishes. **Le Grenier, t** +33 (0)4 79 06 37 79 is a typical Savoyard restaurant.

In Val Claret, **Le Caveau, t** +33 (0)4 79 06 52 32, has 'very good food and very reasonable prices'. For Savoyard setting and food, try **Grattalu, t** +33 (0)4 79 06 30 78, and **Brasserie du Petit Savoyard, t** +33 (0)4 79 06 36 23. **Daffy's Café, t** +33 (0)4 79 06 38 75, is a popular Tex-Mex. **Le Ski d'Or, t** +33 (0)4 79 06 51 60, offers gourmet cuisine, and **Myako, t** +33 (0)4 79 06 34 79, is a sushi restaurant. **La Pizzeria 2000, t** +33 (0)4 79 06 38 49, has great pizzas, fondue and raclette.

Party

In Le Lac, **Le Café de la Poste** and **The Red Lion** are lively watering holes. In Val Claret, **Grizzly's Bar**, decorated with stuffed and carved bears, has lots of character. **Crowded House** lives up to its name. **The Fish Tank** is also popular. **Sub Zero** and **Blue Girl** are the discos. In Lavachet, **Harri's Bar** and **TC's** are equally busy.

Sleep

Le Lac:
- ****Les Suites de Montana**, t +33 (0)4 79 40 01 44, are sumptuously decorated apartments with an outdoor heated pool and a games room.
- ***Hotel Alpaka Lodge**, t +33 (0)4 79 06 45 30, *www.alpaka.com*, is comfortable. Its bar offers 'an unbelievable array of cocktails'.
- ***Les Campanules**, t +33 (0)4 79 06 34 36, *www.campanules.com*, is chalet-style and has been owned by the same family since 1958.
- ***Hotel Le Lévanna**, t +33 (0)4 79 06 32 94, *www.levanna.com*, is a new family hotel that opened last winter.
- **Hotel L'Arbina**, t +33 (0)4 79 06 34 78, *www.arbina.net*, is well positioned and has a wonderful restaurant.

Val Claret:
- ****L'Ecrin des Neiges**, t +44 (0)870 750 6820, *www.ernalow.co.uk*, are comfortable and convenient apartments, with a mini spa complex and swimming-pool.
- ****Hotel Le Ski d'Or**, t +33 (0)4 79 06 51 60, has a gastronomic restaurant, Thalasso spa and gym.
- **Hotel La Vanoise**, t +33 (0)4 79 06 31 90, *www.hotelvanoise.com*, has doorstep skiing and inviting rooms.

Val d'Isère

Profile

Its dedicated fans – and they are legion – consider that Val and adjoining Tignes have the best off-piste skiing in Europe. This high-altitude glacial resort has a reliable snow record and modern lift system. Recommended for complete beginners, strong intermediates and experts – but not for wobbly second-weekers. Busy nightlife, but light on gourmet restaurants for a resort of this size and sophistication

Resort

Val d'Isère combines with neighbouring Tignes to form one of the principal winter playgrounds of Europe. More British skiers go here than to any other resort in the world and amount to 36 per cent of the population during the winter months. Fortunately the French also favour it and prevent it from become altogether anglicized by providing counter-balance.

Val is a cultural and social melting pot for dedicated skiers and riders from all over the world who are drawn by the high, rugged mountains at the head of the beautiful Tarentaise Valley.

The village, which stretches along the road from purpose-built La Daille to the farming outpost of Le Fornet, has smartened its appearance in recent years and can now be described as attractive. Wide pavements have been created where there were previously none. Mature trees have been transplanted to line the main commercial area, and the worst of the concrete edifices of the 1960s have been reclad in soothing wood.

Focal point is Val Village, a cluster of 'old' buildings housing smart boutiques. This was created for the 1992 Winter Olympics

Essentials

Altitude: 1850m (6,068ft)–3456m (11,335ft)
Map: see page M40
Further information: t +33 (0) 4 79 06 06
  60, www.valdisere.com
Lifts in area: 96 in Espace Killy (2
  funiculars, 4 cableways, 45 chairs, 41
  drags) serving 300km of piste
Lift pass: Espace Killy (Val and Tignes)
  adult €192.50, child 5–12yrs €144.50, both
  for 6 days.
Access: Chambéry airport 2hrs, Lyon
  airport 2¼hrs, Geneva airport 2½hrs.
  Station at Bourg-St-Maurice 30km

around the 11th-century church and the
handful of genuine old farmhouses
dating back to when the settlement was a
hunting lodge for the Ducs de Savoie.

Val has grown in all directions in recent
years and even the central area is now
divided into different *quartiers*. Of the two
satellites, La Daille has purpose-built ski
convenience but little character. By
contrast, burgeoning Le Fornet is
becoming an increasingly attractive place
in which to base yourself, although it's a
long walk home to both from the nightlife
that is entirely confined to the centre.

The Train Rouge, the resort's free bus
service, runs with startling efficiency
every few minutes during the day from
one end of the resort to the other. Buses
between Val and Tignes are neither as
frequent or as cheap as you might expect.
Parking is difficult, but having a car is
useful for visiting Sainte-Foy or for trips to
Paradiski (Les Arcs/La Plagne) and La
Rosière.

Val's biggest plus point is its altitude
and geographical situation that create a
snow-sure micro-climate. You can ski here
from late November until early May and
book a holiday in the certainty that you
will not find green fields on arrival.

The piste-skiing is good, but to its
ardent followers it is the easily accessible
deep snow terrain that beckons. This is a
high-mountain area that carries an ever-
present risk of avalanche and should
always be treated with the utmost respect.
Fatal accidents – they happen each winter
– are usually caused by inexperienced or
ignorant skiers and riders ignoring
warnings and venturing off-piste when it
not safe to do so on the principal that 'it
can't happen to me.' It can.

The ski area often takes a full day to
fully reopen after a serious dump, and
wise skiers head off for a day in the
more sheltered and secure powder of
Sainte-Foy. Radio Val d'Isère on 96.1FM
gives bilingual weather and piste-
grooming updates.

Mountain

No fewer than eight entry points give
access to the mountain, thus ensuring
that even during high-season weeks,
when French families are on holiday,
queuing is never a serious problem.

The most convenient and quickest way
into the system is to catch either the
Funival underground funicular from La
Daille or the 30-person jumbo gondola
that also rises to the top of Bellevarde
from near the swimming pool at the foot
of the nursery slopes.

From here a network of pistes and lifts
fan out towards the Rocher du Charvet in
one direction and towards Tignes in the
other. The Tommeuse chair provides a
swift and efficient link to 2704m Tovière,
starting point for a choice of runs down to
Tignes.

Bellevarde is also the start of the OK
downhill course (named after two of Val's
Olympic champions, Henri Oreiller and
Jean-Claude Killy), which brings you over
some moderately demanding but
wonderfully enjoyable terrain all the way
to the Funival station at La Daille.

From the other side of the nursery area in Val, a choice of cable-car or a detachable-chair takes you up Solaise and on towards Le Fornet. From the top of the Manchet chair the long red Mattis run brings you down to the hamlet of Le Laisanant. A new chair-lift this season means you can continue on to Le Fornet without having to take a bus. The high summer ski area at the top of Le Fornet has guaranteed snow-cover.

Dramatic improvements to the lifts at this end of Espace Killy means that you can now ski from Le Fornet to the far corners of Tignes in a single morning. It is important to note that the official piste grading in Val is markedly stiffer than you will find elsewhere. For blue, read red. Intermediates should treat runs that are marked black with considerable caution until they know what is involved.

The nursery slopes in the middle of the village are both good and free, but their position, just off the main descent from Solaise, means that fast-moving traffic often needs to be negotiated when going to and from the novice lift.

Val's *tour de force* lies in its enormous potential for off-piste. Try the Face du Charvet, a steep powder classic accessed from the Grand Pré chair. Danaides, reached from the Solaise Express chair, brings you steeply down through the forest above the town.

No good skier or rider should miss a day-trip to Bonneval-sur-Arc, an attractive little village in the neighbouring Haute Maurienne. The itinerary starts with a 20-minute hike from the top of Le Fornet, followed by a choice of sweeping powder descents over the far side of the ridge. The return journey is best accomplished by a pre-arranged, four-minute helicopter ride for €90 per person. The alternative is a five-hour taxi journey.

Espace Killy is popular with free riders who will find lots of natural gullies and cliffs. La Daille terrain park has a half-pipe and a host of obstacles, as well as two snowcross courses. Riders and twin-tippers also congregate on the Grande Motte above Tignes.

Learn

Val has a dozen ski schools as well as 20 independent individual private instructors. Choosing the right one for your requirements is no easy task.

The **ESF, t** +33 (0)4 79 06 02 34, has a strong presence and offers cutting-edge tuition. But it obstinately maintains a firmly focused Gallic outlook despite the fact that 36 per cent of skiers here are Anglo-Saxon. Consequently it only employs one British instructor.

We strongly recommend **Top Ski, t** +33 (0)4 79 06 14 80, a cult school run by ex-French racer Pat Zimmer, that specialises in teaching and guiding off-piste as well as giving regular lessons and telemark instruction.

We also recommend **The Development Centre**, t + 33 (0)6 15 55 31 56, run by British instructors. **Mountain Masters t**+ 33 (0)4 79 06 05 14, and **Alpine Experience**, t +33 (0)4 79 06 28 81, also have established reputations for teaching off-piste.

The other schools include **Snow Fun**, t +33 (0)4 79 06 22 24, **Ski Concept**, t +33 (0)4 79 40 19 19, **Ogier**, t +33 (0)4 50 479 06 18 93, **Misty Fly**, t +33 (0)4 79 40 08 74, **Tetra Hors Piste**, t +33 (0)4 79 41 97 07, and **Val Glisse**, t +33 (0)4 79 06 00 72. Guiding can be arranged through the **Bureau des Guides**, t +33 (0)4 79 06 94 03, and through ski schools.

Children

For tuition, we recommend **Oxygène**, t +33 (0)4 79 41 99 58, and **Evolution 2**, t+ 33 (0)4 79 41 16 720. **Le Village des Enfants**, t +33 (0)4 79 40 09 81, cares for children from three to eight years with a mix of play and ski lessons. **Le Petit Poucet, t** +33 (0)4 79 06 13 97, collects and delivers children from three years from wherever they are staying. The main ski schools all run courses for children. The Tourist Office, **t**+ 33 (0)4 79 06 06 60, has a list of recommended babysitters.

Lunch

L'Edelweiss, t + 33 (0)6 10 28 70 64, on the blue Mangard piste above Le Fornet, is a fairly new mountain hut with a log fire and good meat and fish. **La Fruitière, t** +33 (0)4 79 06 07 17, situated on the OK run, has excellent spaghetti Bolognese and lamb dishes. The name means 'dairy' and it is suitably decorated with milk churns. **Le Trifollet, t** +33 (0)4 79 41 96 99, and **Les Tufs, t** +33 (0)4 79 06 25 01, further down and at the foot of the OK, are friendly pizza-and-steak alternatives. **Le Signal, t** +33 (0)4 79 06 03 38, at the top of Le Fornet cable-car, has great steaks and a fine *cassoulet*. **Bananas, t** +33 (0)4 79 06 04 23, at the foot of Bellevarde, has good burgers and Tex-Mex, but better bacon-and-eggs. Best lunch in the region is upstairs at **L'Arbina, t** +33 (0)4 79 06 34 78 in Tignes-le-Lac. Specialities include *rognons de veau* and *coquilles St Jacques*.

Dine

Much the best restaurant in Val is no more: Le Chalet du Crêt has been sold as a private home. For a resort of this quality Val is short on gourmet eateries. **La Grande Ourse, t**+ 33 (0)4 79 06 00 19, by the nursery slopes, heads the list. **Le Blizzard, t** +33 (0)4 79 06 02 07, in the hotel of the same name, also has reasonable food in a pleasant atmosphere. **Le 1789, t** +33 (0)4 79 06 17 89, next to the Galérie des Cimes, has an open fire and offers a warm welcome. **La Taverne d'Alsace, t** +33 (0)4 79 06 48 49,

provides traditional French cuisine at reasonable prices.

Party

Le Graal is the new nightclub this season, a replacement for defunct Club 21. **Dick's Tea Bar** remains the most celebrated disco in the Alps. Alternative après-ski centres around **Café Face, Le Petit Danois**, the **Pacific Bar, Le Pub** and the **Saloon Bar** beneath the Hotel Brussels. British teens gather downstairs at **Bananas**.

Sleep

Val is primarily a chalet resort but has a few decent hotels.
****deluxe* Hotel Les Barmes de l'Ours, t** +33 (0)4 79 41 37 00, *www.hotel-les-barmes.com*, is stylish and comfortable, but overpriced.
****deluxe* Eagle's Nest** and **Big Yeti, t** +44 (0)20 8682 5050, *www.scottdunn.com*, are extraordinarily smart chalets in the Les Carats *quartier*.
*****Hotel Le Blizzard, t** +33 (0)4 79 06 02 07, *www.hotelblizzard.com*, has a fine bar area and restaurant, but the bedrooms are disappointing.
*****Hotel Christiania, t** +33 (0)4 79 06 08 25, *www.hotel-christiania.com*, has plenty of atmosphere.
*****Aspen Lodge, t** +44 (0)20 8875 1957, *www.vip-chalets.com*, is an extremely comfortable catered apartment block on the main street.
****Hotel La Savoyarde, t** +33 (0)4 79 06 01 55, *www.la-savoyarde.com*, is conveniently located and has a strong following.
****Hotel Le Tsanteleina, t** +33 (0)4 79 06 12 13, *www.hoteltsanteleina.com*, enjoys a loyal British following.

A number of sumptuous private homes as well as more basic apartments are also available to let by the week through **Val** d'Isère Agence, t +33 (0)4 79 06 73 50, *www.valdisere-agence.com.*

British-owned **Mountain Rooms and Chalets**, t +33 (0)4 79 41 17 43 *www.mrooms.co.uk*, also has a good choice of accommodation.

Valmorel

Profile

Pleasant purpose-built unsophisticated resort with good nursery slopes and modest intermediate skiing. Suits families with young children

Resort

Valmorel is an attractive ski resort that was developed in 1976 almost in architectural protest at the concrete horrors perpetrated a decade earlier elsewhere. It was constructed in a style sympathetic to its mountain setting and over the years it has matured into a family-friendly resort. The large ski area extends into the Maurienne Valley and to the not-so-attractive resort of St-François-Longchamp. It is also linked with the little beginner resort of Doucy-Combelouvière.

Mountain

The skiing stretches in one direction to the 1981m Col du Gollet and to the other across a gorge to mainly intermediate terrain in the Maurienne. The nursery slopes are exceptionally good. The area also lends itself to some excellent off-piste that remains untracked for days after a fresh fall. The snowpark has a half-pipe and boardercross course.

Essentials

Altitude: 1400m (4,592ft)–2550m (8,364ft)
Map: see page M33
Further information: t +33 (0)4 79 09 85 55, *www.valmorel.com*
Lifts in area: 52 in Grand Domaine (2 cableways, 14 chairs, 36 drags) serving 151km of piste
Lift pass: Grand Domaine (covers Valmorel, Doucy Combelouvière and Saint François Longchamp) adult €167, child 5–12yrs €108.50–142, all for 6 days
Access: Chambéry airport 90km. Station at Moûtier 15km

Learn

ESF, t +33 (0)4 79 09 81 86, is the main school, which has a solid reputation, and most instructors speak English. Independent instructors include **Marie-Thérèse Hemart**, t +33 (0)4 79 09 84 67.

Children

Les Piou Piou is a children's club run by the **ESF**, which accepts non-skiers from 18 months and skiers from three to six years.

Lunch

L'Altipiano, t +33 (0)4 79 09 86 31, has *à la carte* specialities, while **The Banquoise 2000**, t +33 (0)4 79 59 10 60, is rustic with a log fire. **Les Mazots**, t +33 (0)4 79 59 10 01, has Savoyard specials including *croûte au fromage*, and **L'Alpage**, t +33 (0)4 79 09 83 81, is a recommended self-service.

Dine

La Grange, t +33 (0)4 79 09 82 51, offers grilled Savoyard cuisine, and **La Marmite**, t +33 (0)4 79 09 83 19, has a cosy atmosphere. **L'Aigle Blanc**, t +33 (0)4 79 09 83 76, in the forest outside the village, has local dishes. **Le Jimbo Lolo, t** +33 (0)4 79 09 82 13, serves tapas and Tex-Mex in a South American atmosphere, **Chez Albert, t** +33 (0)4 79 09 81 77, offers wood-fired pizzas, and **Le Petit Savoyard, t** +33 (0)4 79 06 90 22, has more sophisticated fare.

Party

Le Ski Roc is a wine bar, and **La Cordée** has music. **Les Nuits Blanches** is a disco with two separate rooms called **Le Before** and **L'After**.

Sleep

***Hotel Club du Soleil La Fontaine, t** +33 (0)4 79 09 87 77, is family friendly.
****Hotel du Bourg, t** +33 (0)4 79 09 86 66, *www.hoteldubourg.com*, is the village centre and has been recently renovated.
Chalet-Hotel Edelweiss, t +33 (0)4 79 09 88 08, *www.chalethoteledelweiss.com*, is a gîte, with ten bedrooms and bathrooms.

Val Thorens

Profile

The highest ski village in Western Europe, which has guaranteed snow-cover from before Christmas until after Easter, is part of the giant Trois Vallées area. Not recommended for non-skiers

Resort

This high *station de ski* in the Trois Vallées has grown in a generation from a bland and soulless lift-station-with-apartments into a rather charming village at the end of the 25km road up from Moûtiers. It sits surrounded by a horseshoe of peaks at the end of the

Belleville Valley, with links across the 2850m Mont de la Chambre towards Méribel and Courchevel beyond. However, there is sufficent skiing for all levels to deter most one-week visitors from venturing elsewhere.

These days, the Trois Vallées is a misnomer because the lift system stretches over the 3200m Cime de Caron all the way down to Orelle in the Maurienne Valley. The 3 Vallées Express gondola from here provides a convenient backdoor into the system. Italians can reach Orelle by the Fréjus Tunnel in two hours from Turin or in less than an hour from Sestriere and the resorts of the Milky Way.

New hotels and apartment *résidences* have been designed more in keeping with their mountain environment than the orginal buildings. Val Thorens is a strictly pedestrian resort – you are allowed in to unload but must then park in one of the car parks on the edge of town.

On a sunny day after a fresh snowfall, few places are more inviting than Val Thorens. But when the weather closes in you quickly realize why the locals never chose to build a farming community at this altitude. In flat light the treeless pistes lack any point of reference.

Essentials

Altitude: 2300m (7,544ft)–3300m (10,827ft)
Map: see Méribel page M36
Further information: t +33 (0)4 79 00 08 08, *www.valthorens.com*
Lifts in area: 167 in Trois Vallées (40 cableways, 69 chairs, 58 drags) serving 600km of piste
Lift pass: Trois Vallées adult €204, child 5–13yrs €153.50, both for 6 days
Access: Chambéry airport 2hrs, Lyon airport 2½hrs, Geneva airport 3hrs. Eurostar to Moûtiers station 25km

Mountain

A chair-lift and the swift Bouquetin gondola provide the link to the Col de Chambre and the long run down to Méribel-Mottaret. Pistes lead from the village to the Péclet Funitel gondola, which takes you up to the glacier and to a network of fast chairs and gondolas that criss-cross the mountainside below the ridge separating the Belleville and Maurienne valleys. A gondola and a cable-car, reached by a blue piste below the resort, rise to the 3200m Cime de Caron. This is the starting point for the Combe de Caron, one of the most testing black runs in the area. Wonderful long continuations lead down through 1400m vertical to Les Menuires. For other even longer off-piste runs, like the scenic Itinéraire du Lou, you need the services of a local guide.

From the far side of the Cime de Caron, two chair-lifts take you up to the 2300m Sommet des Pistes, which accesses two high-altitude runs down the Glacier de la Pointe Renod and a snowcross course. Val Thorens' main snow park is on the 2 Lacs piste just above the resort. It has a 110m half-pipe and an assortment of rails and other obstacles. Val Thorens has France's only toboggan course with a 700m verticial drop, reached by the Péclet gondola.

Learn

ESF, t +33 (0)4 79 00 02 86, and the ESI, t +33 (0)4 79 00 01 96, are the main schools. Reporters favour Ski Cool, t +33 (0)4 79 00 04 92, and Pros-Neige, t +33 (0)4 79 01 07 00. A number of other little schools offer specialist courses and guiding. These include Stages Patrick et Eric Berthon, t +33 (0)4 79 00 06 16, which offers bumps and freeride training.

Children

The ESF, t +33 (0)4 79 00 02 86, at Village Le Montana and Le Village Roc, cares for children from three months, with lessons from three years. Stages Zig Zag – Fabienne Pander, t +33 (0)4 79 00 02 66, takes groups of up to eight children (who have at least the ESF Three Star qualification) to a different valley each day.

Lunch

Try La Chaumière, t +33 (0)4 79 00 01 13, Chalet Les 2 Ours, t +33 (0)4 79 01 14 09, and Chalet Génépi, t +33 (0)4 79 00 03 28. L'Oxalys, t +33 (0)4 79 00 20 51 offers the kind of full-blown gastro lunch that precludes afternoon skiing. Etape 3200, t +33 (0)6 07 31 04 14, at the top of the Cime de Caron, has great views.

Dine

Celebrity chef Jean-Michel Bouvier's L'Oxalys, t +33 (0)4 79 00 20 51, and La Table du Rou, t +33 (0)4 79 00 04 78, in the Hotel Le Fitz Roy, are the most gastronomic establishments in town – during high season you need to book in advance. Auberge du Sherpa, t +33 (0)4 79 00 00 70, in Hotel du Sherpa and Le Bellevillois, t + 33 (0)4 79 00 04 33, in Hotel Le Val Thorens are both recommended. La Cabane, t +33 (0)4 79 00 83 84, is an old-style chalet with a warm atmosphere. La Grange de Pierrette, t +33 (0)4 79 00 00 88, is also praised along with Le Panoramic, t +33 (0)4 79 00 04 77 in Hotel Le Bel Horizon.

Party

Popular bars include Le Tango, Ski Rock Café, The Viking Pub and The Frog and Roast Beef. Le Malaysia and The Underground are the late-night venues.

New Generation sports centre, t +33 (0)4 79 00 00 18, has tennis and squash courts, a swimming pool, a gym and a spa.

Sleep

****deluxe** L'Oxalys**, t +33 (0)4 79 00 20 51, www.valthosport.com, is a chalet complex with a gastronomic restaurant.
****Le Fitz Roy**, t +33 (0)4 79 00 04 78, is a magnificent chalet-style hotel with swimming-pool and fitness centre.
***Le Val Thorens**, t +33 (0)4 79 00 04 33, has three restaurants and a lounge with fireplace.
***Le Sherpa**, t +33 (0)4 79 00 00 70, is value-for-money and offers good food.
***Le Portillo**, t +33 (0)4 79 00 00 88, has individually decorated rooms and a gourmet restaurant.
***Le Bel Horizon**, t +33 (0)4 79 00 06 08, is a good-value family option.
Le Val Chavière, t +33 (0)4 79 00 00 33, in the resort centre, is reasonably priced.

Vaujany

Profile

Rural farming village with direct links into the extensive Alpe d'Huez ski area. Excellent for families, intermediates, gourmets and off-piste enthusiasts

Resort

In the late 1980s, Vaujany became unexpectedly wealthy through land sold for France's largest hydro-electric scheme. The villagers swapped tractors for piste-bashers, and converted cowsheds to chalets after Vaujany became a ski resort by building a giant cable-car linking into the giant Alpe d'Huez ski area.

Essentials

Altitude: 1250m (4,101ft)–3330m (10,922ft)
Further information: t +33 (0)4 76 80 72 37, www.vaujany.com
Lifts in area: 86 (16 cableways, 25 chairs, 45 drags) serving 240km of piste
Lift pass: Area (covers Alpe d'Huez and linked resorts, 2 days in Les Deux Alpes, 1 day in La Grave, The Milky Way, Puy-St-Vincent, and Serre Chevalier) adult €187, child 5–15yrs €133, both for 6 days
Access: Grenoble airport 1½hrs, Lyon airport 2hrs

Mountain

Vaujany's hayricks to riches story explains the presence of a 160-person cable-car in this picturesque but no longer sleepy mountain village. The second stage goes up to Dôme des Petites Rousses at 2800m giving direct access to Alpe d'Huez and lifts going up to the 3330m Pic Blanc. A gondola also connects the village to Montfrais.

Learn

The **ESF**, t +33 (0)4 76 80 71 80, is the main ski and board school. **Le Massif**, t +33 (0)6 07 97 38 11. **Christelle Morin**, t +33 (0)6 83 14 05 74, and **V.O. Coaching**, t +33 (0)6 60 27 60 32, also provide lessons.

Children

La Garderie, t +33 (0)4 76 80 77 53, offers daycare for children aged six months to five years, and British tour operator Ski Peak provides a native English-speaking nanny. The **ESF**, t +33 (0)4 76 80 71 80, runs all English-speaking classes during school holidays.

Lunch

Les Airelles, t +33 (0)4 76 80 79 78, at the top of the Montfrais nursery slope, is a family favourite. **Auberge de L'Alpette, t** +33 (0)47 6 80 70 00 .has wonderful omelettes and salads.

Dine

Hotel Rissiou, t +33 (0)4 76 80 71 00 has fine food and wine. **La Remise, t** + 33 (0)4 76 80 77 11 has great pizzas and fondues. **Le Chardon Bleu, t** +33 (0)476 11 03 95 at La Villette is simple but worth the 1km walk.

Party

The **Swallow Bar** is the mandatory resort meeting place for teens and 20-somethings, as well as the **L'Etendard** bar. **Arsen's** Internet café is new. The skating rink and a giant swimming-pool with flumes provide après-ski entertainment.

Sleep

Accommodation is mainly in apartments and in comfortable chalets in Vaujany and in the neighbouring hamlet of La Villette, 1km away.

★★★★**Chalet Saskia, t** +44 (0)1428 608070, *www.skipeak.com*, is a charming stand-alone chalet with exquisite food.

★★★**Résidence La Perle L'Oisans, t** +44 (0)1428 608070, on the higher level of the village, has the most spacious and convenient apartments.

★★**Hotel Le Rissiou, t** +33 (0)4 76 80 71 00, *www.skipeak.com*, offers the best hotel accommodation in the village.

★★**Les Cimes, t** +33 (0)4 76 79 86 50, has small but pleasant rooms.

The Top Resorts: Italy

Arabba

Profile

Best base for the steepest pistes in the otherwise intermediate Sella Ronda ski area. Small village with limited nightlife, unsuitable for non-skiers

Resort

Arabba guards the gateway to the 3342m Marmolada and is the best place in the Sella Ronda for committed skiers and riders.

The village's reputation as a base for serious skiers is built upon the steep north-facing slopes of 2478m Porta Vescovo. An often oversubscribed cable-car serves a choice of challenging black runs, as well as much gentler alternatives leading back to the resort. The Marmolada tour takes you down to the town of Malga Ciapela. A newly renovated three-stage cable-car rises to Punta Rocca at 3269m for a glorious 12km descent all the way back to Malga Ciapela.

Essentials

Altitude: 1600m (5,248ft)–2949m (9,676ft)

Map: see Selva, page M44

Further information: t +39 0436 179130, *www.arabba.it*

Lifts in area: 22 (4 cableways, 13 chairs, 5 drags) serving 54km of piste; 450 lifts in Dolomiti Superski

Lift pass: Dolomiti Superski adult €171–194, child 8–16yrs €120–136, both for 6 days

Access: Verona airport 2½hrs. Station at Belluno 75mins

Learn

The choice lies between **Arabba Ski School**, t +39 0436 79160 and **Rocca-Marmolada**, t +39 0437 722060.

Children

Snow White Village, run by the Arabba Ski School, accepts kids from two years of age on weekdays, t +39 0437 722277.

Lunch

Rifugio Capanna Bill, t +39 0437 722100, near Malga Ciapela offers homemade pasta and grilled meat. **Miky's Grill**, t +39 0436 79119, in the Hotel Mesdì, offers simple lunchtime fare. **Rifugio Plan Boé**, t +39 0436 79339, on the anti-clockwise route, has a suitably rustic atmosphere. **Bec de Roces**, t +39 0436 79193, has a self-service area and an upstairs pizzeria.

Dine

Pizzeria 7 Sass, t +39 0436 780135, is recommended. **Al Tablé**, t +39 0436 79302, specializes in local game. **Al Forte**, t +39 0436 79329, is housed in a late 19th-century Austro-Hungarian fort and has live music on Wednesdays. **Ru de Mont**, t +39 0436 780020, in the satellite village of Renaz, has good pizzas.

Party

Nightlife is muted. **Peter's Bar**, the Sporthotel's **Bacchus Cellar Bar** and **La Treina** are the main bars.

Sleep

★★★★**Sporthotel Arabba**, t +39 0436 79321, *www.sporthotelarabba.com*, has a large pool and a spa offering a full range of treatments.

****Hotel Griffone, t +39 0436 780034, *www.hotelgrifone.com*, is situated outside town on Passo Campolongo.
***Hotel Portavescovo, t +39 0436 79139, *www.portavescovo.it*, has a children's playroom, swimming-pool and gym.
***Hotel Evaldo, t +39 0436 79109, *www.hotelevaldo.com*, is traditional, with an attractive swimming-pool and wellness area.
***Hotel Mesdi, t +39 0436 79119, *www.hotelmesdi.com*, was new last season and has an impressive wellness centre.
***Hotel Olympia, t +39 0436 79135, *www.hotel-olympia.com*, contains apartments and a restaurant.
Chalet Barbara, t +39 0436 780155 is a new all-wood B&B furnished in cosy Alpine style.

Bormio

Profile

Large historic spa town with lots of atmosphere and a small high-altitude ski area. A wide choice of ski and snowboard tuition is available

Resort

Bormio is a large town dating back to Roman times, with a charming pedestrianized centre and a somewhat limited ski area. It has far more of an authentic Italian atmosphere than many comparable resorts and is best suited to couples and families.

Mountain

The resort's greatest plus point is its high altitude that allows skiing to

Essentials

Altitude: 1225m (4,018ft)–3012m (9,879ft)
Further information: t +39 0342 903300, *www.valtellinaonline.com*
Lifts in area: 17 (3 cableways, 7 chairs, 7 drags) serving 40km of piste
Lift pass: Area (covers Bormio, Santa Caterina, Le Motte and Oga) adult €135–159, child from 6yrs €95–110.50, both for 6 days.
Access: Bergamo and Milan airports 3hrs

continue until after Easter. Last winter Bormio successfully hosted the Alpine Skiing World Championships and new lifts are an enduring legacy. Main mountain access is by a two-stage cable-car from the edge of town that takes you up to the Cima Bianca top station via Bormio 2000, a mid-station with a family hotel and a shopping mall. A gondola and quad-chair offer an alternative route. The long descents provide ideal cruising territory for intermediates.

Learn

Of the seven ski schools, **Bormio Alta Valtellina**, t +39 0342 911020 is highly recommended for its friendly, English-speaking instructors.

Children

The ski schools take children from four years, while the crèche at the **Scuola Sci Contea**, t +39 0342 911605 accepts children from three years.

Lunch

Try **La Rocca**, t +39 0342 905083, an old-fashioned hut on the main trail down to Bormio 2000, and **Rododendri Chalet**, t +39 0342 905034, just above 2000.

Dine

La Rasiga, t +39 0342 901541, is a stylishly converted saw mill. Vecchia Combo, t +39 0342 901568, Al Filo, t +39 0342 904771, Osteria dei Magri, t +39 0342 910456, and Kuerc, t +39 0342 904738, are also recommended.

Party

Braulio is a micro-brewery and a wine bar. Lord Byron attracts a young crowd. Gordy's Pub and Sotto-Sotto are popular alternatives. The late-night focus is the King's Club disco. The Rezia Hotel has a jazz café, and Shangri-la has a good choice of cocktails.

Sleep

****Hotel Baita dei Pini, t +39 0342 904346, www.baitadeipini.com, is an excellent hotel, 400m from the gondola.
****Hotel Palace, t +39 0342 903131, www.palacebormio.it, is recently renovated and close to the town centre.
****Hotel Posta, t +39 0342 904753, www.hotelposta.bormio.it, is a former staging inn with an attractive interior.
****Hotel Rezia, t +39 0342 904721, www.reziahotel.it, is in the pedestrianized centre. Its restaurant serves local Valtellina dishes.
***Hotel Funivia, t +39 0342 903242, www.hotelfunivia.it, is close to the lifts and has spacious bedrooms.
***Hotel Nevada, t +39 0342 910888, www.anzibormio.com, is at the foot of the Bormio 2000 cable-car and has comfortable rooms.

Canazei

Profile

An attractive little town that acts as a mass-market base for skiers and riders wanting to explore the Sella Ronda. The remainder of the valley has less crowded skiing and rural villages

Resort

Canazei and adjoining Campitello are the main resorts in the 20km Val di Fassa, a key player in the Sella Ronda circuit, which forms the core of the Dolomiti Superski, the world's largest area lift pass. The valley has been heavily developed for tourism, but with its backdrop of high mountain peaks and heavily wooded lower slopes, it is by no means unattractive.

It takes around two hours to complete the 40km circuit that links Canazei with Selva Gardena, Arabba and Corvara – the principal compass points. It can be skied in either direction. You take 13 lifts clockwise and 15 lifts anti-clockwise. How much time is actually spent skiing depends on your level of proficiency. In

Essentials

Altitude: 1460m (4,790ft)–2949m (9,676ft)
Map: see Selva, page M44
Further information: t +39 0462 602466, www.fassa.com
Lifts in area: 78 (13 cableways, 39 chairs, 26 drags) serving 200km of pistes; 450 lifts in Dolomiti Superski
Lift pass: Dolomiti Superski adult €171–194, child 8–16yrs €120–136, both for 6 days
Access: Verona airport 2hrs. Station at Bolzano 1hr

planning your day you must also allow for possible lift queues. It makes sense to start before 10am and to reach the last of the four main passes by 3.30pm. The lifts close at 5pm – or earlier – in bad weather conditions. Skimap Sella Ronda, available from lift stations and tourist offices, clearly indicates the route and the signposting is good. However, the number of variations and tangental links to other ski areas off the main circuit can be both tempting and confusing.

Other villages in the Val di Fassa valley including Alba, Pozza, Moena and Vigo di Fassa, have their own small and much quieter ski areas that tend to attract multi-generational Italian families rather than an international clientele.

Canazei itself is a hotch-potch of narrow cobbled lanes flanked by old barns, modern hotels, a good choice of restaurants, and a surprisingly wide selection of shops. Visitors are reliant upon the ski or post bus for reaching the lifts from most of the accommodation, but services throughout the valley are efficient. If one of the main access lifts is crowded, you can always stay on the bus and travel to the next.

Mountain

A modern gondola on the edge of Canazei provides the only means of access to the mid-station at Pecol. The seven-minute journey leaves you with a choice of a chair or an 80-person cable-car for formal entry into the Sella Ronda. In theory an intermediate can ski back down to Canazei, but conditions of the south-facing slopes usually limit the opening of this piste to the middle weeks of the season.

Campitello 1440m (4,724ft) acts as an alternative access point. A cable-car takes you up to Col Rodella, from where you either work your way through a sequence of chair-lifts to Passo Sella and Val Gardena beyond, or ski down a pleasant and long intermediate run to Plan Frataces to catch the connection to Passo Pordoi and the anti-clockwise route to Arabba.

Passo Pordoi, midway between Canazei and Arabba, has the steepest piste skiing in the Dolomites and is accessed by the ancient Sass Pordoi cable-car. But this is a variation off the Sella Ronda strictly reserved for truly accomplished skiers.

From the top, you can either return down a truly challenging itinerary run to Passo Pordoi, or follow the difficult Val Lasties to Canazei. Alternatively, you can – with a guide – explore the Val Mesdi. This cuts across the Sella, the giant rounded stump of a mountain at the heart of the famous ski circuit, and brings you down to Colfosco. All these off-piste descents require good snow and stable weather conditions as well as a level of expertise not necessarily required elsewhere in the Sella Ronda.

Canazei and Pozza-based skiers also have the chance to explore Sella Brunech, the lesser-known ski area on the far side of the Fassa Valley, reached by a cable-car from Alba and a gondola from Passa. This is a pleasant and nearly always uncrowded intermediate playground that is augmented by other lifts on Ciampedie on the other side of the valley at Vigo. The further reaches of the valley have other ski opportunities beginning from Carezza and Passo Costalunga as well as from Ronchi above Moena. From here it is possible to delve on skis still further to Passo San Pellegrino and also into the intricate lift system of the Val di Fiemme. Not all links are seamless and the occasional bus journey is necessary.

Learn

None of the various teaching establishments in the valley stands out for its cutting-edge tuition and by no means every instructor speaks fluent English. The schools are **Canazei-Marmolada**, t +39 0462 601211, **Campitello**, t +39 0462 750350, **Vigo di Fassa–Passo Costalunga**, t +39 0462 763125, **Val di Fassa Snowboard**, t +39 0462 600304, **Vajolet Pozza di Fassa**, t +39 0462 763309, and **Moena**, t +39 0462 573770.

Children

Childcare is limited. **Park Bimbo Neve**, t +39 0462 763309, in Pozza is operated by the Vajolet Pozza di Fassa ski school for children over three years. **Kinderland**, t +39 0462 601211, is run by the Canazei-Marmolada ski school and offers daycare for three years and over, and lessons for the over-fours. **Tananai Miniclub**, t +39 0462 764550, in Alba, Canazei and Campitello, are ski and non-ski kindergartens for ages three to ten years.

Lunch

The mountainside is dotted with privately owned huts, and from midday onwards enticing aromas signal the start of lunch, which the Italians see as an essential component of the skiing day. Try **Rifugio Maria**, t +39 0462 601178, on top of Sass Pordoi, which specializes in Trentino cuisine. From its sun terrace it offers some of the best views in the Dolomites. **Refuge Frederich August**, t +39 0462 750133, is on the Col Rodella.

Baita Checco, t +39 335 6563512, above Viga, and **Bellavista**, t +39 0462 763200, 30m from the base cable-car station at Viga, are both worthy lunch spots. **Tobia del Giagher**, t +39 0462 602385, above Alba, and **Buffaure**, t +39 0462 764101, on the piste above Pozza, are also recommended.

Dine

In Canazei most of the best evening restaurants are in hotels. **La Cacciattora**, t +39 0462 601411, has fresh fish shipped in every day. **La Perla's**, t +39 0462 602453, signature dish is *pappardelle* (broad ribbons of pasta) with a game sauce. In Campitello, **La Cantinetta**, t +39 0462 750405, is renowned for its *polenta* with mushrooms and venison. In Pozza, **Al Crocefisso**, t +39 0462 764260, is known for its roast lamb shanks and *porcini* dumplings. Try the house *antipasto* and grilled venison cutlets at **Al Vecchio Mulino**, t +39 0462 764477. **El Pael**, t +39 0462 601433, is another good choice.

In Moena, **Malga Panna**, t +39 0462 573489, is one of the truly outstanding restaurants in the region. Signature dishes include rabbit ravioli with rosemary. **Le Giare**, t +39 0462 764696, is in Pozza. In Vigo, **Hotel Andes**, t +39 0462 764575, has a popular pizzeria and restaurant with fresh pasta dishes.

Party

Nightlife centres around bars in Canazei and Campitello including **Frogs** in Alba, **La Stua dei Ladins**, **Rosengarten**, **The Esso Bar**, **The Husky Bar** and **Kusk** in Canazei, with **da Gulio** and **Ton Tin** in Campitello. The new **Snow Tube** at Alba makes for some fun evening entertainment, and there is a floodlit slope at Pozza.

Sleep

Canazei:
★★★★**Hotel Astoria**, t +39 0462 601302, *www.hotel-astoria.net*, has been run by the same family since the Second World War and provides comfortable rooms and good food.
★★★★**Hotel Croce Bianca & Spa Vivenes**, t +39 0462 60111, *www.hotel*

crocebianca.com, has been in the same
family since 1869 and now houses
an impressive spa and the popular
Husky Pub.

****Hotel La Perla, t** +39 0462 602453,
www.hotellaperla.net, is popular with
British guests and also has an exotic
wellness area.

****Hotel La Cacciatora, t** +39 0462
601411, *www.lacacciatora.it*, situated in
Alba just 100m from the Ciampac cable-
car, has been completely renovated.

***Park Hotel Faloria, t** +39 0462 601118
has small rooms but is reasonably priced
with a fine restaurant.

Campitello:

****Hotel Medil, t** +39 0462 750088,
www.hotelmedil.it, offers the smartest
accommodation, and has a bar with live
music.

***Hotel Alpi, t** +39 0462 750400,
www.hotelalpi.it, is located 400m from
the cable-car and has a ski-bus-stop
outside the door.

Hotel Panorama, t +39 0462 750112,
www.panoramahotel.it, is at the far end
of the village but convenient for the Col
de Lin nursery slope.

Pozzo and Vigo di Fassa:

****Hotel Ladinia, t** +39 0462 764201,
www.hotelladinia.com, in Pozzo, is
recommended.

****Corona Sport & Wellness Hotel**, +39
0462 764211, *www.hotelcorona.com*, in
Vigo, is impressive and was used by
former Olympic slalom Alberto Tomba
as his training base.

Moena:

****Garden Hotel, t** +39 0462 573314,
www.gardenhotel.biz, has an indoor
swimming-pool, and a piano bar.

Cavalese

Profile

Capital of the beautiful Val di Fiemme,
an excellent base for anyone looking for
genuine Dolomite atmosphere coupled
with good Alpine and cross-country skiing

Resort

Cavalese is the capital of the Val di
Fiemme, a heavily wooded valley north of
Trento with nine separate ski areas. The
spruce is prized by furniture makers and,
back in the 1700s, Stradivari strolled
through these woods selecting the raw
material for his violins.

Fiemme is otherwise best known for its
70km cross-country race each January for
6,000 pro-am skiers. The pick of the skiing
is found at Cavalese, and at Predazzo, the
other main town.

Learn

The schools are **Alta Val di Fiemme**,
t +39 0462 502999, **Cermis Cavalese**, t +39
0462 341303, **Alpe di Pampeago**, t +39
0462 813337, and **Passo du Lavaze**, t +39
0462 231830.

Essentials

Altitude: 900m (2,953ft)–2250m (7,382ft)
Further information: +39 0462 241199,
www.valdifiemme.info
Lifts in area: 50 (7 cable-ways, 27 chairs,
16 drags) serving 100km of piste; 450
lifts in Dolomiti Superski
Lift pass: Dolomiti Superski adult
€171–194, child 8–16yrs €120–136, both
for 6 days
Access: Verona airport 2hrs. Station at
Bolzano 1hr

Children

Kinderheim Gardone, t +39 0462 502999, at Predazzo, **Cermislandia**, t +39 0452 235311, at Alpe Cermis and **Asilo della Neve Pampeago**, t +39 0462 813337, all accept children from three years.

Lunch

Try **Rifugio Paion**, t +39 0462 341616, at Alpe del Cermis. **Eurotel Alpe Cermis**, t +39 0462 340572, at the top of the cable-car, has a sunny terrace. **Baita Dosso Larica**, t +39 0462 235411, at Doss dei Laresi, specializes in game. **Baita Gardone**, t +39 0462 503110, at Predazzo, is recommended.

Dine

In Cavalese, **Cantuccio**, t +39 0462 235040, is famous for its lamb dishes. **El Molin**, t +39 0462 340074, housed in an old cowshed, has a huge range of pasta. **Ristorante des Alpes**, t +39 0462 231117, is renowned for its *tortelloni*. In Predazzo, **Hotel Ancora**, t +39 0462 501651, has a fine restaurant. **Saronch**, t +39 0462 503161, specialises in fresh fish.

Party

The **Igloo Bar** at Gardone, the **Siglu** at Doss dei Laresi, and the **Ganischger Alm** at Pampeago are three of the après-hotspots. Later on the action moves to **Mardok** and **El Calderon** pubs in Cavalese, and to **Poldo's** and the **Al Santo** wine bar in Predazzo.

Sleep

Cavalese:
★★★★Hotel Grünwald, t +39 0462 340369, *www.hotelgrunwald.it*, has a piano bar and swimming-pool.

★★★★Hotel La Roccia, t +39 0462 231133, *www.hotellaroccia.it* has a spa.
★★★Hotel Excelsior e Molin, t +39 0462 340403, *www.excelsiorcavalese.com*, is comfortable and friendly.
★★★Orso Grigio, t +39 0462 341481, *www.hotelorsogrigio.it* is the building where Emperor Franz Joseph used to stay in the 19th century.
Predazzo:
★★★★Hotel Ancora, t +39 0462 501651, *www.ancora.it*, offers some of the best accommodation in the valley.
★★★Hotel Sole, t +39 0462 576299, *www.hsole.it*, outside the town at Bellamonte, is child-friendly.

Cervinia

Profile

High-altitude resort with guaranteed snow-cover during a long season. Suits beginners as well as intermediates who will enjoy the long, flattering runs. It is linked to Zermatt in Switzerland and they share a lift pass

Essentials

Altitude: 2050m (6,726ft)–3883m (12,740ft)
Map: see page M43
Further information: t +39 0166 949136, *www.montecervino.it*
Lifts in area: 59 with Zermatt (2 funiculars, 18 cableways, 20 chairs, 19 drags) serving 350km of piste with Zermatt
Lift pass: Area (covers Cervinia, Valtournenche, Zermatt) adult €165–206, child 8–13yrs €103–155, for 6 days
Access: Geneva and Turin airports 2hrs. Station at Châtillon 27km, regular buses to resort

Resort

Cervinia is a high-altitude resort with fabulous long runs and virtually guaranteed snow conditions throughout the winter. It's somewhere Italy should be proud of. Il Duce, Benito Mussolini, felt exactly the same about this and decreed in the 1930s that the then embryo resort should change its name from the Swiss-German-sounding Breuil to Cervinia to reflect the Italianate glory of the mountain above it. Unfortunately most of us think of the Matterhorn rather than Il Cervino when we view the angular peak that adorns more postcards than any other in the world. From the Italian side the peak first climbed by Edward Whymper in 1865 looks unremarkable.

The nucleus of pre-Second World War buildings reflect the austere imperial style of the time, but all that was a long time ago. Cervinia today is a modern ski resort with a hotch-potch of mainly unenterprising architecture created over the past half-century by those who believe that this is Italy's greatest resort.

Actually, it is not. It's a wonderfully ski-friendly playground, dictated by the easy gradient of its seemingly never-ending slopes. These allow beginners and wobbly intermediates to gain enormous confidence in the extensive high-mountain area. At the same time boy- and girl-racers will enjoy the length of the perfectly groomed runs – and if they are bored by the benign gradient, they can always cross the Klein Matterhorn for the more severe pistes of Zermatt.

Valtournenche is an old village 9km by road from Cervinia, but linked into the same ski area.

Mountain

Cervinia's biggest asset is altitude. At 2050m, with slopes rising to 3883m, it is one of Europe's most snow-sure resorts set against a superb glacial backdrop. It's a place where long runs right down to village level are virtually guaranteed from the beginning of December until early May. Summer skiing continues on the glacier throughout the year. Seven lifts serve 21km of prepared piste with an enormous out-of-season vertical drop of 1000m in the right conditions. A terrain park, with a super-pipe and a half-pipe, is open from July until October.

The link to Zermatt and the joint lift pass, engineered after a decade of talks between the two resorts, are of benefit to both parties.

However, don't make the mistake of thinking that by staying in Cervinia you can fully enjoy Zermatt on the cheap – the distances are too great to be able to do more than sample what the Swiss have to offer.

Beginners and lower intermediates will find themselves content with the 28 lifts on the Italian side that extend down to Valtournenche at 1524m. If they want to visit Switzerland during their stay they can invest in a one-day supplement to the local lift pass. It is important to allow plenty of time to make the long journey back up the Klein Matterhorn and over to Italy at the end of the day. The high-altitude link is prone to sudden rupture in adverse weather conditions. The taxi journey from one resort to the other takes six hours – it's better to bivouac for the night in the wrong country.

A gondola and parallel cable-car take skiers up from Cervinia to the mid-mountain hub of 2559m Plan Maison. The base station is an annoying walk up from much of the accommodation. The lazy but longer alternative is to work your way up the lift system by drag-lift from the nursery slopes.

From Plan Maison a network of modern multiple chairs, a gondola and finally a cable-car bring you up to the summer ski area of Plateau Rosa at 3480m. From here you can ski down the Theodulgletscher to Trockener Steg in Switzerland, or return to Cervinia on the 8km Ventina (no.7 on the resort's piste map). This is one of the classic runs of the Alps. For the second- or third-week skier fresh from the nursery slopes, the easy gradient should present no problems. Its completion will give an enormous sense of achievement. For the advanced skier or a rider, a couple of these at the start of the day when the pistes are deserted should reduce the fittest legs to *lasagne*. If you are still hungry, try the descent from the Plateau Rosa to Valtournenche – it's more than twice as long.

The lack of pitch throughout the ski area on the Italian side can be irksome for strong skiers. They will quickly discover that Cervinia has no steep piste skiing at all, just kilometre upon kilometre of blue and red cruising runs. However, it is ideal for novices who can explore the entire mountain after just a week on skis.

In powder conditions there's plenty of good off-piste to be discovered on the shoulder above Cieloalto. Local guides can provide access from the lift system to an enormous number of enjoyable high-altitude descents that can be exceedingly demanding. Heli-skiing is also possible on the Monte Rosa.

The terrain park served by the Fornet chair has a half-pipe and a snowcross course.

Learn

The choice of schools here lies between the traditional **Cervino, t** +39 0166 949034, **Breuil, t** +39 0166 940960, and newer **Matterhorn Cervinia, t** +39 0166 949523. **Valtournenche** has its own ski school, **t** +39 0166 92515. Mountain guides from the local bureau in Cervinia are

much more reasonably priced than their Swiss counterparts, but have equal expertise on the border peaks. Go with **Guide del Cervino, t** +39 0166 948169, or **Heliski Cervinia, t** +39 0166 949267.

Children

Kinderheim, t +39 0166 940201, is a non-ski kindergarten taking children from newborn to eight years old. **Kid Zone, t** +39 0166 940960, is a play area at Plan Maison. Children must be accompanied by an adult. All the ski schools run classes for children from four or five years.

Lunch

Chalet Etoile, t +39 0166 940220, near the Rocce Nere chair-lift, is the best restaurant on the mountain, renowned for its spaghetti with lobster. **Ventina, t** +39 338 6642596, on the way down from Plateau Rosa, has home cooking. **Bontadini, t** +39 335 250312, on the slope of the same name, also received good reviews. **Le Pousset, t** +39 339 6946228, below Laghi Cime Bianche, serves local specialities, as does **Baita Cretaz, t** +39 0166 949914, on the nursery slopes.

Dine

The Hermitage, t +39 0166 948998, has outstanding 'international cuisine' served in an elegant dining room. **Le Bistrot de l'Abbé, t** +39 0166 949060, is smaller and more rustic, but a worthy runner-up. **La Nicchia, t** +39 0166 949842, is smart with rich food. **La Tana, t** +39 0166 949098, is singled out for its game and mushroom dishes. **The Copa Pan, t** +39 0166 949140, is expensive, has a rustic decor, and is rated for its food. **La Maison de Saussure, t** +39 0166 948259, is typical, serving Valdostana specialities in wood-panelled surroundings. Eat tasty pizzas at **Al Solito**

Posto, t +39 0166 949126, and at the classical pizzeria, **Matterhorn, t** +39 0166 948518, another good dining option.

Party

Nightlife is more muted than you might expect in an Italian resort of this calibre. **Lino's Bar**, beside the ice-rink, is everyone's favourite when the lifts close. Cocktails in the **Hotel Edelweiss** are ingenious and intoxicating. **Lo Yeti**, **The Copa Pana**, and **Hostellerie des Guides** are popular, as well as the infamous and ever-crowded **Dragon Bar**.

Sleep

★★★★**Hotel Hermitage, t** +39 0166 948998, *www.hotelhermitage.com*, situated on the edge of town, has the relaxed atmosphere of a country house.

★★★★**Petit Palais, t** +39 01669 49371, is renowned for the quality of its half-board cuisine.

★★★★**Hotel Punta Maquignaz, t** +39 0166 949145, *www.puntamaquignaz.com*, is an attractive hotel close to the drag-lifts,

★★★★**Sertorelli Sport Hotel, t** +39 0166 949797, *www.sertorelli-cervinia.it*, maintains a consistently high standard.

★★★**Hotel Breuil, t** +39 0166 949537, is rated 'clean, spacious and very acceptable'.

★★★**Albergo Grandes Murailles, t** +39 0166 932956, *www.hotelgmurailles.com*, is a homely little hotel in Valtournenche village centre, with 16 large rooms decorated with warm rugs and wrought-iron beds.

★★★**Hotel Jumeaux, t** +39 0166 949044, *www.hotel-jumeaux.com*, is pleasant, and furnished with antiques and period prints.

★★★**Hotel Mignon, t** +39 0166 949344, *www.mignoncervinia.com*, is centrally placed and cosy, with a good restaurant.

Les Neiges d'Antan, t +39 0166 948775, *www.lesneigesdantan.it*, is a few minutes' drive from the lifts by hotel bus. Downstairs the decoration is traditional, while upstairs the bedrooms and bathrooms have been tastefully revamped.

Champoluc

Profile

A linked circuit of unspoilt ski villages in a rustic corner of the Val d'Aosta with plenty of intermediate skiing in Champoluc and Gressoney as well as truly rugged off-piste above Alagna

Resort

Champoluc and the linked villages of Gressoney-La-Trinité, Stafal, and Alagna form an area known as Monterosaski at the north-eastern end of the wide Aosta Valley beneath the towering peak of Monte Rosa. Champoluc and Gressoney are best suited to families, while Alagna is more of a raw mountain experience, a glacial high-altitude ski area that rivals Argentière for its demanding off-piste

Essentials

Altitude: 1568m (5,144ft)–3370m (11,056ft)
Further information: t +39 0125 303111, Alagna only: **t** +44 (0)8701 622 273, *www.monterosa-ski.com*
Lifts in area: 31 (8 cableways, 18 chairs, 5 drags) serving 180km of piste
Lift pass: Aosta Valley (includes La Thuile/ La Rosière, and Courmayeur) adult €146–182, child under 1.30m 50% discount, both for 6 days
Access: Turin airport 1½hrs

opportunities. Catch it while you can –
every season this resort that is so revered
by powderhounds is becoming
increasingly commercial.

However, most of Monterosa Ski is given
over to easy blue and gentle red pistes
that are well connected by a
predominantly modern lift system. It is
worth noting that while the different
resorts are close on the map and easily
reached on skis from one to the other, the
journey by road between any two of them
is at least two hours.

Champoluc dates from the 15th century
and still has some lovely old houses. It has
expanded along the river bank in recent
years with a blossoming of modern hotels
and restaurants, but fortunately it has
managed to retain its village atmosphere.

Gressoney-La-Trinité and larger
Gressoney-St-Jean in the neighbouring
valley are also mountain communities
that have jumped from farming and
forestry to feeding foreigners in the
course of a single generation. Stafal is a
modern purpose-built outpost above
Gressoney-La-Trinité. Alagna, which lies in
Piedmont just beyond the Aosta Valley, is
even more rustic with little wooden
houses with built-in hay frames.

Mountain

Wherever you choose to stay you must
contend with one of the worst lift maps in
Europe and finding your way around relies
more on luck than map-reading skills. All
lifts eventually lead you to Stafal, the focal
point of the ski area, where you turn west
for 2971m Monte Bettaforca and
Champoluc beyond. East takes you to
Passo dei Salati and to Alagna.

Both Gressoney and Champoluc offer
intermediate cruising and the beauty of
the area is that you feel you are going
somewhere each day. Each resort has a
dedicated novice area. Best black itinerary

is the 7km descent from Punta Indren
towards Alagna.

The area suits all standards, although
more accomplished skiers and riders are
advised to stay in – or within easy reach of
– Alagna. Given good snow conditions this
whole area provides some extraordinary
freeriding and couloir skiing, and heli-
skiing is also possible. However, avalanche
danger is ever present and this should not
be attempted without a local guide.

Learn

The schools are **Gressoney-St-Jean, t** +39
0125 355291, **Gressoney Monte Rosa, t** +39
0125 366015, **Alagna, t** +39 0163 922961,
Antagnod, t +39 0125 306641, **Brusson,**
t +39 0340 5410632, and **Champoluc, t** +39
0125 307194. All are generally good, but
English is by no means widely spoken.
Mountain guiding is with **Champoluc,**
t +39 0348 5186479, **Gressoney, t** +39 0125
366139, and **Alagna, t** +39 0163 91310.

Children

Daycare is limited. Champoluc has a
non-ski kindergarten in **Hotel Castor,**
t +39 0125 307117. **Champoluc ski school,**
t +39 0125 307194, accepts children from
five years. At Stafal, **Hotel Monboso, t** +39
0125 366302, cares for children from four
to eight years. In Gressoney, skiers over six
years must join the adult classes. **Alagna**
ski school, t +39 0163 922961, accepts
children from three years.

Lunch

Try **Albergo del Ponte, t** +39 0125
806667, a mountain hut with rooms
above Gabiet that serves delicious pasta.
Rifugio Guglielmina, t +39 0163 91444,
between the Alagna and Gressoney
valleys, has good food and even better
views. **The Belvedere, t** +39 0349 4915130,

at the top of lift 12 has excellent views and traditional cooking. **The Ostafa, t** +39 0339 8180709, at the top of chairs 8 and 9, is known for its homemade pasta.

Dine

In Champoluc, **Le Sapin, t** +39 0125 307598, has good food at reasonable prices. **Favre, t** +39 0125 307131, features local game. **Hotel Villa Anna Maria, t** +39 0125 307128, has reasonable mountain food and an exceptional wine list. **Le Petit Coq, t** +39 0125 307997, at Frachey is elegant-rustic. In Gressoney-St-Jean **Lo Stambecco, t** +39 0125 355201, has fine grilled steaks and lamb. In Stafal, **Capanna Carla, t** +39 0125 366130, serves regional cuisine at reasonable prices in a warm atmosphere. In Alagna, **Fum D'ss, t** +39 0163 922923, has local game with *polenta*. **Ristorante Unione, t** +39 0163 922930, and **Stolemberg, t** +39 0163 923201, are recommended.

Party

The nightlife is what you make it. For families and serious skiers this usually means an early bath and bed. Bars such as **Hirsch Stube** and the **Petit Bar** in Gressoney provide some entertainment. **Disco Gram Parsons** is in Hotel California.

Sleep

Champoluc:
★★★★**Hotel Breithorn, t** +39 0125 308734, *www.breithorn.com*, is smart-rustic with a good spa.
★★★**Hotel Villa Anna Maria, t** +39 0125 307128, *www.hotelvillaannamaria.com*, has 20 individually decorated bedrooms.
★★★**Hotel Castor, t** +39 0125 307117, *www.hotelcastor.it*, is run by a local Englishman and is warmly recommended.

★★★**Hotel California, t** +39 0125 307977, *www.wrpub.it*, is decorated with 1960s music memorabilia. Choose the Bob Dylan Room or the Doors Room.
★★★**Hotel de Champoluc, t** +39 0125 308088, *www.hoteldechampoluc.net*, is recommended.
★★**Hotel Favre, t** +39 0125 307131, *www.tako.it*, is small and well managed with friendly staff.
Alagna:
★★★★**Hotel Cristallo, t** + 39 0163 91285, *www.hotelcristalloalagna.com*, is in the centre near the 16th-century church.
★★★**Pensione Genzianella, t** +39 0163 923921, *www.monterosa4000.it*, has recently been refurbished.
★★★**Albergo Monte Rosa, t** +39 0163 923209, *www.albergomonterosa.com*, was built in 1908 and is still run by the same family.
★★★**Hotel Mirella, t** +39 0163 922965, is a B&B with rooms over a cake shop.
Gressoney valley:
★★★★**Hotel Monboso, t** +39 0125 366302, *www.igrandiviaggi.it*, at Stafal, is recommended.
★★★**Hotel Gasthaus Lysjoch, t** +39 0125 366150, *www.hotellysjoch.com*, in Gressoney-La-Trinité, is a cosily old-fashioned Tyrolean-style chalet.
★★★**Hotel La Gran Baita, t** +39 0125 356441, near Gressoney Weissmatten, is a lovingly restored ancient Walser house.
★★★**Hotel Lo Scoiàttolo, t** +39 0125 366313, *www.htlscoiattolo.com*, in Gressoney-La-Trinité, is comfortable with a warm ambience.

Cortina d'Ampezzo

Profile

Italy's top ski town reigns supreme in a beautiful setting against the backdrop of the craggy peaks of the Dolomites. It suits all levels of skiers, riders and non-skiers who are prepared to swap ski convenience and modern lifts systems for old world charm

Resort

Italy's smartest winter destination, dominated by its magnificent green-and-white bell tower and a glittering confection of grand 19th-century mansions, sits in splendid linguistic defiance of its neighbours, a two-hour drive from Venice.

Despite being variously occupied over the centuries by foreign invaders that have included Bavaria, France, Austria, Italy, Germany and even the Americans in 1945, Cortina has stubbornly maintained a spiritual independence of its own. While the residents of surrounding towns and villages primarily speak Italian or German, native Cortinese cling to their ancient Ladino language to converse among themselves.

The town is surrounded by soaring cathedrals of dolomitic limestone that rise to over 3000m. These distinctive mountains, named after French geologist Deodat de Dolomieu, turn a surreal shade of pink in the final rays of the setting sun. Encroaching twilight is the signal for Cortina to come out to play. A colony of voluminous fur coats and designer ski wear gathers noisily in the Piazza Venezia at the start of the evening *passeggiata*.

The actual business of skiing plays second fiddle to the social sport of seeing and being seen in the elegant boutiques and antique shops that line the Corso Italia, the pedestrianized main street. Much later, the perpetual party atmosphere is transferred to intimate wine bars, expensive restaurants and a smattering of softly lit nightclubs.

The skiing has plenty of appeal for all standards. But one reason for the resort's failure to attract a significant international clientele in recent decades is inevitably related to the lack of regular investment in high-speed mountain transport. A new quad-chair in the Cristallo sector this season is a case of too little, too late.

Cortina Adrenalin Center, t +39 0436 860808 offers alternative snow sports such as bobsleigh and ice-climbing. **Adrenalin Park** behind the bob run has zip-wires with 40 platforms in the trees and is open in the evening.

Mountain

The main skiing is divided into two separate ski areas of Faloria/Staunies and Tofana/Socrepes that can both be reached by old-fashioned cable-cars from either side of town. A busy ski-bus service

Essentials

Altitude: 1224m (4,015ft)–3243m (10,640ft)
Further information: t +39 0436 3231, *www.cortina.dolimiti.com*
Lifts in area: 51 (6 cableways, 29 chairs, 16 drags) serving 140km of piste; 450 lifts in Dolomiti Superski
Lift pass: Dolomiti Superski adult €171–194, child 8–16yrs €120–136, both for 6 days
Access: Venice airport 2hrs. Station at Calalzo-Pieve di Cadore 35km

provides a link to the lifts, but skiing convenience is not a strong feature in Cortina. These two are supplemented by a diverse handful of smaller, unconnected areas as well as a direct link into the Sella Ronda via another ancient cable-car at Passo Falzarego, a 20-minute free bus ride away.

Tofana, the 3243m highest point in the ski area, provides spectacular views. Two chairs from the second stage of the cable-car give access to a collection of blue and red runs. An easy black run links into the more demanding Socrepes sector that can otherwise be reached by a blue run from the top of the first stage of the cable-car.

The bottom of Socrepes is devoted to a benign and scenic nursery area, served by three fixed chairs and three drag-lifts, that curiously resembles a sloping Kensington Gardens. These beginner runs can be reached by bus from the town at Lacedel on the outskirts and at the top of the nursery area at Pocol, 6km from Cortina.

Faloria, reached by a relic of a cable-car, which spans a cliff face on the other side of Cortina, has plenty of intermediate appeal. You can work your way along the mountainside through a sequence of chair-lifts and blue/red runs down to the road at Rio Gere. A modern chair-lift on the far side brings you up to Son Forca and one of the most dramatic runs in the Dolomites. The steep, black Staunies and the fast, red Padeon that it becomes in the lower stages is sandwiched dramatically between two mighty pillars of rock.

Cinque Torri, on the road up to Passo Falzarego, is the pick of the smaller ski areas. The lifts here are mainly modern – another detachable quad was installed last season – and at peak times Cinque Torri offers some of the best and usually least crowded skiing in the region.

Passo Falzarego is the base station for the cable-car that takes you up to Lagazuoi at 2800m for the scenic Hidden Valley run down to Armentarola and a link into the Sella Ronda.

The old lift climbs a cliff face dotted with windows into a rabbit warren of First World War tunnels that connected gun emplacements and observation posts. These can be explored with a guide in summer, but not in winter.

With skiers arriving from both sides of the pass, the queue for the cable-car can last an hour. But the reward is an 8km red roller-coaster that takes you down past a spectacular frozen turquoise waterfall to Armentarola. You have to return to Passo Falzarego and to Cortina by bus.

Learn

Azzurra, t +39 0436 2694, and **Ski Cortina**, t +39 0436 2911, are both recommended by reporters. The others are **Cristallo-Cortina**, t +39 0436 870073, and **Dolomiti-Cortina**, t +39 0436 862264, **Scuola Fondo Ski Cortina**, t +39 0436 2911, and **Morotto**, t +39 0436 862201, are both based at the Fiames Nordic Centre and teach cross-country.

Children

As in most resorts specialist childcare facilities are minimal because Italians tend to take granny with them on holiday. **Gulliver Park Kindergarten**, t +39 340 055 8399 in the Pocol sector cares for children aged from three months to three years.

Lunch

Lunch at **Rifugio Averau**, t +39 0436 4660, in Cinque Torri, heads the list and is famous for its homemade pasta including *pappardelle con funghi* (broad ribbons of pasta with mushrooms). Don't confine your choice to one type of pasta – on request, three are served on a single plate.

Rifugio Duca d'Aosta, t +39 0436 2780, in the Tofana/Socrepes sector is also recommended along with nearby **Rifugio Pomedes, t** +39 0436 862061. **El Sorei, t** +39 0436 877017, also has good food.

Dinner

Dine at Michelin-starred **Tivoli, t** +39 0436 866400, in an intimate ambience enhanced by panelled walls decorated with copper pans and a wood-burning stove in one corner. **El Toula, t** +39 0436 3339, is a converted three-storey hay barn with a rustic atmosphere created by locally carved furniture and sprigged tablecloths. **Leone & Anna, t** +39 0436 2768, is a tiny, romantic Sardinian restaurant that has been pleasing the palates of Cortina for 30 years. **Zanvor, t** +39 0436 860789, and **La Tavernetta, t** +39 0436 868102, are also recommended.

Party

Party in the early evening at the **Enoteca** wine bar, in the bar of the Hotel de la Poste. **DOK-LP26** is a curious mixture of prosciutteria and cocktail bar with live music. It is owned by a millionaire Italian builder who constructed most of Val d'Isère and the new village in Les Arcs – which also has a sister LP26. Other popular bars are **Villa Sandi**, **Brio di Vino** and **El Becalen**. The **VIP Club** at the Hotel Europa and **The Metro Club** liven up after midnight, along with **The Bilbo Club**. **Disco Belvedere** at Pocol has a youthful following.

Sleep

A new airport transfer service operates this year from Venice and from Treviso (to connect with Ryanair). The service is free of charge to some hotels and at a rate of €18 return to others.

★★★★**Hotel Ancora, t** +39 0436 3261, *www.hotelancoracortina.com*, situated in the heart of the Corso Italia, is convenient for the nightlife. Its Terrazza Viennese is a resort meeting place.

★★★★★**Hotel Cristallo, t** +39 0436 881111, *www.cristallo.it*, is situated a five-minute uphill walk from the centre. Rooms are decorated in Gustavian style with hand-painted woodwork and delicate frescoes.

★★★★★**Miramonti Majestic Grand, t** +39 0436 4201, *www.geturhotels.com*, situated 2km out of town is an imposing *fin de siècle* palace. It has a wellness centre and a large indoor pool.

★★★★**Hotel de la Poste, t** +39 0436 4271, *www.delaposte.it*, also in the pedestrianized centre, is an old coaching inn and another resort rendezvous that has been run for generations by the Manaigo family. Some of the rooms are rather small, but the bathrooms are large.

★★★★**Parc Hotel Victoria, t** +39 0436 3246, *www.hotelvictoriacortina.com*, has a solid reputation and is conveniently situated at the beginning of the Corso Italia.

★★★**Hotel Aquila, t** +39 0436 2618, *www.aquilacortina.com*, at the far end of the Corso Italia, is family-run and friendly with an indoor swimming-pool.

★★★**Hotel Menardi, t** +39 0436 2400, *www.hotelmenardi.it*, is a mid-19th-century farmhouse. Its original decoration incorporates the Menardi family's memorabilia.

★★★**Hotel Olimpia, t** +39 0436 868524, *www.hotelolimpiacortina.com*, is a reasonably priced and centrally situated B&B.

Corvara

Profile

Attractive, sophisticated village with great hotels and superb restaurants that acts as a convenient base for exploring the Sella Ronda

Resort

Corvara is a sprawling but sophisticated little town that makes one of the most convenient bases from which to explore the Sella Ronda. It has on-mountain links towards Arabba in one direction and Selva in the other, while off the circuit, you can ski to La Villa, San Cassiano and Armentarola.

Mountain

The modern Boè gondola takes you towards Arabba on the clockwise circuit of the Sella Ronda. It is also the most efficient means of reaching Corvara's own ski area as well as the extensive sunny slopes that it shares with San Cassiano, Armentarola and La Villa.

From near the gondola base, a quad-chair takes you on the anti-clockwide route towards Colfosco and Selva. The

easy blue and reds around Corvara are perfect for intermediates. However, many of the lifts away from the circuit are frustratingly slow.

Learn

Corvara-Ladinia, t +39 0471 836126, and **Colfosco**, t +39 0471 836218, schools both have good reputations.

Children

Skikinderland, t +39 0471 836126, cares for children from two years.

Lunch

Try **Capanna Nera/Neger Hütte**, t +39 0471 836138, at the bottom of the Pralongia piste. **Baita La Marmotta**, t +39 0471 836125, and **Punta Trieste**, t +39 0471 836643, are both on Pralongia. **Mesoles,** t +39 0471 836023, near Colfosco, is also recommended.

Dine

Stua di Michl, t +39 0471 836132, is the Michelin-starred restaurant in Hotel La Perla. The 16th-century **Stüa dl'Jagher**, t +39 0471 836085, in Hotel Sassongher has the atmosphere of the hunting lodge it once was. **La Tambra**, t +39 0471 836281, specializes in Mediterranean cuisine. **Hotel Alisander**, t +39 0471 836055, is renowned for fresh fish. **Stüa Ladina** in the Sporthotel Panorama, t +39 0471 836083, provides local cuisine.

Party

Grillkeller Adler and the **Veranda Keller** are noisy. Piano bars in **Hotel Sassongher**, La Perla and **Table** are more sophisticated. Popular **Posta Zirm Taverna** is the late-night spot.

Essentials

Altitude: 1568m (5,144ft) – 2949m (9,676ft)
Map: see Selva, page M44
Further information: t +39 0471 836176, *www.altabadia.org*
Lifts in area: 52 in Alta Badia (9 cableways, 29 chairs, 14 drags) serving 130km of piste; 450 lifts in Dolomiti Superski area
Lift pass: Dolomiti Superski adult €171–194, child 8–16yrs €120–136, both for 6 days
Access: Verona airport 2½hrs

Sleep

****La Perla, t** +39 0471 831000,
www.romantiklaperla.it, has walls
adorned with carved angels and floors
covered with Oriental rugs.

****Posta Zirm Hotel, t** +39 0471 836175,
www.postazirm.com, is a resort meeting
place, with a spa and pool designed to
Feng Shui principles.

****Hotel Sassongher, t** +39 0471 836085,
www.sassongher.it, is traditional with a
sound reputation.

***La Plaza, t** +39 0471 836011,
www.laplaza.it, is recommended.

***Hotel Grand Ciasa, t** +39 0471 836138,
www.granciasa.com, in Colfosco, is
recommended.

Courmayeur

Profile

**Lovely old town on the Italian side of
the Mont Blanc Tunnel, with dramatic
scenery but limited piste skiing. Suits
novices, low intermediates and experts.
Superb restaurants both on and off the
slopes and a lively nightlife**

Resort

Courmayeur is one of the great ski and
climbing villages of the Alps, an ancient
community situated just below the Italian
end of the Mont Blanc Tunnel at the foot
of the mightiest mountain in Western
Europe. Like nearby Chamonix, its
proximity by *autoroute* to Geneva airport
makes it popular with weekenders from
other countries, while Italians from Turin
arrive in numbers on Friday evenings.
Despite being no more than a 20-minute
drive from Chamonix, Courmayeur has an

entirely different weather pattern thanks
to the towering intervening presence of
Mont Blanc. The snow is not always as
good on the Italian side, but Courmayeur
gets much more sunshine during the
course of the winter.

The heart of the old village is the
cobbled and pedestrianized Via Roma that
is lined with boutiques, bars, delicatessens
and expensive interior decoration and
antique shops. Steep and narrow cobbled
alleyways lead off on either side. Eating is
the alternative occupation to skiing, with
Courmayeur boasting the best mountain
restaurants of any Italian resort as well a
delightful choice of evening eateries. Its
downside is the main arterial road that
separates the town from the ski area.
Choose where you stay with care to avoid
the midnight chorus of gear changes
from trucks and cars trundling to and
from the tunnel. To get the best out of the
skiing in the region you need a car. It's
best to invest in the more expensive
regional lift pass that also covers other
resorts in the Aosta Valley such as Pila,
Champoluc and Gressoney, as well as La
Thuile and linked La Rosière in France.

Mountain

A cable-car from Courmayeur provides mountain access to Plan Chécrouit, the main hub of this moderately compact ski area facing Mont Blanc. A blue piste brings you down again to the valley – not to the cable-car but to Dolonne on the far side of the main road from where you must take a bus to return to Courmayeur. Therefore it is better to download by cable-car at the end of the day, but skis and boots can be left at Plan Chécrouit. You can also reach the mountain by another cable-car from Entrèves, nearer to the tunnel, or by chair-lift from Zerotta in the Val Veny.

From Plan Chécrouit, a small network of lifts takes you up to Col Chécrouit at 2256m. Two ancient cable-cars rise to higher Cresta Youla and Cresta d'Arp. The latter is the 2755m starting point for some outstanding off-piste runs that take you down through 1500 of vertical to Dolonne or through the scenic Vallon de Youla to the village of la Balme just outside La Thuile at the foot of the Petit-St-Bernard pass. These itinerary runs require no special technical skills, but it's easy to get lost and the risk of avalanche is ever present. It makes sense to ski them with a local guide.

Other lifts from Plan Chécrouit bring you to the shoulder of 2343m Mont Chétif for the pick of Courmayeur's piste skiing – mainly red and black runs leading down towards the Val Veny with magnificient views of Mont Blanc.

A dedicated nursery slope served by the Chiecco drag-lift at Plan Chécrouit is in a secluded position on the edge of the piste. But novices and wobbly second-weekers must otherwise contend with a heavy amount of traffic converging on the mid-mountain station. More easy slopes are to be found at the top of the Maison Vieille chair-lift.

In the right snow conditions, Val Veny slopes offer hours of entertainment, with a few surprisingly challenging pistes such as the black Pista dell'Orso and Diretta. However, accomplished skiers and riders will soon tire of the limited piste skiing available from Plan Chécrouit.

They should head to the other side of Courmayeur to ride the three-stage Mont Blanc cable-car at La Palud, near the village of Entrèves. This takes you all the way up to Punta Helbronner at 3462m where you can descend the Vallée Blanche to Chamonix – without having to negotiate the infamous ice-steps on the French side. A cluster gondola connects Punta Helbronner to the Aiguille du Midi enabling you to make your way back to Italy by lift, or on skis by the Toula Glacier.

A number of descents of varying difficulty and danger are possible on the Italian side of Mont Blanc and you are strongly recommended to use a local guide. Spectacular heli-skiing is also possible from a number of fixed drops above the Val Veny. There is a snowcross course served by the Plan de la Grabba chair and a new rail park by the Le Greye drag above Plan Chécrouit. Val Ferrat, at the foot of the Grandes Jorasses a few minutes' drive from Courmayeur, is the setting for 30km of spectacular cross-country trails.

Learn

Monte Bianco, t +39 0165 842477, and **Courmayeur, t** +39 0165 848254, are the main schools. Both have a sound reputation for teaching modern technique. However, not all instructors are fluent English speakers. **Interski, t** +44 (0)1623 456333, is a British tour operator with its own school. Guiding is available from **Società delle Guide Alpine di Courmayeur, t** +39 0165 842064, and heli-skiing with **Air Vallée, t** +39 0165 869814.

Children

Kinderheim, t +39 0165 842477 at Plan Chécrouit cares for children from six months to 12 years with an alternative pick-up and drop-off point at the foot of the cable-car. Both Italian ski schools give lessons to children from four years.

Lunch

Courmayeur has the best value-for-money mountain eateries anywhere in the world. **Rifugio Maison Vieille, t** +39 0337 230979, serves grilled meat and fine pasta and has a big wood-burning stove. **Hotel Christiania, t** +39 0165 843572, at Plan Chécrouit is a gastronomic delight. **Chiecco, t** +39 347 2800579, is warmly recommended. **La Grolla, t** +39 0165 869095, on the Val Veny side has lots of atmosphere and fine cuisine. On the Mont Blanc side, **Rifugio Pavillon, t** +39 0165 844090, at the top of the first stage of the cable-car, has a sunny terrace and great food. **Rifugio Torino, t** +39 0165 844034, at the second stage, is also recommended.

Dine

Pierre Alexis 1877, t +39 0165 843517, is the top eatery in town and has a particularly extensive wine list. **Cadran Solaire, t** + 39 0165 844609, is a close contender for cuisine and atmosphere. **Mont Frèty, t** +39 0165 841786, and **La Terrazza, t** +33 0165 843330, are also recommended. **La Maison de Filippo, t** +39 0165 869797, in the suburb of Entrèves, is an exercise in unparalleled gluttony; it offers a fixed-price menu of more than 30 courses.

Party

The **American Bar** and the **Bar Roma** with its comfortable sofas and armchairs, are busy throughout the evening. **Cadran Solaire** attracts the smart crowd while the **Red Lion** is a more basic pub. **Les Privé, Bar Posta** and **Bar delle Guide** both have lots of atmosphere. I **Maquis** in Entrèves is the best nightspot. **Jimmy Night Café, Planet** and **Poppy's** are the others.

Sleep

****Gran Baita, t** +39 0165 844040, *www.sogliahotels.com*, is comfortable but inconveniently positioned outside the town.

****Hotel Pavillon, t** +39 0165 846120, *www.pavillon.it*, has a swimming-pool and a sauna.

****Royal e Golf, t** +39 0165 831611, *www.royalegolf.com*, is close to the centre.

***Hotel Courmayeur, t** +39 0165 846732, *www.hotelcourmayeur.com*, is welcoming, with an open fire in the sitting room.

***Bouton d'Or, t** +39 0165 846729, *www.hotelboutondor.com*, is a firm favourite in a quiet location close to the centre. It doesn't have a restaurant but arranges half-board in a choice of restaurants.

***Auberge de la Maison, t** +39 0165 869811, *www.aubergemaison.it*, in the quiet little hamlet of Entrèves, has attractively decorated rooms, and friendly owners.

***Hotel Dolonne, t** +39 0165 846674, *www.hoteldolonne.com*, is a luxury family hotel in the hamlet of the same name. It has some interesting antiques and log fires.

***Hotel Meublé Laurent, t** +39 0165 846687, *www.meublelaurent.com*, is traditional, cosy and clean.

Kronplatz

Profile

A ski area rather than a single resort in the South Tyrol that has the most sophisticated network of gondolas in the world, but is largely unknown outside Italy and Germany

Resort

Kronplatz is one of the great secrets of the South Tyrol. It is the top Italian ski resort for Germans, but remains virtually unknown elsewhere. The dome-shaped mountain, also known as Plan de Corones, is a ski area rather than a single centre. Accommodation is in the nearby town of Bruneck (Brunico) and in a dozen small villages around the mountain base. Only St Vigilio di Marebbe is Italian-speaking.

Mountain

Kronplatz has a remarkable 19 gondolas – most of them state-of-the-art. Along with 12 chairs and drags they are capable of ferrying enormous numbers of skiers to the summit. Most of the descents are undemanding, but the black Sylvester and the Herrneg roller-coaster provide challenge. Mountain access by gondola is from Olang, Reischach or St Vigilio.

Learn

Olang-Rasen, t +39 0474 592091, teaches new technique in a friendly manner. The other schools are **Kronplatz**, t +39 0474 548474, **San Vigilio**, t +39 0474 501049, **Sporting Al Plan**, t +39 0474 501448, **Cima**, t +39 0474 497216, and **Gsieser Tal**, t +39 0474 948142.

Essentials

Altitude: 900m (2,953ft)–2275m (7,464ft)
Further information: t +39 0474 555447, *www.kronplatz.com*
Lifts in area: 31 (19 cableways, 6 chairs, 6 drags) serving 85km of piste; 450 lifts in Dolomiti Superski area
Lift pass: Dolomiti Superski adult €171–194, child 8–16yrs €120–136, both for 6 days
Access: Innsbruck airport 1hr 45mins. Station at Bruneck 10mins

Children

Croniworld, t +39 0474 548474, on the summit, cares for children from three to eight years. The villages of Olang-Rasen and St Vigilio both have kindergartens.

Lunch

CAI-Hütte, t +39 0474 554836, at the top of the Kronplatzbahn, is good value. **Ciola Grill, t** + 39 0474 501701, above St Vigilio, is recommended.

Dine

In Olang, **Pizzeria Petrus, t** +39 0474 496202, and **Christl, t** +39 0474 498212, are praised. In San Vigilio, **Fana Ladina, t** +39 0474 501175, specializes in Ladino cuisine. In Bruneck, **Zum Goldener Löwen, t** +39 0474 555834, is popular.

Party

In Reischach, German-style après-ski begins before the lifts close at **Après Ski Tenne, Igli Bar Gigger, K1** and **Pub Hardimitz'n**. Olang has a similar scene at **Ski Toni** and **Skistadl**. Lively **Igloo** is in St Vigilio. Bruneck has a more cosmopolitan choice of bars and discos.

Sleep

Olang:

★★★★Hotel Mirabell, t +39 0474 496191, *www.mirabell.it*, has a first-rate spa.

★★★★Hotel Post, t +39 0474 496127, *www.post-tolderhof.com*, has comfortable rooms and a separate six-bedroom Art Nouveau villa.

St Vigilio:

★★★★Wellness Hotel Almhof Call, t +39 0474 501043, *www.almhof-call.com*, has a swimming-pool built into the rocks.

★★★★Parc Hotel Posta, t +39 0474 501010, *www.parchotel-posta.com*, is family-friendly.

Bruneck:

★★★★Royal Hotel Hinterhuber, t +39 0474 541000, *www.royal-hinterhuber.com*, is traditional.

★★★★Hotel Petrus, t +39 0474 548263, *www.hotelpetrus.com*, has a warm atmosphere.

Livigno

Profile

Most remote and cheapest of all Alpine resorts, with good beginner and limited intermediate skiing. The town's duty-free status encourages an alcohol-fuelled nightlife

Resort

Duty-free Livigno is the cheapest and also the most inaccessible of all mainstream resorts in the Alps. Its fiscal privileges date back to 1600 and were confirmed by Napoleon in 1805 and the EC in 1960. The resort can compete comfortably on price with Andorra

Essentials

Altitude: 1820m (5,970ft)–2797m (9,177ft)
Further information: t +39 0342 052200, *www.livignoweb.com*
Lifts in area: 65 in Alta Valtellina (6 cableways, 28 chairs, 31 drags) serving 110km of piste
Lift pass: Alta Valtellina adult €138–163, child under 15yrs €97–113, both for 6 days
Access: Zurich airport 5hrs, Bergamo 4hrs. Station at Tirano 2½hrs.

although the Pyrenean principality has the edge on skiing and accessibility.

Nevertheless, Livigno is a great beginner area for anyone who wants to discover skiing or snowboarding without huge financial commitment.

The village is divided into the four hamlets of Santa Maria, San Antonio, San Rocco and Trepalle. Of these, San Antonio is the main resort rendezvous with the majority of hotels, bars and restaurants.

Mountain

On south-east-facing Carosello a gondola rises to 3000m and five chairs, including the new Federia, serve undulating slopes above the tree-line. The area is ideally suited to beginners who take their first slide on skis on a dozen nursery drags on Carosello. Intermediates will enjoy the steeper slopes on Monte Sponda and Il Mottolino.

Learn

The ski schools are **Top Club Mottolino**, t +39 0342 970822, **Azzura**, t +39 0342 996683, **Inverno/Estate**, t +39 0342 996276, **Livigno Italy**, t +39 0342 996767, and **Sci Livigno**, t +39 0342 996887.

Children

Peribimbi, t +39 0342 970711 cares for
non-skiers from 18 months to three years.
M'eating Point, t +39 0342 9997408
accepts children from three years. The ski
schools provide lessons from four years.

Lunch

Try **La Costaccia**, t +39 0342 997264 for
its outdoor barbecue. **Tea da Borch**, t +39
0342 997016, below Carosello, is
recommended.

Dine

The Michelin-rated **La Pioda**, t + 39 0342
997610 is close to San Rocco church. **La
Rusticana**, t +39 0342 996047 is renowned
for its pizzas. **La Vecchia Lanterna**, t +39
0342 996103 has lots of atmosphere and
is good value.

Party

Tea del Vidal and **Galli's** are the busiest
bars. **Kokodi** and **Il Cielo** provide the late-
night entertainment.

Sleep

★★★★**Hotel Amerikan**, t +39 0342 996521,
www.amerikan.it, has a wellness centre.
★★★★**Hotel Concordia Lungolivigno**, t +39
0342 990100, *www.lungolivigno.com*,
has attractive rooms.
★★★★**Hotel Intermonti**, t +39 0342 972100,
www.valfin.it, is in four chalets on the
hillside.
★★★★**Hotel Spöl Charme and Relax**, t +39
0342 996105, *www.hotelspol.it*, is in the
town centre with a good spa.
★★★**Hotel Villaggio San Carlo**, t +39 0342
972000, *www.valfin.it*, is set in seven
chalets linked by internal corridors.

Madonna di Campiglio

Profile

Smart, traditional resort with good
snowboarding that attracts wealthy
skiers from Verona, Venice and Milan.
Excellent hotels, good restaurants and a
lively nightlife, but lack of kindergarten
means it is not suited to families with
small children

Resort

Madonna has a traditional charm and
village ambience that attracts a curious
combination of older skiers and young
snowboarders who return here year after
year – one in search of easy cruising and
bodily comforts, the other for some of the
best riding in Italy. The first chair-lift
opened for business here in 1948 and it
has been a popular resort with an
international clientele since the 1960s. In
what is already considered an expensive
resort by Italian standards prices have
steadily risen since the introduction of
the euro.

Essentials

Altitude: 1520m (4,987ft)–2505m (8,219ft)
Further information: t +39 0465 447501,
www.campiglio.it
Lifts in area: 21 (5 cableways, 11 chairs,
5 drags) serving 90km of piste; 140 lifts
in whole Skirama region serving 340km
of piste
Lift pass: Superskirama adult €167–188.50,
child 8–15yrs €135–151.50
Access: Verona airport 2½hrs. Station at
Trento 80km

The village fathers have now solved the problem of through traffic that used to plague the resort. A bypass has returned it to the congenial little mountain community that it used to be. New buildings blend well with the old. Its wealthy guests demand and get a high standard of hotels. You can eat well here and, for those who live life in the fast track, the nightlife is livelier than in most other Italian resorts. Racing driver Michael Schumacher is a regular visitor who beats his minders around the resort's go-kart track when not skiing.

The resort is situated in the Brenta Dolomites, well to the west of the Sella Ronda, and is not included in the giant Dolomiti Superski lift pass. It is reached by a 75km serpentine climb from the Brenner–Verona *autostrada* through galleried tunnels and past spectacular drops. Along with Cortina d'Ampezzo Madonna attracts more glitterati than any other resorts in Italy. Like Cortina, not all its smart clientele venture on to the slopes. Shopping and eating out have both been raised to an art form, while skating on the scenic little lake provides alternative activity. Madonna is much smaller than Cortina, but has a considerably more modern lift system and far better snowboarding facilities. The first terrain park was created here as long ago as 1993, and committed riders from all over the country gather each winter in the current park in the Grosté area.

Mountain

Madonna is officially rated the top resort in Italy for piste-grooming. This makes it popular with its slightly older than average clientele who revel in some of the most flattering slopes of the Dolomites. What at first sight appear to be three entirely separate ski areas covering the slopes on three sides of the village, are in fact cunningly linked at valley level. The link is created by a snow-cannon-maintained piste that winds from one area to the other beneath a series of road bridges. A link to neighbouring Pinzolo is also being built.

The first area, 5 Laghi, is reached by a five-minute cable-car ride from the centre of the village. This takes you up to a *rifugio* of the same name, the starting point for an easy blue run that brings you to the Patascoss quad-chair. The 3-Tre piste from the top has a couple of sharp bends and dramatic changes in gradient. On the lower half of the mountain this red run turns a wicked shade of black as it becomes the notorious Canalone Miramonti, which used to be used as a World Cup course. The bottom half can also be reached by a double chair-lift. The run is floodlit for night skiing.

From the northern end of town, a modern 12-person gondola takes you up to Pradalago at 2100m, the largest of the three ski areas. It is linked to the neighbouring resorts of Marilleva and Folgarida. Direct return to the resort is by the always challenging Amazzonia black, which crosses beneath the gondola. Less accomplished skiers and riders take the blue Pradalago Facile run, which follows a much gentler line around the shoulder. Two quad-chairs and a couple of drags access a pleasant mixture of easy and intermediate runs on Pradalago. Skiers heading for Marilleva and Folgarida, in the larger Skirama area, follow the red Genziana piste down to Malga Vigo.

The third area of Monte Spinale/Grosté is on the opposite side of the valley and is reached by a two-stage gondola from the east side of town. At 2443m this is the high point of the ski area. Cima Grosté and Corna Rossa, two short red pistes at the top, are served by a new six-person chair. The linked area of Monte Spinale can also be reached by gondola from the resort. Spinale direttissima, beneath the gondola, is one of the most enjoyable black runs in the resort.

Learn

The eight schools here all compete vigorously with each other for customers but none stands out as being better than any of the rest. In general, the standard of teaching in Italian resorts does not reflect the enormous advances in equipment that has led to basic changes in technique. The school are **Adamello Brenta**, t +39 0465 443412, **Campiglio**, t +39 0465 446272, **Campo Carlo Magno**, t +39 0465 443222, **5 Laghi**, t +39 0465 441650, **Des Alpes**, t +39 0465 442850, **Nazionale**, t +39 0465 443243, **Professional Snowboarding**, t +39 0465 443251, and **Rainalter**, t +39 0465 443300.

Children

All the ski schools offer lessons for children, but there is currently no kindergarten. Babysitting can be arranged through the tourist office.

Lunch

Try **Cascina Zeledria**, t +39 0465 440303, just above the woods on Pradalago below Piste No.7. Artini, the owner, is a well-known local chef specializing in regional Trentino dishes. If you are lucky, you will get a tow by snowmobile back up to the piste. **Giorgio Graffer**, t +39 0465 440 539, on the blue run down from the top of Grosté, is a classic mountain refuge with homemade local dishes. **Rifugio Malga Montagnoli**, t +39 0465 443355, at the bottom of Marchi black run on Monte Spinale, is one of the better self-service mountain restaurants in the area.

Dine

Dine at **Da Alfiero**, t +39 0465 440117, which is known for its homemade spaghetti dishes and for lamb cutlets in balsamic vinegar with asparagus. **Al Sottobosco**, t +39 0465 440737, is a kilometre from town, but worth the journey for its *pappardelle ai mirtilli e funghi porcini* (broad ribbons of pasta with blueberries and porcini mushrooms). **Artini**, t +39 0465 440122, is famed for its *risotto ai funghi* and its chocolate *crêpes*. **Al Sarca**, t +39 0465 440287, has wonderful homemade salami, grilled alpine trout, and *panna cotta* with woodland fruits. **Antico Focolare**, t +39 0465 441686, has a warm ambience and serves typical Trentino dishes including venison and *polenta* with gorgonzola and mushrooms. **La Locanda degli Artisti**, t +39 0465 442980, has lots of atmosphere and good food at low prices.

You can take a ride by snowcat at night to eat in **Cascina Zeledria** or three other cowsheds that have been converted into mountain restaurants – **Malga Montagnoli**, t +39 0465 443355, **Boch**, t +39 0465 440465, and **Malga Ritorto**, t +39 0465 442470.

Party

Bar Suisse, **La Cantina del Suisse** and the **Franz-Josef Stube** are the main après-ski haunts. **The Zangola**, situated in a converted cow shed 3km out of town, is one of the most famous discos in the Alps.

Sleep

* ★★★★**Alpen Suite Hotel**, t +39 0465 440100, *www.alpensuitehotel.it*, has 28 one-bedroom suites, each with its own sitting room.
* ★★★★**Hotel Bertelli**, t +39 0465 441 013, *www.hotelbertelli.it*, dates back to the

1930s. Completely rebuilt in 1999, it is a traditional family hotel situated just 50m from the Pradalago cable-car.

★★★★Biohotel Hermitage, t +39 0465 44 1558, *www.chalethermitage.com*, has been in the Maffei family for over 100 years and has been refurbished as an eco hotel. It is situated over a kilometre from the resort but operates a bus service to the lifts and shops. Local dishes and homemade pasta are a speciality of the restaurant.

★★★★Hotel Relais Club des Alpes, t +39 0465 440000, *www.relaisdesalpes.it*, is also in a ski-in ski-out position in the middle of the resort.

★★★★Hotel Lorenzetti, t +39 0465 441404, is on the edge of the piste and on the outskirts of the village.

★★★★Palace Hotel, t +39 0465 441004, *www.savoiapalace.com*, 50m from the Cinque Laghi cable-car, is a favourite with British visitors.

★★★★Spinale Club Hotel, t +39 0465 441116, *www.editeltn.it/hotelspinale*, is situated close to the resort centre and the skiing.

★★★Hotel Bellavista, t +39 0465 441034, *www.bellavistacampiglio.it*, has a friendly atmosphere and is opposite the Pradalago cable-car station.

★★★Grazia Hotel Plaza, t +39 0465 443100, is comfortable and conveniently located in the village centre.

Ortisei

Profile

Lowest and one of the most attractive of the Val Gardena villages, with links into both the Sella Ronda and the scenic Alpe de Siusi ski areas

Essentials

Altitude: 1236m (4,055ft)–2949m (9,676ft)
Map: see Selva page M44
Further information: t +39 0471 796328, *www.valgardena.it*
Lifts in area: 83 (10 cableways, 36 chairs, 37 drags) serving 176km of piste; 450 lifts in Dolomiti Superski
Lift pass: Dolomiti Superski adult €171–194, child 8–16yrs €120–136, both for 6 days
Access: Verona airport 2hrs. Station at Bolzano 1hr

Resort

Ortisei in the Val Gardena is a pretty alternative to nearby Selva. You can enjoy the skiing of the Sella Ronda but also have direct access to the more secluded Alpe di Siusi. Pastel-painted and ornately frescoed buildings flank the pedestrianized main street and central piazza. Escalators and walkways provide easy access to the lifts.

Mountain

A long gondola, followed by a cable-car, takes you up over a dramatic cliff face to 2518m Seceda. From here, you can either return to Ortisei, or continue to Pla da Tieja above Santa Cristina. This is the terminal for the new underground funicular that effectively links Ortisei into the Sella Ronda and beyond.

On the southern edge of Ortisei, reached by a new pedestrian bridge, a gondola acts as the gateway to the Alpe di Siusi. From the top station, you can reach Compatsch on the Alpe di Siusi plateau where a handful of modern hotels have sprung up in recent years.

Learn

Ortisei, t +39 0471 796153 and **Saslong**, t +39 0471 786258 schools provide adequate instruction.

Children

Ortisei Ski School Miniclub cares for children from two years. **Hotel Cavallino Bianco Miniclub**, t +39 0471 783333, cares for children from one month to 12 years.

Lunch

Try **Sofie Hütte**, t +39 335 5271240, at Seceda and **Rifugio Col Raiser**, t +39 0471 796302, above Pla da Tieja. On the Alpe di Siusi side, stop at the **Sanon Hütte**, t +39 0471 727002, or **Mont Seuc** at the top of the gondola.

Dine

Anna Stuben, t +39 0471 796315, in the Hotel Gardena-Grödnerhof, serves local specialities. **Tubladel**, t +39 0471 796879, is in a converted hay barn. **La Rosticceria**, t +39 335 6174467, is renowned for its grilled meat and fish. **Concordia**, t +39 0471 796276, smokes its own game and ham. **Vedl Mulin**, t +39 0471 796089, is a popular pizzeria.

Party

Seceda and **Siglu**, at the Cavallino Bianco, are the main après-ski rendezvous.

Sleep

★★★★**Hotel Adler**, t +39 0471 775050, *www.hotel-adler.com*, is an elegant place with an impressive spa.
★★★★**Hotel Cavallino Bianco**, t +39 0471 783333, *www.cavallino-bianco.com*, has

the most comprehensive child facilities of any ski resort.
★★★★★**Hotel Gardena-Grödnerhof**, t +39 0471 796315, *www.gardena.it*, was completely rebuilt in 2001.
★★★★**Hotel Hell**, t +39 0471 796785, *www.hotelhell.it*, is situated in a heavenly ski-in, ski-out position.
★★★**Hotel Arnaria**, t +39 0471 796649, *www.arnaria.com*, is a family-run pension.
★★★**Hotel Digon**, t +39 0471 797266, *www.hoteldigon.com*, is recently renovated.

Passo Tonale

Profile

Unprepossessing high-altitude village with snow-sure skiing from late October until early May, as well as year-round summer skiing on the Presena Glacier

Resort

Passo Tonale is situated at the western end of the Val di Sole and its high altitude

Essentials

Altitude: 1883m (6,178ft)–3069m (10,069ft)
Further information: t +39 0364 903838, *www.valdisole.net*
Lifts in area: 28 (1 cableway, 19 chairs, 7 drags) serving 100km of piste
Lift pass: Area (includes Madonna di Campiglio, Marilleva/Folgarida and five other resorts) adult €167–188.50, child from 8yrs €99–114. All for 6 days
Access: Verona airport 2½hrs. Station at Edolo 30mins

makes it one of the most snow-sure resorts in Italy. National ski teams train here and it has a strong international following. The resort opens from late October until the beginning of May, but summer skiing continues throughout the year on the Presena Glacier.

Mountain

Passo Tonale has plenty of beginner and intermediate terrain, with access by cable-car to Passo Paradiso, where a chair and three drags bring you to the 3069m summit. From here, long runs lead back to the village over high-altitude terrain. On the other side of the main road, the south-facing slopes are served by a sequence of chairs and drags over undulating pastures. One chair takes you to the old smuggling route of Passo Contrabbandieri at 2681m. You can ski down to the village of Ponte di Legno, which has easy terrain. A gondola link is planned, but for the present skiers must return by bus.

Learn

Tonale-Presena, t +39 0364 903991, Pontedilegno-Tonale, t +39 0364 903943, and Castellaccio, t +39 0364 900302, have good reputations. 6punto9, t +39 335 803604, is the snowboarding specialist.

Children

Miniclub, t +39 0364 900501, in Hotel Miramonti cares for non-resident children from newborn to three years. It will also offer free daycare for older children if they are hotel guests. Fantaski, t +39 0364 903991, is the ski kindergarten.

Lunch

Ristorante Erica, t +39 0364 91460, at the foot of the Paradiso cable-car and Capanna Presena, t +39 0463 758299, at the top are both recommended.

Dine

Try Ristorante Rododendro, t +39 0364 900259, and Serodine, t +39 0364 903724. Reporters praised pizzeria Antares, t +39 0364 903789, and Il Focalare, t +39 0364 903790.

Party

The resort is friendly and unpretentious. Try the Umbrella Bar after skiing. Baita Faita and Nico's are popular resort rendezous. Disco-Pub Miramonti and Heaven are usually crowded. Antares has live music, and Bar Paninoteca Cantuccio stays open until 6am.

Sleep

****Grand Hotel Miramonti, t +39 0364 900501, www. miramonti.com, is the best hotel in town.

***Hotel La Mirandola, t +39 0364 903933, is in old hospice up the mountain with snowmobile transport until 2am.

***Hotel Orchidea, t +39 0364 903935, www.hotelorchidea.net is a comfortable family-run establishment.

***Hotel Panorama Edelweiss, t +39 0364 903789, www.panoramaedelweiss.com, offers good food.

San Cassiano

Profile

Small, sophisticated village that shares its intermediate ski area with larger La Villa. Both are renowned for their designer hotels and gourmet restaurants

Resort

San Cassiano is a quiet, sophisticated village just off the main Sella Ronda circuit. Larger La Villa shares its immediate ski area, which is linked to Armentarola and Corvara. They make an attractive holiday base but links to and from the Sella Ronda from San Cassiano are frustratingly slow.

Mountain

Mountain access from San Cassiano and La Villa is by gondola and, even during peak season, queues are rare. In San Cassiano the lift station is a 10-minute walk from the centre but the main hotels operate a courtesy minibus service. The immediate ski area consists of gentle pistes above and below the tree-line that are ideally suited to beginners and to intermediates who want the feeling of 'going somewhere' each day.

Learn

The choice lies between **San Cassiano**, t +39 0471 849491, **La Villa**, t +39 0471 847258 **Pedraces**, t +39 0471 839648, and **Dolomites**, t +39 0471 844018, ski schools.

Children

La Villa ski school runs a kindergarten and miniclub. **Dolomites ski school** has a playground on Piz La Villa. **Casa Bimbo,** t +39 0471 838096, in **Pedraces** cares for babies and children up to 11 years.

Lunch

Try **Rifugio Scotoni**, t +39 0471 847330, above Armentarola for barbecued meat. Also recommended is the nearby **Capanna Alpina**, t +39 0471 847330. **Malga Saraghes**, t +39 335 7897164, above San Cassiano, has outstanding homemade pasta.

Essentials

Altitude: 1537m (5,043ft)–2949m (9,676ft)
Map: see Selva, page M44
Further information: t +39 0471 849422, *www.altabadia.org*
Lifts in area: 52 in Alta Badia (9 cableways, 29 chairs, 14 drags) serving 130km of piste; 450 lifts in Dolomiti Superski
Lift pass: Dolomiti Superski adult €171–194, child 8–16yrs €120–136, both for 6 days
Access: Verona airport 2½ hrs

Dine

In San Cassiano, **St Hubertus**, t +39 0471 849500, and **La Siriola**, t +39 0471 849445, have Michelin stars. In La Villa, **Ciastel Colz**, t +39 0471 84 7511, serves South Tyrol cuisine with gourmet flair.

Party

The **Rosa Alpina** and **Siriola** both have wine bars. **Franz de la Vedla** and **Hug's bar** are both popular meeting places. In La Villa the evening action is centred around **Durni's Pub** and **La Bercia**.

Sleep

San Cassiano:

★★★★Rosa Alpina, t +39 0471 849500, *www.rosaalpina.it*, epitomises the new wave of first-rate hotels being established in the Dolomites.

★★★★Dolomiti Wellness Hotel Fanes, t +39 0471 849470, *www.hotelfanes.it*, offers good child reductions.

★★★Hotel Conturines-Posta, t +39 0471 849464, *www.conturines.it*, is family-run.

La Villa:

★★★★Ciastel Colz, t +39 0471 84 75 11, *www.colz.siriolagroup.it*, is a magnificently restored early 16th-century castle with four bedrooms.

★★★La Majun, t +39 0471 847030, *www.lamajun.it* has quirky interior design and a swimming-pool lined with flagstones.

★★★Hotel La Villa, t +39 0471 847035, *www.hotel-lavilla.it*, has a wellness area.

Sauze d'Oulx

Profile

Important value-for-money component of the giant Milky Way ski area with plenty of high-mileage cruising, decent restaurants and wild nightlife. Suits 20- and 30-somethings in search of piste and party

Resort

Sauze d'Oulx has a longstanding and justified reputation as one of the winter party capitals, a place where pub culture takes precedence, despite valiant attempts over many years by the village fathers to engineer a more family-oriented environment. Sauze is one of the main resorts of the 88-lift Milky Way circuit that straddles the border with France and provides a mighty 400km of groomed runs. Much the best skiing in the region is found here, but the privilege of playing principal host to the XX Winter Olympics next February goes to nearby Sestriere. Instead Sauze must be content with being the venue for the aerials and moguls competitions.

The original medieval town has considerable charm but the more recent buildings adjacent to the slopes are far from sympathetic to their beautiful mountain environment. Skiing here inevitably involves a lot of walking, and the resort bus service is not included in the weekly lift pass.

Mountain

The Milky Way will benefit considerably from being chosen to host the Games, but beyond a new piste and lift for the freestyle events and some improved snowmaking, Sauze is not a major beneficiary.

From the village, a sequence of chair-lifts take you up to the mid-mountain hub of Sportinia for access to Cesana and

Essentials

Altitude: 1509m (4,951ft)–2507m (8,225ft)

Map see page M48

Further information: t +39 0122 850700, *www.comune.sauzedoulx.to.it*

Lifts in area: 88 in Milky Way (5 cableways, 38 chairs, 45 drags) serving 400km of piste

Lift pass: Milky Way (covers Montgenèvre, Sestriere, Sauze d'Oulx and other smaller resorts) adult €145–163, child 8–12yrs €72.50–81.50, both for 6 days

Access: Turin airport 60mins. Station at Oulx 5km, regular buses to resort

Sestriere. Other lifts rise from the village to Clotes and the open slopes of Pian della Rocca, as well as to the secluded and nearly always uncrowded sector beneath 2540m Mont Genevris. On busy high-season weekends, this is where you where you will find the locals. The Sauze d'Oulx slopes face west and north, and the majority of them are below the tree-line. Sportinia is in effect a higher satellite with hotels, restaurants and good nursery slopes.

The resort quite wrongly has a 'novice' label attached to it. In fact, the majority of the runs are graded intermediate, and it is an excellent playground for accomplished skiers and riders looking for high mileage. Some of the best skiing is found between Sportinia and Sansicario. Good skiers will also want to journey on across the Monti della Luna to Montgenèvre in France. The new gondola linking Sestriere with Monte Fraiteve also allows for a swift return from Sestriere to Sauze. However, anyone thinking of staying in Sauze this February and commuting on skis to watch the main Alpine events will be disappointed. Sestriere has announced plans to restrict its lift system on race days to racers and their entourage.

Learn

Scuola Sauze d'Oulx, t +39 0122 858084, has an excellent reputation for teaching up-to-date technique. The others are Sauze Project, t +39 0122 858942, and Sauze Sportinia, t +39 0122 850218. Not all instructors speak good English. Guide Alpine Valsusa, t +39 0335 398984, and Elisusa Heli-skiing, t +39 0122 623162, are the off-piste specialists.

Children

Piccolo Dumbo, t +39 347 691 3531, and La Cinciarella, t + 39 328 6445146, accept children from 13 months. All the ski schools offer children's lessons from four years.

Lunch

Chalet Il Capricorno, t +39 0122 850273, at the top of the Clotes piste, is renowned for chef Maria Rosa Sacchi's handmade ravioli and is much the best restaurant on the mountain. Ciao Pais, t +39 0122 850280, at Clotes is recommended. Capanna Kind, t +39 0122 850206, and La Tana dell'Orso, t +39 0122 850226, at Sportinia are favourites with reporters.

Dine

Del Falco, t +39 0122 858063, and Del Borgo, t + 39 0122 858318, have a warm atmosphere and good food. Gran Villar, t + 39 0122 858822, and La Griglia, t + 39 0122 850344, are also recommended.

Party

The New Scotch Bar at the foot of the slopes is a resort institution.

Wine Bar Gran Trun and Village Café have live bands. The Grotto, the bar of Hotel Derby, and The Cotton Club are ever popular. Osteria dei Vagabondi has live music. Schuss Disco, Gina-Il Bandito, Paddy McGinty's and Queen's Lounge are the late-night venues.

Sleep

★★★★Il Capricorno, t +39 0122 850273, is a comfortable boutique hotel in an isolated position on the Clotes piste.

★★★★Gran Baita, t +39 0122 850183, is praised as 'excellent – very clean, the staff are pleasant'.

★★★★Hotel Relais des Alpes, t + 39 0122 859747, www.gestioniabc.it, in the resort centre, was recently renovated.

****La Torre, t** +39 0122 859816, is one of Sauze's most comfortable establishments, although we have mixed reports of the half-board food.

***Hotel Miravalle, t** +39 0122 858530, *www.gestioniabc.it*, has been recently refurbished and has excellent cuisine.

***Hotel Sauze, t** +39 0122 850285, *www.gestioniabc.it*, near the Clotes piste, has been completely refurbished.

***Hotel Splendid, t** +39 0122 850172, *www.gestioniabc.it*, is in a quiet position, with a swimming-pool.

***Hotel Stella Alpina, t** +39 0122 858731, *www.stellalpinahotel.it*, is slope-side with a good atmosphere. The owner's wife is British.

***Parc Hotel Gran Bosco, t** +39 0122 850166, *www.sauzedoulx.org/granbosco*, 1km out of town, has a courtesy bus, good food and friendly staff.

****Hotel Meublé Gran Trun, t** +39 0122 850016, has simple rustic-style rooms above the wine bar of the same name, and suits night- owls but not families.

****Hotel Hermitage, t** +39 0122 850385, *www.sauzedoulx.org/hermitage*, on the piste at Clote, is clean and comfortable.

****Hotel Miosotis, t** +39 0122 850288, *www.gestioniabc.it*, is conveniently situated for lifts to Clotes and Sportinia.

Chalet Faure, t +39 0122 859760, *www.chaletfaure.it*, is full of atmosphere, with some split-level bedrooms and a spa.

Selva Gardena

Profile

One of the best-known resorts of the vast Sella Ronda ski circuit. The resort has good family facilities and some good mountain restaurants

Resort

Selva, also known as Wolkenstein, is a rather bland resort that stretches without a heart along the busy road between Bolzano and Corvara and links almost seamlessly to neighbouring villages of Santa Cristina and Ortisei. However, the high number of hotel beds and rental chalets coupled with direct access into the Sella Ronda make it a popular and convenient base from which to explore the core of the Dolomites

Selva is the setting each December for the Val Gardena Downhill, traditionally one of the earliest European venues of the season for the Men's World Cup. Britain's Konrad Bartelski famously took second place on the podium here back in 1981.

This does much to publicise the resort but gives a false impression that the skiing here is demanding. In fact the area is best suited to beginners, intermediates and to families looking for a bustling resort with a moderate amount of nightlife and plenty of alternative activities.

Essentials

Altitude: 1563m (5,128ft)–1800m
Map: see page M44
Further information: t +39 0471 795122 *www.valgardena.it*
Lifts in area: 83 in Selva Val Gardena (1 funicular, 9 cableways, 36 chairs, 37 drags) serving 175km of piste. 450 in Dolomiti Superski area
Lift pass: Dolomiti Superski adult €171–194, child 8–16yrs €120–136, both for 6 days
Access: Innsbruck airport 120km, Verona airport 2½hrs

Mountain

Selva is one of the four compass point of the Sella Ronda, the 40km circuit around the Gruppo Selle massif. It takes around two hours of lifts to complete in either direction, plus or minus the joker factor of any queues. You take 13 lifts on the clockwise route and 15 lifts on the anti-clockwise. The amount of time actually spent skiing can be remarkably short – depending on your level of proficiency. You really don't need to be an accomplished skier to complete it. Anyone who has skied for three weeks should be able to achieve it, but you do need a moderate level of fitness.

Skiers travelling clockwise from Selva take a chair-lift followed by a long gondola up to 2300m Dantercepies to begin the long descent towards Colfosco and Corvara beyond. Anti-clockwise skiers and riders take the Ciaminoi gondola for the easy piste down to Plan de Gralba in the direction of Passo Pordoi and Arabba. You can also leave the circuit to explore the Val di Fassa.

The Ciaminoi downhill course – it is an intermediate piste when not prepared for racing – brings you down to Santa Cristina and the terminal for the new Val Gardena Ronda Express, an underground funicular that gives skiers direct access to Ortisei's ski area. Ciaminoi and the adjoining Mont de Seura sector – reached this winter by a new quad-chair – provide some of the most scenic and enjoyable skiing in the valley.

Nursery slopes served by half-a-dozen short drags just above the resort provide a near perfect playground for the large number of beginners who come to Selva.

Learn

In Selva, the choice lies between **2000**, t +39 0471 773125 and **Ski & Boarders'**

Factory, t +39 0471 794257. We have mixed reports of both. In Santa Cristina **CIR**, t +39 0471 790184, and **Santa Cristina**, t +39 0471 792045, are less internationally oriented.

Children

Casa Bimbo, t +39 348 870 0661, run by the Santa Cristina school cares for children from 18 months. All the schools offer children's classes. Reporters praise the nursery slopes as 'brilliant'.

Lunch

Try **L'Medel**, t +39 0471 795235, on the piste of the same name. It is decorated with local mountain antiques. **Piz Sella**, t +39 0471 794115, is a wood-panelled restaurant with a warm atmosphere. **Rifugio Emilio Comici**, t +39 0471 794121, above Plan de Gralba, specialises in fresh fish. **Baita Panorama**, t +39 0471 795372, on the Dantacepies piste above Selva, has good homely fare.

Dine

Le Stuben, t +39 0471 795555, in Hotel Alpenroyal, offers a choice of five dining rooms, each with a different ambience ranging from Alpine hut to formal 17th-century country house. **Armin's Grillstube** in the Hotel Armin, t +39 0471 795347, has fine steaks. **Al Cervo**, t +39 0471 795086, **La Bula**, t +39 0471 795208, **Rino**, and **Stübele** are popular pizzerias. In Santa Cristina, **Bistro Susi**, t +39 0471 793703, is warmly recommended, along with **Da Peppi**, t +39 0471 793335.

Party

Laurinkeller, t +39 0471 795059, is the long-established resort rendezvous.

Umbrella Bar, t +39 0417 772200, in front
of Hotel Wolkenstein, and Igloo Bar, t +39
0471 795135, are ever crowded. In Santa
Cristina Crazy Pub, t +39 0338 6370581,
and Bar 2000, t +39 0471 793693 are the
liveliest bars.

Sleep

Selva:
*****Alpenroyal Sporthotel Gourmet &
Relax, t +39 0471 795555,
www.alpenroyal.com, has giant
swimming-a pool housed in an all-glass
conservatory The Eghes Spa offers an
exhaustive range of treatments.
****Acadia Beauty & Relax, t +39 0471
774444, www.acadia.it, has been run by
the Prinoth family for four generations.
****Granvara Sport & Wellness hotel,
t +39 0471 795250, www.granvara.com, is
in a quiet position on the edge of piste.
The owner also runs the 2000 ski
school.
****Sporthotel Gran Baita, t +39 0471
795210, www.hotelgranbaita.com, has
been looking after skiers since 1953.
****Sporthotel Maciaconi, t +39 0471
793500, www.hotelmaciaconi.com, has a
large pool, sauna and solarium.
***Hotel Armin, t +39 0471 795347,
www.hotelarmin.com, is friendly.
***Albergo Gruppo Sella, t +39 0471
795182, www.grupposella.com, situated
a couple of kilometres outside Selva at
Plan de Gralba, is owned by a former
Italian World Cup racer.
***Hotel Wolkenstein, t +39 0471 772200,
www.wolkenstein.it, is strong on après-
ski which can last deep into the night.
Santa Cristina:
****Alpenhotel Plaza, t +39 0471 793463,
www.alpenhotelplaza.com, is a new
hotel in the centre of the village.
****Hotel Diamant Port & Wellness, +39
0471 796780, www.hoteldiamant.it, is set
in an extensive private park.

***Charme-Hotel Uridi, t +39 0471 793215,
www.uridi.it, is recommended.

Sestriere

Profile

Setting this winter for the main Alpine
events in the Turin Winter Olympics, a
slightly austere high altitude ski village in
the Milky Way. Suits intermediates in
search of high-mileage cruising

Resort

Sestriere was purpose-built as a ski
resort in 1934 by the Agnelli family, which
founded Fiat. This winter it hosts the lion's
share of the Alpine events in the XX
Winter Olympics. To the consternation of
the Swiss, Turin was chosen over Sion in
Switzerland on the final ballot.
Discounting tales of jiggery-pokery, the
Turin bid – with Sestriere earmarked for
the Blue Riband events – was probably the
best on the table. It had the backing of
the Agnelli family and the promise of full
Fiat sponsorship.

Essentials

Altitude: 2035m, 6,675ft)–top 2823m,
(9,262ft)
Map: see page M48
Further information: t +39 0122 353099,
www.sestriere.it
Lifts in area: 88 in Milky Way (5 cableways,
38 chairs, 45 drags) serving 400km of
piste
Lift pass: Milky Way (covers Montgenèvre,
Sestriere, Sauze d'Oulx and other
smaller resorts) adult €145–163, child
8–12yrs €72.50–81.50, both for 6 days
Access: Turin airport 1½hrs. Station at Oulx
30 mins, buses to resort

But since then both Agnelli brothers who were successive chairmen of Fiat have died and the car company has fallen on hard times. Sestriere has soldiered solidly on with its preparations. New lifts have been built and a magnificent downhill course should provide the required thrills and spills. But you can't help but feel that the chassis has a design fault and the carriage work of the Fiat Games is failing to shine as it should. However, the Italians may well come right on the day – as they did for the Alpine World Skiing Championships in 1997.

Anyone planning to visit the Milky Way this February should note that skiing over from a neighbouring resort to watch events will not be feasible. While past hosts of the Winter Olympics have been actively at pains to point out that recreational skiing continues unaffected during the fortnight of the Games, Sestriere plans to close its lifts on race days to all but racers and their entourage.

Sestriere is the capital of the Milky Way or Via Lattea, an alliance of villages that straddle the Italian/French frontier between Turin and Briançon. The Olympic venue has the highest and most challenging skiing in the region, along with a level of sophistication that is lacking in neighbouring Sauze d'Oulx. When Giovanni Agnelli originally built the resort, the high-altitude site he chose had a good snow record. However, in these times of climate change, cover is not as reliable as it used to be.

The village is dominated by the twin towers of the original smart Torre and Duchi d'Aosta hotels. Club Med operated them for many years but has dropped Sestriere this season. A whole new athletes' village has been built just below the resort.

Mountain

The Milky Way in general and Sestriere in particular have benefited from preparations for the Olympics. A new eight-person gondola now connects Cesana to Sansicario in only eight minutes instead of 30 on the old Pariol and Forte chairs. Hopefully a 60-person cable-car will be completed in time, connecting the ancient outlying town Pragelato to Borgata.

The old, slow Trebials chair between Borgata and Sestriere has been upgraded to a detachable-quad. The Garnel drag-lift has by replaced by a chair from the Olympic Village up to Alpette, with a tunnel beneath the giant slalom piste. At Claviere, a new detachable quad-chair connects La Coche to Colle Bercia and lots more snow-cannon have been installed.

Sestriere's skiing is split into the Monte Motta and Monte Sises sectors. Both are reached by quad-chairs and offer skiing for all standards. The beginner slopes just above the village are particularly good, and Sestriere has a terrain park with a half-pipe and a snowcross course.

Best powder run in the Milky Way is the Rio Nero, which follows a river gully down to the Oulx–Cesana road from Monte Fraiteve. Heli-skiing is possible on the top of Valle d'Argentera and Val Thures.

Learn

Sestriere has four ski schools of which **Scuola Nazionale Sci Sestriere, t** +39 0122 77060 is much the largest, with focus on making lessons enjoyable. The others are **Borgata, t** +39 0122 77497, **Extrème, t** +39 0122 76214, and **Olimpionica, t** +39 0122 76116. Guiding can be arranged through **Guide Alpine Sestriere, t** +39 0335 6601940.

Children

Asilo Neve, t +39 0122 755444, cares for
children from two years and over.

Lunch

Try **Rifugio Alpette, t** +39 0122 755505,
for fresh pasta, **Chisonetto, t** +39 0122
76094, is renowned for its polenta. **La
Brua, t** +39 0122 76000, at **Grangesises** is
good, **La Gargotte, t** +39 0122 76888, is
expensive but worth it. **Lou Brachettes,
t** +39 0122 77598, and **La Tana della Volpe,
t** +39 335 362054, at the top of the
Banchetta cable-car is also recommended.

Dine

Ristorante Du Grand-Père, t +39 0122
755970, in the hamlet of Champlas
Janvier, specializes in local Piedmont
dishes. **Antica Osteria, t** +39 0122 785300,
in Pragelato, close to the site of the
proposed cable-car, is a converted
cowshed with a vaulted ceiling. **Le
Lanterne, t** +39 0122 795283, in
Grangesises, and **Pinky Pizzeria, t** +39 0122
76441, are recommended.

Party

Après-ski is quiet during the week but
picks up at weekends when young and
wealthy *Torinos* are in town. The **Kandahar**
bar beneath the Hotel du Col is stylish and
friendly. The infamous **Irish Igloo** and
Tabata provide the late-night
entertainment, spliced by inevitable
vodka-and-Red Bull.

Sleep

★★★★**Grand Hotel Sestriere, t** +39 0122
76476, *www.grandhotelsestriere.it*, has
been recently restored with a fine spa.

★★★★**Hotel Cristallo, t** +39 0122 750707,
www.newlinehotels.com, has small
rooms but a large new swimming-pool.
★★★★**Il Fraitevino, t** +39 0122 76022,
www.hotelilfraitevino.it, is in the centre
of town
★★★**Hotel Biancaneve, t** +39 0122 755176,
www.newlinehotels.com suits families.
★★★**Hotel Banchetta, t** +39 0122 70307,
www.sestriere2000.com, in the satellite
of Borgata, is in a peaceful position
200m from the lift.

La Thuile

Profile

The Italian half of a large intermediate
ski area shared with La Rosière in France,
renowned for the quality of its snow and
its restaurants

Resort

La Thuile is situated in a remote corner
of the Aosta Valley at the foot of the Petit-
St-Bernard Pass to France, which is closed
in winter. It was once a grim mining town
that has embraced tourism with

Essentials

Altitude: 1441m (4,728ft)–2641m (8,665ft)
Further information: t +39 0165 884179,
www.lathuile.it
Lifts in area: 37 (1 cableway, 17 chairs, 19
drags) serving 150km of piste
Lift pass: Aosta Valley (includes La Rosière,
Champoluc-Gressoney-Alanga) adult
€146–182, child under 1.30m 50%
discount, both for 6 days
Access: Turin and Geneva airports 2hrs.
Station at Pré-St-Didier 15mins, regular
buses from station

enthusiasm, although not all its new buildings are sympathetic to their beautiful mountain environment. The good snow record can sometimes provide outstanding off-piste skiing when other resorts have little to offer. The skiing is linked to La Rosière in France.

Mountain

A cableway and a parallel chair rise over wooded terrain to the mid-mountain station of Les Sucres at 2200m. A network of further lifts climb to the French border. This is a demanding ski area, with a predominance of steep reds and the , occasional black. Heli-skiing is possible on the Ruitor Glacier. La Thuile has good nursery slopes, a terrain park and half-pipe.

Learn

Instruction is restricted to **La Thuile** ski school, **t** +39 0165 884123, which was founded in 1964.

Children

Il Grande Albero, **t** +39 0165 884986, accepts children from newborn to three years. Ski school **Miniclub**, **t** +39 0165 884123, takes children from four years.

Lunch

Try **Rifugio Lo Riondet**, **t** +39 0165 884006, on the piste from the pass. **La Bricole**, **t** +39 0165 884149, is in an attractive old house at the bottom of the lifts. **L'Eden**, **t** +39 0165 885348, provides outstanding food, and **La Meleze**, **t** +39 0165 885553, above the gondola station, is new.

Dine

A La Lune, **t** +39 0165 884964, has Tuscan cooking. **Le Rascard**, **t** +39 0165 88499, serves innovative cuisine including chocolate pizza. **La Fordze**, **t** +39 0165 884800, specializes in grilled meat and game. **La Bricole**, **t** +39 0165 884149, is traditional, **La Lisse**, **t** +39 0165 884167, serves local specialities and **La Raclette**, **t** +39 0165 884541, is recommended.

Party

'Do not go out in search of entertainment,' warned a reporter, 'because you will be disappointed.' What there is includes **Bar La Buvette**, **La Bricolette**, **La Cage aux Folles** and **La Bricole** for dancing.

Sleep

- ★★★★**Planibel Hotel and Aparments**, **t** +39 0165 884541, *www.tivigest.com*, is a giant complex with pool, disco and shops.
- ★★★**Chalet Alpina**, **t** +39 0165 884187, is a rustic hotel 200m from the lifts.
- ★★★**Chalet Eden**, **t** +39 0165 885050, is renowned for its food.
- ★★★**Hotel du Glacier**, **t** +39 0165 884137, is convenient and has been refurbished.
- ★★★**Les Granges**, **t** +39 0165 883048, 3km out of town, has home cooking.
- ★★**Entrèves**, **t** +39 0165 884134, is a recently restored family hotel.

The Top Resorts: Scandinavia

07

Åre, Sweden

Profile

Scandinavia's only truly world-class downhill ski resort, suited to all standards of skier and snowboarder, as well as families who are not on a strict budget

Essentials

Altitude: 384m (1,259ft)–1420m (4,659ft)
Further information: t +46 (0)647 17700, *www.skistar.com*
Lifts in area: 43 (1 funicular, 2 cableways, 9 chairs, 31 drags) serving 93km of piste
Lift pass: adult SEK 1,545, child 8–15yrs SEK1,235, both for six days
Access: Östersund airport 90mins

Resort

Åre is the largest resort in Scandinavia, with skiing that matches many resorts in the Alps both for the length of its runs, the gradient, and the extent of the terrain. It will be the setting for the 2007 World Skiing Championships and a new downhill course is being created. The skiing is spread across different villages that are linked on-mountain and by ski bus. Confusingly, two of these – Duved and Åre Björnen – seek resort status in their own right, but Åre Village is the international player.

Mountain

A detachable quad and a six-seater chair take skiers from the valley to the top station in under four minutes. From here a network of lifts criss-crosses the mountainside both above and below the treeline. A tow behind a snowcat brings experienced skiers and riders to the 1420m summit of Åreskutan, starting point for a rewarding off-piste descent. Slopes are open for night skiing until 8pm for much of the season. Cross-country skiing is also a popular pastime with 56km on trails on the shores of the lake.

Learn

Beginners are well served by the **Åre ski school,** +46 (0)771 840000, which enjoys a sound reputation and is staffed entirely by fluent English-speakers.

Children

The village crèche, t +46 (0) 647 17700, cares for non-skiing children from three to five years. The ski school kindergarten offers tuition from three years.

Lunch

Try **Ullådalsstugan,** t +46 (0)647 53171, and **Hummelstugan,** t +46 (0)647 53284. You can buy reindeer burgers from Lapps in front of their teepees at Stendalen.

Dine

Villa Tottebo, t +46 (0)647 50620, is an old hunting lodge specializing in reindeer steaks. **Marmite,** t +46 (0)647 50240, has gourmet cuisine. **Liten Krog,** t +46 (0)647 52200, is recommended for its reasonably priced pizzas.

Party

Skiers' Bar at the Hotell Diplomat, **Fjällgården,** and **Werséns Bar** are packed when the lifts close. **Bygget** at Årefjällby is the best nightspot.

Sleep

Accommodation can be booked through a central office, **t** +46 (0)647 17700.
Luxury:
Hotell Diplomat Åregarden, **t** +46 (0)647 17800, *www.diplomathotel.se*, is close to the lifts.
Moderate:
Holiday Club Åre, **t** +46 (0)647 12000, *www.holidayclub.se*, is one of the biggest ski hotels in Sweden, with bowling and an adventure pool with 67m of winding waterslide.
Hotell Fjällgården, **t** +46 (0)647 14500, *www.fjallgarden.se*, is slope-side.
Park Inn Tott Hotell, **t** +46 (0)647 15000, *www.totthotell.com*, has a huge spa with 17 treatment rooms.

Geilo, Norway

Profile

Traditional resort with impressive cross-country skiing and limited but relaxed downhill skiing for beginners to intermediates

Essentials

Altitude: 800m (2,624ft)–1178m (3,864ft)
Further information: **t** +47 3209 5900, *www.geilo.no*
Lifts in area: 19 (5 chairs, 14 drags) serving 40km of piste
Lift pass adult Kr1,030–1,210, child 7–15yrs Kr770–905, both for 6 days
Access: Fagernes airport 2hrs, Oslo airport 4½hrs

Resort

Geilo is one of the best family resorts in Scandinavia, a village well known to avid cross-country skiers as one of the centres of the famous Hardangehrvidda Plateau, with a total of 220km of loipe in the immediate area of the resort. Geilo is also known as the European capital of kite-surfing and last season hosted the world championships.

Mountain

With a vertical drop of only 373m, the resort is best suited to beginners, low intermediates, and families. The two main ski areas are inconveniently situated on either side of a wide valley, with the resort in the centre.

Most of the skiing is at Geilohovda, while the Vestlia area is best for novices. A third area at Kikut has a quad-chair and a drag-lift. Reporters enthuse about the friendliness of the locals and the fact that the slopes are uncrowded. Geilo has a terrain park at Fugleleiken and a smaller one at Vestlia.

Learn

Per Bye, **t** +47 3209 0650, and **Geilolia**, **t** +47 3209 0000, are the two excellent schools. 'This is a top resort for novice instruction,' enthused one reporter, 'No arrogant show-off instructors here – just honest, nice and well qualified people who actually want you to get better'.

Children

The much-praised **Trollklubben**, **t** +47 3209 5518, kindergarten at Vestlia cares for children from newborn to seven years.

Hemsedal, Norway

Lunch

Stugu and **Toppen** cafés, t +47 3209
00 00, for both, serve basic fare, but no
alcohol until after 3pm. The sun terrace of
the stately **Dr Holms Hotel**, t +47 3209
5940, is a lunchtime rendezvous.

Dine

The rustic-style **Hallingstuene**, t +47
3209 1250, specializes in game. **Peppe's
Pizza**, t +47 3209 1815, is the cheaper
alternative.

Party

Jegerbaren and **Lille Blå** are popular
and lively. **Recepten Pub** in the Dr Holmes
Hotel and the **Pianobaren** in the Highland
have plenty of ambience. **Highdance** is
the disco.

Sleep

All accommodation can be booked
through a central number, t +47 3209
5940.
Luxury:
Dr. Holms Hotel, t +47 3209 5940,
www.drholms.no, has been the focal
point of the resort for 100 years.
Moderate/budget:
Ustedalen Hotel, t +47 3209 0111,
www.usterdalen.no, is a comfortable
family-run establishment 700m from
the resort centre.
Park Inn Highland Hotel, t +47 3209 6100,
www.highland.no, is recommended for
families.
Vestlia Resort, t +47 3208 7200,
www.vestlia.no, in the Vestlia ski area,
has excellent food.
Bardøla Hyttegrend are 22 log cabins set
in the woods, each with four bedrooms,
two bathrooms, and a cosy sitting room.

Profile

Best downhill skiing in Norway, suited
to all standards of skier as well as
families. Has an excellent terrain park for
snowboarders and twin-tip skiers

Resort

Hemsedal has the most challenging
downhill skiing in Norway. The resort is
divided into the self-contained Skisenter
at the base of the mountain and the
original community of Hemsedal two
miles away. Plans are on the drawing
board to link the two by gondola. At the
moment they are connected by a free
ski bus.

Mountain

The skiing is suited to all standards
with some genuinely steeper terrain
served by an eight-seater chair, including
the Hjallerløypa run, which deserves its
double-black classification. Reidarskaret
is a challenging off-piste itinerary that
evolves from a precipitous couloir. You are

Essentials

Altitude: 650m (2,133ft)–1497m (4,911ft)
Further information: t +47 3205 5030,
www.hemsedal.com
Lifts in area: 21 (6 chairs, 15 drags) serving
42km of piste
Lift pass: adult Kr1,320, child 7–15yrs
Kr1,060, both for 6 days
Access: Oslo airport 3½hrs

advised to take a guide who will arrange for a taxi to bring you back to the resort. However, there is also plenty of benign terrain for novices and intermediates. Night skiing until 9pm is possible four days a week until mid-March.

The resort now has two terrain parks. The 600m main park, considered to be one of the best in Europe, has two half-pipes and a quarter-pipe. The recently-extended second one in the Trollskogen area is aimed at new riders.

Learn

Hemsedal Ski School, t +47 3205 5067, has a good reputation. **Solheisen Ski and Snowboard School, t** +47 4130 5094, is an alternative learning centre at Solheisen, a ten-minute drive away. Its three lifts are included in the Hemsedal lift pass.

Children

A large new children's area with five easy runs makes this one of the best resorts in Scandinavia for kids. Ski passes and helmet rental are free for under sevens. **The Trollia crèche, t** +47 3205 5300, beside the slopes cares for childen from three months.

Lunch

Try **Harahorn, t** +47 3206 2380, mid-mountain. Cafés at Hemsedal Village include **Kremen Kafe, t** +47 3206 0237, and **Café Kakaotwo, t** +47 9509 5811.

Dine

The restaurant at **Hotel Skarsnuten, t** +47 3206 1700 serves gourmet food. **Norlandia Skogstad Hotel, t** +47 3205 5000, **Peppes Pizza, t** +47 3205 9557, and the **Hemsedal Café, t** +47 3205 5410, are recommended.

Party

Garasjen is the main meeting place. **The Skogstad Piano Bar** and **Hemsedal Café** are also always crowded.

Sleep

For accommodation contact Hemsedal Booking, t +47 3205 5060.
Luxury:
Skarsnuten Hotell, t +47 3206 1700, *www.skarsnutenhotel.no*, is at 1000m, linked by chair to the Mountain Village.
Norlandia Skogstad Hotell, t +47 3205 5000, *www.norlandia.no/skogstad*, in Hemsedal village, has a nightclub and swimming pool and is the centre for nightlife.
Good:
Hemsedal Hotell, t +47 3205 5400, *www.gohemsedal.com*, is situated at Tuv, midway between Hemsedal and the lifts.

Levi, Finland

Profile

Offbeat resort in the Arctic Circle with a long snow-sure season. Suits beginners and intermediates, with a wide choice of non-skiing activities, but limited nightlife

Essentials

Altitude: 400m (1,312ft)–531m (1,742ft)
Further information: t +358 (0)16 641 246, *www.levi.fi*
Lifts in area: 26 (1 cableway, 25 drags) serving 60km of piste
Lift pass: adult g66–132, child under 12yrs g39.50–79.50
Access: Kittilä airport 10mins

Resort

Finland's only truly international ski resort has guaranteed snow from mid-October until mid-May, which explains why Rossignol has one of its four worldwide equipment test centres here.

Levi is situated in magical surroundings in a pine forest 161km from Rovaniemi, the capital of Finnish Lapland.

From November to January the sun fails to make it over the horizon and when not pitch dark, the resort is bathed in soft twilight. Some 15 runs are floodlit from 10am to 8pm by sodium lamps, which give the winter landscape a surreal tint. By night, the Northern Lights dance across the sky. After New Year the hours of daylight increase, and in Spring the ski area is open without lights until 8pm.

Mountain

This is a modest ski area with short runs down all sides of the dome-shaped mountain, best-suited to beginners, low intermediates and families. A modern gondola acts as the backbone of the 26-lift system. The resort has a super-pipe and a separate terrain park with half-pipe and a snowcross course.

Other activities include 230km of cross-country skiing, a visit to a Lapp farm for reindeer rides, snowmobiling, dog-sledding, and ice-diving.

Learn

Levi Ski School, t +358 (0)16 641 655, has an excellent reputation and lessons include the use of lifts.

Children

Tenavatokka, t +358 (0)16 641 377, cares for skiing and non-skiing kids from three years. Adjoining **Children's Land** has three baby-lifts. Children under seven wearing helmets can ski free.

Lunch

Try **Battery Grill t** +358 (0)16 641 346, **The Carlsberg Pub, t** +358 16 641 313, **Alpine Café Paulig, t** +358 (0)16 641 314, and **Luvattumaa, t** +358 (0)40740 0925.

Dine

Most guests eat in their hotels where reindeer rules the menu. **Fun Action Fondue, t** +358 (0)400 503278, is what it says it is. **Levin Gastro, t+** 358 (0)16 644 884, is a gourmet experience. **Levin Bistro,** t +358 (0)16 644 125, is a pizzeria.

Party

The Seika nightclub and **Joiku Karaoke Bar** are both in Spa Hotelli Levitunturi. **Disco Beige** is the alternative.

Sleep

Accommodation can be booked through a central office **t** +358 (0)16 639 3300.
Luxury:
Hotelli K5 Levi, t +358 (0)16 639 1100, *www.k5levi.fi*, has minimalist decoration and private saunas or hot-tubs in each room.
Spa Hotelli Levitunturi, t +358 (0)16 646 301, *www.hotellilevitunturi.fi*, has a swimming pool, five restaurants, and a nightclub.
Moderate:
Levi Centre Hullu Poro, t +358 (0)16 6510 100, *www.hulluporo.fi*, meaning 'crazy reindeer', has comfortable a rooms – some with private saunas.

The Top Resorts: Spain

Baqueira– Beret

Profile

Spain's smartest resort set amid dramatic Pyrenean scenery and patronized by King Juan Carlos. A wide choice of restaurants and nightlife

Resort

Baqueira–Beret is one of the great skiing secrets of Europe, a sophisticated ski resort on the French side of the Spanish Pyrenees that Spain has so far managed to keep to itself. The reason for its lack of international profile has been the shortage of hotel and apartment beds in and around Baqueira (Beret is just a linked base area and car park).

The resort is situated above the old town of Viella at the head of the beautiful Val d'Aran, a two-hour drive from Toulouse. But its image is about to change. One new hotel has already been built, work has started on two others, and Baqueira seems set to realize a major international profile. For those of us who have quietly enjoyed its skiing over the years, this is a shame – but in today's competitive market ski resorts must evolve or die. The window between unspoilt mountainsides and commercial exploitation is unfortunately narrow.

Baqueira has already acquired serious chic status. King Juan Carlos and wealthy families from Madrid and Barcelona have holiday homes here. The King, who is an excellent skier and who learnt his skills here, can be seen enjoying himself on the mountain throughout the season whenever affairs of state permit.

Essentials

Altitude: 1500m (4,920ft)–2510m (8,235ft)
Further information: t +34 973 63 90 10, www.baqueira.es
Lifts in area: 30 (19 chairs, 11 drags) serving 93km of piste
Lift pass: adult €191, child 6–11yrs €120, both for 6 days
Access: Toulouse airport 2hrs

The original purpose-built edifices of the 1970s are made of functional concrete. However, recent additions are in much more pleasing, in keeping with the resort's dramatically beautiful setting on the road that leads to the high Bonaigua Pass. Spanish is the main language, but Aranese, Catalan, and French are spoken.

Anyone not used to the Spanish way of doing things needs to understand the timetable. For indigenous guests, skiing is something you rarely contemplate before 10.30am. Lunch is at 2pm or even 3pm, followed by a last run to the base area. Rioja-and-*tapas* last until 7pm when the bars empty – and everyone goes to bed. Dinner *en famille* is at 10pm or at 11pm for grown-ups, and the nightclubs start to warm up around 2am.

Mountain

A new gondola opens this December as the main means of mountain access, replacing a strange quad-chair that you rode without skis (you slotted them into the back of the chair in front). It begins from just below the chair – with an altered piste to accommodate it – and ends at the same mid-mountain station at 1800m. At first glance such expenditure seems unnecessary. The Spanish are slow to ski each morning and rush-hour queues are almost unheard of. However, the gondola is designed to cope with the extra traffic envisaged from two hotels at the base, to be completed for 2006–7.

Snow cannon installed on the front face for this season will greatly assist piste maintenance at the beginning and the end of the season – although Baqueira has notched up an outstanding record for good snow cover in recent years

The moderately extensive ski area covers four linked mountains that offer a substantial vertical drop of 1000m. Most is given over to comfortable cruising terrain, but there are all sorts of variants, with some sharp little drop-offs at the edge of runs, and plentiful off-piste opportunities with a guide. Where Goats Tumble, Baqueira's most infamous couloir, can test even experienced powderhounds.

Learn

Baqueira Ski School, t +34 973 63 90 10, has 200 ski instructors, but don't expect many of them to speak fluent English.

Children

Baqueira has **Snowparks** for kids of three months to three years opposite the Bosque ski-lift at 1800, **t** +34 606 544132, opposite the control tower in Beret, **t** +34 606 544134, and next to the Hotel Montarto at 1500, **t** +34 973 645448.

Lunch

Apart from a handful of self-services, the choice includes **Cap del Port, t** +34 973 250082, a gothic folly, which offers haute cuisine 200m from Bonaigua village. **Restaurant 1800, t** +34 973 645202, is at the foot of the Baqueira Plain chair and serves Aranese and Catalan cuisine.

Dine

Esquiro, t +34 973 645430, specializes in hearty Aranese dishes. **La Borda Lobato,**

t +34 973 645708 majors in roast suckling pig and whole baby lamb carved at the table. **Urtau, t** +34 973 641815, in nearby Arties, is warmly recommended for its variety of duck dishes and crêpes. **Casa Irene, t** +34 973 644364, in Arties, has excellent fresh fish and grilled meat.

Party

Nightlife starts late in Spain. **Tiffany's** is the popular nightclub. Others include **Tuc Nere**, and **Viella Dance Club** in Viella.

Sleep

*****Melia Royal Tanau Boutique Hotel, **t** +34 973 644446, *www.solmelia.com*, has a chair-lift to the slopes.

****Parador de Arties, t +34 973 640801, *www.paradores-spain.com*, is in the hamlet of Arties; traditional design with wooden beams in all bedrooms.

*****Rafaelhoteles La Pieta, t +34 973 645550, *www.rafaelhoteles.com*, with its bell tower and Aranese design, has a swimming pool.

****Hotel Casa Irene, t +34 973 644364, *www.innsofspain.com*, is also in Arties. It has spacious and rustic rooms and a good restaurant serving local specialities.

****Hotel Chalet Bassibe, t +34 973 645152, *www.valderuda-bassibe.com*, is up at Baqueira 1700.

****Hotel Montarto, t +34 973 639001, *www.montarto.com*, boasts two restaurants, a swimming pool, and children's entertainment.

***Hotel Orri, t +34 973 646086, *www.husa.es*, located in the small village of Tredòs 2km from Baqueira, offers free transport to the slopes.

**Hotel Tuc Blanc, t +34 973 644350, *www.hoteltucblanc.com*, is conveniently set at the foot of the slopes.

The Top Resorts: Switzerland

09

Andermatt

Profile

Quaint and picturesque non-mainstream resort that is the reserve of serious skiers and riders looking for steep pistes and plenty of challenging powder runs

Resort

Andermatt has a low profile as an international resort. Outside Switzerland it is known only to that dedicated three per cent of skiers whose enjoyment of the sport lies mainly in exploring ungroomed slopes well away from the village in which they are staying.

Andermatt does have machine-prepared runs, but it also has enormous off-piste potential and is renowned for its reliable snow cover. Its isolated position in the Urseren Valley by the Gotthard pass and road tunnel makes it an unlikely winter destination. The Swiss army has adopted it over many years as a major training centre for its alpine troops who have never fought a war against any of its neighbours. Rather austere barrack blocks mar the otherwise sympathetic village architecture, but National Service troops along with that three per cent of international powderhounds form the backbone of the local economy.

Mountain

The Gemsstock is the main ski area reached from Andermatt by a two-stage cable car that takes you up to the top of the Gurschengletscher at 2963m. From here a famous Bernard Russi-designed run brings you all the way back down to Andermatt. Another marginally easier

Essentials

Altitude: 1445m (4,740ft)–2965m (9,725ft)
Further information: t +41 (0)41 887 1454, www.andermatt.ch
Lifts in area: 35 in Gottard–Oberalp (1 funicular, 3 cableways, 10 chairs, 21 drags) serving 166km of piste
Lift pass: Gottard–Oberalp (covers Andermatt, Oberalp, Sedrun and Disentis) Adult CHF230, child (from 6yrs) CHF115
Access: Zurich airport 1½hrs by car. By rail 2hrs, station in resort

piste takes you down the St Anna glacier to the mid-mountain station, Gurschen.

The separate ski area of Gütsch, reached by a two-stage chair lift on the other side of the resort and by a train that goes up to the 2044m Oberalppass, is overall less challenging but still has some demanding slopes. Two other areas, Hospental and Realp, provide further advanced and intermediate terrain.

Learn

Snowsports School Andermatt, t +41 (0)41 887 1240) is the only learning academy. **Bergschule Uri,** t +41 (0)41 872 09 00, **Bergschule Montanara,** t +41 (0)41 878 1259, and **Alpine Sportschule Gotthard,** t +41 (0)41 883 1728 all provide guiding.

Children

Snowsports School Andermatt accepts children from four-and-a-half years.

Lunch

Try **Bergrestaurant Gurschen,** t + 41 (0)41 887 1618, for wholesome fare at reasonable prices, and **Bergrestaurant Nätschen-Gütsch, t** +41 (0)41 887 1352.

The **Bahnhofbuffet, t** +41 (0)41 888 0050, is recommended. **Tre Passi, t** +41 (0)41 887 0088, is good for venison and wild boar. **Postillion, t** +41 (0)41 887 1044, and **Spycher, t** +41 (0)41 887 1753, are also praised. In Hospental, try **Zum Dörfli**, **t** +41 (0)41 887 0132.

Party

Baroko Music Bar and **Dancing Gotthard** are the liveliest spots. Others to try are **Ochsen, Barry Bar, Piccadilly Pub**, and **Bar La Curva**.

Sleep

***Activ Kronen Hotel Andermatt, t** +41 (0)41 887 0088, *www.kronenhotel.ch*, is a family-run hotel.

***Drei Könige & Post, t** +41 (0)41 887 0001, *www.3koenige.ch*, is a quiet hotel in the middle of town with a wellness centre.

***Monopol-Metropol, t** +41 (0)41 887 1575, *www.monopol-andermatt.ch*, has simple rooms, some with kitchenettes.

***Hotel Schweizerhof, t** +41 (0)41 887 1189, *www.schweizerhof-andermatt.ch*, is central and its restaurant specializes in Italian cooking and fondues.

***Hotel Sonne, t** +41 (0)41 887 1226, *www.hotelsonneandermatt.ch*, is two minutes' walk from the Gemsstock cable car.

Crans-Montana

Profile

Large town with smart hotels and elegant boutiques. Suits epicurean intermediates in search of certain snow, and is one of the best resorts for snowboaders

Resort

Skiing began in 1911 in Crans and the adjoining village of Montana when British pioneer Sir Arnold Lunn organized the first genuine downhill in skiing history. He chose this scenic little resort, partly because of its long vertical drop from the Plaine Morte glacier. More importantly, his father Henry had been running golf holidays for the previous five years and had already established the necessary local contacts.

Crans Montana had already built a reputation from the 1890s as a centre for tuberculosis clinics. During the early days, invalid and sportsman sat uneasily side by side in the resort's cafés and restaurants. Today a large proportion of the hotels still

Essentials

Altitude: 1500m (4,920ft)–3000m (9,840ft)
Further information: t +41 (0)27 485 0404, *www.crans-montana.ch*
Lifts in area: 33 (6 cableways, 6 chairs, 21 drags) serving 140km of piste
Lift pass: adult CHF274, child 6–15yrs CHF164, both for 6 days
Access: Sion airport 30 mins, Geneva airport 1¼hrs. Station at Sierre 15km, bus to resort

offer health treatments with dietary restaurants and doctors on hand to prescribe treatments, much to the bemusement of young snowboarders who congregate here for some of the best riding facilities in Switzerland.

Crans, Montana, and neighbouring Aminona are in an enviable position on a sunny plateau above the Rhône Valley dotted with larches and lakes. However, they have grown together in an urban sprawl along several kilometres of main road that is often clogged with traffic. The fresh alpine air, for which it originally won acclaim, carries more than a healthy share of carbon monoxide. However, a funicular from the valley town of Sierre takes only 12 minutes to reach Crans and has done much to alleviate the traffic problem, particularly at weekends. Swiss has direct flights from London Heathrow to Sion, which is only a 30-minute bus ride from the resort.

Mountain

Crans Montana is a pleasant family ski area that suits intermediates who are happy to take a few cruising runs amid spectacular scenery before settling down to a long lunch on a sunny terrace. Former 007 Roger Moore, a long-time resident, falls happily into this bracket. It also has good nursery slopes, but advanced skiers will soon tire of the lack of challenging gradients. The only officially graded black run is a bumpy fall-line pitch under the Toula chair that does not really justify its colour. Possible itinerary routes from the Plaine-Morte glacier include an enjoyable run down to the lake at Zeuzier. By walking through tunnels – a torch is needed – and skiing down a summer road, you can reach the ski area of the neighbouring purpose-built resort of Anzère. Novice skiers get a care-free introduction to the sport on nursery slopes served by three drag-lifts on the golf course at Crans.

Crans Montana and Amonina have terrain parks, and there is a half-pipe at Cry d'Err.

Learn

Swiss Snowsports Schools in Crans, t +41 (0)27 485 9370, and Montana, t +41 (0)27 481 1480, both have worthy reputations. **Ski & Sky**, t +41 (0)27 485 4250, is a much-praised alternative. **Stoked**, t +41 (0)27 480 2421, used to be just a dedicated riding academy but now also teaches skiing. **Air Glacier**, t +41 (0)27 329 1415, and **Helicopter Services**, t +41 (0)27 327 3060, offer heli-skiing.

Children

Fleurs des Champs, t +41 (0)27 481 2367, the kindergarten next to Hotel Eldorado in Montana, accepts children from three months to seven years on weekdays only and is recommended. **Zig-Zag**, t +41 (0)27 481 2205, also in Montana, takes children from 18 months. The **Jardin des Neiges**, t +41 (0)27 481 1480, is at the Grand Signal mid-station, and **Crans Ski School kindergarten**, t +41 (0)27 485 9370, is beside the tubing slope.

Lunch

The resort has 13 mountain eateries, including the delightful but expensive **Merbé**, t +41 (0)27 481 2297, and **Plumachit**, t +41 (0)27 481 2532, which has great atmosphere and food at better prices. **Cabane des Violettes**, t +41 (0)27 481 3919, is a genuine touring hut which provides simple meals.

Dine

In Crans try **Nouvelle Rôtisserie**, t +41 (0)27 481 1885, and the **La Bergerie du Cervin**, t +41 (0)27 481 2180, which specializes in raclette, fondue, and other cheesy dishes. In Montana, **Gastronomic l'Ours**, t +41 (0)27 485 9333, has lots of atmosphere and good food. **La Diligence**, t +41 (0)27 485 9985, is renowned for its Middle Eastern cuisine, and **Au Gréni**, t +41 (0)27 481 2443, a Roger Moore favourite, serves gourmet fare at film-star prices. **Rhapsodie**, t +41 (0)27 481 1155, is new.

Party

Bars include **The Cuban Punch**, which has salsa and samba music. **Le Monki's** is new, **Amadeus** attracts a young crowd, and **Le New Pub** is on the edge of a lake. Teenagers flock to Montana's **Number-Two** for late drinking. **Absolut** and **Le Barocke** are the discos.

Sleep

Crans:
- ★★★★★**Hostellerie du Pas de l'Ours**, t +41 (0)27 485 9334, *www.relaischateaux. com*, is a stylish hotel.
- ★★★★★**Hotel Royal**, t +41 (0)27 481 3931, *www.hotel-royal.ch*, has a wellness centre with a good pool.
- ★★★★★**Grand Hotel du Golf**, t +41 (0)27 481 4242, *www.grand-hotel-du-golf.ch*, is elegant and discreet.
- ★★★**Hotel Mont-Blanc**, t +41 (0)27 481 3143, on a hill above Crans, has striking views and 13 spacious bedrooms.
- **Domaine de la Baronne**, t +44 (0)870 787 1785, *www.oxfordski.com*, built in the 1950s outside the village, is more Florentine palazzo than Heidi chalet. It sleeps 14 in splendour.

Montana:
- ★★★**Hotel St-George**, t +41 (0)27 481 2414, *www.hotel-st-george.ch* offers good food and service but small rooms.
- ★★★**Hotel de la Prairie**, t +41 (0)27 481 4421 is chalet-style with lovely views from the breakfast table.

Davos

Profile

Glorious pistes amid spectacular scenery in the place where alpine skiing began over a century ago. The large town shares its Parsenn ski area with Klosters. Good for snowboarders, suits all standards of skier

Resort

Davos is a spa town that has a life beyond skiing. Each winter it receives worldwide exposure when global movers and shakers, along with a small army of protesters, gather for the World Economic Forum. While the likes of Blair, Bush and Bill Gates are airing their predictions in the conference centre, skiers and riders

Essentials

Altitude: 1560m (5,117ft)–2844m (9,328ft)
Map: see page M49
Further information: t +41 (0)81 415 2121, *www.davos.ch*
Lifts in area: 53 in Davos/Klosters area (2 funiculars, 13 cableways, 9 chairs, 29 drags) serving 370km of piste
Lift pass: adult CHF282, child 6–17yrs CHF94–189, both for 6 days
Access: Zurich airport 2½hrs, station in Davos Dorf and Davos Platz

are just as importantly engaged on the mighty mountain above.

The Parsenn is one of Europe's classic ski areas, where the sport first developed in the early 1880s when a local businessman imported a pair of the new 'Norwegian snowshoes' from Oslo. They quickly became the teenage rage and a local carpenter busily carved copies. A British woman resident who had lived in Norway showed them how to turn the planks. The trend soon caught the attention of the large foreign community in Switzerland's top sanatorium resort for victims of tuberculosis.

It might have ended there but for the timely presence of the man who was about to become Britain's first ski writer. Arthur Conan Doyle, who created Sherlock Holmes, had brought his terminally ill wife to Davos in the hope of a cure. During the many months of her treatment he became hooked on skiing. He wrote about his experiences in *Strand* magazine and encouraged a whole generation of well-to-do Brits to come out and try skiing for themselves. The Davos English Ski Club built its first refuge for members in 1906.

Nearly half a century slipped by before the first mountain railway was built and then in 1934 a local man came up with the invention of the drag-lift within weeks of a similar contraption being designed in Alpe d'Huez in France. Davos never looked back. As antibiotics put the sanatorium business into decline, winter sports became increasingly big business.

The town – the highest in Western Europe – is by no means attractive. Large hotels that are urban rather than Alpine in construction and character straggle along the roadside for a couple of kilometres from the railway half of Davos Dorf to Davos Platz. Where you stay is of crucial important to ski convenience. Of the two sectors Davos Dorf is best for

skiing, while Davos Platz has most of the shops, restaurants, and nightlife. Regular buses run the loop of the one-way system, but it can be a long walk home to Davos Dorf late at night.

Mountain

The Parsenn is the largest and the most famous - but not the only - ski area. Jakobshorn, reached from Davos Platz, is popular with snowboarders. It has two half-pipes, a snowcross course, and night-riding. The outlying areas of Pischa and Rinerhorn are both worth visiting when the Parsenn is crowded during peak weeks of the season

However, the Parsenn is the main course. Take the recently rebuilt first stage of the Parsennbahn funicular from Davos Dorf, followed by the six-person chair to the Weissfluhjoch for the start of the first run of the day. The alternative slow second stage of the train has yet to be refurbished and should be avoided. From Weissfluhjoch a short cable car also takes you up a further 180m vertical to the 2844m Weissfluhgipfel, the highest point in the area. A network of lifts and mainly intermediate runs stretches across the mountainside to Klosters. All the different lift companies in the area are now amalgamated and one electronic pass serves the whole region.

From the Weissfluhgipfel you can ski 12km with a 2000m vertical drop down to the farming hamlets of Küblis and Serneus from where you can return to Klosters and then to Davos by train. Anyone who can ski parallel can do it, and in mid-season when the snow is at its best, it's a great way to end the day.

This is not an ideal resort for complete beginners. Madrisa is too far away (suitable only for Klosters-based skiers). The Bolgen beginner slopes at the bottom of the Jakobshorn are the best bet. Bünda in Davos Dorf is steeper. At the other end of the scale of expertise, the best black run starts from the top of the Parsenn and descends through the Meierhofer Tälli to the hamlet of Wolgang between Klosters and Davos. Still more demanding itinerary routes on the other side of the Parsenn take you down to Klosters.

In the right snow conditions off-piste opportunities abound and this is a great area for ski touring. Conan Doyle wrote vividly of crossing the Maienfeld Furka Pass to Arosa, and you can follow in his tracks if you are prepared for a four-hour climb and a three-hour train journey home again. Davos is also big on cross-country skiing with 75km of trails at Jakobshorn as well as in the Dischma and Sertig valleys. Shopping is a major après-ski activity with a wide range of shops as befits a rich town of this international calibre.

Learn

Swiss Snowsportschool, t +41 (0)81 416 2454, offers ski and board. **New Trend, t** +41 (0)81 413 2040, specializes in off-piste tours with emphasis on the use of safety equipment. **Top Secret Ski & Board Freestyle School, t** +41 (0)81 413 4043, and British-run **White Heat, t** +44 (0)20 8989 3281, also concentrate on off-piste instruction.

Children

Swiss Snowsportschool, t +41 (0)81 416 2454, is praised for its children's classes from three years on Bolgen and Bünda, with lunch and lifts included in the price, and a **Bobo Wonderland playground**, in both areas. **New Trend, t** +41 (0)81 413 2040, accepts children from four years. **Kinderschatzalp, t** +41 (0)81 415 5151, and **Wallis Kidsclub, t** +41 (0)81 417 9333, are both for kids from three years.

Lunch

Chalet Güggel, t +41 (0)81 413 5148, on Jakobshorn is a welcoming mountain hut with the best *Rösti* in the region. **Hotel Kulm, t** +41 (0)81 417 0707, built in 1864 in the hamlet of Wolfgang, is a favourite of Price Charles. **Gallo Rosso** at the Weissfluhjoch, **t** +41 (0)81 417 6611, and **Bruhin's Weissfluhgipfel, t** +41 (0)81 417 6644, are both praised.

Dine

Hubli's Landhaus, t +41 (0)81 417 1010, which has a Michelin star, the **Magic Mountain, t** +41 (0)81 415 3747, in the Waldhotel Bellevue, and the **Stübli, t** +41 (0)81 410 1717, in Hotel Flüela are the gourmet choices. Also try **Zauberberg, t** +41 (0)81 415 4201, in Hotel Europe. The **Goldener Drachen, t** +41 (0)81 414 9797, is a Chinese eatery in the Hotel Bahnhof Terminus, and **Ahaan-Thai, t** +41 (0)81 413 6044, is another Oriental offering in Hotel Stela at Davos Platz, the **Pöstli, t** +41 (0)81 415 4500, in the Morosani Posthotel, serves light Swiss cuisine and fish dishes.

Party

Popular bars include **Chämi** and **Ex-Bar**. **Café Schneider** in Davos Platz and **Café Weber** in Davos Dorf are traditional coffee houses with mouthwatering cakes. Skating on Europe's largest natural ice-rink at Davos Dorf attracts a large après-ski crowd. Swiss league and international ice hockey matches are staged at the Sports Centre. The **Cabanna Club** is the late-night venue. Riders hang out in the disco of the **Hotel Bolgenschanze**.

Sleep

*****Hotel Steigenberger Belvédère,
t +41 (0)81 415 6000,
www.davos.steigenberger.ch, above
Platz, is traditional.

****Hotel Flüela, t +41 (0)81 410 1717,
www.fluela.ch, opposite the railway
station in Dorf has a spa, swimming
pool, and piano bar.

****Turmhotel Victoria, t +41 (0)81 417
5300, *www.victoria-davos.ch*, in Dorf, is
recommended for its health and fitness
centre, and good food.

****Waldhotel Bellevue, t +41 (0)81 415 37
47, *www.waldhotel-bellevue.ch*, is a
traditional hotel in Platz.

****Arabella Sheraton Hotel Waldhuus,
t +41 (0)81 415 3747, in Platz is chalet-
style and family-friendly.

****Arabella Sheraton Seehof, t +41 (0)81
415 9444, has the fastest internet
connection in Switzerland – Bill Gates
stays here.

****Hotel Sunstar Park, t +41 (0)81 413
1414, *www.sunstar.ch*, receives much
repeat booking – the guest book reveals
people who have been back eight times.

ArtHaus Hotel Quisisana, t +41 (0)81 413
5104, *www.arthaushotel.ch*, is inspired by
the owner's art collection. All the rooms
are individually decorated.

Chalet-Hotel Larix, t +41 (0)81 413 1188,
www.hotel-larix.ch, is an attractive chalet-
style hotel run by a British couple.
Bedrooms are all individually designed.

Engelberg

Profile

**High-altitude snow-sure resort in
Central Switzerland within easy reach of**

Zurich and Luzern that is popular with
snowboarders and younger skiers

Resort

Engelberg, above the beautiful lakeside
city of Luzern, is better known in Calcutta
than it is in London or New York. In recent
years it has become a location for Bollywood
movies. Thousands of Indian fans flock
here each summer to tread in the
footsteps of their heroes on the flower-
decked lower slopes of the 3238m Titlis.

In winter, Engelberg puts away its
poppadoms and returns to the familiar
guise of traditional ski resort that it first
adopted before and immediately after the
Second World War when it was one of the
most fashionable ski centres in Europe.
Engelberg has seen renewed success in
recent years – thanks to new lifts, a good
snow record, and a concerted effort to
attract young snowboarders and freeriders.

Mountain

Beginners and families with small
children head for the sunny slopes of
Brunni, reached by a cable car followed by
fixed-grip chair from just above the town.

The main Titlis ski area on the other side
of town is reached by a modern gondola
or a parallel, high-season combination of
funicular and cable car. The second stage

of the gondola rises over sheer cliffs to Trübsee at 1800m where a chair lift conveys you over the frozen lake towards Jochstock at 2564m and the terrain park. Alternatively you continue on up by cable car towards the summit of Titlis. The last stage is completed in the Rotair revolving cable car with panoramic views. Off-piste itineraries include the Laub, a powder bowl with a leg-burning 1120m vertical drop.

Learn

The excellent **Skischule Engelberg-Titlis**, t +41 (0)41 639 5454, has the monopoly. **Snowboard School Engelberg**, t +41 (0)41 639 5455, and **Boardlocal Snowboard Engelberg**, t +41 (0)41 637 0000, are for riders.

Children

Skischule Engelberg-Titlis, t +41 (0)41 639 5454, accepts skiers from three years. **Hotel Edelweiss**, t +41 (0)41 639 7878, and **Hotel Ramada**, t +41 (0)41 639 5858, both have crèches.

Lunch

Titlis-Stübli, t +41 (0)41 639 5080, has high-altitude gourmet cuisine, **Untertrübsee**, t +41 (0)41 637 1226, and **Ritz**, t +41 (0)41 637 2212, at Gerschnialp are both rated for standard cheesy mountain fare. **Brunnihütte**, t +41 (0)41 637 3732, at Brunni has good home cooking.

Dine

Spannort, t +41 (0)41 637 2626, is traditionally Swiss. **Axels**, t +41 (0)41 639 5087, serves French cuisine. **Alpenclub**, t +41 (0)41 637 1243, is warmly recommended.

Party

Head for **The Spindle**, the **Yukatan**, or the smarter **Hotel Eden**.

Sleep

★★★★**Ramada Hotel Regina Titlis**, t +41 (0)41 639 5858, *www.treff-hotels.de*, is a modern hotel with a swimming pool.
★★★★**Hotel Waldegg**, t +41 (0)41 637 1822, *www.waldegg-engelberg.ch*, is set well above the town and houses one of the resort's leading restaurants.
★★★**Hotel Europe – Europaischer Hof**, t +41 (0)41 639 7575, *www.hoteleurope.ch*, is in a 1905 Art Nouveau building.
★★★**Hotel Spannort**, t +41 (0)41 637 2626, *www.spannort.ch*, is family-run.
★★★**Hotel Terrace**, t +41 (0)41 639 6666, *www.terrace.ch*, was built in 1904 above the town.

Flims

Profile

One of Switzerland's largest and most snowsure ski areas that is virtually unknown internationally. Good choice of hotels, popular with snowboarders, not the best resort for non-skiers

Essentials

Altitude: 1100m (3,609ft)–3018m (9,902ft)
Further information: t +41 (0)81 920 9200, *www.alpenarena.ch*
Lifts in area: 30 (11 cableways, 7 chairs, 12 drags) serving 220km of piste
Lift pass: CHF306, child 6–17yrs CHF102–204, both for 6 days
Access: Zurich airport 2hrs

Resort

Flims and neighbouring Laax in the Graubunden have been spa resorts since the 1880s and ski resorts since 1962 when the glacier above them was first developed for skiing. Together with the picturesque farming village of Falera they form the 220km Alpenarena, one of the largest ski circuits in the Alps.

Flims is made up of the two quite separate hamlets of Flims Dorf ('ski convenient') and Flims Waldhaus ('isolated from the ski area, but better choice of hotels'). Laax is also a bus ride away from the lifts but has Laax Murschetg, a more ski-friendly satellite built around the base station. Murschetg has become a serious destination for snowboarders who congregate at the Riders' Palace hotel. Falera is a much smaller and more rural community, but with a direct lift link into the system. A ski bus connects all the accommodation and base stations.

Mountain

The skiing takes place on the 3018m Voralb Glacier and on the slopes of four other interconnected peaks. Much of it is above the tree line and suited to skiers of all standards, but particularly intermediates in search of long cruising runs. There is also plenty of steeper terrain, divided by bands of rock and steep gullies in the Siala and Cassons sectors. A long itinerary from the glacier descends 2000m to the remote hamlet of Ruschein Ladir.

The top of the glacier is the starting point for the annual Weisse Schuss, a 14km pro-am downhill race that ends in Flims Dorf. The undulating FIS downhill course from Crap Sogn Gion down to Laax–Murschetg provides plenty of scope for boy and girl races, but no great technical difficulty when not prepared

for racing. A more challenging descent is the Platt'Alva itinerary from Nagens or the black Sattel from Voralb down to Alp Ruschein.

The Alpenarena attracts a high percentage of snowboarders who gather at the terrain parks and half-pipes on the glacier and at Crap Sogn. It is also a major centre for cross-country skiing with trails along the valley from Flims and through the nearby villages of Trin and Sagogn. Higher altitude loipe are also located in the Bargis Valley.

Learn

The mainstream **Snowsports School**, t +41 (0)81 927 7171, and **Snowboard Fahrschule**, t +41 (0)81 927 7155, have branches in Flims, Laax and Falera.

Other schools in Flims Dorf are **Alpine Action Unlimited**, t +41 (0)81 936 7474, **EuroBoard**, t +41 (0)81 281 8183, **EuroSki**, t +41 (0)79 683 5642, **Rock and Snow**, t +41 (0)78 679 7153, **Roland Tuchschmid**, t +41 (0)79 742 6677, **Touchdown** t +41 (0)78 830 5960, and **Yetis**, t +41 (0)79 635 3767.

Other schools in Flims Waldhaus are **Mountain Fantasy**, t +41 (0)81 936 7077, and **Swissraft**, t +41 (0)81 911 5250. In Laax **Inspiraziun Grischun**, t +41 (0)76 391 6894, is recommended.

Children

Swiss Snowsports School, t +41 (0)81 927 7171, runs a kindergarten for children from two years, with ski lessons from four years. **Park Hotels Waldhaus**, t +41 (0)81 928 4848, and **Hotel Adula**, t +41 (0)81 928 2828, both run crèches for guests. In Flims Dorf, **Annina Hägler**, t +41 (0)79 791 5221, runs a non-ski kindergarten.

Lunch

Try **Startgels Alpenrose**, t +41 (0)81 911 5848, **Naraus Enzian**, t +41 (0)81 911 5878, **Segneshütte**, t +41 (0)81 927 9925, and **Cassonsgrat Edelweiss**, t +41 (0)81 911 5898. **Capalari Mountain Hostel**, t +41 (0)81 927 7373, at Crap Sogn Gion is recommended. **Elephant**, t +41 (0)81 927 7390, at Crap Masegn and **Tegia Larnags**, t +41 (0)81 927 9910, are the gourmet choices.

Dine

Recommended restaurants include **La Clav**, t +41 (0)81 928 2828, in Hotel Adula, and **Clavau Vegl**, t +41 (0)81 911 3644, in Flims Dorf for regional specialities. Pizzeria **Pomodoro**, t +41 (0)81 911 1062, and **Pizzeria La Dolce Vita**, t +41 (0)81 928 1440, in Flims Waldhaus are singled out. In Laax, **Romana**, t +41 (0)81 921 5055, specializes in Balkan cuisine and **Riva**, t +41 (0)81 921 5353, has good cheese dishes. **Casa Seeli**, t +41 (0)81 921 30 48, in Falera is praised.

Party

In Flims Dorf, **Iglu Music Bar** and **Legna Bar** are main rendezvous. **Living-room Flims** is less frenetic. In Flims Waldhaus, **Bellendavista Bistro Bar** is popular. In Laax, **Casa Veglia** is the disco favourite with occasional live concerts. **Rider's Club and Gallery** at the DesignHotel Riders Palace is where snowboarders congregate for parties, concerts and shows. **The Crap Bar** is also rated.

Sleep

Flims:
- ***** **Park Hotel Waldhaus**, t +41 (0)81 928 4848, *www.parkhotel-waldhaus.ch*, is a giant hotel complex set in five buildings linked by underground walkways.
- **** **Hotel Adula**, t +41 (0)81 928 2828, *www.adula.ch*, in Flims Dorf, has good children's facilities and La Mira spa.
- **** **Albana Sporthotel**, t +41 (0)81 927 2333, *www.albana-flims.ch*, is convenient for the slopes.
- **** **Sunstar Hotel Surselva**, t +41 (0)81 928 1800, *www.sunstar.ch/flims*, in Waldhaus, has a swimming pool and wellness centre. Children under 16 years pay only CHF1 per year of age per night.
- *** **Ayurveda-Wohlfühlhotel Fidazerhof**, t +41 (0)81 920 9010 in Fidaz, has minimalist-design rooms and a spa offering Ayurvedic treatments.

Laax:
- *** **Hotel Posta Veglia**, t +41 (0)81 921 4466, *www.poestlilaax.ch*, has attractive panelled rooms with hand-painted furniture.
- *** **Hotel La Siala**, t +41 (0)81 927 2222, *www.lasiala.ch*, in the farming hamlet of Falera has an indoor swimming pool.
- *** **Riders Palace DesignHotel**, t +41 (0)81 927 9700, *www.riderspalace.com*, is an unusual blend of designer hotel and backpacker hostel with different rooms for different budgets.

Grindelwald

Profile

Busy and sophisticated village beneath the mighty Eiger that attracts a cosmopolitan crowd to its large and mainly intermediate ski area

Resort

Grindelwald is one of the world's oldest and most cosmopolitan ski resorts. The first British ski pioneers came to this corner of the Bernese Oberland in the 1880s. They were drawn by the awesome beauty of the Eiger, the Schreckhorn, and the Wetterhorn that tower above it – and by the newly-built rack-and-pinion mountain railway that not only provided easy access but acted as the first ski lift. Despite its network of cableways, chair- and drag-lifts the railway still today forms the backbone of the lift system in the linked Jungfrau region that Grindelwald shares with Wengen and Mürren.

Visitors from all over the world – and Japan in particular – come here to ride the train that rises though the north face of the Eiger to the 3454m Jungfraujoch, the highest station in Europe. Trains run with typical Swiss precision to a printed timetable. New rolling stock is being introduced this season, but reporters complain that rail is an annoyingly slow means of uphill transport that cuts into skiing time.

Mountain

Grindelwald has its own ski area of First that is reached by gondola from the village. It takes you up to the sunny mid-mountain station of Bort. From Schreckfeld two drags provide high-altitude novice terrain and a couple of

Essentials

Altitude 943m (3094ft)–2501m (8,206ft)
Map see page M53
Further information: t +41 (0)33 854 1212, www.grindelwald.com
Lifts in area: 41 in Jungfrau Top Ski Region (5 funiculars, 7 cableways, 15 chairs, 14 drags) serving 213km of piste
Lift pass: Jungfrau (covers Grindelwald, Mürren, Wengen) adult CHF288, child 6–19yrs CHF144–230, both for 6 days
Access: Zurich airport 2hrs, Geneva airport 3hrs. Station in resort

chairs continue up to Oberjoch at 2501m. Most of the skiing is easy intermediate, but a long black run from the top of the Egg drag-lift follows the line of the gondola back to the resort and is of considerable challenge. However, the main ski area is Kleine Scheidegg beneath the north face of the Eiger. Grindelwald shares these intermediate slopes with Wengen and a train runs from the base station at Grund up the mountain and over the shoulder to Wengen on the far side. Halts along the way provide access to runs on both sides. From Kleine Scheidegg itself, on top of the shoulder, a further train or a drag-lift brings you up to the Eigergletscher, the high point of the joint ski area and starting point for two notorious black runs – Blackrock and Oh God. Off-piste opportunities abound, with high-altitude drops possible on the surrounding glaciers and peaks by helicopter and fixed-wing aircraft. This is high alpine terrain and a guide should be used at all times.

A gondola also rises from Grund to the 2230m Männlichen ridge that separates the two resorts. From here you can work your way through a sequence of chair lifts and easy pistes to the Lauberhorn, starting point for one of the classic World Cup downhill courses. Grindelwald has a terrain park at Bargelegg.

Learn

The Jungfrau should be a perfect location for complete novices, but we cannot recommend it because of the restrictive hours offered by the mainstream **Swiss Snowsports School**, t +41 (0)33 853 5200. It gives mornings-only group lessons from Sunday to Friday. Guiding is through **Swiss Snowsports and Mountaineering School Grindelwald**, t +41 (0)33 854 1280.

Children

Kinderclub Bodmi, t +41 (0)33 853 5200, cares for non-skiing children from three years in its play area by the nursery slopes. **Kinderhort Sunshine**, t +41 (0)79 592 0209, accepts children from one month old at Männlichen. **Kinderhort Murmeli**, t +41 (0)33 853 0440, at First accepts children from six months.

Lunch

Brandegg on Kleine Scheidegg, t +41 (0)33 853 1057, is world renowned for its apple fritters. **Jagerstübli**, t +41 (0)33 853 1131, below Männlichen, is a farmhouse with a cosy atmosphere. **Hotel Aspen**, t +41 (0)33 854 4000, above Grund is 'sunny and welcoming'. **Berghaus**, t +41 (0)33 853 3651, at Bort is reasonably priced. **Hotel Wetterhorn**, t +41 (0)33 853 1218, on the way down to Grindelwald, is recommended.

Dine

Adlerstube, t +41 (0)33 854 7777, in the Sunstar is family friendly, with a large play area. **La Marmite**, t +41 (0)33 853 3553, in Hotel Kirchbühl, **The Derby-Bahnhof**, t +41 (0)33 854 5461, and **Schmitte**, t +41 (0)33 853 2202, in Hotel Schweizerhof are recommended. Kreuz & Post's **Challi-**

Stübli, t +41 (0)33 854 5492, and **Gade**, t +41 (0)33 854 1020, in Hotel Eigerblick are also praised.

Party

Downtown Park has DJs and regular live bands. **Challi-Bar**, **Cava-Bar**, and **Espresso** are resort meeting-places. **Gepsi-Bar** has live music and attracts an older clientele. **Mescalero** and the **Plaza** are the late-night venues.

Sleep

★★★★★**Grand Regina Alpin WellFit Hotel**, t +41 (0)33 854 8600, *www.grandregina.ch*, is decorated with antiques, and has a spa.

★★★★**Romantik Hotel Schweizerhof**, t +41 (0)33 853 2202, *www.hotel-schweizerhof.com*, was built in 1892 and retains its traditional character.

★★★★**Hotel Kreuz & Post**, t (0)33 854 5492, *www.kreuz-post.ch*, has a wellness centre, dancing-bar, and good food.

★★★★**Hotel Spinne**, t +41 (0)33 854 8888, *www.spinne.ch*, contains three restaurants and a disco.

★★★★**Sunstar-Hotel**, t +41 (0)33 854 7777, *www.sunstar.ch/grindelwald*, is opposite the First gondola, has a spa, and sleeps 400.

★★★**Hotel Alpenhof**, t +41 (0)33 853 5270, *www.alpenhof.ch*, is piste-side and three minutes' walk from the centre.

★★★**Hotel Bodmi**, t +41 (0)33 853 1220, *www.bodmi.ch*, on the nursery slopes, only accepts individual bookings and no groups.

★★★**Hotel Derby**, t +41 (0)33 854 5461, *www.derby-grindelwald.ch*, is family-run and in the town centre.

★★★**Chalet-Hotel Gletschergarten**, t +41 (0)33 853 1721, *www.hotel-gletschergarten.ch*, is close to the piste, with wood-panelled public rooms and

suites, and comfortable modern
bedrooms.
***Hotel Hirschen, t +41 (0)33 854 8484,
www.hirschen-grindelwald.ch, has been
in the same family since 1870 and is
known for its cooking.

Gstaad

Profile

**Quaint village with an exclusive hotel
and smart chalets that were once the
haunt of celebrities, but its low altitude
limits snow cover in these uncertain
winters of global warming**

Resort

This was once the winter home of the
rich and the famous. In the 1970s you
could easily find yourself sharing a chair-
lift with Liz Taylor, Richard Burton, Julie
Andrews or Roger Moore. But times – and
more significantly, climates – change. By
the standards of 21st-century ski resorts,
the skiing is limited in challenge. Nearly
half of it is graded as easy. Uncertain
snow cover at this low altitude has driven
the next generation of celebrities to seek
fresh pastures. The village understandably
argues that the volume of skiing covered

by the regional lift pass compensates for
the absence of demanding gradient. Nearby
Les Diablerets glacier, which has a top height
of 2979m, always provides limited skiing
even in the driest winters. Rougemont
offers some challenging skiing.

Mountain

Gstaad's own skiing takes place in the
separate Wispile and Eggli areas on either
side of the village with a top height of less
than 2000m. The mainly easy blue runs here
and on the other nearby pastures offer
limited challenge – and limited snow cover
for much of the winter. Ski buses to the
surrounding villages of Saanenmöser and
Schönried St Stephan, Zweisimmen,
Lauenen, Gsteig, Saanen and Château d'Oex
are all included in the regional lift pass.

Terrain parks are located on Eggli, at
Hornberg above Saanenmöser, and at
Rinderberg above Zweisimmen. More
than 140km of cross-country tracks line
the valley floor.

Learn

The choice lies between **Gstaad
Snowsports**, t +41 (0)33 744 1865,
Snowsports Saanenland, t +41 (0)33 744
3665, and **Alpinzentrum Gstaad
Snowsports**, t +41 (0)33 744 1044.

Children

All the ski schools offer lessons.
Babysitting is available through the
tourist office.

Lunch

Try **Chemistube**, t +41 (0)33 722 2240,
above St Stephan, **Gobeli**, t +41 (0)33 722
1219, at Rinderberg, **Kübelialp**, t +41 (0)33
744 9898, near the mid-station at
Saanersloch, **Berghaus Rellerli**, t +41 (0)33

Essentials

Altitude: 1050m (3,445ft)–2979m (9,744ft)
Further information: t +41 (0)33 748 8737,
www.mountainrides.ch/www.gstaad.ch
Lifts in area: 62 (15 cableways, 17 chairs, 30
drags) serving 250km of piste
Lift pass: Region top card adult CHF266,
child from 6yrs CHF139, both for 6 days
Access: Geneva airport 1½hrs, station in
resort

748 8722, above Schönried, and **Berghaus Wasserngrat**, t +41 (0)33 748 9622, at Wasserngrat.

Dine

In Gstaad, Robert Speth, Gault Millau Swiss Chef-of-the-Year, presides over the kitchen in the **Chesery**, t +41 (0)33 744 2451, built in 1962 by the Aga Khan. **Rooster Bar**, t +41 (0)79 481 6561, in Hotel Gsaaderhof serves Thai food. **Spoon de Neige** in the sixteenth-century Chlösterli, t +41 (0)33 748 7979, is warmly recommended. **Hüsy**, t +41 (0)33 722 1056, in Zweisimmen specializes in fresh fish. Erich Baumer's **Sonnenhof**, t +41 (0)33 744 1023 in Saanen has great food and a warm ambience.

Party

In Gstaad, The Palace Hotel's **GreenGo** nightclub is the place to see and be seen. The locals meet at **Richi's Pub**. Other haunts include **Hush**, managed by Roger Moore's son, Geoffrey, **Stall-Bar Chlösterli**, **La Cave**, and **Rialto Bar**.

Sleep

*****Palace Hotel**, t +41 (0)33 748 5000, made famous by Peter Sellers in *The Pink Panther* looks likes a fairytale castle.
*****Grand Hotel Park**, t +41 (0)33 748 9800, is the opulent alternative.
****Hotel Bernerhof**, t +41 (0)33 748 8844, is conveniently close to the train station.
****Hotel Christiania**, t +41 (0)33 744 5121, has individually designed bedrooms.
Hotel Olden, t +41 (0)33 744 3444, is family-run and cosy.
Posthotel Rössli, t +41 (0)33 748 4242, *www.posthotelroessli.ch*, is in the village centre and has pine-panelled rooms and a restaurant which serves traditional local fare.

Klosters

Profile

Attractive traditional resort that shares the Parsenn ski area with Davos. Well-groomed slopes for intermediates and tough off-piste, along with some memorable mountain restaurants

Resort

Despite its high international profile largely created by the annual visits of Prince Charles and his sons, Klosters clings tenaciously to its roots as a typical Swiss alpine village that combines tourism with the more serious business of farming. Unlike Davos, its much larger and more cosmopolitan sister that shares the Parsenn ski area, Klosters entertains fame and embraces fortune but has never knowingly sought either. Of course, this unassuming air is exactly what attracts people like Prince Charles and the wealthy bankers from Zurich's Bahnhofstrasse who form an important part of its upmarket clientele. The farming community has been welcoming tourists ever since the first British skiers showed up here in 1904, drawn by the steeper ski slopes at this end of the Parsenn.

Essentials

Altitude: 1192m (3,911ft)–2844m (9,328ft)
Map: see page M49
Further information: t +41 (0)81 410 2020, *www.klosters.ch*
Lifts in area: 53 in Davos/Klosters area (2 funiculars, 13 cableways, 9 chairs, 29 drags) serving 370km of piste
Lift pass: adult CHF282, child 6–17yrs CHF94–189, both for 6 days
Access: Zurich airport 2½hrs, stations in Klosters Dorf and Klosters Platz

Like Davos, the resort is divided into two sectors. Klosters Platz around the main railway station is the village centre, with most of the hotels, shops, restaurants, and access to the Parsenn. Klosters Dorf, also on the railway line but a couple of kilometres away, is a more remote outpost around the base of the Madrisa gondola. A regular bus service connects the two. Trains between Klosters and Davos are included in the regional lift pass.

Mountain

Klosters' own area, Madrisa, has some of the best beginner slopes in this part of Switzerland but is too often dismissed as just a novice ski area. A painfully slow gondola followed by two more lifts brings you to the start of Prince Charles' favourite run – follow the piste to the Alpi hut, fork left on to the steep black No.10 on the map. A long path by a dramatic river gully brings you back to the gondola base. From the top of Madrisa you can ski, with a guide, to Gargellen in Austria.

However, for most skiers and riders the Parsenn is the main course. Mountain access from Klosters Platz is by the two-stage Gotschna cable car. Much the most challenging pistes and itinerary routes are to be found at this end of the Parsenn. Several spectacular and demanding runs such as the usually wickedly mogulled Drostobel lead back down through the trees to Klosters.

A network of lifts and pistes takes you across the Parsenn to the Weissfluhjoch above Davos and the still higher 2844m Weissfluhgipfel. From here you can ski 12km through 2000m vertical down to the outlying villages of Küblis and Serneus. It is a fine way to end the day, with a drink at bottom before catching the train back up the valley to Klosters.

Snowboarders find a frustrating number of flats in the centre of the Parsenn. They tend to congregate in the separate Davos ski areas of Jakobshorn which has a terrain park, two half-pipes and a snowcross course.

Learn

Saas Ski and Snowboard School, t +41 (0)81 420 2233, has mainly young instructors with fluent English. Swiss Snowsports School, t +41 (0)81 410 2828, is the competition. Boardriding Klosters, t +41 (0)81 420 2662, and Bananas, t +41 (0)81 422 6660, are the boarding specialists. Guiding is with Adventure Skiing, t +41 (0)81 422 4825, Berger Jürg, t +41 (0)81 422 3636, and through the ski schools.

Children

Kids Land t +41 (0)81 410 2170 at Madrisa is for non-skiers from two years, while the Snow Garden, t +41 (0)81 410 2828, based in the Sports Centre at Klosters Platz, is for skiers over four years.

Lunch

Berghaus Erika, t +41 (0)81 422 1117, in the hamlet of Schlappin on the black run down from Madrisa, is warmly recommended for its *Rösti*. Reporters complain that the famous Schwendi Houses, rustic huts on the Parsenn that have long been a mainstay of Klosters lunchtime scene, have dropped their standards and are overpriced. Best bet is the Schwendi Ski und Berghaus, t +41 (0)81 422 1289. Gotschna, t +41 (0)81 422 1428 at Serneus is a welcome sight after the long run down. Schifer Berghaus, t +41 (0)81 332 1533 has good food and a cheerful atmosphere.

Dine

Celebrity chef, Beat Bolliger, runs his Michelin-starred restaurant in **Hotel Walserhof, t** +41 (0)81 410 2929, which is the top dining spot in town. In high season you must book well in advance. **Chesa Grischuna, t** +41 (0)81 422 2222, maintains a high standard. **The Wynegg, t** +41 (0)81 422 1340, serves wholesome mountain fare in pleasant surroundings.

Party

The Gotschnabar, next to the cable-car station, has been totally rebuilt and is the latest après-ski meeting point. **Steinbock Bar**, **Chesa Grischuna**, and **The Piano Bar** in the Silvretta Parkhotel are usually lively. Later on Prince Harry's favourite, **Casa Antica**, is the hotspot. Try also **Kir Royal**, **The Rössli Bar**, and **The Mountain Pub** in Klosters Dorf.

Sleep

★★★★Hotel Alpina, t +41 (0)81 410 2424, *www.alpina-klosters.ch*, is a well-positioned hotel with a small swimming pool and a restaurant serving 'creative cooking'.

★★★★Chesa Grischuna, t +41 (0)81 422 2222, *www.chesagrischuna.ch*, has been welcoming guests since 1938, and retains its rustic style.

★★★★Eugenia, t +44 (0)20 7384 3854, *www.descent.co.uk*, is a handsome villa with vast bedrooms, oak panelled walls, beautiful marble and stripped wood floors, and impressive pillared fireplaces.

★★★★Hotel Pardenn, t +41 (0)81 423 2020, *www.pardenn.ch*, is central yet quiet, with a swimming pool and a restaurant that has vegetarian options.

★★★★Hotel Vereina, t +41 (0)81 410 2727, *www.vereinahotel.ch*, has more suites than bedrooms, a huge pool and exquisite basement spa.

★★★★Hotel Walserhof, t +41 (0)81 410 2929, *www.walserhof.ch*, has an excellent restaurant and royal patronage.

★★★★Silvretta Parkhotel, t +41 (0)81 423 3435, *www.silvretta.ch*, has large rooms, a wellness centre, and children's Flipper Club.

★★★Hotel Rustico, t +41 (0)81 410 2288, *www.the-rustico-klosters.ch*, has bedrooms that are individually decorated and serves Asian-Japanese food in its restaurant.

Hotel Wynegg, t +41 (0)81 422 1340 is a cosy old hotel run along the lines of a large chalet for its mainly British guests.

Mürren

Profile

Chocolate-box pretty, car-free village with some steep skiing for strong intermediates and advanced skiers. This is not the ideal resort for beginners

Resort

Back in 1911, Henry Lunn, an entrepreneurial lawn tennis equipment

Essentials

Altitude: 1650m (5,412ft)–2971m (9,748ft)
Map: see page M53
Further information: t +41 (0)33 856 8686, *www.wengen-muerren.ch*
Lifts in area: 12 (2 railways, 2 cableways, 5 chairs, 4 drags). 41 in Jungfrau Top Ski Region serving 213km of piste
Lift pass: Jungfrau (covers Grindelwald, Mürren, Wengen) adult CHF288, child 6–19yrs CHF144–230, both for 6 days
Access: Zurich airport 3hrs, Geneva airport 4hrs. Station in resort

salesman, launched a new career for himself as the first ski package tour operator in this delightful Swiss village above Lauterbrunnen in the Bernese Oberland.

He persuaded the Jungfrau Railway to keep the line open during the winter, rented the Palace Hotel and asked the 'right' sort of Englishmen – those who had been privately educated – to come and join him. He never actually skied himself. His son Sir Arnold, founder of modern ski racing - and, in turn, his son Peter – continued the association. Sir Arnold's Kandahar Ski Club made its home here in 1922 and a strong relationship with Britain has continued until the present day.

The car-free village is the perfect example of a quaint Swiss alpine community with Heidi-esque chalets and dramatic views of the Eiger, the Mönch, and the Jungfrau. The village is perched on a balcony 550m above the valley and is reached either by a funicular and mountain railway from Lauterbrunnen, or by cable car from Stechelberg and Gimmelwald. Mürren shares its lift pass with Wengen and Grindelwald, which can be reached by train. However distances are big and the trains are slow. Most Mürren-based skiers tend to remain in their own 12-lift territory dominated by the 2970m Schilthorn.

Mountain

The skiing here suits all standards – but, despite the vociferous protestations of committed Mürrenites, there is not much of it. A chair lift from the edge of the village and a drag above serve undulating intermediate runs on the 2145m Schiltgrat. A funicular from the village gives access to a nursery slope at Allmendhubel and further reds as well as an easy blue back to the village. The Winteregg sector, reached by train from

Mürren or by piste and chair from Allmendhubel, has easy, open pistes. In good snow conditions it is possible to ski all the way down to Lauterbrunnen.

Serious skiers and riders take the cable car from the village up to Birg and then the final stage to the Piz Gloria revolving restaurant on the 2970m summit of the Schilthorn. The black descent is one of the classic runs of the Alps and starting point for the annual pro-am Inferno Race, which goes down to Winteregg or even Lauterbrunnen when conditions permit. The top section can become heavily moguled later in the day. The Muttlern and Kandahar chairs beneath Obere Hubel, allow further skiing without having to descend to the cable car.

Off-piste opportunities abound, but it is essential to take a guide. Tschingelchrachen off the Schilthornbahn is steep and technically demanding, but prone to avalanche. Others include Hidden Valley from the summit of the Maulerhubel to Grutsch, and the Blumental.

Learn

The **Swiss Ski and Snowboard School**, **t** +41 (0)33 855 1247, has no competition, but the level of instruction is surprisingly high. Group ski lessons are limited to two hours each morning from Monday to Saturday. Snowboard group lessons are afternoon-only, from Monday to Friday.

Children

Snowgarten, t +41 (0)33 856 8686, behind Hotel Jungfrau, cares for non-skiing children from 18 months to five years with free nappies and a pick-up service from hotels on request.

Lunch

The revolving **Piz Gloria**, t +41 (0)33 826 0007, on the summit of the Schilthorn, was made famous in the 1968 Bond film, *On Her Majesty's Secret Service*, and is worth a visit even if the views are more spectacular than the cuisine. The **Schilthornhütte**, t +41 (0)78 788 5767, on the way down, serves simple mountain fare. **Gimmelen**, t +41 (0)33 855 1366, is renowned for its cheesy dishes and *Apfelküchen*. **Sonnenburg**, t + 41 (0)33 855 1127, is praised for its *Rösti*.

Dine

Hotel Eiger Stübli, t + 41 (0)33 856 5454, **Hotel Alpenruh**, t +41 (0)33 856 8800, and the **Eiger Guesthouse**, t +41 (0)33 856 5460, are all recommended, along with **Hotel Edelweiss**, t +41 (0)33 856 5600, and the **Stägerstübli**, t +42 (0)33 855 1316. **Kandahar Snack**, t +41 (0)33 855 8695, offers good light meals.

Party

The **Ballon Bar** in the Anfi Palace, **The Pub** in the Eiger Guesthouse, and the **Tächi Bar** in Hotel Eiger are the main meeting-places. The **Blüemlichäller** disco in Hotel Blumental and **The Inferno** disco in the Anfi Palace are crowded in high season.

Sleep

****Anfi Palace**, t +41 (0)33 856 9999, *www.muerren.ch/palace*, dates back to the Edwardian days of Henry Lunn, when it housed its first tourists.
****Hotel Eiger**, t +41 (0)33 856 5454, *www.hoteleiger.com*, across the road from the railway station, is the only hotel with its own indoor pool.
***Hotel Alpenruh**, t +41 (0)33 856 8800, *www.hotelschilthorn.ch*, at the Schilthornbahn end of the village, has a good restaurant and great views.
***Hotel Blumental**, t +41 (0)33 855 1826, *www.muerren.ch/blumental*, has been recently renovated.
***Hotel Edelweiss**, t +41 (0)33 856 5600. *www.edelweiss-muerren.ch*, is friendly and well positioned.
***Hotel Jungfrau**, t +41 (0)33 856 6464, *www.hoteljungfrau.ch*, is a friendly place, with an annexe called Haus Mönch across the road.
*Eiger Guesthouse**, t +41 (0)33 856 5460, formerly the Belmont, has Swiss-Scottish owners, low prices, and a relaxed atmosphere.

Saas-Fee

Profile

Traditional village offering year-round glacier skiing. Terrain is best suited to beginners, low intermediates, and ski tourers. Popular resort for snowboarding

Essentials

Altitude: 1800m (5,904ft)–3600m (11,811ft)
Further information: t +41 (0)27 958 1858, *www.saas-fee.ch*
Lifts in area: 22 (1 funicular, 7 cableways, 1 chair, 13 drags) serving 100km of piste
Lift pass: Saasertal CHF327, child 6–16yrs CHF275, both for 6 days
Access: Geneva airport 4hrs, Sion airport 1½hrs. Station at Visp or Brig, hourly bus connection

Resort

Saas-Fee is an ancient village in a supreme high-altitude setting, surrounded by a horseshoe of no less than 13 peaks of 4000m. Blackened chalets interspersed with modern hotels, fashion boutiques, and ski shops line its narrow car-free streets. Its high altitude allows skiing on the glacier from the beginning of July through to the start of the winter season in November. Despite its year-round tourism, Saas-Fee somehow manages to maintain an innocent charm often lacking in major resorts. The handful of powerful village families who still run it have been known to favour image over commercial gain. The resort once famously reneged on its lucrative contract to stage the British University Ski Championships over worries that the alcoholic après-ski intake of contestants and supporters might upset the sensibilities of older guests. You can still buy fresh milk by the pail, the lift system is modern and efficient, and it has some of the best nursery slopes in Switzerland.

However such alpine bliss has its drawbacks. The glacial terrain is as hostile as it is beautiful. Much of the mountainside is littered by giant *séracs* and wide crevasses that beckon anyone who is foolish enough to leave the marked piste without a local guide. Such treacherous topography means that the pistes themselves are inevitably limited in scope and reporters complain that for a resort of this size there is simply not enough skiing or riding for a whole week. The separate outlying hamlets of Saas-Almagell and Saas-Grund provide a little more variety. Saas-Fee also has a a whole mountain, served by a gondola, that is reserved for tobogganing. Cars must be left in car parks on the outskirts of the resort and transport is confined to electric ski buses and taxis.

Mountain

Access is by cable cars from either end of the resort, which take you to the mid-mountain station of Morenia. A further cable car continues to 3000m Felskinn, starting point for the Metro-Alpin, the world's highest underground funicular. This brings you up to Allalin at 3500m, just below the highest point of the ski area. A gondola from the village, followed by a cable car and a sequence of drag-lifts, provides a slower alternative passage to the top of the mountain. Despite the full range of colour codings, neither of the main routes back down offers much challenge. A network of other lifts – mainly drag-lifts because of the itinerant nature of the glacier – give access to more short runs. The separate Plattjen sector, reached by gondola from the village, provides more intermediate skiing and a floodlit piste for night skiing. Saas-Fee has a terrain park and half-pipe served by the Mittaghorn drag reached from Morenia. There is also a half-pipe and snowcross course in the summer ski area.

Learn

The overtly staid **Swiss Ski and Snowboard School, t** +41 (0)27 957 2348, has the monopoly for skiing, but faces a formidable rival for riding instruction in the **Eskimo Snowboardschool, t** +41 (0)27 957 4904. In the past, the Swiss school has been heavily criticized for being old-fashioned and not keeping abreast of modern technique. However, the standard of teaching is said to be much improved and most instructors speak good English.

Children

Murmeli, t +41 (0)27 957 4057 in Hotel Artemis offers daycare for children aged one month to six years, and **Glückskäfer,**

t +41 (0)79 225 8154 provides babysitting in your hotel or apartment.

Lunch

The **Metro-Alpin** revolving restaurant, t +41 (0)957 1771, at Mittelallalin has great views and average food. **Berghaus Plattjen**, t +41 (0)79 5666926, serves fine *Rösti*. Try also **Egginer Morenia**, t +41 (0)957 1881, **Längfluh**, t +41 (0)957 2132, and the **Gletschergrotte**, t +41 (0)957 2160. Many skiers return to the village at lunchtime.

Dine

Vernissage, t +41 (0) 27 958 1904, is a new restaurant and après-ski complex opened this season by avant-garde Zermatt artist and designer Heinz Julen. **Cheminée**, t +41 (0) 27 957 2748, **Cäsar Ritz**, t +41 (0)27 958 1900 in the Ferien art Resort, and the Michelin-rated **Fletschhorn Waldhotel**, t +41 (0)27 957 2131, are warmly recommended. **Boccalino**, t +41 (0)27 957 1731, and **Don Ciccio**, t +41 (0)27 957 4020, are good pizzerias.

Party

Après-ski is wild. Busy bars include **Alpen-Pub**, **Happy Bar**, **Metro-Bar**, **Nesti's Ski-Bar**, and **Hozwurm**. Later on the action switches to **Vernissage**, **Crazy Night**, **John's Pub**, and **Popcorn The Snowboard Joint** in Hotel Dom.

Sleep

*****Ferienart Resort & Spa**, t +41 (0)27 958 1900, has six restaurants and a new health and fitness centre.

****Hotel Metropol**, t +41 (0)27 957 1001, is run on Feng-Shui principles with bio and Finnish saunas as well as a disco.

****Gourmet & Wellnesshotel Schweizerhof**, t + 41 (0)27 958 7575, has a waterfall in the lounge and reception rooms decorated in Belle Epoque style.

****Allalin Relais du Silence**, t +41 (0)27 957 1815, is in a peaceful setting and has lots of atmosphere.

***Fletschhorn Waldhotel**, t +41 (0)27 957 2131, *www.fletschhorn.ch*, set in the woods above Saas-Fee, houses a modern art gallery and an outstanding wine cellar.

***Unique Hotel Dom**, t +41 (0)27 957 51 01, is a central snowboarders' rendezvous, with a state-of-the-art Sony sound system in every room.

St Moritz

Profile

One of the world's most famous resorts with beautiful scenery, great hotels, gourmet restaurants, superb shops, and a wide range of other winter sports

Essentials

Altitude: 1800m (5,904ft)–3303m (10,834ft)

Map: see page M52

Further information: t +41 (0)81 837 3333, *www.stmoritz.ch*

Lifts in area: 57 (1 funicular, 10 cableways, 18 chairs, 27 drags) serving 350km of piste

Lift pass: Upper Engadine (covers Celerina, Pontresina, St Moritz, Sils Maria, Silvaplana and 1 day in Livigno) adult CHF262–332, child 6–15yrs CHF131–166, both for 6 days

Access: Zurich airport 3–4hrs, station in resort

Resort

The first home of winter sports in the Alps has been an important spa town since the Middle Ages and has never knowingly lost an opportunity to market itself internationally. The brand name, synonymous with wealth and high-living, is protected by trademark in 50 countries around the world. As long ago as 1519, Pope Leo X was offering full absolution for every Christian who visited the healing mineral springs.

Reliable weather in the Engadine Valley brought summer visitors, but it wasn't until 1864 that hotelier Johannes Badrutt hit upon the idea of a creating a winter season. That September he overheard four Englishmen lamenting the fact that they must soon return to London for the winter and would be back again the following July. He suggested they returned in January and wagered that if they experienced fewer sunny days in winter than in summer he would pay for their accommodation. Johannes was on a statistical winner – and the rest is history.

They skated on the frozen lake and tobogganed on a steep slope that was to become the Cresta Run. Today it remains the most machismo and dangerous of all winter sports. The private and still British-run St Moritz Tobogganing Club continues to maintain a sexist men-only stance as it has done for more than 100 years.

Socially well-connected beginners can launch themselves head first down the ice on a heavy metal skeleton toboggan on four mornings a week from Christmas to the end of February. They achieve speeds of around 100kph.

The Cresta should not be confused with bobsleigh. St Moritz has the one remaining natural ice run that is rebuilt each winter with nine serpentine bends snaking down to Celerina. Skating and curling are also important activities that take place on the frozen lake. Not all alternative sports involve sliding – golf, polo, horse-racing, show jumping, greyhound racing, and even cricket are played and watched by St Moritz's hedonistic clientele.

The resort is divided into two communities. St Moritz Bad lies along the shore of the lake, while St Moritz Dorf is the higher town centre. Surprisingly for a place with such an impeccable pedigree, the architecture is far from being aesthetically pleasing. The beauty of the place lies not in the views of the resort itself but in the vista from it.

Mountain

Skiing is only one of the many winter activities offered by St Moritz, but the area is extensive, with sufficient variety and challenge to please most skiers and riders. The regional lift pass covers 57 lifts in villages scattered across the Upper Engadine. These include Celerina, Pontresina, Silvaplana and Sils Maria. They are by no means all connected.

St Moritz's own skiing takes place on Corviglia, reached by a cable car from St Moritz Bad or by a funicular from St Moritz Dorf. It can also be accessed by chair from Suvretta and by gondola from Celerina. A 100-person cable car continues on up to Piz Nair at 3057m.

Corvatsch, on the other side of the valley, and reached by bus, is of greater interest to advanced skiers and riders. It is reached from Sils Maria, Silvaplana and Surlej.

The third outlying main area of Diavolezza-Lagalb rises to a snowsure 3000m and is reached from St Moritz by bus or train. A long itinerary run from the top of Diavolezza, considered to be one of the Alpine classics, winds down over heavily crevassed glacial terrain to Morteratsch.

High prices restrict the number of young riders who can afford to come to St Moritz, but those that do find some outstanding terrain. Diavolezza is great for freeriding. The terrain park and half-pipe at Corviglia is accessed by the Munt da San Murezzan chair.

Cross-country skiing is as popular as the downhill variety, with tracks through the pine forest and along the shores of the lake. The annual pro-am 42km Engadine Marathon attracts thousands of Langlaufers and is a highlight of the European cross-country calendar.

Learn

Swiss Snowsports School, t +41 (0)81 830 0101, and **Suvretta**, t +41 (0)81 836 3600, are both recommended, along with **Wave Snowboard School**, t +41 (0)81 837 5353, in Celerina. A high number of the resort's wealthy guests book private guides, which has resulted in the establishment of a number of specialist organisations: **AAA**, t +41 (0)81 832 2233, **Bergsteigerschule Pontresina**, t +41 (0)81 838 8333, and the **St Moritz Experience**, t +41 (0)81 833 7714. **Heli Bernina** t +41 81 852 4677, and **Heliswiss**, t +41 (0)81 852 3535, can arrange heli-skiing.

Children

Hotel Schweizerhof, t +41 (0)81 837 0707, has daycare for children over three years, as does **Badrutt Palace Hotel**, t +41 (0)81 837 1000. **Suvretta House's Teddy Bear Club**, t +41 (0)81 836 36360, has a kindergarten for small guests from 12 months old, and a children's restaurant. **Kempi Kids Club**, t +41 (0)81 838 3838, in the Grand Hotel des Bains Kempinski officially takes children from three years, although it will also care for guests' babies. All the ski schools take children from four years.

Lunch

On Corviglia, La Marmite, which has a justified reputation as the best (and most expensive) high altitude lunching experience in the Alps is now known as **Mathis Food Affairs**, t +41 (0)81 833 6355. Owner Reto Mathis continues to serve caviar and truffle-rich dishes in the stately style pioneered a generation ago by his father Hartly. **Chasellas**, t +41 (0)81 833 3854, **Trutz**, t +41 (0)81 833 7030, and **Chamanna**, t +41 (0)79 682 5080, are all owned by the Suvretta House Hotel and are warmly recommended along with **Salastrains**, t +41 (0)81 833 3867.

Dine

Chesa Veglia, t +41 (0)81 837 2800, serves Engadine specialities and fine pizzas. **Jöhri's Talvo** at Champfer, t +41 (0)81 833 4455, is renowned for its local venison and game. **Nobu**, t +41 (0) 81 837 2624 has opened in Badrutt's Palace Hotel for gourmet sushi and other Japanese cuisine, and **The Sunny Bar** at the Kulm, t +41 (0) 81 836 8000, also serves sushi. **Trutz**, t + 41 (0)81 836 3737, is open for evening fondue and raclette. **The Grischuna** at the Hotel Monopol, t +41 (0)81 837 0404, is warmly recommended.

Party

Hanselmann's in St Moritz Dorf is a 100-year-old coffee house that is a resort meeting place after skiing, serving pastries and delectable ice cream. Moroccan-themed **King's Club**, t +41 (0)81 837 1000, is the top nightclub. **Diamond** is the new place in town, with a lounge, restaurant and club. **Vivai**, **Cascade**, and **Cava** in the Hotel Steffani are rated. **Devil's Place** bar at Hotel Waldhaus am See has the world's biggest range of malt whisky and receives a mention in *Guinness World Records*. The **Stübli** at the

Schweizerhof has late-night dancing on tables, and after 10pm is 'so crowded that you could not possibly fall off'. The **Muli Bar** hosts Country and Western music, **Bobby's Bar** is for the under-20s.

Sleep

★★★★★**Grand Hotel des Bains Kempinski,** t +41 (0)81 838 3838, in St Moritz Bad has a renowned spa, the smartest wine bar in town, and a casino.

★★★★★**Badrutt's Palace Hotel,** t + 41 (0)81 837 1000, with its landmark tower, is the most famous establishment housing seven restaurants and the King's Club.

★★★★★**Kulm Hotel,** t +41 (0)81 836 8000, is the customary choice of Cresta riders.

★★★★★**Suvretta House,** t +41 (0)81 836 3636, has a spa, skating-rink, nursery slope, its own ski lift, and ski school.

★★★★★**Hotel Carlton,** t +41 (0)81 836 7000, is the smallest of the five-stars with a more intimate country-house atmosphere.

★★★★**Hotel Schweizerhof,** t +41 (0)81 837 0707, is renowned for its Acla and Clavadatsch restaurants and its basement Hofkeller.

★★★★**Hotel Steffani,** t +41 (0)81 836 9696, is a traditional family-owned hotel in the centre of town with the resort's oldest restaurant.

★★★**Hotel Waldhaus am See,** t +41 (0)81 833 7676, is comfortable and world famous for its whisky collection, but is situated a brisk walk from the town centre.

★★★**Hotel Arte,** t +41 (0)81 837 5858, in St Moritz Dorf has nationally-themed bedrooms including Engadine, Australian, Japanese, Venetian, and Mexican.

Verbier

Profile

Switzerland's overall most challenging skiing both on and off-piste. Some excellent chalet accommodation, and a magnet for party-goers and snowboarders

Resort

Verbier lacks the pedigree of Davos or the aristocratic resorts of the Bernese Oberland that in Edwardian times became the original winter playgrounds for wealthy foreign skiers from Britain and elsewhere. The first lift, a Heath Robinson petrol-driven affair that pulled a sledge 200 vertical metres, wasn't opened until 1946. In those austere times, British and, indeed, German skiers were still otherwise engaged. Another 11 years passed before the Attelas cable car was built, and only then could Verbier could propertly describe itself as a ski resort.

Progress towards becoming one of the world's most famous and challenging winter destinations has been paved with periods when lack of reinvestment in the mountains threatened its status. But Verbier today is a thriving modern resort with an improved lift system and some extraordinarily challenging pistes, as well as a clutch of stomach-churning steep couloirs and limitless powder terrain.

Verbier is linked by lift and and an expensive electronic pass to neighbouring Thyon, Veysonnaz, and Nendaz. Together they form the Four Valleys, an uneasy alliance that should not be compared to the French Trois Vallées. In practice few Verbier-based skiers bother to journey into the far corners of the area where the lifts are primitive. More importantly, the pick of the slopes are found close to home on Mont Fort and Mont-Gelé.

Essentials

Altitude: 1500m (4,920ft)–3330m (10,925ft)
Map: see page M50
Further information: t +41 (0)27 775 3888, www.verbier.ch
Lifts in area: 89 in Four Valleys (16 cableways, 27 chairs, 46 drags) serving 412km of piste
Lift pass: Four Valleys (covers Bruson, Nendaz, Thyon, Verbier, Veysonnaz) adult CHF319, child 6–15yrs CHF223, both for 6 days
Access: Geneva airport 2–3hrs. Station at Le Châble 30mins by car or 10mins by cableway

The village itself, situated above the valley town of Le Châble 10km from Martigny, is a not particularly sightly blend of apartment blocks and chalets centred around a *place centrale* and dominated by a 1962 church with a 20m spire. Only 1,170 of the 12,000 beds are in hotels and little of the accommodation offers doorstep skiing. Overall the resort best suits accomplished skiers and riders looking for steep slopes and a bottomless nightlife.

Mountain

Access to Verbier's main ski area is a bus ride from Médran or a short walk from the Place Centrale. From here two gondolas rise to the 2200m mid-mountain hub of Les Ruinettes. A gondola also comes up from Le Châble and day-visitors are encouraged to use this rather than drive up to the resort.

A long-awaited new lift – a combination of gondola and chair lift – that is scheduled to open this winter, links Les Attelas to 2260m La Chaux where the Jumbo cable car rises to 2950m Col des Gentianes and finally to Mont Fort, the top of the ski area at 3330m. This will allow skiers from Geneva arriving at Le Châble rail station to reach Mont-Fort in 50 minutes.

The alternative route from Les Ruinettes is to take the Funispace gondola up to 2740m Attelas. From here, you either take the cable car up to the demanding slopes of Mont-Gelé, descend towards Les Ruinettes, or continue on into the Lac des Vaux sector. The black piste from the top of Mont Fort demands considerable concentration, particularly in icy conditions. Verbier is also famous for its ski itineraries that are patrolled but not groomed. Most notorious of these is Tortin, a steep, wide slope that is often dangerous to access because of exposed rocks at the top.

The standard of skier and rider in Verbier is high. Within hours of a fresh snowfall you will find tracks on even the most impossible-looking slopes, and runs such as Stairway to Heaven and Hidden Valley give the appearance of having been pisted. The north face of Mont Fort, with its B52 and Poubelle variants, is routinely skied, despite its hair-raising entry.

Not all the skiing is so radical. Les Ruinettes offers plenty of easier blue runs as does the resort's second ski area of Savoleyres, reached by gondola from the other side of town. The skiing here has been improved with a detachable six-person chair. It benefits from sunny south-facing slopes towards Verbier and longer, better runs down its back side to La Tzoumaz.

Novices make their first turns on a short nursery slope on the golf course and at Les Esserts. You can learn to ski in Verbier, but there are easier places in the Alps to do so. Verbier is a major centre for snowboarding. There is a giant terrain park at Les Chaux with separate snowcross and freestyle sectors, and a bar at the base area.

Learn

Verbier has a wide choice of ski schools, all with good reputations. **Powder Extreme, t** +41 (0)76 479 8771, was new last season. British-run **Altitude, t** +41 (0)27 771 6006, is highly rated: 'The best lessons I have ever had,' said one reporter. **European Snowsport, t** +41 (0)27 771 6222, offers courses for just six skiers including off-piste and women-only clinics. **La Maison du Sport, t** +41 (0)27 775 3363, is the official resort ski school. **Adrénaline, t** +41 (0)27 771 7459, and **No Limits, t** +41 (0)27 771 5556, are the remaining competition. **Bureau des Guides** at La Maison du Sport and **La Fantastique, t** +41 (0)27 27 771 4141, are the mountain-guiding companies. **Air Glaciers, t** +41 (0)27 329 1415, is the heli-skiing operation.

Children

Kid's Club, t +41 (0)27 775 3363, for skiers over four years, is run by La Maison du Sport at the Moulins nursery site, which has its own lift and restaurant. **Les Schtroumpfs, t** +41 (0)27 771 6585, also at Moulins, offers daycare for little ones aged three months to seven years.

Lunch

Cabane du Mont Fort, t +41 (0)27 771 7191, is a popular mountain refuge off the La Chaux piste, and **Cabane du Tortin, t** +41 (0)27 288 1153, serves heart-warming food. **Chez Dany, t** +41 (0)27 771 2524, in the woods below the Ruinettes chair, is a resort institution. **Au Vieux Verbier, t** +41 (0)27 771 1668, at Médran is famed for its beef flambéed at your table. On Savoleyres, **La Marlénaz, t** +41 (0)27 771 5441, is off-piste and has a good sun terrace, **La Marmotte, t** +41 (0)27 771 6834, specialises in *Rösti*, and **Le Sonalon, t** +41 (0)27 771 7271, is popular. **Chez Simon, t** +41

(0)27 306 8055, is atmospheric and non-smoking.

Dine

Roland Pierroz at the Hotel Rosalp still has the finest international cuisine in town. The hotel's brasserie, **La Pinte, t** +41 (0)27 771 6323, for both, is informal and less expensive. **Le Caveau, t** +41 (0)27 771 2226, has raclette and fondues. The restaurant in **Hotel Montpelier, t** +41 (0)27 771 6131, offers outstanding cuisine. **Appartement, t** +41 (0)27 27 771 6200, in Chalet d'Adrien specializes in French-international cuisine. **Chez Martin, t** +41 (0)27 771 2252, and **Al Capone, t** +41 (0)27 771 6774, serve pizzas. **Netsu, t** +41 (0)27 771 6272, is Japanese and **Chez Kamai, t** +41 (0)27 771 7628, is Indian.

Party

This is a party place, especially at weekends when wealthy players from London and Geneva hit town. **Le Farinet** in the Place Centrale is the most popular venue as the lifts close. Young skiers and snowboarders crush into the glass-sided terrace bar with live music. 30-somethings chill out inside over a bottle of wine in leather armchairs. **Offshore** with its pink VW Beetle centrepiece is a great place for après-ski drinks, and **Le Fer à Cheval** is busy by mid-afternoon. Resort staff flock to **Pub Mont Fort** for its cheap drinks. Later on, sophisticated **Crok No Name** provides the warm-up act for the night clubs of which the London- and Manhattan-priced **Farm Club** is still the leader. Moroccan-themed **Casbah** beneath Hotel Farinet, is an alternative. **Taratata** (known as Tara's) attracts a younger crowd. Clubs stay open until 4am.

Accommodation

*****Le Chalet d'Adrien, t** +41 (0)27 771 6200, *www.chalet-adrien.com*, in Savoleyres, is small with individually decorated rooms, two restaurants and a spa.

****Hotel Montpelier, t** +41 (0)27 771 6131, *www.hotelmontpelier.ch*, is inconvenient for the lifts but has attractive bedrooms and an indoor swimming pool.

****Hotel Rosalp, t** +41 (0)27 771 6323, *www.rosalp.ch* contains the resort's best restaurant and a spa that specializes in skin-ageing prevention.

****Hotel Vanessa, t** +41 (0)27 775 2800, *www.verbier.ch/vanessa*, is convenient, family-friendly, with good food.

***Hotel Bristol, t** +41 (0)27 771 6577, *www.bristol-verbier.ch*, is conveniently positioned and houses a disco on the first floor.

***Le Mazot, t** +41 (0)27 775 2121, owned by former ski racer, Serge Tacchini, is small and pleasant.

***Hotel Phenix, t** +41 (0)27 771 6844, *www.hotelphenix.pagesjaunes.ch*, is comfortable and central.

***Hotel Verbier, t** +41 (0)27 771 6688, *www.hotelverbier.ch*, in the village square, has a cosy sitting room.

****Hotel Garbo, t** +41 (0)27 771 6272, *www.hotelgarbo.com*, has two restaurants – French and sushi – and is well positioned.

The Bunker, t +41 (0)27 771 6602, *www.thebunker.ch*, next to the sports centre, attracts a large number of young people to its good-value dormitory accommodation.

Chalet Mozart, t +44 (0)20 7385 8050, *www.skiverbier.com*, sleeps two and is one of the most romantic chalets in the Alps.

Villars

Profile

An underrated area for beginners, intermediates and families with easy airport access from Geneva. Its low altitude means snow cover is unpredictable, but Les Diablerets glacier is open all year

Resort

Villars is one of the original resorts in the Alps that first attracted British skiers, largely because it is one of the few places in Switzerland where foreigners can buy property in their own right without serious restriction.

Snow cover at this low altitude is uncertain for much of the season, but the skiing is ideal for unadventurous intermediates and families who come here in large numbers to enjoy gentle slopes and magnificent scenery above the Rhône Valley in the beautiful Vaudois Mountains.

The resort shares its ski area with Les Diablerets, a large village with mainly chalet accommodation and a 3209m glacier where limited skiing is always possible even in the driest of winters.

Essentials

Altitude: 1300m (4,265ft)–2113m (6,932ft)
Further information: t +41 (0)24 495 3232, *www.villars.ch* / +41 (0)24 492 3358, *www.diablerets.ch*
Lifts in area: 48 (1 funicular, 6 cableways, 11 chairs, 30 drags) serving 215km of piste
Lift pass: Area (covers Villars, Les Diablerets and Gryon) adult CHF255, child 5–15yrs CHF153, both for 6 days
Access: Geneva airport 1½hrs

Mountain

Mountain access from Villars is by a cableway or by rack-and-pinion mountain railway that lead to Roc d'Orsay and the mid-mountain station of Bretaye at 1806m. A second gondola from the outlying hamlet of Barboleusaz provides an alternative means of mountain access.

From Bretaye a sequence of lifts and pistes leads across Les Chaux des Conches into the Diablerets sector, with a choice of runs down from 1949m Meilleret and 1727m Les Mazots to Vers L'Eglise and Les Diablerets itself. From here a gondola climbs the gentle pastureland to Isenau for some easy blue and slightly more challenging red runs. A bus takes you to Col du Pillon for the gondola up to the glacier which can also be reached by cable-car and chair from Reusch near Gstaad. The long run from the top takes you down the Combe d'Audon to Oldenalp at 1840m from where you can ride two chairs back up again in order to descend by cable car to Cold du Pillon and a bus back to Les Diablerets for the homeward journey to Villars. Terrain parks are at Bretaye and Les Chaux.

Learn

Villars Ski School, t +41 (0)24 495 4545, uses the graduated length method of teaching. **Riderschool, t** +41 (0)24 495 1600, is the dedicated boarder academy. **Gryon, t** +41 (0)24 498 2434, is warmly recommended. **Swiss Ski and Snowboard School, t** +41 (0)24 495 2210, is the traditional option, **Handicapt Sports & Loisirs, t** +41 (0)24 498 1028, is a sit-ski learning centre with a worldwide reputation. Off-piste guiding is available through **Villars Expérience, t** +41 (0)24 495 4138, and the ski schools. **Swiss Ski and Snowboard School, t** +41 (0)24 492 2002, is where to learn in Les Diablerets.

Children

Snowli – the Swiss school's kindergarten, and **Villars Ski School** both teach children from three years at Bretaye. **La Trottinette, t** +41 (0)24 495 8888, down in the village, cares for non-skiers from two months to six years. In Les Diablerets, the **Swiss Ski and Snowboard School** has a kindergarten from four years. **Hotel Le Chamois, t** +41 (0)24 492 2653, has an in-house kindergarten, and **Diablodocus Park** is part of the ski and snowboard school, offering lessons and childcare.

Lunch

Try **Hotel du Lac de Bretaye, t** +41 24 495 2192, and **Les Mazots** at Meilleret, **t** +41 24 492 1023. **Le Col de Bretaye, t** +41 (0)24 495 2194, and **Les Chaux, t** +41 (0)24 498 1187 are both recommended and **Les Chevonnes, t** +41 (0)24 495 2131, is in a lovely lakeside setting at Bretaye.

Dine

Les Ecovets, t +41 24 495 2378, specializes in regional dishes. **Le Vieux Villars, t** +41 24 495 2525, is renowned for its fondue and raclette. **Le Soleil, t** +41 24 495 4530, is a new gourmet restaurant. **Pasta & Basta, t** +41 (0)24 495 1818, in Chesières, **Le Sporting, t** +41 (0)24 495 1313, in Villars, and **L'Escale, t** +41 (0)24 498 1215, at Gryon below Les Chaux are cheaper alternatives. In Les Diablerets, **Auberge de la Poste, t** +41 (0)24 492 3124, and **Café des Diablerets, t** +41 (0)24 492 0909, serve regional specialities.

Party

Après-ski includes live rock and pool at **Café Central** in Villars or **Harabee Café** in Barboleuse, and drinking at **Charlie's Bar,**

L'Alchemiste, **Murphy's Wine Bar,** the Jazz or **Blues Bar** in Villars, or at **Ragot d'Elfe** in Gryon. Dance the night away at **El Gringo** in Villars. Les Diablerets' nightlife is quiet and centres around a few bars and discos, including **La Diabletine** bar and internet café, **Atomix Bar, B'Bar** disco in Mon Abri, and **Pote Saloon** which is the other disco. **Les Vioz** is a good place for a *vin chaud* after the last run down.

Sleep

Villars:

- ★★★★★**Grand Hotel du Parc,** t +41 (0)24 492 2828, *www.parcvillars.ch,* contains a choice of gastronomic and regional restaurants.
- ★★★★**Eurotel Victoria,** t +41 (0)24 492 3131, *www.forum.ch/eurotel-victoria-villars,* is in the village centre and has spacious rooms.
- ★★★★**Hotel du Golf,** t +41 (0)24 492 3838, *www.hotel-golf.ch,* is central, with attractive rooms and a wellness area.
- ★★★★**Hotel La Renardière,** t +41 (0)24 495 2592, *www.larenardiere.ch,* has a home-from-home ambience and lovely wood-panelled bedrooms.
- ★★★**Hotel Alpe Fleurie,** t +41 (0)24 492 3464 is a chalet-style hotel in the resort centre.
- ★★★**Hotel Ecureuil,** t +41 (0)24 492 3737, *www.hotel-ecureuil.ch,* has been run by the same family for over 50 years and is child-friendly.
- ★**Hotel Les Papillons,** t +41 (0)24 495 3484, between Villars and Gryon, is a small chalet-style B&B with attractive bedrooms.
- **Whitepod,** t +41 (0)79 744 6219, *www.whitepod.com,* is a luxury village of geodesic domes with wood-burning stoves and real beds.

Les Diablerets:

- ★★★★**Eurotel-Victoria,** t +41 (0)24 492 3721, *www.eurotel-victoria.ch,* is the biggest

hotel with large modern rooms and an indoor swimming pool.

- ★★★★**Hotel des Diablerets,** t +41 (0)24 492 0909, *www.hoteldesdiablerets.ch,* is in the village centre.
- ★★★**Hotel Le Chamois,** t +41 (0)24 492 265, *www.hotelchamois.ch,* is family-friendly with its own kindergarten.

Wengen

Profile

A car-free traditional resort with a large intermediate ski area linked to Grindelwald. Recommended for beginners and intermediates, as well as off-piste skiers, but not for families with small ski-age children

Resort

Wengen is one of the Edwardian cradles of modern skiing. Foreign – mainly British – visitors first arrived here in the late 19th century to gaze at the mighty peaks of the Eiger, Mönch, and Jungfrau – and they

Essentials

Altitude: 1274m (4,180ft)–2320m (7,612ft)
Map: see page M53
Further information: t +41 (0)33 855 1414, *www.wengen-muerren.ch/ www.wengen.com*
Lifts in area: 41 in Jungfrau Top Ski Region (5 funiculars, 7 cableways, 15 chairs, 14 drags) serving 213km of piste
Lift pass: Jungfrau (covers Grindelwald, Mürren, Wengen) adult CHF288, child 6–19yrs CHF144–230, both for 6 days
Access: Zurich airport 3hrs, Geneva airport 4hrs. Station in resort

came by train. The Jungfraubahn, the rack-and-pinion railway in the beautiful Bernese Oberland, was one of the engineering feats of the new Iron Age, climbing eventually through the granite heart of the Eiger to the 3454m Jungfraujoch, the highest railway station in Europe. It is now a Unesco World Natural Heritage site that attracts tourists throughout the year from all over the world and notably Japan.

From 1911 the rail company took the commercial decision to keep the network open in winter and sports-minded visitors quickly discovered that it could be used as a ski lift. Not all of these hardy tweed-clad pioneers approved of such easy uphill transport. The believed it offended the principle of 'no pain, no gain' and detracted from the achievement of skiing downhill. But in February 1925 the Downhill Only Club was formed in Wengen by British skiers to race against their Kandahar rivals encamped at Mürren on the other side of the Lauterbrunnen Valley. Both clubs are happily alive, active, and as big rivals as ever in the 21st century.

Today the railway connecting the three resorts of Wengen, Grindelwald, and Mürren still acts as the backbone of the shared Jungfrau ski region, along with a network of conventional ski lifts.

Car-free Wengen sits on a sunny ledge nearly 500m above Lauterbrunnen and is reached only by rail in winter. Electric taxis and a few licensed motor vehicles provide the in-resort transport. The main street stretches back from the station to a modest collection of hotels, shops, restaurants, a giant skating-rink, and family-friendly nursery slopes. Hotels and private homes line the steep mountainside above.

In recent years, Wengen has lost some of its faded Edwardian ambience in favour of the high-tech demands of a modern ski resort. Nevertheless it remains a tranquil Alpine backwater best suited to

intermediate piste skiers and riders looking for distance over challenging gradient against one of the world's most spectacular mountain backdrops.

Sadly, the failure of the Swiss Ski School to offer afternoon group lessons makes it an inconvenient destination for families with small children. Despite excellent conditions here in 2004–5, the region has had a sketchy snow record over the past decade, making early booking Christmas and late Easter skiing something of a lottery.

Mountain

'One of the most breathtaking places I have skied in,' said one reporter, 'One of the most picturesque resorts in the world,' said another, and 'The only place I have found where I can truly relax and enjoy my skiing'.

The commute up to the main skiing at Kleine Scheidegg is unquestionably more relaxing and scenic than the daily grind into Manhattan or the City of London. Swiss trains run to a precise timetable, with halts along the way. From Kleine Scheidegg you can drop back towards Wengen or take a run down the far side to Grindelwald. Trains also continue down to Grindelwald as well as up to the 2320m Eigergletscher. This is the highest point from which you can ski. The train then disappears behind the rock face and takes foot passengers on to the Jungfraujoch. Don't miss this excursion (the final section is not included in the lift pass), which stops at the famous windows in the North Face of the Eiger. From here mountain guides have launched dramatic rescue operations to save climbers stranded on the treacherous Eigerwand.

Alternative mountain access from Wengen is provided by a cable car that rises to the 2230m Männlichen ridge separates the Lauterbrunnen and

Grindelwald valleys. From here, a network of pistes and lifts brings you up to Kleine Scheidegg and the Eigergletscher. Long runs also continue down to the rail station at Grund near Grindelwald.

Each January, Wengen is the setting for the Lauberhorn, the longest – as well as one of the most celebrated and testing – downhill race in the World Cup Calendar. When not prepared for racing, the course that begins at the top of the Wixi chair, provides a glorious 4.5km red descent back to Wengen. Advanced skiers and riders will find that even the handful of runs marked black on the piste map lack real challenge, however, the opportunities for lift-accessible off-piste are enormous. The dramatic White Hare, which begins from the foot of the Eigerwand and is reached from Eigergletscher, is a favourite. Wengen has a terrain park with a variety of jumps and obstacles, served by the Wixi chair. Mürren is included in the lift pass and linked by train but not by piste. A day trip is viable, but distances are big and the trains are slow.

Learn

Swiss Ski School, t +41 (0)33 856 2022, gives three-hour morning group lessons from Sunday to Friday, as well as private lessons at any time. Privat Ski and Snowboard School, t +41 (0)33 855 5005, offers private tuition from young English-speaking instructors.

Children

Swiss Ski and Snowboard School, t +41 (0)33 856 2022, runs morning-only group lessons, which makes life difficult for parents with small skiers who consequently never get the chance to explore far afield. Both the Swiss and Privat Ski School, t +41 (0)33 855 5005, offer private afternoon lessons. However

these constitute an expensive form of childcare and don't solve the problem of lunchtime babysitting. Playhouse Wengen, t +41 (0)33 855 1414, cares for non-skiers from 18 months to seven years.

Lunch

Hotel Jungfrau, t +41 (0)33 855 1622, at Wengernalp has outstanding views from the terrace and the best food on the mountain. Brandegg, t +41 (0)33 853 1057, is famous for its apple fritters. Kleine Scheidegg Bahnhof, t +41 (0)33 828 7828, is a hotel and good restaurant as well as a station. Mary's Café, t +41 (0)33 855 2775, at the foot of the Lauberhorn race course, has wholesome and reasonably priced fare such as *Suppentopf* (beef and vegetable stew topped with cheese). Try also Allmend, t +41 (0)33 855 5800, for cheese fondue, Eigergletscher, t +41 (0)33 828 7888, and Männlichen, t +41 (0)33 853 1068.

Dine

With a few notable exceptions, restaurants in Wengen are almost all located in hotels. Da Sina, t +41 (0)33 855 3172, is a lively pizzeria. Hirschenstübli, t +41 (0)33 855 1544, in the Hotel Hirschen is renowned for its *fondue chinoise*. Hotel Berghaus, t +41 (0)33 855 2151, has a fish restaurant, and the Bernerhof, t +41 (0)33 855 2721, serves good fondue and raclette.

Party

At the end of the day, skiers and riders gather around the outdoor Brunner Snowbar on the home run. The last trains up the mountain are packed with families heading to Wengernalp for the 4km toboggan run back to the village. Mary's Café is ever popular. Later on the action moves to Tanne Bar, Sina's Pub, Tiffany, the Underground, and Chilis.

Sleep

****Beausite Park Hotel, t** +41 (0)33 856 5161, *www.parkwengen.ch*, is in a peaceful location next to the Männlichen cableway above town. It has a leisure area with swimming pool.

****Hotel Regina, t** +41 (0)33 856 5858, *www.wengen.com/regina*, is a stately old hotel housing two good restaurants and rooms from a bygone age.

****Hotel Sunstar, t** +41 (0)33 856 5111, *www.sunstar.ch/wengen*, is one of the most conveniently placed hotels, containing family duplexes and a swimming pool. 'A model of Swiss efficiency,' enthused one reporter.

***Hotel Alpenruhe Kulm, t** +41 (0)33 856 24 00, is set beside the woods with lovely views.

***Hotel Brunner, t** +41 (0)33 855 2494, *www.wengen.com/hotel/brunner*, is ski-in, ski-out above the village, and family-friendly.

***Hotel Eiger, t** +41 (0)33 855 1131, *www.eiger-wengen.ch*, is well positioned and a longtime British favourite.

***Hotel Falken, t** +41 (0)33 856 5121, *www.hotelfalken.com*, is one of the resort's original Edwardian hotels and decorated with historic photographs. Rooms are quaintly old-fashioned.

****Hotel Bernerhof, t** +41 (0)33 855 2721, is said to be 'very friendly and the food is good'.

Zermatt

Profile

Ancient, historic climbing town with lashings of Alpine charm, snow-sure skiing, luxury accommodation and the best mountain restaurants in the Alps.

Suits all standards of skier and rider, as well as non-skiers

Resort

Zermatt is no stranger to change. Ever since Victorian mountaineer Edward Whymper controversially conquered the Matterhorn in 1865, with four of his companions falling to their deaths on the downward journey, Zermatt has regularly reinvented itself as a tourist destination. Most recently this has been in the form of a high-tech ski resort by building a modern lift system to slowly replace the old network of sardine-can cable cars and drag-lifts that had changed precious little during the previous 40 years. At the same time is has developed a range of smart hotels and sumptuous restaurants on the mountain that have few rivals anywhere else in the world.

The bustling little town, set at 1620m above the valley town of Visp, attracts well-heeled skiers and snowboarders who want to combine snowsports with excellent eating and nightlife. Faithful followers include Michael Douglas, Robbie

Williams, Ronan Keating, Tom Cruise, King Juan Carlos, Diana Ross, Sir Paul McCartney, Nicole Kidman, and Peter Gabriel, along with members of Pink Floyd and Dire Straits.

The town – actually it is no more than a large village, its size dictated by limited avalanche-safe building territory – dates back to the Middle Ages. Old blackened barns stand beside modern hotels and smart boutiques and farmers still tend to their chickens and goats within 200m of the resort centre. Transport is by myriad high-speed electric taxis and an electric ski bus system. These reduce noise and air pollution but can cause a dangerous traffic hazard to pedestrians.

Zermatt's ski area is linked via the Klein Matterhorn to Cervinia in Italy and the two resorts share a lift pass. Skiing continues here 365 days a year at 3900m on the border with Italy, with seven lifts and a vertical drop in summer of 1000m. The terrain park has a super-pipe and a half-pipe open from the second week of July until the end of October.

Mountain

The skiing divides into three basic areas, two of them properly linked and the third tenuously so. Improvements to the lifts system have been dramatic in recent years since the various separate lift companies amalgamated.

Focus for experienced skiers and riders is on the Trockener Steg – Klein Matterhorn – Schwarzsee sector that is linked across the Plateau Rosa to Cervinia in Italy. The Matterhorn Express gondola provides fast access to Furi and Schwarzsee. A cable car from Furi takes you up to 2939m Trockener Steg, and another continues up to the Klein Matterhorn at 3820m. The area provides a wide range of scenic and occasionally demanding snow-sure intermediate skiing with magnificent views of the mighty Matterhorn. On sunny days, Zermatt-based skiers head over the top for the long intermediate run to Cervinia and an Italian lunch at half the price of Switzerland. Distances are huge and it is important to allow plenty of time for the return journey. Missing the last lift involves a six-hour taxi journey or, more sensibly, an overnight stay in a B&B.

The second area of Sunnegga is reached by an underground funicular from near the centre of town that takes you up to 2288m. A new combination cableway this season – half gondola, half six-pack chair – brings you on up to Blauherd, replacing the slow old cable car. The Sunnegga sector has some demanding pistes including the black roller coaster, Obere National FIS, as well as more benign red descents to the valley.

From 3103m Rothorn above Blauherd the area links via a long scenic piste and the Gant cable car to the third sector of Gornergrat. This can also be accessed from the resort by a slow surface train that winds gently up the mountainside. Hohtälli above Gant and parallel Rote Nase-Stockhorn are the starting points for some of the best advanced pistes in the resort including the notorious Stockhorn descent to Triftji. However, these runs are often closed until mid-January because of insufficient snow.

The whole of Zermatt has enormous off-piste potential, with heli-skiing possible on the Monte Rosa and the Alphubeljoch. Snowboarding is a serious business with free-riding popular beneath Hohtälli. The winter terrain park is served by the Furggsattel lift above Trockener Steg.

Learn

Since the establishment of **Stoked The Ski and Snowboard School, t** +41 (0)27 967 7020, Zermatt is no longer a resort to avoid for complete novices. Its young, international team was the first to provide the competition that the old and staid **Swiss Ski and Snowboarding School, t** +41 (0)27 966 2466, sorely lacked. British-run **Summit Ski & Board School, t** +41 (0)27 967 0001, was a successful newcomer last season and quickly established a faithful following among all nationalities. **Independent Swiss Snowboard Instructors, t** +41 (0)27 967 7067, offers dedicated riding tuition. **Alpin Center, t** +41 (0)27 966 2460, provides guiding and **Air Zermatt, t** +41 (0)27 966 8686, heli-skiing.

Children

Summit, t +41 (0)27 967 0001 takes children in groups of six from six years, with New School courses for teenagers. Stoked's **Snowflakes Kids Club, t** +41 (0)27 967 4340, at the top of the Matterhorn Express at Schwarzee cares for children from four years with lessons and play. **Snowli Snow Club, t** +41 (0)27 966 2466, run by the Swiss School is a kindergarten for four- to six-year-olds at Riffelberg. **Nico Kids Club, t** +41 (0)27 966 0777, in Hotel Nicoletta accepts kids from two to eight years on weekdays. Childminding for children from two years is available at **Kinderclub Pumuckel, t** +41 (0)27 966 5000, in Hotel La Ginabelle six days a week. **Kinderparadies, t** +41 (0)27 967 7252, cares for infants from three months and runs a babysitting service until 10pm. A list of recommended childminders is available from the tourist office.

Lunch

No resort in the world has a more enticing – and expensive – collection of welcoming mountain huts offering gourmet fare.
Chez Vrony, t +41 (0)27 967 2552, in Findeln is renowned for its *Rösti*, spicy fish soup, and spaghetti with prawns and wild

mushrooms. The ancient hamlet of **Zum See, t** +41 (0)27 967 2045 houses a restaurant of the same name, serving delicious albeit pricey cuisine such as carpaccio of tuna with olive oil and lemon juice, Thai-style duck breast with basmati rice, and giant prawns with curry sauce and noodles. **Blatten, t** +41 (0)27 967 2096, below Furi, has 'fantastic *Rösti*'. Also at Furi is **Simi, t** +41 (0)27 967 2695, with a wood grill and serving Valais dishes at reasonable prices. **Alphittä, t** +41 (0)27 967 2114, at Riffelalp is wood-panelled and offers local specialities. **Fluhalp, t** +41 (0)27 967 2597, en route to Gant, offers fine food and the best views of the Matterhorn. **Stafelalp, t** +41 (0)27 967 3062, specializes in *Rösti* and sweet omelettes. **Pizzeria Cervino, t** +41 (0)27 967 1812, at Trockner Steg has 'no charm whatseoever, but the pizzas were excellent and cooked on a traditional wood-burning fire'. Wherever you go, even in low season, it is essential to book in advance.

Dine

Le Mazot, t +41 (0)27 966 0606, specializes in lamb cooked on an open grill. **Le Gitan, t** +41 (0)27 968 1940, has its own 'gypsy kebabs' and succulent giant prawns. The rustic **Schäferstube, t** +41 (0)27 966 7605, in Hotel Julen has lamb from its own flock.
Rua Thai, t +41 (0)27 966 6181, in Hotel Albana Real has authentic Thai cuisine. **Casa Rustica, t** +41 (0)27 967 4858, has meat fondues and homely fare. **Mood's, t** +41 (0)27 967 8484, has a glass floor and gourmet nouvelle cuisine. **Myoko, t** +44 (0)27 966 8739, is an authentic sushi restaurant in the Seilerhaus.

Party

'Après-ski is OK but not wild,' said one reporter. **Hennustall** is *the* piste-side bar on the way down from Furi. **Papperla** is always bursting at the seams at the end of the skiing day. **Elsie's Bar**, by the church, is a crowded but atmospheric place to go for champagne and oysters. **The Post Hotel** complex caters for everybody: upstairs is **Papa Caesar's** bar, downstairs is **Pink** with jazz, **Le Village** plays house music, and **Le Broken** is the traditional disco. The former owners of the Post have moved to Robbie Williams' favourite restaurant, **Mood's**, taking their loyal clientele with them. **Schneewittchen** is another popular meeting-place. **Hotel Alex** nightclub attracts a 30-plus age group. Artist Heinz Julen's **Vernissage** is full of atmosphere with an art gallery, eclectic mix of ancient Valais furniture and light fittings made from recycled bicycle parts and bath plugs.

Sleep

★★★★★Grand Hotel Zermatterhof, t +41 (0)27 966 6600, *www.matterhorn-group.ch*, once a favourite of both Audrey Hepburn and Walt Disney, is a glamorous hotel with all its rooms recently refurbished with wood-panelling and murals.

★★★★★Mont Cervin Palace, t +41 (0)27 966 8888, w*ww.seiler-hotels.ch*, founded in 1851, has recently opened a three-storey Daniel Steiner Beauty Spa. It has some brand new suites, and a wine cellar housing 10,000 bottles.

★★★★★Riffelalp Resort 2222, t +41 (0)27 966 0505, *www.zermatt.ch/riffelalp*, is a luxurious mini-resort at Gornergrat with an indoor pool with whirlpool and Europe's highest outdoor pool.

★★★★Hotel Alex, t +41 (0)27 966 7070, *www.hotelalexzermatt.com*, an Alpine-Byzantine mélange, has individually-designed 'artistic' rooms, swimming pool and spa.

★★★★Hotel Alpen Resort, t +41 (0)27 966 3000, *www.alpenresort.com*, has family

rooms and suites, as well as a spa, swimming pool, gym, and an indoor tennis court.

★★★★Hotel Ambassador, t +44 (0)27 966 2611, *www.ambassador-zermatt.ch*, is comfortable, traditional, and rated 'excellent' by reporters.

★★★★Hotel La Ginabelle, t +41 (0)27 966 5000, *www.la.ginabelle.ch*, is family-friendly with a kids club.

★★★★Seiler Hotel Monte Rosa, t +41 (0)27 966 0333, a favourite of Sir Winston Churchill and the base from which Edward Whymper, the Victorian mountaineer, set off to conquer the Matterhorn, is extremely central and guests can use the Mont Cervin spa.

★★★★Seiler Hotel Nicoletta, t +41 (0)27 966 0777, *www.seiler-hotels.ch*, offers guests the use of the Mont Cervin spa with swimming pool, and has its own kids club.

★★★★Hotel Sonne, t +41 (0)27 966 2066, *www.sonne.masch.com*, is family-run and chalet-style, with a wellness centre and a good restaurant.

★★★Hotel Biner, t +41 (0)27 966 5666, *www.hotel-biner-zermatt.ch*, near the railway station, has been recently renovated using all natural materials and offers five-star facilities including a spa with huge swimming pool.

★★★Hotel Perren, t +41 (0)27 966 5200, *www.hotel-perren.ch* has been welcoming guests since 1937 and has a relaxed and informal atmosphere.

Chalet Zaphir and Chalet Louise, t +44 (0)20 8682 5050, *www.scottdunn.com*, are luxury chalet-apartments sleeping 10 each, created by celebrated Swiss designer Heinz Julen.

Chalet Zen, t +44 (0)20 7384 3854, *www.descent.co.uk*, one of only a handful of stand-alone chalets available to rent in Zermatt, is decorated with antique furniture, rugs and paintings.

The Top Resorts: USA

Aspen, Colorado

Profile

One of the top resorts in North America with skiing and snowboarding for all standards. The historic town has a wide choice of restaurants, shops and nightlife. Neighbouring Snowmass is the less expensive accommodation base

Essentials

Altitude: 7,945ft (2422m)–12,518ft (3815m)
Map: see page M57
Further information: t +1 970 925 1220, www.aspensnowmass.com
Lifts in area: 37 (1 cableway, 30 chairs, 6 drags) serving 4,893 acres of terrain
Lift pass: Area (covers all 4 mountains) adult $190–267, child 7–17yrs $162–229, both for 6 days
Access: Aspen airport 10mins, Denver airport 3½hrs, Eagle County/Vail airport 90mins

Resort

Aspen is too often dismissed by skiers who have never been there as a pretentious Hollywood-on-ice, a place for poseurs rather than pisteurs. In fact, nothing could be further from the truth. The reason why so many famous people make their home or take their holidays here is because they are fanatical skiers or riders who want some of the best facilities and challenging slopes that America has to offer. Stars with whom you may find yourself riding the gondola or a chair include Jack Nicholson, Michael Douglas, Melanie Griffiths and Antonio Banderas.

It is a wealthy town that was founded on money – back in the 1880s Aspen was briefly the silver-mining capital of the world. Its 14-year reign as a boom town ended in 1893 with the US adoption of the gold standard and by the early 1930s its population of 12,000 had plummeted to 350. But then came the discovery of 'white gold' and Aspen's rebirth as a ski town.

Its legacy from those early years is a collection of fine Victorian buildings including Hotel Jerome, the original inn. They all been beautifully restored and more recent additions are constructed in sympathetic period style.

Some 200 shops range from art galleries and designer boutiques like the new Prada store to sportswear outlets and beauty salons. No other resort in America has such a wonderful range of restaurants.

Property prices match Manhattan and London and the cost of living is higher than in any other major ski destination in North America. That said, Aspen is no more expensive than Courchevel 1850 or Val d'Isère. This is not a place for budget skiers and riders but, as in France, with a little careful research it is possible to enjoy a holiday here without spending a fortune.

The town centre at the foot of Aspen Mountain – also known as Ajax – is relatively compact. An efficient bus service connects outlying hotels as well as the three other ski areas of Buttermilk, Aspen Highlands, and Snowmass. Snowmass (nine miles) and Highlands (three miles) are alternative places to base yourself if the town with its shops, restaurants, and nightlife is not a priority.

Work has started on a new base village for Snowmass, which will make it a much more attractive option, with 246 hotel-style units, 349 condos, ten town homes, two luxury hotels as well as shops and restaurants. The new base should be connected this season by an open cabriolet gondola to the existing Snowmass Mall.

You can fly direct to Aspen from Denver. The airport is only three miles from town. It's worth noting that the route is heavily booked during the winter and flights must be arranged well in advance.

Mountain

The skiing is divided into four separate areas linked by ski bus. Furthest apart are Aspen Mountain and Snowmass (20 minutes). Each has its own character.

Buttermilk is a benign beginner and family area with lots of easy green runs served by the West Buttermilk Express and some marginally more taxing routes back to the base down the front face. The eastern side of the mountain is given over to runs marked black on the piste map, although they should present few difficulties to anyone who has just learned to ski parallel. An enormous terrain park is accessed by the Summit Express and runs from top to bottom.

Snowmass is the largest and most underrated sector which is suited to everyone from beginner to expert. It has a vertical drop of 3,904ft (1190m), one of the longest in North America. The upper mountain is mostly for advanced skiers with some truly steep terrain such as the Cirque headwall. Elk Camp and Big Burn have plenty of intermediate runs.

The new Sam's Knob Express lift opens this winter as part of $45 million of mountain improvements to complement the Base Village. It will take skiers and riders 1,030ft to the top of Sam's Knob in nine-and-a-half minutes with a midway stop to access beginner runs. Plans for 2006–7 include a giant children's centre and a new gondola from the base to Elk Camp. Pipeline Park, served by the Burlingame chair, has three half-pipes and a warming yurt.

Aspen Highlands has some of the most radical terrain in America. Beginner and intermediate runs are found on the lower part of the mountain, but generally this is not a place for the faint-hearted. Highland Bowl, Steeple Chase and Olympic Bowl have awesome reputations. This season it all gets even better with the opening of a series of vertiginous runs served by the new Deep Temerity lift to the skier's left of Highland Bowl.

Aspen Mountain, immediately above the town and served by the venerable Silver Queen gondola, is also the domain of strong skiers. It is riddled with short, sharp and quite steep, double-black-diamond chutes, including the famous 'dump runs' such as Bear Paw, Short Snort and Zaugg Dump, which were created by miners' spoil. Walsh's is considered to be the most challenging.

Face of Bell leading down into Spar Gulch usually provides excellent tree-skiing. You don't have to be a double-diamond addict to ski on Aspen Mountain – you can ski top to bottom on blue runs – but the Little Nell approach to the gondola is quite steep and can be icy when covered in artificial snow. Aspen Mountain Powder Tours offers skiing and riding off the back of the mountain.

Learn

Ski and Snowboard School of Aspen/Snowmass, t +1 970 925 1227, has branches on all four mountains. Courses include Too Cool For School teen skiing, **Aspen Adventures, t** +1 970 925 7625, and **Aspen Mountain Powder Tours, t** +1 970 920 0720.

Children

The ski school runs a full children's programme and kids aged 12 years and under must wear helmets. **Kids Room, t** +1 701 456 7888, provides childcare in town and a kindergarten, **t** +1 970 925

1227, is at each mountain base. At Snowmass, **Snow Cubs, t** +1 970 923 0563, caters for children aged from eight weeks with lessons from 18 months. **Big Burn Bears, t** + 1 970 923 0570, or the **Grizzlies, t** +1 970 923 0580, are clubs for older children. At Buttermilk, **Powder Pandas, t** +1 970 923 1227, cares for three- to six-year olds.

Lunch

Buttermilk has **Bumps, t** + 1 970 920 0991, at the base and the **Cliffhouse, t** +1 970 925 1220, at the top of the Summit Express.

At Snowmass, try **Gwyn's High Alpine, t** +1 970 923 51880, for grilled game and homemade desserts. **Sam's Knob, t** +1 970 925 1220, has good pasta and views of the Big Burn. **Ullrhof, t** +1 970 923 5143, is warmly recommended for its burgers, elk medallions, and Thai shrimp. **Up 4 Pizza, t** +1 970 925 1220, is quick and cheerful.

At Highlands, **Cloud Nine Alpine Bistro, t** +1 970 923 8715, is a small gourmet restaurant with magnificent views of the Maroon Bells. On Aspen Mountain, **Bonnie's, t** +1 970 925 1220, has wonderful white bean chilli and *apfelstrudel*. **Ajax Tavern, t** +1 970 920 9333, by the Silver Queen gondola, has good food and is great for people-watching. **Benedict's, t** +1 970 920 6971, at the top of the gondola, is also recommended.

Dine

Most restaurants are expensive, but if you are prepared to eat at the bar you are served the same food in smaller portions at a greatly reduced price.

In Aspen, **Mezzaluna, t** +1 970 925 5882, serves pizza and other Italian cuisine. **Kenichi, t** + 1 970 920 2212, **Takah Sushi, t** +1 970 925 8588, and **Matsuhisa,**

t +1 970 544 6628, all serve Japanese food. **Olives Aspen, t** + 1 970 920 7356, in the St Regis Resort serves Mediterranean-inspired American food. **La Cocina, t** +1 970 925 9714, **Little Annie's, t** +1 970 925 1098, **Mother Lode, t** +1 970 925 7700, and **Wild Fig, t** +1 970 925 5160, are all warmly recommended. **Jimmy's, t** +1 970 925 6020, is said to be 'posh but not too posh'. In Snowmass, try **Mountain Dragon, t** +1 970 923 3576 and **Sage Bistro, t** +1 970 923 0923, at the Snowmass Club.

Party

The **Jerome Bar** or J-Bar is a popular resort rendezvous. **The Ajax Tavern** is always crowded at the end of the skiing day. **Elevation**, Jimmy's, the **Mogador**, and **Club Chelsea** attract a sophisticated after-dinner crowd. **Shooters** is a Country and Western saloon with live bands. **Mezzaluna** serves inexpensive beers and pizza. The health-conscious head for **The Aspen Club and Spa** or the **Remede Spa** in the St Regis Resort. Those who have celebrity friends or are prepared to pay for temporary membership gather in the exclusive **Caribou Club**.

Sleep

Aspen:
Luxury:
Hotel Jerome, t +1 970 920 1000, *www.hoteljerome.com*, is the original Victorian inn.
The Little Nell, t +1 970 920 4600, *www.thelittlenell.com*, is a five-star resort institution at the base of Aspen Mountain.
St Regis Resort Aspen, t +1 970 920 3300, *www.stregisaspen.com*, also at the base, has received a $35-million makeover this year and has a new spa.

Moderate/budget:

Aspen Mountain Lodge, t +1 970 925 7650 *www.aspenmountainlodge.com*, has a pool and a hot tub.

Hotel Durant, t +1 970 925 8500, *www.durantaspen.com*, is two blocks from the centre and includes breakfast.

Innsbruck Inn, t +1 970 925 2980, is a favourite with the budget-conscious.

Limelite Lodge, t +1 970 925 3025, *www.limelite-lodge.com*, is centrally located and good value.

St Moritz Lodge, t +1 970 925 3220, *www.stmoritzlodge.com*, has triple-bed dormitories as well as regular rooms.

Snowmass:

Moderate/budget:

Chamonix Inn, t +1 970 923 3232, *www.snowmass.ski.com*, has piste-side rental units with a pool.

Crestwood Inn, t +1 970 923 2450, *www.snowmass.ski.com*, are three-bedroom condos and townhouses.

Silvertree Hotel, t +1 970 923 3520, *www.silvertreehotel.com*, is Snowmass' only full-service ski-in ski-out hotel.

Snowmass Club, t +1 970 923 5600, *www.snowmassclub.com*, is a smart condo complex.

Snowmass Inn, t +1 970 923 4302, *www.snowmassinn.com*, is family-owned and adjacent to the Village Mall.

Stonebridge Inn, t +1 970 923 2420, *www.stonebridgeinn.com*, has slope-side hotel rooms and suites.

Beaver Creek, Colorado

Profile

An upmarket choice for families with a good snow record and an excellent ski school. Not ideal for those on a budget

Resort

'Couldn't believe the luxury,' said one reporter, 'Why walk when you can stand on a motorized walkway'. Beaver Creek is an elegant family resort situated at the end of a private road, a 20-minute drive from its sister resort of Vail. The two are under the same giant corporate ownership and run a joint ski school and unlinked lift system, but there the similarity ends. While Vail is big and brash, Beaver Creek is more compact, with an intimate atmosphere and plenty of slope-side accommodation.

Essentials

Altitude: 8,100ft (2,470m)–11,440ft (3488m)

Map: see Vail, page M60

Further information: t +1 970 845 9090, *www.beavercreek.com*

Lifts in area: 14 (13 chairs, 1 drag) serving 1,625 acres of terrain

Lift pass: Colorado Ticket (covers Arapahoe Basin, Beaver Creek, Breckenridge, Keystone, Vail) adult $164–375, child 5–12yrs $151–190, both for 6 days

Access: Denver airport 2½hrs, Eagle County/Vail airport 45mins

The resort exudes an air of wealth and sophistication that is reflected in its luxurious hotels, magnificent condos, designer boutiques and plethora of art galleries. Excellent childcare facilities and a scenic network of easy runs that are as immaculately groomed as its visitors consistently win it awards as one of America's top family resorts.

The Colorado Ticket lift pass entitles skiers to use the lift systems in Vail, Breckenridge and Keystone as well as the small but challenging ski area of Arapahoe Basin. Shuttle buses operate between Beaver Creek, Vail, Breckenridge and Keystone at a nominal charge.

Mountain

This substantial ski area includes the linked villages of Bachelor Gulch and Arrowhead. Main mountain access from Beaver Creek is by the Centennial Express chair, which takes you up to Spruce Saddle, the mid-mountain station. From here the Birds of Prey Express chair continues on to the summit of the ski area. You can also take the Bachelor Gulch Express from Bachelor Gulch or the Arrow Bahn Express from Arrowhead, and work your way along the adjoining mountains.

The beginner areas are at the base of the Haymeadow, at the top of the Birds of Prey Express lift, and at Arrowhead. Long, cruising intermediate trails are the hallmark of Beaver Creek's skiing. The cross-mountain journeys to Bachelor Gulch and Arrowhead enable you to feel you are going somewhere, as opposed to the more usual American experience of skiing variations of the same terrain over and over again.

The Birds of Prey downhill course is one of the most testing in the business. When you stand on the aptly named Brink, the mountain falls away at a stomach-churning 45 degrees. Screech Owl and

Osprey are usually heavily mogulled, while Royal Elk Glades is a steep double-black-diamond run from the top of the mountain. The Rose Bowl lift also serves a choice of black-diamond trails.

The resort has three terrain parks that attract as many twin-tipped skiers as they do snowboarders. Park 101, situated on Upper Sheephorn, is designed for park novices. Zoom is for accomplished riders, and has a half-pipe as well as the full range of rails, hips and spines.

Early in the morning on new snow days in high season, the local powderhounds ignore Vail's inevitably crowded back bowls and head for Grouse Mountain. This provides some truly spectacular trails between the trees and along the edge of the ski area boundary.

Learn

Beaver Creek Ski and Snowboard School, t +1 970 845 5300, is consistently praised for the teaching quality and the friendliness of its instructors. The resort offers a large disabled skiing programme.

Children

Beaver Creek ranks as one of the top US resorts for families ('one of the best resorts we've ever been to with our children'). **Small World Play School**, t +1 970 845 5325, is the non-skiing kindergarten. It provides all-day care for children from three years of age.

Lunch

Owing to the well-heeled nature of its clientele, Beaver Creek takes lunch more seriously than many American resorts – but unfortunately the public are unable to share the best part of it. At lunch-time **Beano's Cabin**, t +1 970 949 9090, remains a private club. The same applies to **Zach's**

Cabin, t +1 866 395 3185 (Pacific Rim cooking), and **Allie's Cabin**, t +1 970 845 5762, which has some fine wines. 'The few accessible outlets are heavily subscribed', said one reporter, 'and the best option is to return to the resort for lunch'. **Beaver Creek Tavern** offers gourmet burgers, and the **Broken Arrow Café** in Arrowhead has 'home-made soup and enormous club sandwiches'.

Dine

Splendido at the Chateau t +1 970 845 8808, offers 'Rocky Mountain cooking' and is the ultimate in fine dining, while **SaddleRidge**, t +1 970 845 5762, houses a museum of Western memorabilia and serves game and seafood. **Allie's**, t +1 970 845 5762, and **Zach's**, t +1 866 395 3185, are open by night to all. **Beano's Cabin**, t +1 970 949 9090, reached by motorized sleigh, has memorable five-course meals. **Mirabelle**, t +1 970 949 7728 has a Belgian owner/chef. **traMonti**, t +1 970 949 5552, serves 'exciting new dishes', including lobster ravioli, and **Toscanini**, t +1 970 845 5590, is Italian. **The Blue Moose**, t +1 970 845 8666, is a New York-style pizzeria.

Party

The **Coyote Café**, **Beaver Creek Chophouse** and **Dusty Boot Saloon** capture the main crowd, along with the **Beaver Creek Tavern** and **McCoy's** for live music. **The Black Family Ice Rink** is open until 10pm.

Sleep

*****The Charter**, t +1 970 949 6660, www.thecharter.com, at the base, has two restaurants, a spa and indoor pool.
*****Park Hyatt Resort & Spa**, t +1 970 949 1234, beavercreek.hyatt.com, has a renowned spa and two restaurants.

*****Ritz-Carlton**, t +1 970 748 6200, www.ritzcarlton.com, is at the base of Bachelor Gulch and boasts a magnificent spa.
*****SaddleRidge**, t +1 970 845 5990, www.beavercreekresortproperties.com, consists of separate two-bedroom chalets furnished with Ralph Lauren fabrics and Western antiques.
****Inn at Beaver Creek**, t +1 970 845 5990, theinnatbc.coloradoreservation service.com, is slope-side and adjacent to the Strawberry Park Express lift.
****Trapper's Cabin**, t +1 970 845 5900, www.trapperscabincolorado.com, is a rustic hideaway in the trees sleeping ten people, reached on skis or by snowmobile.

Breckenridge, Colorado

Profile

Lively old mining town with a good nightlife. Large ski area with reliable snow conditions, but short runs. Snowboarding is popular. Time needed to acclimatize at this extremely high altitude

Resort

Breckenridge earned its inclusion in the map of the world in July 1887 when miners Tom Grove and Harry Lytton stumbled across a nugget of gold that weighed an astonishing 13lb 7oz. Tom's Baby, as it was christened, was the culmination of a ten-year mining boom that created the attractive Victorian town that is now one of Colorado's top ski destinations and still the most popular with overseas skiers.

Essentials

Altitude: 9,600ft (2927m)–12,998ft
  (3962m)
Map: see page M62
Further information: t +1 970 453 5000,
  www.breckenridge.com
Lifts in area: 19 (15 chairs, 54 drags) serving
  2,208 acres of terrain
Lift pass: Colorado Ticket (covers Arapahoe
  Basin, Beaver Creek, Breckenridge,
  Keystone, Vail) adult $164–375, child
  5–12yrs $151–190, both for 6 days
Access: Denver airport 90mins, Eagle
  County/Vail airport 1hr

The legacy of the boom years of the 19th century is a number of fine pastel-painted weatherboarded buildings along Main Street, the focal point of the resort with its wide range of shops and restaurants. Others have been created in a sympathetic style, while the late 20th-century ski-in ski-out accommodation around the ski base is more utilitarian with few concessions to architectural frivolity. The skiing and riding is suitable for all standards but – the resort would beg to differ – is best for intermediates. Breckenridge shares a lift pass with Keystone, Vail, Beaver Creek, and Arapahoe Basin, all of which are within easy reach. They are linked by a free bus service to Keystone and the local challenging ski area of A-Basin. Daily transport subsidized by the joint lift company connects Breckenridge with Vail and Beaver Creek, which are slightly further away. During a week or ten-day stay here you are strongly advised to explore further afield.

Visitors arriving at Denver from either coast or from overseas can easily reach Breckenridge in just 90 minutes but it is easy to forget the enormous change in altitude. This, combined with low humidity can cause dehydration and headaches that are exacerbated by

exercise. Don't overdo it on your first day, drink plenty of water, and abstain from alcohol until your body has had a chance to acclimatize. Snow cover in Breckenridge is usually the most abundant of all the Vail resorts.

Mountain

'Breckenfridge' is its apt nickname. The mercury can plunge at this high altitude and in mid-winter you need technical ski clothing to be comfortable. The skiing takes place on four side-by-side peaks in the Ten Mile Range alongside the town. Someone devoid of imagination originally named them Peaks 10, 9, 8, and 7 and no-one else has so far found the courage to change them.

For the present, easiest access is by the Quicksilver Super 6 from the top of town that takes you up Peak 9 and into the system. All the peaks are well-linked on mountain. In the future, skiers and riders will be able to access Peak 8 direct from Main Street and parking lots rather than by bus. Work has already started on the ambitious Skyway Skiway, which won't be completed until 2006–7.

From the top of the Quicksilver, easy runs fan out to the Falcon SuperChair on Peak 10, the starting point for a network of predominantly advanced runs with some testing mogul-fields. It is also possible to ski to the Mercury and Beaver Run SuperChairs on Peak 9, which has some of the most inviting cruising in the resort, plus Gold King, a terrain park designed for learner freeriders. Peak 7 is built for cruising, with huge rollers on all seven new trails.

The opening of the SuperConnect lift has reduced queuing by integrating the ski area efficiently. It has eased access to Peak 8, otherwise currently reached by shuttle bus or the venerable Snowflake dog-leg chair from the edge of town.

The Vista Haus mid-station is the focal point for the chair lifts that serve the network of blue and black trails on the lower slopes of Peak 8. The Independence SuperChair has extended Breckenridge's boundaries into a glade area cut from the forest on the lower slopes of Peak 7 that is suited to intermediates.

Breckenridge's expert terrain, created as a result of local demand for more 'European-style off-piste', covers the wide open upper slopes on Peaks 7, 8 and 9. The T-Bar takes snow-users into Peak 8's double-black-diamond zone, comprising Horseshoe, Contest, North and Cucumber Bowls, all of them ungroomed. Beyond that you're on your own, hiking over 12,000ft to the radical Peak-top runs. Whale's Tail and Peak 7 Bowl are 1,500ft vertical above the T-Bar, but the sterner test is Peak 8's Imperial Bowl, a 2,700ft vertical rise from the same starting point. This also accesses the Lake Chutes, which have slopes of up to 50 degrees.

Breckenridge was the first resort in Colorado to allow snowboarding and remains popular with riders who form 25 per cent of the winter clientele. The four dedicated areas include the Freeway Terrain Park and the Breckenridge Super-Pipe, which are equally attractive to twin-tippers.

Learn

Breckenridge Ski & Ride School, t +1 970 453 3272, has an excellent reputation with a wide range of courses, including some for teens and 50+.

Children

Breckenridge Children's Center, t +1 970 453 3258, offers slope-side crèches for kids from two months at Peak 8 and Peak 9. Both have pagers for parents to hire, provide lunches and offer a non-skiing,

outdoor snow-play programme. Advance reservations are essential during the busiest weeks.

Breckenridge Ski & Ride School accepts children from three years and is praised by reporters: 'I would definitely recommend Breckenridge to families with children who require warm coaxing into having lessons'.

Lunch

This is not a ski area for gourmets whose ideal skiing day involves a hard morning and lazy afternoon at a laden table. You can eat well in town, but good food on the mountain is harder to come by. Restaurants listed below without numbers belong to the resort, t +1 970 453 5000.

On Peak 9, **Le Bistro de Paris**, t +1 970 453 2572, is less burger-oriented, reasonably priced, and much the best bet. **Ten Mile Station**, at the top of the Quicksilver Chair, has a heated outdoor deck, a mining-themed food court, and a barbecue in fine weather. On Peak 8, **Border Burritos** at the Bergenhof has good-value salads and tacos, **The Vista Haus** food court at the top of the Colorado SuperChair has a great view of the Continental Divide, while the food is less spectacular.

Dine

Breckenridge has a choice of some 50 restaurants. In high season, booking is essential. **Hearthstone**, t +1 970 453 1148, is a converted Victorian brothel with loads of atmosphere and a creative Western menu. Try the granola-crusted elk chops. **South Ridge Seafood Grill**, t +1 970 547 0063, has oysters flown in daily from Chesapeake Bay. **The Blue River Bistro**, t +1 970 453 6974, and **Café Alpine**, t +1 970 453 8218, are fine-dining destinations. **Steak and Rib**, t +1 970 453 0063, is recommended.

Mi Casa, t +1 970 453 2071, is a good-value Mexican restaurant, and **Columbine Café, t** +1 970 547 4474 offers nutritious breakfasts. **The Red Orchid, t** +1 970 453 1881, specializes in Mandarin and Szechwan fare, **Mountain Flying Fish, t** +1 970 453 1502, and **Wasabi, t** +1 970 453 8311, are sushi restaurants, and **My Thai, t** +1 970 547 2887, is the fourth oriental offering. Italian eateries include **St. Bernard, t** +1 970 453 2572, **Fatty's, t** +1 970 453 9802, and **Giampetro, t** +1 970 453 3838. **Pierre's Riverwalk Café, t** +1 970 453 0989, blends American and French cuisine. If you don't want to go out **Gourmet Cabby, t** +1 970 543 7788, will deliver food and drink from 30 restaurants to your condo.

Party

This is a lively town with young skiers and riders determined to party away the hours not spent on the mountain. **Mi Casa** serves mean jugs of Margaritas: Try also **Breckenridge Brewery, Sherpa & Yeti, Gold Pan Saloon** (the oldest bar in the US west of the Mississippi), **Downstairs at Eric's, Ullr's Sports Grille,** and **Gracy O'Malleys. Julius Caesar** is a British-style pub.

Sleep

Breckenridge offers spacious rather than deluxe hotels, two large condominium resorts, several smaller apartment buildings and restored Victorian inns.
- ***Beaver Run Resort, t** +1 970 453 6000, *www.beaverrun.com,*is a 500-room ski-in ski-out condo complex praised for its 'excellent facilities'.
- ***Breckenridge Mountain Lodge, t** +1 970 453 2333, *www.breckenridgemountainlodge.com,* provides budget accommodation at the end of Main Street, offering an 'Old West bed and breakfast experience'.

- ***Great Divide Lodge, t** +1 970 453 4500, *www.greatdividelodge.com,* is near Peak 9 base and is one of the only full-service hotels.
- ***Lodge and Spa, t** +1 970 453 9300, *www.thelodgeatbreck.com,* is five minutes' from town with a shuttle bus to the slopes.
- ***The Mountain Thunder Lodge, t** +1 888 547 8092, *www.mtnthunderlodge.com,* contains comfortable studios, condos and suites below Peak 8.

The Canyons, Utah

Profile

Ten-year-old purpose-built resort with convenient and extensive skiing for all standards. A good choice for foodies, including a superb mountain restaurant

Resort

The Canyons is one of three side-by-side ski areas an easy 40-minute drive from Salt Lake City. Leave the highway at Kimball Junction and you come first to The Canyons, followed by Park City Mountain Resort and then Deer Valley. Linking all three would involve the construction of just one lift. Rivalry has so far prevented this, but for 2005–6 the three have come a step closer by launching a joint adult and children's pass for foreign visitors that is only sold through tour operators, with a single rate throughout the season.

Essentials

Altitude: 6,800ft (2073m)–9,990ft (3045m)
Further information: t +1 435 649 5400, *www.thecanyons.com*
Lifts in area: 15 (2 cableways, 12 chairs, 1 drag) serving 3,500 acres of terrain
Lift pass: Three Resort International adult $345, child 7–12yrs $193, both for 6 out of 10 days. Other lengths of stay and single resort passes also available
Access: Salt Lake City airport 40mins

The Canyons is the relative newcomer. It has developed over a decade from a small, local ski area into what is now the fifth largest ski resort in the United States, with the facilities to attract international skiers and boarders. The Utah Olympic Park, adjoining The Canyons, has a bob-sleigh and luge track. It is also one of the few places in the world where beginners can try their hand at ski-jumping.

From the purpose-built village, the Flight of the Canyons gondola rapidly conveys skiers and riders to the Red Lodge Pine mid-station. Lifts fan out from here in all directions across the mainly tree-covered mountainside. The skiing suits all standards with lots of easy cruising runs as well as some more demanding terrain reached by the Super Condor Express and the Ninety Nine 90 Express at the 9,990ft summit of the ski area. This season Dreamcatcher, a new quad-chair with a 1,600ft vertical drop, adds 200 acres of intermediate and advanced gladed runs. The Canyons now has two terrain parks for beginners and experts that are accessed by the Sun Peak lift.

Kimball Junction, just outside the resort, has a large collection of designer outlet stores with attractive prices.

Learn

The Canyons Ski & Snowboard School, **t** +1 435 615 3449, offers group and private tuition, and courses such as learn-to-ski packages, clinics with Olympic athletes, and telemark.

Children

The Canyons Ski & Snowboard School offers children's tuition, and **The Canyons Little Adventures Center, t** +1 435 615 8036, provides daycare for children from six weeks to four years.

Lunch

The Lookout Cabin, **t** +1 436 615 2892, at the top of the Golden Eagle and Short Cut chairs is an unexpected gastronomic treat, a European-style mountain hut with a sophisticated menu and friendly service. Other mountain eateries, **t** +1 435 649 5400 for all, include **Red Pine Lodge**, at the top of the gondola, which has pizzas and deli-sandwiches; **Sun Lodge**, at the base of the Sun Peak Express, which is less crowded and majors on grilled meat; and **Westgate Grill**, in the village, which has lots of atmosphere and an all-American menu.

Dine

The Cabin, **t** +1 435 615 8060, in The Canyons Grand Hotel is one of the best dining options in the region. Try the seafood mixed grill or the rack of venison. Join an evening excursion by snowcat to **The Viking Yurt, t** +1 435 615 9878, for a five-course Scandinavian dinner. **Grub Steak**, **t** +1 435 649 8060, is renowned for its fresh fish and Angus beef. **Loco Lizard Cantina**, **t** +1 435 645 700, at Kimball Junction is a contemporary Mexican restaurant.

Party

Late-night bars conform to the strictures of a private club licence in Utah, but temporary membership is easily obtained. **Doc's at the Gondola** is the main bar at The Canyons. In Park City, try **J.B. Mulligans Club and Pub**, **Wasatch Brew Pub Cantina** and **The Star Bar at Plan B** for live bands.

Sleep

All accommodation can be booked on **t** +1 800 472 6309, *www.the canyons.com.* *Luxury/Moderate/Budget:*
The Canyons Grand Hotel (formerly The Grand Summit Resort) is an impressive slope-side complex, with a spa and outdoor swimming pool.
The Sundial Lodge has a rooftop hot tub and a new heated outdoor pool.
The Miner's Club, **t** +1 435 615 8900, has elegant two- to four-bedroom condos.
Holiday Inn Express Park City, **t** +1 435 658 1600, *www.hiexpress.com,* is a budget-priced option at Kimball Junction.

Copper Mountain, Colorado

Profile

Recently developed car-free resort with good facilities for families with young children. The skiing suits all standards and snowboarding is a particular strength. Currently still one the best-kept secrets of Colorado

Resort

Since 1998 skiers driving north on Highway I-70, from one sleek Vail-owned resort to the other, cast barely a glance to their left at what, for over five years, was a construction site dominated by cranes. But now the steel gantries and booms have gone and Copper has emerged from its seemingly endless $400-million makeover since it was acquired by giant resort developer Intrawest. The new car-free base is set around four lodges and plazas with a good range of shops and restaurants.

Copper is no newcomer to skiing. It first opened as a ski area back in 1972. It has one of the best snow records in Colorado and the terrain suits all standards of skier and boarder, with plenty of powder opportunities.

Mountain

Copper is a serious snowboarding destination. Kidz terrain park, located near the top of the American Flyer lift, is for novices and has a mini-pipe. Night Riders Jib Park by the Burning Stones Plaza is floodlit on Friday and Saturday evenings. Catalyst is the main park with three distinct lines for different levels and a super-pipe. New park zones under the American Flyer lift link up with Kidz and Catalyst to form a top to bottom park run.

Essentials

Altitude: 9,712ft (2926m)–12,313ft (3767m)
Further information: **t** +1 970 968 2882, *www.coppercolorado.com*
Lifts in area: 21 (15 chairs, 6 drags) serving 2,450 acres of terrain
Lift pass: adult $236–275, child 6–13yrs $144–154, both for 6 days
Access: Denver airport 90mins

The mountain summit is reached in eight minutes by the Super Bee chairlift.The shape of the mountain naturally allows for one of the best designed ski areas in the United States. The tree-lined trails become more difficult as you move towards the left of the piste map. Thus, advanced skiers and boarders tend to stick to the main face of Copper Peak and beginners will find little beyond their capabilities on the other side of the resort. In between, the terrain is mainly intermediate. Copper Bowl and Spaulding Bowl provide some of the best off-piste skiing in Colorado, with the latter full of natural jumps and lips for riders.

Learn

Ski & Ride School, t +1 866 841 2481, is at the Village and at Union Creek and offers a range of special courses including freestyle, Bumps Busters, and Women's Wednesdays. Over The Hill Gang, t +1 970 968 3059, was founded here in 1976 for the over-45s and arranges guiding for different levels.

Children

Kids Jump Start, t +1 866 841 2481, at the Ski & Ride School offers lessons from three to 15 years. Copper Freeride Camp, t +1 866 385 0144, is a weekend course for ages 12 to 18 years. Belly Button Babies, t +1 970 968 2882, accepts children from six weeks to two years, and Belly Button Bakery provides indoor and outdoor play for children from two to four years.

Lunch

Try Double Diamond, t +1 970 968 2880, in the Fox Pine Inn for fried fish on Fridays. The Blue Moose, t +1 970 968 9666, by the American Eagle lift serves New York-style pizzas and salads. Creekside, t +1 970 968 2033, is a local favourite offering 'hand-tossed' pizzas as well as pasta and BBQs.

Dine

Alexander's, t +1 970 968 2165, is new, featuring contemporary cuisine and fine wines. Salsa Mountain Cantina, t +1 970 968 6300, serves home-made Mexican cuisine, and Imperial Palace, t +1 970 968 6688, serves low-cholesterol low-sodium Chinese dishes without any additives.

Party

Endo's Adrenaline Café is popular for après-ski. Pravda is a Russian vodka bar with the contemporary atmosphere of the Cold War Soviet era. JJ's Rocky Mountain Tavern has live entertainment. Copper Mountain Racquet and Athletic Club offers excellent facilities.

Sleep

Most of the accommodation is in apartments with location the main choice to be made. Call t +1 888 219 2441 for all reservations.

The Village at Copper is the newest village and is well placed for the beginner and intermediate terrain as well as most of the dining and shopping. East Village is at the base of the intermediate to expert terrain. Accommodation quality choices range from Platinum (with heated swimming pool, underground parking, fitness facilitites), through Gold (with hot tub), Silver (spaciously designed) to Bronze (most affordable). The Cirque is Copper's newest Platinum-level lodging.

Crested Butte, Colorado

Profile

Attractive old town set a short drive away from the ski area base. Some excellent steep and deep off-piste and a well-regarded ski school. Its drawback is difficult international access

Resort

First thing you need to know about Crested Butte is how to pronounce it. A butte (as in 'beaut-iful') is a stand-alone mountain that provides the town with a reputation for challenging skiing that stretches far beyond Colorado. The small Victorian town is no newcomer to the ski scene. Miners from Scandinavia were competing in jumping and downhill races here at least a decade before Alpine skiers attempted their first awkward turns in the Swiss Alps. The January 1887 edition of *Outing* magazine gave graphic details of a team skiing competition that had taken place in Crested Butte the previous year.

The resort is under new ownership and currently undergoing a major development plan. However, its remote location has meant that until now Crested Butte has remained something of a backwater. Visitors must first fly into Denver, catch a connecting flight to Gunnison and then a 30-minute transfer to the resort. For those coming from overseas it is not always possible to complete the journey in a single day. The ski area is located three miles from the town. Some 40 original buildings have been restored to their Victorian glory and others have been constructed in sympathetic style. Reporters warn of the need to acclimatize to the resort's high altitude.

Future plans involve a $57-million makeover that includes a new base area village called Mountaineer Square with 93 homes and the construction of a convention centre in the first phase.

Mountain

Crested Butte has some of the steepest lift-served terrain in North America and regularly hosts ski-extreme competitions. Most, but not all, of the mountain is suited to competent skiers and riders in search of new and challenging experiences. Main mountain access from the new Mountaineer Village is by the Red Lady Express and Silver Queen lifts. The first gives access to plenty of intermediate terrain, while the second takes you up into steep double-diamond territory.

The Prospect lift, new last season, carries skiers from the Prospect housing development to the top of the Goldlink and Painter Boy lifts.

This season sees an extensive landscaping of the base area, and the replacement of the T-bars with a fixed grip quad.

The resort is a favourite with snowboarders. The Canaan terrain park, served by the Paradise lift has a host of jumps and rails and a super-pipe.

Learn

Crested Butte Ski and **Snowboard School, t** +1 970 349 2252, offers workshops on turning skills, all-terrain and ski-racing.

Children

Kids Ski and **Snowboard World, t** +1 970 349 2259, runs Baby Bears kindergarten for potty-trained toddlers, and Cuddly Bears is from 13 months. Lessons are given from three years. The facilities in the Kids' Corral area have been updated.

Lunch

On the mountain, **Ice Bar** and **Restaurant, t** +1 970 349 2275, offers fine dining and exotic martinis. **Andiamo** in the Paradise Warming Hut, **t** +1 970 349 2274, has sound Italian cuisine and good service.

Dine

Recommended restaurants include **Buffalo Grille & Saloon, t** +1 970 349 9699, and **Black Whale Restaurant & Pub, t** +1 970 349 0480. **The Secret Stash, t** +1 970 349 6245, is a 100-year-old miners' cabin with Japanese-style seating and serving Asian BBQ wings and gourmet pizzas. **Le Bosquet Restaurant, t** +1 970 349 5808, offers fine dining. **Lil's Land & Sea, t** +1 970 349 5457, serves an eclectic menus of seafood, game and sushi. **Izzy's, t** +1 970 349 5630, is new and specializes in stuffed Mediterranean crêpes.

Party

Hot-spots include **Talk of the Town, Kochevar's,** and the **Eldo**. The **Firehouse Grill** is renowned and operated by local firefighters. **Performing Arts** is the local theatre, with drama, music and comedies.

Sleep

★★★★**The Grand Lodge, t** +1 970 349 8000, *www.sheratoncrestedbutte.com*, at the base area, is the finest full-service hotel in the resort and has an indoor swimming pool.
★★★**The Nordic Inn, t** +1 970 349 5542, *www.nordicinncb.com*, is a friendly family-run ski lodge.
Purple Mountain Lodge B&B and Spa, t +1 970 349 5888, *www.purple mountainlodge.com*, with five individually decorated rooms, offers massage and a hot tub.

Deer Valley, Utah

Profile

Glitzy upmarket resort renowned for the immaculate grooming of its trails and guest alike, but with some surprisingly challenging skiing. Snowboarding is still not permitted

Resort

Deer Valley is the furthest from Salt Lake City of a trio of major resorts reached by a 40-minute drive to Kimball Junction. Its carefully nurtured reputation as the smartest – and most expensive – ski

Essentials

Altitude: 6,570ft (2003m) – 9,570ft (2917m)
Further information: t +1 435 649 1000, *www.deervalley.com*
Lifts in area: 21 (1 cableway, 20 chairs) serving 1,825 acres of terrain
Lift pass: Three Resort International adult $345, child 7–12yrs $193, both for 6 out of 10 days. Other lengths of stay and single resort passes also available
Access: Salt Lake City airport 40mins

destination in America has done nothing to endear it to hardcore skiers who instinctively dismiss it as a place for middle-aged lower intermediates who are only happy if every wrinkle has been surgically removed from the slopes.

In fact, this is an unfair age-ist misconception: the mountain at Deer Valley offers plenty of challenge for advanced skiers – but not for snowboarders. You don't have to be old or rich as Croesus to ski here, although the latter helps. The resort remains a founding member of the tiny clutch of destinations around the world where snowboarding is still banned.

Deer Valley lies one mile to the south-east of Park City, up a winding mountain road lined with multi-million-dollar homes. It is so exclusive that the staff who unload the skis from your car and carry them to the snow won't accept tips. Any visit here should include days in Park City Mountain Resort (so close that skiers illegally go under the rope from one to the other) and The Canyons on the other side of the town of Park City.

Linking all three would involve the construction of just one lift. Rivalry has so far prevented this, but for 2005–6 the three have come a step closer by launching a joint adult and children's pass for foreign visitors that is only sold

through tour operators, with a single rate throughout the season.

Mountain

Main mountain access from the car parks at Snow Park Lodge is by two parallel high-speed chairs that bring you up to Silver Lake Lodge mid-mountain hub. From here you can make your way up to lots of easy cruising terrain on Flagstaff Mountain and Empire Canyon. Two new chairs were opened last season on Flagstaff. The 9,400ft peak of Bald Mountain, reached by the Wasatch Express lift, is the starting point for some more challenging black-diamond terrain. The Daly Chutes and Daly Bowl, accessed from Empire Canyon, are steep powder tests.

Riders may be noticeable by their absence, but twin-tippers have their own Trick 'n' Turn rail park and a skiercross course on Empire Canyon.

Learn

The Deer Valley Ski School, t +1 435 645 6648, offers group and private lessons as well as Women on Wednesdays, and Men on Thursdays.

Children

Deer Valley Children's Center, t + 1 435 645 6648, cares for children from two months to 12 years. Deer Valley Ski School accepts children from four to 12 years, with clubs for different age groups and Teen Equipe lessons for 13- to 17-year-olds.

Lunch

For restaurants listed without numbers call, t +1 435 649 1000.
You can arrange a private lunch for two to 15 people at **Sunset Cabin**, t +1 435 645

6650, tucked away off Sunset run. At
Royal Street Café at Silver Lake Lodge
try the Vermont cheddar burger or the
shrimp and lobster margarita appetizer
served in a margarita glass. Try **Bald
Mountain Pizza** at Silver Lake Lodge,
Empire Canyon Grill as well as **Snow
Park** for burgers and chilli.

Dine

Deer Valley has four evening restaurants:
the **Seafood Buffet, t** +1 435 645 6632, at
the Snow Park Lodge, which is warmly
recommended, **The Mariposa, t** +1 435
645 6715, at Silver Lake Lodge which offers
fine dining, **Royal Street Café, t** +1 435 645
6724, at Silver Lake, and **Fireside Dining**,
t +435 645 6632, in the Empire Canyon Lodge.

Party

The **Après Ski Lounge** at the Snow Park
Lodge in Deer Valley is popular after
skiing, but the best of the nightlife is on
Historic Main Street in Park City, which
has some 70 shops, bars and restaurants.

Sleep

Luxury:
The Lodges at Deer Valley, t +1 435 615
2600, is a condominium hotel built in
Old West style with views across the
Snow Park Ponds.
Goldener Hirsch Inn, t +1 435 649 7770, is
an Austrian-style hotel with a fine
restaurant.
Stein Eriksen Lodge, t +1 435 649 3700,
www.goldernhirschinn.com, at Silver Lake
Village has a Scandinavian ambience
and is named after the Norwegian
legend who won gold at the 1954 Oslo
Olympics and is 'father' of Deer Valley.
The Chateaux at Silver Lake, t +1 435 649
4040, is an elegant condo hotel with
French country decor.

Heavenly, California/ Nevada

Profile

Quirky resort straddling the California-
Nevada border, with spectacular views of
Lake Tahoe as well as the desert. Suits
beginners and intermediates, as well as
party-goers and gamblers

Resort

Heavenly has reinvented itself since it
was bought by Vail Resorts and started
to receive the lavish annual funding that
is the hallmark of America's richest resort
company. The development of a village
around the base of the gondola has
created an identity that it previously
lacked as the detached ski area of the
brash gambling town of South Lake
Tahoe. This is the largest of the 15 resorts
that fringe the shores of Lake Tahoe, the
second largest and most beautiful alpine
lake in the world after Titicaca in Peru. Its
position, straddling the frontier between
two states, gives it an intriguing split
personality.

From the top of the mountain you can
choose to ski in Nevada, with views of the
arid vastness of the Nevada Desert, or to
head for the Californian side overlooking
the lush beauty of Lake Tahoe.

The choice of where to stay is equally
contrasting and largely depends on
which side of the stateline lies your
accommodation. California's is more
tranquil with a peaceful waterfront and
simple single-storey homes. Nevada's
South Lake Tahoe has monstrous casino

Essentials

Altitude: 6,500ft (1982m)–10,067ft
(3068m)
Further information: t +1 775 586 7000,
www.skiheavenly.com
Lifts in area: 27 (2 cableways, 19 chairs,
6 drags) serving 4,800 acres of terrain
Lift pass: adult $241–311, child 5–12yrs
$53–120, both for 6 days
Access: Reno airport 90mins, Sacramento
airport 2hrs, San Francisco airport 4hrs

hotels where the ground floors are given over to 24-hour slot machines. The third choice is the slightly more skier-orientated Heavenly Village at the gondola base.

Mountain

The gondola takes you up to a sunny balcony at just over 9,000ft with great views of the lake. The alternative is to start by chair or cable-car from California Lodge or on the Nevada side from Stagecoach Lodge or Boulder Lodge. The upper Californian side is generally fast, blue, cruising terrain with more difficult runs higher up, but plenty of easy cruising runs descend to mid-mountain. Most of the trails are ideally suited to intermediates – long cruisers bordered by banks of pine trees and enhanced by the stunning view of the lake. You can take the Sky Express chair and try Liz's or Betty's, then head to Nevada for the Big Dipper, Sand Dunes, Perimeter and Galaxy runs – the Nevada face consists mainly of blue trails.

The most advanced skiing and riding is found in Mott Canyon and Killebrew Canyon. Steep chutes are cut through the trees, with runs such as Snake Pit, Widowmaker, and the difficult Boundary Chutes. Links between the two sides involve a number of annoying flats that

bring complaints from snowboarders. Heavenly has four terrain parks and a super-pipe.

Learn

Resort-owned **Heavenly Ski School**, t +1 775 586 7000 x 6206, has the monopoly here. Quality of teaching is always a lottery. One reporter complained that his teacher was Argentinian and had only a rudimentary grasp of English.

Children

The Daycare Center, t +1 775 586 7000 x 6912, takes non-skiers from six weeks. The ski school accepts children from three years.

Lunch

On the California side, try **Café Blue** at the first stop on the gondola and **Adventure Peak Grill** at the top. **Lakeview Lodge** offers unrivalled views of Lake Tahoe and **Sky Deck** has a daily barbecue. On the Nevada side, **Slice of Heaven** at the Stagecoach base-lodge is Italian, while **Black Diamond Cantina** at Boulder Lodge offers Mexican fare. For information on restaurants telephone t +1 775 586 7000.

Dine

In South Lake Tahoe, **The Summit**, t +1 775 588 6611, in Harrah's is one of America's top 100 restaurants. **Fire + Ice**, t +1 530 542 6650, cooks fresh dishes to order. **The Naked Fish,** t +1 530 541 3474, offers outstanding sushi and **The Chart House,** t +1 775 588 6276, is more expensive but has wonderful views. **The Red Hut,** t +1 775 588 7488, **Ernie's Coffee Shop,** t +1 530 541 2161, and **Heidi's Pancake House,** t +1 530 544 8113, all offer 'powder breakfasts'.

Party

Traditional après-ski is limited. **Fire + Ice** at the gondola base is the main resort rendezvous. Otherwise you must head into South Lake Tahoe and try your hand at the green baize tables. As in Las Vegas, a by-product of casino culture is a wide range of cabaret acts and concerts featuring famous American and occasionally international artists.

Sleep

Luxury:
Tahoe Seasons Resort, t +1530 541 6700, *www.tahoeseasons.com*, complex is within walking distance of the lifts at the California base.
Moderate:
Caesars Tahoe, t +1 702 588 3515, *www.caesars.com*, has six restaurants including the Roman Feast Buffet, and houses Club Nero Nightclub, a lagoon-style swimming pool, and a wedding chapel.
Harrah's Lake Tahoe, t +1 702 588 6611, *www.harrahs.com*, is a large casino-hotel at South Lake Tahoe.
Tahoe Lakeshore Lodge & Spa, t +1 530 541 2180, *www.tahoelakeshorelodge.com*, on the South Shore, has a view of the lake from every room, all of which are spacious and decorated with lodgepole pine furniture.
Embassy Suites Hotel, t +1 530 541 4418, is close to the gondola and has an indoor pool.
Moderate:
Harveys Resort & Casino, t +1 775 588 2411, *www.harrahs.com*, is located close to Heavenly's gondola base. It houses eight restaurants, ten cocktail lounges, health club and the ubiquitous wedding chapel.
Best Western Station House Inn, t +1 530 542 1101, *www.stationhouseinn.com*, has a shuttle-bus to the skiing, and features some 'spa rooms'.

Jackson Hole, Wyoming

Profile

Some of North America's most challenging trails and steepest backcountry terrain. Stay in the town of Jackson with its Wild West ambience, or for ski convenience at Teton Village. Wide range of moderate to extreme luxury accommodation

Resort

Along with powder bums from all over the world, Jackson Hole manages to draw a glitteringly wealthy clientele worthy of Switzerland's St Moritz or France's Megève, and the reason for this lies in Jackson's long history of dude ranching.

City Slickers have been answering the call of the wild in the Tetons ever since 1908 when rancher Louis Joy discovered that the urban rich would pay good money for chuck-waggon fare, lumpy mattresses and saddle sores. Little and much has changed since dude-ranching was overtaken by skiing.

The mighty Tetons remain unchallenged in their wild beauty.

Jackson Hole rancher Struthers Burt once wrote: 'You must search for the loveliness of America. It is not obvious, it is scattered. But when you find it, it touches you and binds you to it like a great secret oath taken in silence'. Presumably he was looking out of his window at the time.

The mountain range is captivating from the moment you step from the plane at Jackson Hole airport, where the runway is

Essentials

Altitude: 6,311ft (1924m)–10,135ft (3135m)
Map: see page M58
Further information: t +1 307 733 2292,
  www.jacksonhole.com
Lifts in area: 11 (2 cableways, 9 chairs)
  serving 2,500 acres
Lift pass: adult $225–361, child 14yrs and
  under $113–179, both for 6 days
Access: Jackson Hole airport 15mins from
  Jackson, 35mins from Teton Village

fringed by huge herds of grazing elk and the occasional enormous moose.

'It matched the vision I had of what beautiful is,' said Harrison Ford who forsook Hollywood for his 800-acre ranch here and has become part of the community. The occasional injured skier is astonished to find that his or her rescuer in a Bell 407 helicopter is Ford himself who has been known to spring into action when called out by the ski patrol.

A 15-minute car-ride from the airport takes you to the quaint cowboy town of Jackson. The jet-lagged visitor usually assumes that the steep, groomed trails immediately above the town are his ski destination. Wrong. This mountain is the small and entirely separate resort of Snow King.

Jackson Hole Mountain Resort is located a further 20-minute drive away at Teton Village on the far side of the Snake River, an enticing trout stream that coils across the valley floor.

This leaves you with a dilemma as to where to base yourself. Both have hotels of equal stature. But the convenience of doorstep skiing has to be weighed against the shops, restaurants, and nightlife of Jackson. If you can't make up your mind, you can stay in rural tranquillity between the two. Personally we now favour Teton Village since it has expanded into a real resort rather than just a base station. The

police take a dim view of drink-driving and if you enjoy an evening out in Jackson it makes sense to travel by bus or taxi.

Some 8,000 elk and a host of celebrities, including Russell Crowe, Uma Thurman, Ralph Fiennes, Sandra Bullock and Jack Nicholson, agree that this is the best place in the Rockies to spend all or part of the winter. The winning combination of spectacular scenery, yester-year cowboy values and what we consider to be some of the best skiing in North America make the long journey from Europe worthwhile.

To the chagrin of purist powderhounds Teton Village has doubled in size in recent years. The establishment of such exotic hotels as the Amangani and the Four Seasons has brought a new breed of winter visitor who is not necessarily wedded to the mountainside from first to last lift. To the astonishment of local diehards, some have even been seen out of ski clothes and carrying boutique shopping bags at lunchtime rather than a pair of fat powder skis.

Focus in the quaint town of Jackson is on the main square with its archway made from hundreds of antlers naturally shed by elk in their winter reserve. Others have tried, but only Jackson – and Telluride on a smaller scale – has succeeded in welding the dusty gun-slinging charisma of a Western frontier town to the high-tech facilities of a modern ski resort.

Mountain

Jackson Hole is ambrosia for snow gourmets. You don't have to be an expert to enjoy it, but it sure helps. Much of the terrain is best described as 'difficult' to 'very difficult', although an increased amount of intermediate skiing can now be found on Apres Vous, the much more benign of the two adjoining mountains.

It is hard to imagine that a resort with only 11 lifts can produce such excitement, but as one reporter put it 'I am certain I could ski here every day for a whole season and never tire of the ever-changing and challenging terrain'.

For this one last winter the Aerial Tram, a venerable cable car, still takes you up to the 10,449ft summit of Rendezvous for Corbet's Couloir, a notorious heart-stopping gully reached by a 13ft jump off a cornice. However, the resort has given notice of its impending retirement during the course of 2006. Currently insufficient funds mean that there are no plans for its replacement, although no doubt this will be reviewed. A whip-round among the celebrities who ride it each winter would doubtless produce sufficient loose change to build a new one.

The top of the windswept peak is the start of one of the longest vertical drops in the United States served by a single lift. The upward journey is accompanied by warnings of potential dangers. The full range of bowls and chutes is radical in the extreme. However, in all but the most difficult snow conditions, confident intermediates will have no trouble in picking out manageable descents – provided they remember that, in Jackson, expert-only, double-black-diamond trails take no prisoners. The Hobacks are a series of side-by-side and seemingly endless off-piste itineraries that will test the strongest legs.

The Bridger gondola provides access to the intermediate area between the two mountains as well as to much of the terrain served by the cable car. A 20-minute hike up the Headwall opens up Casper Bowl. A further short walk takes you out of the resort area to Granite Bowl, a magnificent mile-long powder field followed by a wilderness traverse back to base, but it is avalanche-prone and so should not be attempted without a guide, transceivers and shovels. The same applies to Cody Peak and Rock Springs Bowls off Rendezvous Mountain.

The second mountain of Apres Vous is prime beginners' territory, with a beginner network of runs at the bottom served by the Teewinot quad, and more demanding, intermediate terrain at the top, which is served by the Apres Vous quad. A new triple chair introduced this winter will ease intermediate traffic on the Bridger gondola by providing a link to the Caspar Bowl lift from the top of the Eagle's Rest chair. The adjacent freestyle terrain park and half-pipe is as popular with twin-tippers as it is with riders.

Learn

Jackson Hole Mountain Sports School, t +1 307 733 2292, has an outstanding reputation. Courses include Learn to Turn, Mountain Masters, and Race Clinics. The demanding Steep and Deep Camp provides a safe introduction to Jackson's radical terrain. **Jackson Hole Alpine and Backcountry Guide Service**, t +1 307 739 2663, offers off-piste guiding. **High Mountain Heli-skiing**, t +1 307 733 3274, is another option.

Children

The slope-side **Kids' Ranch**, t +1 307 733 2292, has its own dedicated corral complete with a magic carpet lift and Fort Wyoming playground. It offers childcare from six months to three years, and ski programmes for three- to 14-year-olds. **Annie's Nannies**, t +1 307 733 8086, and **Babysitting by the Tetons**, t +1 307 730 0754, are the options available for non-skiers.

Keen teens can join **Team Extreme**, t +1 307 733 2292, a demanding four-day clinic for skiers and snowboarders aged from 12 and 17 years, which is aimed at children who have outgrown regular ski school.

Lunch

On-mountain lunches never used to be a strong feature, but the **Four Seasons** t +1 307 734 5040, slope-side terrace is a welcome gourmet reward for a hard morning in the Hobacks. A new restaurant is scheduled to open this winter at the top of the gondola. The other lunchtime venues worth considering are the **Mangy Moose**, t +1 307 733 4913, and upstairs at the **Alpenhof**, t +1 307 733 3242.

Dine

In Teton Village, the **Westbank Grill** in the Four Seasons has an international menu and cosy atmosphere. The **Mangy Moose**, t +1 307 733 4913, is a family favourite set in a vast barn. **GameFish**, t +1 307 732 6040, in the Snake River Lodge and Spa focuses on fish and smoked game, and **Masa Sushi**, t +1 307 732 2962, at Teton Pines golf course serves Japanese fare. **Calico**, t +1 307 733 2460, is a good-value Italian family restaurant on Teton Village Road. In Jackson, try **Nikai Sushi**, t +1 307 734 6490, and **Koshu's Wine Bar**, t +1 307 733 5283, which is popular with the locals. **Old Yellowstone Garage**, t +1 307 734 6161, is top-of-the-range Italian. Signature dishes at the **Snake River Grill**, t +1 307 733 0557, include smoked tuna carpaccio and pan-roasted Idaho trout. **Rendezvous Bistro**, t +1 307 739 1100, is run by the son of Snake River Grill's owner. Intimate **Wild Sage**, t +1 307 733 2000, at the Rusty Parrot is the first four-diamond restaurant in Wyoming.

Party

The slope-side **Peak** in the Four Seasons Resort attracts skiers at the end of the day, but Teton Village has little life after dark, with lights out almost everywhere by 11pm. **The Snake River Brewing Company** is popular with the locals. Those in search of serious drinking should head for the **Million Dollar Cowboy Bar** on Jackson's Town Square. This huge saloon has stools made from Western saddles, live music and pool tables, all of which is dominated by a stuffed grizzly bear. The local paper will tell you where to find live music each night – for example **The Stagecoach** in the nearby village of Wilson has music on Thursday evenings and the **Mangy Moose** in Teton Village is on Saturdays. A word of warning: Jackson is strict about licensing laws, which forbid anyone under 21 to go to bars; over-21s must carry ID to show when asked.

Sleep

Teton Village
Luxury:
Amangani, t +1 307 734 7333, *www. amangani.com*, is a veritable palace set on a bluff halfway between Teton Village and Jackson town. Rooms are minimalist with ample use of black resin, animal hide and pale wood floors, as well as beautiful black slate bathrooms and wrap-around balconies.
Four Seasons Resort, t +1 307 734 5040, *www.fourseasons.com/jacksonhole*, has the best location of any hotel here. It is decorated with works of art by Miró and Giacometti and has slate floors and animal-hide upholstery. The substantial bedrooms and family-sized suites all have connecting marble bathrooms, and there is a kids' club and games room, state-of-the-art spa and fitness centre.
Moderate:
Rusty Parrot Lodge t +1 307 733 2000, *www.rustyparrot.com*, in Jackson has a welcoming atmosphere with old terracotta floors, Persian rugs and an open fire in the lobby.

Spring Creek Resort, t +1 307 735 8833, *www.springcreekresort.com*, is next to the Amangani and contains traditional condos.

Snake River Lodge & Spa, t +1 307 732 6000, *snakeriverlodge.rockresorts.com*, is at the foot of the ski area and owned by Vail Resorts. It has a pleasant lobby and lounge area but dated rooms. The spa includes an attractive indoor-outdoor swimming pool among the rocks.

Teton Club, t +1 307 734 9777, *www.tetonclub.com*, is a very comfortable condo development in Teton Village with maid service and spa.

Teton Mountain Lodge, t +1 307 734 7111, *www.tetonlodge.com*, at Teton Village, is the newest lodge that is ideal for families. The condos contain cosy bedrooms and modern kitchens with huge fridges.

Teton Village Condos, t +1 307 733 3990, are spacious, well equipped, and a free bus ride from the slopes.

The Wort Hotel, t +1 307 733 2190, *www.worthotel.com*, a comfortable stagecoach inn close to the main square in Jackson, is the best situated in town.

Keystone, Colorado

Profile

As well as easy access from an international airport, the attractive purpose-built village has the largest night-skiing operation in North America

Resort

Keystone has been a Colorado community since the 1880s and is the

Essentials

Altitude: 9,300ft (2835m)–12,200ft (3719m)
Further information: t +1 970 496 4386 (UK t +44 (0)1708 224773), *www.keystone.snow.com*
Lifts in area: 15 (2 cableways, 11 chairs, 2 drags) serving 81 miles (130km) of piste
Lift pass: Colorado Ticket (covers Arapahoe Basin, Beaver Creek, Breckenridge, Keystone, Vail) adult $164–375, child 5–12yrs $151–190, both for 6 days
Access: Denver airport 75mins

only resort of that vintage that does not owe its existence to gold or silver strikes. For a while in those heady days, Old Keystone was the end of the line for the Denver, South Park (yes, of cartoon fame), and Pacific railroad. Not a lot happened here again until the 1960s when an enterprising group of developers persuaded the US Forest Service to let them build a ski resort. Its location, only 75 miles on I-70 from Denver made it attractive to local skiers. The establishment of what is now the largest floodlit night-skiing operation in North America appealed to city workers who could drive out after work as well as at weekends.

In the 1990s Keystone underwent a complete makeover, with a new resort village constructed by Canadian ski property giant developer Intrawest. The result is a friendly family resort divided into the linked 'villages' of Lakeside and River Run. It has considerable atmosphere for somewhere that has been largely purpose-built. Keystone also has a substantial amount of intermediate skiing of its own and shares a lift pass with nearby Breckenridge and Arapahoe Basin as well as Vail and Beaver Creek, which are slightly further afield. The first two are linked by a free ski bus and there is subsidized daily transport to the others. Skiers or riders spending a week or more here are strongly advised to explore the other Vail resorts as well as separate Copper Mountain.

Mountain

Skiing takes place on three interlinked mountains that lie one behind the other and each is progressively more challenging.

Main mountain access to Dercum, the closest peak to the resort, is by gondola or multiple chair from River Run. Alternatively start from the other end of the strung-out resort with the Argentine chair from Mountain House. The easy and intermediate cruising runs on Dercum are floodlit for night-skiing. The gondola continues across to the summit of the second mountain, North Peak, which offers slightly more challenging terrain. Pistes and a quad-chair connect to the Outback at 12,220ft, which has steeps, trees and lots of bumps. From the top of the lift you can hike up the truly challenging South and North Bowls – but you need to be fit and acclimatized for a climb at this altitude.

Keystone's beginner and advanced terrain parks are located on the front side of Dercum Mountain in Pack Saddle Bowl.

Learn

Keystone Ski and Ride School, t +1 970 496 4170, offers group and private lessons.

Children

Keystone Children's Center and **Snowplay Programs**, t +1 970 496 4181, cares for babies from just two months at River Run and at the Mountain House base area.

Lunch

The Alpenglow Stube, t +1 800 354 4386, is the highest *haute cuisine* in North America. Signature dishes include *ragoût* of blue crab, and duck *foie gras* with roast garlic hummus.

Dine

Ski Tip Lodge, t +1 877 625 1540, offers four-course menus. Almost as rustic is the 1930s **Keystone Ranch**, which serves 'Colorado Frontier and fine-dining, fusion cuisine'. **Champeaux**, t +1 970 496 2316, at Keystone Lodge in Lakeside Village serves French country cuisine.

Party

Great Northern Tavern, **Kickapoo Tavern**, and **Inxpot** provide snacks and après-ski entertainment, while **Snake River Saloon** has pool and live music. **Parrot Eyes** at River Run serves tacos, margaritas and draft beer.

Sleep

All accommodation can be booked through central reservations, t +1 970 496 4386.
Ski Tip Lodge, t +1 877 625 1540, *www.skitiplodge.com*, is an original and charming stagecoach inn. It offers B&B with a separate restaurant, and is a bus ride from the resort.
Keystone Ranch, t +1 877 204 7881, *www.keystoneranch.com*, is also a bus ride away from the skiing and offers good food.
Keystone Lodge, t +1 970 496 2316, has been recently renovated with smart guest rooms and loft suites.

Killington, Vermont

Profile

Chilly East Coast resort with phenomenal snowmaking capability and recommended ski school. Good accommodation, but resort lacks a village centre

Resort

Killington is usually the first resort in the US to open each November and the last to close in May or June. The reason for this has nothing to do with nature's bounty, but with the most sophisticated snowmaking system on the planet. The resort claims 250 inches of natural snow each winter but this doesn't always fall to order. Instead, cannons mounted on 'giraffe' poles can blanket 1,182 acres with sufficient artificial cover to open terrain on all seven of its peaklets without a flake of the real thing.

Arriving by car on a crisp blue-sky day you may notice with gloom that the only clouds in the sky hang over your destination. But that's no cloud – just a prescribed mix of crystalized air-and-water falling from hundreds of snow cannon in the world's biggest broadside. Not only the pistes but the surrounding forest is laden with man-made snow that is manufactured in a dozen different qualities from adhesive base layers to fluffy finishes.

Killington's main shortcoming is that it lacks a heart – any one area that you can truly call the resort centre. Hotels, bars and restaurants sprawl along the five-mile approach road from the highway. Reporters warn that it can be bitterly cold here in mid-winter. The resort shares a lift pass with the neighbouring attractive little resort of Pico. Despite years of promises, a mountain link between the two has yet to be established.

Mountain

Killington claims to have skiing on seven mountains, but this is creative topography. The reality is one – 4,241ft Killington Peak, which has six shoulders. Together they form a naturally shaped ski area that extends for miles across a heavily wooded mountainside with a number of isolated condo-clad base areas. Snowshed, at the top of the road from the highway, is the main one with a clutch of high-speed chairs providing mountain access.

The much lower base of Skyship is served by a two-stage heated gondola that brings you up to Skye Peak 450ft below the top of the ski area. Killington suits all standards of skier and rider but the emphasis is on quantity rather variety – so many of the gladed runs have the same pitch that it is often hard to differentiate between them. The most demanding runs are to be found on the front face of Killington Peak, reached by the K1 Express gondola and on lower Bear Mountain. Killington is popular with snowboarders and has three terrain parks with a super-pipe and a snowcross course.

Essentials

Altitude: 1,165ft (354m)–4,241ft (1293m)
Further information: t +1 802 422 1330, *www.killington.com*
Lifts in area: 31 (3 cableways, 22 chairs, 6 drags) serving 45 miles of trails
Lift pass: adult $264–396, child $194–290, both for 6 days
Access: Burlington airport 2hrs, Boston airport 3hrs

Learn

The **Perfect Turn Ski School**, t +1 802 422 1234, uses the graduated length teaching method and has a good reputation for imparting the basics.

Children

Friendly Penguin Day Care, t +1 802 422 6222, is for kids aged six weeks to 23 months at the Ramshead Family Center and for up to six years at the Grand Hotel. Children as young as two years can join **First Tracks** for lessons, and **SnowZone** is ski or ride tuition for 13 to 18 years, t +1 800 923 9444 for all.

Lunch

Mountain Top Inn, t +1 802 483 6737, is traditional American. **Peak Restaurant**, t +1 802 422 6780, is a cafeteria on Killington Peak.

Dine

'Killington has a low-end feel to it. There are dozens of places to eat but the quality is generally moderate,' reports one journalist. **Hemingway's**, t +1 802 422 3886, near the Skyship base serves good food but it is expensive. Other eateries include award-winning **Cascades**, t +1 802 422 3731, which has a casual atmosphere. **Casey's Caboose**, t +1 802 422 3539, serves traditional American. **Kong Chow**, t +1 802 775 5244, and **Sushi Yoshi**, t +1 802 422 4241, offer Asian dishes. **Santa Fe Steakhouse**, t +1 802 422 2124, is recommended. **The Wobbly Barn**, t +1 802 422 6171, has some of the best steaks and seafood in the area. **Peppers**, t +1 802 422 3177, in Killington Mall is reminiscent of a 1940s diner and is a good place for breakfast.

Party

Pickel Barrel on Killington Road is the hub of the evening action, with big-name bands playing every weekend. **Mogul's Pub** is also on Killington Road. **The Wobbly Barn** is where Killington's nightlife first began and still features world-class rock 'n' roll acts.

Sleep

Snowshed base is the best place to stay if you don't have a car.
Inn of the Six Mountains, t +1 800 228 4676, *www.sixmountains.com*, is close to the nightlife and a short drive from the base lodges. A courtesy taxi service is provided.
Killington Grand Resort Hotel, t +1 802 422 1330, *www.killington.com*, is a slope-side condominium-hotel.
Butternut on the Mountain, t +1 800 524 7654, *www.bestlodging.com*, is a no-smoking property with an indoor swimming pool, games room.
Vermont Inn, t +1 888 636 8107, *www.vermontinn.com*, is an 1840s farmhouse 10 miles out of town, offering individually decorated rooms, some with fireplaces or hot tubs.

Mammoth, California

Profile

Large but remote high-altitude ski area for all standards, with good sunshine and snow records. Particularly recommended for snowboarders

Resort

Skiing is no newcomer to the high Sierra Nevada mountain range that lies behind California's sunny coastline. As winter storms sweep in from the Pacific Ocean they attract some 400 inches of snow each winter, resulting in a season that lasts from November until June – or even July 4 in 2005. Back in the 1850s, some 30 years before skiing started in Switzerland, immigrant Scandinavian miners were using Lapp hunting skis as winter transport and weekend recreation.

Mammoth, named after the Mammoth Mining Company, which staked claim to the mountain after the discovery of gold here in 1878, has some of the best and most weather-reliable skiing in California. When it is not snowing, the sun shines for an average of 300 days each year. Mammoth it is, the largest single mountain ski and ride destination in North America.

The drawback is that it is a long way from anywhere. The local airstrip has been rebuilt but plans for services from Chicago and Dallas have so far failed to materialize.

Outside the main US holiday dates the resort is quiet mid-week, although young Los Angelinos drive up for the weekend in large numbers. Mammoth ski resort is just above the town of Mammoth Lakes and has been expanded at a cost of $830 million in recent years. The focal point is the two-year-old Village at Mammoth, which is the best place to begin and end your skiing day. The village is linked by gondola to the ski area.

A regular free shuttle bus runs to and from the ski-area bases at Main Lodge, Canyon Lodge and Juniper Springs and there is also a bus service to Mammoth Lakes. June Mountain, 20 miles away, is owned by Mammoth, shares the lift pass, and has easy intermediate runs in a spectacular setting.

Mountain

The Village Gondola takes you up to Canyon Lodge, giving access to some easy beginner and intermediate terrain as well as some testing double-diamonds such as Grizzly, Viva and Avalanche Chutes. However, the most challenging slopes are reached by the two-stage gondola from Main Lodge, which brings you up to Panorama Lookout at 11,053ft. From here and from Chair 23 you can traverse and drop into some phenomenal chutes and bowls such as Hangman's Hollow, Cornice Bowl and Beyond the Edge. The lower half of the mountain has plenty of cruising terrain and some good novice slopes but, overall, Mammoth is a mountain that will please good skiers and riders in search of testing gradients and fresh challenges.

Snowboarders are particularly at home in Mammoth and the Unbound terrain parks are considered among the best in North America with a super-pipe and a super-duper pipe. JM2 at June Mountain has spines, pipes and rails.

Learn

Mammoth Ski and Snowboard School, t +1 760 934 0745, offers courses including teen skiing, Women Only and skiing for

Essentials

Altitude: 7,953ft, (2424m)–11,053ft (3369m)
Further information: t +1 760 934 0745, *www.mammothmountain.com*
Lifts in area: 27 (3 cableways, 22 chairs, 2 drags) serving 3,500 acres of terrain
Lift pass: Area (Mammoth and June Mountain) adult $238–403, child 7–18yrs $118–301, both for 6 days
Access: Los Angeles airport 5½hrs, Reno airport 3hrs

the disabled. **A J Kitt's Ski & Race Camp**, t +1 760 934 2571, organizes slalom and GS training. Off-piste guiding is through **Mammoth Mountaineering School**, t +1 760 924 9100.

Children

Small World Child Care, t +1 760 934 0646, looks after children from newborn to 12 years with ski or snowboard lessons for older ones.

Lunch

'Pretty poor' was how one reporter described the food available on the mountain. Choices include the **Mill Café**, t +1 760 934 2571, **Mountainside Grill**, t +1 760 934 0601, in the Mammoth Mountain Inn, and the **Yodler Restaurant and Pub**, t +1 760 934 2571 x 2234. In The Village at Mammoth try **Hennessey's**, t +1 760 934 8444, and **Lakanuki Café**, t +1 760 934 7447. **Parallax**, t +1 760 934 2571 x 3118, at McCoy Station serves Pacific Rim and Mediterranean cuisine.

Dine

Skadi, t +1 760 934 3902, and **Nevado's**, t +1 760 934 4466, offer gourmet fare. **Ocean Harvest**, t +1 760 934 8539, specializes in seafood. **Matsu**, t + 1 760 934 8277, offers an eclectic Far Eastern menu, including Thai and Chinese specialities. **Chart House**, t +1 760 934 4526, and **The Mogul**, t +1 760 934 3039, have fine steaks. **Alpenrose**, t +1 760 934 3077, offers cheese fondue. Other dining options in the Village include **Hennessey's**, t +1 760 934 8444, and **Pita Pit**, t +1 760 924 7482.

Party

Dublin's is a traditional-style Irish pub with the addition of 50 TVs lining the

walls. If you want to dance the night away, go to **Fever**, the new nightspot inside Dublin's. **Lakanuki** is a hip mountain 'tiki bar' where you can try hula dancing in your ski boots while sipping tropical drinks. **Unbound** is a cool place to buy a new snowboard or hang out after a day in the terrain park. **Canyon Lodge** regularly has live bands. **The Clocktower** in Alpenhof Lodge and **Whiskey Creek** are popular meeting-places in town.

Sleep

All accommodation can be reserved on t +1 760 934 0745.
Luxury/moderate:
The Village at Mammoth, t +1 800 421 7005, *www.intrawestmammoth.com*, condos include Lincoln House, White Mountain Lodge, and Grand Sierra Lodge.
Alpenhof Lodge, t +1 760 934 8558, *www.alpenhof-lodge.com*, is within easy access of the skiing and the town.
Mammoth Mountain Inn, t +1 760 934 2581, *www.mammothmountain.com*, is at the Main Lodge base,
Austria Hof Lodge, t +1 760 934 2764, *www.austriahof.com*, at the ski area base is good value, with some units containing fireplaces and hot tubs.
Canyon Lodge, Juniper Springs and **Sunstone Lodges**, t +1 760 924 1102, *www.mammothcondos.com*, offer slope-side self-catering.
Mammoth Lakes:
Shilo Inn Suites, t +1 760 934 4500, *www.shiloinns.com*, are conveniently located on Main Street.
June Mountain:
Double Eagle Resort & Spa, t +1 760 648 7004, *www.double-eagle-resort.com*, has a full-service spa, pool and health club.

Park City, Utah

Profile

Convenient resort for airport access, with a wide choice of nearby resorts. Good skiing for all levels and an excellent snow record. Recommended for gourmets

Resort

The Victorian mining town of Park City plays host to three of the most important ski resorts in Utah and is home of the finest and driest powder snow in the world. All three are located side-by-side on a five-mile stretch of mountainside an easy 40-minute drive from Salt Lake City. In the middle lies Park City Mountain Resort directly above the attractive old town of Park City. It is flanked by Deer Valley and The Canyons.

Linking them would involve the construction of just one lift. Rivalry has so far prevented this, but for 2005–6 the three have come a step closer by launching a joint adult and children's pass for foreign visitors that is only sold through tour operators, with a single rate

Essentials

Altitude: 6,900ft (2104m)–10,000ft (3049m)
Further information: t +1 435 649 8111, *www.parkcitymountain.com*
Lifts in area: 14 (14 chairs) serving 3,300 acres of terrain
Lift pass: Three Resort International: adult $345, child 7–12yrs $193, both for 6 out of 10 days. Other lengths of stay and single resort passes also available
Access: Salt Lake City airport 40mins

throughout the season. You can buy individual passes, but the new ticket offers a considerable saving on window prices.

The heart of Park City is steep Main Street, lined with restored Victorian buildings and home to the Wasatch Brewery, the Egyptian Theater and a host of art galleries, boutiques, restaurants, bars and coffee shops. Mountain Resort at the foot of the pistes is a moderately well-designed complex on three levels, with shops, cafés and accommodation, set around a skating rink and a car park.

Mountain

Main mountain access is by two detachable six-person chairs that take 12 minutes to reach the Summit House Restaurant. Alternatively, you can get there by riding a triple-chair from the top end of town. It's a far automated cry from the early 1960s when the first skiers travelled up on an underground mine train before being brought to the surface on a hoist lift. The skiing is much more varied and challenging than is indicated by the lift map. The lower half of the mountain has plenty of easy intermediate terrain but much of it is given over to steepish gladed blacks. The top half, served by McConkey's Six-pack and the Jupiter lift, is a more serious proposition with an abundance of double-diamond chutes and bowls and still more off-piste opportunities for those prepared to hike along Pinecone Ridge.

Anyone spending a week or more here – Park City is a sensible accommodation base – is advised to not only explore Deer Valley and The Canyons but also Snowbird and Alta, which are a 45-minute drive away.

Learn

Park City Ski & Snowboard School, t +1 435 649 5496, has a justified reputation for some of the best cutting-edge technical instruction in the US, as befits the town that is official home of the US ski team. Strong skiers and riders should try the **Mountain Experience** programme for exploring Jupiter Peak. Guided off-piste can be arranged through **Park City Powder Cats**, t +1 435 649 6596, **Ski Utah Interconnect Tour**, t +1 801 534 1907, and **Wasatch Powderbird Guides Heli-skiing**, t +1 801 742 2800.

Children

Park City Mountain Resort has no childcare facilities, but the town has no less than three non-ski kindergartens: **Annie's Nannies**, t +1 435 615 1935, **Creative Beginnings**, t +1 435 645 7315, and **Guardian Angel**, t +1 435 783 2662. The ski school provides lessons from three years.

Lunch

Legacy Lodge has grills and fresh fish. **Summit House** near the top of the Bonanza lift has pizzas, grills and a large deck with views of Park City and beyond. **Mid-Mountain Lodge**, near the base of the Pioneer and McConkey lifts, is a modified version of an old miner's home with pasta, pizza and chilli. Further information on t +1 435 649 8111.

Dine

Chenez, t + 1 435 940 1909, is a new French restaurant with an intimate ambience. **Zoom**, t +1 435 649 9108, owned by Robert Redford, is an old favourite, with Californian cuisine. **Wahso**, t +1 435 615 0300, is an Asian restaurant styled on Shanghai in the 1930s. **Chimayo**, t +1 435 649 6222, serves South-Western cuisine. **Grappa Italian Café**, t +1 435 645 0636, features

traditional Tuscan dishes. **Claimjumper Steakhouse**, t +1 435 649 8051, is a carnivore's delight, and **Kampai Sushi**, t +1 435 649 0655 offers Japanese cuisine. **350 Main**, t +1 435 649 3140, has fresh seafood, while **The Riverhorse** on Main, t +1 435 649 3536, is hip American.

Party

This the Mormon heartland but, contrary to popular belief, it is far from 'dry.' However, in a restaurant you may not be offered the wine list unless you ask for it. Liquor laws require pubs to be privately licensed, but temporary membership is easily obtained – the barman usually asks a local to 'sponsor' the stranger. Try **Legends at The Resort** in the Legacy Lodge at the base area. **No Name Saloon** displays the local Park City Rugby Club memorabilia on its walls. **J.B. Mulligans Club and Pub**, and **Wasatch Brew Pub Cantina** are popular. **The Star Bar at Plan B** features live bands.

Sleep

Luxury:
Hotel Park City, t +1 435 200 2000, *www.hotelparkcity.com*, is an all-suite hotel in the style of a grand national park lodge of the early 1900, and a leading Small Hotel of the World
Silver King, t +1 435 649 5500, *www.silverkinghotel.com*, is a smart condo hotel one mile from Main Street.
The Yarrow Resort Hotel, t +1 435 649 7000, *www.yarrowresort.com*, is a full-service hotel adjacent to the Holiday Village Mall.
Moderate:
Lodge at Mountain Village, t +1 435 649 8111, *www.parkcitymountain.com*, is a full-service hotel at the base area.

Marriott's Summit Watch, t +1 435 647
4100, *www.marriott.com*, is conveniently
located at the lower end of Main Street.
Park City Marriott, t +435 649 2900,
www.parkcitymarriott.com, is situated
one mile from the downtown area.
Radisson Inn, t +1 435 649 5000,
www.radisson.com, has spacious rooms
and mountain views.
Budget:
Angel House Inn, t +1 435 647 0338,
www.angelhouseinn.com, has nine rooms,
each modelled on a different angel.
Best Western Landmark Inn, t +1 435 649
7300, *www.bwlandmarkinn.com*,is five
miles out of town at Kimball Junction,
but good value.
Holiday Inn Express Park City, t +1 435 658
1600, also at Kimball Juncton, is another
budget-priced option.

Snowbird and Alta, Utah

Profile

Two contrastingly different, linked resorts
for accomplished skiers and riders that
attract the best powder snow in the world.
Snowboarding is not permitted in Alta

Resort

It is hard to find two more different
resorts than Snowbird and adjoining Alta
in Little Cottonwood Canyon, a 40-minute
uphill drive from Salt Lake City. But, strangely,
they admirably complement each other.
Their alliance has created a formidable

European-style ski circuit with two villages
separated by some of the most exciting and
radical terrain in North America. The canyon
– Brigham Young and his 143 Mormon
pioneers came this way in 1847 from
Nebraska to found their city beside the
great salt lake – is home to Champagne
Powder. These talcum-like flakes are freeze-
dried in their passage above the desert from
the Pacific Ocean. They land here in the
winter in copious quantities.

This annual phenomenon persuaded
Texan oilman-turned-mountaineer Dick
Bass to build Snowbird in the 1970s.
Unfortunately, he chose the utilitarian
concrete architecture of high-rise Tignes
in France as a role model. Cliff Lodge with
its 11-storey atrium dominates the resort.
Snowbird Center, departure point for the
Aerial Tram, a dated but renovated cable
car, is the official heart of the village. The
open space is surrounded by other nearby
accommodation blocks and shops on three
levels. Snowbird is no beauty, but very ski-
convenient. Under its maximum-tog duvet
of snow it is by no means unappealing.

Little Alta, higher up the canyon, is an
altogether different proposition, a handful
of lodges providing simple but exclusive
accommodation favoured by 'old money'
Americans and new money wannabees.
Both hark back to halcyon Hemingway-
esque days when handsome couples in
cable-knit sweaters and white polo-necks

sat around the fireplace at the end of day drinking mulled wine, while wooden skis were stretched and leather lace-up boots dried in the boiler room below. Skiing started in Alta in the 1930s and the first lodge was built in 1939.

The lifts all used to be fixed double-chairs that gave the formidable ski area an atmosphere reminiscent of St Anton in 1960. However, while retro-skiing has proved to be big business, ever-aloof Alta has been unable to ignore some of the refinements to the original invention of the wheel. Since its relatively recent alliance with Snowbird after decades of bitter rivalry, a couple of detachable quads – to the chagrin of Alta purists – have surreptitiously crept in to the system.

Mountain

The joint area is a world-class point of pilgrimage for anyone who is hooked on sliding down mountains and knows how to do it at a reasonably high level. The continued ban in Alta on snowboarding makes it a more suitable destination for those who prefer two planks to one. The gradient of the double-diamonds and the off-piste in both resorts, backed by usually sensational snow cover, has few rivals in North America. There is a reasonable amount of lower intermediate terrain in both resorts, as well as good novice slopes. Snowbird has a new super-pipe on the Big Emma run next to the Big Emma terrain park. The main terrain park is located by the Baby Thunder lift.

Main access from Snowbird is by cable car straight up to 11,000ft Hidden Peak. Importantly, there are two easy routes down from the top. Better skiers and riders will head for Upper Cirque or Silver Fox, as well as High Baldy Traverse and the steep descents of Thunder Bowl. Mineral Basin, 500 acres of prime alpine terrain, provides the gateway to Alta.

Main mountain access from Alta is by the Collins quad, gateway to an enormous range of intermediate and advanced runs back down the mountain and across to the Sugarloaf quad. A glance at the lift map shows a complete absence of double-black-diamond runs. Don't be deceived – it's just Alta's quirky way of doing things. They printed the first map decades before such gradings were invented and see no reason to change. Some of the most demanding terrain is reached from the Supreme triple-chair, and the most challenging routes are not on the lift map – you need to ask the locals. Also try the Ski Utah Interconnect, a guided day tour from Deer Valley to Snowbird via Solitude, Brighton and Alta.

Learn

Snowbird Mountain School, t +1 801 933 2170, has a sound reputation and the full range of ski and snowboard courses. **Alf Engen Ski School, t** +1 801 359 1078, is named after America's greatest skier of the 1930s, who taught skiing here in 1945–6. Guiding is with the **Ski Utah Interconnect Tour, t** +1 801 534 1907, or **Wasatch Powderbird Guides Heli-skiing, t** +1 801 742 2800.

Children

Camp Snowbird, t +1 801 933 2256, at Cliff Lodge looks after children from six weeks to 12 years. **Mountain School, t** +1 801 933 2170, at Camp Snowbird gives lessons from three years.

Alta's Alf Engen Ski School, t +1 801 359 1078, provides children's lessons. **Alta Lodge Kids' Program, t** +1 801 742 3500, is aimed at its four- to ten-year-old residents and provides transport to and from ski school, as well as après-ski activities. **Alta Children's Center, t** +1 801 742 3042, offers daycare.

Lunch

The only eating place on the mountain at Snowbird is **Mid-Gad Restaurant, t** +1 801 933 2245. Serious lunchers must return to the base.

On the slopes at Alta, **Alf's Restaurant, t** +1 801 799 2295, serves lunch and snacks, while **Collins Grill, t** +1 801 799 2297, features French cuisine. **Albion Grill, t** +1 801 742 2500, is a cafeteria at Albion base area. **Alta Lodge, t** +1 801 742 3500, at Wildcat Base serves breakfast, lunch and dinner. **The Shallow Shaft, t** +1 801 742 2177, is one of the top restaurants in the US.

Dine

Snowbird has a dozen restaurants; the **Aerie, t** +1 801 933 2160, at Cliff Lodge, serves continental cuisine, **The Keyhole, t** +1 801 933 2025, specializes in South-western food and the **Wildflower Restaurant, t** +1 801 933 2230, at Iron Blosam Lodge offers gourmet pizzas.

Alta's best food is served at **Alta Lodge, t** +1 801 742 3500, where Chef Paul Raddon has presided for more than 30 years and wealthy guests from Boston and New York dine at communal tables. **Goldminer's Daughter, t** +1 801 742 2300, serves New Mexican fare at the mountain base.

Party

At Snowbird, **Aerie Lounge & Sushi Bar, The Wildflower Lodge, Lodge Bistro Lounge,** and **The Keyhole Cantina** are the main meeting-places. **The Tram Club** at Snowbird Center has billiards, video games, live music and 13 televisions. **The Aerie** has live jazz on Wednesdays and Saturdays.

In Alta, après-ski is limited to the slope-side hot tub or the screening of black-and-white ski films, followed by drinks around a roaring log fire. Guests at Alta Lodge swap tales in the **Sitzmark Club.**

Sleep

Snowbird, **t** +1 801 742 2222, for all reservations.

Cliff Lodge is the smartest address, with a major spa, a rooftop swimming pool and what claims to be the world's largest collection of Oriental rugs. The Cliff Club in the west wing has 54 three-room suites furnished in Mission style.

Lodge at Snowbird, by the cable car, is the original lodge, completely renovated, with an outdoor pool and hot tub.

The Inn has simple studios, suites and an outdoor pool.

Iron Blosam Lodge is geared towards families, with its own spa and pool.

Alta:

Alta Lodge, t +1 801 742 3500, renovated in 1990, is a charming place that has been attracting visitors since 1939.

Alta Peruvian Lodge, t +1 801 742 3000, has a swimming pool.

Rustler Lodge, t +1 801 742 2200, has a heated outdoor pool.

Alta Chalets, t +1 866 754 2426, are seven lovely ski-in ski-out log homes and chalets, ranging from four to eight bedrooms.

Squaw Valley, California

Profile

Scenic Lake Tahoe resort with good intermediate terrain as well as steep slopes. Also particularly good for snowboarding. For those with transport, the evening dining choices in the area are superb

Resort

Squaw Valley, despite a virtual absence of lifts at the time, managed, with a little help from Walt Disney, to convince the Olympic Committee that it should host the 1960 Winter Olympics, which were the first to be televised. Jean Vuarnet of France won gold in the downhill and went on to re-invent sunglasses. Squaw Valley has never looked back. The resort sits in natural splendour on the north shore of beautiful Lake Tahoe, home to 15 alpine resorts and eight cross-country centres with over 100 lifts in 17,520 acres of skiable terrain. Squaw has the best of it.

Its new Intrawest-built village provides the base area that it previously lacked, while no one has ever questioned the quality of the skiing. You need a car to explore the other Lake Tahoe resorts included in the Interchangeable lift pass.

Tahoe City, a ten-minute drive away, is a small town providing an alternative bed base with considerable atmosphere and some appealing restaurants.

Mountain

No less than seven lifts, including the Gold Coast Funitel gondola, give mountain access from the village, while the Squaw Valley Creek triple-chair provides an eighth way into the system. Val d'Isère in the French Alps is the only other ski destination with comparable diversity. The lifts lead up to six peaks: Granite Chief, Snow King, KT22, Squaw Peak, Emigrant and Broken Arrow. The area is divided into three sectors with the 32 lifts, rather than the runs, colour-graded. All the main lifts on KT22, Squaw Peak and Granite Chief are black-diamond, while those on Snow King and Emigrant are blue. Intermediates will find a huge amount of skiing – the highlight is a three-mile trail from the

Essentials

Altitude: 6,200ft, (1890m) – 9,050ft (2,758m)
Further information: t +1 530 583 6985, *www.squaw.com*
Lifts in area: 32 (3 cableways, 25 chairs, 4 drags) serving 4,000 acres of terrain.
Lift pass: Interchangeable (covers Alpine Meadows, Heavenly, Kirkwood, Northstar-at-Tahoe, Sierra-at-Tahoe, Squaw Valley) adult $241–311, child 5–12yrs $53–120, both for 6 days
Access: Reno 1hr, San Francisco 4hrs

High Camp area to the mountain base. However, Squaw was birthplace of the American extreme skiing movement and offers a comprehensive menu of steep chutes. The most radical terrain is found off KT22, Headwall, Cornice II and Granite Chief chair-lifts.

Three terrain parks and three half-pipes, as well as exciting freeride terrain, make this a serious destination for snowboarders. All are accessed by the gondola or cable car. Start in Belmont, move on to Central Park (floodlit at night), and then into the jumps and rails of Mainline Park.

Learn

Squaw Valley Ski and Snowboard School, t +1 530 581 7263, has a sound reputation. A new beginner double-chair built last winter make the learning process more enjoyable.

Children

Squaw Kids Children's Center, t +1 530 581 7166, takes children from three to 12 years. Squaw Kids Ski & Snowboard School, t +1 530 581 7263, gives lessons from four years.

Lunch

The resort has dozens of eateries and bars both on the mountain and in the base village. These include the **Gold Coast**, t +1 530 583 6985 for all, at the top of the Funitel in Squaw Valley, which features a barbecue, restaurants and bars on three levels. **Crossroads Café** is its newest addition, serving sandwiches and salads. **High Camp**, t +1 530 583 2555, boasts six different restaurants and bars, and the main dining room is open at night.

Dine

Dining in the area offers a huge choice of venues. Restaurants in the new Village include **PlumpJack Balboa Café**, t +1 530 583 5850, which is an 'American bistro' and **Fireside Pizza Co**, t +1 530 584 6150, offering gourmet pizzas 'with a sourdough crust and farm-fresh toppings'. **High Sierra Grill**, t +1 530 584 6100, has steaks and salads, and **Mamasake** sushi bar, t +1 530 584 0110, is a real treat. **Zenbu Tapas Lounge**, t +1 530 583 9900, upstairs in the Olympic House, has late-night 'Asian Tapas' and dancing. **Glissandi**, t +1 530 583 6300, in the Resort at Squaw Creek, is a high-priced Italian.

Ten minutes' drive away in Truckee are **Java Sushi**, t +1 530 582 1144, **China Garden Restaurant**, t +1 530 587 7625, and **Blue Agave Mexican Restaurant**, t +1 530 583 8113. **Cottonwood**, t +1 530 587 571, has seafood and live jazz.

In Tahoe City, **Wolfdale's**, t +1 530 583 5700, has 'Flavors of the West & Far East'. **Yama Sushi**, t +1 530 583 9262, is affordable and fun. **Bacchi's Inn** t +1 530 583 3324, is Italian, **Christy Hill**, t +1 530 583 8551, overlooking the lake, serves Californian cuisine with a French influence. **Sunnyside**, t +1 530 583 7200, serves seafood. **Izzy's Burger Spa**, t +1 530 583 4111, has great views and **Rosie's Café**, t +1 530 583 8504, is friendly.

Party

Bar One in the Olympic House features music, pool and karaoke. Other post-slope options include **Le Chamois** at Village Green, **PlumpJack Balboa Café** in the Village and **Red Dog Bar & Grill** at Far East Center. **High Camp** is open until 9pm with a Snowtubing Arena and Olympic Ice Pavilion in winter and Swimming Lagoon & Spa during the spring. For something a little different, try the **Altitude Oxygen Bar & Aqua Massage**, which is said to 'reverse stress and render hangovers null and void'.

Sleep

****Resort at Squaw Creek**, t +1 530 583 6300, *www.squawcreek.com*, is a luxury ski-in, ski-out complex near the base with spa, swimming pool, ice rink and five in-house restaurants.

****Squaw Valley Lodge**, t +1 530 583 5500, *www.squawvalleylodge.com*, is ski-in ski-out and contains condos with kitchens and hot tubs.

****The Village at Squaw Valley**, t +1 530 584, 1000 contains smart and well-equipped condos in the new base village. Shared facilities include a movie room, games room and billiards lounge.

PlumpJack Squaw Valley Inn, t +1 800 323 7666, dates back to 1959 and was upgraded in 1995 with attractively minimalist decoration and a renowned restaurant.

Olympic Village Inn, t +1 530 583 1576, served as the home to many of the 1960 Olympic athletes but was remodelled in 1982. It contains one-bedroom suites with kitchenettes and a shuttle bus to the ski base.

Tahoe City and Truckee provide alternative bed bases for visiting other resorts in the area.

Steamboat, Colorado

Profile

A Wild West town set apart from the ski area base. The resort offers a good choice of restaurants. The ski area suits families and beginners, and is particularly good for snowboarders

Resort

The unlikely name of Steamboat Springs originated when three French fur trappers exploring the River Yampa at the foot of Rabbit Ears Pass in 1865 thought they heard the chugging sound of a paddle-steamer – only to discover that it was actually the sound of the bubbling local mineral springs.

A lot of water has gone under the bridge since then and Steamboat has built a reputation as a Wild West ski town famous for its annual Cowboy Downhill when the skills of skiing and ranching come together. After negotiating a slalom course, competitors must first lasso a mountain host and then saddle a horse, before crossing the finishing line on skis. It produces a dramatic, and often hilarious, spectacle.

The history of skiing here goes back to 1914 when a bricklayer called Carl Howelsen organized a ski carnival and won every event. He possibly failed to mention that he had already won 14 trophies for ski jumping in his native Norway. Steamboat is an area that suits all standards of skier but is particularly suited to intermediates. Steamboat resort lies three miles from the town of Steamboat Springs and both offer a choice of hotels and condos.

Mountain

Main mountain access is by a gondola from the base area, This is a large resort with skiing on six linked peaks in the Routt National Forest: Mounts Werner, Sunshine, Storm, Thunderhead and Christie Peaks and Pioneer Ridge. It all adds up to 142 trails with a vertical drop of 3,688ft (1124m). Routt County's winter snowfall is traditionally measured by the number of fence wires it covers. *Three Wire Winter*, a quarterly journal produced by the local high school, is so called because in a typical winter, snow 30 inches deep will cover all three of the lower fence wires. In a seriously good winter, with snow depths of over 40 inches, the snow will cover the fourth.

This is home of some of Colorado's best powder and in a good winter the off-piste opportunities are exceptional. The modern lift system is backed up by extensive snowmaking. The resort is popular with riders and the 66ft Mavericks super-pipe is the longest in North America.

Learn

Steamboat Ski and **Snowboard School**, t +1 970 871 5375, has a good reputation as befits a school that claims to have produced more Olympians than any

Essentials

Altitude: 6,900ft (2103m)–10,568ft (3221m)
Further information: t +1 970 879 6111, *www.steamboat.com*
Lifts in area: 20 (1 cableway, 18 chairs, 1 drag) serving 2,939 acres of terrain
Lift pass: adult $246–312, child 6–12yrs $222–253, both for 6 out of 8 days
Access: Eagle Airport 2hrs, Denver airport 3 hrs

other in the world. It incorporates the Billy Kid Performance Center, founded by the resort's most famous champion, which provides specialized coaching to get skiers off the 'intermediate plateau'. **Steamboat Powdercats**, t +1 970 871 4260, offers 10,000 acres of cat-skiing terrain only 20 minutes from the town on Buffalo Pass

Children

The Kids Vacation Center, t +1 970 871 5375, accepts non-skiing children from six months and arranges ski lessons for older children.

Lunch

The most sophisticated lunch option is **Hazie's**, t +1 970 871 5150, at the top of the gondola, which serves New American cuisine. **Ragnar's**, t +1 970 871 5191, at Rendezvous Saddle, specializes in seafood, game, and beef. Try also **Gondola Pub & Grill**, t +1 970 879 4448, at Gondola Square.

Dine

At Steamboat Resort, **The Butcher Shop**, t +1 970 879 2484, has been feeding carnivores for 34 years. **The Cabin**, t +1 970 871 5550, features contemporary Colorado cuisine; try the Rocky Mountain Lamb Shanks. **La Montana**, t +1 970 879 5800, has Tex-Mex.

At **Steamboat Springs**, **Antares**, t +1 970 879 9939, **Giovanni's**, t +1 970 879 4141, and the **Steamboat Yacht Club**, t +1 970 879 4774, are all recommended. **Yama Chan's**, t +1 970 879 8862, is a great sushi restaurant. **The Cottonwood Grill**, t +1 970 879 2229, has tasty Pacific Rim cuisine.

Party

Skiers gather at the **Slopeside Grill** and **The Tugboat** in Times Square, as well as at **Mahogany Ridge** in downtown Steamboat Springs. Other popular bars include **Chaps** in the Grand Resort Hotel, **Bear River Bar & Grill**, **Dos Amigos**, and **Levelz**.

Sleep

Steamboat base area
Luxury:
Bear Claw, t +1 970 879 6100 is a smart condo complex.
Sheraton Steamboat, t +1 970 879 2220, *www.sheraton.com/steamboat* has Western decor.
Steamboat Grand Resort & Conference Center, t +1 970 871 5500, *www.steamboatgrand.com,*has a spa and fitness centre, a themed restaurant, and 327 rooms.
Torian Plum, t +1 970 879 8811, offers comfortable furnished suites at the base area.
Budget:
Fairfield Inn, t +1 970 870 9000, has reasonably-priced rooms close to the skiing.
Steamboat Springs
Moderate/budget:
Alpiner Lodge, t +1 970 879 1430, is a low-cost Tyrolean-style lodge within walking distance of the shops and restaurants.
Hampton Inn & Suites, t +1 970 871 8900, *www.hamptonsteamboat.com*, is a new hotel located midway between the resort and downtown.
The Harbor Hotel, t +1 970 879 1522, has simple rooms at budget prices.

Stowe, Vermont

Profile

A classic New England village surrounded by beautiful scenery, which suits all standards. Not all of the accommodation is convenient for the slopes and nightlife is quiet

Resort

Back in February 1914 when war clouds were gathering over Europe, a librarian from Dartmouth College called Nathaniel L. Goodrich made the first recorded descent on skis down Mount Mansfield. 'It was,' he said, 'a lot of fun and very satisfying. But my stops – voluntary and otherwise – were very frequent'. What he achieved was rather greater than personal satisfaction. He had set in motion the future prosperity of the charming 18th-century New England town of Stowe.

The trouble with Stowe is that the skiing takes place a full six miles from either Mount Mansfield or smaller and tamer Spruce Peak beside it. Hotels line the route, but wherever you stay is inconvenient for the skiing, the nightlife – or both. You need a car, but note that the police take a zero-tolerance stance on drink-driving. However, all that is set to change as Stowe Mountain Resort develops a new $400-million village at Spruce Peak that will act as a bed base for both mountains. Work has already started, but it will take ten years to complete.

Stowe is the most patrician of all East Coast resorts with a pedigree going back to the 1920s and 1930s. It attracts wealthy Bostonians and New Yorkers, as well as

Essentials

Altitude: 1,300ft (396m)–3,640ft (1109m)
Further information: t +1 802 253 3000, www.stowe.com
Lifts in area: 11 (1 cableway, 8 chairs, 2 drags) serving 63km of terrain
Lift pass: adult $174–250, child 6–12yrs $83–174, both for 6 days
Access: Montreal airport 2¼hrs, Boston airport 3¼hrs, Burlington 40mins

ten per cent of its skiers from Britain. The appeal lies in the quintessential Vermont town with its red-and-white weatherboarded houses set around a steepled white church on attractive Main Street, where most of the shops and restaurants, as well as some of the hotels are located.

Mountain

Stowe probably needs to do more than build a couple of new lifts to access beginner and intermediate terrain – if the development at Spruce Peak is to become what is euphemistically billed as 'a dynamic alpine village with world-class amenities'. The Little Spruce Double, which has been carrying skiers up the mountain since 1963, has been replaced by a high-speed quad. From Spruce you can reach Smugglers' Notch ski area on the other side of the mountain, but the two do not share a lift pass and are not officially linked.

Anyone who has mastered the basics on Spruce will quickly want to progress to the 'real' skiing, which takes place a short shuttle-bus ride away on Mount Mansfield. Two fast lifts serve nearly all the trails. An eight-person gondola up to the Cliff House Restaurant offers a choice of mainly blue runs down, while the Cliff Trail links with the main part of Mansfield. On this sector a high-speed quad carries skiers to the self-service Octagon Café & Gallery, with superb views.

The main course on the mountain is the Front Four, a choice of fall-line double-diamond runs, which are steep and often glazed with ice. It is rightly said that if, in these testing conditions, you can stand up on, and ski gracefully down, Starr, Liftline, National and Goat, you can ski just about any pisted trail in the world.

Learn

Stowe Ski & Snowboard School, t +1 802 253 3000, offers group and private lessons.

Children

Cubs Daycare Center, t +1 802 253 3000, takes children from six weeks to six years.

Lunch

The Cliff House Restaurant, t +1 802 253 3000, at the Gondola Summit was renovated in summer 2005. Fireside Tavern, t +1 802 253 3656, at the slope-side Inn at the Mountain, serves salads, grilled sandwiches, regional specials, and light appetisers at lunchtime.

Dine

Partridge Inn, t +1 802 253 8000, serves seafood in a typical New England ambience. Next door Pie in the Sky, t +1 802 253 5100, serves good-value wood-fired pizzas. Blue Moon Café, t +1 802 253 7006 features innovative cuisine based on seafood and game. Olive's Bistro, t +1 802 253 2033, has hand-painted murals and eclectic Mediterranean-Pacific cuisine. Cactus Café, t +1 802 253 7770, takes an

imaginative approach to Mexican and American cuisine. Red Basil, t +1 802 253 4478, offers a mix of Thai dishes and sushi.

Party

José's Cantina at Midway Lodge and The Den at Mansfield Base Lodge are busy when the lifts close. In town, The Shed Brewery is the liveliest place. Rusty Nail Bar & Grille offers live weekend entertainment and pool tables. The Matterhorn has pool, darts and video games, as well as a sushi restaurant.

Sleep

Luxury:
Top Notch Resort & Spa, t +1 802 253 8585, *www.topnotch-resort.com,* has rooms decorated in sprigged English country-house style, and a spa that is rated one of the best in the country.
The Trapp Family Lodge, t +1 802 253 8511, *www.trappfamily.com,* four miles out of town, is an opulent Tyrolean-style lodge containing the Mountain Kids Club and Activity Center providing activities for children. The Von Trapp Suite was once the private residence of Maria von Trapp.
Moderate:
Golden Eagle Resort, t +1 802 253 4811, *www.stoweagle.com,* along the road from Stowe, is friendly and offers accommodation for every budget, from comfortable rooms to large suites with fireplace and whirlpool bath.
The Green Mountain Inn, t +1 802 253 7301, *www.greenmountaininn.com,* has been welcoming guests since 1833. It has an outdoor heated pool, two restaurants and a health club.
Honeywood Inn and Lodge, t +1 800 659 6289 or t +44 (0)800 085 7730, from UK, *www.honeywoodinn.com,* offers B&B accommodation at the Inn, with patchwork quilts, lacy pillows and

curtains, and the Lodge has high ceilings and four-poster beds.

Inn at the Mountain, t +1 802 253 3656, *www.stowe.com/lodging/inn.php,* is the resort's only slope-side accommodation, offering 33 rooms and suites.

Stoweflake Mountain Resort & Spa, **t** +1 802 253 7355, *www.stoweflake.com* ,houses two restaurants, a world-class spa and state-of-the-art fitness centre.

Sun Valley, Idaho

Profile

Charming resort based around an old Idaho mining town with a laid-back atmosphere. Good intermediate skiing, great restaurants and nightlife

Resort

The Rockies' oldest ski resort is completely confusing to the newcomer until you master the geography in this remote and delightful corner of Idaho. Sun Valley, created in 1936 by Averell Harriman, chairman of the Union Pacific Railroad, as an all-American answer to St Moritz, Megève, and St Anton is the name of the star-struck village at the base of a pimple of a mountain with five lifts, ten beginner and low intermediate runs and a vertical drop of just 628ft.

Sun Valley Lodge, made of poured concrete coloured to resemble wood, is the grand hotel in a rural village near the base that was constructed to house the big names of Hollywood. Ernest Hemingway wrote his earth-moving epic *For Whom The Bell Tolls* in room 206,

which is kept as a museum. The room is surprisingly cramped by 21st-century ski resort standards. Sun Valley Inn is a later addition in similar style within the extensive manicured grounds. A small number of smart shops and restaurants compliment the carefully maintained original resort image.

It's all good historical fun, but the real skiing that you have come all this way to experience – and it is indeed a long way across the desert from anywhere to Sun Valley – lies not on little Dollar but on Bald Mountain a mile away to the west. This is directly above the quaint but vibrant Victorian mining town of Ketchum, much the most convenient place to stay. It would be a mistake, but you could easily spend an enjoyable week here without even visiting actual Sun Valley and little Dollar Mountain – and you still may find yourself riding a chair with Clint Eastwood, Tom Hanks or Arnold Schwarzenegger who comes here whenever Californian governmental duties allow.

Mountain

In skiing terms, Sun Valley's biggest claim to fame is that it invented the chair lift. In the heat of August in 1936 a system for shifting stems of bananas onto ships in Panama was installed. However, no allowance was made for

Essentials

Altitude: 5,750ft (1753m)–9,150ft (2789m) bottom
Further information: t +1 208 622 4111, *www.sunvalley.com*
Lifts in area: 18 (18 chairs) serving 2,045 acres of skiable terrain
Lift pass: adult $235–378, child under 12yrs $132–214, both for 6 out of 7 days
Access: Sun Valley Airport 20mins

the snowfall and sub-zero temperatures of the Rockies, and by the the start of the season it had completely ground to a halt. Lifts today are of more reliable design and Bald Mountain also has one of the world's most extensive automated snowmaking systems.

The skiing here suits all standards, but especially intermediates. Main mountain access is by quad-chair from River Run Plaza at one end of the town or from Warm Springs Day Lodge at the other. Both take you up to the Look Out restaurant where you can take a wide choice of routes back down or ride a triple chair to the 9,150ft summit for some challenging bowl skiing. The most demanding runs are in Easter Bowl. Snowboarding is popular, with a half-pipe on Lower Warm Springs.

Learn

Sun Valley Ski and Snowboard School, t +1 208 622 2289, has a fine reputation and regularly has Austrian instructors.

Children

Sun Valley Playschool, t +1 208 622 2288 takes children aged six months to six years.

Lunch

For further information on restaurants listed without individual telephone number call t +1 208 622 4111.

The Roundhouse, t +1 208 622 2371, at the top of the Exhibition and Cold Springs lift, offers a proper gourmet lunch in a warm atmosphere and is much the best place to eat. **Look Out** and **Seattle Ridge Lodge** are the above-average, self-service alternatives, along with **River Run Plaza** and **Warm Springs Day Lodge** at the bottom of Bald Mountain. At Sun Valley,

Gretchen's, t +1 208 622 2144, has pasta and salads. **Trail Creek Cabin**, t +1 208 622 2135, one-and-half miles east of Sun Valley and reached by sleigh or on cross-country skies, features prime rib, chops and an open log fire.

Dine

In Ketchum, **Michel's Christiania**, t +1 208 726 3388, is a French restaurant renowned for its *truite aux amandes* and *tournedos au Stilton*. **Chandler's**, t +1 208 726 1776, has Hawaiian *ahi* tuna, Alaskan halibut and local elk tenderloin. **Felix's**, t +1 208 726 1166, has Spanish Andalusian cuisine. **The Pioneer Saloon**, t +1 208 726 3139 – Clint Eastwood's favourite – is cheerful, much cheaper, and serves steaks. **Sushi on Second**, t +1 208 726 5181, is warmly recommended.

At Sun Valley, **Bald Mountain Pizza**, t +1 208 622 2143, has fine hand-tossed pizzas and a children's games room, **The Ram**, t +1 208 622 2225 has local trout and lamb as well as fresh seafood.

Party

Whiskey Jacques' on North Main in Ketchum has dancing and live music. **The Cellar Pub** is what is says it is. At Sun Valley, **The Boiler Room** has comedy shows, live bands and karaoke nights. **Duchin Lounge** is the piano bar in the Lodge.

Sleep

Luxury:
Sun Valley Lodge, t +1 208 622 4111, *www.sunvalley.com*, has a smart old-money atmosphere.
Sun Valley Inn, t +1 208 622 4111, *www.sunvalley.com*, is the slightly later addition that has been completely refurbished.

Les Saisons, t +1 208 727 1616, is warm and welcoming and contains condos with hickory wood floors, as well as a small spa and gym.

Thunder Spring, t +1 208 726 6060, *www.thunderspring.com,* contains impressive condos: bedrooms have wrought-iron bed frames, sitting rooms have polished wood floors and sofas with oversized velvet cushions and open-plan kitchens. There is a 25-m heated outdoor pool, and the 40,000sq-ft Zenergy centre houses a state-of-the-art gym, two indoor tennis courts and squash courts.

Knob Hill Inn, t +1 208 726 8010, *www.knobhillinn.com,* is a European style Relais et Chateaux hotel.

Moderate:

Best Western Kentwood Lodge, t +1 208 726 4114, *www.bestwestern.com/ kentwoodlodge* is within easy reach of shops, nightlife and Bald Mountain.

Clarion Inn of Sun Valley, t +1 208 726 5900, *www.resortswest.net,* has spacious rooms and is centrally situated in Ketchum.

Taos, New Mexico

Profile

Quirky resort in desert surroundings with steep skiing and good ski-school tuition, but banned to snowboarders

Resort

Even by the diverse standards of America, skiing scattered across a 2,500-mile continent Taos – surrounded by the magical peaks of the Sangre de Cristo mountains – is a glorious one-off. Like D.H. Lawrence, Georgia O'Keeffe and Wild West frontiersman Kit Carson who all lived here, you don't have to ski to enjoy it, but you can have a lot more fun if you do. The original 1,000-year-old town with its adobe buildings and dominant Native American culture has been inspiring writers, artists and musicians for more than a century. The skiing – snowboarding is still not allowed here – takes place an 18-mile drive away up the road from the cactus and sage of the desert floor, into the alpine pines of the Carson National Forest.

Taos Ski Valley (TSV) has a distinctly European atmosphere and, given that it sits on the same latitude as Rome, it usually has copious amounts of high-quality snow. It was this giant white basin that German-born Swiss Ernie Blake spotted from the window of his Cessna as he flew over the mountains in 1954. He took one look from the ground and moved there the following year to found the resort, which is still run by the family today.

The resort is a collection of lodges and condo buildings that line the banks of the Rio Hondo creek, linked by bridges and walkways near the base of what at first – and at second – glance looks like an extraordinarily steep mountain.

Essentials

Altitude: 9,207ft (2807m)–11,819ft (3603m)

Further information: t +1 505 776 2291, *www.skitaos.org*

Lifts in area: 11 (11 chairs) serving 1,294 acres of terrain

Lift pass: adult $324, child 7–12yrs $192, both for 6 days

Access: Santa Fe 75mins, Albuquerque airport 2hrs 15mins

'Don't panic,' says the sign at the bottom of Al's run, the fall-line mogul field beneath the chair lift, 'you are looking at 1/90th of Taos Ski Valley. We have easy skiing too'.

Mountain

The resort insists that Taos suits all standards of skier. But, while there is some good novice terrain and excellent ski instruction, this is a place for skiers who like their mountains steep and deep, or heavily mogulled between snow dumps. It seems strange that somewhere so far from Colorado can offer some of the toughest double-black-diamond skiing in North America. Oster and Stauffenberg, two of the most respected of these trails off the High Traverse are named after the German officers who plotted against Hitler – a statement of Ernie Blake's anti-Nazi stance during the Second World War. British skier Sir Arnold Lunn, founder of slalom racing, is also remembered by his own trail. The terrain park for twin-tippers is located on Maxie's run under lift no. 7. It has a couple of big jumps, rails and a quarter-pipe.

Learn

Ernie Blake Ski School, t +1 505 776 2291 x 1355, provides tuition with a full range of courses and has an excellent reputation.

Children

Ernie Blake Ski School has a maximum class size of nine pupils. Little ones aged six weeks to three years are cared for by Bebekare and Kinderkare and skiers join Junior Elite. Kids' nights with entertainment and teen party nights are regularly organized.

Lunch

Rhoda's Restaurant, t +1 505 776 2291, slope-side in the Resort Centre, serves soups and sandwiches at lunchtime. The Phoenix Grill, at the base of the quad-chair in Kachina Bowl, is the perfect spot for enjoying lunch and watching skiers go by. The Whistlestop Café, t +1 888 285 8920, at the base of no. 6 lift and close to the no. 2 quad, is the place to get a quick pizza or soup. The Bavarian, t +1 505 776 8020, is mid-mountain and – despite its name – looks like it is in Alpbach or Kitzbühel, with carved wooden furniture, staff in dirndl dresses and warmth provided by a tiled fireplace oven.

Dine

Rhoda's Restaurant, t +1 505 776 2291, features steaks, prime rib, salads, pasta, chicken and seafood at affordable prices. De la Tierra, t +1 505 758 3502, at El Monte Sagrado Living Resort & Spa serves regional and seasonal American dishes and has an impressive wine list. Doc Martin's Restaurant, t +1 505 758 1977, at the Historic Taos Inn at Taos, is an acclaimed fine-dining establishment. Michael's Kitchen, t +1 505 758 4178, in Taos seves New York steaks and Tex-Mex. Lambert's of Taos, t +1 505 758 1009, serves contemporary American cuisine.

Party

The Martini Tree Bar, upstairs at Tenderfoot Katie's, is the hot place for après-ski action. Adobe Bar at Taos Inn features twice-weekly jazz evenings and flamenco on Sundays. Thunderbird Lodge hosts live jazz.

Sleep

Luxury:

El Monte Sagrado Living Resort & Spa,
t +1 505 758 3502, *www.elmontesagrado.
com,* in Taos town, offers 36 elegant
suites and 'casitas' with decor inspired
by Native American culture and local
artists. The property has an exquisite
spa and two restaurants.

Moderate:

St Bernard Hotel & Condos, t +1 505 776
2251, *www. stbernardtaos.com,* in TSV,
is owned by Jean Mayer – technical
director of the ski school. Rooms are
normally fully booked for the season
by early August. The hotel contains a
kids club.

Inn at Snakedance, t +1 505 776 2277,
www.innsnakedance.com, is a no-
smoking hotel with modern rooms,
located 10 yards from the lifts.

Sagebrush Inn & Conference Center,
t +1 505 758 2254, *www. sagebrushinn.
com,* in Taos town, is an adobe building
housing an impressive collection of
Indian rugs and artefacts. The inn has
been hosting visitors since the 1920s
when the elite of New York and the
East Coast would stop at Taos en route
to Arizona.

Rio Hondo Condos, t +1 505 776 2347,
www.hondoproperties.com, between
Taos town and TSV, features 'casitas' –
one-bedroomed guesthouses with
bathroom, living room, two fireplaces
and a hot tub.

Quail Inn Ridge Resort, t +1 505 776 2211,
www.quailridgeinn.com, four miles
from TSV, is in an adobe building and
features a desert ambience, tennis
courts and an outdoor swimming pool.

Telluride, Colorado

Profile

**Lovely old town with a wide choice
of restaurants. Gondola to separate
mountain village with further
accommodation. Suits intermediate
to advanced skiers and highly rated
for snowboarding**

Resort

The old mining town of Telluride, tucked
away in a remote corner of the San Juan
mountains, has a more colourful history
and more present-day charm than any
resort in North America. In 1889 Butch
Cassidy and the Sundance Kid relieved the
San Miguel Valley Bank of $24,000. Jack
Dempsey washed dishes in a brothel here
before finding his fists full of dollars
elsewhere. In the 1890s Telluride built a
power station and became the first town
in the world to be lit by alternating
electrical current. At the height of the
gold rush 5,000 miners crowded into a
town that supported one hotel and 100
brothels. Most probably it took its name
either from tellurium, a non-metallic

Essentials

Altitude: 8,725ft (2660m)–12,247ft
(3734m)
Further information: t +1 866 287 5015,
www.tellurideskiresort.com
Lifts in area: 18 (3 cableways, 13 chairs,
2 drags) serving 1,700 acres of terrain
Lift pass: adult $414, child 6–12yrs $222,
both for 6 out of 8 days
Access: Montrose airport 75mins

element in gold and silver ore or, less probably, from 'to hell you ride.'

The extra-wide streets, with their beautifully preserved Victorian buildings, including the New Sheridan Hotel and the original courthouse, were designed so that a carter could turn a full team of oxen without difficulty. Modern traffic regulations limit speed to 15mph and cars give way to pedestrians. The old town is connected by gondola to the purpose-built Mountain Village Resort, four miles away by road. This provides a ski-convenient bed base, but lacks the charm of its venerable parent.

In the late 1980s, Telluride caught the eye of Hollywood investors as it developed as a ski resort, attracting stars looking for an as yet uncommercialized *Aspen*. Many have since moved on, but their presence helped to forge Telluride into one of the smartest destinations in America, with shops and restaurants of commensurate quality – and price. The modest-sized ski area suits all standards with plenty of easy terrain, as well as some demanding steep chutes.

Mountain

The free gondola rises steeply from the edge of town and dog-legs down from the top station to Mountain Village. The backbone of the skiing is See Forever, a rolling blue run from Guiseppe's Restaurant at 11,890ft down to the village at 9,540ft. The whole area is made up of gladed runs with a good pitch for intermediate cruising. The sector immediately above the town is steeper with some tough fall-line options such as Kant-Mak-M, Spiral Stairs, and East and West Drain. Further challenging runs are served by the Gold Hill lift. The expansion into Prospect Bowl a few years ago greatly added to Telluride's appeal. A short hike from the top accesses La Rosa,

Genevieve and Crystal – three of the steep double-black-diamonds in the resort.

Telluride Air Garden terrain park, served by the gondola from Mountain Village, has a new monster super-pipe.

Learn

Telluride's Ski & Snowboard School, **t** +1 970 728 7507, offers adult group and private lessons as well as women's ski courses and adaptive skiing.

Children

The Children's Nursery, **t** +1 970 728 7531, is part of the Ski & Snowboarding School and is for kids aged two months to three years. The ski school also offers lessons for skiers from three to 12 years, and a nightly activities programme for five to 12-year-olds. **Mountain Village Nursery**, **t** +1 970 728 7533, and **Annie's Nannies**, **t** +1 970 728 2991, are the alternatives for babysitting. **The Ski & Snowboarding School** provides special teen programmes.

Lunch

On-mountain dining is in a choice of five venues. **Allred's**, **t** +1 970 728 7474, provides regional American dishes and fine wines. Try the Maine lobster bisque Asian and the spiced Muscovy duck. **Giuseppe's**, **t** +1 970 728 7503, has a cosy atmosphere and **Big Billie's**, **t** +1 970 728 7556, offers 'friendly family fare. **Gorrono Ranch**, **t** +1 970 728 7566, is located on a late 19th centtury Basque sheep herder's homestead, and at **That Pizza Place**, **t** +1 970 728 7499, you can bake your own pizza.

Dine

Restaurants are one of Telluride's great strengths. **Rustico, t** +1 970 728 4046, in Telluride and **La Piazza del Villaggio, t** +1 970 728 8283, in Mountain Village are both owned by Italian-born Paolo Canclini and offer fresh-made pasta, wood-fired pizzas, and one of the largest selections of Italian wines in Colorado. **Brown Dog, t** +1 970 728 8046, is the hippest new pizza joint in town. **Honga's Lotus Petal, t** +1 970 728 5134, features an extensive selection of Asian cuisine. **Bluepoint Grill, t** +1 970 728 8862, a block from the gondola base, is a hip seafood and steak house. **Harmon's, t** +1 970 728 3773, located in Telluride's historic train depot, serves modern American cuisine. **9545 Restaurant, t** +1 970 728 5678, at the Inn at Lost Creek, serves 'fine American cuisine with Rocky Mountain flair' using organic ingredients.

Party

Ski to the **Crunchy Porcupine** for cocktails. In town you can sip a martini at the **Noir Bar** in the Bluepoint restaurant, decorated with leather sofas, faux fur bench seats, and a leopard-spotted carpet. **Fly Me to the Moon Saloon** has live music.

Sleep

Luxury:
Camel's Garden, t +1 888 772 2635, *www.camelsgarden.com*, is right next to the gondola station. It has 35 rooms and a spa.
Inn at Lost Creek, t +1 970 728 5678, *www.innatlostcreek.com*, is at Mountain Village and contains individually decorated rooms with deluxe kitchenettes.
Hotel Telluride, t +1 866 468 3501, *www.thehoteltelluride.com*, is a stylish new boutique hotel housing an aromatherapy day spa. All bedrooms and suites contain feather beds with down duvets and embroidered sheets.
Wyndham Peak Resort & Golden Door Spa, t +1 800 789 2220, *www.thepeaksresort.com*, is the ultimate luxury ski-in ski-out hotel at Mountain Village with an impressive 42,000sq-ft spa.

Moderate:
The New Sheridan Hotel, t +1 800 200 1891, *www.newsheridan.com*, has been welcoming guests since 1891, four years after Telluride was founded. It is decorated in Victorian style and has a handsome mahogany bar. Its restaurant serves elk, ostrich and venison.
Ice House Lodge & Condos, t +1 800 544 3436, *www.icehouselodge.com*, is modern, central, smart and convenient for the gondola station. Adjoining the lodge are 16 luxury two- and three-bedroom condos.

Vail, Colorado

Profile

Faux-Tyrolean village with smart hotels and restaurants. The extensive ski area has a reliable snow record, excellent ski school and substantial off-piste. A good choice for well-heeled families and skiers and riders of all levels

Resort

For most visitors, Vail is the one resort that is close to perfection. A large and easily accessible mountain offers beginner and intermediate trails immediately above the village that are nightly groomed in to pristine condition. The back side is given over to hundreds of acres of lift-accessed, off-piste terrain that, after a fresh snow dump, becomes one of the world's greatest winter playgrounds.

The resort itself, built in neo-Bavarian and Tyrolean style, promises a sophisticated winter wonderland borrowed from a Christmas card – and manages to deliver. Luxurious hotels are complemented by an outstanding array of restaurants and, by American standards, a busy nightlife.

The only people disatisfied with this rose-tinted view of a snow-sure corner of Colorado are the three per cent of expert skiers and riders who find the gradient too tame in a destination that is more moneyed than mogulled. Chamonix or Jackson Hole it is not. This is skiing at its most shamelessly comfortable, a state of affairs that would doubtless have been appreciated by eccentric Irish Baronet 'Lord' St George Gore when he passed through present-day Vail on a hunting trip in 1855 with no skis but with 112 horses and 50 dogs. While slaughtering 2,000 buffalo, 1,600 elk and 100 bears, he slept every night in a brass bed. The hedonistic trappings of his camp included a commode with a fur-lined seat, a library of rare books, and a silver dinner service.

Vail resort annually injects huge sums of cash into maintaining itself as the premier showcase of American skiing. In a move of which the likes of Tignes in France should take note, it has started work on razing the ugly 1970s buildings in the satellite of Lionshead as part of $380-million redevelopment programme.

Where you stay is important for reaching shops and restaurants, but not the slopes. The resort sprawls for seven miles along the busy I-70 freeway. The

Essentials

Altitude: 8,120ft (2475m)–11,570 ft (3,526m)
Map: see page M60
Further information: t +1 970 476 9090, *www.vail.com*
Lifts in area: 34 (1 cableway, 24 chairs, 9 drags) serving 5,289 acres of terrain
Lift pass: Colorado Ticket (covers Arapahoe Basin, Beaver Creek, Breckenridge, Keystone, Vail) adult $164–375, child 5–12yrs $151–190, both for 6 days
Access: Denver airport 2½hrs, Eagle County airport 40mins

various lodging components are linked by an efficient bus service. Vail shares its lift pass with Beaver Creek ten miles to the west, as well with Breckenridge, Keystone, and the small high-altitude ski area of Arapahoe Basin. A subsidized bus service runs between the resorts.

Mountain

Main mountain access is by the Vistabahn Express chair from Vail Village, but five other lifts at different points along the valley offer alternative routes. As a result lift queues are rarely a problem. From the Mid-Vail hub lifts and pistes fan out all along the front face of the mountain, offering an extraordinarily wide range of terrain. It is essentially an intermediate paradise spiced with some vicious bump runs such as Highline, Blue Ox and the infamous Roger's Run.

The Back Bowls, accessed from the top of the mountain, are ideally suited to beginner and inexperienced deep-snow skiers, who get a chance to find their feet in a controlled and lift-served environment with a mainly modest pitch. Nevertheless, it is rewarding for anyone to make fresh tracks here, with plenty of chutes, drop-offs and tree skiing to be found once you know where to look.

Beyond the bowls lies Blue Sky Basin, Vail's most prized possession. This 645-acre area houses some truly stupendous off-piste served by the Skyline Express and Pete's Express lifts.

The Minturn Mile is an itinerary route that in the right snow conditions takes you down through some scenic and challenging terrain to the small town of Minturn; margaritas or pitchers of beer at the Saloon make a pleasant end to the outing.

Beginner areas are located at Golden Peak and at Eagle's Nest where there is also an activity centre – open in the evenings – with tubing, skating and snowmobiling. The Golden Peak terrain park features a 400ft super-pipe with 18ft walls. There is also a smaller park on Bwana, which has jumps and rails.

Learn

Vail/Beaver Creek Ski and Snowboard School, t +1 970 476 3239, has a formidable reputation as an excellent, albeit expensive, learning academy. Courses include dedicated classes for teenagers, women's clinics, terrain park, and skiing for the disabled.

Children

Small World Play School, t +1 970 479 3285, at Golden Peak and at Lionshead is the non-ski kindergarten for children aged from eight weeks to six years. **Children's Ski and Snowboard School, t** +1 970 479 3280, at **Golden Peak** and **t** +1 970 479 4450, at Lionshead arranges classes for children from three to 12 years.

Lunch

Game Greek Restaurant, t +1 970 479 4275, offers American-French fusion cuisine. **Blue Moon, t** +1 970 479 4530, at Eagle's Nest has a relaxed atmosphere and specials such as Smoked duck *quesadilla* and Blackened catfish stuffed with a black bean-mango salsa. **Larkspur, t** +1 970 479 8050, in the Golden Peak base lodge has American cooking with a rustic French influence. **Cucina Rustica, t** +1 970 476 5011, at the Lodge at Vail has an excellent and reasonably-priced buffet. **Two Elk Lodge, t** +1 970 476 9090, on the ridge separating the Front Face from the China Bowl and Blue Sky Basin, is a huge self-service with Oriental dishes such as sushi and stir-fry with noodles or rice as well as the ubiquitous burger 'n' fries. **Bart & Yeti's, t** +1 970 474 2754, at Lionshead is all-American. **Pepi's, t** +1 970 476 4671, has fine *moules marinière* and *Wienerschnitzel*. **Los Amigos, t** +1 970 476 5847, is a long-established Mexican restaurant.

Dine

Nozawa, t +1 970 476 9355, in the West Vail Lodge has great sushi.

Terra Bistro, t +1 970 476 6836, has an eclectic menu with Oriental-Italian fusion cuisine. **Montauk Seafood Grill, t** +1 970 476 2601, serves oysters flown in daily from both coasts, and Dungeness crab. **Russell's, t** +1 970 476 6700, offers fine steaks and seafood. **Campo de Fiori, t** +1 970 476 8994, specializes in pasta and risotto. **La Tour, t** +1 970 476 4403, is a celebrated French restaurant. Try the seared *foie gras* and the black truffle-scented pheasant breast. **Mezzaluna, t** +1 970 477 4410, has modern Italian-American cuisine. **Up The Creek, t** +1 970 476 8141, on the banks of Gore Creek, is renowned for its fresh fish, duck and pasta. **May Palace**, t +1 970 476 1657, is a good Chinese restaurant. **The Lancelot**, t +1 970 476 5828, specializes in prime rib. **The Wildflower**, t +1 970 476 5011, in the Lodge at Vail, is considered one of the top restaurants in Colorado. **Pazzo's Pizzeria**, t +1 970 476 9026, has sensibly priced pizzas and pasta.

Party

Chill out at the **Blue Moon** bar at Eagle's Nest after tubing, ski-biking, orienteering and a choice of other après-ski activities at **Adventure Ridge** at the top of the Eagle Bahn gondola. **Mickey's Piano Bar** at the Lodge is where to spot celebrities. **The Red Lion** in Bridge Street is the most popular après-ski bar with live music. **The Tap Room & Sanctuary** has dining and dancing. Numerically named **8150** is a fashionable nightclub. The **Ore House** offers happy-hour prices.

Sleep

Luxury:
The Lodge at Vail, t +1 970 476 5011, *www.lodgeatvail.com*, on the edge of the piste, is owned by the resort and remains one of the best addresses in the resort.
Sonnenalp Resort, t +1 970 476 5656, *www.sonnenalp.com*, is an elegant Bavarian-inspired hotel built in 1979 and still one of Vail's top places to stay.
Moderate:
Evergreen Lodge, t +1 970 476 7810, *www.evergreenvail.com*, located between Lionshead and Vail Village, heads the second rank.
Vail Marriott Mountain Resort & Spa, *www.marriott.com*, t +1 970 476 4444, at Lionshead, is a convenient and comfortable base.
Roost Lodge, t +1 970 476 5451, *www.roostlodge.com*, has been recently

renovated and is a good-value place to stay in West Vail.
Vail Mountain Lodge and Spa, t +1 970 476 0700, *www.vailmountainlodge.com*, has been revamped and is highly recommended.
Antlers at Vail, t +1 970 476 2471, *www.antlersvail.com*, is a condo hotel on Gore Creek that recently underwent a $20-million refurbishment.

Winter Park, Colorado

Profile

Unsophisticated family resort with plenty of advanced skiing, reasonably price accommodation and a short airport transfer. Not recommended for night owls

Resort

Winter Park is the closest major ski destination to Denver and currently at the start of a mighty 15-year rebuild. The municipally owned ski area has now been leased to Canadian giant Intrawest over a 50-year period. Central to the expansion plan is the new Village at Winter Park Resort beside the base area, which will have 1,500 residential units and 24 shops and restaurants. The company is investing $70 million in the first phase, which includes the creation of a scenic lake from the Fraser River that runs through the base area. Completion of this initial project is scheduled for the start of the 2008–9 winter season.

All this augurs well for the future, but the problem for the present is that the town of Winter Park is an inconvenient

Essentials

Altitude: 9,000ft (2743m)–12,050ft (3677m)
Further information: t +1 970 726 1564, *www.skiwinterpark.com*
Lifts in area: 21 (19 chairs, 2 drags) serving 2,770 acres of terrain
Lift pass: adult $234–270, child 6–13yrs $132, both for 6 days
Access: Denver Airport 90mins, ski train from Denver 2hrs 15mins

Learn

Winter Park Resort Ski & Snowboard School, t +1 800 729 7907, runs a full range of courses.

Children

Kids Adventure Junction Center, t +1 970 726 1564, provides free pagers for parents and cares for non-skiing children from eight weeks to six years.

Lunch

Doc's Roadhouse, t +1 970 722 5450, at Zephyr Mountain Lodge, specializes in prime rib, Club Car, t +1 970 726 5514, at the Mary Jane Center and the Dining Room at the Lodge at Sunspot, t +1 970 726 1446, are the main mountain options.

two miles from the skiing. Plans to link the mountain to the town by gondola are included in the master plan but still seem to be a decade away. A regular bus service operates between the two but finishes at 10.30pm.

Mountain

Winter Park offers extensive terrain for all levels of skier and rider. The area naturally divides into two main sectors. Winter Park has beginner, intermediate and expert trails with main access by the Zephyr Express quad. More demanding Mary-Jane, named after a popular local prostitute of the 1920s, features hard bump skiing, some tree-level romps, as well as some expert double-diamond chutes from Vasquez Cirque. Main access is by the Summit Express, which has been replaced for this season by a high-speed six-pack. Sorensen Park is a new five-acre learning area. Winter Park has three terrain parks and a 450ft super-pipe. Neighbouring Berthoud Pass no longer operates as a ski area, but the off-piste runs from the top of the pass are superb. You will need a local guide and a strategically parked car.

Dine

Untamed Steakhouse, t +1 970 726 1111, has creative Colorado cuisine and live entertainment. Carlos and Maria's, t +1 970 726 9674, offers good Mexican food. Deno's Mountain Bistro, t +1 970 726 5332, serving steaks and seafood, is a resort institution. Fontenot's Cajun Café, t +1 970 726 4021, features Cajun dishes. New Hong Kong, t +1 970 726 9888, offers Szechwan, Mandarin, Cantonese and Thai specials.

Party

The Derailer Bar at West Portal Station is busy as the lifts close, but Winter Park is a family destination with limited après-ski entertainment. Try Buckets Saloon, Smokin' Moe's, Moffat Station Restaurant and Brewery, Randi's Irish Saloon and Winter Park Pub.

Sleep

Luxury:

For further information and reservations call **t** +1 970 726 5587.

Zephyr Mountain Lodge provides rustic contemporary style accommodation beside the lifts.

Moderate/Budget:

Beaver Creek Condos is a comfortably furnished complex a seven-minute shuttle ride from the slopes and five minutes from shops and restaurants.

Iron Horse Resort is the original condo complex with an outdoor pool.

Super 8 Motel, t +1 970 726 8088, close to the resort centre, features a 14-person indoor hot tub.

Winter Park Mountain Lodge has been extensively refurbished and is situated three minutes by shuttle bus from the base area.

A–Z of World Resorts

Abetone, Italy
t +39 0329 4207373, *www.abetone.org*
Altitude 1390m (4,560ft)–1900m (6,233ft)
Lifts 25
Tour operators Alpine Tours, Erna Low,
SkiBound
Appennine resort within easy reach of
Florence and Pisa.

Abondance, France
t +33 (0)4 50 73 02 90,
www.valdabondance.com
Altitude 930m (3,050ft)–1800m (5,906ft)
Lifts 207 in Portes du Soleil
Tour operator Interhome
Small historic village 7km from La Chapelle
d'Abondance. A regular bus service links the
village with the Portes du Soleil area.
Abondance has its own small ski area. Hotels
include **La Rocaille**, t +33 (0)4 50 73 01 74, **Hotel
Les Touristes**, t +33 (0)4 50 73 02 15, and
Le Ferraillon, t +33 (0)4 50 73 07 75.

Adelboden and Lenk, Switzerland
Adelboden t +41 (0)33 673 8080,
www.adelboden.ch
Lenk t +41 (0)33 733 3131, *www.lenk.ch*
Altitude 1068m (3,503ft)–2357m (7,733ft)
Lifts 56 in area
Tour operators Interhome, Kuoni, Swiss Travel
Service.
The unspoilt village of Adelboden consists of
chalets set on a sunny terrace below the
Wildstrubel massif. Neighbouring Lenk is a spa
village, and the two resorts share a 170km
intermediate ski area with a good selection of
mountain restaurants. 'By the end of February
or early March there is always good snow,
sunshine, few queues, and not many Brits',
said one reporter.

Alagna, Italy
See *Champoluc*, page 155
Tour operators Alpine Answers Select,
Momentum, Original Travel, Ski 2, Ski
Weekend

Alpbach, Austria
Page 15
Tour operators Crystal, Inghams, Interhome,
Made to Measure

Alpe d'Huez, France
Page 84
Tour operators Airtours, Alpine Answers
Select, Alpine Elements, Club Med, Crystal,
Direct Ski, Erna Low, First Choice, French
Freedom, French Life, Frozen Planet,
Inghams, Interhome, Lagrange, Made to
Measure, Mark Warner, Momentum, Neilson,
On The Piste, Panorama, Ski Activity, Ski
Arrangements, SkiBound, Ski Expectations,
Ski France, Ski Freshtracks, Ski Independence,
Ski Miquel, Ski Supreme, Skiworld, Thomson,
Tops, Wasteland

Alpendorf, Austria
See *Wagrain and the Salzburger Sportwelt*,
page 48

Alpine Meadows, California, USA
t +1 530 583 4232, *www.skialpine.com*
Tour operator Ski the American Dream
Altitude 6,835ft (2083m)–8,637ft (2633m)
Lifts 14
Challenging small ski area next to Squaw
Valley on Lake Tahoe with 2,400 acres of
terrain suited to intermediate and advanced
skiers and riders.

Alta, Utah, USA
See *Snowbird and Alta*, page 256
Tour operators Ski All America, Ski the
American Dream, Ski Independence

Alta Pusteria, Italy
t +39 0474 913156, *www.three-peaks.info*
Altitude 1310m (4,298ft)–2000m (6,562ft)
Lifts 27
Seven small Alpine ski areas within the
Hochpustertal, which is a popular cross-
country destination. Some 200km of trails
begin around the scenic village of Sesto and
charming Moso in the Val di Sesto, and around
the thriving Tyrolean village of Dobbiaco and
the ancient historic town of San Candido in
the Val Pusteria. These head south-west to the
quiet Val Fiscalina, with striking views of the
Tre Cime di Lavaredo (the Three Peaks) en
route. A popular trail also leads south from
Dobbiaco to Cortina d'Ampezzo. **Berghotel
Tirol**, t +39 (0)474 710386 is the hotel of choice
in Sesto and **Hotel Villa Stefania**, t +39 0474

913588 is a small hotel with a good restaurant in San Candido.

Altenmarkt, Austria
See *Wagrain and the Salzburger Sportwelt*, page 48
Tour operator Interhome

Alyeska, Alaska, USA
t +1 907 754 1111, *www.alyeskaresort.com*
Altitude 250ft (76m)–3,939ft (1200m)
Lifts 9
Tour operators Frontier Ski, Ski All America
Alaska's steep peaks offer excellent heli- and snowcat-skiing and fabulous scenery and have made this a cult destination for ski extremists. The cable-car conveniently starts inside the Alyeska Prince Hotel, t +1 907 754 1111.

Andalo, Italy
t +39 0461 585570,
  www.aptdolomitipaganella.com
Altitude 1040m (3,412ft)–2125m (6,972ft)
Tour operators Equity/Rocket Ski, PGL,
  SkiBound
Lifts 18
Town dating back to the 12th century with pleasant intermediate skiing. This is the place where the World Cup started.

Andermatt, Switzerland
Page 192
Tour operators Momentum, Switzerland Travel
  Centre (Plus Travel)

Anzère, Switzerland
t +41 (0)27 399 2800), *www.anzere.ch*
Altitude 1500m (4,921ft)–2420m (7,940ft)
Lifts 11
Tour operator Interhome
Purpose-built neighbour of Crans-Montana and Aminona with 1970s apartment buildings and a loyal Swiss following.

Aonach Mor, Scotland
See *Nevis Range*, page 305
Tour operator Skisafe Travel

Aosta, Italy
See *Pila*, page 308
Tour operator Crystal

Apex, BC, Canada
t +1 250 292 8222, *www.apexresort.com*
Altitude 5,197ft (1575m)–7,197ft (2180m)
Lifts 4
Tour operators Frontier Ski, Ski Safari
Little-known village in the Okanagan Valley offering high-quality skiing without the crowds. The resort is 30 minutes' drive up a private road from the town of Penticton, and an hour from Kelowna airport. The varied runs include blues and easy black-diamonds on the front face, with the highest chair accessing some short and steep trails. Recommended hotels include **The Coast Inn Apex, t** +1 250 979 3939, **Saddleback Lodge, t** +1 250 292 8118, and the low-cost **Double Diamond Hostel, t** +1 250 292 8256.

Aprica, Italy
Pleasant family resort 170km from Milan with 50km of piste.
t +39 0342 746 113, *www.apricaonline.com*
Altitude 1181m (3,875ft)–2361m (7,746ft)
Lifts 19
Tour operators Club Europe, PGL, SkiBound

Arabba, Italy
Page 146
Tour operators Inghams, Neilson, Original Travel, Ski Expectations

Arapahoe Basin, Colorado, USA
t +1 970 496 7077, *www.arapahoebasin.com*
Altitude 10,780ft (3283m)–13,050ft (3967m)
Lifts 5
Tour operators Ski Activity, Ski the American
  Dream, SkiBound
Arapahoe Basin (A-Basin) is a small high-altitude ski area with certain snow until May. Most of the trails suit beginners to intermediates, with the Pallavicini bump run one of the longest and steepest in North America. The nearest accommodation base is six miles away at Keystone. A-Basin shares a lift pass with Vail, Keystone, Breckenridge and Beaver Creek.

Arcalis, Andorra
See *Pal-Arinsal*, page 8

Les Arcs, France
Page 86

Tour operators Airtours, Alpine Answers
Select, Alpine Elements, Club Med,
Corporate Ski Company, Crystal, Direct Ski,
Equity/Rocket Ski, Erna Low, Esprit, First
Choice, French Freedom, French Life, Frozen
Planet, Inghams, Interhome, Lagrange, Made
to Measure, Momentum, Neilson, On The
Piste, PGL, Ski Activity, Ski Adventures, Ski
Amis, Ski Arrangements, Ski France, Ski
Freshtracks, Ski Independence, Skiworld,
Thomson, Total Ski, Wasteland

Ardent, France
Tour operator Family Ski Company
Small village in the Portes du Soleil ski area.

Åre, Sweden
Page 183
Tour operators Neilson/Neilson School
Groups, Nortours

Argentière, France
Page 92
Tour operators AWWT, Board and Lodge,
Colliniege, Erna Low, French Life, Interhome,
Lagrange, McNab, Mountain Retreats, Ski
Hillwood, Ski Scott James, Ski Freshtracks, Ski
Weekend, White Roc Weekends

Arinsal, Andorra
See *Pal-Arinsal*, page 8
Tour operators Airtours, Crystal, Direct Ski,
First Choice, Inghams, Neilson, Panorama,
SkiBound, Ski Wild, Thomson

Arosa, Switzerland
t +41 (0)81 378 7020, *www.arosa.ch*
Altitude 1800m (5,904ft)–2653m (8,702ft)
Lifts 13
Tour operators Interhome, Kuoni, Made to
Measure, Momentum, Powder Byrne, Swiss
Travel Service, Switzerland Travel Centre
(Plus Travel), White Roc Weekends
This pretty village offers the all-round winter-
sports holiday with skiing for beginners to
intermediates. Reporters rated the pistes as
'mainly wide, varied and really good fun to ski'.
A new half-pipe opened last season.
Recommended hotels include five-star **Arosa
Kulm, t** +41 (0)81 378 8888 and **Tschuggen
Grand Hotel, t** +41 (0)81 378 9999. **Hotel
Cristallo, t** +41 (0)81 378 6868 has bedrooms

with four-posters, attractive **Hotel Arlenwald,
t** +41 (0)81 377 1838 has just eight rooms and is
ski-in ski-out. Stylish **Hotel Eden, t** +41 (0)81
377 0261 has individually decorated bedrooms
with a theatrical theme. **Hotel Alpensonne,
t** +41 (0)81 377 1547 is another good choice.

Aspen and Snowmass, Colorado, USA
Page 227
Tour operators Alpine Answers Select,
American Ski Classics, AWWT, Carrier,
Crystal, Elegant Resorts, Erna Low, Lotus
Supertravel, Made to Measure, Momentum,
Rocky Mountain Adventures, Seasons in
Style, Ski Activity, Ski All America, Ski the
American Dream, Ski Expectations, Ski
Freshtracks, Ski Independence, Ski Safari, Ski
Solutions, Skiworld, Thomson, Trailfinders,
United Vacations, Virgin

Auffach, Austria
See *Niederau*, page 30

Auris-en-Oisans, France
t +33 (0)4 76 80 13 52, *www.auris-en-
oisans.com*
Altitude 1600m (5,249ft)–3330m (10,922ft)
Lifts 85 in linked area
Tour operator Lagrange
Purpose-built Auris is linked into the Alpe
d'Huez ski area and is well placed for day trips
to Les Deux Alpes, Serre Chevalier and La Grave.

Auron, France
t +33 (0)4 93 23 02 66, *www.auron.com*
Altitude 1165m (3,822ft)–2450m (8,038ft)
Lifts 12
Tour operators Club Pavilion/Concept, French
Life, Lagrange
Traditional resort with a good atmosphere,
linked to St-Etienne de Tinze and only 90km
from Nice. The ski area provides good
intermediate skiing on 130km of piste, with
a recommended terrain park and ice-
skating rink.

Aussois, France
t +33 (0)4 79 20 42 21, *www.aussois.com*
Altitude 1500m (4,921ft)–2750m (9,022ft)
Lifts 10
Aussois is an easily accessible resort situated
on a wide sunny plateau at the foot of the

3697m Dent Parrachée in the Maurienne Valley. The old village with its traditional stone-and-slate houses, shared in winter by man and beasts, is built around the central 'place' with its fountain and communal oven. The skiing is best suited to beginners and intermediates looking for easing cruising runs amid spectacular scenery. The village shares a joint lift pass with nearby La Norma and Valfréjus. It has 35km of cross-country trails.

Autrans, France

t +33 (0)4 76 95 30 70, www.ot-autrans.fr
Altitude 1050m (3,445ft)–1710m (5,610ft)
Lifts 12
Tour operator Lagrange
Small and attractive low-altitude ski area in the Vercors.

Aviemore, Scotland

See *Cairngorm Mountain (Aviemore)*, page 284
Tour operator Skisafe Travel

Avoriaz, France

Page 88
Tour operators Airtours, Chalet Snowboard, Club Med, Crystal, Direct Ski, Erna Low, First Choice, French Freedom, French Life, Frozen Planet, Kuoni, Momentum, Neilson, On The Piste, Original Travel, Ski Arrangements, Ski Freshtracks, Ski Independence, Thomson, White Roc Weekends

Axalp, Switzerland

See *Meiringen*, page 301

Axamer Lizum, Austria

t +43 (0)5125 9850, www.innsbruck.info
Altitude 874m (2,867ft)–2343m (7,687ft)
Lifts 10
Tour operators Crystal, Neilson School Groups, PGL, SkiBound, Thomson
The small modern resort offers the best skiing and snowboarding within easy reach of Innsbruck. Axamer is one of the top snowboarding destinations in Austria.

Bad Gastein and Bad Hofgastein, Austria

See *Gasteinertal*, page 16

Tour operators Crystal, First Choice, Inghams, Interhome, Made to Measure, SkiBound, Ski Miquel, Ski Wild

Bad Kleinkirchheim and St Oswald, Austria

t +43 (0)4240 8212, www.badkleinkirchheim.at
Altitude 1080m (3,543ft)–2000m (6,560ft)
Lifts 26
Tour operators Alpine Tours, Crystal, PGL, SkiBound, Sloping Off, Solo's
Bad Kleinkirchheim (BKK) is the home resort of Austrian racing legend Franz Klammer. The 90km intermediate ski area is linked with the village of St Oswald. Accommodation includes five-star Thermenhotel Ronacher, t +43 (0)4240 282, which has a good spa.

Banff-Lake Louise, Alberta, Canada

Page 56
Tour operators Alpine Answers Select, American Ski Classics, AWWT, Crystal, First Choice, Frontier Ski, Inghams, Lotus Supertravel, Made to Measure, Momentum, Neilson/Neilson School Groups, Nonstopski, Rocky Mountain Adventures, Seasons in Style, Ski Activity, Ski All America, Ski the American Dream, Ski Arrangements, SkiBound, Ski Freshtracks, Ski Independence, Ski Safari, Skiworld, Solo's, Thomson, Trailfinders, United Vacations, Virgin

Bansko, Bulgaria

Page 77
Tour operators Balkan Holidays, Direct Ski, First Choice, Inghams, Neilson/Neilson School Groups, Panorama, Thomson

Baqueira Beret, Spain

Page 189
Tour operator Ski Miquel

Bardonecchia, Italy

t +39 0122 99032, www.montagnedoc.com
Altitude 1290m (4,232ft)–2750m (9,022ft)
Lifts 24
Tour operators Corporate Ski Company, Crystal, Erna Low, Momentum, Neilson, Ski Arrangements, Ski High Days, Thomson
The busy market town is by the entrance to the Fréjus Tunnel and close to the resorts of Montgenèvre and Sestriere. It offers good

value. 'The resort is very child-friendly and the pistes are well groomed. Many times I never saw another soul on the whole run down to the bottom,' enthused a reporter. Three ski areas offer some challenging skiing with few crowds, and a choice of 11 mountain restaurants. The resort has recently added a new chair-lift and an eight-seater gondola.

Barèges and La Mongie, France

Barèges t +33 (0)5 62 92 16 00,
  www.bareges.com
La Mongie t +33 (0)5 62 91 94 15,
  www.bagneresdebigorre-lamongie.com
Altitude 1250m (4,100ft)–2350m (7,708ft)
Lifts 43 in linked area
Tour operators Borderline, Lagrange, Pyrenean
  Mountain Tours, Tangney Tours
Barèges and La Mongie make up the largest ski area in the Pyrenees, sharing pistes suited to all standards on both sides of the Col du Tourmalet. There is virtually no queuing due to a new fast six-seater chair. La Mongie is the better base for complete beginners, with 'lots of off-piste the locals don't seem to use'. The one-street spa village of Barèges has more atmosphere than its neighbour. Recommended hotels in Barèges include the two-star **Hotel Igloo, t** +33 (0)5 62 92 68 10, which has been refurbished and has a good brasserie, and **Hotel Alphée, t** +33 (0)5 62 92 68 39, offering cheap and tasty food. **Hotel Europe, t** +33 (0)5 62 92 68 04 is also recommended. Accommodation in La Mongie includes three-star **Le Pourteilh, t** +33 (0)5 62 91 93 33 and **Résidence Le Montana, t** +33 (0)5 62 91 99 99.

Bariloche, Argentina

See *Gran Catedral (Bariloche)*, page 292

Beaver Creek, Colorado, USA

Page 230
Tour operators AWWT, Carrier, Crystal, Elegant
  Resorts, Made to Measure, Seasons in Style,
  Ski Activity, Ski All America, Ski the American
  Dream, Ski Independence, Ski Safari, Ski Wild,
  United Vacations

Le Bettex, France

See *St Gervais*, page 127

Big Mountain, USA

t +1 406 862 2900, *www.bigmtn.com*

Altitude 4,500ft (1372m)–7,000ft (2134m)
Lifts 13
Tour operators AWWT, Ski Independence
Large ski area at Whitefish, close to the Canadian border, with 3,000 acres of mainly bowl- and tree-skiing.

Big Sky, Montana, USA

t + 1 406 995 5000, *www.bigskyresort.com*
Altitude 6,800ft (2073m)–11,150ft (3398m)
Lifts 17
Tour operators AWWT, Momentum, Ski
  Activity, Ski the American Dream, Ski
  Independence, Ski Safari
Up-and-coming resort with uncrowded high-altitude skiing for all standards, situated 45 miles from Bozeman and 18 miles from Yellowstone National Park. The skiing takes place on three mountains with 150 marked runs in 3,600 acres of skiable terrain. The main action is on 11,150ft Lone Mountain reached by the Lone Peak Tram. Runs from the top include the steep Big Couloir, a vertiginous fall-line descent that requires considerable concentration. The Gullies and the exposed south face can be almost as challenging. The lower half of the mountain, together with the adjoining peaks of Andersite and Flat Iron provide plenty of intermediate gladed skiing. The 1,300ft terrain park is the longest in Montana and has a half-pipe. Combined with neighbouring Yellowstone Club, to which it is linked, it would arguably be one of the biggest ski resorts in the USA. However, you have to be a multi-millionaire property owner to ski at strictly private Yellowstone. **Big Sky Snowsports School, t** + 1 406 995 5743 has a sound reputation. Best hotel is **The Summit at Big Sky**. **Shoshone Condominium Hotel** has comfortable units with fireplaces. **Powder Ridge Cabins** are rustic-style with hand-hewn log finishes and three or four bedrooms (**t** + 1 406 995 5000 for all reservations).

Big White, BC, Canada

Page 59
Tour operators AWWT, Crystal, Frontier Ski,
  Made to Measure, Momentum, Ski Activity,
  Ski All America, Ski the American Dream, Ski
  Freshtracks, Ski Independence, Ski Safari

Bled, Slovenia

See *Bohinj*, page 78

Tour operators Crystal, Balkan Holidays, Thomson, Waymark

Blue Cow, Australia
See *Perisher-Blue*, page 307

Bohinj, Slovenia
Page 78
Tour operators Balkan Holidays, Crystal, Just Slovenia, Thomson

Bolzano, Italy
t +39 0473 279 457, *www.ortlerskiarena.com*
Altitude 1459m (4,787 ft)–2070m (6,791ft)
Lifts 74 in Ortler Skiarena
Valley town that offers accessible nearby skiing at Meran 2000, Rittner Horn and a host of other resorts. Hotel choices include **Parkhotel Laurin**, **t** +39 0471 311000, **Hotel Kohlern**, **t** +39 0471 329978 and **Park-Hotel Holzner**, **t** +39 0471 345231, all with excellent restaurants.

Borca, Italy
See *Macugnaga*, page 300

Borgata, Italy
t +39 0122 755449, *www.montagnedoc.it*
Altitude 1840m (6,035ft)–2823m (9,262ft)
Lifts 93 in the Milky Way
Hamlet adjoining Sestriere in the Milky Way that acts as an alternative tranquil bed base.

Bormio, Italy
Page 147
Tour operators Equity/Rocket Ski, Neilson School Groups, PGL, Ski Arrangements, Sloping Off

Borovets, Bulgaria
Page 79
Tour operators Airtours, Balkan Holidays, Crystal, Direct Ski, First Choice, Frozen Planet, Inghams, Interhome, Neilson/Neilson School Groups, Panorama, Thomson

Les Bottières, France
See *Le Corbier*, page 288

Bourg-St-Maurice, France
See *Les Arcs*, page 86
Tour operators Neilson School Groups, Vanilla Ski

Breckenridge, Colorado, USA
Page 232
Tour operators Alpine Answers Select, Alpine Tracks, American Ski Classics, AWWT, Crystal, Erna Low, Inghams, Made to Measure, Neilson, Rocky Mountain Adventures, Ski Activity, Ski All America, Ski the American Dream, Ski Expectations, Ski Freshtracks, Ski Independence, Ski Safari, Ski Solutions, Ski Wild, Skiworld, Thomson, Trailfinders, United Vacations, Virgin

Briançon, France
See *Serre Chevalier*, page 129
Tour operator Lagrange

Brides-les-Bains, France
t +33 (0)4 79 55 20 64, *www.brides-les-bains.com*
Altitude 1400m (4,593ft)–2952m (9,685ft)
Lifts 198 in Trois Vallées
Tour operators Airtours, AWWT, Erna Low, First Choice, French Life, Lagrange, Peak Retreats, SkiBound, Ski Independence, Skiweekends
An alternative spa town choice for those wishing to ski the Trois Vallées ski area on a budget. 'Friendly and accessible' was how one reporter described it. It is linked by a gondola to Méribel. The town has 21 hotels including **Grand Hotel des Thermes**, **t** + 33 (0)4 79 55 38 38.

Brienz, Switzerland
See *Meiringen–Hasliberg*, page 301

Brighton, Utah, USA
t +1 801 532 4731, *www.skibrighton.com*
Altitude 8,755ft (2668m)–10,750ft (3277m)
Lifts 8
Tour operator Ski the American Dream
Utah's oldest ski area was founded in 1936 and is located 45 minutes by road from Salt Lake City. Attractive resort best suited to intermediates. Brighton has some of the most extensive night skiing in the country, with over 22 trails floodlit until 9pm six days per week. **The Brighton Lodge**, **t** +1 800 873 5512 x 236, *www.brightonresort.com* is slope-side and friendly.

Brixen-im-Thale, Austria
t +43 (0)5334 8433, *www.brixenimthale.at*

Altitude 800m (2,624ft)–1829m (6,001ft)
Lifts 93 in SkiWelt
Traditional Tyrolean village near Kitzbühel, linked by gondola into the SkiWelt.

Bruson, Switzerland

t +41 (0)27 776 1682, *www.verbier.ch*
Altitude 1100m (3,543ft)–2445m (8,022ft)
Lifts 89 in Four Valleys
Small uncrowded resort near Verbier with some steep powder skiing. Bruson has a couple of hotels, and some apartments on the mountain.

Cairngorm Mountain (Aviemore), Scotland

t +44 (0)1479 810363, *www.cairngorm mountain.com*, *www.ski.visitscotland.com*
Altitude 550m (1,804ft)–1100m (3,608ft)
Lifts 17
Tour operator Ski Norwest
Aviemore is Britain's best-known ski resort – despite the fact that it is not a ski resort at all. The action takes place on Cairngorm Mountain, ten miles to the east. Main mountain access is by funicular, and the skiing and riding are surprisingly challenging when conditions allow. However, in these troubled winters of global warming, the days of regular cover throughout most of the season are a distant memory. The skiing at Cairngorm can be comparable to that of an Alpine resort of similar size, but booking in advance is a risky business. Aviemore, the nearest town, is located about 120 miles north of Edinburgh and Glasgow on the A9. Recommended places to stay include the three-star **Cairngorm Hotel**, t +44 (0)1479 810233 and the **Hilton Coylumbridge Hotel**, t +44 (0)1479 810661.

Campitello, Italy

See *Canazei*, page 148
Tour operators Direct Ski, Neilson

Campo Felice, Italy

t +39 06 943 00001, *www.campofelice.it*
Altitude 1410m (4,626ft)–2065m (6,775ft)
Lifts 14
Little resort with a good lift system and five restaurants, linked to village of Rocca di Cambio and within a one-hour drive of Rome.

Canazei, Italy

Page 148
Tour operators Direct Ski, Equity/Rocket Ski, First Choice, Inghams, Interhome, Neilson, Thomson

Canillo, Andorra

See *Soldeu-El Tarter*, page 11

The Canyons, Utah, USA

Page 235
Tour operators AWWT, Ski All America, Ski the American Dream, Ski Independence, Ski Safari, Skiworld, United Vacations

Cardrona, New Zealand

See *Wanaka (Cardrona and Treble Cone)*, page 325

Les Carroz, France

t +33 (0)4 50 90 00 04, *www.lescarroz.com*
Altitude 1140m (3,740ft)–2480m (8,134ft)
Lifts 72 in Grand Massif
Tour operators Altitude Holidays, Erna Low, French Life, Lagrange, Peak Retreats, Ski Independence
One of the main resorts of the Grand Massif that is centred around Flaine. 'This is a gem,' enthuses one reporter, 'it oozes charm.' 'Genuinely friendly people', and 'a nice ordinary French village – you don't have to pay the earth for a cup of coffee', were the other favourable comments. The village is more architecturally appealing than Flaine and attracts families and weekend visitors. The cableway and chair are reached by efficient ski-bus from the village centre, and are within easy reach of hotels such as **Les Airelles**, t +33 (0)4 50 90 01 02, **Les Belles Pistes**, t +33 (0)4 50 90 00 17 and **Croix de Savoie**, t +33 (0)4 50 90 00 26. The old village has been renovated and apartment blocks including **MGM**, t +44 (0)20 7584 2841 have been added in keeping with the resort's style.

Castelrotto (Kastelruth), Italy

t +39 0471 706333, *www.castelrotto.com*
Altitude 1060m (3,478ft)–2180m (7,152ft)
Lifts 24 in Alpe di Suisi
Tour operator Inntravel
Village of the South Tyrol at the end of the Val Gardena near Ortisei with nearby access to

Alpe di Siusi and Sella Ronda. Nearby Zanseralm is a resort dedicated to snow-shoeing. **Hotel Cavallino d'Oro, t** +39 0471 706337 is an ancient and pretty little hotel with quaint decoration. A ski-bus takes you to Alpe di Siusi under 30 minutes away.

Cauterets, France

t +33 (0)5 62 92 50 50, *www.cauterets.com*
Altitude 1000m (3,280ft)–2350m (7,710ft)
Lifts 15
Tour operators Lagrange, Leisure Direction
Small spa town 40km from Lourdes Tarbes airport, offering skiing mainly for beginners and intermediates. This takes place in the rather exposed Cirque du Lys bowl. A cable-car takes you up and brings you back again at the end of the day. One reporter complains of the 'very limited skiing' while another rates it 'ideal for novices'. Nearby Pont d'Espagne is a separate ski area with four lifts and 37km of cross-country trails. Recommended three-stars in Cauterets include **Hotel Bordeaux, t** +33 (0)5 62 92 52 50 and **Hotel-Résidence Aladin, t** +33 (0)5 62 92 60 00.

Cavalese, Italy

Page 151
Tour operators Alpine Tours, First Choice, SkiBound, Thomson

Celerina, Switzerland

t +41 (0)81 830 0011, *www.celerina.ch*
Altitude 1720m (5,643ft)–3057m (10,030ft)
Lifts 56 in area
Tour operator Made to Measure
Quiet alternative to St Moritz, with old fres-coed houses and access on skis to the Corviglia ski area. **Cresta Kulm, t** +41 (0)81 836 8080, **Chesa Rosatsch, t** +41 (0)81 837 0101 and offbeat **Hotel Misani, t** +41 (0)81 833 3314 with its themed bedrooms, are the hotels of choice.

Cervinia, Italy

Page 156
Tour operators Alpine Answers Select, Club Med, Crystal, Elegant Resorts, First Choice, Inghams, Interhome, Momentum, Ski Arrangements, SkiBound, Ski Freshtracks, Ski Solutions, Thomson

Cesana-Sansicario, Italy

t +39 0122 89202, *www.montagnedoc.it*
Altitude 1350m (4,428ft)–2823m (9,262ft)
Lifts 92 in Milky Way
Cesana, setting for the Olympic Bobsleigh and Biathlon events, has been given something of a face-lift for the 2006 games. The attractive, albeit slightly shabby, 12th-century village is set on a busy road close to the Montgenèvre Pass. The chair-lifts accessing the skiing are a long walk from the village centre.
Accommodation includes **Hotel Chaberton, t** +39 0122 89147. Halfway up the mountain lies the purpose-built village of Sansicario, made up mainly of apartment buildings and a shopping mall. The recommended place to stay here is **Hotel Rio Envers, t** +39 0122 811333.

Chamonix, France

Page 92
Tour operators Alpine Answers Select, Alpine Elements, Alpine Tracks, Alpine Weekends, AWWT, Bigfoot Travel, Barelli Ski, Board and Lodge, Concept Chalets, Classic Ski, Club Med, Club Pavilion/Concept, Collineige, Concept Chalets, Corporate Ski Company, Crystal, Direct Ski, Erna Low, Esprit, First Choice, Flexiski, French Freedom, French Life, Frozen Planet, High Mountain Holidays, Inghams, Interhome, Lagrange, Made to Measure, Momentum, Mountain Leap, Mountain Retreats, Neilson, Original Travel, Oxford Ski Company, Peak Retreats, Ski Activity, Ski Arrangements, Ski Expectations, Ski France, Ski Independence, Ski Solutions, Ski Weekend, Skiweekends, Snow Safari, Thomson, White Roc Weekends

Champagny-en-Vanoise, France

See *La Plagne*, page 120
Tour operators Barelli Ski, Erna Low, Lagrange, Made to Measure, Ski Independence

Champéry, Switzerland

t +41 (0)24 479 2020, *www.champery.ch*
Altitude 1053m (3,455ft)–2350m (7,708ft)
Lifts 206 in Portes du Soleil
Tour operators Alpine Answers Select, Corporate Ski Company, Made to Measure, Momentum, Oak Hall, White Roc Weekends
Traditional village that is the main Swiss resort in the trans-frontier Portes du Soleil ski

area. A large cable-car whisks you up to the mid-mountain station at Planachaux. Alternative access is by a new six-seater covered chair from Grand-Paradis up to Planachaux. In town, attractive wooden chalets, hotels, shops and restaurants line the main street, but the resort is finally beginning to modernise with a new ice hall featuring regular ice-hockey matches and a revamped sports centre. Recommended places to stay include comfortable **Hotel Suisse, t** +41 (0)24 479 0707, **Hotel National, t** +41 (0)24 479 1130 and **Hotel Beau-Séjour, t** +41 (0)24 479 5858. **Auberge du Grand-Paradis, t** +41 (0)24 479 1167) is well regarded, while **Hotel la Rose des Alpes, t** +41 (0)24 479 2303 and **Pension La Mattaz, t** +41 (0)24 479 2002 are good value.

Champex-Lac, Switzerland

t +41 (0)27 783 2828, *www.champex.ch*
Altitude 1470m (4,823ft)–2188m (7,178ft)
Lifts 4
Charming small resort close to Verbier but not sharing its lift pass. The skiing is limited but never crowded, with some excellent tree-skiing. **Hotel Belvédère, t** +41 (0)27 783 1114 is full of character.

Champoluc, Italy

Page 155 `
Tour operators Alpine Answers Select, Alpine Tracks, Crystal, Momentum, Ski Expectations, Ski 2

Champoussin, Switzerland

t +41 (0)244 76 83 00, *www.portesdusoleil.com*, *www.royalalpageclub.com*
Altitude 1680m (5,512ft)–2350m (7,708ft)
Lifts 211 in Portes du Soleil
Tour operator Esprit
Champoussin in the Portes du Soleil is a mini-resort of modern, rustic-style buildings. Most are apartments, but the focal point is **Résidence Royal Alpage Club, t** +41 (0)244 76 83 00, a hotel containing swimming-pool, games room, disco and kindergarten.

Chamrousse, France

t +33 (0)4 76 89 92 65, *www.chamrousse.com*
Altitude 1700m (5,577ft)–2255m (7,398ft)
Lifts 26
Tour operators Erna Low, Lagrange

A rather unattractive but ski-convenient collection of buildings on the mountainside a 30-minute drive from Grenoble. The resort, scene of Jean-Claude Killy's clean sweep in the 1968 Grenoble Olympics, attracts a mainly French clientele and is popular with visitors from the city at weekends. **Hotel Bellevue, t** +33 (0)4 76 89 97 73 is at the foot of the slopes. **Hotel L'Hermitage, t** +33 (0)4 76 89 93 21 is rated, along with the simpler **Hotel Virage, t** +33 (0)4 76 89 90 63 and **La Datcha, t** +33 (0)4 76 89 91 40.

La Chapelle d'Abondance, France

t +33 (0)450 73 51 41, *www.portesdusoleil.com/station/chapelle*
Altitude 1010m (3,313ft)–1700m (5,577ft)
Lifts 207 in Portes du Soleil
Tour operators Ski Addiction, Ski La Côte
The old straggling farming village is 6km from Châtel. On one side of the road two long chairs take you up to Crêt Béni, on the other side a gondola and chair take you to Châtel and Torgon. **Hotels Les Cornettes, t** +33 (0)450 73 50 24 houses one of the area's best restaurants, and **Alti 1000, t** +33 (0)450 73 51 90 also has a swimming-pool.

Château d'Oex, Switzerland

t +41 (0)26 924 25 25, *www.chateau-doex.ch*
Altitude 1050m (3,445ft)–2979m (9,744ft)
Lifts 62
Tour operator Alpine Tours
Small and attractive village sharing Gstaad's 250km ski area, and popular with hot-air-balloon enthusiasts. Accommodation includes **Gourmet-Hotel Ermitage, t** +41 (0)26 924 60 03 and **Pension Le Vieux Chalet, t** +41 (0)26 924 6879.

Châtel, France

t +33 (0)4 50 73 22 44, *www.chatel.com*
Altitude 1200m (3,936ft)–2350m (7,708ft)
Lifts 207 in Portes du Soleil
Tour operators First Choice, Freedom Holidays, Frozen Planet, Interhome, Lagrange, Momentum, Peak Retreats, Ski Addiction, Skialot, Ski Arrangements, Ski Independence, Ski Rosie, Snowfocus, Tops
The small farming village of Châtel is set in the vast Portes du Soleil ski area. Not a lot of planning has gone into the development of

the village, which consists of buildings scattered up towards the Morgins Pass and Switzerland, and along the valley to the Linga lift with its access to Avoriaz. Reporters complain that lifts in the Super-Châtel sector are 'somewhat tired'. **Hotel Fleur de Neige**, t +33 (0)4 50 73 20 10 is a restaurant with rooms. **Hotel Castellan**, t +33 (0)4 50 73 20 86 is reknowned for its food, and **Hotel Les Rhododendrons**, t +33 (0)4 50 73 24 04 is in the best position.

Le Chazelet, France
t +33 (0)476 79 95 73,
  www.lagrave-lameije.com
Altitude 1500m (4,921ft)–2100m (6,890ft)
Lifts 1
Close to the extreme skiing at La Grave, on the north face of the Meije, are the three more moderate areas of Le Chazelet, Villar d'Arène and the Col du Lautaret, which are ideal for beginners. If you are staying in La Grave, this is the nearest place to find ski tuition for adults and children.

Clavière, Italy
t +39 0122 878856, www.claviere.it
Altitude 1760m (5,773ft)–2293m (7,523ft)
Lifts 92 in Milky Way
Tour operators Crystal, Equity/Rocket Ski, First Choice, SkiBound, Ski High Days
Set on the Franco-Italian border, the village is made up of a handful of hotels and shops. Clavière is linked into the giant Milky Way ski area, with access to the skiing above Montgenèvre and Cesana Torinese and easy home runs. Accommodation includes the **Grand Albergo Clavière**, t +39 0122 878787, **Passero Pellegrino**, t +39 0122 878914, **Pian del Sole**, t +39 0122 878085 and **Savoia**, t +39 0122 878803. Ski-in ski-out **Sporthotel Sagnalonga**, t +39 0122 878856 is rated for its swimming-pool. 'The hotel is in a perfect position and really cosy,' said one reporter, 'and the snow-mobile ride up to the hotel at night was a great bonus for the kids.'

La Clusaz, France
Page 95
Tour operators Classic Ski, Crystal, Interhome, Lagrange, Made to Measure, Ski Activity, Ski Arrangements, SkiBound, Skitopia, Ski Weekend, Snowlife

Les Coches, France
See La Plagne, page 120
Tour operators Family Ski Company, Finlay's, French Life, Lagrange, Mountain Sun, Ski Independence

Colfosco, Italy
See Corvara, page 161

El Colorado, Chile
See Valle Nevado, page 322

Compaccio (Compatsch), Italy
t +39 0471 704122, www.schlern.info
Altitude 1236m (4,055ft)–2949m (9,676ft)
Lifts 24 in Alpe di Suisi
Tour operators Equity/Rocket Ski, Inntravel
Small high-altitude hamlet above Ortisei with skiing in the Alpe di Siusi (Seiseralm) and a back-door link into Sella Ronda ski area. Ski-in ski-out **Hotel Urthaler**, t +39 0471 727919 is a temple to all that is fresh and understated in hotel design of today.

Les Contamines-Montjoie, France
t +33 (0)4 50 47 01 58, www.lescontamines.com
Altitude 1164m (3,818ft)–2500m (8,202ft)
Lifts 24
Tour operators Classic Ski, Club Europe, Frozen Planet, Interhome, Lagrange, Ski Arrangements, Ski Weekend
The resort may be little known internationally, but it has a loyal following. Set a short distance from Megève, the long straggling village is based on one side of the river while the skiing is the opposite side. The lift access is a 1km walk from the town centre, although a frequent bus service provides welcome transport. It is immediately after a fresh snowfall when Les Contamines comes into its own, offering some delightful off-piste skiing. Three-stars **Hotel La Chemenaz**, t +33 (0)4 50 47 02 44 is said to be friendly with good food, and **Chalet-Hôtel Camille Bonaventure**, t +33 (0)4 50 47 23 53 is new.

Copper Mountain, Colorado, USA
Page 237
Tour operators American Ski Classics, AWWT, Crystal, Equity/Rocket Ski, Erna Low, Neilson/Neilson School Groups, Ski Activity, Ski All America, Ski the American Dream,

SkiBound, Ski Independence, Ski Safari, Thomson, United Vacations, Virgin

Le Corbier, France

t +33 (0)4 79 83 04 04, *www.le-corbier.com*
Altitude 1550m (5,085ft)–2600m (8,530ft)
Lifts 76 in area
Tour operators Equity/Rocket Ski, Erna Low, Interhome, Lagrange, Ski Independence
Le Corbier is part of one of the largest ski areas in the Maurienne Valley, sharing 225km of terrain with the neighbouring resorts of Les Bottières, St Jean d'Arves, St-Sorlin d'Arves and La Toussuire. The skiing is ideal for beginners and lower intermediates. Most of the accommodation in Le Corbier is in apartments. It also has a couple of two-stars: **Hotel Mont Corbier**, t +33 (0)4 79 56 70 27 in the centre and **Le Grillon, t** +33 (0)4 79 56 72 59, 3km away towards Villarembert.

Coronet Peak, New Zealand

See *Queenstown (Coronet Peak and The Remarkables)*, page 310

Corrençon, France

See *Villard-de-Lans*, page 324

Cortina d'Ampezzo, Italy

Page 158
Tour operators Alpine Answers Select, Corporate Ski Company, Crystal, Elegant Resorts, Inghams, Made to Measure, Momentum, Original Travel, Ski Arrangements, Ski Equipe, Ski Expectations, Ski Freshtracks, Ski Solutions, Thomson, White Roc Weekends

Corvara, Italy

Page 161
Tour operators Momentum, Neilson, Pyrenean Mountain Tours

Courchevel, France

Page 96
Tour operators Airtours, Alpine Answers Select, Alpine Elements, Alp Leisure, Corporate Ski Company, Crystal, Direct Ski, Elegant Resorts, Erna Low, Esprit, Finlay's, First Choice, Flexiski, French Freedom, French Life, Frozen Planet, Inghams, Jeffersons, Kaluma, Lagrange, Le Ski, Lotus Supertravel,

Made to Measure, Mark Warner, Momentum, Mountain Leap, Neilson, Oxford Ski Company, PGL, Scott Dunn Ski, Seasons in Style, Silver Ski, Simply Ski, Ski Activity, Ski Amis, Ski Arrangements, Ski Deep, Ski Expectations, Ski France, Ski Independence, Ski Link, Ski 'n' Action, Ski Olympic, Ski Solutions, Ski Val, Ski Weekend, Skiworld, Thomson, Total Ski, White Roc Weekends

Courmayeur, Italy

Page 162
Tour operators Alpine Answers Select, Alpine Weekends, Corporate Ski Company, Crystal, First Choice, Inghams, Interhome, Interski, Mark Warner, Momentum, Ski Arrangements, Ski Expectations, Ski Solutions, Ski Weekend, Thomson, White Roc Weekends

Crans-Montana, Switzerland

Page 193
Tour operators Corporate Ski Company, Crystal, Inghams, Interhome, Kuoni, Made to Measure, Momentum, Oxford Ski Company, PGL, Ski Freshtracks, Swiss Travel Service, Switzerland Travel Centre (Plus Travel)

Crested Butte, Colorado, USA

Page 239
Tour operators AWWT, Club Med, Ski Activity, Ski the American Dream, Ski Safari, United Vacations

Crest-Voland, France

See *Notre-Dame-de-Bellecombe*, page 305 and *Les Saisies*, page 313

Les Crosets, Switzerland

t +41 (0)24 477 2077, *www.lescrosets.com*
Altitude 1660m (5,445ft)–2350m (7,708ft)
Lifts 207 in Portes du Soleil
The hamlet of Les Crosets sits in the heart of the Portes du Soleil and is highly rated by riders. It has its own snowboard school and terrain park. This is not the most appealing of resorts and is best suited to serious skiers and boarders who favour early nights. **Hotel Télécabine, t** + 41 (0)24 479 0300 is simple with good food.

Dachstein Glacier, Austria

See *Wagrain and the Salzburger Sportwelt Amadé*, page 48

La Daille, France
See *Val d'Isère*, page 136

Davos, Switzerland
Page 195
Tour operators Alpine Answers Select, Alpine Weekends, Corporate Ski Company, Flexiski, Frozen Planet, Headwater, Inghams, Interhome, Kaluma, Kuoni, Made to Measure, Momentum, PGL, Ski Expectations, Ski Freshtracks, Ski Gower, Swiss Travel Service, Switzerland Travel Centre (Plus Travel), White Roc Weekends

Deer Valley, Utah, USA
Page 240
Tour operators American Ski Classics, Momentum, Ski All America, Ski the American Dream, Ski Independence, Ski Safari

Les Deux Alpes, France
Page 100
Tour operators Airtours, Chalet Snowboard, Club Med, Crystal, Erna Low, First Choice, French Life, Frozen Planet, Inghams, Interhome, Lagrange, Made to Measure, Mark Warner, McNab, Momentum, Neilson, Panorama, Peak Retreats, Ski Activity, Ski Arrangements, Ski Independence, SkiBound, Ski Supreme, Skiworld, Thomson, Tops, Wasteland

Les Diablerets, Switzerland
See *Villars*, page 217
Tour operators Crystal, Equity/Rocket Ski, Interhome, Momentum, PGL, Ski Gower, Sloping Off, Solo's, Swiss Travel Service, Switzerland Travel Centre (Plus Travel), Thomson

Dienten, Austria
See *Maria Alm*, page 300

Dobbiaco, Italy
See *Alta Pusteria*, page 278
Tour operators Headwater, HF Holidays, Ramblers, Waymark

Durango, Colorado, USA
t +1 970 247 9000, *www.durangomountain resort.com*

Altitude 8,793ft (2680m)–10,822ft (3299m)
Lifts 10
Tour operator Ski Independence
Durango Mountain Resort in southern Colorado is a purpose-built, alpine-style resort with an old-town ambience. The skiing takes place on Purgatory Mountain. The resort makes an ideal two-centre trip combined with Telluride, which is just two and a half hours' drive away. Snowboarders and twin-tippers are well catered for with the Paradise Freestyle Arena and the Pitchfork Terrain Park. The Adaptive Sports Association is one of the best ski schools for disabled skiers in the USA. Hotels include **Purgatory Village Hotel, t** +1 970 385 2100, **The Inn at Durango Mountain,** **t** +1 970 247 9669, and **Sheraton Tamarron Resort, t** +1 970 259 2000. The **Twilight View Condos** are recommended.

Eichenhof, Austria
See *St Johann in Tirol*, page 40

Ellmau, Austria
t +43 (0)5358 2301, *www.ellmau.at*
Altitude 820m (2,690ft)–1829m (6,001ft)
Lifts 93 in SkiWelt
Tour operators Airtours, Crystal, Inghams, Interhome, Neilson/Neilson School Groups, Ski Astons, Ski Wild, Thomson
The largest resort of the SkiWelt offers good access into the lift system and a wide choice of accommodation. **Hotel Christoph, t** +43 (0)5358 3535, a five-minute walk from the main lift, has spacious rooms. **Hotel Hochfilzer, t** +43 (0)5358 2501 and **Sporthotel Ellmau, t** +43 (0)5358 3755 are both four-stars. The deluxe **Relais & Châteaux Der Bär, t** +43 (0)5358 2395 has a spa.

Encamp, Andorra
See *Soldeu*, page 11

Engelberg, Switzerland
Page 198
Tour operators Alpine Answers Select, Corporate Ski Company, Crystal, Inntravel, Interhome, Kuoni, Made to Measure, Momentum, Oak Hall, Ski Gower, Swiss Travel Service, Switzerland Travel Centre (Plus Travel), Waymark, White Roc Weekends

Entrèves, Italy
See *Courmayeur*, page 162

Espace Diamant, France
See *Notre-Dame-de-Bellecombe*, page 305

Espace Killy, France
See *Val d'Isère*, page 136 and *Tignes*, page 133

Falls Creek and Mount Hotham, Australia
Falls Creek t +613 5758 3224, *www.fallscreek.com.au*
Mount Hotham t +613 5759 4444, *www.hotham.com.au*
Altitude 1450m (4,757ft)–1861m (6,105ft)
Lifts 13
These are the major resorts in Victoria, sharing a lift pass and linked by a six-minute heli-copter ride. Falls Creek Alpine Resort is four hours' drive from Melbourne on the edge of the Bogong High Plains. A European-style, ski-in ski-out village has accommodation among the gum trees. Australia's largest snowmaking system covers the main trails, and the resort has a good terrain park.
Mount Hotham is the highest alpine resort in Victoria, with most of the skiing taking place below the village. Dinner Plain, Mount Hotham's architect-designed sister village, provides good-value accommodation 10km from the mountain but linked by free ski-bus.

Le Fayet, France
See *St-Gervais*, page 127

Fernie, BC, Canada
Page 60
Tour operators Alpine Answers Select, American Ski Classics, AWWT, Crystal, Frontier Ski, Inghams, Made to Measure, Momentum, Neilson, Nonstopski, Ski Activity, Ski All America, Ski the American Dream, Ski Arrangements, Ski Freshtracks, Ski Independence, Ski Safari, Skiworld, Virgin

Fieberbrunn, Austria
t +43 (0)5354 563330, *www.pillerseetal.at*
Altitude 800m (2,625ft)–2020m (6,627ft)
Lifts 11
Tour operators Snowscape, Thomson, Tyrolean Adventures

Small and attractive ski area near St Johann in Tirol with a reputation for good snow and a network of long, easy tree-level runs. **Austria Trend Sporthotel Fontana, t** +43 (0)5354 56453 and **Hotel-Pension Lindauerhof, t** +43 (0)5354 56382 are convenient for the skiing, while **Schloss Rosenegg, t** +43 (0)5354 56201 is a 14th-century castle with bedrooms reached by spiral staircase, dungeons, and an armoury linked by an underground passageway.

Filzmoos, Austria
See *Wagrain and the Salzburger Sportwelt*, page 48
Tour operator Inghams

Finkenberg, Austria
See *Mayrhofen*, page 26
Tour operator Crystal

Flachau, Austria
See *Wagrain and the Salzburger Sportwelt*, page 48
Tour operators Interhome, Made to Measure

Flaine, France
Page 102
Tour operators Alpine Answers Select, Altitude Holidays, Classic Ski, Crystal, Erna Low, French Freedom, French Life, Inghams, Lagrange, Momentum, Neilson, On The Piste, PGL, Ski Arrangements, Ski Freshtracks, Ski Independence, Thomson

Flims, Switzerland
Page 199
Tour operators Alpine Answers Select, Corporate Ski Company, Frozen Planet, Interhome, Made to Measure, Momentum, Powder Byrne, Swiss Travel Service, Switzerland Travel Centre (Plus Travel), White Roc Weekends

Flumet, France
See *Notre-Dame-de-Bellecombe*, page 305 and *Les Saisies*, page 313

Folgarida, Italy
t +39 0463 901280, *www.valdisole.net*
Altitude 1300m (4,265ft)–2505m (8,219ft)
Lifts 47 in area
Tour operators Equity/Rocket Ski

Purpose-built resort linked to Marilleva, and to Madonna di Campiglio, which is 9km away. A total of 120km of linked skiing, popular with budget skiers and school groups.

La Foux d'Allos, France
See *Pra-Loup*, page 309
Tour operator Club Europe

Font-Romeu, France
t +33 (0)468 30 68 30, *www.font-romeu.fr*
Altitude 1700m (5,577ft)–2250m (7,382ft)
Lifts 26
Tour operators Lagrange, Solo's
Important resort in the Pyrenees, 90km from Perpignan. The skiing and purpose-built ski station are 4km from the old village and linked by gondola. The pistes are best suited to beginners, lower intermediates and families. Weekend queueing can be a problem. There are two dozen hotels and pensions, including three-stars **Hotel Carlit, t** +33 (0)468 30 80 30, **Le Grand Tetras, t** +33 (0)468 30 01 20, **La Montagne, t** +33 (0)468 30 36 44 and **Sun Valley, t** +33 (0)468 30 21 21.

Fulpmes, Austria
See *Neustift and the Stubaital*, page 29
Tour operator Crystal

Galtür, Austria
t +43 (0)5443 8521, *www.galtuer.com*
Altitude 1585m (5,200ft)–2300m (7,546ft)
Lifts 10
Tour operators Crystal, First Choice, Inghams, Made to Measure
Small resort with considerable atmosphere close to Ischgl. It suffered terribly in the February avalanches of 1999, but has since rebuilt its tourist trade with considerable success. Galtür's pistes are at Wirl, an outpost five minutes away by a free and frequent shuttle bus. The skiing is gentle and well suited to beginners and families; the area is also a notable centre for ski-touring. The family-run **Fluchthorn Hotel, t** +43 (0)5443 8202 offers a warm welcome in a central loca-tion. **Hotel Post, t** +43 (0)5443 84220 is convenient.

Gargellen, Austria
t +43 (0)5557 6303, *www.gargellen.at*
Altitude 1430m (4,692ft)–2300m (7,546ft)
Lifts 8
Tour operator Made to Measure
The chalet-style village in the Montafon area is close to the border with Switzerland and attacts a loyal international clientele. Hotels include the four-star **Madrisa, t** +43 (0)5557 6331, which was built as a country house at the beginning of the 20th century and opened as a hotel in the 1920s. **Hotel Heimspitze, t** +43 (0)5557 63190 is also rated. The resort has a modern eight-person gondola, and free ski-buses link Gargellen with the neighbouring resorts of Gaschurn and St Gallenkirch.

Garmisch-Partenkirchen, Germany
t +49 8821 1806,
www.garmisch-partenkirchen.de
Altitude 710m (2,330ft)–1330m (4,364ft)
Lifts 32 in Zugspitze
Tour operators Interhome, Moswin's Germany
The towns of Garmisch and Partenkirchen are surrounded by striking scenery and lie beneath the Zugspitze, Austria and Germany's highest mountain. Partenkirchen is an ancient Roman town dating back to 15 BC, while Garmisch has frescoed medieval houses. The towns were linked for Hitler's 1936 Winter Olympics. The ski area is made up of five mountains and offers 15km of the only glacier skiing in Germany. Although Garmisch has 18km of undemanding piste, the majority of runs are best suited to intermediate skiers and riders, with a terrain park featuring a super-pipe. The mountain can be accessed from three starting places, including a cable-car and cog railway from Garmisch. The glacier can also be reached from the village of Ehrwald in Austria. Hotels include five-star **Reindl's, t** +49 8821 943870 and the four-star **Hotel Alpina, t** +49 8821 7830.

The Gasteinertal, Austria
Page 16

Geilo, Norway
Page 184
Tour operators Alpine Tracks, Crystal, Headwater, Inntravel, Neilson/Neilson School Groups, Thomson

Les Gets, France

Page 117

Tour operators Descent International, Equity/Rocket Ski, First Choice, Gourmet Chalet Company, Lagrange, Made to Measure, Momentum, Oxford Ski Company, Peak Retreats, Reach4theAlps, Ski Activity, Ski Expectations, Ski Famille, Ski Hillwood, Ski Independence, Ski-n-Do, Total Ski, Wasteland, Wood Advent Farm

Glencoe and Glenshee, Scotland

Glencoe **t** +44 (0)1855 851226, *www.ski-glencoe.co.uk*

Glenshee **t** +44 (0)1339 41320, *www.ski-glenshee.co.uk*

Altitude 304m (1,000ft) – 1109m (3637ft)

Tour operator (Glenshee) Skisafe Travel

Glencoe is the orginal UK resort and has the longest black run in Scotland, while Glenshee has the largest lift system in Britain. However both are victims of the changing European weather pattern and suffer from lack of snow for much of the winter. When it does fall, both can offer good skiing, but it is impossible to book a holiday in advance and be certain of sufficient cover. Both have excellent ski schools. Near Glencoe recommended accommodation is the **Macdonald Hotel, t** +44 (0)1855 831539 and **Invercoe Highland Holiday Cottages, t** +44 (0)1855 811210. Near Glenshee, recommended hotels include **Callater College Hotel, t** +44 (0)1339 741275, **Braemar Lodge at Braemar t** +44 (0)1339 741627, **Dalmunzie House Hotel,** t +44 (0)1250 885224 and the **Spittal Hotel, t** +44 (0)1250 885215.

Going, Austria

t +43 (0)5358 2438, *www.going.at*

Altitude 800m (2,624ft)– 1892m (6,207ft)

Lifts 93 in SkiWelt

Tour operators Interhome, Neilson, Solo's

Linked into the SkiWelt area, Going has some stunning views and a good nursery slope. One of the village highlights is five-star **Hotel Stanglwirt, t** +43 (0)5358 2000, which has a Lipizzaner riding school.

Golden, BC, Canada

See *Kicking Horse*, page 62

Gosau, Austria

See *St Wolfgang*, page 313

Grächen, Switzerland

t +41 (0)27 955 60 60, *www.graechen.ch*

Altitude 1615m (5,330ft)–2890m (9,537ft)

Lifts 13

Tour operator Interhome

Chalet-style village close to Saas-Fee and Zermatt. The ski area is accessed by a choice of two gondolas.

Gran Catedral (Bariloche), Argentina

t +54 2944 423776, *www.bariloche.com*

Altitude 1050m (3,445ft)–2050m (6,725ft)

Lifts 32

Tour operators Andes, Exsus, Lotus Supertravel

San Carlos de Bariloche, in Patagonia, is home to Gran Catedral – Argentina's oldest and most famous ski resort – better known as Bariloche. It is a large, attractive resort not far from the Chilean border.

Sophisticated Bariloche is South America's biggest resort, boasting a modern lift system, 50 trails, a vertical drop of 1000m and the largest snowmaking system in South America. The area provides intermediate slopes with high-speed cruising and abundant off-piste. Hotels include the five-star **Panamericano,** *www.panamericanobariloche.com* and four-stars **Hotel Nevada, t** +54 2944 522778, *www.nevada.com.ar* and **Hotel Edelweiss,** **t** +54 2944 445500, *www.edelweiss.com.ar.*

Le Grand Bornand, France

t +33 (0)4 50 02 78 00, *www.legrandbornand.com*

Altitude 950m (3,120ft)–2100m (6,890ft)

Lifts 39

Tour operators Interhome, Lagrange, Ski Arrangements

Charming village with extensive skiing comprising some 90km of piste, and offering something for all levels. The main ski station is at Le Chinaillon. The picturesque Col des Annes offers motorway cruising. From Lachat, at 2100m, the piste stretches out to the gentle slopes of Joyere. Snowboarders have some designated pistes and the new Aiguille Mountain terrain park provides a good playground. La Clusaz is an easy drive away.

Grand Targhee, Wyoming, USA

t +1 307 353 2300, *www.grandtarghee.com*

Altitude 8,000ft (2438m)–10,230ft (3118m)

Lifts 8

Tour operators AWWT, Ski Safari
This small purpose-built resort is just inside the Wyoming border and 47 miles from Jackson Hole. It boasts a wonderful snow record, which is why the main attraction is snowcat-skiing and -boarding. If you can't get a space on a snowcat, the resort's 2,000-acre ski area offers some challenge and plenty of powder. Prices are considerably lower than in *Jackson Hole*, and accommodation (**t** +1 800 827 4433 for booking office) includes **Teewinot Lodge**, **Targhee Lodge** and **Sioux Lodge Condominiums**.

Grand Valira, Andorra
See *Pas de la Casa* page 10 and *Soldeu* page 11

Grau Roig, Andorra
See *Pas de la Casa*, page 10

La Grave, France
Page 105
Tour operators Interhome, Lagrange, Momentum, Peak Retreats, Ski Arrangements

Gressoney, Italy
See *Champoluc*, page 155
Tour operators Alpine Answers Select, Crystal, Momentum, Ski Expectations

Grindelwald, Switzerland
Page 202
Tour operators Corporate Ski Company, Crystal, Elegant Resorts, Inghams, Interhome, Jeffersons, Kuoni, Made to Measure, Momentum, PGL, Powder Byrne, Seasons in Style, Ski Freshtracks, Solo's, Swiss Travel Service, Switzerland Travel Centre (Plus Travel), Thomson, White Roc Weekends

Grossarl, Austria
Small village with ski area linked to Dorfgastein.

Gstaad, Switzerland
Page 204
Tour operators Corporate Ski Company, Headwater, Made to Measure, Momentum, Seasons in Style, Ski Astons, Ski Expectations, White Roc Weekends

Guthega, Australia
See *Perisher-Blue*, page 307

Hafjell, Norway
See *Lillehammer*, page 299
Tour operator Crystal

Happo'one and Hakuba Valley, Japan
t +44 (0)20 7734 6870, *www.snowjapan.com*
Altitude 760m (2,493ft)–1830m (6,007ft)
Lifts 33
The pretty village of Happo'one is the biggest ski area in the Nagano Prefecture's resort-studded Hakuba Valley, and arguably the best ski resort in the country. The valley lies 200km from Tokyo, to which it is linked by the *shinkansen* (bullet train). The resort has some striking scenery, challenging terrain and longer-than-average runs. Accommodation includes **Hotel Omoshiro Hasshinchi**, **t** +81 0261 72 6663 at the resort base. The **Hotel Lady Diana & St George's**, **t** +81 0261 75 3525 is also rated.

Hasliberg, Switzerland
See *Meiringen-Hasliberg*, page 301

Haus-im-Ennstal, Austria
t +43 (0)3686 22340, *www.en.skiamade.com*
Altitude 750m (2,460ft)–2015m (6,611ft)
Lifts 64 in area
Tour operator Oak Hall
Haus is a peaceful little farming village linked into the Schladming ski area. **Hotel Gasthof Herrschaftstaverne**, **t** +43 (0)3686 2392 has a spa, traditional **Dorfhotel Kirchenwirt**, **t** +43 (0)3686 2228 is in the village centre. **Gasthof Reiter**, **t** +43 (0)3686 2225 is a delightful old chalet, and the **Panoramahotel Gürtl**, **t** +43 (0)3686 2383 is family-run.

Heavenly, California/Nevada, USA
Page 242
Tour operators American Ski Classics, AWWT, Equity/Rocket Ski, Erna Low, Neilson, Ski Activity, Ski All America, Ski the American Dream, SkiBound, Ski Freshtracks, Ski Independence, Ski Safari, Skiworld, Thomson, Trailfinders, United Vacations

Hemsedal, Norway
Page 185

Tour operators Alpine Tracks, Crystal, Neilson/Neilson School Groups, Thomson

Hinterthal and Hintermoos, Austria
See *Maria Alm*, page 300

Hintertux, Austria
See *Tux im Zillertal*, page 321

Hochsölden, Austria
See *Sölden*, page 45

Hopfgarten, Austria
t +43 (0)5335 2322, *www.hopfgarten.com*
Altitude 622m (2,040ft)–1829m (6,001ft)
Lifts 93 in SkiWelt
Tour operators Contiki, First Choice, PGL
The traditional village of Hopfgarten in the SkiWelt circuit is dominated by the twin yellow towers of its impressive church, yet despite its friendly atmosphere few British are attracted to the resort. The village is popular with Australians and New Zealanders. Accommodation includes **Aparthotel Hopfgarten**, t +43 (0)5335 3920 and **Sporthotel Fuchs**, t +43 (0)5335 2420.

Les Houches, France
Page 106
Tour operators Barelli Ski, Erna Low, French Life, Interhome, Lagrange, Peak Retreats, Ski Expectations, Ski Weekend, Snow Safari

Huez, France
t +33 (0)4 76 11 44 44, *www.alpedhuez.com*
Altitude 1120m (3,674ft)–3330m (10,922ft)
Lifts 85 in Alpe d'Huez area
Old town below Alpe d'Huez resort and connected by cable-car. **Hotel L'Ancolie**, t +33 (0)4 76 11 13 13 is a renovated farmhouse with a recommended restaurant.

Hungerburg, Austria
See *Innsbruck*, opposite

Igls, Austria
t +43 (0)5125 9850, *www.innsbrucktourist.info*
Altitude 900m (2,953ft)–2247m (7,372ft)
Lifts 6
Tour operators Inghams, Made to Measure
The small village of Igls is set 5km from Innsbruck towards the Europabrücke and the

Italian border. The skiing is limited, with the Olympic downhill run (of Franz Klammer fame) presenting the only real challenge. The village is made up of traditional hotels and coffee houses, some bracing winter walks, and the Olympic bob-run which is open to the public. **Sporthotel Igls**, t +43 (0)5123 77241 has good food, the five-star **Schlosshotel**, t +43 (0)5123 77217 is highly recommended, and **Hotel Batzenhäusl**, t +43 (0)5123 8618 is very comfortable.

Inneralpbach, Austria
See *Alpbach*, page 15

Innsbruck, Austria
t +43 (0)5125 9850, *www.innsbruck.info*
Altitude 580m (1,903ft)–2334m (6,250ft)
Lifts 60 in six ski areas
Tour operators Corporate Ski Company, Direct Ski, Ramblers
Innsbruck is usually described as a minor ski resort, but its real significance is as a base for visiting the well-known resorts of the Tyrol and the Arlberg by bus or car. Hungerberg is the home ski area just outside the city, set on the steep south-facing slopes of the Hafelekar. The city's best hotel is the five-star **Europa-Tyrol**, t +43 (0)5125 9310. Four-stars include **Hotel-Restaurant Goldener Adler**, t +43 (0)5125 71111, **Hotel Penz**, t +43 (0)5125 75657, and **Romantikhotel Schwarzer Adler**, t +43 (0)5125 87109. **Hotel Weises Kreuz**, t +43 (0)5125 94790 is a 500-year-old hotel where Mozart stayed as a child.

Interlaken, Switzerland
t +41 (0)33 826 53 00, *www.interlakentourism.ch*
Altitude 796m (2,612ft)–2971m (9,748ft)
Lifts 41 in Jungfrau Top Ski Region
Tour operators Kuoni, Ski Astons
Sophisticated and attractive Interlaken is positioned between two lakes at the foot of the dramatic Eiger, Mönch and Jungfrau mountains. The town provides a good base for mixed groups including non-skiers who would rather stay in a bustling town than in a ski resort. From the centre it is a short train ride to Lauterbrunnen where you can catch the cable-car to Mürren, or a train to Wengen and Grindelwald. The best place to stay is

outwardly traditional **Grand Hotel Victoria-Jungfrau, t** +33 (0)828 2828, which has a state-of-the-art spa and strikingly minimalist rooms in a special spa wing.

Ischgl, Austria

Page 19

Tour operators Alpine Answers Select, Crystal, First Choice, Frozen Planet, Inghams, Made to Measure, Momentum, Original Travel, Ski Solutions, Ski Wild

Isella, Italy

See *Macugnaga*, page 300

Isola 2000, France

t +33 (0)4 93 23 15 15, *www.isola2000.com*
Altitude 1800m (5,904ft)–2610m (8,561ft)
Lifts 22
Tour operators Club Pavilion/Concept, Crystal, Erna Low, French Life, Lagrange, Leisure Direction, PGL, Ski Arrangements

The purpose-built resort of Isola offers 120km of piste and was built by a British property company in the 1960s. Isola is the most southerly ski area in France but it is a particularly good place to find late-season snow. Created with families in mind, Isola has a decent collection of shops, bars, no-frills apartments and hotels, and a large, sunny nursery area. British skiers make up a large portion of the winter business, with many owning apartments in the resort. The ski area is limited, but varied enough for beginners, families with young children, and undemanding intermediates. The original building, the unattractive and soulless Front de Neige Centre, is right on the slopes. More aesthetically pleasing wood-clad additions behind it improve the resort's appeal. **Hotel Le Chastillon, t** +33 (0)4 93 23 26 00 and **Hotel Diva, t** + 33 (0)4 93 23 17 71 are the four-stars, while three-stars **Hotel de France, t** +33 (0)4 93 02 17 04 and **Hotel Pas du Loup, t** +33 (0)4 93 23 27 00 are also recommended.

Itter, Austria

t +43 (0)5335 2670, *www.skiwelt.at*
Altitude 703m (2,306ft)–1829m (6,001ft)
Lifts 93 in SkiWelt

Itter is a small village with just 850 tourist beds, but a fast gondola nearby with no queues for the uphill journey, plus the longest run in the SkiWelt (8.5km), make it a quiet and good-value alternative to Söll. **Sporthotel Tirolerhof, t** +43 (0)5335 2690 has a bowling alley.

Jackson Hole, Wyoming, USA

Page 244

Tour operators Alpine Answers Select, American Ski Classics, AWWT, Carrier, Crystal, Inghams, Lotus Supertravel, Momentum, Neilson, Seasons in Style, Ski Activity, Ski All America, Ski the American Dream, Ski Freshtracks, Ski Independence, Ski Safari, Skiworld, Trailfinders, United Vacations, Virgin

Jasper, Alberta, Canada

t +1 780 852 3816, *www.skimarmot.com*
Altitude 5,534ft (1686m)–8,534ft (2601m)
Lifts 8
Tour operators Crystal, Frontier Ski, Inghams, Made to Measure, Neilson/Neilson School Groups, Ski Activity, Ski All America, Ski the American Dream, SkiBound, Ski Independence, Ski Safari, Virgin

Arguably the most beautiful Canadian resort – and the most northerly – is set among the forests, glaciers, frozen lakes and waterfalls of Jasper National Park. The small but varied ski area is based at Marmot Basin, 20 minutes' drive out of town. The terrain is made up of open bowls, with steep chutes and glades cut through the trees. Eagle Ridge, Sugar Bowl and Birthday Bowl offer the most challenging skiing. **Chateau Jasper, t** +1 780 852 5644 is a comfortable place to stay.

June Mountain, California, USA

See *Mammoth*, page 251

Kandersteg, Switzerland

t +41 (0)33 675 8080, *www.kandersteg.ch*
Altitude 1200m (3,937ft)–1920m (6,299ft)
Lifts 7
Tour operators Headwater, HF Holidays, Inghams, Inntravel, Kuoni, Swiss Travel Service, Waymark

The charming village in the Bernese Oberland is popular with cross-country skiers and boasts 75km of loipe. But it also has some commendable Alpine skiing for beginners. Hotels include the five-star **Royal Park**, t +41 (0)33 675 8888, the four-stars **Waldhotel Doldenhorn, t** +41 (0)33 675 8181 with a well-ness centre and sister hotel **Landgasthof Ruedihus, t** + 41 (0)33 675 8181, both full of atmosphere. Three-star **Victoria Ritter, t** +41 (0)33 675 8000 is also recommended.

Kaprun, Austria
See *Zell am See* and *Kaprun*, page 52
Tour operators Airtours, Crystal, Direct Ski, Esprit, First Choice, Interhome, Neilson/Neilson School Groups, PGL, Ski Astons, Ski Wild, Thomson

Kelchsau, Austria
See *Söll and the SkiWelt*, page 46

Ketchum, Idaho, USA
See *Sun Valley*, page 265

Keystone, Colorado, USA
Page 248
Tour operators American Ski Classics, AWWT, Crystal, Erna Low, Frozen Planet, Ski Activity, Ski All America, Ski the American Dream, Ski Independence, Ski Safari, Thomson, United Vacations

Kicking Horse, BC, Canada
Page 62
Tour operators Alpine Answers Select, AWWT, Crystal, Frontier Ski, Made to Measure, Ski All America, Ski the American Dream, Ski Independence, Ski Safari

Killington, Colorado, USA
Page 250
Tour operators American Ski Classics, Crystal, Equity/Rocket Ski, Inghams, Neilson School Groups, Ski Activity, Ski All America, Ski the American Dream, Ski Arrangements, SkiBound, Ski Independence, Ski Safari, Solo's, Thomson, Trailfinders, United Vacations, Virgin

Kimberley, BC, Canada
t +1 250 427 4881, *www.skikimberley.com*
Altitude 4,035ft (1230m)–6,500ft (1981m)
Lifts 9
Tour operators Frontier Ski, Frozen Planet, Inghams, Ski Activity, Ski the American Dream, Ski Independence, Ski Safari

The log-cabin-style ski village is a five-minute drive from the Tyrolean-style town of Kimberley at the foot of the Purcell Mountains and ideal for a two-resort holiday combined with Fernie. The front face offers gentle slopes, while the backside area provides more chal-lenge. There is night-skiing two nights a week on the longest floodlit trail in the country. In the rather spread-out ski village the choice of accommodation includes ski-in, ski-out **Polaris, t** +1 877 286 8828 and **Trickle Creek Residence Inn by Marriott, t** +1 877 282 1200.

Kirchberg, Austria
t +43 (0)5357 2309, *www.kirchberg.at*
Altitude 850m (2,788ft)–2000m (6,562ft)
Lifts 57
Tour operators Airtours, Direct Ski, First Choice, Interhome, Neilson
Kirchberg shares the Hahnenkamm and the ski safari to Pass Thurn with nearby Kitzbühel and from this winter is linked by a new eight-person cable-car to the 1956m Gampen above Westendorf in the SkiWelt. This should create a single mammoth circuit of 150 lifts and over 400km of skiing, but you still have to take a bus from Westendorf to Brixen or Hopfgarten. A new wide piste has been created back down on the Kirchberg side. One- and two-day lift passes are valid in both areas this season but you need to buy separate passes for longer stays. Kirchberg lacks the medieval charm of Kitzbühel but has considerable character. It has its own nursery area on the Gaisberg. **Tiroler Adler, t** +43 (0)5357 2327 is not particu-larly convenient but is one of the best hotels in town. **Hotel Alexander, t** +43 (0)5357 2222 and **Hotel Metzgerwirt, t** +43 (0)5357 2128 are recommended. **Restaurant Rosengarten** in **Hotel Taxacherhof, t** +43 (0)5357 2527 is run by one of Austria's celebrated young chefs.

Kitzbühel, Austria
Page 21
Tour operators Airtours, Corporate Ski Company, Crystal, Direct Ski, Elegant Resorts, First Choice, Inghams, Interhome, Made to Measure, Momentum, Neilson/Neilson School Groups, Original Travel, Panorama, PGL, Seasons in Style, Ski Activity, SkiBound, Ski Freshtracks, Ski Solutions, Ski Wild, Snowscape, Thomson, Tyrolean Adventures

Kleinarl, Austria
See *Wagrain and the Salzburger Sportwelt*, page 48

Klosters, Switzerland
Page 205
Tour operators Descent International, Flexiski, Inghams, Kuoni, Made to Measure, Mountain Leap, Oxford Ski Company, PGL, Powder Byrne, Seasons in Style, Ski Expectations, Ski Freshtracks, Ski Solutions, Swiss Travel Service, White Roc Weekends

Kranjska Gora, Slovenia
t +386 (0)4588 1768, *www.kranjska-gora.si*
Altitude 810m (2,667ft)–1630m (5,348ft)
Lifts 20
Tour operators Balkan Holidays, Crystal, First Choice, Inghams, Just Slovenia, Solo's, Thomson
This is Slovenia's best-known resort – but not necessarily its best. The village, set in a pretty flat-bottomed valley between craggy wooded mountains, has considerable charm and a level of sophistication that puts it on a par with any similar-sized Austrian or Italian resort. The 30km of skiing served by five chair-lifts and 15 drag-lifts lacks the variety and challenge of some of the other less famous resorts. However, Kranjska is an ideal base for beginners and early intermediates. The ski school, the Alpine Ski Club, has an excellent reputation, and the 5km toboggan run is not to be missed. Stay at the four-star **Hotel Kompas**, or at the four-star **Hotel Lek**. The recommended alternatives are **Hotel Larix**, **Hotel Prisank**, **HIT Casino** and **Hotel Spik**. The **Razor apartments** are situated 200m from the lifts. Accommodation can be booked centrally t +386 (0)4588 1768 or through a tour operator.

Kronplatz, Italy
Page 165

Krvavec, Slovenia
t +386 (0)425 25 930, *www.rtc-krvavec.si*
Altitude 1450m (4,757ft)–1971m (6,466ft)
Lifts 12
Tour operator Just Slovenia
Ski area within a few minutes' drive of Ljubljana airport. The network of runs served by chair-lifts from the top of the modern access-gondola happily resembles a modest North American resort. In mid-winter you can even ski the whole way to the valley floor. The ski area has no village, but you can stay in the **A&S Hotel Krvavec**, t +386 (0)420 19 152, *www.hotel-as.com*. Some 90 per cent of the trails are covered by snow-cannon.

Kühtai, Austria
t +43 (0)5239 5222, *www.kuehtai.co.at*
Altitude 2020m (6,627ft)–2520m (8,268ft)
Lifts 12
Tour operators Crystal, Inghams
A pretty little Tyrolean village offering 40km of piste and a lack of queues. **Jagdschloss Kühtai**, t +43 (0)5239 5201, five minutes from the village centre, was once a hunting lodge and today is a hotel brimming with character.

Kvitfjell, Norway
See *Lillehammer*, page 299

Lake Louise, Alberta, Canada
See *Banff-Lake Louise*, page 56
Tour operators AWWT, Ski Safari

Lake Tahoe, California, USA
See *Heavenly*, page 242 and *Squaw Valley*, page 259

Lauterbrunnen, Switzerland
t +41 (0)37 856 8568, *www.wengen-muerren.ch*
Altitude 796m (2,612ft)–2971m (9,748ft)
Lifts 41 in Jungfrau Top Ski Region
Tour operators Oak Hall, Re-lax Holidays, Ski Miquel
Lauterbrunnen is the railway junction town near Interlaken that provides a cheap alternative to the better-known resorts of Mürren and Wengen. Hotels offer a convenient, if rather characterless, base from which to explore the skiing in this corner of the Bernese Oberland. Mürren, reached by a steep rack-and-pinion railway, is the easier to get to. Try three-star **Hotel Schützen**, t +41 (0)33 855 2032 and **Hotel Silberhorn**, t +41 (0)33 856 2210.

Lech, Austria
Page 23
Tour operators Alpine Answers Select, Alpine Tracks, Crystal, Elegant Resorts, Erna Low, Flexiski, Inghams, Kaluma, Made to Measure, Momentum, Original Travel, Seasons in Style, Ski Activity, Ski Expectations, Total Ski, White Roc Weekends

The Lecht, Scotland
t +44 (0)1975 651440, www.lecht.co.uk
Altitude 643m (2,109ft)–793m (2,600ft)
Lifts 14
Scotland's smallest ski area has a network of short lifts on both sides of the A939 Cock Bridge–Tomintoul road. It lies 56 miles west of Aberdeen and about 45 miles from Glenshee and Cairngorm. The area is best suited to beginners and intermediates living within reasonable driving distance. The longest run is 900m. The nearest accommodation is the **Allargue Arms**, t +44 (0)1975 651410, three miles away at Corgarff.

Las Leñas, Argentina
t +54 262 747 1100 (in Buenos Aires 1 313 1300), www.laslenas.com
Altitude 2240m (7,349ft)–3431m (11,257ft)
Lifts 11
Tour operators AWWT, Exsus, Scott Dunn Latin America
Las Leñas can be the most challenging resort in South America. But it depends entirely upon the weather and the operation or closure of a single lift. If there is sufficient stable snow and little enough wind to open the avalanche-prone Marte chair then strong skiers and riders are in for the finest feast in the southern hemisphere. The lift provides the only mechanized access to some extraordinary off-piste with plunging powder bowls and vertiginous couloirs. The area is exposed to avalanche danger and dotted with cliffs. It's the kind of place where you never follow lone tracks to see where they go and a local guide is essential. On the other hand, if the Marte chair is closed, Las Leñas reverts to being a fun but bland Andean resort – a tree-less wilderness that is not necessarily worth the 90-minute flight from Buenos Aires to Malargue and the one-hour bus transfer. You can also fly to San Rafael, a three-hour drive from the resort. All accommodation is in

hotels and lodges within a short walk or ski of a lift. The five-star **Hotel Piscis**, t +54 262 747 1100 is the most luxurious, featuring what claims to be the highest ski-resort casino in the world. **The Aries**, t +54 262 742 7120 has its own cinema.

Lenk, Switzerland
See *Adelboden and Lenk*, page 278

Lenzerheide and Valbella, Switzerland
t +41 (0)81 385 1120, www.lenzerheide.ch
Altitude 1500m (4,920ft)–2865m (9,397ft)
Lifts 34 in area
Tour operator Made to Measure
These linked resorts at either end of the beautiful Heidsee have considerable charm and lots of mainly intermediate skiing. They used to attract a high number of British families but have declined in popularity for no discernible reason. The lift system has been steadily updated. None of the terrain is particularly difficult, and it makes a pleasant holiday centre where most of the clientele are Swiss. It is best suited to families and intermediate skiers and riders. Recommended hotels include the four-star **Sunstar**, t +41 (0)81 384 0121 and **Romantik Guarda Val**, t +41 (0)81 385 8585. Valbella has less charm. Both the four-star **Posthotel Valbella**, t +41 (0)81 384 1212 and the **Valbella Inn**, t +41 (0)81 384 3636 are recommended.

Leogang, Austria
t +43 (0)6583 8234, www.leogang-saalfelden.at
Altitude 800m (2,625ft)–2096m (6,877ft)
Lifts 55 in area
Tour operators Inntravel, Tyrolean Adventures
The village is a collection of ten farming hamlets with a modern gondola taking you to Berghaus Asitz at 1758m, where a quad-chair and six-seater chair link into the Saalbach-Hinterglemm area. Four-star **Hotel Salzburgerhof**, t +43 (0)6583 7310 is convenient.

Levi, Finland
Page 186
Tour operators Inghams, Nortours

Leysin, Switzerland
t +41 (0)24 494 2244, www.leysin.ch
Altitude 1330m (4,363ft)– 2200m (7,218ft)
Lifts 15

Tour operators Interhome, Sloping Off, Switzerland Travel Centre (Plus Travel)

The village above the town of Aigle has historically been associated with finishing schools, health clinics and cut-price student holidays. Today it is also one of the top resorts in Switzerland for snowboarders with the advantage of the 50km area having virtually no drag-lifts. 'Uncrowded – once or twice in January we were the only people on the piste,' said one reporter. **Garderie Arc en Ciel**, t +41 (0)24 494 1200 cares for children from newborn to seven years.

Best-situated accommodation is the four-star **Hotel Classic-Terrasse**, t +41 (0)24 493 0606 with spacious rooms, and the simpler **Bel-Air**, t +41 (0)24 494 1339. **The Hiking Sheep**, t +41 (0)24 494 3535 is a renovated Art Deco building run as a hostel with good dormitories.

Lillehammer, Norway

t +47 612 89800, *www.lillehammerturist.no* , *www.hafjell.com*

Altitude 200m (656ft)–1050m (3,444ft)

Lifts 11

Tour operators Crystal, Direct Ski, Nortours, Original Travel, Waymark

Lillehammer is cosy little town with a single main street of weatherboard houses that was a surprising (given that it has such limited skiing) but successful choice for the 1994 Winter Olympics. The closest skiing is 15 minutes away at Hafjell. Kvitfjell, 50km from Lillehammer, has only 18km of pistes but provides more demanding terrain. **Radisson SAS Lillehammer**, t +47 612 86000, **Rica Victoria**, t +47 612 50049 and **First Hotel Breiseth**, t +47 612 47777 are all recommended.

Livigno, Italy

Page 166

Tour operators Airtours, Direct Ski, Equity/Rocket Ski, Inghams, Interhome, Neilson, Panorama, Ski Arrangements

Long-Zhu Erlongshan, China

t +86 451 791 3640

Altitude 266m (872ft)–1371m (4,500ft)

Lifts 4

This is the second most important resort in the Heilongjiang province after larger Yabuli.

It is situated at Bin Xian, 56km from Harbin. The ski area is currently being developed by the Beijing Long-Zhu Leisure Group, which is pumping millions of dollars into mountain facilities.

Loveland, Colorado, USA

t +1 303 571 5580, *www.skiloveland.com*

Altitude 10,600ft (3231m)–13,010ft (3965m)

Lifts 11

This small, high ski resort competes annually with Killington to be the first US resort to open at the end of October or in early November. It is set on the Continental Divide 53 miles west of Denver and 12 miles east of Silverthorne. The resort is a local favourite due to its reliable snow-cover and low prices. The most convenient accommodation is **Silver Mine Lodge**, t +1 877 733 2656 in Silver Plume 10 miles from Loveland, at **Georgetown Mountain Inn**, t +1 569 3201 at Georgetown 12 miles away, or at **Peck House**, t +1 569 9870 in Empire 14 miles away.

Luosto, Finland

t +358 16 624 367, *www.luosto.fi*

Altitude 203m (665ft)–531m (1,750ft)

Lifts 4

Tour operator Canterbury Travel

Geographically in the centre of Lapland, Luosto is easily accessible from Rovaniemi airport. The resort has seven pistes that are best suited to families. Pyhä is 20km away and offers a further ten pistes and four lifts. Luosto offers 74km of cross-country trails, 25km of which are floodlit. Other activities in the area include snowmobile or reindeer safaris through the forest, snowshoe hiking, and dinner in a kota (Sámi teepee). Don't miss a visit to Lampivaara amethyst mine, and watch the Northern Lights through the glass-roofed Pohjan Kruunu kota.

Stay in the village of log cottages or in the new **Hotel Luostontunturi** that houses an 'amethyst spa'.

Macugnaga, Italy

t +39 0324 65119, *www.macugnaga-online.it*

Altitude 1327m (4,353ft)–2984m (9,790ft)

Lifts 12

Tour operators Neilson/Neilson School Groups

This resort is made up of five villages: Borca, Isella, Pecetto, Pestarena and Staffa. They are set at the foot of the Monte Rosa, close to the Swiss border and two hours' from Turin. The skiing is mainly of intermediate level. Due to the resort's proximity to the border, many of the buildings are Swiss in style. The dozen hotels include **Hotel Dufour, t** +39 0324 65529 in Staffa's main square, and **Hotel Zumstein, t** +39 0324 65490.

Madesimo, Italy

t +39 0343 53015, *www.madesimo.com*
Altitude 1530m (5,018ft)–2984m (9,790ft)
Lifts 19
Tour operators Frozen Planet, Inghams
This attractive old village with narrow streets and a scattering of converted farmhouses has a considerable international following among families who want a quiet resort offering plenty of snow-sure intermediate skiing. It lies close to the Swiss border, a two-hour drive from Bergamo and it is possible to take a day-trip from here to St Moritz. The skiing in the Valle Spluga ski area is mostly intermediate and takes place on the usually uncrowded slopes of the Pizzo Groppera, with long trails leading into neighbouring Valle di Lei. The area boasts mostly red runs and some challenging black, including the famous Canelone run. Hotels include four-star **Emet, t** +39 0343 53395, family-run **Andossi, t** +39 0343 57000, **Hotel Harlequin, t** +39 0343 53005 which is well located, and **Hotel Cascata e Crystal, t** +39 0343 53108 with a swimming-pool and mini-club.

Madonna di Campiglio, Italy
Page 167
Tour operators Crystal, Direct Ski, Equity/Rocket Ski, First Choice, Inghams, Interhome, Ski Arrangements, Ski Expectations, Ski Freshtracks, Solo's

Mammoth, California, USA
Page 251
Tour operators American Ski Classics, AWWT, Crystal, Made to Measure, Ski Activity, Ski All America, Ski the American Dream, Ski Independence, Ski Safari, United Vacations Virgin

Mariborsko Pohorje, Slovenia
t +386 (0)260 36 554, *www.pohorje.org*
Altitude 325m (1,066ft)–1347m (4,419ft)
Lifts 20
Maribor is Slovenia's second largest city and the modest slopes above it are home each January to the Golden Fox Trophy, one of the most important events in the Women's World Cup calendar. The 80km of trails are backed up by snow-cannon and low temperatures usually ensure top to bottom skiing. Stay at the base in the luxurious five-star **Hotel Habakuk, t** +386 (0)230 08 100, *www.termemb.si* or the more modest three-star **Hotel Tisa, t** +386 (0)260 36 100.

Marilleva, Italy
t +39 0463 901280, *www.valdisole.net*
Altitude 1300m (4,265)–2505m (8,219ft)
Lifts 47 in area
Tour operators Interhome, PGL
Purpose-built resort linked to Folgarida and to Madonna di Campiglio which is 9km away. A total of 120km of linked skiing, popular with budget skiers and school groups.

Marble Mountain, Newfoundland, Canada
t +1 709 637 7601, *www.skimarble.com*
Altitude 33ft (10m)–1,791ft (546m)
Lifts 4
Tour operators Club Pavilion/Concept, Frontier Ski
Small 175-acre ski area with a large annual snowfall of 16ft (5m). Marble is part of the foothills of the Appalachians above the Humber River, which cuts a winding path through the valley to the Bay of Islands. The scenery is beautiful but temperatures low.

Maria Alm, Austria
t +43 (0)6584 7816, *www.mariaalm.at*
Altitude 800m (2,625ft)–2000m (6,562ft)
Lifts 39
Tour operators Club Europe, Ski Astons
This unspoilt village close to Zell am See is dominated by a church boasting the highest spire in Salzburgerland and has won awards as the region's most beautiful village. Lots of inter-mediate skiing linked to Saalfelden, Hinterthal, Hintermoos, Dienten, and Mühlbach. It is included in the giant Ski Amadé lift pass.

Marmot Basin, Alberta, Canada
See *Jasper*, page 295

La Massana, Andorra
See *Pal-Arinsal*, page 8
Tour operator First Choice

Le Massif, Québec, Canada
t +1 418 632 5876, *www.lemassif.com*
Altitude 118ft (36m)–2,644ft (806m)
Lifts 5
Tour operators Frontier Ski, Ski All America, Ski the American Dream, SkiBound, Ski Safari
Le Massif is under new ownership and the mountain is currently undergoing a Can$5 million makeover to turn it into a four-seasons resort. As a ski centre it has the unusual attribute of being upside down. You park your car at the top of the mountain and ski all the way down to take the first lift. The resort and mountain are perched on the bank of the mighty St Lawrence, a 45-minute drive from Québec City and have one of the most enchanting views of any ski destination in the world. So steep is the angle of descent down the principal run that you feel that at any moment you are liable to tumble off the mountain and on to the majestic ice flows of the river far below. The resort suits all standards of skier and is used as a training centre by the Canadian national team.

Mayrhofen, Austria
Page 26
Tour operators Crystal, Equity/Rocket Ski, First Choice, HF Holidays, Inghams, Neilson/Neilson School Groups, Ski Activity, Ski Astons, Ski Freshtracks, Ski Wild, Snowcoach, Thomson

Megève, France
Page 108
Tour operators Alpine Answers Select, Classic Ski, Corporate Ski Company, Erna Low, French Life, Frozen Planet, Interhome, Lagrange, Leisure Direction, Made to Measure, Momentum, Mountain Leap, Original Travel, Peak Retreats, Simon Butler Skiing, Ski Arrangements, Ski Barrett-Boyce, Ski Expectations, Ski Independence, Ski Solutions, Stanford Skiing, White Roc Weekends

Meiringen-Hasliberg, Switzerland
t +41 (0)33 972 5050, *www.alpenregion.ch*
Altitude 1061m (3,481ft)–2433m (7,982ft)
Lifts 22
Tour operators Kuoni, PGL
Meiringen-Hasliberg is the key component of four linked villages that form the Alpen Region in the Bernese Oberland, between Lucerne and Interlaken. Brienz, Axalp, Hasliberg and Meiringen offer modest intermediate ski areas set against an awesome Alpine backdrop. Meiringen is known to all Sherlock Holmes fans for the Reichenbach Falls, where Sir Arthur Conan Doyle's character fell to his untimely death during his final struggle with arch-villain Moriarty. The Alpen Region is great for riding, with natural obstacles that form Switzerland's first 'natural snowboard park'. In Meringen, **Alpin Sherpa**, t +41 (0)33 972 5252, **Parkhotel du Sauvage**, t +41 (0)33 971 4141 and three-star **Sporthotel Sherlock Holmes**, t +41 (0)33 972 9889 are recommended. In Hasliberg try the **Bären**, t +41 (0)33 971 6022 and the **Bellevue**, t +41 (0)33 971 2341. In Brienz, recommended places to stay include **Hotel Brienz**, t +41 (0)33 951 3551 and **Grandhotel Giessbach**, t +41 (0)33 952 2525.

Les Menuires, France
Page 111
Tour operators Club Med, Erna Low, Family Ski Company, First Choice, French Freedom, French Life, Interhome, Neilson, PGL, Silver Ski, Ski Arrangements, SkiBound, Ski Olympic, Ski Independence, Ski Supreme, Skitopia, Wasteland

Meran 2000, Italy
t +39 0473 279457, *www.hafling.com*
Altitude 1650m (5,413ft)–2300m (7,546ft)
Lifts 7 in resort, 74 in Ortler Skiarena
The South Tyrol village, close to Bolzano, is 30 minutes' drive from the ski area with its 36km of piste served by two cableways and six other lifts. The resort is part of the Ortler Skiarena, with 13 unconnected resorts on one lift pass. Some 260km of piste is served by eight cableways and 66 chairs and drags. Hotels in Meran 2000 are headed by **La Pergola Residence**, t +39 0473 201435 on a hillside outside the village. It opened last August and was designed by Matteo Thun, whose signature

style is clear lines and wide-open spaces, using wood, stone, glass and traditional wickerwork. Guests tell the kitchen what they want to eat using organic products straight from the farm. Other hotels include **Romantik Hotel Staffler**, **t** +39 0472 771136, **Grand Hotel Palace**, **t** +39 0473 271000, **Hotel Sissi**, **t** +39 0473 231062, and **Castel Fragsburg**, **t** +39 0473 244071.

Méribel, France
Page 113
Tour operators Airtours, Alpine Action, Alpine Answers Select, Alpine Elements, Alp Leisure, AWWT, Belvedere Chalets, Bonne Neige, Club Med, Cooltip, Corporate Ski Company, Crystal, Descent International, Direct Ski, Elegant Resorts, Erna Low, First Choice, Four Winds Meriski, Flexiski, French Freedom, French Life, Inghams, Interhome, Kaluma, Lagrange, Lotus Supertravel, Made to Measure, Mark Warner, Momentum, Mountain Leap, Neilson, Oxford Ski Company, PGL, Purple Ski, Scott Dunn Ski, Seasons in Style, Silver Ski, Simply Ski, Ski Activity, Ski Amis, Ski Basics, Ski Blanc, Ski Cuisine, Ski Expectations, Ski France, Ski Freshtracks, Ski Independence, Ski Olympic, Ski Solutions, Ski Weekend, Skiworld, Snowcoach, Snowline, Thomson, Total Ski, VIP, Wasteland, White Roc Weekends

Mieders, Austria
See *Neustift and the Stubaital*, page 29

The Milky Way, Italy
See *Clavière*, page 287; *Montgenèvre*, page 115; *Sauze d'Oulx*, page 174; *Sestriere*, page 178

Mittersill, Austria
See *Kitzbühel*, page 21

Moena, Italy
See *Canazei*, page 148

La Mongie, France
See *Barèges and La Mongie*, page 282
Tour operators Lagrange, Tangney Tours

Montafon, Austria
See *Gargellen*, page 291
Tour operator Made to Measure

Montalbert, France
See *La Plagne*, page 120
Tour operators French Life, Interhome, Lagrange

Montchavin, France
See *La Plagne*, page 120

Montgenèvre, France
Page 115
Tour operators Airtours, Club Europe, Crystal, Equity/Rocket Ski, French Life, Lagrange, Leisure Direction, Neilson, SkiBound, Ski Etoile

Monte San Vigilio, Italy
t +39 0473 561770, *www.lana.net*
Lifts 2
From the town of Lana, a cable-car with real leather seats – a 1970s replacement of the original cabin built in 1912 – takes you up to a lone building in the small ski area of Monte San Vigilio. The building is **Hotel Vigilius**, **t** +39 0473 556600, which is a true mountain hideaway oozing understated elegance. The Asian-European-fusion spa has an infinity swimming-pool. Skiing is on a choice of three lifts outside the door or a ride down the cable-car and on to the more extensive resorts of Val d'Ultimo (20 minutes' drive) or Val Senales (75 minutes).

Montriond, France
t +33 (0)450 79 12 81, *www.portesdusoleil.com*
Altitude 950m (3,116ft)–2350m (7,708ft)
Lifts 211 in Portes du Soleil
Montriond is a suburb of Morzine, with no real centre and a collection of simple, good-value hotels. A bus links the village to the gondola that accesses the Portes du Soleil ski area. The British Alpine Ski and Snowboarding School has a branch in the resort.

Mont-Sainte-Anne, Québec, Canada
t +1 418 827 4561, *www.mont-sainte-anne.com*
Altitude 575ft (175m)– 2,625ft (800m)
Lifts 15
Tour operators Frontier Ski, Ski All America, Ski the American Dream, SkiBound, Ski Safari
This is one the best ski areas in eastern Canada, situated only a half-hour drive from Québec City, with lots of intermediate slopes of a respectable gradient that are interspersed

with much more challenging double-black-diamonds. As all destinations in Québec, the mercury can plummet unbelievably low in mid-winter and occasionally the resort considers it is just too dangerously cold to open the lifts. But Canadians wrap up well in technical clothing and take low temperatures in their stride. On weekdays city-dwellers pop out to catch a few runs after work. Some 15 trails are floodlit for night-skiing in what is the biggest illuminated vertical drop (2,000ft) in Canada.

Chateau Mont-Sainte-Anne, t +1 418 827 5211 is at the base area, and the **Chalets Mont-Sainte-Anne, t** +1 418 827 5776 condominium complex is nearby.

Morgins, Switzerland
t +41 (0)24 477 2361, *www.morgins.ch*
Altitude 1350m (4,428ft)–2000m (7,710ft)
Lifts 211 in Portes du Soleil
Tour operators Ski Morgins, Ski Rosie
Morgins is a laid-back resort a short distance from Châtel on the Swiss–French sideof the Portes du Soleil circuit. Most of the accommodation is in chalets and apartments. The two-stars are **Hotel La Reine des Alpes, t** +41 (0)24 477 11 43 and **Hotel Beau-Site, t** +41 (0)24 477 11 38.

Morillon, France
t +33 (0)4 50 90 15 76, *www.ot-morillon.fr*
Altitude 700m (2,296ft)–2480m (8,134ft)
Lifts 78 in Grand Massif
Tour operators Altitude Holidays, Erna Low, French Life, Lagrange, Peak Retreats
The old village of Morillon in the beautiful Giffre Valley has a 16th-century church and is linked by road or gondola to the purpose-built satellite of Morillon 1100 ('in a fantastic position'). Together they have some 10,000 visitor beds and make a popular second-home resort for the French. Morillon has seven of its own lifts and is linked into the Grand Massif ski area, of which Flaine is the best-known resort. Two-star **Hotel Le Morillon, t** +33 (0)4 50 90 10 32 has a recommended restaurant.

Morzine, France
Page 117
Tour operators Alpine Answers Select, Alpine Escapes, Alpine Tracks, Alpine Weekends, AWWT, Chalet Chocolat, The Chalet

Company, Chalet Snowboard, Challenge Activ, Corporate Ski Company, Crystal, Esprit, First Choice, French Life, Frozen Planet, Inghams, Lagrange, Made to Measure, Momentum, Mountain Highs, Neilson School Groups, PGL, Reach4theAlps, Ski Activity, Ski Arrangements, SkiBound, Ski Chamois, Ski Expectations, Ski Independence, Snowline, Thomson, Trail Alpine, White Roc Weekends

Moso, Italy
See *Alta Pusteria*, page 278

Mount Buller, Australia
t +61 35777 6077, *www.mtbuller.com.au*
Altitude 1390m (4,559ft)–1804m (5,917ft)
Lifts 22
Mount Buller is the major area for Melbourne-based skiers, located a three-and-a-half-hour (250km) drive north-east from the city. It has the largest lift capacity in the country. There are some long cruising runs, as well as some genuine black-diamond runs. The scenery is impressive, with panoramic views across the gum forests. **The Breathtaker Hotel, t** +61 35777 6377 is Australia's first mountain spa hotel. The **Schuss Lodge, t** +61 35777 6007 is a small hotel with great views.

Mount Hotham, Australia
See *Falls Creek and Mount Hotham*, page 290

Mount Hutt, New Zealand
t +64 (0)3 302 8811, *www.mthutt.co.nz*
Altitude 1585m (5,200ft)–2075m (6,808ft)
Lifts 9
New Zealand's best-known resorts is a 35-minute drive from Methven and 90 minutes from Christchurch airport. It has wonderful views across the Canterbury Plains and is normally the first resort to open in Australasia each winter. Although the weather is unpredictable, the skiing can be excellent and Mount Hutt has some of the most extensive snowmaking in this part of the world.The village of Methven has a good choice of accommodation.

Mount Ruapehu, New Zealand
t +64 (0)7 892 3738, *www.mtruapehu.com*
Altitude 1605m (5,266ft)–2322m (7,616ft)
bottom

Lifts Turoa 9, Whakapapa 14

Mt Ruapehu is in the midst of North Island's Tongariro National Park and is the country's biggest and busiest ski area. It comprises Whakapapa on the north-western side of the volcano, and Turoa, on the south-western slopes.

Mt Ruapehu is renowned for its unpredictable weather – on a good day the skiing can be excellent but during a wet and windy white-out the visibility can be so poor that the resort is barely skiable. Happy Valley is New Zealand's largest beginner area, tucked away from the main slopes at Whakapapa. It normally opens in mid-June before the rest of the area.

Turoa shares a pass and has Australasia's biggest vertical drop of 720m. Unfortunately there is no easy way to get from resort to resort on snow. Turoa is always the last resort in the country to close in early November, and offers fabulous spring skiing.

Whakapapa village, 6km from the mountain, boasts the smart and pricey **Grand Château, t** +64 (0)7 892 3809, while the cheaper **Skotel, t** +64 (0)7 892 3719 is nearby. **Adventure Lodge & Motel, t** +64 (0)7 892 2991 with a spa, and **Howard's Lodge, t** +64 (0)7 892 2827 are at National Park Village 22km away, but convenient for both ski fields.

Lively Ohakune provides a wide choice of accommodation including **Powderhorn Chateau, t** +64 (0)7 385 8888.

Mühlbach, Austria
See *Maria Alm*, page 300

Mürren, Switzerland
Page 207
Tour operators Inghams, Kuoni, Made to Measure, Momentum, Ski Freshtracks, Ski Solutions, Swiss Travel Service, Switzerland Travel Centre (Plus Travel)

Naeba, Japan
t +44 (0)20 7734 6870, *www.snowjapan.co.uk*
Altitude 900m (2,953ft)–1800m (5,905ft)
Lifts 28
This is one of the busiest ski areas in the Niigata Prefecture in the northern Japanese Alps, with 24-hour skiing. It is presided over by the **Naeba Prince, t** +81 25 789 2211 – the

world's largest ski hotel containing a shopping mall, spa, amusement centre and over 40 restaurants. At weekends, when packed bullet trains and buses disgorge their human cargo, an absurd number of skiers floods the slopes – the record stands at 40,000 in one weekend – so at least at 4am there is some chance of finding a place to turn.

Nakiska, BC, Canada
t +403 256 8473, *www.skinakiska.com*
Altitude 5,003ft (1524m)–7,415ft (2215m)
Lifts 4
Tour operator Ski the American Dream
Small ski area just 83km from Calgary and a venue for the 1988 Olympics.

Nasserein, Austria
See *St Anton*, page 37
Tour operator Albus Travel

Nassfeld, Austria
t +43 (0)4285 8241, *www.skiarena.at*, *www.hermagor.com*
Altitude 600m (1969ft)–1500m (4,921ft)
Lifts 40
Tour operators PGL, Ski Wild
The Carinthian resort offers mainly intermediate skiing and claims to have the longest cable-car in the Alps – the Millennium-Express is 6000m and takes 17 minutes to climb from the valley. However, the resort is increasing in popularity, which means crowds during peak season.

The 11 four-stars include **Alpen Adria, t** +43 (0)4282 2666, **Berghotel Presslauer, t** +43 (0)4285 209 and **Hotel Berghof, t** +43 (0)4285 8271. **Cube**, *www.cube-hotels.com* is a new concept in hotels that combines function with cutting-edge design. The building doesn't have rooms: it has minimalist 'cube boxes'. Each box has its own 'showroom' used to dry clothing and store sports equipment. Cube doesn't have any stairs: it has 'gateways'. The whole building is constructed in glass and concrete, with the maximum use of light.

Nelson, BC, Canada
See *Whitewater*, page

Nendaz, Switzerland
t +41 (0)27 289 5589, *www.nendaz.ch*

Altitude 1365m (4,478ft)–3330m (10,925ft)
Lifts 89 in Four Valleys
Tour operators Frozen Planet, Interhome, OTP
Nendaz is a cheaper alternative bed-base to
Verbier, although access into the Four Valleys
skiing from here is complicated. A free ski-bus
operates between Nendaz and Siviez.

Neuberg, Austria
See *Wagrain and the Salzburger Sportwelt*,
page 48

Neustift, Austria
Page 29
Tour operators Alpine Tours, Esprit, Made to
Measure, Ski Astons

Nevis Range, Scotland
t +44 (0)1397 705825 snow info/t +44 (0)1397
703781 tourist info, *www.nevisrange.co.uk*,
www.ski.visitscotland.com
Altitude 655m (2,148ft)–1221m (4,006ft)
Lifts 12
This is Scotland's premier ski resort, a compact
but challenging ski area that is reached by a
modern six-seater gondola. It is situated near
Ben Nevis – Britain's highest peak – seven
miles north of the ancient town of Fort
William which provides accommodation. You
can also find B&Bs in the pretty nearby
hamlet of Torlundy. In good snow conditions
Nevis (sometimes known as Aonach Mor) can
offer just as good skiing as its Alpine counterparts of similar size. The Braveheart chair
accesses the back bowls of the Coire Dubh,
which provide outstanding off-piste opportunities after a fresh snowfall. However, like all
Scottish resorts Nevis Range suffers from lack
of regular cover in these troubled times of
global warming. Nineteenth-century
Inverlochy Castle, t +44 (0)1397 702177 is a
convenient place to stay.

Niederau, Austria
Page 30
Tour operators Airtours, Direct Ski, First Choice,
Inghams, Interhome, Neilson/Neilson School
Groups, Panorama, PGL, Thomson

La Norma, France
t +33 (0)4 79 20 31 46, *www.la-norma.com*
Altitude 1350m (4,429ft)–2750m (9,022ft)
Lifts 18

Tour operators Erna Low, Interhome, Lagrange,
Leisure Direction, Peak Retreats
Car-free family ski resort in the Maurienne
Valley.

Northstar-at-Tahoe, California, USA
t +1 530 562 1010, *www.northstarattahoe.com*
Altitude 6,330ft (1929m)–8,610ft (2624m)
Lifts 17
Tour operators Ski the American Dream,
SkiBound, United Vacations

Notre-Dame-de-Bellecombe, France
Altitude 1150m (3773ft)–2070m (6,791ft)
Lifts 72 in area
Tour operators Peak Retreats, SkiBound
Pretty village in the rural Val d'Arly between
Megève and Albertville with a distinctive
bulb-shaped bell tower that dates back to the
11th century. Ski area is linked to Flumet and
Praz-sur-Arly. From this winter it is also
connected to Les Saisies and Crest-Voland as
part of the Espace Diamant area.

Nozawa Onsen, Japan
t +44 (0)20 7734 6870, *www.snowjapan.co.uk*
Altitude 560m (1,837ft)–1650m (5,414ft)
Lifts 29
The neighbour to better-known Shiga Kogen
is an attractive spa village with old-world
charm. The busy, narrow streets are marred by
traffic and imbued with the aroma of sulphur
from the 13 public hot-spring bath-houses. The
slopes are reached by a steep uphill walk,
followed by two long escalators. The ski
terrain is varied with some steep pitches.
Accommodation is mainly in *ryokans* (inns)
and small hotels, with **Kameya Ryokan**, t +82
269 852124 recommended.

Obendorf, Austria
See *St Johann in Tirol*, page 40

Oberau, Austria
See *Niederau*, page 30
Tour operators Inghams, Neilson

Obergurgl-Hochgurgl, Austria
Page 31
Tour operators Airtours, Corporate Ski
Company, Crystal, Esprit, First Choice,
Inghams, Made to Measure, Momentum,

Neilson, Panorama, Ski Activity, Ski Expectations, Ski Freshtracks, Ski Solutions, Thomson

Oberlech, Austria

See *Lech*, page 23

Oberndorf, Austria

See *St Johann in Tirol*, page 40
Tour operator Tyrolean Adventures

Obertauern, Austria

Page 33
Tour operators Alpine Answers Select, Club Europe, Direct Ski, Inghams, SkiBound, Snowscape, Thomson

Oppdal, Norway

t +47 724 00470, *www.oppdal.com*
Altitude 545m (1,788ft)–1300m (4,265ft)
Lifts 16
One of Norway's most northerly and largest downhill resorts, 120km south of Trondheim, Oppdal has three ski areas: Stölen, Hovden and Vangslia, some good off-piste skiing, and 60km of cross-country trails. **Quality Hotel Oppdal, t** +47 724 00700 is in the village centre, **Nor Alpin Hotel, t** +47 724 04700 is recommended, and **Vangslia Fjelltun, t** +47 724 00801 contains piste-side log-built apartments.

Orcières-Merlette, France

t +33 (0)4 92 55 89 89, *www.orcieres.com*
Tour operators French Life, Interhome, Lagrange
Remote purpose-built resort with an almost exclusive French clientele in the southern French Alps 45 minutes from Gap.

Ordino, Andorra

See *Pal-Arinsal* page 8

Les Orres, France

t +33 (0)4 92 44 01 61, *www.lesorres.com*
Altitude 1550m (5,085ft)–2720m (8,924ft)
Lifts 23
Tour operators Equity/Rocket Ski, Lagrange, Sloping Off
Pleasant resort in the southern French Alps with 88km of skiing in heavily wooded terrain.

Ortisei, Italy

Page 170
Tour operators Inghams, Interhome

Oz-en-Oisans, France

t +33 (0)4 76 80 78 01, *www.oz-en-oisans.com*
Altitude 1350m (4,429ft)–3330m (10,922ft)
Lifts 84 in area
Tour operators Erna Low, Lagrange, Ski Activity, Ski Independence, Skiworld, Wasteland
The purpose-built village of Oz Station is set above the old village of Oz-en-Oisans and provides a back door into the *Alpe d'Huez* lift system. The small **Hotel Le Hors Piste, t** +33 (0)4 76 79 40 25 is the only hotel.

Pal, Andorra

Page 8
Tour operator Direct Ski

Pamporovo, Bulgaria

t +359 2 987 97 78, *www.bulgariatravel.org*
Altitude 1450m (4,757ft)–1925m (6,316ft)
Lifts 8
Tour operators Balkan Holidays, Crystal, Direct Ski, First Choice, Inghams, Pamporovo, Panorama, Solo's, Thomson
The small resort is 85km from the attractive old town of Plovdiv. Most of the accommodation is in the handful of hotels straggling between the centre and the lift station. At the top of the mountain of Snezhanka is the Bulgarian telecom tower. Pamporovo boasts an average of 272 sunny days each year, although it does not always snow on the other days. Lift queues are rare, except for a 15-minute spell in the morning when all the ski school classes set off together. Ski school instructors are said to speak 'great English'. It is advisable to book hotels through one of the many tour operators to the resort. Reporters criticize hotel food. **Hotel Orlovets** was newly built in 2005, with a swimming-pool and spa facilities. **Hotel Finlandia** is of a good standard but lacking in atmosphere. **Hotel Murgavets** has a spa with fitness room, whirlpool, massage and beauty treatments. **Hotel Snezhanka** is said to be 'very cosy' with good food. **Hotel Perelik** is basic but clean – avoid rooms above the disco that closes at 3am. The hotel also houses Pamporovo's main shopping centre. The après-ski is lively.

Panorama, BC, Canada
Page 65
Tour operators Inghams, Oak Hall, Ski Activity, Ski All America, Ski the American Dream, Ski Independence

Park City, Utah, USA
Page 254
Tour operators Alpine Answers Select, American Ski Classics, AWWT, Crystal, Equity/Rocket Ski, Momentum, Ski Activity, Ski All America, Ski the American Dream, Ski Independence, Ski Safari, Skiworld, Thomson, United Vacations

Paradiski, France
See *Les Arcs*, page 86; *Peisey-Vallandry*, below; *La Plagne*, page 120

La Parva, Chile
See *Valle Nevado*, page 322
Tour operators Andes, Scott Dunn Latin America

Pas de la Casa, Andorra
Page 10
Tour operators Airtours, Crystal, Direct Ski, First Choice, Inghams, Lagrange, Neilson, Panorama, Thomson

Passo Tonale, Italy
Page 171
Tour operators Airtours, Alpine Tours, Club Europe, Crystal, Direct Ski, Equity/Rocket Ski, First Choice, Inghams, Neilson/Neilson School Groups, PGL, SkiBound, Sloping Off, Thomson

Pecetto, Italy
See *Macugnaga*, page 300

Peisey-Vallandry, France
t +33 (0)4 79 07 94 28,
www.peisey-vallandry.com
Altitude 1350m (4,428ft)–3226m (10,581ft)
Lifts 144 in Paradiski
Tour operators Alpine Elements, Club Med, Erna Low, Esprit, French Life, Lagrange, Ski Hiver, Ski Independence, Ski Olympic, Snow Monkey Chalets
Vallandry and the other low-lying villages of Peisey and Nancroix in Paradiski used to be regarded as a tree-level bolthole in bad weather. The only other winter visitors were a few French families who stayed here to avoid the commercial realities of the true *stations de ski*.

All that changed in December 2003 with the opening of the £12 million Vanoise Express, a double-decker cable-car linking Les Arcs to La Plagne. These two major resorts now form the single ski area of Paradiski with 420km of piste.

The delightful village of Vallandry, with its wide and well-groomed pistes, is situated just below the cable-car station. From this quiet little base, your biggest decision each day is whether to ski the slopes of Les Arcs or to take the link and explore La Plagne. What Vallandry offers that larger resorts cannot is a true village ambiance, for the village still boasts more cows than people.

The village has 80 chalets, some low-rise apartments, and a couple of hotels. **L'Orée des Cimes**, t +44 (0)870 750 6820 is a new MGM development, and a four-star **Club Med** village is due to open this season.

Pestarena, Italy
See *Macugnaga*, page 300

Perisher-Blue, Australia
t +61 26459 4419, *www.perisherblue.com.au*
Altitude 1605m (5,264ft)–2034m (6,672ft)
Lifts 47
Perisher in New South Wales is part of the largest ski area in Australia and is linked to Blue Cow, Guthega and Smiggins. You get there by driving up the Kosciuszko Road, or better by train – the Skitube takes you through 10km of tunnels on a 20-minute journey to Perisher and Blue Cow from Bullocks Flat. Snowcats take you from the Perisher terminal to your lodge.

The country's first eight-person chair was installed here. Blue Cow has a high proportion of advanced terrain, and more than half the trails are intermediate. Excelerator is the longest run in the Perisher-Blue area. Guthega has some short challenging runs and its half-pipe is rated the best in Australia. The whole area has recently been the subject of a Aus$750,000 makeover.

Perisher Valley Hotel, t +61 26459 4455 is said to offer the best accommodation. **Perisher Manor**, t +61 26457 5291 is ski-in ski-out, and smoking is banned at **The Lodge**, t +61 26457 5341 at Smiggins.

Pila, Italy

t +39 0165 521148, *www.pila.it*
Altitude 1750m (5,741ft)–2750m (9,022ft)
Lifts 12
Tour operators Crystal, Interski, Momentum, Thomson

Pila is a compact but surprisingly challenging ski area with pistes of mainly intermediate level, but with lots of accessible off-piste. The gentle blue run, Grimond, is enjoyable for beginners, while The Wall is a long run that provides a challenge for experts. An impressive gondola links with the regional capital of Aosta in 18 minutes, making it feasible to commute. The old Roman town, although blighted by commercial development, has a delightful pedestrianised centre. Accommodation in Pila includes ski-in ski-out **Hotel Etoile de Neige**, t +39 0165 521541 and **Hotel Printemps**, t +39 0165 521246, while in Aosta you can stay at **Hotel Europe**, t +39 0165 236363 in the centre.

Pitztal, Austria

t +43 (0)5414 86999/5413 8288 (Pitztaler Glacier), *www.tiscover.at/pitztal*
Altitude 2880m (9,446ft)–3440m (11,283ft)
Lifts 11

The Pitztal region in the Tyrol is made up of four villages, with St Leonhard the main accommodation base close to the Pitztaler Glacier and Rifflsee ski area. The skiing at Rifflsee is for all standards. The glacier skiing is accessed by funicular and the highest gondola in Austria. The area has a wide range of hotels, including the four-star ski-in ski-out **Alpinhotel**, t +43 (0)5413 86361 at the glacier base station.

La Plagne, France

Page 120
Tour operators Airtours, Alpine Answers Select, Club Med, Crystal, Equity/Rocket Ski, Esprit, First Choice, French Life, Frozen Planet, Inghams, Interhome, Lagrange, Made to Measure, Mark Warner, Momentum, Neilson, On The Piste, Ski Activity, Ski Amis,

Ski Arrangements, SkiBound, Ski Expectations, Ski France, Ski Freshtracks, Ski Independence, Ski Olympic, Ski Supreme, Skiworld, Thomson

Plan-Peisey, France

See *Les Arcs*, page 86

Poiana Brasov, Romania

Page 81
Tour operators Airtours, Balkan Holidays, Frozen Planet, Inghams, Neilson/Neilson School Groups, Solo's

Pont d'Espagne, France

See *Cauterets*, page 285

Ponte di Legno, Italy

See *Passo Tonale*, page 171

Pontresina, Switzerland

t +41 (0)81 838 8300, *www.pontresina.com*
Altitude 1800m (5,904ft)–2978m (9,770ft)
Lifts 56 in St Moritz area
Tour operator Made to Measure

Pontresina is midway between the Diavolezza and Corviglia ski areas of St Moritz. **Grand Hotel Kronenhof**, t +41 (0)81 842 0111 is a five-star, **Saratz Hotel**, t +41 (0)81 839 4000 is a four-star that mixes traditional with modern design. **Kochendorfer's Albris**, t +41 (0)81 838 8040 is a relatively inexpensive three-star. **Hotel Steinbock**, t +41 (0)81 842 6371 is comfortable.

Portes du Soleil, France

See *Avoriaz*, page 88; *Champéry*, page 285; *Châtel*, page 286; *Morgins*, page 303; *Morzine*, page 117

Portillo, Chile

t +56 2 263 0606, *www.skiportillo.com*
Altitude 2512m (8,241ft)–3348m (10,984ft)
Lifts 15
Tour operators Andes, AWWT, Crystal, Exsus Travel, Lotus Supertravel, Momentum, Scott Dunn Latin America, Ski Safari

Chile's oldest ski area is the best-known resort but not necessarily the best resort in South America. It affable American-born owner runs the hotel and mountain with impeccable efficiency. Portillo lies 160km north of Santiago on the frontier with Argentina. The brilliant yellow Hotel Portillo sits in a deep cleft in the Andes on the shore of the beautiful Laguna de Inca surrounded by towering peaks including 6960m Aconcagua, the highest mountain in the southern hemisphere.

The sophisticated hotel attracts both the United States and Austrian national teams who spend part of each off-season training here. Their hi-tech presence is in sharp contrast to the bygone era that lingers in the lakeside dining-room, harking back to winters when Harris tweed plus-fours rather than latex cat-suits were worn at breakfast. The walls are covered in antique leather, and waiters wear bow-ties and formal red jackets. The number of guest in the whole resort is limited to just 450. The food is outstanding, service is exemplary, but most of the rooms are rather small. Free daycare and après-ski activities are provided for children aged three to six years, with lessons available from three years. Tio Bob's is the only mountain restaurant with a daily selection of grilled meats and salads. The main dining room in the hotel specialises in Chilean seafood.

The skiing is suited to all standards, with plenty of intermediate terrain as well as some dramatically steeper slopes. The two infamous *va et vient* lifts – multiple drag-lifts without pylons designed by Poma to access steep avalanche-prone slopes – tow you up the mountain at a knee-juddering 22kph. 'The only drawback is that the slopes are limited in variety and size, and you can cover the whole lot in a day,' said a reporter.

Pradollano, Spain
See *Sierra Nevada*, page 316

Pragelato, Italy
t +39 0122 740011, *www.pragelatoresort.com*
Altitude 2035m (6,675ft)–2823m (9,262ft)
Lifts 88 in Milky Way
This old village 10km by road down the valley from Sestriere has been given a face-lift as the ski jumping venue and an accommodation base for the Olympics. A new cable-car is to connect it to Sestriere and accommodation is in the new **Pragelato Resort**, t +39 0122 740011, *www.pragelatoresort.com*, which has 205 chalet-style units with a spa. **Antica Osteria**, t + 39 0122 785300, a converted cowshed with a vaulted ceiling, is the best restaurant in the region.

Pralognon-la-Vanoise, France
t +33 (0)4 79 08 79 08, *www.pralognon.com*
Altitude 1400m (4,593ft)–2350m (7,710ft)
Lifts 12
Tour operators Erna Low, Lagrange, Ski Independence
Attractive family resort with good cross-country skiing and modest alpine skiing between Courchevel and La Plagne.

Pra-Loup, France
t +33 (0)4 92 84 10 04, *www.praloup.com*
Altitude 1600m (5,249ft)–2500m (8,202ft)
Lifts 53 with La Foux d'Allos
Tour operators Equity/Rocket Ski, French Life, Lagrange, Leisure Direction
Pra-Loup shares a ski area with neighbouring La Foux d'Allos. The skiing takes place on two main mountains, accessed by cable-car from the top of the village of 1600. Pra-Loup has a wide choice of beginner and intermediate runs, including a variety of open-bowl skiing, good tree-level runs and extensive off-piste. Weekend queueing can, however, be a problem. The resort is divided into the two villages of 1500 and 1600, which are linked by chair and made up of a collection of 1960s hotels and apartments. Try **Hotel Club Les Bergers**, t +33 (0)4 92 84 14 54 or **Hotel Le Prieuré**, t +33 (0)4 92 84 11 43.

Puy-St-Vincent, France
t +33 (0)4 92 23 35 80, *www.puystvincent.com*
Altitude 1400m (4,593ft)–2750m (9,022ft)
Lifts 16
Tour operators Erna Low, Interhome, Lagrange, Snowbizz Vacances
Puy-St-Vincent (PSV) is an established resort that was extremely popular with British families in the 1970s. It is located 20km from Briançon on the edge of the Ecrins National Park. Its micro-climate usually ensures secure late-season snow-cover, along with 300 days of sunshine per year. As one reporter put it: 'Excellent for families, much quieter than other more famous resorts even at peak times.' PSV 1400 is an unspoilt mountain village connected by a double chair and a drag to PSV 1600. Newer *résidences*, a few chalets and shops and restaurants have been built on the edge of the piste, and the higher village is the better bet if you want doorstep skiing.

The 67km of piste in the small but challenging area has enough variety to suit all standards, although most runs are classified as blue or red. From PSV 1600, two chair-lifts give easy access to the main skiing, and queues are rare outside school holidays. The resort has a small terrain park that is floodlit at night, and a cross-country track.

The best of the apartments here are in the **Mona Lisa** building. Three-star **Hotel Saint Roche**, t +33 (0)492 23 32 79, is down at 1400.

Pyhä, Finland
See *Luosto*, page 299

Québec City, Canada
t +1 418 649 2608, *www.quebecregion.com*
Altitude Stoneham: 695ft (420m)–2,075ft (632m)/Mont-Sainte-Anne: 575ft (175m)–2,625ft (800m)
Lifts Stoneham 8, Mont-Sainte-Anne 15
Tour operators Carrier, Crystal, Neilson School Groups, Virgin, Waymark
Romantic, beautifully preserved – and reasonably priced – Québec acts as a bed-base from which to explore the nearby ski areas, each of which is worth a day or two's exploration. A regular shuttle-bus operates between the city, Stoneham (20-minute drive) and Mont-Sainte-Anne (30 minutes away). Le Massif (30 minutes) offers dramatic piste views of the frozen St Lawrence River. The city was built in 1608 and its cobbled streets added in the 18th century. The city has a wide choice of restaurants, shops, art galleries, and is home to a thriving club scene. The **Fairmont Chateau Frontenac**, t +1 418 692 3861 is a prominent hotel at the heart of the city overlooking the St Lawrence River.

Queenstown (Coronet Peak and The Remarkables), New Zealand
Coronet Peak t +64 (0)3 442 4634
The Remarkables t +64 (0)3 442 4617, *www.queenstown-nz.co.nz*
Altitude 1200m (3,937ft)–1957m (6,421ft)
Lifts 10
Six resorts come under the marketing umbrella of the Southern Lakelands, based around Queenstown and Wanaka. Queenstown is a lively and picturesque lakeside town situated in the south-west of the

South Island. It is flanked by two separate resorts. The traditional but modernised resort is Coronet Peak, with six lifts providing a variety of good all-round skiing. The nursery slope now claims the longest magic carpet lift (146m) in the world. The resort has recently installed a new six-seater chair.

The Remarkables was constructed more recently. The resort is visually exciting, but has fewer options than Coronet Peak. From Queenstown, The Remarkables range seems impossibly steep, but the ski area is in gentle bowls. The **Remarkables Lodge**, t +64 (0)3 442 2720 is highly rated and closest to the resort.

Radstadt, Austria
See *Wagrain and the Salzburger Sportwelt*, page 48

Ramsau, Austria
Tour operators HF Holidays, Inntravel
Small village near Schladming that is strong on cross-country skiing.

Rauris, Austria
t +43 (0)6544 20022, *www.rauris.net*
Altitude 950m (3,114ft)–2200m (7,253ft)
Lifts 10
Tour operator Crystal
Old gold mining village with beginner and family skiing in the Hohe Tauern mountains between the Gasteinertal and Zell am See.

Reberty, France
See *Les Menuires*, page 111

Red Resort, BC, Canada
Page 66
Tour operators AWWT, Frontier Ski, Nonstopski, Ski Independence, Ski Safari

Reith, Austria
See *Alpbach*, page 15

The Remarkables
See *Queenstown (Coronet Peak and The Remarkables)* opposite

Riksgränsen, Sweden
t +46 980 400 800, *www.riksgransen.nu*
Altitude 500m (1,640ft)–909m (2,982ft)
Lifts 5

Tour operators Nortours, Original Travel
The resort in Swedish Lapland is 300km into the Arctic Circle yet just 90 minutes from Stockholm. This far north the sun doesn't set during midsummer (mid-May to mid-June), so you can ski, snowboard or heli-ski until the early hours. **Hotel Riksgränsen,** t +46 980 400 800 is the accommodation of choice with a spa and swimming-pool.

Risoul, France
Page 123
Tour operators Crystal, First Choice, Interhome, Lagrange, Leisure Direction, Neilson School Groups, On The Piste, Ski Arrangements, SkiBound, Ski Independence, Wasteland

Rittnerhorn (Corno Renon), Italy
t +39 0471 352993, *www.ortlerskiarena.com*
Altitude 1530m (5,020ft) – 2070m (6,791ft)
Lifts 3, 74 in Ortler Skiarena
To the north of Bolzano is a small village that is especially good for families, with 8km of piste, one gondola and three drag-lifts. The resort is part of the Ortler Skiarena, with 13 unconnected resorts covered by one lift pass. A total 260km of piste is served by eight cableways and 66 chair- and drag-lifts.

Rocca di Cambio, Italy
See *Campo Felice*, page 284

Rohrmoos, Austria
t +43 (0)3687 61147, *www.rohrmoos.at*
Altitude 870m (2,854ft)–1850m (6,070ft)
Lifts 46 in Schladming area
The spread-out satellite of Schladming has ski-in ski-out accommodation and is unchallenging. Try **Hotel Austria,** t +43 (0)3687 61444, **Hotel Seiterhof,** t +43 (0)3687 61194 or **Hotel Waldfrieden,** t +43 (0)3687 61487, all of which are good value. Smarter **Hotel Schwaigerhof,** t +43 (0)3687 61422 is on the edge of the piste and has a swimming-pool. **Hotel Schütterhof,** t +43 (0)3687 61205 is recommended.

La Rosière, France
Page 125
Tour operators Crystal, Erna Low, Esprit, Interhome, Leisure Direction, Ski Amis, Ski Arrangements, Ski Independence, Ski Olympic, Thomson

Ruapehu, New Zealand
See *Whakapapa and Turoa*, page 326

Saalbach-Hinterglemm, Austria
Page 35
Tour operators Airtours, Alpine Answers Select, Board and Lodge, Club Europe, Crystal, Direct Ski, Equity/Rocket Ski, First Choice, Inghams, Interhome, Neilson, Panorama, PGL, Ski Activity, Ski Astons, SkiBound, Thomson

Saalfelden, Austria
See *Maria Alm*, page 300

Saas-Fee, Switzerland
Page 209
Tour operators Alpine Answers Select, Crystal, Erna Low, Esprit, Inghams, Interhome, Kuoni, Made to Measure, Momentum, Oak Hall, OTP, PGL, Ski Freshtracks, Ski Independence, Ski Solutions, Swiss Travel Service, Switzerland Travel Centre (Plus Travel), Thomson, Total Ski

St Anton, Austria
Page 37
Tour operators Airtours, Alpine Answers Select, Corporate Ski Company, Crystal, Direct Ski, Elegant Resorts, Esprit, First Choice, Flexiski, Frozen Planet, Kaluma, Inghams, Interhome, Lotus Supertravel, Made to Measure, Mark Warner, Momentum, Neilson, Original Travel, Seasons in Style, Simply Ski, Ski Activity, Ski Equipe, Ski Expectations, Ski Solutions, Ski St Anton, Ski Total, Ski Val, Ski Wild, Skiworld, Snowscape, Solo's, Thomson, White Roc Weekends

St Christoph, Austria
t +43 (0)5446 22690,
www.stantonamarlberg.com
Altitude 1800m (5,906ft)–2811m (9,222ft)
Lifts 82 on Arlberg Ski Pass
Tour operators Elegant Resorts, Flexiski, Jeffersons, Kaluma, Made to Measure, Momentum, Powder Byrne, Scott Dunn Ski, Seasons in Style
St Christoph is a delightful village directly linked into St Anton ski area. It consists of a small collection of restaurants and hotels, of

which the luxury **Arlberg-Hospiz**, **t** +43 (0)5446 2611 is the most famous and comfortable. St Christoph has five other hotels as well as the **Bundes Ski Academy**, where future ski and snowboard instructors are trained. The resort is a peacful alternative to bustling St Anton.

St-Christophe-en-Oisans, France

Small village linked off-piste with La Grave. See page 105

Sainte-Foy, France

Page 126
Tour operators Alpine Answers Select, Alpine Elements, Alpine Weekends, Erna Low, Frozen Planet, Leisure Direction, Peak Leisure, Ski Arrangements, Ski Independence

St-François-Longchamp, France

See *Valmorel*, page 140
Tour operators Erna Low, French Life, Interhome, Lagrange, Peak Retreats, Ski Independence

St-Gervais, France

Page 127
Tour operators Erna Low, French Life, Interhome, Lagrange, Leisure Direction, Peak Retreats, PGL, Snowcoach

St-Jean d'Arves, France

See *Le Corbier*, page 288
Tour operators Crystal, First Choice, French Life, Peak Retreats, Ski France, Thomson

St-Jean-d'Aulps, France

Independent village in Portes du Soleil ski area.

St Johann im Pongau, Austria

See *Wagrain and the Salzburger Sportwelt*, page 48

St Johann in Tirol, Austria

Page 40
Tour operators Crystal, Direct Ski, Ski Wild, Snowscape, Thomson

St-Lary, France

t +33 (0)5 62 39 50 81, *www.saintlary.com*
Altitude 830m (2,723ft)–2515m (8,251ft)
Lifts 32
Tour operators French Life, HF Holidays, Lagrange, Leisure Direction
This village, located 80km from Lourdes, is typically Pyrenean with stone-built houses and one narrow main street. The skiing is suitable for beginners to intermediates, and it takes four minutes to walk from the village centre to the cable-car to St-Lary Pla d'Adet, a small modern ski station with some accommodation. This is linked by road and by lift to an alternative base at St-Lary La Cabane. The fourth base area of St-Lary Espiaube is also reached by road, or on skis from Soum de Matte. The ski area is mainly treeless and lacks variety. It extends into the neighbouring Auron Valley and up the snow-sure glacier on Mont Pichaleye.
Hotel Mercure Coralia, **t** +33 (0)5 62 99 50 00, **Hotel La Terrasse Fleurie**, **t** +33 (0)5 62 40 76 00 and **Les Arches**, **t** +33 (0)5 62 49 10 10 are all recommended, while **Hotel Christiania**, **t** +33 (0)5 62 98 40 62 is new. At Espiaube, **Hotel La Sapinière**, **t** +33 (0)5 62 98 44 04 provides reasonable accommodation.

St-Martin-de-Belleville, France

Page 128
Tour operators Les Chalets de St Martin, Erna Low, First Choice, Kaluma, Leisure Direction, Ski Independence, Skitopia, Thomson

St Michael, Austria

t +43 (0)6477 8913, *www.stmichael-lungau.at*s
Altitude 1100m (3,609ft)–2411m (7,910ft)
Lifts 38
Tour operators Alpine Tours, Club Europe, Equity/Rocket Ski
Pretty, traditional village and intermediate ski area near Obertauern on the border of Salzburgerland and Carinthia.

St Moritz, Switzerland

Page 211

Tour operators Alpine Answers Select, Club Med, Corporate Ski Company, Elegant Resorts, Flexiski, Inghams, Interhome, Jeffersons, Kuoni, Made to Measure, Momentum, Oak Hall, Original Travel, Oxford Ski Company, Powder Byrne, Scott Dunn Ski, Seasons in Style, Ski Gower, Ski Solutions, Swiss Travel Service, Switzerland Travel Centre (Plus Travel)

Saint-Nicolas-de-Véroce, France

See *St-Gervais*, page 127

St-Sorlin-d'Arves, France

t +33 (0)4 79 59 71 77, *www.saintsorlindarves.com*
Altitude 1550m (5,085ft)–2620m (8,595ft)
Lifts 75
Tour operators Crystal, First Choice, French Life, Lagrange, Leisure Direction, Peak Resorts, Peak Retreats, SkiBound, Ski France, Ski Independence, Thomson, Wasteland
Quaint mountain village of carefully preserved Savoyard farmhouses and long-established shops built around an early 17th-century Baroque church in the Maurienne Valley. The village is part of the 310km Les Sybelles ski area linked to St-Jean, Le Corbier and La Toussuire. It holds the coveted 'Les P'tits Montagnards' label for good children's facilities. The skiing is best suited to intermediates and has two terrain parks and 16km of cross-country trails. See also Le Corbier, page 288

St Wolfgang, Austria

t +43 (0)6138 8003, *www.stwolfgang.at*
Altitude 550m (1,800ft)–1600m (4,763ft)
Lifts 8
Tour operators Crystal, First Choice, Inghams, Thomson
The village at the centre of Austria's lake district acts as a pleasant base for those wishing to ski the modest Postalm plateau, a magnificent 35-minute drive. Additional skiing is available at Gosau, an hour away. St Wolfgang's nursery slope is just outside the village.

Les Saisies, France

t +33 (0)4 79 38 90 30, *www.lessaisies.com*
Altitude 1650m (5,413ft)–1941m (6,368ft)
Lifts 72
Tour operators Classic Ski, Erna Low, French Life, Lagrange, Leisure Direction, Peak Retreats, Ski Independence
Les Saisies sits in a delightfully scenic position on the ridge dominating the Arly and Beaufortain valleys in a beautiful area of woodland and Alpine pastures 30km from Albertville that is sometimes called the French Tyrol. It is primarily a cross-country resort with 80km of loipe, but it also boasts 34 Alpine pistes, of which more than half are on easy tree-lined slopes. 'A great resort for families,' said one reporter, but 'not many English-speaking instructors' complained another. Accommodation is headed by three-star **Hotel Le Calgary**, t +33 (0)4 79 38 98 38 in the village centre, with a health club, swimming-pool and gourmet restaurants.
Les Saisies first attracted international fame when it was chosen as the venue for cross-country skiing for the 1992 Winter Olympics. From this winter Les Saisies is linked by two chair-lifts into the new Espace Diamant, a ski area of 72 lifts covering 140km of piste that connect the neighbouring resorts of Crest-Voland, Notre-Dame-de-Bellecombe, and Flumet. Les Saisies also provides a back-door entrance to Les Contamines.

Sälen, Sweden

t +46 (0)28 018700, *www.skistar.com*
Altitude 366m (1,201ft)–620m (2,034ft)
Lifts 77
The town of Sälen, 53km from the better-known resort of Trysil, has a range of ski areas close by. These are Lindvallen, which is linked to smaller Högfjället, and two more linked resorts of Tandådalen and Hundfjället. Yet more small resorts include Kläppen and Stöten. Most of the pistes are of intermediate standard, although there are over 30 black runs in the area. The Trollskogen – or Enchanted Forest – at Hundfjället is a children's forest trail featuring 400 trolls in theatrical stage sets complete with sound-effects. Lindvallen has the first ski-in, ski-out McDonald's. **Högfjälls Hotel**, t +46 (0)28

087000, *www.salen-hotell.se* is a comfortable piste-side hotel in the area, with facilities that include a spa and a sushi restaurant.

Salzburger Sportwelt, Austria
See *Wagrain*, page 48

Samnaun, Switzerland
t +41 (0)81 868 5858, *www.samnaun.ch*
Altitude 1840m (6,035ft)–2864m (9,394ft)
Lifts 44 in Ischgl-Samnaun area
Samnaun lives off its duty-free status and its linked skiing with Ischgl. The resort has a loyal Swiss following. Hotels include **Chasa Montana**, **t** +41 (0)81 861 9000, *www.hotelchasamontana.ch*, **Hotel Post**, **t** +41 (0)81 861 9200 and **Hotel Silvretta**, **t** +41 (0)81 86 1 95 00.

Samoëns, France
t +33 (0)4 50 34 40 28, *www.samoens.com*
Altitude 700m (2,296ft)–2480m (8,134ft)
Lifts 78 in Grand Massif
Tour operators Altitude Holidays, French Life, Interhome, Lagrange, Peak Retreats, Ski Independence
The resort is linked into the Grand Massif ski area, of which Flaine is the major resort. It is easily accessible, just 45 minutes' drive from Geneva and an easy drive from Calais. 'There is a real warmth about the village,' enthused a reporter. However it is fairly quiet in the evenings. Traditional bars and restaurants abound in this 'authentic French village'. The long-awaited Red Devil Gondola now whisks you up from Samoëns 720 to the ski area at 1600m in eight minutes. Hotels include three-star **Neige et Roc**, **t** +33 (0)4 50 34 40 72 and **Hotel Les Drugères**, **t** +33 (0)4 50 34 43 84, which has good food. The B&Bs **Chez Bobeau**, **t** +33 (0)4 50 34 98 95 and **Les Gîtes de Plampraz**, **t** +33 (0)4 50 34 95 98 are recommended. For something a little different, try **Le Chateau du Bérouze**, **t** +33 (0)4 50 34 95 72, a charming old manor house run by a New Zealand couple.

San Candido, Italy
See *Alta Pusteria*, page 278
Tour operator Waymark

San Cassiano, Italy
Page 173

Tour operators Momentum, Mountain Sun, Powder Byrne

San Martino (Reinswald), Italy
t +39 0471 623091, *www.sarntal.com*, *www.reinswald.com*
Altitude 1570m (5,151ft)–2460m (8,071ft)
Lifts 5 in resort, 74 in Ortler Skiarena
The South Tyrol village, in the Val Sarentino, has a modern gondola and three drag-lifts serving some 12km of piste. The resort is part of the Ortler Skiarena, with 13 small resorts covered by one lift pass. A total 260km of piste is served by eight cableways and 66 chair- and drag-lifts. For skiing at San Martino you can stay 15 minutes' drive away at the charming Hotel **Bad Schörgau**, **t** +39 0471 623048.

San Martino di Castrozza, Italy
t +39 0439 768867, *www.sanmartino.com*
Altitude 1450m (4,757ft)–2385m (7,825ft)
Lifts 17
San Martino is on the eastern edge of the Trentino Dolomites, surrounded by wild forest with soaring mountain peaks above. In 1700, the violin-maker Stradivari used to go into the same woods to select the spruce for his violins. Skiing started at San Martino di Castrozza in the early 1930s, and it has developed into three separate areas (two of which are linked). The resort lacks high-season queues and snowboarders, and has the charm of a low-profile ski station, although the majority of lifts are old-fashioned and slow. Accommodation includes four-star **Hotel Savoia**, **t** +39 0439 68094 and three-star **Hotel-Residence Colfosco**, **t** +39 0439 68224.

Santa Caterina, Italy
t +39 0342 935598, *www.valtellinaonline.com*
Altitude 1738m (5,702ft)–2725m (8,940ft)
Lifts 8
Tour operators Airtours, Neilson School Groups
The quiet village, 30 minutes by bus from Bormio, is ideal for families and beginners. It is set up a mountain road that is a dead-end in winter when the Gavia Pass is closed. Local skiing is on the north-east-facing slopes of the Sobretta. The higher slopes are fairly steep and there are some intermediate trails through the trees. Comfortable **San Matteo Hotel**, **t** +39 0342 925121 has good food.

Sauze d'Oulx, Italy
Page 174
Tour operators Airtours, Club
Pavilion/Concept, Crystal, First Choice,
Inghams, Momentum, Neilson, Panorama,
Ski Arrangements, Ski Freshtracks, Ski High
Days, Thomson

Savognin, Switzerland
t +41 (0)81 659 16 16, *www.savognin.ch*
Altitude 1200m (3,937ft)–2715m (8,907ft)
Lifts 17
Attractive village close to St Moritz and Davos.
It has recently added a cutting-edge new **Cube
Hotel**, *www.cube-hotels.com* (see Nassfeld)

Scheffau, Austria
t +43 (0)5358 7373, *www.scheffau.com*
Altitude 752m (2,467ft)–1829m (6,001ft)
Lifts 93 in SkiWelt
Tour operators Crystal, Esprit, Neilson/Neilson
School Groups, PGL, Ski Astons, Ski Wild,
Thomson
Hotel residents in Scheffau are given priority
in the queue for the sometimes-crowded
eight-person gondola, which links into the
giant SkiWelt circuit. **Hotel Alpin Scheffau**,
t +43 (0)5358 85560 has comfortable rooms
and a swimming-pool. The resort is a quieter
alternative to popular Söll.

Schladming, Austria
Page 41
Tour operators Alpine Answers Select, Crystal,
Equity/Rocket Ski, Interhome, Neilson School
Groups, Oak Hall, PGL, SkiBound, Sloping Off

Schlick 2000, Austria
See *Neustift and the Stubaital*, page 29

Schönberg, Austria
See *Neustift and the Stubaital*, page 29

Schwendau, Austria
Small village close to Mayrhofen.

Seefeld, Austria
Page 43
Tour operators Crystal, Direct Ski, Headwater,
Inghams, Interhome, Thomson, Waymark

Seiseralm, Italy
See *Alpe di Siusi*, page

Sella Ronda, Italy
See *Arabba*, page 146; *Canazei and the Val di
Fassa*, page 148; *Corvara*, page 161; *San
Cassiano*, page 173; *Selva Gardena*, page 176

Selva Gardena, Italy
Page 176
Tour operators Alpine Answers Select, Crystal,
Esprit, First Choice, Inghams, Momentum,
Neilson, Ski Arrangements, Ski Expectations,
Thomson, Total Ski

Serfaus, Austria
t +43 (0)5476 62390, *www.serfaus.com*
Altitude 1427m (4,682ft)–2684m (8,806ft)
Lifts 53 in area
Tour operators Alpine Tours, Made to Measure
Smart Serfaus attracts a mainly Austrian,
German and Dutch clientele to its beginner
and intermediate slopes and its luxury hotels.
The village is car-free and has an unusual
underground railway, which runs on air cushions rather like a hovercraft. This transports
snow-users from the far end of the village to
the ski lifts and contributes to the resort's
serene atmosphere. Serfaus specialises in
health treatments, with five spa hotels
including the **Löwe and Bär**, t +43 (0)5476
6058, **Wellnesshotel Cervosa**, t +43 (0)5476
62110 and **Wellnesshotel Schalber**, t +43
(0)5476 6770. The ski area is linked to the
villages of Fiss and Ladis.

Serrada-Folgaria, Italy
t +39 0464 720538, *www.folgariaski.com*
s1169m (3,835ft)–2060m (6,758ft)
Lifts 42
Tour operators Equity/Rocket Ski, Neilson
School Groups, PGL, SkiBound, Sloping Off
Good-value mainly beginner and easy intermediate ski area in the Dolomites that is
popular with school groups. Folgaria is made
up of seven hamlets of which Serrada has the
low-cost accommodation.

Serre Chevalier, France
Page 129
Tour operators Alpine Elements, Club Med,
Crystal, Equity/Rocket Ski, Erna Low, First
Choice, French Life, Frozen Planet, Hannibals,
Inghams, Interhome, Lagrange, Momentum,
Neilson/Neilson School Groups, Ski Activity,
Ski Arrangements, SkiBound, Ski

Expectations, Ski Independence, Ski Miquel, Skitopia, Sloping Off, Thomson

Sestriere, Italy

Page 178

Tour operators Alpine Answers Select, Crystal, Equity/Rocket Ski, First Choice, Inghams, Interhome, Momentum, Neilson, Ski Arrangements, Thomson

Shiga Kogen, Japan

t +44 (0)20 7734 6870, *www.snowjapan.co.uk*
Altitude 1228m (4,028ft)–2305m (7,562ft)
Lifts 71
This is Nagano's largest ski area, and was the venue for the majority of ski events at the 1998 Winter Olympics. It is a mixture of 21 different ski bases, served by 71 lifts, dotted over six interlinked mountains. None of the sectors is big or particularly difficult; in Alpine terms, the whole area would make up just three or four linked resorts of reasonable size. A competent skier or rider could cover all the terrain in a couple of days. Accommodation includes **Villa Alpen, t** +81 269 34 2731, which has its own ski school and equipment rental shop in the Sun Valley resort, and **Hotel La Neige Higashikan, t** +81 261 72 7111 at Shiga Kogen.

Sierra-at-Tahoe, California, USA

t +530 659 7453, *www.sierrattahoe.com*
Altitude 6,640ft (2024m)–8,852ft (2698m)
Lifts 9
Tour operator Ski the American Dream
Lake Tahoe resort set in 2,000 acres with plenty of sunny intermediate skiing and no fewer than six terrain parks with two half-pipes for skiers and riders.

Sierra Nevada, Spain

t +34 958 24 91 00, *www.sierranevadaski.com*
Altitude 2100m (6,888ft)–3470m (11,385ft)
Lifts 19
Tour operator Thomson
The Andalucian resort of Sierra Nevada is 32km from Granada, and offers mainland Europe's most southerly skiing. The presence of a ski resort here seems at complete odds with the nearby resorts of Marbella and Malaga, under two hours away. The purpose-built and somewhat charmless village of Pradollano is where most skiers stay. The ski area is vulnerable to bad weather, the mountain range is often exposed to high winds, and skiing is as likely to be interrupted by too much snow as too little. But when conditions are good, the skiing can be excellent and is best suited to beginners and intermediates. On a clear day you can from the top across to North Africa. During fiesta time the resort can be crowded due to its proximity to Granada and the Costa del Sol.
Accommodation includes **Hotel Sol Melia Sol y Nieve, t** +34 958 48 03 00 and the four-star **Sol Melia Sierra Nevada, t** +34 958 48 04 00, both of which are convenient and pleasant. Four-star **Hotel Maribel, t** +34 958 24 91 11 is highly rated.

Silver Star, BC, Canada

Page 67

Tour operators Alpine Answers Select, AWWT, Crystal, Frontier Ski, Ski Activity, Ski All America, Ski the American Dream, Ski Independence, Ski Safari

Sinaia, Romania

t +40 1 614 5160 or +44 (0)207 224 3692, *www.romaniantourism.com*
Altitude 855m (2,805ft)–2219m (7,280ft)
Lifts 10
Sinaia is a spa town where the Romanian royal family used to spend their summers after King Karol I built beautiful Peles Castle in the 1870s. Its once-smart hotels and casinos have an air of faded grandeur. The skiing is basic, but the setting is delightful. The long and easy runs down the front of the mountain are poorly marked and therefore challenging in uncertain visibility. The main area is on exposed slopes behind the mountain. Four-star hotels include **New Montana, t** +40 244 312 751, **Hotel Anda, t** +40 244 306 020 and the recently renovated **Palace Hotel, t** +40 244 312 051. Three-star **Hotel Sinaia, t** +40 244 311 551 is also rated.

Siviez, Switzerland

t +41 (0)27 289 5589, *www.nendaz.ch*
Altitude 1730m (5,676ft)–3330m (10,925ft)
Lifts 89 in Four Valleys
Tour operator Interhome

Sunny Siviez is a budget option for those wanting to ski the Four Valleys. A high-speed chair links to the Gentianes–Mont-Fort cable-cars of Verbier. Accommodation is in one hotel, a soulless apartment block and a youth hostel.

Sixt Fer à Cheval, France

t +33 (0)450 34 49 36, *www.sixtferacheval.com*
Altitude 1600m (5,248ft)–2480m (8,134ft)
Lifts 73 in Le Grand Massif
Tour operators Lagrange, Peak Retreats
The small 9th-century village of Sixt in the Grand Massif ski area is linked via the Piste des Cascades, a 14km blue trail, from the resort of Flaine.

SkiWelt, Austria
See *Söll and the SkiWelt*, Page 43

Smiggins, Australia
See *Perisher-Blue*, page

Smugglers' Notch, Vermont, USA

t +1 800 451 8752, *www.smuggs.com*
Altitude 1,030ft (314m)–3,640ft (1109m)
Lifts 8
Tour operators Neilson School Groups, Virgin
The resort has carved a niche for itself in the family market, but you would not choose to come to 'Smuggs' if you did not have small children. The key is convenience, with the lifts and accommodation within a 1,000ft radius, and apartments designed with families in mind. Smuggs is a small, unadorned village consisting mainly of condos.
Morse is the beginners' mountain, conveniently situated in the village centre. Another novice area, Morse Highlands, is set halfway up the mountain. More adept skiers move on from Morse to the other two mountains, which are reached by bus or on skis. Madonna Mountain offers some pleasant trails, and Sterling has long intermediate runs.
Snow Sport University, t +1 802 644 1293 is the highly respected ski and snowboard school. But children are what Smuggs is all about, and they are cared for at Treasures Child Care Center, t +1 800 451 8752, which features under-floor heating and giant fish tanks.

Snowbird and Alta, Utah, USA
Page 256

Tour operators Alpine Answers Select, American Ski Classics, AWWT, Momentum, Ski All America, Ski the American Dream, Ski Independence, Ski Safari, United Vacations

Snow King, Wyoming, USA

t +1 307 733 5200, *www.snowking.com*
Altitude 6,237ft (1901m)–7,808ft (2380m)
Lifts 4
This small ski area is confusingly in Jackson town but quite separate from Jackson Hole resort. The quiet ski area offers ample scope for a day's (or night's) skiing. The closest accommodation is the Snow King Resort Hotel and Condominiums, t +1 307 733 5200 at the base.

Snowmass, USA
See *Aspen and Snowmass*, page 227

Solda (Sulden), Italy

t+39 0473 737060, *www.sulden.com*
Altitude 1905m (6,185ft)–2625m (8,612ft)
Lifts 11
The South Tyrol village with its 11 lifts and 40km of piste offers some extensive skiing and is also home to the magnificent four-star Hotel Post, t +39 0473 613024 with an indoor pool and spa. The resort is part of the Ortler Skiarena, with 13 separate resorts sharing one lift pass. A total 260km of piste is served by eight cableways and 66 chair- and drag-lifts.

Sölden, Austria
Page 45
Tour operators Airtours, Frozen Planet, Panorama, Neilson, Thomson

Soldeu, Andorra
Page 11
Tour operators Airtours, Club Pavilion/Concept, Crystal, Direct Ski, First Choice, Inghams, Lagrange, Neilson, Panorama, Ski Freshtracks, Ski Wild, Thomson

Solitude Mountain Resort, Utah, USA
t +1 801 534 1400, *www.skisolitude.com*
Altitude 7,988ft (2435m)–10,035ft (3059m)
Lifts 8
Tour operators Ski the American Dream, Ski Independence

Solitude is located 45 minutes' drive from Salt Lake City in the heart of Big Cottonwood Canyon in Utah's Wasatch National Forest. The underrated, ski-in ski-out resort is family owned and full of charm. Some 50 per cent of the trails are rated intermediate.

All accommodation (t +1 801 536 5707 for reservations) is of a good standard, with comfortable ski-in, ski-out apartments in **Creekside Lodge** and **Powderhorn Lodge**, as well as at the four-star **Inn at Solitude**, which houses the St Bernard's restaurant and a spa. **The Crossings** townhouses are well equipped. **Silver Fork Lodge, t** +1 801 533 9977 in the Wasatch National Forest overlooks **Solitude**.

Söll, Austria

See *Söll and the SkiWelt*, page 46

Tour operators Airtours, Crystal, Direct Ski, First Choice, Inghams, Neilson/Neilson School Groups, Panorama, PGL, Ski Activity, Ski Astons, Ski Freshtracks, Ski Hillwood, Ski Wild, Thomson

Squaw Valley, California, USA

Page 259

Tour operators American Ski Classics, AWWT, Ski All America, Ski the American Dream, Ski Expectations, Ski Independence, Ski Safari, United Vacations

Staffa, Italy

See *Macugnaga*, page 300

Steamboat, Colorado, USA

Page 261

Tour operators American Ski Classics, Crystal, Erna Low, Lotus Supertravel, Made to Measure, Ski Activity, Ski All America, Ski the American Dream, Ski Independence, Ski Safari, Skiworld, Thomson, United Vacations, Virgin

Stoneham, Quebec, Canada

t +1 418 848 2415, *www.ski-stoneham.com*
Altitude 695ft (420m)–2,075ft (632m)
Lifts 8

Tour operators Frontier Ski, Ski All America, Ski the American Dream, SkiBound, Ski Safari

Stoneham is known for having the most extensive night-skiing in Canada. Its 17 illuminated trails are open daily from 3pm to 10pm,

making it popular with local skiers from Québec City on weekday evenings. With 32 trails spread over four mountains, Stoneham is one of the three largest ski areas in the province. It boasts three terrain parks, including a super-pipe with 17ft walls, and a 1km-long boardercross course. **Stoneham Hotel, t** +1 418 848 2411 is the only lodging at the base.

Stowe, Vermont, USA

Page 263

Tour operators American Ski Classics, Crystal, Erna Low, Neilson School Groups, Ski All America, Ski the American Dream, Ski Arrangements, SkiBound, Ski Independence, Ski Safari, Trailfinders, United Vacations, Virgin

Stubaital, Austria

See *Neustift and the Stubaital*, page 29

Stuben, Austria

t +43 (0)5582 399, *www.stuben.com*
Altitude 1407m (4,616ft) –2811m (9,222ft)
Lifts 82 on Arlberg Ski Pass

The village is called after the warm parlour – or *Stube* – of a solitary house on the Arlberg Pass where pilgrims used to shelter in the eighteenth century. Only 32 houses have been added since, and Stuben has just 104 residents and 650 guest beds. Four-star **Hotel Post, t** +43 (0)5582 7616 was where mail-coach drivers changed horses for the steep journey up the pass. With its small collection of five hotels and restaurants, Stuben is an ideal base for exploring St Anton and the Arlberg.

Sun Peaks, BC, Canada

Page 68

Tour operators Alpine Answers Select, AWWT, Crystal, Frontier Ski, Made to Measure, Ski Activity, Ski All America, Ski the American Dream, Ski Freshtracks, Ski Independence, Ski Safari

Sun Valley, Idaho

Page 265

Tour operators AWWT, Ski Activity, Ski All America, Ski Independence, Ski Safari

Sundance, Utah, USA

t +1 801 225 4107, *www.sundanceresort.com*
Altitude 6,100ft (1,859m)–8,250ft (2,515m)
Lifts 4
Tour operators Ski All America, Ski the American Dream, Ski Independence, Ski Safari
This traditional little Utah resort, created by film star Robert Redford, has old boardwalks and an atmosphere of a bygone era. It is a 55-minute drive from Salt Lake City and lift queues are rare. Sundance offers a variety of terrain ranging from wide, open trails to bowl skiing and is recommended for families. Accommodation is in the elegant-rustic **Sundance Cottages, t** +1 801 225 4107.

Sunday River, Maine, USA

t +1 207 824 3000, *www.sundayriver.com*
Altitude 800ft (244m)–3,140ft (957m)
Lifts 18
Tour operators American Ski Classics, Crystal, Ski the American Dream, SkiBound, Ski Independence, Ski Safari, Virgin
Sunday River, six miles north of Bethel in Maine, is one of the largest East Coast resorts. The picturesque state suffers at times from sparse natural snow, but given low temperatures this is of little consequence thanks to the snow-cannon that can cover up to 92 per cent of the total terrain. 'A good selection of runs,' said a reporter. 'The resort offers blacks and double-blacks with steep inclines.' The quality of the skiing compares favourably with that of a medium-sized Alpine resort. Fortunately, Sunday River is far enough from New York not to suffer from the overcrowding to which other Vermont resorts are prone. Sunday River is flanked at one end by the **Grand Summit Hotel, t** +1 207 824 3500 and at the other by the **Jordan Grand Resort, t** +1 207 824 5000. In between lies the base area beneath a ridge of eight peaks offering a variety of terrain. 'Après-ski is non-existent with the village of Bethel a ghost town at night with the exception of a few pokey bars,' complained a reporter.

Les Sybelles, France

See *Le Corbier*, page 288; *St-Jean-d'Arves*, page 312; *St-Sorlin-d'Arves*, page 313 and *La Toussuire*, page 320.

La Tania, France

Page 132
Tour operators Airtours, Alpine Action, Alpine Answers Select, Crystal, Erna Low, First Choice, French Freedom, French Life, Frozen Planet, Lagrange, Le Ski, Momentum, Neilson, Silver Ski, Ski Activity, Ski Amis, Ski Arrangements, Ski Deep, Ski France, Ski Freshtracks, Ski Independence, Ski Power, Skiweekends, Snowline, Thomson

Taos, New Mexico, USA

Page 267
Tour operators AWWT, Ski Activity, Ski the American Dream, Ski Independence

El Tarter, Andorra

See *Soldeu-El Tarter*, page 11
Tour operators Airtours, Direct Ski, First Choice, Panorama

Telfes, Austria

See *Neustift and the Stubaital*, page 29

Telluride, Colorado, USA

Page 269
Tour operators American Ski Classics, AWWT, Crystal, Lotus Supertravel, Ski All America, Ski the American Dream, Ski Independence, Ski Safari, United Vacations

Termas de Chillán, Chile

t +562 233 1313, *www.andesweb.com*
Altitude 1800m (5,900ft)– 2500m (8,200ft)
Lifts 9
Tour operators Andes, Elegant Resorts, Exsus Travel, Momentum, Scott Dunn Latin America, Ski Safari
South America's most exotic resort is set against a backdrop of smoking volcanoes and bubbling sulphur springs, 480km south of Santiago and 80km east of Chillán. The resort boasts some of the country's longest runs, with some 28 groomed trails spread across varied terrain. The excellent off-piste includes the 14km Shangri-La run, and Pirigallo – one of the resort's most celebrated itineraries, which comes complete with fumaroles belching sulphur fumes.
The Gran Hotel, t +562 233 1313 has expensive ski-in ski-out accommodation and a steaming indoor/outdoor swimming-pool fed by pipes

from the volcano. Reporters recommend renting a cabin in the village, which at US$20 per day is cheaper than any of the hotels.

Thierbach, Austria

See *Niederau*, page 30

Thredbo, Australia

t +61 2 6459 4100, *www.thredbo.com.au*
Altitude 1365m (4,478ft)– 2037m (6,683ft)
Lifts 12

Thredbo, in the Kosciuszko National Park of New South Wales, is Australia's leading resort. It was founded in the early 1950s by Austrian and Czech immigrants who helped build the Snowy Mountain hydroelectric scheme. Aussies make either a six-hour drive from Sydney or the two-and-a-half-hour journey by road from Canberra, but you can also fly to Cooma, 80km away.

The lifts serve some of the best intermediate terrain in the country and this is consequently Australia's nearest equivalent to a European ski resort – with the addition of gum trees. Four quads among the dozen lifts whisk skiers and boarders above the tree-line. From here you progress to the summit on T-bars, which are better suited to the altitude's windier conditions. Because the snow record is unpredictable, the resort has invested heavily in snowmaking, and boasts the largest system in the southern hemisphere.

Hotels include **The Alpenhorn, t** +61 (0)2 6457 6223, **Black Bear Inn, t** +61 (0)2 6457 6216, **Candlelight Lodge, t** +61 (0)2 6457 6049, **High Country Mountain Resort, t** +61 (0)2 6456 2511, and **Thredbo Alpine Hotel, t** +61 (0)2 6459 4100, which has a new-look pub called **The Pub**. Nearby **Crackenback Farm, t** +61 (0)2 6456 2198 is a four-star country guesthouse. **Eagle's Nest**, at the top of the Kosciuszko Express, is the highest mountain restaurant in Australia and sometimes opens for sunset dinners. Reporters rated the resort 'astonishingly expensive for what it offers'.

La Thuile, Italy

Page 180

Tour operators Alpine Answers Select, Crystal, Inghams, Interski, Momentum, Neilson, Ski Arrangements, Thomson

Thyon-Les Collons, Switzerland

t +41 (0)27 281 27 27, *www.thyon-region.ch*
Altitude 1500m (4,920ft)–3330m (10,925ft)
Lifts 89 in Four Valleys

The unexpected piste-side community is situated at the top of the Mayen-de-l'Ours gondola. It is little more than a collection of apartment blocks and a hotel linked into the Four Valleys ski area, of which Verbier is the major resort.

Tignes, France

Page 133

Tour operators Alpine Answers Select, Alpine Elements, Chalet Iguana, Club Med, Corporate Ski Company, Crystal, Direct Ski, Erna Low, Esprit, First Choice, French Life, Frozen Planet, Inghams, Interhome, Lagrange, Made to Measure, Mark Warner, Momentum, Neilson, On The Piste, Ski Activity, Ski Amis, Ski Arrangements, SkiBound, Ski Expectations, Ski France, Ski Freshtracks, Ski Independence, Ski Olympic, Ski Solutions, Ski Supreme, Skitopia, Ski Val, Skiworld, Snowstar, Thomson, Total Ski, Wasteland, White Roc Weekends

Torgon, Switzerland

t +41 (0)24 481 3131, *www.torgon.ch*
Altitude 1100m (3,608ft)–2350m (7,708ft)
Lifts 207 in Portes du Soleil
Tour operator Interhome

Torgon is one of the least-visited resorts of the Portes du Soleil, a small purpose-built Swiss outpost of 1960s A-frame buildings on a sunny balcony above the Rhône and close to Lac Léman. It is reached on skis either from Châtel or from La Chapelle d'Abondance. Accommodation is in modest apartments. The resort is best-suited to families looking for a quiet off-beat holiday spot with no other distractions apart from skiing.

La Toussuire, France

t +33 (0)4 79 83 06 06, *www.la-toussuire.com*
Altitude 1800m (5,905ft)–2620m (8,596ft)
Lifts 75

Tour operators Erna Low, French Life, Interhome, Lagrange

Village in the 310km Les Sybelles ski area in the Maurienne Valley, linked to St-Jean, Le Corbier and St-Sorlin.

Trafoi, Italy

t +39 0473 613015, *www.inmontagna. net/trafoi.htm*
Altitude 1570m (5,151ft)–2550m (8,366ft)
Lifts 74 in area
Little Trafoi in the South Tyrol has only four lifts and 15km of piste but plenty of other skiing within a short drive of the village and included in the same lift pass. The resort is part of the Ortler Skiarena, with 13 unconnected resorts covered by one lift pass. There is a total 260km of piste in the area. Three-star **Hotel Madatsch** t +39 0473 611767 at Trafoi is a comfortable spot in which to base yourself.

Treble Cone, New Zealand

See *Wanaka (Cardona and Treble Cone)*, page 325

Tremblant, Québec, Canada

Page 70
Tour operators Crystal, Elegant Resorts, Equity/Rocket Ski, Erna Low, Frontier Ski, Inghams, Lotus Supertravel, Neilson/Neilson School Groups, Ski All America, Ski the American Dream, SkiBound, Ski Independence, Ski Safari, Ski Wild, Thomson, Trailfinders, United Vacations, Virgin

The Trois Vallées, France

See *Brides-les-Bains*, page 96; *Courchevel*, page 111; *Les Menuires*, page 113; *Méribel*, page 128; *St-Martin-de-Belleville*, page 132; *La Tania*, page 132; *Val Thorens*, page 141

Trysil, Norway

t +47 624 51000, *www.trysil.com*
Altitude 600m (1,969ft)–1132m (3,714ft)
Lifts 25
Tour operators Alpine Tracks, Neilson School Groups
Norway's largest ski area is ideal for families. 'An awesome resort,' said reporters, 'Waiting times at lifts were very small.' Trysil is situated a two-and-a-half-hour drive from Oslo and has some of the most reliable snow-cover in Norway. The village is not picturesque compared to Alpine resorts and does not offer much après-ski. Its pistes spread across the wooded slopes of Trysilfjellet and run 75 is rated for adventurous skiers and boarders. Instruction is highly rated and teachers are said to speak good English.

The excellent accommodation is in hotels, apartments, and the many new *hyttes* (cabins). **Trysilfjell Aparthotel,** t +47 624 52350 is on the slopes. **Norlandia Trysil Hotel,** t +47 624 50833 and **Trysil-Knut,** t +47 624 48000 are based in the old village of Trysil, 2km away from the slopes. Reporters recommend avoiding staying in the Fageråsen area as the slopes there are 'quite flat'.

Turoa, New Zealand

See *Mount Ruapehu*, page 303

Tux im Zillertal, Austria

t +43 (0)5287 8506, *www.tux.at*
Altitude 1500m (4,920ft)–3250m (10,663ft)
Lifts 21 on Hintertux Glacier
Tux im Zillertal is made up of five villages in the Tuxer valley, the main one of which is Hintertux. It boasts the steepest glacier skiing in Austria and is usually open 365 days a year (20km of the piste is open all summer). It also offers the most advanced skiing and snowboarding on the otherwise low-altitude Zillertal Superskipass.
The glacier is prone to overcrowding in winter when conditions are poor elsewhere, but hotel guests receive priority in the lift queue. Nowhere on the glacier is the skiing particularly challenging, with most runs groomed and free of bumps. However, the pistes are considered to be the best year-round downhill training ground in Europe, and national teams spend much of their summer here.
The handful of modern, four-star hotels in Hintertux includes **Hotel Bergfried,** t +43 (0)5287 87239, which has a swimming-pool surrounded by rock walls.

Vail, Colorado, USA

Page 271
Tour operators American Ski Classics, Alpine Answers Select, Alpine Tracks, AWWT, Carrier, Crystal, Elegant Resorts, Erna Low, Inghams, Lotus Supertravel, Made to Measure, Momentum, Neilson, Rocky Mountain Adventures, Seasons in Style, Ski Activity, Ski All America, Ski the American Dream, Ski Expectations, Ski Freshtracks, Ski Independence, Ski Safari, Ski Solutions, Ski Wild, Skiworld, Thomson, Trailfinders, United Vacations, Virgin

Val Cenis, France
t +33 (0)4 79 05 23 66, *www.valcenis.com*
Altitude 1400m (4,593ft)–2800m (9,186ft)
Lifts 22
Tour operators AWWT, Erna Low, Lagrange,
MGS Ski, Peak Retreats, Snowcoach
The old unspoilt villages of Lanslebourg and
Lanslevillard in the Haute Maurienne join
together to form the resort of Val Cenis. The
villages have a traditional community ambience. The skiing is for all standards,
particularly beginners to intermediates. The
eight two-star hotels include **La Vieille Poste**,
t +33 (0)4 79 05 93 47 and **Le Val Cenis**, t +33
(0)4 79 05 80 31.

Val di Fassa, Italy
See *Canazei*, page 146

Val di Fiemme, Italy
See *Cavalese*, page 151
Tour operators Neilson School Groups,
Ramblers, Waymark

Val d'Isère, France
Page 136
Tour operators Airtours, Alpine Answers
Select, Alpine Weekends, Club Med,
Corporate Ski Company, Crystal, Descent
International, Direct Ski, Elegant Resorts,
Erna Low, Esprit, Flexiski, Finlay's, First
Choice, French Freedom, French Life, Frozen
Planet, Inghams, Interhome, Lagrange, Le Ski,
Lotus Supertravel, Made to Measure, Mark
Warner, Momentum, Mountain Leap,
Neilson, On The Piste, Oxford Ski Company,
Scott Dunn Ski, Silver Ski, Simply Ski, Ski
Activity, Ski Amis, Ski Arrangements,
SkiBound, Ski Expectations, Ski France, Ski
Freshtracks, Ski Independence, Ski Olympic,
Ski Solutions, Ski Supreme, Ski Val, Ski
Weekend, Skiworld, Snowline, Thomson,
Total Ski, Val d'Isère à la Carte, VIP,
Wasteland, White Roc Weekends, YSE

Val d'Ultimo, Italy
See *Monte San Vigilio*, page 302

Val Fiscalina, Italy
See *Alta Pusteria*, page 278

Valfréjus, France
t +33 (0)4 79 05 33 83, *www.valfrejus.com*

Altitude 1550m (5,085ft)–2737m (8,980ft)
Lifts 12
Tour operators Erna Low, Lagrange, Peak
Retreats
The modern resort of Valfréjus is built around
the old wood-and-stone hamlet of Charmaix
above the town of Modane. The skiing is
mainly above the treeline on steep and sometimes mogulled slopes. **Hotel Club MMV Le
Valfréjus**, t +33 (0)4 92 12 62 12 is a Savoyard-
style three-star in the centre of the village,
while **Le Grand Vallon**, t +33 (0)4 79 05 08 07 is
a two-star with good views.

Valle Nevado, Chile
t +56 2 206 0027, *www.vallenevado.com*
Altitude 2860m (9,383ft)–3670m (12,040ft)
Lifts 11
Tour operators Andes, Crystal, Exsus Travel,
Lotus Supertravel, Momentum, Scott Dunn
Latin America, Ski Safari
Valle Nevado was constructed by the French in
the 1980s and is situated just 64km from
Santiago, making it the closest resort to a
capital city. The resort is linked by lift to the
resorts of La Parva and El Colorado to create a
small-sized version of an Alpine ski circuit. A
variety of slopes offer mainly intermediate
skiing, and experienced skiers and riders can
also take advantage of some of the world's
best-value heli-skiing which goes up to a
breathtaking 5000m. Reporters rated the
pistes 'pretty well maintained'.
The most comfortable accommodation is in
Hotel Valle Nevado. The slightly cheaper
options are **La Puerta del Sol** and **Tres Puntas**
(bookings advisable through tour operators).
La Parva is an enclave of smart holiday homes
for wealthy city dwellers, while **El Colorado** is a
purpose-built base for the adjoining old
village of Farellones. Due to the extremely
high altitude, visitors arriving from sea level
may feel some discomfort for the first few
days and are advised to drink plenty of water
and refrain from drinking alcohol.

Vallnord, Andorra
See *Pal-Arinsal* page 8

Valloire, France
t +33 (0)4 79 59 03 96, *www.valloire.net*
Altitude 1430m (4,690ft)–2600m (8,528ft)
Lifts 33

Tour operators Crystal, Erna Low, Ski France, French Life, Lagrange, Peak Retreats, SkiBound, Ski Independence, Thomson
The large and attractive village of Valloire is set in an isolated bowl above the Maurienne Valley. It is still very much a traditional French farming community without a lot of nightlife. The skiing, linked to Valmeinier, is divided between three areas on adjacent mountains accessed by two gondolas a few minutes' walk from the village centre. The ski area is mainly intermediate with some long runs. 'If you want to learn, go somewhere else,' warned a snowboarder; 'the pistes are better suited to skiing than boarding, as even the green runs are very narrow.' Accommodation includes three-stars **Les Oursons**, t +33 (0)4 79 59 01 37 with a swimming-pool, **Grand Hotel de Valloire et du Galibier**, t +33 (0)4 79 59 00 95 opposite the lifts, **Hotel Rapin**, t +33 (0)4 79 59 06 02 which contains gastronomic restaurant **Le Matafan**, and a wide range of chalets and apartments.

Valmeinier, France

t +33 (0)4 79 59 53 69, *www.valmeinier.com*
Altitude 1430m (4,690ft)–2600m (8,528ft)
Lifts 33
Tour operators Crystal, Erna Low, French Freedom, French Life, Lagrange, Neilson School Groups, On The Piste, Ski Independence, Snowcoach, Thomson
The skiing is linked to that of Valloire in the Maurienne Valley (see above). 'Not really suitable for complete beginners, and the attitude of the ESF is cavalier to say the least', complained a reporter. Accommodation choices include **Auberge Le Grand Fourchon**, t +33 (0)4 79 59 21 01, **Hotel L'Aigle**, t +33 (0)4 79 59 24 31 with an outdoor hot tub, and **Hotel Club Les Carrettes**, t +33 (0)4 79 59 25 45 which provides full-board, a mini-club and evening entertainment.

Valmorel, France

Page 140
Tour operators Crystal, Erna Low, French Life, Neilson/Neilson School Groups, Ski Amis, Ski Independence, Ski Supreme, Thomson

Val Senales (Schnalstal), Italy

t +39 0473 662171, *www.schnalstal.com*

Altitude 2005m (6,578ft)–3250m (10,663ft)
Lifts 12
The principal destination in the Ortler Skiarena, with 13 unconnected resorts all covered by one lift pass. A total 260km of prepared piste is served by eight cableways and 66 chair- and drag-lifts. This is the main village of the scenic Vinschgau and base for one of Europe's largest year-round ski areas with guaranteed snow, six lifts in summer at the top of the Ghiacciai cable-car and another five in winter. **Berghotel Grawand**, t +39 0473 662118, located at 3212m on the glacier, is a simple two-star hotel that houses the only on-mountain eatery and a small museum dedicated to Ötzi, the Neolithic man found preserved in the ice above the ski area in 1991. Other hotels include three-star **Hotel Schwarzer Adler**, t +39 0473 669652, which has been in the same family for four generations.

Val Thorens, France

Page 141
Tour operators Airtours, Alpine Elements, Club Med, Crystal, Erna Low, First Choice, French Freedom, French Life, Frozen Planet, Inghams, Interhome, Lagrange, Made to Measure, Momentum, Neilson, Ski Activity, Ski Amis, Ski Arrangements, Ski Expectations, Ski France, Ski Freshtracks, Ski Independence, Ski Solutions, Ski Supreme, Skiworld, Thomson, Total Ski, Wasteland

Valtournenche, Italy

t +39 0166 92055, *www.cervinia.it*
Altitude 1524m (5,000ft)–3883m (12,740ft)
Lifts 59 with Zermatt
The old village is 9km by road from Cervinia, but linked into the same ski area. Valtournenche provides good-value accommodation in a genuine village ambience unspoilt by tourism. **Albergo Grandes Murailles**, t +39 0166 932956 is a small hotel with lots of atmosphere.

Vars 1850, France

t +33 (0)4 92 46 51 31, *www.vars-ski.com*
Altitude 1850m (6,068ft)–2750m (9,020ft)
Lifts 57 with Risoul
Tour operators Erna Low, Interhome, Lagrange, Neilson School Groups, Tops, Wasteland

Vars 1850 is larger, less attractive and not as welcoming to the non-French as neighbouring Risoul 1850. The old village is linked by drag-lift to the modern station, but you have to walk across town to reach the Vars gondola and chair to Risoul 1850. Beginners can learn in the village where there are two drags and some gentle green runs. Intermediates have a good choice of runs above and below the treeline, and some wide-open bowl skiing.

Vaujany, France
Page 143
Tour operators Erna Low, Lagrange, Peak Retreats, Ski Independence, Ski Peak

Vent, Austria
t +43 (0)5254 8193, *www.vent.at*
Altitude 1900m (6,234ft)–2680m (8,793ft)
Lifts 4
The small village has just 900 beds but offers some good off-piste skiing. The seven hotels include **Familyhotel Vent, t** +43 (0)5254 8102, which houses a kindergarten. A free ski-bus links with Sölden and Obergurgl.

Verbier, Switzerland
Page 214
Tour operators Alpine Answers Select, Corporate Ski Company, Crystal, Descent International, Erna Low, First Choice, Flexiski, Inghams, Interhome, Kaluma, Lotus Supertravel, Made to Measure, Momentum, Mountain Leap, Oxford Ski Company, Peak Ski, The Powder Co, Simply Ski, Ski Activity, Ski Expectations, Ski Freshtracks, Ski Independence, Ski Solutions, Ski Verbier, Ski Weekend, Ski with Julia, Skiworld, Swiss Travel Service, Thomson, Total Ski, White Roc Weekends

Veysonnaz, Switzerland
t +41 (0)27 207 1053, *www.veysonnaz.ch*
Altitude 1400m (4,593ft)–3330m (10,925ft)
Lifts 89 in Four Valleys
This resort, used as a training base by the Swiss national team, is reached by a winding 13km mountain road from Sion. It is part of the 412km Four Valleys circuit and provides a useful back-door into the steeps of Mont Fort. A new eight-person gondola brings you up to the mid-station and Veysonnaz's own consid-

erable ski area can also be accessed from a second base area 3km away by road at Mayen-de-l'Ours. A bus connects the two. **Hotel Magrappé, t** +41 (0)27 207 1817 is comfortable and friendly.

Villard-de-Lans, France
t +33 (0)4 76 95 10 38, *www.ot-villard-de-lans.fr*
Altitude 1160m (3,806ft)–2170m (7,119ft)
Lifts 29
Tour operators AWWT, Interhome, Lagrange
This rural French community attracts weekend skiers from nearby Grenoble rather than an international clientele. The pistes, best suited to beginners and low intermediates, are at Côte 2000 – a rather unappealing *station de ski* situated a 2km bus ride from the resort. Together with the resort of Corrençon, Villard-de-Lans is also a popular venue for cross-country skiing. Recommended hotels include three-star **Le Christiania, t** +33 (0)4 76 95 12 51, **Le Dauphin, t** +33 (0)4 76 95 95 25) and two-star **Les Bruyères, t** +33 (0)4 76 95 11 83.

Villard-Reculas, France
t +33 (0)4 76 80 45 69, *www.villard-reculas.com*
Altitude 1500m (4,921ft)–3330m (10,922ft)
Lifts 84 in area
Tour operator La Source
This isolated farming hamlet is perched on the mountainside below Alpe d'Huez and above the valley town of Bourg-en-Oisans. A quad chair-lift links it to the top of Signal de L'Homme and the rest of the large Alpe d'Huez circuit, which includes Vaujany, Auris and Oz-en-Oisans. Accommodation is at **Hotel Beaux Monts, t** +33 (0)4 76 80 43 14 and in a few converted barns.

Villaroger, France
See *Les Arcs*, page 86
Tour operator Optimum Ski

Villars, Switzerland
Page 217
Tour operators Club Med, Corporate Ski Company, Crystal, Erna Low, Inghams, Interhome, Kuoni, Made to Measure, Momentum, Original Travel, OTP, PGL, Ski Independence, Ski Solutions, Ski Weekend, Swiss Travel Service, Switzerland Travel Centre (Plus Travel), Thomson

Vorderlansersbach, Austria
Small village up the valley from Mayrhofen.

Voss, Norway
t +47 565 20800, www.visitvoss.no
Altitude 91m (300ft)–945m (3,100ft)
Lifts 9
Tour operators Alpine Tracks, Crystal, Inghams, Neilson School Groups
Despite its low altitude, Voss provides a reasonable ski area for beginners and lower intermediates, but it can become busy at weekends. 'Extremely quiet slopes and very well groomed,' enthused a reporter; 'The mountain is deserted during the week,' said another. But 'On the minus side, very poor mountain restaurants – cheeseburgers pall a little after six days and there is no beer on the mountain'. For more experienced skiers and boarders, the resort has three black runs and some off-piste. Cross-country skiers will not be disappointed with 60km of prepared loipe close to the centre, with more on offer in the valleys around the area. Hotel Fleischer, t +47 565 20500 is traditional.

Wagrain, Austria
Page 48

Waidring, Austria
t +43 (0)5353 5242, www.tiscover.com/waidring
Altitude 780m (2,558ft)–1860m (6,102ft)
Lifts 8
Tour operators Thomson, Tyrolean Adventures
This unspoilt village is less under 20km away from St Johann in Tyrol and is situated in the same snow pocket as Fieberbrunn. The peaceful resort is known for its family skiing, with convenient nursery slopes in the village centre. The main skiing is at Steinplatte, 4km from the village and ideal for beginners and intermediates. Hotel Waidringerhof, t +43 (0)5353 5228 has a swimming-pool, and the central Hotel Tiroler Adler, t +43 (0)5353 5311 is also rated.

Wanaka (Cardrona and Treble Cone), New Zealand
Cardrona t +64 (0)3 443 8651
Treble Cone t +64 (0)3 443 7443
www.cardrona.com, www.lakewanaka.co.nz, www.treblecone.co.nz
Altitude Cardrona 1670m (5,479ft)–2060m (6,759ft), Treble Cone 1200m (3,936ft)–1860m (6,102ft)
Lifts 9 in Cardona and Treble Cone
Wanaka is an alternative bed-base to Queenstown from which to explore the main South Island skiing. From here, the ski areas of Cardrona and Treble Cone, as well as the Waiorau Nordic Ski Area and the Wanaka Snow Park (New Zealand's first whole-mountain terrain park) are all within a 30-minute drive. The road between Queenstown and Wanaka is sealed, but reporters warn it is 'a test of nerves', making the other Southern Lakelands resorts of Coronet Peak and The Remarkables even more accessible.
Cardrona's ski field is well suited to beginners and intermediates with several wide and gentle slopes. It is known for its dry snow and reliable season, which runs from late June until early October. The area boasts the country's largest terrain park and four half-pipes.
Wanaka is also the gateway to Treble Cone, with 'scenery that has to be seen to be believed'. One of the country's top resorts, it boasts New Zealand's first six-seater chair. Advanced skiers – and snowboarders in particular – are well catered for but the area is quite limited for beginners. The area's best off-piste is found by hiking 20 minutes to the summit. There is good heli-skiing nearby in the Harris Mountains.

Wengen, Switzerland
Page 219
Tour operators Club Med, Crystal, Inghams, Interhome, Kuoni, Made to Measure, Momentum, Oak Hall, Ski Expectations, Ski Freshtracks, Ski Solutions, Swiss Travel Service, Switzerland Travel Centre (Plus Travel), Thomson

Westendorf, Austria
Page 50
Tour operators Inghams, Interhome, Thomson

Whakapapa, New Zealand
See Mount Ruapehu, page 303

Whistler, BC, Canada
Page 72

Tour operators Alpine Answers Select, American Ski Classics, AWWT, Carrier, Crystal, Elegant Resorts, Equity/Rocket Ski, Erna Low, First Choice, Frontier Ski, Frozen Planet, Inghams, Lotus Supertravel, Made to Measure, Momentum, Neilson, Rocky Mountain Adventures, Seasons in Style, Ski Activity, Ski All America, Ski Freshtracks, Ski Safari, Ski the American Dream, Ski Arrangements, SkiBound, Ski Expectations, Ski Independence, Ski Miquel, Ski Solutions, Ski Wild, Skiworld, Solo's, Thomson, Total Ski, Trailfinders, United Vacations, Virgin

Whitewater, BC, Canada

t +1 250 354 4944, www.skiwhitewater.com, www.nelsonbc.ca
Altitude 5,400ft (1646m)–6,700ft (2042m)
Lifts 3
Tour Operators Frontier Ski, Ski Safari
Whitewater is a pleasant little ski area close to the atmospheric Victorian town of Nelson. Its two lifts give direct access to challenging trails through the trees as well as some great – but avalanche-prone – off-piste. Some 20 per cent of the terrain is made up of easy runs, while the remainder is divided equally between intermediate and advanced skiing.
But the real attraction is Nelson. The lakeside town, close to the Montana border, was the point of arrival in Canada for hundreds of hippies fleeing the draft during the Vietnam War. Some of them travelled no further. **Inn the Garden, t** +1 250 352 3226 is a recommended B&B.

Wildschönau, Austria

See *Niederau*, page 30

Winter Park, Colorado, USA

Page 275
Tour operators American Ski Classics, AWWT, Crystal, Equity/Rocket Ski, Erna Low, Lotus Supertravel, Neilson/Neilson School Groups, Ski Activity, Ski All America, Ski the American Dream, SkiBound, Skiworld, Ski Independence, Thomson, United Vacations, Virgin

Wirl, Austria

See *Galtür*, page 291

Yabuli, China

t +86 451 345 5088, www.yabuliskiresort.com
Altitude 1374m (4,508ft)–1944m (6,378ft)
Lifts 9
Yabuli is China's most important resort. It was initially developed at a cost of $210m, and was the venue for the 1996 Asian Winter Games. Situated 194km north-west of the city of Harbin, the resort is open 120 days a year and is attempting to double its present ski terrain. However, development is being held back by an apparent lack of agreement between the government and the ten Chinese investors. The longest run is 5km and there is a vertical drop of 600m. Yabuli is also the location for a separate ski area used until now for competitions and by army skiers. There is a plan to link the two areas to create China's most extensive ski area. The hotel of choice is four-star **Windmill Villa, t** +86 451 345 5168 close to the slopes.

Yellowstone Club, Montana, USA

t +1 406 995 4900,
www.theyellowstoneclub.com
Altitude 7160ft (2182m)–9,860ft (3005m)
Lifts 13
The world's only private ski resort covers an area of 6,000 acres of perfectly manicured piste – that's an area bigger than Breckenridge – but you'll never see more than 30 people on the slopes on a busy day. Of the total 12 lifts, 11 are high-speed covered chairs, the pistes are so smooth that you never see a pebble or a mogul. The ski area is supplemented by neighbouring Big Sky, with its 11 lifts and 150 runs that can be skied by YC members but not vice versa.
To join you have to be proposed by another member. Then you have to buy property here, with prices starting at $795,000. Three lodges – Rainbow, Warren Miller and Timberline – house restaurants, bars, and a ski shop. Some 20 lovely little log cabins are available to members' friends and to prospective buyers.

Zakopane, Poland

t +48 18 2020400, www.zakopane.pl
Altitude 838m (2,749ft)–2301m (7,549ft)
Lifts 16
Tour operators Interhome, Poltours

Skiing has been popular in Zakopane for over a hundred years. The earliest international ski competition took place here in 1910. The resort offers plenty of scope, from beginner runs to the more difficult. The best skiing can usually be found in the Kasprowy Wierch area.

Zao, Japan

t +44 (0)20 7734 6870, *www.zao-spa.or.jp, www.snowjapan.com*
Altitude 780m (2,599ft)–1736m (5,696ft)
Lifts 42
Zao, in the Yamagata Prefecture, retains its spa-town charm in spite of being one of the biggest resorts in Japan. It is located two and a half hours from Tokyo by *shinkansen* (bullet train), and its slopes are reached by ancient cable-car. They are famous throughout the country because of a huge forest of 'snow-ghosts' – fir trees that become encrusted with hoar frost and snow to form a vast collection of monster shapes. Some 90 per cent of this large ski area is suited to beginners and inter-mediates, and the resort has little to entice advanced skiers. Accommodation is mainly in traditional *ryokan* inns, which include the recommended **Zao Onsen Eko**, t +23 6949533.

Zauchensee, Austria

See *Wagrain and the Salzburger Sportwelt Amadé*, page 48
Tour operators Ski Hillwood, Sloping Off

Zell am See, Austria

See *Zell am See and Kaprun*, page 53
Tour operators Airtours, Club Europe, Crystal, Direct Ski, Erna Low, First Choice, Inghams, Interhome, Neilson/Neilson School Groups, PGL, Ski Activity, Ski Astons, SkiBound, Ski Freshtracks, Ski Wild, Snowscape, Thomson

Zell am Ziller, Austria

t +43 (0)5282 22810, *www.zell.at*
Altitude 1250m (4,101ft)–2505m (8,219ft)
Lifts 55 in area
Tour operators Equity/Rocket Ski, Neilson School Groups, PGL, Ski Astons, Sloping Off
Zell am Ziller is the second most substantial valley resort in the Zillertal area after Mayrhofen. The two areas, Kreuzjoch or Gerlosstein, are set away from the town. Kreuzjoch is reached by swift, eight-person

gondola, and Gerlosstein has twin cable-cars. There is an influx of visitors from Germany each weekend. Four-star **Sport und Wellnesshotel Theresa**, t +43 (0)5282 22860 and three-star **Hotel Englhof**, t +43 (0)5282 3134 are rated.

Zermatt, Switzerland

Page 222
Tour operators Alpine Answers Select, Corporate Ski Company, Crystal, Descent International, Elegant Resorts, Frozen Planet, Inghams, Interhome, Kuoni, Lotus Supertravel, Made to Measure, Momentum, Oak Hall, OTP, Powder Byrne, Scott Dunn Ski, Seasons in Style, Simply Ski, Ski Expectations, Ski Freshtracks, Ski Independence, Ski Solutions, Swiss Travel Service, Switzerland Travel Centre (Plus Travel), Thomson, Total Ski, White Roc Weekends, Zermatt Holidays

Zillertal 3000, Austria

See *Mayrhofen*, page 26

Zug, Austria

See *Lech and Zürs*, page 23

Zürs, Austria

See *Lech and Zürs*, page 23
Tour operators Alpine Answers Select, Corporate Ski Company, Crystal, Elegant Resorts, Inghams, Kaluma, Made to Measure, Momentum, Powder Byrne, Seasons in Style

Directory

Tour Operators

The 200 ski and board operators listed below offer inclusive ski and board holiday packages, but you should be aware that not all of them are fully bonded. Before parting with any money it makes sense to discover what would happen in the event of a company going bust before you travel or while you are abroad. One extra safeguard, which may entitle you to a refund in such an event, is to pay by credit card direct to the company rather than to a travel agent.

Airtours Ski & Snowboard: Holiday House, Sandbrook Park, Sandbrook Way, Rochdale OL11 1SA
t +44 (0)870 241 8964,
www.airtours.co.uk, www.mytravel.com
Mass-market UK subsidiary of Mytravel, with hotel, chalet and apartment holidays in Andorra, Austria, Bulgaria, Canada, France, Italy and Romania
Albus Travel: Hill Farm Barn, Angel Hill, East Stonham, Stowmarket IP14 5DP
t +44 (0)1449 711 952,
www.albustravel.com
Holidays with flights to four chalets in Nasserein near St Anton, Austria
Alp Leisure: La Nouvaz, 73120 Courchevel, France
t +33 (0)479 00 59 42, *ww.alpleisure.com*
Tailor-made luxury holidays to privately owned chalets in Méribel and Courchevel 1850. Chalets available all year round
Alpine Action: Marine Suite, The Old Town Hall, Southwick BN42 4AX
t +44 (0)1273 597 940,
www.alpineaction.co.uk
Small family-run operator with chalets in Méribel and La Tania
Alpine Answers Select: The Business Village, 3–9 Broomhill Road, London SW18 4JQ
t +44 (0)208 871 4656,
www.alpineanswers.co.uk

Well-established tailor-made arm of specialist ski travel agency
Alpine Elements: Lyon House, 160–166 Borough High Street, London SE1 1JR
t +44 (0)8700 111 360,
www.alpineelements.co.uk
Luxury and standard catered ski and snowboard chalet holidays in France
Alpine Escapes: 4 Clayfarm Road, New Eltham, London SE9 3PS **t** +33 (0)6161 22880, *www.alpine-escapes.com* Small family-run company with two chalets in Morzine available all year round
Alpine Tours: The Ardmour Group, Berkshire College, Burchetts Green, Berks SL6 6QR
t +44 (0)1628 826 699,
sales@alpinetours.co.uk
Long-established schools and groups operator to Austria, Italy, Switzerland and Spain
Alpine Tracks: 40 High Street, Menai Bridge, Anglesey LL59 5EF
t +44 (0)1248 717 440,
www.alpine-tracks.com
Chalet and hotel holidays in Champoluc, Lech, Morzine, Breckenridge, and Vail
Alpine Weekends: 95 Dora Road, London SW19 7JT
t +44 (0)20 8944 9762,
www.alpineweekends.com
Bespoke breaks in France, Italy and Switzerland, with off-piste, heli-skiing and ski-touring
Altitude Holidays: Suite 787, 2 Old Brompton Road, London SW7 3DQ
t +44 (0)870 870 7669,
www.altitudeholidays.com
Chalets and apartments, catered and self-catered in Flaine, Les Carroz, Samoëns and Morillon
American Ski Classics: PO Box 250, Twickenham, TW1 2XX
t +44 (0)20 8392 6660,
www.americanskiclassics.com
Hotels and apartments in over 20 resorts in North America

Andes: 37A St Andrews Street, Castle Douglas DG7 1EN
t +44 (0)1556 503 929,
www.andes.org.uk
South American skiing and climbing specialist, with holidays and ski-tours to Chile and Argentina

AWWT: 1 Lonsdale Gardens, Tunbridge Wells TN1 1NU
t +44 (0)1892 511 894,
www.awwt.co.uk
Tailor-made holidays to North America

Balkan Holidays: Sofia House, 19 Conduit Street, London W1S 2BH
t +44 (0) 845 130 1114,
www.balkanholidays.co.uk
Mass-market operator to Bulgaria, Slovenia, Serbia and Romania

Balkan Tours: 61 Ann Street, Belfast BT1 4EE
t +44 (0)28 9024 6795,
www.balkan.co.uk
Long-established holiday specialist to Bulgaria and Romania, with direct flights from Belfast and Dublin

Barelli Ski: 19 Sefton Park Road, St Andrew's, Bristol BS7 9AN
t +44 (0)870 220 1500,
www.barelliski.co.uk
Accommodation-only holidays to 20 chalets in Chamonix, Les Houches and Champagny-en-Vanoise

Barwell Leisure: The Coach House, Elm Road, Chessington, KT9 1AW
t +44 (0)20 8786 3071,
www.barwell.co.uk
Specialist to Humber Valley Resort in Newfoundland

Belvedere Chalets: Peach House, Gangbridge Lane, St Mary Bourne SP11 6EW
t +44 (0)1264 738 257,
www.belvedereproperties.net
Small specialist platinum disc operator with top-of-the-market catered chalets in Méribel

Bigfoot Travel: 186 Greys Road, Henley-on-Thames, Oxon RG9 1QU

t +44 (0)870 300 5874,
www.bigfoot-winters.com
Hotels, chalets and apartments in the Chamonix Valley

Board and Lodge: 18c Belsize Grove, London NW3 4UN
t +44 (0)20 7419 0722,
www.boardnlodge.com
Snowboarding holidays in Argentière, Chamonix and Saalbach

Bonne Neige Ski Holidays: PO Box 42, Crewe CW2 7FH
t +44 (0)1270 256 966,
www.bonne-neige-ski.com
Small independent tour operator, with two luxury chalets and hotel accommodation in Méribel

Borderline: Les Sorbiers, 65120 Barèges, France
t + 33 (0)562 92 68 95,
www.borderlinehols.com
Well-established operator with own hotel and self-catering properties in Barèges in the French Pyrenees

Canterbury Travel: 42 High Street, Northwood HA6 1BL
t +44 (0)1923 822 388,
www.laplandmagic.com
Lapland specialist with holidays to Luosto in Finland

Carrier North America: Church Street, Wilmslow SK9 1AX
t +44 (0)1625 547 040, *www.carrier.co.uk*
Luxury tailor-made holidays in Aspen, Beaver Creek, Jackson Hole, Vail, Québec and Whistler

Chalet Chocolat: Glebe Cottage, Philleigh, Truro TR2 5NB
t +44 (0)1872 580 814,
www.chalet-chocolat.co.uk
Luxury catered chalet in Morzine

The Chalet Company: Résidence Sabaudia, Les Bois Venants, 74110 Morzine, France
t +44 (0)871 717 4208,
www.thechaletco.com
Accommodation-only holidays in eight luxury catered chalets in Morzine

Chalet Iguana: Unit 8, 151 The High Street,
Southampton SO14 2DS
t +44 (0)800 849 3011,
www.chaletiguana.com
Luxury catered chalet in Tignes

Chalet Snowboard: 31 Aldworth Avenue,
Wantage OX12 7EJ
t +44 (0)870 800 4020,
www.chaletsnowboard.com.uk
Specialist snowboard holidays and
freestyle camps based in company's
own chalets in Morzine and Avoriaz.
Summer camps in Les Deux Alpes

Les Chalets de St Martin: Chalet Rousette,
73440 St-Martin-de-Belleville, France
t +33 (0)479 08 91 77,
www.leschalets.co.uk
Catered chalet in St-Martin-de-Belleville

Challenge Activ: Chalet Flori, L'Ele,
Montriond 74110, France
t +44 (0)871 717 4113,
www.challenge-activ.com
Activity holiday specialist with catered
chalet in Morzine

Classic Ski: Ober Road,
Brockenhurst SO42 7ST
t +44 (0)1590 623 400,
www.classicski.co.uk
Established operator with holidays in
the French Alps including tuition for
singles and couples over 50yrs, weekday
flights and flexible-length stays

Club Europe: Fairway House, 53
Dartmouth Road, London SE23 3HN
t +44 (0)800 496 4996,
www.club-europe.co.uk
Schools operator with ski programmes
in Austria, France and Italy

Club Med: 1st Floor, Gemini House,
10–18 Putney Hill, London SW15 6AA
t +44 (0)845 367 6767,
www.clubmed.co.uk
Club villages in France, Switzerland,
Italy, Japan and the USA. Flights, transfers, full-board accommodation, ski pass,
tuition, après-ski entertainment and
insurance all included in the price, as
well as childcare in many resorts

Club Pavilion/Concept Holidays:
The Mezzanine, 56 Landsdowne Place,
Hove BN3 1FG
t +44 (0)870 241 0427,
www.conceptholidays.co.uk
Specialists in low-cost ski and weekend
breaks

Collineige: 30–32 High Street,
Frimley GU16 7JD
t +44 (0)1276 24262, www.collineige.com
Large portfolio of catered and uncatered
chalets in Chamonix and Argentière.
Guiding/instruction and on request.
Chalets available winter and summer

Concept Chalets: 3 Cholswell Court,
Shippon, Abingdon OX13 6HX
t +44 (0)1865 390 807,
www.conceptchalets.com
Luxury catered chalet with spa in
Chamonix

Contiki: Wells House, 15 Elmfield Road,
Bromley BR1 1LS
t +44 (0)20 8290 6422, www.contiki.com
Holidays for 18–35s in Hopfgarten,
Austria, by coach or air

Cooltip Mountain Holidays: Ashcourt,
Main Street, Long Riston, Hull HU11 5JF
t +44 (0)1964 563 563,
www.cooltip.com
Small operator with catered chalet-
apartments in Méribel

The Corporate Ski Company: Olympic
House, 196 The Broadway,
Wimbledon SW19 1RY
t +44 (0)20 8542 8555,
www.thecorporateskicompany.co.uk
Corporate ski trips to major resorts in
the Alps

Crystal Holidays: King's Place, 12–42 Wood
Street, Kingston-upon-Thames KT1 1SH
t +44 (0)870 160 6040,
www.crystalski.co.uk
Mass-market operator with UK's largest
choice of resorts and properties
throughout Europe, North and South
America

Descent International: Riverbank House,
Putney Bridge Approach,

London SW6 3JD
t +44 (0)20 7384 3854,
www.descent.co.uk
Luxury operator positioned at the
extreme upper end of the chalet market,
with properties in Courchevel, Les Gets,
Megève, Méribel, Val d'Isère, Gstaad,
Klosters, Verbier and Zermatt
See page M37

Directski.com: Block 10–4,
Blanchardstown Corporate Park,
Dublin 15, Ireland
t +44 (0)800 587 0945,
www.directski.com
Major Dublin-based online operator
with holidays to Andorra, Austria,
Bulgaria, France, Italy and Norway
See page M13

Elegant Resorts: The Old Palace,
Chester CH1 1RB
t +44 (0)1244 897 333,
www.elegantresorts.co.uk
Worldwide 4- and 5-star deluxe hotel
and chalet tour operator with an
established reputation in skiing
See page M61

Elemental Adventure: Kitts Farm, Churt
GU2 2PH
t +44 (0)870 738 7838, *www.eladv.com*
Heli-skiing in Alaska, Canada, Greenland,
Himalayas and Russia

Equity Ski: Dukes Lane House, 47 Middle
Street, Brighton BN1 1AL
t +44 (0)1273 299 299,
www.equityski.co.uk
All-inclusive ski holidays to 34 resorts in
Austria, France, Italy, Switzerland and
North America

Erna Low: 9 Reece Mews, London SW7 3HE
t +44 (0)870 750 6820/t +44 (0)20 7584
7820 (brochure line), *www.ernalow.co.uk*
The oldest independent ski tour operator, with wide selection of apartments
in France, Switzerland, Austria and Italy,
as well as hotels. Also ski programme to
selected resorts in North America and
spa holidays to a wide range of resorts
See inside front cover

Esprit Ski: 185 Fleet Road, Fleet GU51 3BL
t +44 (0)1252 618 300,
www.esprit-holidays.co.uk
Family specialist to 17 resorts in Austria,
France, Italy and Switzerland, with dedicated nurseries, ski classes and activity
clubs

Exsus Travel: 23 Heddon Street,
London W1B 4BQ
t +44 (0)20 7292 5050, *www.exsus.com*
Specialist tailor-made operator to South
America, with luxury accommodation

Family Ski Company: Bank Chambers,
Walwyn Road, Colwall,
Malvern WR13 6QG
t +44 (0)1684 540 333,
www.familyski.co.uk
Family ski specialist with dedicated facil-
ities for children three months to 14yrs.
Catered chalets in Portes du Soleil,
Paradiski and the Trois Vallées

Finlays: 2 Abbotsford Court Business
Centre, Kelso TD5 7BQ
t +44 (0)1573 226 611, *www.finlayski.com*
Long-established small Scottish chalet
company with a dedicated following in
Courchevel, Val d'Isère and Paradiski

First Choice Ski: First Choice House,
London Road, Crawley RH10 2GX
t +44 (0)870 754 3477,
www.firstchoice.co.uk/ski
Mainstream winter sports operator with
a collection of chalets, hotels and apartments across Europe and North America

Flexiski: Olivier House, 18 Marine Parade,
Brighton BN2 1TL
t +44 (0)870 909 0754, *www.flexiski.com*
Luxury arm of First Choice Ski (see
above), with holidays of variable length
to chalets and hotels in Austria, France
and Switzerland. *See* page M3

Four Winds Meriski: 1st Floor, Carpenters
Buildings, Carpenters Lane,
Cirencester GL7 1EE
t +44 (0)1285 648 518,
www.fourwindsresorts.com
New incarnation of established luxury
family chalet operator in Méribel

Freedom Holidays: PO Box 46, Petworth GU28 9ZX
t +44 (0)1798 861 881,
www.freedomholidays.co.uk
Tailor-made weekends and weeks in apartments, chalets and hotels in Châtel in the Portes du Soleil

French Freedom Holidays: 44 Newdown Road, Southpark, Scunthorpe DN17 2TX
t +44 (0)1724 290 660,
www.skifrance4less.co.uk
Self-drive and fly-drive holidays to the northern French Alps, specializing in Chamonix and Val d'Isère

French Life Ski: Spring Mill, Earby, Barnoldswick, Lancs BB94 0AA
t +44 (0)870 197 6963,
www.frenchlifeski.co.uk
Budget ski holidays for the independent traveller, mainly focused on self-drive to the French Alps. Also short breaks

Frontier Ski: 6 Sydenham Avenue, London SE26 6UH
t +44 (0)20 8776 8709,
www.frontier-ski.co.uk
Canadian specialist with a dedicated following

Frozenplanet.co.uk:
t +44 (0)7947 331 606,
www.frozenplanet.co.uk
Online operator offering ski and snowboard holidays worldwide

Gourmet Chalet Company: 15 Scalebor Square, Burley-in-Wharfedale, Ilkley LS29 7SP
t +44 (0)871 218 0480,
www.gourmet-chalet.com
Luxury catered chalet in Les Gets with transfers

Hannibals: Farriers, Little Olantigh Road, Wye, Ashford TN25 5DQ
t +44 (0)1233 813 105,
www.hannibals.co.uk
Established specialist operator with hotels, chalets and self-catering apartments in Serre Chevalier

Headwater Holidays: The Old School House, Chester Road, Northwich CW8 1LE
t +44 (0)1606 720 199,
www.headwater.com
Cross-country ski programme in France, Italy, Austria, Switzerland and Scandinavia, winter discovery weeks in North America,

HF Holidays: Imperial House, Edgware Road, London NW9 5AL
t +44 (0)20 8905 9558,
www.hfholidays.co.uk
Group holidays with instruction in cross-country skiing and snowshoeing in Austria, France, Italy and Switzerland

High Mountain Holidays: 39 Bartholomew Close, Ducklington OX29 7UJ
t +44 (0)1993 775 540,
www.highmountain.co.uk
Chamonix specialist with apartments, hotels and eight chalets. Weekends and short stays, off-piste courses

Huski Chalet Holidays: 63a Kensington Church Street, London W8 4BA
t +44 (0)20 7938 4844, www.huski.com
Long-established Chamonix chalet operator, also offering hotels, apartments and weekend skiing

Inghams: 10–18 Putney Hill, London SW15 6AX
t +44 (0)20 8780 4433,
www.inghams.co.uk
Major tour operator with chalets and hotel holidays in 90 resorts in 12 countries. Top end of the mass market but also has separate luxury programme with scheduled flights

Inntravel: Nr Castle Howard, York YO60 7JU
t +44 (0)1653 617 906,
www.inntravel.co.uk
Cross-country, snowshoeing and Alpine skiing in Austria, Italy, France, Switzerland, Spain, Scandinavia and USA

Interhome: 383 Richmond Road, Twickenham TW1 2EF
t +44 (0)20 8891 1294,
www.interhome.co.uk
Swiss company (part of

Hotelplan/Inghams group) with a large database of self-catering ski-drive chalets and apartments throughout the Alps

Interski: Acorn Park, Commercial Gate, Mansfield NG18 1EX

t +44 (0)1623 456 333, *www.interski.co.uk* Long-established schools operator to Courmayeur and the Aosta Valley. Also has own BASI ski school and equipment rental.

James Orr Heliski: 12 Rose & Crown Walk, Saffron Walden CB10 1JH

t +44 (0)1799 516 964, *www.heliski.co.uk* Established agent for heli-skiing holidays in Canada

Jeffersons Private Jet Holidays: Mill House, Millers Way, London W6 7NA

t +44 (0)870 850 8181, *www.jeffersons.com* Short breaks by private jet to selected resorts with own airstrip (Courchevel, Grindelwald, Lech, St Christoph am Arlberg, St Moritz). Limousine transfers and luxury accommodation

Just Slovenia: The Barns, Woodlands End, Mells, Frome BA11 3QD

t +44 (0)1373 814 230, *www.justslovenia.co.uk* Specialist tour operator offering tailor-made holidays to Slovenia

Kaluma Travel: 1st Floor Offices, 263 Putney Bridge Road, London SW15 2PU

t +44 (0)870 442 8044, *www.kalumatravel.co.uk* Luxury ski holiday specialist in France, Austria and Switzerland. Also flexible-length trips and weekend breaks *See page M31*

Kuoni Travel: Kuoni House, Deepdene Avenue, Dorking RH5 4AZ

t +44 (0)1306 747 000, *www.kuoni.co.uk* Long-established mainstream hotel operator to Switzerland

Lagrange: 168 Shepherds Bush Road, London W6 7PB

t +44 (0)20 7371 6111, *www.lagrange-holidays.co.uk*

British branch of giant French operator with a wide range of self-catering accommodation in 100 resorts in the Alps and the Pyrenees. *See page M29*

Le Ski: 25 Holly Terrace, Huddersfield HD1 6JW

t +44 (0)870 754 4444, *www.leski.com* Family-run chalet company with a long-established pedigree to Courchevel 1650, Val d'Isère and La Tania. Offers childcare, free ski guiding and owns a complex of six chalets in Val d'Isère. *See page M31*

Leisure Direction: Image House, Station Road, London N17 9LR

t +44 (0)20 8324 4042, *www.leisuredirection.co.uk* Established ski-drive operator to 36 French resorts

Lotus Supertravel: Sandpiper House, 39 Queen Elizabeth Street, London SE1 2BT

t +44 (0)20 7962 9933, *www.supertravel.co.uk* High-quality chalets and tailor-made holidays to Europe and North America

Made To Measure Holidays: 1 South Street, Chichester PO19 1EH

t +44 (0)1243 533 333, *www.mtmhols.co.uk* Long-established operator specializing in tailor-made and flexible holidays to a wide range of resorts in Europe and North America

Mark Warner: 10 Old Court Place, London W8 4PL

t +44 (0)870 770 4226, *www.markwarner.co.uk* Family holiday specialist with over 30 years' experience, offering chalet-hotel holidays with childcare and adult-only holidays in eight major French resorts, as well as Courmayeur and St Anton. *See inside back cover*

McNab Mountain Sports: Harbour House, Crinen, Lochgilphead PA31 8SW

t +44 (0)1546 830 243, **t** +33 (0)450 54 22 84, *www.mcnab.co.uk*, *www.kommunity.com* Off-piste snowboarding courses and technical clinics based at catered chalet in Argentière. Also summer freestyle/freeride snowboard camps in Les Deux Alpes

MGS Ski: 109 Castle Street, Saffron Walden CB10 1BQ
t +44 (0)1799 525 984, www.mgsski.com
Small, well-established family operator offering apartments in Val Cenis in France

Momentum Ski: 162 Munster Road, London SW6 6AT
t +44 (0)20 7371 9111,
www.momentumski.com
Tailor-made operator specializing in weeks and weekends to the Alps and North America, together with a corporate programme. Italy and Switzerland are a particular strength
See page M47

Moswin's Germany: The Birds Building, Fleckney Road, Kibworth LE8 0HJ
t +44 (0)870 062 5040,
www.moswin.com
Holidays in Garmisch-Partenkirchen in Germany

Mountain Highs: Apt. 2, Le Bretalet, La Crusaz, 74110 Morzine, France
t +44 (0)121 550 9321,
www.mountainhighs.co.uk
Three catered chalets in Morzine, with optional ferry crossings, transfers and childcare

Mountain Leap: 25 Eccleston Square, London SW1V 1NS
t +44 (0)20 7931 0621,
www.mountainleap.com
Tailor-made holidays to Chamonix, Courchevel, Megève, Méribel, Val d'Isère, Klosters and Verbier. Also large groups and corporate hospitality events

Mountain Retreats: Guilton Ash, Tile Barn, Woolton Hill, Newbury RG20 9UU
t+44 (0)1635 253 946,
www.mountainretreats.co.uk
Small company offering luxury catered ski-in, ski-out accommodation in Chamonix Valley

Mountain Sun: Fillis Cottage, The Street, Kingston near Lewes BN7 3NT
t +44 (0)7941 196 517,
www.mountainsunltd.com
Catered chalets in Les Coches and San Cassiano

Mountain Tracks: The Business Village, 3 Broomhill Road, London SW18 4JQ
t +44 (0)20 8877 5773,
www.mountaintracks.co.uk
Off-piste trips and hut-to-hut ski-touring in the Alps and Canada

Neilson: Locksview, Brighton Marina, Brighton BN2 5HA
t +44 (0)870 333 3347, www.neilson.co.uk
Major tour operator with hotels, apartments and chalets in 10 countries including Andorra, Austria, Bulgaria, France, Italy, Norway, Romania and Sweden and North America. The company is part of Thomas Cook. See page M23

Neilson School Groups: Locksview, Brighton Marina, Brighton BN2 5HA
t +44 (0)870 333 3620,
www.neilsonschools.com
Schools and adult groups operator

Nonstopski: Shakespeare House, 168 Lavender Hill, London SW11 5TF
t +44 (0)870 241 8070,
www.nonstopski.com
Learn-to-be-a-ski-instructor courses in Banff, Fernie and Red Mountain in Canada

Nortours: 31–35 Kirby Street, London EC1N 8TE
t +44 (0)870 744 7305,
www.nortours.co.uk
Scandinavian specialist offering holidays to Finland, Norway and Sweden

Oak Hall Skiing and Snowboarding: Oak Hall, Otford TN15 6XF
t +44 (0)1732 763 131, www.oakhall.co.uk
Christian holidays for 20s and 30s to Austria, Canada and Switzerland

On The Piste: 28 Great King Street, Macclesfield SK11 6PL
t +44 (0)1625 503 111,

www.onthepiste.com
French Alps specialist offering tailor-made travel for school groups, students and adults by coach or air

On The Piste Holidays (OTP): 2 Oldfield Court, Cranes Park Crescent, Surbiton KT5 8AW
t +44 (0)871 871 8034, www.otp.co.uk
Holidays to Nendaz, Saas-Fee, Villars and Zermatt

Optimum Ski: Chalet Tarentaise, Le Pré, 73640 Villaroger, France
t +44 (0)8702 406 198, www.optimumski.com
BASI trainer-run ski courses in Villaroger near Les Arcs with accommodation in large chalet

Original Travel Company: Crombie Mews, 11a Abercrombie Street, London SW11 2JB
t +44 (0)20 7978 7333, www.originaltravel.co.uk
Upmarket short-break specialist offering heli-skiing, ski-touring and off-piste in Austria, France, Italy, Switzerland and Sweden

The Oxford Ski Company: Field Cottage, Hazelton, Rodmarton, Cirencester GL7 6PG
t +44 (0)870 787 1785, www.oxfordski.com
Tailor-made luxury holidays for private and corporate clients in luxury private chalets in France and Switzerland

Panorama Holidays: Panorama House, Vale Road, Portslade BN41 1HP
t +44 (0)870 750 5060, t +44 (0)870 241 5026 (24hr brochure line), www.panoramaski.co.uk
Budget-priced chalets, hotels and apartments in Andorra, Austria, France and Italy, part of the Mytravel group

Peak Leisure: The Old Post Office, Steventon, Basingstoke RG25 3BA
t +44 (0)870 760 5610, www.peak-leisure.co.uk
Independent catered chalet in Ste-Foy, flexible-length stays with transfers

Peak Retreats: 2.4 Central Point, Kirpal Road, Portsmouth, PO3 6FH
t +44 (0)870 770 0408, www.peakretreats.co.uk
French Alps specialist for self-catering chalets, apartments and family-run hotels in offbeat resorts

Peak Ski: White Lilacs House, Water Lane, Bovingdon HP3 0NA
t +44 (0)1442 832 629, www.peakski.co.uk
Independent operator offering catered chalets in Verbier

PGL Ski: Alton Court, Penyard Lane, Ross-on-Wye HR9 5GL
t +44 (0)870 162 6622, www.pgl.co.uk
Major schools operator to Austria, France, Italy, Switzerland and USA

Poltours: 20 The Avenue, London W13 8PH
t + 44 (0)208 810 5625, www.poltours.co.uk
Tailor-made ski holidays to Zakopane in Poland

The Powder Co: Case Postale 1454, Verbier 1936, Switzerland t +44 (0)777 185 0609, t +41 (0)79427 9778, www.thepowderco.com
Luxury chalets in Verbier

Powder Byrne: 250 Upper Richmond Road, London SW15 6TG
t +44 (0)20 8246 5300, www.powderbyrne.com
Luxury family ski holidays to Austria, France, Italy, France and Switzerland, with exclusive children's clubs and crèches

Powder Skiing in North America: 61 Doneraile Street, London SW6 6EW
t +44 (0)20 7736 8191, www.canadianmountainholidays.com
Agent for CMH Heli-ski in Canada, with international flights

Purple Ski: Hamilton Cottage, Chapel Hill, Speen HP27 0SL
t +44 (0)1494 488 633, www.purpleski.com
Small luxury chalet operator in Méribel

Pyrenean Mountain Tours: 2 Rectory Cottages, Wolverton, Tadley RG26 5RS

t +44 (0)1635 297 209, www.pyrenees.co.uk
Small operator with ski, ski-touring and snowshoeing holidays to hotels and self-catering apartments in Barèges in the French Pyrenees and Corvara in the Dolomites

Ramblers Holidays: PO Box 43, Welwyn Garden City AL8 6PQ
t +44 (0)1707 331 133, www.ramblersholidays.co.uk
Walking holidays specialist with group cross-country holiday programme to Achenkirch and Innsbruck in Austria, Dobbiaco and Val di Fiemme in Italy

Reach4theAlps: Chalet Sol Re, Essert La Pierre, 74430 St Jean d'Aulps, France
t +44 (0)1382 731 719, www.reach4thealps.com
Independent chalet company offering a high standard of catered accommodation with chalets in Morzine and Les Gets

Re-lax Holidays: 2 Shirley Road, Enfield EN2 6SB
t +44 (0)20 8360 1185, www.re-laxholidays.co.uk
Holidays to hotel in Lauterbrunnen, with flights or self-drive

Rocket Ski: Dukes Lane House, 47 Middle Street, Brighton BN1 1AL
t +44 (0)1273 262 626, www.rocketski.com
Online booking service for components of holidays to Austria, France, Italy and North America

Rocky Mountain Adventures: 6 Denstone, Woolton, Liverpool L25 8SJ
t +44 (0)870 366 5442, www.rockymountain.co.uk
Full-season chalet holidays in Aspen, Breckenridge, Vail, Banff and Whistler

Scott Dunn Ski: Fovant Mews, 12 Noyna Road, London SW17 7PH
t +44 (0)20 8682 5050, www.scottdunn.com
Upmarket operator with a portfolio of luxury catered chalets in Courchevel

1850, Méribel, Val d'Isère and Zermatt. Also runs its own childcare operation. *See* page M41

Scott Dunn Latin America: Fovant Mews, 12 Noyna Road, London SW17 7PH
t +44 (0)20 8682 5030, www.scottdunn.com
Holidays to major resorts in Argentina and Chile

Seasons in Style: Telegraph House, 246 Telegraph Road, Heswall CH60 7SG
t +44 (0)151 342 0505, www.seasonsinstyle.co.uk
Five-star worldwide hotel operator with a ski programme to Austria, France, Switzerland, USA and Canada

Silver Ski: Conifers House, Grove Green Lane, Maidstone ME14 5JW
t +44 (0)1622 735 544, www.silverski.co.uk
No-nonsense catered chalets in Paradiski, Trois Vallées and Val d'Isère

Simon Butler Skiing: Portsmouth Road, Ripley GU23 6EY
t +44 (0)870 873 0001, www.simonbutlerskiing.co.uk
Holidays to chalet-hotels in Megève, including instruction

Simply Ski: Kings Place, 12–42 Wood Street, Kingston upon Thames KT1 1SG
t +44 (0)20 8541 2209, www.simplyski.co.uk
Worldwide villa specialist with chalet operation to Courchevel, Méribel, Val d'Isère, Verbier, Zermatt and St Anton. Also offers childcare facilities

Ski 2: The Old Forge, High Street, Twyford SO21 1RF
t +44 (0)1962 713 330, www.ski-2.com
Champoluc specialist, offering total flexibility of travel dates and length of stay, with its own crèche and ski school

Ski Activity: Lawmuir House, Methven PH1 3SZ
t +44 (0)1738 840 888, www.skiactivity.com
Chalets, hotels and apartments in 11 resorts in France, as well as in St Anton, Verbier, and 25 resorts in North America

Ski Addiction:
t +44 (0)1580 819 354,
www.skiaddiction.co.uk
Holidays in Châtel and La Chapelle
d'Abondance in the Portes du Soleil.
Short breaks, and instruction

Ski Adventures: 14a Graham Road,
Malvern WR14 2HN
t +44 (0)1684 560 707,
www.skiadventures.co.uk
Piste-side catered chalet accommodation in Les Arcs 1600

Ski All America: 117 St Margarets Road,
Twickenham TW1 2LH
t +44 (0)870 167 6676,
www.skiallamerica.com
Chalets, hotels and apartments in a
large portfolio of resorts in North and
South America

Skialot: 119 Apple Grove, Enfield EN1 3DB
t + 44 (0)845 004 3622, *www.skialot.com*
Catered chalet in Châtel, with draught
beer on tap from chalet's own micro-
brewery

Ski the American Dream: 31 Beaufort
Court, Admirals Way, Waterside,
South Quay, London E14 9XL
t +44 (0)870 350 7547,
www.skidream.com
The UK's original independent ski
holiday specialist operator to North
America. *See* page M63

Ski Amis: 122–126 High Road,
London NW6 4HY
t +44 (0)20 7692 0850,
www.skiamis.com
Well-established company offering
catered and self-catered apartments
and chalets in the French Alps

Ski Arrangements: The Reading Rooms,
Sandy Lane, Crich, Matlock DE4 5DE
t +44 (0)8700 110 565,
www.skiarrangements.com
Flexible-length ski holidays to France,
Italy and Canada, staying in apartments,
chalets and hotels

Ski Astons: Clerkenleap, Broomhall,
Worcester WR5 3HR

t +44 (0)1905 829 200,
www.skiastons.co.uk
Schools specialist with all-inclusive holidays to resorts in Austria and
Switzerland

Ski Barrett-Boyce: 3 Mayfields, Brighton
Road Lower Kingswood KT20 6QZ
t +44 (0)1737 831 184, *www.skibb.com*
Family-run company offering chalet
holidays in Megève, with instruction and
childcare

Ski Basics: 95 West Avenue, Oldfield Park,
Bath BA2 3QB
t +44 (0)1255 444 143,
www.skibasics.co.uk
Méribel specialist with eight chalets,
offering ski courses with Inspired to Ski

Ski Beat: Metro House, Northgate,
Chichester PO19 1BE
t +44 (0)1243 780 405, *www.skibeat.co.uk*
Long-established operator with chalets
with childcare in, Méribel, Paradiski, La
Tania and Val d'Isère

Ski Blanc: 89 Palmerston Road, Buckhurst
Hill, Essex IG9 5NH
t +44 (0)20 8502 9082,
www.skiblanc.co.uk
Small operator with a range of catered
chalets in Méribel-Les-Allues

Ski Bon: 6 St Paul's Terrace,
Northampton NN2 6ET
t +44 (0)1604 247 723, *www.skibon.com*
Holidays to two catered chalets in
Méribel, with self-drive, sleeper-coach
travel or airport transfers

SkiBound: Olivier House, 18 Marine
Parade, Brighton BN2 1TL
t +44 (0)870 900 3242,
www.skibound.co.uk
Market leader for school trips to Austria,
France, Italy and North America. Part of
the First Choice group

Ski Chamois: 18 Lawn Road,
Doncaster DN1 2JF
t +44 (0)1302 369 006,
www.skichamois.co.uk
Small chalet-hotel operator in Morzine,
with own childcare programme

Ski Cuisine: 49 Burgess Road, Southend-on-Sea SS1 3AX
t +44 (0)1702 589 543,
www.skicuisine.co.uk
Small company with six gourmet-catered chalets in Méribel

Ski Deep: 5 The Orchard, St Johns Hill Road, Woking GU21 7RF
t +44 (0)1483 722 706, *www.skideep.com*
Catered chalets in Courchevel and La Tania, with instruction

Ski Equipe: 79 London Road, Alderley Edge, Cheshire SK9 7DY
t +44 (0)870 444 5533,
www.ski-equipe.co.uk
Small operator with chalets and hotels in Cortina d'Ampezzo and St Anton

Ski Etoile: Glebelands, Clun, Shropshire SY7 8JH
t +44 (0)1588 640 442,
www.skietoile.co.uk
Flexible holidays to Montgenèvre with hotels, chalets and apartments

Ski Expectations: Jasmine Cottage, Manor Lane, Great Chesterford CB10 1PJ
t +44 (0)1799 531 888,
www.skiexpectations.com
Small tailor-made hotel and catered chalet operator to major resorts in Europe, Canada and North America

Ski Famille: Unit 10, Chesterton Mill, French's Road, Cambridge CB4 3NP
t +44(0)845 644 3764,
www.skifamille.co.uk
Specialist family-run chalet operator for families in Les Gets, with free childcare programme

Ski France: Unit 14, Croydon House Business Centre, 1 Peall Road, Croydon CR0 3EX
t +44 (0)870 787 3402,
www.skifrance.co.uk
Travel by rail, air or self-drive to France, with chalets, hotels and apartments

Ski Freshtracks: The White House, 57–63 Church Road, Wimbledon, London SW19 5SB
t +44 (0)845 458 0784,
www.skifreshtracks.co.uk
Ski Club of Great Britain's programme where you can ski or snowboard with a group of similar ability for weeks, weekends or on specialist courses. Carefully selected leaders, instructors and guides. *See* page M4

Ski Gower: 2 High Street, Studley B80 7HJ
t +44(0)1527 851 411, *www.skigower.co.uk*
Tailor-made holidays in Switzerland for schools and groups

Ski High Days: Fire Clay House, Netham Road, Bristol BS5 9PJ
t +44 (0)117 955 1814,
www.skihighdays.com
Group tour operator with an increasingly large presence in Sauze d'Oulx, Clavière and Bardonecchia in Italy

Ski Hillwood: Lavender Lodge, Dunny Lane, Chipperfield WD4 9DD
t +44 (0)1923 290 700,
www.hillwood-holidays.co.uk
Long-established specialist family operator with childcare programme to Söll and Zauchensee in Austria, Les Gets and Argentière in France

Ski Hiver: 119A London Road, Waterlooville PO7 7DZ
t +44 (0)2392 428 586,
www.skihiver.co.uk
Catered chalets with childcare in Peisey-Nancroix and Plan-Peisey in Paradiski

Ski Independence: 5 Thistle Street, Edinburgh EH2 1DF
t +44 (0)845 310 3030, *www.ski-i.com*
Largest independent operator to USA and Canada, with hotels, chalets and apartments in 40 resorts. Also extensive programme to 30 French and 4 Swiss resorts, with option to fly or drive for week or weekend stays

Ski La Côte: 33 Dale Road, Welton, Brough HU15 1PE
t +44 (0)1482 668 357,
www.ski-la-cote.karoo.net
Catered chalet in La Chapelle d'Abondance, with airport transfers, but not flights

Ski Link: Chalet La Pige, Allée des Cerisiers, Le Praz St Bon, 73120 Courchevel, France
www.ski-link.co.uk
Online operator with catered chalets and hotels in Courchevel

Ski Miquel: 73 High Street, Uppermill, Oldham OL3 6AP
t +44 (0)1457 821 200,
www.miquelhols.co.uk
Long-established chalet, hotel and apartment operator to Bad Gastein, Alpe d'Huez, Serre Chevalier, Baqueira-Beret in Spain, Lauterbrunnen in Switzerland, and Whistler.
See page M21

Ski Morgins: The Barn House, 1 Bury Court Barns, Wigmore HR6 9US
t +44 (0)1568 770 681,
www.skimorgins.com
Small specialist operator to Morgins in Switzerland

Ski 'n' Action: Maison Beaufort, rue des Beauforts, Le Praz, Courchevel 73120, France
t +44 (0)1707 251 696,
www.ski-n-action.com
Catered chalet in Le Praz Courchevel 1300

Ski-n-doo: Les Clos, 74260 Les Gets, France
t +44 (0)871 900 8126,
www.ski-n-doo.com
Upmarket catered chalets in Les Gets

Ski Norwest: 8 Foxholes Cottages, Foxholes Road, Horwich, Bolton BL6 6AL
t +44 (0)1204 668 468,*www.skinorwest.com*
Weekend and midweek ski and snowboarding breaks to Scotland

Ski Olympic: PO Box 396, Doncaster DN5 7YS
t +44 (0)1302 328 820,
www.skiolympic.com
Chalets and hotels in seven French resorts, including own chalet-hotel at Vallandry in Paradiski

Ski Peak: Barts End, Crossways Road, Grayshott GU26 6HD
t +44 (0)1428 608 070, *www.skipeak.com*

Small, dedicated operator with its own chalets and apartments and its own hotel in Vaujany in the Alpe d'Huez ski area. Provides a British nanny for the local crèche. Chalets available all year round.
See page M24

Ski Power: The Gables, Coopers Hill Road, Nutfield RH1 5PD
t +44 (0)1737 823 232,
www.skipower.co.uk
Three catered chalets in La Tania

Ski Rosie: L'Alpage 8B, route du Petit Châtel, 74390 Châtel, France
t +33 (0)450 81 31 00, *www.skirosie.com*
Long-established operator with one catered chalet in Morgins, apartments and hotels in Châtel

Ski Safari: 1 Amber House, St Johns Road, Hove BN3 2EZ
t +44 (0)1273 224 060, *www.skisafari.com*
North America expert with high-quality hotels and apartments. Self-drive adventures a speciality. Also holidays in Chile

Skisafe Travel: Unit 4, Braehead Estate, Old Govan Road, Renfrew PA4 8XJ
t +44 (0)141 812 0925,
www.osatravel.co.uk
Family-run operation in Aviemore, Aonach Mor and Glenshee

Ski Scott James: Byre Cottage, Sessay, Thirsk YO7 3BE
t +44 (0)1845 501 139,
www.skiscottjames.co.uk
Catered chalets in Argentière, with off-piste courses

Ski Solutions à la Carte: 84 Pembroke Road, London W8 6NX
t +44 (0)20 7471 7777,
www.skisolutions.com
Tailor-made arm of specialist ski travel agency, with hotels and apartments in all major resorts in the Alps and North America. Staff have intimate knowledge of the resorts and properties

Ski St Anton: Avon House, Albany Park Estate, Frimley Road, Camberley GU16 7PL

t +44 (0)1276 61072, *www.skistanton.net*
One-resort specialist with hotels, luxury catered chalets and flexible-length holidays

Ski Supreme: 24 Howard Court, Neraton Estate, East Kilbride G74 4QZ
t +44 (0)1355 260 547, *www.skisupreme.co.uk*
Self-drive and accommodation-only holidays in France

Skitopia: 40 Lemon Street, Truro TR1 2NS
t +44 (0)1872 272 767, *www.skitopia.com*, *www.skitopia.biz*
Hotel and chalet holidays to the French Alps and Italy for schools and adults

Ski Val: The Ski Barn, Middlemoor, Tavistock PL19 9DY
t +44 (0)870 746 3030, *www.skival.co.uk*
Catered chalets and chalet-hotels in Courchevel, Tignes, Val d'Isère and St Anton

Ski Verbier: 25 The Coda Centre, 189 Munster Road, London SW6 6AW
t +44 (0)20 7385 8050, *www.skiverbier.com*
Well-established upmarket operator in Verbier, with 14 catered chalets and its own 4-star hotel. Chalets available all year round.
See page M51

Ski Weekend: Darts Farm Village, Topsham, Exeter EX3 0QH
t +44 (0)870 060 0615, *www.skiweekend.com*
Weekends and short breaks combined with high-mountain guiding and specialist courses, to Chamonix Valley and other destinations in Switzerland and Italy. Corporate programme also available

Skiweekends: 4 Post Office Walk, Fore Street, Hertford SG14 1DL
t +44 (0)870 442 3400, *www.skiweekends.com*
Budget weekend and short break specialist. Coach and air packages to Brides-les-Bains, La Tania and Chamonix

Ski Wild: Corner Cottage, Woodlands Lane, Stoke d'Abernon, Surrey KT11 3QA
t +44 (0)870 746 9668, *www.skiwild.co.uk*
Tailor-made holidays in Andorra, Austria, France and North America

Ski with Julia: East Lodge Farm, Stanton, Broadway WR12 7NH
t +44 (0)1386 584 478, *www.skijulia.co.uk*
Three catered chalets in Verbier

Skiworld: Skiworld House, 3 Vencourt Place, London W6 9NU
t +44 (0)870 241 6723 (Europe), **t** +44 (0)870 787 9720 (North America), *www.skiworld.ltd.uk*
Largest independent ski tour operator, with major chalet programme in the Alps and North America

Sloping Off: 47 Middle Street, Brighton BN1 1AL
t +44 (0)1273 886 888, *www.sloping-off.co.uk*
Schools and groups operator to resorts in Austria, France, Italy and Switzerland

Snowbizz Vacances: 69 High Street, Maxey PE6 9EE
t +44 (0)1778 341 455, *www.snowbizz.co.uk*
Small, long-established operator to Puy-St-Vincent in France, with extensive childcare and own ski-school programme with race-training for children 10–16yrs

Snowcoach: 146–148 London Road, St Albans AL1 1PQ
t +44 (0)1727) 866 177, *www.snowcoach.co.uk*
Specialist ski and snowboard operator offering high-quality accommodation and good-value holidays to France and Austria

Snowfocus: Chalet La Fonnaille, 74390 Châtel, France
t +44 (0)1392 479 555, *www.snowfocus.com*
Two catered chalets for weeks and weekend breaks in Châtel

Snowlife: Chanson de la Mer, rue de la Falaise, Trinity, Jersey JE3 5BD
t +44 (0)1534 863 630,
www.snowlife.co.uk
Catered chalet with childcare in La Clusaz

Snowline: Collingbourne House, 140–142 Wandsworth High Street, London SW18 4JJ
t +44 (0)870 112 3118,
www.snowline.co.uk
Well-established chalet operator with wide range of catered properties in Morzine, Méribel, La Tania and Val d'Isère. Childcare service with private nannies in Trois Vallées, plus crèche in Val d'Isère

Snow Monkey Chalets: Maison Rose, 73210 Peisey-Nancroix, France
t +44 (0)20 7387 0095,
www.snowmonkeychalets.co.uk
Comfortable catered chalets in Paradiski

Snow Safari: 1351 route des Chavants, 74310 Les Houches, France
t +33 (0)450 54 56 63,
www.chaletsavoy.com
Small chalet specialist to Chamonix Valley with mountain guiding and instruction.

Snowscape: 108 Wylds Lane, Worcester WR5 1DJ
t +44 (0)1905 357 760,
www.snowscape.co.uk
Weekly and flexible holidays to Austria for groups and individuals

Snowstar Holidays: 38 Nicola Close, South Croydon CR2 6NB
t +44 (0)870 068 6611,
www.snowstarholidays.com
Catered chalet holidays in Tignes

Solo's Holidays: 54–58 High Street, Edgware HA8 7EJ
t +44 (0)870 072 0700,
www.solosholidays.co.uk
Holidays for singles in 14 resorts in Austria, France, Italy, Switzerland, Romania, Bulgaria, Slovenia, Canada and USA

La Source: 14 The Grove, Brookmans Park, Hatfield AL9 7RN
t +44 (0)1707 655 988,
www.lasource.org.uk
Luxury catered chalet in Villard Reculas near Alpe d'Huez

Stanford Skiing: 479 Unthank Road, Norwich NR4 7QN
t +44 (0)1603 477 471,
www.stanfordskiing.co.uk
Long-established specialist operator with chalets and hotels in Megève.
See page M35

Swiss Travel Service: Bridge House, 55–59 High Road, Broxbourne EN10 7DT
t +44(0)870 191 7175,
www.swisstravel.co.uk
Major hotel operator to 19 resorts in Switzerland. Travel by scheduled flight with rail transfers, or by rail or car from UK

Switzerland Travel Centre (Plus Travel): 30 Bedford Street, London, WC2E 9ED
t +44 (0)20 7420 4900, *www.stc.co.uk*
Specialist hotel operator to 16 Swiss resorts

Tangney Tours: 3 Station Court, Borough Green TN15 8AF
t +44 (0)1732 886 666,
www.tangney-tours.com
Pilgrim charter operator to Lourdes, with a small ski programme in nearby Barèges in the French Pyrenees

Thomson Ski & Snowboarding: King's Place, 12–42 Wood Street, Kingston-upon-Thames KT1 1JY
t +44 (0)870 606 1470,
www.thomson-ski.co.uk
Major tour operator to over 80 resorts in 11 countries, with group discounts and childcare facilities

Tops Ski Chalets and Club Hotels: Lees House, 21 Dyke Road, Brighton BN1 3GD
t +44 (0)1273 774 666,
www.topstravel.co.uk
Chalets and club-hotels in Alpe d'Huez, Châtel, Les Deux Alpes and Vars

Total Ski: 185 Fleet Road, Fleet GU51 3BL
t +44 (0)870 163 3633, *www.skitotal.com*
Large portfolio of catered chalets in
14 resorts in Austria, France, Italy,
Switzerland and Canada

Trail Alpine: Cordelia House, James Park,
Dyserth, Rhyl LL18 6AG
t +44 (0)870 750 6560,
www.trailalpine.co.uk
Small operator with a chalet in Morzine

Trailfinders: 194 Kensington High Street,
London W8 7RG
t +44 (0)845 050 5900,
www.trailfinders.com
Largest independent travel company in
UK, with tailor-made programmes to
resorts including Banff-Lake Louise,
Whistler, Breckenridge, Heavenly and
Killington

Tyrolean Adventures: 56 Poynder Road,
Corsham SN13 9LZ
t +44 (0)777 976 4858,
www.tyroleanadventures.com
Small operator offering holidays by
coach, inclusive of ski pass and ski hire,
based at a hotel in Hochfilzen near
Kitzbühel. Discounts for those choosing
to fly or using their own transport

United Vacations: PO Box 377,
Bromley BR1 1LY
t +44 (0)870 606 2222,
www.unitedvacations.co.uk
Tour operator arm of United Airlines,
offering a tailor-made service to 25
resorts across USA and Canada

Val d'Isère à la Carte: La Hure, rue de la
Motte, St Martins, Guernsey GY4 6ER
t +44 (0)1481 236800,
www.skivaldisere.co.uk
Tailor-made holidays and booking
service for all components of holidays to
Val d'Isère, but not flights

Vanilla Ski: Avoca Cottage, Woodside
Road, Chiddingfold GU8 4RJ
t +44 (0)1932 860 696,
www.vanillaski.com
Catered chalet near Bourg-St-Maurice,

with day trips organized to nearby
resorts

VIP: Collingbourne House,
140–142 Wandsworth High Street,
London SW18 4JJ
t +44 (0)8701 123 119,
www.vip-chalets.com
Well-established luxury chalet operator
with a large portfolio of properties in Val
d'Isère and Méribel. Childcare service
with private nannies in both resorts,
plus crèche in Val d'Isère

Virgin Snow: The Galleria, Station Road,
Crawley RH10 1WW
t +44 (0)870 990 4212,
www.virgin.com/holidays
The tour-operator arm of Virgin Atlantic.
Offers hotel and fly-drive holidays to 22
resorts across North America

Wasteland Ski Company: 9 Disraeli Road,
London SW15 2DR
t +44 (0)870 844 4644,
www.wastelandski.com
The largest student operator with
dedicated events team. Works with over
100 University snowsports clubs in UK.
Also good-value chalets for graduates

Waymark Holidays: 44 Windsor Road,
Slough SL1 2EJ
t +44 (0)1753 516 477,
www.waymarkholidays.com
Long-established cross-country ski
operator to hotels in Austria, France,
Italy, Switzerland, Norway, Finland,
Slovenia, USA and Canada

White Roc Weekends: 69 Westbourne
Grove, London, W2 4UJ
t +44 (0)20 7792 1188,
www.whiteroc.co.uk
Weekend and longer tailor-made
holidays for individual and corporate
clients to Austria, France, Italy, Spain and
Switzerland, with a choice of 25 resorts
and an emphasis on characterful,
good-quality hotels

Wood Advent Farm: Roadwater, Exmoor
National Park, TA24 0RR
t +44 (0)1984 640 920,

www.skilesgets.com
Catered chalet in Les Gets
YSE: The Business Village, Broomhill Road, London SW18 4JQ
t +44 (0)20 8871 5117, *www.yseski.co.uk*
Large Val d'Isère specialist with a wide range of chalets, from comfortable to luxurious, with travel by charter flights
Zermatt Holidays: 3920 Zermatt, Switzerland
t +41 (0)27 968 1130, *www.zermattholidays.com*
Resort specialist with chalets and apartments, including long-term rentals

Ski Travel Agents

Alpine Answers
t +44 (0)20 8871 4656, *www.alpineanswers.co.uk*
Also a tour operator
Chalet World Ski
t +44 (0)1743 231199, *www.chaletworldski.co.uk*
Chalet agents to major Alpine resorts
Chalet World (London)
t +44 (0)20 7373 2096, *www.chaletworld.co.uk*
Agency for tour operator chalets
Erna Low
t +44 (0)20 7584 2841, *www.ernalow.co.uk*
Agent for Paradiski, Intrawest Europe and MGM apartments. Also a tour operator
The First Resort
t +44 (0)87 0055 6300, *www.thefirstresort.com*
Online holiday booking, cheap flights and information for snow-users
Ifyouski
www.ifyouski.com
Online agency
Iglu
t +44 (0)20 8542 6658, *www.iglu.com*
Online travel and accommodation

Packyourskis
t +44 (0)18 9267 3406, *ww.packyourskis.com*
Online agents for ski destinations and flights
Independent Ski Links
t +44 (0)19 6453 3905, *www.ski-links.com*
Agency offering holidays to the Alps and North America
Momentum Ski
t +44 (0)20 7371 9111, *www.momentumski.com*
London-based agency, also a tour operator
Mountain Beds
t +44 (0)20 7924 2650, *www.mountainbeds.co.uk*
Apartment bookings for Verbier
Ski Deals
t +44 (0)80 0027 3158, *www.skideals.com*
Online holiday agency
Ski McNeill
t +44 (0)28 9066 6699, *www.skimcneill.com*
Small independent ski travel agency
Ski Solutions
t +44 (0)20 7471 7700, *www.skisolutions.com*
The original ski travel agency, also a tour operator
Ski & Surf
t +44 (0)20 8958 2418, *www.skisurf.com*
Independent ski travel agency
Ski Travel Centre
t +44 (0)141 649 9696, *www.skitravelcentre.co.uk*
Scotland's biggest ski travel agency
Snow Finders
t +44 (0)18 5846 6888, *www.snowfinders.com*
Independent ski travel agency
Snowhounds
t +44 (0)1243 788 487, *www.snowhounds.co.uk*
Ski specialist agency arm of Ski Beat
Snow-Line
t +44 (0)87 0050 7025, *www.snow-line.co.uk*

Large and long-established ski travel
agency
World Ski & Travel
  t +44 (0)870 043 4122,
  www.worldski.co.uk
  Specialist ski travel agency

Travelling by Air

Airlines
Air Canada
  t +44 (0)87 0220 1111, *www.aircanada.ca*
Air France
  t +44 (0)87 0142 4343,
  www.airfrance.co.uk
Air 2000/First Choice
  t +44 (0)870 900 3213,
  www.firstchoice.co.uk
Alitalia
  t +44 (0)87 0544 8259,
  www.alitalia.co.uk
American Airlines
  t +44 (0)20 7365 0777, *www.aa.com*
Austrian Airlines
  t +44 (0)87 0124 2625, *www.aua.com*
bmibaby
  t +44 (0)870 264 2229,
  www.bmibaby.com
British Airways
  t +44(0)870 850 9850, *www.ba.com*
Continental Airlines
  t +44 (0)12 9377 6464,
  www.continental.com
Delta Airlines
  t +44 (0)8 0041 4767, *www.delta.com*
easyJet
  t +44 (0)905 821 0905, *www.easyjet.com*
Excel Airways
  t +44 (0)870 169 0169, *www.xl.com*
Flybe
  t +44 (0)871 700 0535, *www.flybe.com*
Jet 2
  t +44 (0)870 737 8282, *www.jet2.com*
JMC/Thomas Cook
  t +44 (0)870 750 5711,
  www.thomascook.com

Lufthansa
  t +44 (0)845 773 7747,
  www.lufthansa.com
Monarch Airlines
  t +44 (0)1582 40 0000,
  www.flymonarch.com
Northwest Airlines
  t +44 (0)870 507 4074, *www.nwa.com*
Mytravel/Airtours
  t +44 (0)870 241 5333,
  www.mytravel.com
Ryanair
  t +44 (0)871 246 0000, *www.ryanair.com*
Swiss International Airlines
  t +44 (0)845 601 0956, *www.swiss.com*
Thomsonfly
  t +44 (0)800 107 1517,
  www.thomsonfly.com
United Airlines
  t +44 (0)845 844 4777,
  www.unitedairlines.co.uk
Virgin Atlantic Airways
  t +44 (0)1293 74 7747,
  www.virgin-atlantic.com
Zoom
  t +44 (0)870 240 0055,
  www.flyzoom.com

Travel extras
First Luggage
  t +44 (0)845 270 0670,
  www.firstluggage.com
  Take the hassle out of travelling by
  having your skis and suitcases collected
  from your home and delivered to any
  European ski resort
Holiday Extras
  t +44 (0)870 844 4186,
  www.holidayextras.co.uk
  A selection of over 100 hotels
  (with/without parking), 55 car parks and
  23 lounges at 26 airports across the UK,
  as well as chauffeur transfers, car hire to
  and from the airport, foreign exchange
  and travel insurance

Travel Supermarket
www.travelsupermarket.com
Price comparisons for flights
and car hire

Travelling by Car

Breakdown insurance
AA Five Star Services
t +44 (0)800 444500, *www.theaa.com*
Autohome
t +44 (0)800 371280,
www.autohome.co.uk
Britannia Rescue
t +44 (0)800 591 563,
www.britanniarescue.com
Direct Line Rescue
t +44 (0)845 246 8702,
www.directline.com
Europ Assistance
t +44 (0)1444 442211,
www.europ-assistance.co.uk
Green Flag National Breakdown
t +44 (0)845 767 0345,
www.greenflag.com
Mondial Assistance
t +44 (0)208 681 2525,
www.mondial-assistance.co.uk
RAC Travel Services
t +44 (0)800 550055, *www.rac.co.uk*

Channel crossings
Brittany Ferries
t +44 (0)870 366 5333,
www.brittanyferries.com
Portsmouth–Caen
Eurotunnel
t +44 (0)870 535 3535,
www.eurotunnel.com
Folkestone–Calais
Norfolkline
t +44 (0)870 870 1020,
www.norfolkline.com
Dover–Dunkerque
P&O Ferries
t +44 (0)870 598 0333,
www.poferries.com

Seafrance
t +44 (0)870 571 1711, *www.seafrance.com*
Dover–Calais
Stena Line
t +44 (0)870 570 7070,
www.stenaline.com
Harwich–Hook of Holland

Ski roof-boxes
Karrite Europe
t +44 (0)1440 760000, *www.karrite.co.uk*
The Roof Box Company
t +44 (0)1539 621884, *www.roofbox.co.uk*
Thule
t +44 (0)1275 340404, *www.thule.co.uk*

Snow chains
AA
t +44 (0)870 550 0600, *www.theaa.com*
Brindley Chains
t +44 (0)1925 825555,
www.brindley-chains.co.uk
Polar Automotive
t +44 01892 519933,
www.snowchains.com
RAC
t +44 (0)800 550055, *www.rac.co.uk*
Rud Chains
t +44 (0)1227 276611, *www.rud.co.uk*
Snowchains
t +44 (0)1732 884408,
www.snowchains.co.uk

Travelling by Rail

Eurostar
t +44 (0)8705 186 186, *www.eurostar.com*
A weekly overnight service leaves
London Waterloo on Friday evening,
arriving in the Tarentaise valley the
following morning. The return train
departs on Saturday evening. An additional daytime service departs on
Saturday morning, in each direction
Rail Europe
t +44 (0)870 1244646,
www.raileurope.co.uk or *www.sncf.com*

Agents for tour operators' chartered Snowtrain, which leaves Calais on Friday night, arriving in the French Alps on Saturday morning, and departs on Saturday evening, arriving in Calais Sunday morning

Also agents for SNCF couchette service departing Paris Gare du Nord for the Alps on Friday evening, arriving Saturday morning, and leaving the Alps on Saturday evening, arriving Sunday morning. Services connect with Eurostar to London Waterloo but involve a change of train, though not of station

Also agents for SNCF daily and couchette Intercity services to the French Alps from Paris Gare de Lyon

National Tourist Offices

Andorran Delegation
t +44 (0)20 8874 4806, www.andorra.ad
Argentinian Embassy
t +44 (0)20 7318 1300,
embar.ru@btconnect.com
Australia
t (09068) 633235 (brochure line),
www.australia.com
Austria
t +44 (0)84 5101 1818, www.austria.info
Bulgaria
t +44 (0)20 7584 9400,
www.bulgariaski.com
Canada
t (09068) 715000 (brochure line),
www.travelcanada.ca
Chile
t +44 (0)20 7580 1023, www.visitchile.org
Czech Republic
t (09063) 640641 (brochure line),
www.visitczechia.cz
Finland
t +44 (0)20 7365 2512,
www.visitfinland.com
France
t (09068) 244123 (brochure line),
www.franceguide.com, www.skifrance.fr

Italy
t +44 (0)20 7408 1254, www.enit.it
Japan
t +44 (0)20 7734 9638,
www.seejapan.co.uk
New Zealand
t (09050) 606060,
www.newzealand.com
Norway
t (09063) 022003 (brochure line),
www.visitnorway.com
Romania
t +44 (0)20 7224 3692,
www.romaniatourism.com
Scotland
t +44 (0)13 1332 2433,
www.visitscotland.com
Slovenia
t +44 (0)87 0225 5305, www.slovenia.info
Spain
t +44 (0)20 7486 8077,
www.tourspain.co.uk, www.spain.info
Sweden
t +44 (0) 0800 3080 3080 (international freephone), www.visit-sweden.com
Switzerland
t +44 (0) 0800 1002 0030 (international freephone), www.myswitzerland.com
United States
Switchboard t +44 (0)20 7499 9000
Visa Information Line t +44 (0)9068 200 290 (24hr), www.unitedstatesvisas.gov
California
www.visitcalifornia.com
Colorado
www.visitcolorado.com
Maine
www.visitmaine.com
Nevada
t +44 (0)87 0523 8832 (brochure line),
www.visitnevada.com
New England
www.skinewengland.com
New Hampshire
www.visitnh.gov
Rocky Mountain International
t +44 (0)9063 640655,
www.rmi-realamerica.com

Ski-related Organizations

Association of British Tour Operators to France (ABTOF)
t +44 (0)1989 769140,
www.holidayfrance.org.uk

Association of British Travel Agents (ABTA)
t +44 (0)20 7637 2444, www.abta.com

Association of Independent Tour Operators (AITO)
t +44 (0)20 8744 9280,
t +44 (0)870 751 8080 (brochure line),
www.aito.co.uk

The Back Up Trust
t +44 (0)20 8875 1805,
www.backuptrust.org.uk
Charity for disabled skiing

British Alpine Racing Academy
t +44 (0)191 5847619,
www.alpine-racing.co.uk
Summer and winter race training for adults and children in Europe, New Zealand and North America

British Association of Ski Patrollers
t +44 (0)1855 811443, www.basp.org.uk
Safety officers at Scottish resorts and UK artificial slopes

British Association of Snowsport Instructors (BASI)
t +44 (0)1479 861717, www.basi.org.uk

British Bobskeleton Association
t +44 (0)1225 323696
www.british-bobsleigh.com

British Bobsleigh Association
t +44 (0)1225 386802,
www.british-bobsleigh.com

British Mountain Guides
t +44 (0)1834 871694, www.bmg.org.uk

British Ski Academy
t +44 (0)20 8399 1181, t +33 450 544059,
www.britskiacad.org.uk

British Ski Club for the Disabled
t +44 (0)1747 828515, www.bscd.org.uk

Freestyle Snowsports
www.freestylesnowsports.co.uk

Ski Club of Great Britain
t +44 (0)845 458 0780, www.skiclub.co.uk
The leading club for British skiers

Snowsport Industries of Great Britain
t +44 (0)131 557 3012,
www.snowlife.org.uk

Snowsport England
t +44 (0)121 501 2314,
www.snowsportengland.org.uk

Snowsport GB
t +44 (0)131 445 7676,
www.snowsportgb.com

Snowsport Wales
t +44 (0)2920 561904,
www.snowsportwales.net

Snowsport Scotland
t +44 (0)131 445 4151,
www.snowsportscotland.org

The Uphill Ski Club of Great Britain
t +44 (0)1479 861272
www.uphillskiclub.co.uk
Club for disabled skiers

World Ski & Snowboard Club
t +44 (0)870 043 4122,
www.worldski.co.uk

Artificial Snow Slopes

Tamworth SnowDome, Staffordshire
t +44 (0)8705 000011,
www.snowdome.co.uk

Xscape Snowzone, Castleford, West Yorkshire
t +44 (0)871 222 5671, www.xscape.co.uk

Xscape Snozone, Milton Keynes
t +44 (0)871 222 5670, www.xscape.co.uk

Dry slopes
A full list of the 70 slopes is available from the Ski Club of Great Britain

Bearsden Ski Club, Glasgow
t +44 (0)141 943 1500,
www.skibearsden.co.uk

Gloucester Ski and Snowboard Centre
t +44 (0)8702 400375,
www.gloucesterski.co.uk

Hemel Ski Centre, Hemel Hempstead
t +44 (0)1442 241321,
www.hemel-ski.co.uk

Llandudno Ski and Snowboard Centre
t +44 (0)1492 874707,
www.llandudnoskislope.co.uk

Midlothian Ski Centre, Edinburgh
t +44 (0)131 445 4433
Rossendale Ski Centre, Lancashire
t +44 (0)1706 226457,
www.ski-rossendale.co.uk
Sheffield Ski Village
t +44 (0)114 276 9459,
www.sheffieldskivillage.co.uk
Wycombe Summit, High Wycombe
t +44 (0)1494 474711,
www.wycombesummit.com

Ski Recruitment Agencies

Free Radicals
www.freeradicals.co.uk
Jobs in the Alps
www.jobs-in-the-alps.com
Natives
t +44 (0)870 046 3377, www.natives.co.uk
Ski Connection
www.skiconnection.co.uk
Voovs.com Ltd
t +44 (0)1707 396511, www.voovs.com

Gap-year Skiing

Bunac / Gap Canada
t +44 (0)20 7251 3472, www.bunac.org
Student work opportunities in
North America
Nonstopski
t +44 (0)870 241 8070,
www.nonstopski.com
Intensive instruction in Fernie, Red
Mountain and Banff, with the aim of
qualifying as a Level 1 Canadian ski or
board instructor
Peak Leaders
t +44 (0)1337 860079,
www.peakleaders.co.uk
Gap-year instructor courses
Ski Le Gap
t +44 (0)800 328 0345,
www.skilegap.com
Instructors' programme in Tremblant for
UK gap-year students

Clothing and Equipment Retailers

For a full list see www.snowlife.org.uk
Blacks
t +44 (0)800 214890, www.blacks.co.uk
Boardwise
t +44 (0)8707 504421,
www.boardwise.com
Ellis Brigham
t +44 (0)161 833 0746,
www.ellis-brigham.com
47 Degrees
t +44 (0)20 7384 1747,
www.47degrees.com
Sheactive
t +44 (0)207 836 0440,
www.sheactive.co.uk
Snow + Rock
t +44 (0)845 100 1011,
www.snowandrock.com

Weather and Snow

www.avalanches.org
Collective avalanche warning site for
Europe
www.lawine.at
Avalanche warnings for Austria
www.meteo.fr
French weather forecasts
www.skiclub.co.uk
Snow reports and six-day weather
forecasts on more than 250 resorts
across Europe and North America
www.slf.ch
Avalanche warnings for Switzerland
www.snow-forecast.com
Worldwide snow data

Ski Travel Insurance

American Express
t +44 (0)800 028 7573,
www.americanexpress.co.uk
BIBA
t +44 (0)870 950 1790, www.biba.org.uk

Columbus Direct
  t +44 (0)845 330 8518,
  www.columbusdirect.com

Direct Travel Insurance
  t +44 (0)845 605 2700,
  www.direct-travel.co.uk

Endsleigh Insurance Services
  t +44 (0)800 028 3571,
  www.endsleigh.co.uk

Europ Assistance
  t +44 (0)1444 444692,
  www.europ-assistance.co.uk

Fogg Travel Insurance
  t +44 (0)1623 631331,
  www.fogginsure.co.uk

Insure & Go
  t +44 (0)870 901 3674,
  www.insureandgo.com

James Hampden
  t +44 (0)870 220 0634,
  www.primary1.co.uk

Liverpool Victoria
  t +44 (0)1202 292333,
  www.liverpool-victoria.co.uk

Medicover
  t +44 (0)870 735 3600,
  www.medi-cover.co.uk

Mondial Assistance
  t +44 (0)20 8681 2525,
  www.mondial-assistance.co.uk

MPI
  t +44 (0)1428 664265,
  www.mpibrokers.com

MRL Insurance Direct
  t +44 (0)870 876 7677,
  www.mrlinsurance.co.uk

Options
  t +44 (0)870 876 7878,
  www.optionsinsurance.co.uk

Primary Insurance
  t +44 (0)870 220 0634,
  www.primaryinsurance.co.uk

Ski Club of Great Britain
  t +44 (0)8700 759 759, *www.skiclub.co.uk*

Snowcard Insurance Services
  t +44 (0)1327 262805,
  www.snowcard.co.uk

Sportscover Direct
  t +44 (0)845 120 6400, t +44 (0117) 922
  6222, *www.sportscover.co.uk*

Travel & General Group
  t +44 (0)845 345 2487,
  www.tagdirect.co.uk

WorldSki
  t +44 (0)870 043 4122,
  www.worldski.co.uk

Worldwide Insure
  t +44 (0)870 112 8100,
  www.worldwideinsure.com

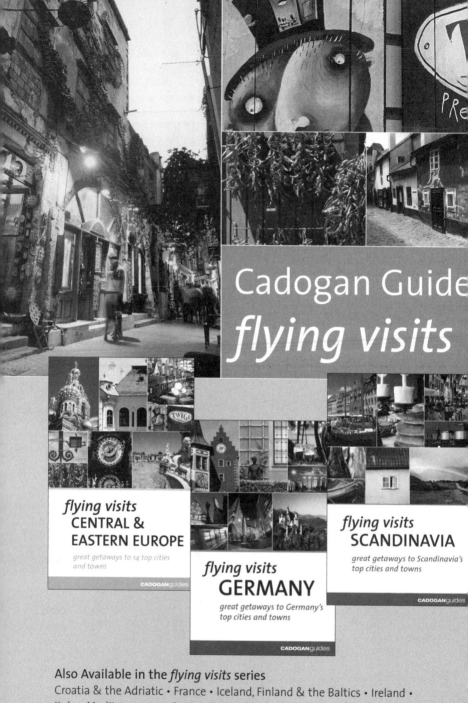

Cadogan Guide
flying visits

flying visits
**CENTRAL &
EASTERN EUROPE**

*great getaways to 14 top cities
and towns*

CADOGANguides

flying visits
GERMANY

*great getaways to Germany's
top cities and towns*

CADOGANguides

flying visits
SCANDINAVIA

*great getaways to Scandinavia's
top cities and towns*

CADOGANguides

Also Available in the *flying visits* series
Croatia & the Adriatic · France · Iceland, Finland & the Baltics · Ireland ·
Italy · Mediterranean · Spain · Switzerland

CADOGANguides
well travelled **well read**